Christianity and the Law of Migration

This collection brings together legal scholars and Christian theologians for an interdisciplinary conversation responding to the challenges of global migration.

Gathering 14 leading scholars from both law and Christian theology, the book covers legal perspectives, theological perspectives, and key concepts in migration studies. In Part 1, scholars of migration law and policy discuss the legal landscape of migration at both the domestic and international level. In Part 2, Christian theologians, ethicists, and biblical scholars draw on the resources of the Christian tradition to think about migration. In Part 3, each chapter is co-authored by a scholar of law and a scholar of Christian theology, who bring their respective resources and perspectives into conversation on key themes within migration studies.

The work provides a truly interdisciplinary introduction to the topic of migration for those who are new to the subject; an opportunity for immigration lawyers and legal scholars to engage Christian theology; an opportunity for pastors and Christian theologians to engage law; and new insights on key frameworks for scholars who are already committed to the study of migration.

Silas W. Allard, Senior Fellow in Law and Religion, Center for the Study of Law and Religion, and Doctoral Student, Graduate Division of Religion, Emory University, Atlanta, Georgia, USA.

Kristin E. Heyer, Professor of Theological Ethics and Director of Graduate Studies, Boston College, Boston, Massachusetts, USA.

Raj Nadella, Samuel A. Cartledge Associate Professor of New Testament, Columbia Theological Seminary, Decatur, Georgia, USA.

Law and Religion
Series Editor
Professor Norman Doe
Director of the Centre for Law and Religion, Cardiff University, UK
Series Board
Carmen Asiaín
Professor, University of Montevideo, Uruguay
Paul Babie
Professor and Associate Dean (International), Adelaide Law School, Australia
Pieter Coertzen, Chairperson
Unit for the Study of Law and Religion, University of Stellenbosch, South Africa
Alison Mawhinney
Reader, Bangor University, UK
Michael John Perry
Senior Fellow, Center for the Study of Law and Religion, Emory University, USA

The practice of religion by individuals and groups, the rise of religious diversity, and the fear of religious extremism, raise profound questions for the interaction between law and religion in society. The regulatory systems involved, the religion laws of secular government (national and international) and the religious laws of faith communities, are valuable tools for our understanding of the dynamics of mutual accommodation and the analysis and resolution of issues in such areas as: religious freedom; discrimination; the autonomy of religious organisations; doctrine, worship and religious symbols; the property and finances of religion; religion, education and public institutions; and religion, marriage and children. In this series, scholars at the forefront of law and religion contribute to the debates in this area. The books in the series are analytical with a key target audience of scholars and practitioners, including lawyers, religious leaders, and others with an interest in this rapidly developing discipline.

Titles in this series include:

Law and the Christian Tradition in Modern Russia
Edited by Paul Valliere and Randall A. Poole

Christianity and the Law of Migration
Edited by Silas W. Allard, Kristin E. Heyer, and Raj Nadella

For more information about this series, please visit: www.routledge.com/Law-and-Religion/book-series/LAWRELIG

Christianity and the Law of Migration

Edited by Silas W. Allard, Kristin E. Heyer, and Raj Nadella

Produced by the Center for the Study of Law and Religion, Emory University

LONDON AND NEW YORK

First published 2022
by Routledge
2 Park Square, Milton Park, Abingdon, Oxon OX14 4RN

and by Routledge
605 Third Avenue, New York, NY 10158

Routledge is an imprint of the Taylor & Francis Group, an informa business

© 2022 selection and editorial matter, Silas W. Allard, Kristin E. Heyer, and Raj Nadella; individual chapters, the contributors

The right of Silas W. Allard, Kristin E. Heyer, and Raj Nadella to be identified as the authors of the editorial material, and of the authors for their individual chapters, has been asserted in accordance with sections 77 and 78 of the Copyright, Designs and Patents Act 1988.

All rights reserved. No part of this book may be reprinted or reproduced or utilised in any form or by any electronic, mechanical, or other means, now known or hereafter invented, including photocopying and recording, or in any information storage or retrieval system, without permission in writing from the publishers.

Trademark notice: Product or corporate names may be trademarks or registered trademarks, and are used only for identification and explanation without intent to infringe.

British Library Cataloguing-in-Publication Data
A catalogue record for this book is available from the British Library

Library of Congress Cataloging-in-Publication Data
Names: Allard, Silas W., editor. | Heyer, Kristin E., 1974– editor. | Nadella, Raj, editor.
Title: Christianity and the law of migration / edited by Silas W. Allard, Kristin E. Heyer, and Raj Nadella.
Description: Abingdon, Oxon ; New York, NY : Routledge, 2021. | Series: Law and religion | Includes bibliographical references and index.
Identifiers: LCCN 2021012311 (print) | LCCN 2021012312 (ebook) | ISBN 9780367486693 (hardback) | ISBN 9781032049526 (paperback) | ISBN 9781003042198 (ebook)
Subjects: LCSH: Emigration and immigration law—United States. | United States—Emigration and immigration—Religious aspects—Christianity.
Classification: LCC KF4819 .C47 2021 (print) | LCC KF4819 (ebook) | DDC 342.7308/2—dc23
LC record available at https://lccn.loc.gov/2021012311
LC ebook record available at https://lccn.loc.gov/2021012312

ISBN: 978-0-367-48669-3 (hbk)
ISBN: 978-1-032-04952-6 (pbk)
ISBN: 978-1-003-04219-8 (ebk)

Typeset in Galliard
by Apex CoVantage, LLC

Contents

List of contributors	viii
Preface and acknowledgments	x
Foreword: displacement and trauma	xii
EMILIE M. TOWNES	

Introduction: law and theology in the age of migration	1
SILAS W. ALLARD	

PART 1
The law of migration
9

1	**Exclusion, admission, and deportation: categorical evolution and normative challenges**	11
	DANIEL KANSTROOM	

2	**The institutionalization of inequality: lower-skilled and undocumented workers in immigration law**	29
	ENID TRUCIOS-HAYNES	

3	**In defense of chain migration**	51
	BILL ONG HING	

4	**The state of the law on refugees, asylees, and stateless persons**	69
	MICHELE R. PISTONE	

5	**Borders: sites of exclusion, sites of engagement**	87
	SILAS W. ALLARD	

vi *Contents*

6 Immigrant integration and disintegration in an era
of exclusionary nationalism 105
DONALD M. KERWIN

7 True faith, allegiance, and citizenship 126
ROSE CUISON-VILLAZOR

PART 2
Theology and migration 145

8 Different kinds of foreignness: the Hebrew Bible's
terminology for foreigners 147
SAFWAT MARZOUK

9 Embrace, ambivalence, and theoxenia: New Testament
perspectives on hospitality to strangers 165
RAJ NADELLA

10 Toward a theology of migration 179
LUIS N. RIVERA-PAGÁN

11 When the poor knock on our door: a theological response
to unwanted migration 195
GEMMA TULUD CRUZ

12 The theopolitics of the migrant: toward a coalitional and
comparative political theology 212
ULRICH SCHMIEDEL

13 Migration, social responsibility, and moral imagination:
resources from Christian ethics 230
KRISTIN E. HEYER

PART 3
Dialogues 249

14 "No more deaths": religious liberty as a defense for
providing sanctuary for immigrants 251
ROSE CUISON-VILLAZOR AND ULRICH SCHMIEDEL

Contents vii

15 A vision of integration rooted in hospitality 276
DONALD M. KERWIN AND SAFWAT MARZOUK

16 Labor, inequality, and globalization: legal and theological
perspectives on vulnerable migrant workers 292
GEMMA TULUD CRUZ AND ENID TRUCIOS-HAYNES

17 Empire, displacement, and the Central American refugee crisis 312
BILL ONG HING AND RAJ NADELLA

18 Empathy, legitimacy, faith, and the dangerously uncertain
future of migration 332
KRISTIN E. HEYER AND DANIEL KANSTROOM

Index 349

Contributors

Silas W. Allard, Senior Fellow in Law and Religion, Center for the Study of Law and Religion, and Doctoral Student, Graduate Division of Religion, Emory University, Atlanta, Georgia, USA

Gemma Tulud Cruz, Senior Lecturer in Theology, Australian Catholic University, Melbourne, Australia

Rose Cuison-Villazor, Interim Dean, Professor of Law, and Chancellor's Social Justice Scholar, Rutgers Law School, Newark, New Jersey, USA

Kristin E. Heyer, Professor of Theological Ethics and Director of Graduate Studies, Boston College, Boston, Massachusetts, USA

Bill Ong Hing, Professor of Law and Migration Studies, Director of the Immigration and Deportation Defense Clinic, University of San Francisco, San Francisco, California, USA

Daniel Kanstroom, Professor of Law, Faculty Director of the Rappaport Center for Law and Public Policy, Codirector of the Center for Human Rights and International Justice, and Thomas F. Carney Distinguished Scholar, Boston College, Boston, Massachusetts, USA

Donald M. Kerwin, Executive Director, Center for Migration Studies, New York, New York, USA

Safwat Marzouk, Associate Professor of Old Testament, Union Presbyterian Seminary, Richmond, VA, USA.

Raj Nadella, Samuel A. Cartledge Associate Professor of New Testament, Columbia Theological Seminary, Decatur, Georgia, USA

Michele R. Pistone, Professor of Law, Director of Clinic for Asylum, Refugee, and Emigrant Services (CARES), Founding Faculty Director of Villanova Interdisciplinary Immigration Studies Training for Advocates (VIISTA), Villanova University, Villanova, Pennsylvania, USA

Luis N. Rivera-Pagán, Henry Winters Luce Professor of Ecumenics and Mission, Emeritus, Princeton Theological Seminary, Princeton, New Jersey, USA

Contributors   ix

Ulrich Schmiedel, Lecturer in Theology, Politics, and Ethics, University of Edinburgh, Edinburgh, Scotland, UK

Emilie M. Townes, Dean of the Divinity School and Distinguished Professor of Womanist Ethics and Society, Vanderbilt University, Nashville, Tennessee, USA

Enid Trucios-Haynes, Professor of Law, Director of the Muhammad Ali Institute for Peace and Justice, and Codirector of the Brandeis Human Rights Advocacy Program, University of Louisville, Louisville, Kentucky, USA

Preface and acknowledgments

This volume, *Christianity and the Law of Migration*, is one of several new introductions to Christianity and law commissioned by the Center for the Study of Law and Religion at Emory University. Each of these introductions is an anthology written by leading scholars from across relevant disciplines. Each volume has historical, doctrinal, and comparative materials designed to uncover Christian sources and dimension of familiar legal topics, to encourage a cross-disciplinary conversation between law and Christian theology, and to think about the role and impact of law on the Christian tradition. Each volume is authoritative but accessible, calibrated to reach students, scholars, and instructors in law, divinity, graduate, and advanced college courses as well as educated readers from various fields interested in the interaction of law and Christianity. This volume joins several others in print or press: *Christianity and Law* (2008); *Christianity and Human Rights* (2010); *Christianity and Family Law* (2017); *Christianity and Natural Law* (2017); *The Profession of Ecclesiastical Lawyers* (2019); *Christianity and Global Law* (2020); *Christianity and Criminal Law* (2020); *Christianity and Economic Law* (2021); *Christianity and the Laws of Conscience* (2021); *Christianity and International Law* (2021); *Christianity and Constitutionalism* (2021); *Christianity and Private Law* (2021). The editors express our thanks to John Witte Jr. for his vision and leadership in imagining, soliciting, guiding, and fundraising for this series of books, including this one.

This and several other volumes in the field of law and Christianity were made possible by the generous support of the McDonald Agape Foundation. We thank the foundation leadership—particularly the late Ambassador Alonzo McDonald and Mrs. Suzie McDonald, who created the foundation, as well as the new foundation president and chairman, Peter McDonald—for their benefaction, leadership, and dedication to this work.

The editors are deeply grateful to all the contributors, who have been wonderful conversation partners throughout the development of this book. We were privileged to work with such a committed, creative, and courageous group of scholars. Cross-disciplinary conversation is often difficult and fraught, and joint authorship can be a perilous exercise. The contributors to this volume not only rose to the challenge but also embraced the vision we put forward of the potential for dialogue between law and theology on a vital issue of our time. Furthermore, the manuscript of this volume was finalized in the summer and fall of 2020, during the disruptions and difficulties of the COVID-19 pandemic. We thank the contributors for their persistence and perseverance in bringing this volume to fruition when the demands of teaching, scholarship, and everyday life were so much more difficult.

We also thank the many others who helped bring this volume into being. We are grateful to the faculty and staff at the Center for the Study of Law and Religion and Columbia Theological Seminary, especially Sandra Tilley, Karen Wishart-Christian, and Michael Thompson, who helped make possible the 2019 workshop and conference, "Migration and Border Crossings," where the contributors began the conversations that would become this book. We are grateful to Anita Mann for handling the financial arrangements for the book; to Tallulah Lanier for assistance in citation checking; to Gary Hauk for his excellent copyediting; and to Mark Douglas, editor of *@This Point*, for granting us permission to reprint Emilie M. Townes's essay as the foreword to this book. Finally, we thank Norman Doe for accepting this book into the distinguished Law and Religion series at Routledge, and Alison Kirk, Emily Summers, and their colleagues at Routledge for shepherding the volume to publication.

Silas W. Allard, Emory University
Kristin E. Heyer, Boston College
Raj Nadella, Columbia Theological Seminary

Foreword
Displacement and trauma[1]

Heart of Jesus full of love and mercy, watch over my sister and brother migrants. Have pity on them and protect them; they suffer mistreatment and humiliations on their way, looked on as dangerous by most, and marginalized for being foreigners. Help us to respect them and appreciate their dignity. Touch with your goodness the hearts of we who see them pass by. Take care of their families until they return home, not with broken hearts but with their hopes fulfilled. May it be so.

Altar is a small town in northern Mexico, about 60–80 miles south of Nogales, Arizona.

Altar has become something of a gathering place for people migrating from the south

folks will spend a bit of time there, preparing for the next hard leg of the journey

they will pack their backpacks, carrying a little food and as much water as they can carry for the journey across the unforgiving landscape of the Sonoran desert

rather than stem the tide of folks crossing into the United States

the U.S. government's decision to pour more money and resources into sealing off the border has resulted in making the journey into the United States more difficult, more dangerous, more expensive, and more profitable

---

1 This foreword was delivered as keynote address to the Migration and Border Crossings Conference at Columbia Theological Seminary, Decatur, GA, February 7–9, 2019. It was originally published as Emilie M. Townes, "Displacement and Trauma," *@ThisPoint* 13, no. 2 (2019), www.ctsnet.edu/at-this-point/displacement-trauma/. It is reprinted here with the permission of the author and the editor of *@ThisPoint*.

Foreword xiii

on the town square in Altar sits a Catholic cathedral

the congregation at Mass changes every day because so many people are just
passing through
it is a parish that bears witness, daily, to the plight of the migrant

hanging just inside this church for all who enter to see is the prayer I began
with, which is also repeated every time the gathered community celebrates
mass[2]

it is recited as people leave for the north into the dangers or cartels, border
patrols, bandits, the desert with its dangers of dehydration or hypothermia
then possible discovery, deportation or repatriation to rest and prepare for the
next attempt at crossing

such is the migrant journey for far too many on our southern border

I

as I have said elsewhere:

the times we are in are a hot mess or a postmodern Shakespearean fresh hell

in other words—

we are living in a society in which our economic outlook is one of steady
growth—we are in what some experts call a goldilocks economy

growth is not too hot, causing inflation or too cold, creating a recession

while jobs are not materializing as promised and hoped for and tax cuts have
a decided edge

the middle fifth of earners got about $950—nice but hardly huge
the bottom fifth got about $60
and in a world where housing and health care are soaring
an extra $60 or $1.15 a week—is near meaningless

the list of things we worry about and organize about are a vexing mix:

abortion
gay marriage
marital rape

---

2 Thanks to Viki Matson, Assistant Professor of the Practice of Ministry and Director of Field
Education at Vanderbilt Divinity School, who shared the prayer and the story behind it in a
faculty meeting, February 1, 2019, Nashville, TN.

xiv *Foreword*

> planned parenthood funding
> LGBT adoption rights
> gender identity
> policing
> #lives matter
> government mandates
> religious freedom act
> education
> women in combat
> mass incarceration
> death penalty
> gender workplace diversity
> confederate flag and monuments
> euthanasia
> health care
> safe spaces
> First Amendment
> immigration
> and much more

we have allowed the ideas of "post truth" and "alternative facts" that began as laughing points that have turned into policy points that become legal points such that some of us need not apply for justice or mercy

given the uproar going on all around us, as I was writing this talk, I noticed that there are two conferences that have created a particular kind of buzz this spring semester for the students, faculty, and staff at Vanderbilt Divinity School and perhaps in the spaces and places you live and work in

> one is a conference being sponsored by the Office of Religious Life at Princeton University in March—Christianity and White supremacy: heresy and hope
> the other is this one—migration and border crossings

there's also annual conferences like the Samuel Dewitt Proctor conference whose theme is "the cry of black blood: the call to sacred memory"

> and on the more conservative side, there is the Brehm Conference—"worship, theology and the arts in a divided world" and the Shepherds' Conference for men in church leadership—"faithful"

and denominationally, the United Methodists are meeting in a little less than 3 weeks for a called General Conference that will center on human sexuality

> the sense of fear and hope for this conference is tangible—even for those of us who live and work in a nondenominational theological school

Foreword xv

after all, VDS is only 1 block away from the United Methodist General Board of Higher Education and Ministry

it is impossible to miss the care and concern from there and in area churches

these conferences represent, I think, the various conversations we are attempting to have within our faith communities, our circles of accountability, our personal commitments, our striving toward a discipleship of depth and breadth

that does not settle for a stultifying status quo of inequalities wrapped in the dull colors of iniquity and spit

as we look out on and live into the worlds we travel in or the ones we seek to understand

and I begin by naming these pieces of our daily puzzle of living not as a kind of yardstick for our various conversations through religious lenses

but rather to remind us that this conference is set in a much larger context that we dare not forget or neglect

a context that is built on memory and hope, dreams and nightmares, vitriol and healing balm, calls to circle the wagons and those who are opening the doors wide and filling in the moats of hatred

because we not only aim for a better day, we are moving ever closer to the new heaven and new earth as we work with the holy each and every day through acts both large and small

II

so, when I turn to this conference and the topic I have been asked to reflect on in this closing keynote, "displacement and trauma," I find the topic to be an interesting turn to take to send us on our way

over the last couple of days, we have explored the causes, processes, and effects of global migration—the journey of the migrant, causes of migration, processes of migration, and consequences of migration in our plenary times
the conference organizers have been true to their word that this conference would

1 [To] bring together leading scholars from various disciplines and religious backgrounds as well as ecclesial leaders to explicate political, theological/ethical, and religious issues pertaining to immigration and border-crossings.
2 [To] offer quality resources that faith communities can draw upon as they seek to engage these issues faithfully-on both intellectual and

xvi *Foreword*

practical levels. These resources would include curriculum-related material and possibly lectures, and presentations posted on YouTube.

3 [To] suggest to faith communities concrete ways for participatory praxis at local and national levels.
with workshops on pedagogies, worship and preaching, organizing, immigration policies and law, pastoral care, best practices, getting in line

and oh, the networking and side conversations we have had

and the deep listening many if not most of us have engaged in

so, in many ways, to talk about displacement and trauma as we prepare to end brings us back to the beginning of our time together

though with an important difference: we have become a community of sorts that has been through something together

and hopefully we have some new insights or different angles of vision or committed ourselves to our next

perhaps some of us have come to understand a different viewpoint with more empathy rather than bare ideology
and we are beginning our goodbyes and hoping, I pray, that we will find ways to live into what we have learned by taking it back to our home spaces and working with others to take more seriously, where we have not, that we are to welcome the stranger at the gate in our communities and into our lives

III

so, how do we welcome the stranger at our southern gate?

what fuels the fear and hatred and hording of resources that makes some folks *acceptable* migrants and others a dark horde of violence?

how do we, as I think we have tried to do in our time together, find a faith-filled theology and ethical muscle that we turn away from a lexicon of terror that creates social, political, religious, and legal categories to include or exclude those who have been forced from their country

their homes

to escape war or persecution or the lack of jobs

for I think that part of what we point to when we pair displacement and trauma is what is going on in us as much, if not more, than what is happening to migrants

the crisis I see at the border is a humanitarian one
not one that threatens U.S. sovereignty and security

in the last half decade, while immigration at the U.S. border has dropped significantly compared with earlier years, the profile of migrants has

Foreword xvii

changed in ways that the U.S. immigration system has never been designed to address

> instead of young men and seasonal workers, most of whom migrated from Mexico, the majority of people now arriving are asylum-seeking families from Central America
>
> this past November, more than twenty-five thousand families crossed the U.S. border—the highest such monthly total on record
>
>> they were fleeing the violence, poverty, and rampant political corruption that have made parts of Honduras, El Salvador, and Guatemala virtually uninhabitable

the crisis at our border is a refugee crisis that is difficult, if not impossible to fix at our border with a wall

> and the reality is that the United States alone cannot fix this refugee crisis
>
> it will need the efforts of the countries in the region working together

by refusing to see the reality that the change in who is crossing our southern border are asylum seekers we are able to ignore the law that these migrants must be allowed to present their claims to immigration agents

> that children cannot be detained for more than 20 days

our catch and release response for migrant families has now moved to punishing asylum seekers and attempting to dismantle what we already have in place, inadequate as it is

> these scare tactics simply have not worked—deterrence has failed and we need to shift how we handle this refugee crisis
>
> and more importantly deal with it *as* a refugee crisis rather than casting brown bodies as a threat to national security
>
>> or the reason why we refuse to offer a living wage to millions of workers
>> or the alleged cause of the rise in crime in the United States

thinking about displacement and trauma begins, for me, with acknowledging that what we have is not a border-security crisis

> it's a crisis created by the fact that we need more asylum officers, immigration judges, beds that are suitable for families, and better coordination between ICE, customs and border protection, and U.S. citizenship and immigration services

it is little wonder that we are in the midst of this particular mess as we remember the complex troubling milieu we are in

xviii *Foreword*

IV

displacement and trauma (especially when we link them together) are creations of the fantastic hegemonic imagination that rests in all of us

> this is an imagination that encourages us to see one another through stereotypes and innuendos
> an imagination that is arrogant about our ignorance
> and denies that we are often afraid of what we do not know or understand and hesitant to take on educating ourselves
>
>> because it just might mean that we will have to open up our hearts, minds, souls, bodies, communities, religious homes to a full-blown spring cleaning of the spirit
>> in other words—we will have to change

taking my cues from Astrid Scheuermann[3] who writes about migration in Europe, I translate her into our context and am suggesting that the reason there is a fear about our southern border that we don't have for the north

> is, in part, because we want migrants from the south to want to be just like us
> and we place all the responsibility of adaptation on these migrants and refugees without acknowledging the stress and trauma that these folks have already been through
>
>> and what we put them through if they do manage to make it into the United States because of inadequate resources or misplaced emphasis on solutions that make problems rather than solve them, political posturing, and ignoring our own laws and regulations that creates a situation that piles these stressors and trauma they engender high and deeper

if we demonize them, as too many of the federal public narratives I hear do, then we do not have to acknowledge that migrants from the south and other countries may have experienced the destruction of their homes, violent acts perpetrated again loved ones, or have been victims of violence or life-threatening situations themselves

> and sometimes U.S. foreign policy has helped fuel this destruction

displacement kicks in when folks are cast off to fend for themselves while waiting for their asylum hearings or border agents have separated families—parents and children—and no one seems to know who is where

> and let me say that this is far too reminiscent of what happened during slavocracy in this country—children became pawns, caged, expendable, unaccounted for except for on the tote boards of slave bills of sale

---

3 Astrid Scheuermann, "Misinterpreting Integration: Displacement and Trauma," *PETRIe*, accessed December 18, 2020, www.petrieinventory.com/misinterpreting-integration-displacement-and-trauma/.

Foreword xix

so, as we end by talking about what happens to folks in post-migration—displacement and trauma

> I do so by turning to the power of lament, communal lament that may help guide our way

V

I am often struck

> as a sometimes archetypical grumpy and never quite satisfied ethicist
> with the drive we have as meaning-makers and moral agents to address vexing moral problems like migration and immigration
> and that we turn them into problems instead of opportunities to exercise the gift of God's grace in our lives

our need for order sometimes drives us into acts of justice

> sometimes acts of ill-conceived passions
> sometimes acts of ethical hubris
> sometimes acts of moral strength and resilience
> sometimes acts of great care and compassion
> sometimes brave acts—even when we do not have a burning bush to guide our way

in short, we humans are a rather creative lot

> we never quite know what we will do next at times
> and just when we think we've got ourselves figured out, we go and commit the unfathomable

dealing with displacement and trauma

> is not a linear process
> not exactly a loop
> not wholly a curly-q

perhaps it is a sense of urgency that shapes our concern

> a cosmic rumbling that is relentless in its precision in interrupting, disrupting, changing our lives and countless others

although the prophets of the Hebrew Bible are some of my favorite challenging/disturbing/disrupting reading—both as an ethicist and a person of faith

> I do not envy their task

xx *Foreword*

for they take on human predictabilities and unpredictabilities because of divine
    mandate
and this is not my idea of a particularly good time

but I find that their response to exile and despair are a profound biblical mooring
for my moral musings today

for they are guides for how do we respond to the questions of What ought we
    do? How ought we be? What is happening?

the prophets Ezekiel and Micah help ground me biblically as I think about displacement (when people either move or are moved from their homes) and trauma
(a deeply distressing or disturbing experience)
Ezekiel forces us to consider what it means when we cannot lament

and what forces of nature or the divine are at work that prevent us from form-
    ing our frustration and outrage into familiar groans of anguish

of loss
of chaos
of dawning awareness
of plotting faith-filled response

is this truly the way to re-forming us by placing us into a cataclysm of the primal
where reason and rationality hold no sway?
we are not allowed to structure, to order the loss
instead we must twist and turn into the collapse of our efforts to reach out in
faith and deep mission
and you and I are left with the horror of questions formed out of absolute con-
fusion or confounding competing narratives and frustrations that we have when
we are observers at the accident scene

and we begin to realize that the wail of sirens in the background is not the
    rescue squad that promises to help the wounded
no, those siren wails are coming from us

we are the questioners in modern and postmodern smugness at times

that is now worn thin by the shock and horror of realizing we have become
    like Shelley's Frankenstein—not the monster, but its creator

rather than escape into neat discourses or familiar rituals

we *must* make meaning out of the devastation that displacement and trauma
    wreaks in the lives of migrants

Foreword xxi

rather than ignore the ways that we must step forward, perfectly and imperfectly to respond in deep faithfulness when our brothers and sisters need us

Micah—the advocate of pure worship and social justice

speaks judgment, divine forgiveness, and hope

we can ponder notions of the good with him

the ways in which it can be seen as a supreme end
the ways in which it can be juxtaposed to justice
the ways in which it can be inseparable from the inner person

and we should never forget the power of stories

they can help establish identity and location
they locate us in time—past, present, future
they can also clarify accountability

in Micah's hands, the power of stories and the concept of the good join forces such that the good is something that the people should already know

what must we do to contribute to the good: do justice, love mercy, have an attitude of humility?
these concrete acts, these practices are the stuff of moral formation for Micah

not liturgies that are actually self-condemning or worse

displeasing to God

both Ezekiel and Micah remind us that we have the ability to grow and change
yes, both have witnessed the problem side of growth and change

and call for the faithful side of this to show its face in our actions

these are not easy tasks and they certainly are not for the weak of will or faith to engage in
I am reminded of something the British philosopher, Mary Midgley, points out

"it is the ideas we actually live by that we most need to understand"[4]

I think these prophets remind us of this on a continual basis
for as Midgley goes on to note, just being a part of a culture is not enough to make us understand it morally[5]

---

4 Mary Midgley, *Can't We Make Moral Judgements?* (New York: St. Martin's Press, 1991), 13.
5 Ibid., 89.

xxii   *Foreword*

but when all is said and done—we are the interpreters of our cultures and we are its meaning-makers and we are the ones who must speak out of our faith rather than that which comforts only us

> too often, we are ill-equipped to take up the challenge of understanding what it is we have helped to create
>
> and what we have such a vested interest in maintaining

so, we have gathered to open up the shutters of the windows of our souls

> to think through, feel through, talk through, act through how we can be present and alert when it comes to migration and border crossings

it is often in the exile of displacement and despair of trauma that we are shaken from our nocturnes of mediocrity and faithlessness

> and our jazz riffs of injustice and annihilation

VI

these two biblical guides call forth a much larger ethical playground than we tend to live our lives in from day to day

so I turn to them because prophets have a nasty habit of reminding us of what we already know—that when faced with the humanity of what we do when we would build a wall instead of opening a door

they remind us that we are not to be the poster children of the status quo and that we must turn to a bone-deep faith

> its depths *and* its shallows

> and recognize that if we have a faith that only rests on the familiar and the known, this does not get us to the radical reordering of the new heaven and new earth we are to seek to proclaim and work with God to bring in

if we continue to use the same moral playbook to guide our actions

> we will, at best, only come up with updated versions of the same beliefs and practices that got us in the conundrum to begin with

salvation, which is God's business, does not come very often in status quo moral formulations

> at least not in the hands of these prophets

Foreword   xxiii

so, what must we do to move into our faith?

I argue this afternoon that we take our cues from Ezekiel and begin by finding the lament, the moral clarity within us

> for in the Hebrew Bible laments mark the *beginning* of the healing process
>> that allows us to begin to see what we must do to be faithful

if we learn anything from prophets like Ezekiel and Joel, it is to know that the healing of brokenness and injustice

> the healing of social sin and degradation
> the healing of fractured relationships
> the healing of spiritual doubts and fears
> the healing of body, individual and corporate

begins with an unrestrained lament of faith to the God of faith that we need help

> that we can't respond to the shameful ways in which we do not welcome the
>> strangers at our southern gates by our individual fears and worries alone
> we ache, with every fiber of our being, with grief and sorrow and guilt
> we need some *divine* help that allows us to confess that which we have done
>> and that which we have not done

Claus Westermann maintains that no worship observance in ancient Israel is better known to us today than the rite of lament.[6] It is the cry of distress that is so powerful, this lament. For as Ezekiel and Micah present situations of crisis, of distress, the lament comes forth in potent language that is unequivocal in its anguish. It is only a rending of the heart such as this that Westermann notes belongs to the events of deliverance.[7]

Walter Brueggemann tells us that lament is formful.[8] By putting our suffering into the form of lament, we first have to acknowledge that we are going through some mess. Lament helps us put words to our suffering and our frustrations and outrage. For when we can name it, we begin to see the contours of allowing our faith to help us *into* how we can address the journey of the migrant, the causes of migration, the processes and consequences of migration—to do helpful, faithful acts of justice in responding to deep human need.

---

6 Claus Westermann, *The Psalms: Structure, Content and Message*, trans. Ralph D. Gehrke (Minneapolis: Augsburg Publishing House, 1980), 32.

7 Claus Westermann, "The Role of Lament in the Theology of the Old Testament," *Interpretation: A Journal of Bible and Theology* 28, no. 1 (1974): 20–38, 21.

8 Walter Brueggemann, "The Formfulness of Grief," *Interpretation: A Journal of Bible and Theology* 31, no. 3 (1977): 263–75, 265. Although Brueggemann uses the word grief in this essay, I believe that his remarks also closely parallel the process of lament in Joel.

xxiv *Foreword*

Lament enables us and even requires of us to acknowledge and to experience our suffering or the suffering of others. Lament in our contemporary world helps us ask questions of justice and righteousness.

You see, the formfulness of communal lament has a deep moral character for us today. I believe that we are drawn to explore anew what lament can mean for us as a part of understanding displacement and trauma and how to effectively address them when we seek to shape responsive ministries for migrants—and for ourselves. I want to stress the importance of communal lament as we do this. We must tell the truth of what is going on with the various truths, half-truths, alternative facts, and outright lies when it comes to migration and immigration.

I have tried to begin this conversation one last time as we prepare to leave this place. For you and I have been doing a communal lament in our time together already. And in this lament, I end with a word about hope that we learn from Micah and then, finally, a word about home.

VII

a disclaimer: the reality is that all forms of ethical reflection tend to forget that human actions, our actions and those of others, are incomplete

> we are constrained and free, good and evil, historical and ahistorical beings
> the world of Cartesian dualisms fails to capture the dynamic quality of the moral life

the challenge for me as an ethicist is to remember that at the end of the day decision-making is not as easy *or* as difficult as it seems

> and that there is an intangible quality that can sustain us in all of our contingent wanderings

I believe that this is hope

Hope places us in the wonderful and maddening tension between the sometimes-harsh realities of the present and the vision of the new heaven and new earth that helps fuel our acts of justice and mercy. Engaging hope is to seek to live our faith in the face of the difficult reality that far too many of us live in whirlpools of catastrophe and it is up to us to help folk who live this and seek to flee from it for the promise of a better day.

Acts of justice and mercy embrace all of humanity for it is our kinship and relationship with God and with one another. Through this embrace, we are transformed body and spirit, individuals and society, persons and cosmos, time and eternity.[9]

---

9 Gustavo Gutiérrez, *A Theology of Liberation: History, Politics, and Salvation*, rev. ed., trans. Sister Caridad Inda and John Eagleson (Maryknoll: Orbis Books, 1988), 85.

Foreword xxv

This is not the seductive siren call of rampant individualism that has taken hold in many of our lives, and in far too many public policies and religious pronouncements. I am talking about community here. So, the faith we proclaim, the faith we seek is not perfect—for perfection is not the point. It is not to be hoarded like an ill-gotten possession. It is one that if found in a deep, deep hope that refreshes us as God's relentless love for us, regardless, touches *all* of humanity in a caress that is neither sentimental nor spiritualized.

allowing hope to shape our acts of justice and mercy in displacement and trauma is a bold thing to do

I think

because it can, and perhaps must, conjure up the ghosts, the terrors in our lives

that come as dancing specters
haunting goblins
moaning trolls

who remind us again and again

that we are far too human
to try to do this life all by ourselves
and we cannot always be in control or seek to be in control

you see I think lament can be a good thing

because lament is often the sign that we are seeking

yearning
chasing hope

not just a hope in the divine

but the hope that God loves us
God rocks us
God cares for us
God will heal us

but perhaps not in the ways we expect or want

hope means we have opened our eyes, hearts, minds, souls, very spirits

and now see and feel and touch and smell

the joy and the agony living in the fractures of creation

xxvi *Foreword*

that is the irony of hope

for in our yearning for it

we often walk far away from it as we try to come home to it
we often live into the small and narrow spaces of life that stunt our growth

and demand far too little of us
because far too little is expected from us
or far too little gives us comfort

hope is one more piece to the fabric of the universe

one more way to signal this restless journey we are on
one more sign that Emmaus is not the end of the journey

but its beginning

you see, I don't think hope is the end product on the assembly line of our lives

no, I think it is simply a part of the journey

part of the way in which we come to know God's way in our lives with a richness
that ripens and ripens and ripens

a richness that often disquiets us when we learn that there are things we *can*
do to humanize our nation's response to migrants

and not only migrants, but the great variety of who we are along lines of
race and ethnicity, gender, sexuality, sexual orientation, theological view
point, political persuasion, ableness, and so much more

this richness often disrupts our comfort and our certainty

and this richness that lets us know that that we are *not* alone as a child of God

and an enormous part of our task as members of faith communities is to
make sure that no one is alone or caged or marked as less than because
we must be there as witnesses and disciples

perfect and deeply imperfect
and we demand restored humanity

acts of justice and mercy

for those who have made one of the most difficult decisions they will make in
their lives—to leave their homes in search for a safer, better life

it can mean lobbying our elected officials to honor our shared responsibility
to protect the rights of refugees, asylum seekers, and migrants

Foreword xxvii

it can mean pressuring our government to properly process asylum claims with diligence and fairness so that families and individuals are not left in limbo or worse, locked away in detention centers for years

it means working to see that migrants are being protected from exploitation and abuse by their employers or by traffickers

it means remembering that "migrant" or "asylum seeker" are temporary names—they do not reflect the person behind the label, and it is that person for whom we must fight at all the borders that get constructed in our society

and this only happens if we allow *ourselves* to practice the faith-act of lament and allow our days to be shaped by hope rather than walking around the rib bones of nothingness

lament can be a gateway *into* hope

and hope, in this case, is another way to say faith
a faith that is forged on the hard work of living it

rather than having it handed to us in doctrine or dogmatics

lament, earnest and soul-deep searching, can hold us when we begin again and again

to step out of the folds of old wounds

and live anew as we refuse to let the howling specters of displacement and trauma keep us from reaching into ourselves as we stretch out our arms in welcome

VIII

a lament that calls forth hope names our sister and brother migrants is a search for home—to go from displacement to a place of one's own that is more than a cot in a camp that dangerously mimics the Japanese internment camps of World War II

home is a place for health, healing, identity formation, resistance, celebration, transformation

not only for one, but for all

that is the place where the "real lives" the "real worlds" of peoples take place

it is not the obscene depiction of evil hordes of drug dealers and criminals and murderers caravanning from the south or middle eastern terrorists

bringing with them crime and terror

it is the place where the realities of the journey that has been travelled and the journey yet to come provide a place for folk to be themselves rather than a statistic or sound bite or photo op

xxviii *Foreword*

it is the place that acknowledges the trauma of fear and loathing and violence yet insists on providing an alternative space that is a launching pad for an ornery refusal to let these things become the only thing in their or our narrative
it is the place of core resistance to devaluing oppressions

and, oh yes, home is a place of rest

a place where we get things done, sometimes alone, but mostly with others
a place that we are still learning to create in a world that features a suffocating regime of galloping inequalities

it is the place of Morrison's dancing mind

Neruda's light and darkness
Walker's world in our eye
Marquez's yellow flower
Sanchez's house of lions
Luiselli's dream
Danticat's Krik?, Krak!

it is a place, that we are building, life by life as we allow the voices within our communities

the young and the old
the lesbian and the gay
the propertied and the propertyless
the heterosexual and the celibate
the dark and the light
the bisexual and the transgender,
the female and the male
the conservative and the radical
the undocumented and the documented
the thoughtful and the clueless

all these and more
to speak, to breath free air, to live lives to their fullest

and learn a communal hope that teaches us as we learn

to love the eyes
backs
hands
mouths

feet
shoulders
arms
necks
inside parts
lungs
life-holding wombs
life-giving private parts
hearts
spirits
souls
      of everyone

may it be so

Emilie M. Townes

Introduction
Law and theology in the age of migration

Silas W. Allard

There are more people on the move today than at any point in human history. The International Organization for Migration estimates that in 1970 there were 84.5 million international migrants, and in 2019 that number had climbed to 271.6 million.[1] The 2019 estimate included 26 million refugees and 4.2 million asylum seekers, according to the United Nations High Commissioner for Refugees.[2] Like international migrants generally, there are now more refugees globally than at any prior time, including the previous refugee apotheosis following the Second World War.[3]

Stephen Castles, Hein de Haas, and Mark J. Miller have dubbed ours the "age of migration."[4] While reflecting the overall growth in human movement, this moniker also denotes the centrality of international migration to the political, social, and economic spheres of the modern world. "International migration," according to Castles, de Haas, and Miller, "ranks as one of the most important factors in global change."[5] This change brings with it both opportunities and challenges. A growing number of transnational networks that can foster global solidarity exist alongside increased xenophobia and nationalism. The ability to protect human rights through refuge and asylum is limited and counteracted by anti-immigrant hostility and violence. Migration's potential to spur economic

---

1 International Organization for Migration, *World Migration Report 2020* (Geneva: International Organization for Migration, 2019), 21. As a proportion of global population, international migration has remained relatively steady over the past 35 years, rising from 2.3 percent in 1970 to 3.5 percent in 2019. Ibid. It is worth noting, however, that 1 percent of the world's population of 7.7 billion is 77 million people—a small number in relative, but not absolute, terms.

2 United Nations High Commissioner for Refugees, *Global Trends: Forced Displacement in 2019* (Copenhagen: UNHCR Global Data Service, 2020), 2.

3 Ibid., 8, 16; UNHCR Statistics Team, FICSS, and David Scott, "Refugees Statistics—Are Refugee Numbers the Highest Ever?" *UNHCR Blog*, August 14, 2018, www.unhcr.org/blogs/statistics-refugee-numbers-highest-ever/.

4 Stephen Castles, Hein de Haas, and Mark J. Miller, *The Age of Migration: International Population Movements in the Modern World*, 5th ed. (Basingstoke, UK: Palgrave Macmillan, 2014).

5 Ibid., 7.

2 Silas W. Allard

growth in destination countries is counterbalanced by concerns over lost economic potential in countries of origin. What marks the age of migration as such is the pervasive role that these challenges and opportunities have in shaping and reshaping the structures and institutions of social and political life.

Human mobility is not, however, a new phenomenon. The human ability to migrate—to leave one's current place of settlement and resettle in a new place—was essential to the dispersal of the human species across the globe. Peter Bellwood has described the earliest migrations as "the founding, through migration, of the human world."[6] Humans have continued to migrate over the intervening millennia, and migration has continued to play an essential role in shaping human life and society. Our contemporary age of migration might be distinguished by attention to three aspects beyond (but underpinning) the sheer scale of human movement in modern times. These three aspects broadly reflect the phenomenon known as globalization.

Jehu Hanciles has described the first aspect of globalization as "the emergence of *global consciousness*: the growing awareness that the world we inhabit is a single (social) place."[7] While forms of internationalization have been developing for millennia, as contact among different peoples and cultures increased, the age of European conquest created an awareness of a single, unified globe, and this awareness was, through the same process, spread to all corners of the globe. Thus, as Hanciles notes, globalization describes "processes of change that transcend territorial limits . . . or cultural differentiations, with the clear implications that the limits of impact and action are the globe itself."[8] This global consciousness has a profound impact on international migration, as can be seen in the colonial, neocolonial, and neoliberal projects of states and corporations, which have established patterns of international migration through conquest, occupation, trade, and labor recruiting (Kristin E. Heyer, Chapter 13). Such consciousness can also be seen in the growth of transnational commercial, familial, and cultural networks among former and prospective migrants, which perpetuate existing and establish new patters of international migration.

The second aspect of globalization is technological innovation. As Castles, de Haas, and Miller note, "Global cultural interchange, facilitated by improved transport and the proliferation of print and electronic media, can also increase migration aspirations," and "falling costs of travel and infrastructure improvements have rapidly increased non-migratory forms of mobility such as tourism,

---

6 Peter Bellwood, "Prehistoric Migration and the Rise of Humanity," in *The Global Prehistory of Human Migration*, eds. Peter Bellwood and Immanuel Ness (Malden, MA: Wiley-Blackwell, 2015), 56.

7 Jehu Hanciles, *Beyond Christendom: Globalization, African Migration and the Transformation of the West* (Maryknoll, NY: Orbis Books, 2009), 17. As Hanciles notes, what we refer to as globalization had historical antecedents to the emergence of a global consciousness, as distant communities were brought into contact by conquest, trade, and migration or consolidated under major empires. Ibid., 16–17.

8 Ibid., 17.

Introduction   3

business trips and commuting."[9] The combined technological developments of the industrial, broadcast, and internet revolutions have combined to further global consciousness and reduce barriers to long-distance travel.

The third aspect of globalization is the hegemony of the nation-state as a form of global political community. The modern nation-state brought together the concepts of sovereignty, nation (or people), and territory, such that it became possible to regulate access to territory and membership in the nation through the mechanism of law (Silas W. Allard, Chapter 5). In other words, in a world ordered politically and legally into states defined by their territorial borders, international migration is fundamentally a question of law (Daniel Kanstroom, Chapter 1; Ulrich Schmiedel, Chapter 12). Furthermore, migration is regulated at the level of state law, such that to migrate in the age of migration means navigating or subverting the layered legal regimes of one's country of origin, destination country, and transit countries. In the latter part of the twentieth century, a body of international law was created to protect migrants of various sorts (Michele R. Pistone, Chapter 4), but this body of international law also ensures the sovereign right of states to control entry into their territory and largely leaves with individual states the power to admit, exclude, and deport. Thus, domestic regimes of immigration law overlap with one another and with international law to form what we are calling the *law of migration*. In this regard, the law of migration as a conceptual framework attempts to take the perspective of migrants—for whom the ability to move or remain is governed by opaquely layered legal regimes that sometimes conflict but often reinforce each other—rather than the perspective of states—for whom these same legal regimes may be unreflexively invoked as the sovereign prerogative to maintain the rule of law.[10]

While global consciousness and technological innovation have tended to further the growth of international migration, the law of migration has attempted (often unsuccessfully) to exert a countervailing force. This is true particularly since the end of the nineteenth century. Until the close of the nineteenth century, the potential to regulate international migration—a potential made possible by the growth of the international system of states—had gone relatively unutilized. But, as Castles, de Haas, and Miller note, "A defining feature of the age of migration is the challenge that some politicians and analysts believe is posed by international migration to the sovereignty of states, specifically to their ability to regulate movements of people across their borders."[11] Thus, the age of migration is marked not only by extensive movement but also by attempts to tighten the regulation of movement, and as people around the world have sought to move greater distances more often, more extensive restrictions on movement have been put into place.

---

9 Castles, de Haas, and Miller, *The Age of Migration*, 7.
10 For a further discussion of this tension, see Silas W. Allard, "Global and Local Challenges to Refugee Protection," *International Journal of Legal Information* 46, no. 1 (2018): 45–52.
11 Castles, de Haas, and Miller, *The Age of Migration*, 5.

4　*Silas W. Allard*

As noted earlier, in the age of migration, international migration and the law that regulates it profoundly shape social life and institutions globally, and this includes the Christian church. As Jennifer Saunders, Elena Fiddian-Qasmiyeh, and Susanna Snyder have written, "religion can be central to migration at a variety of levels and across diverse spaces, from the individual, family, and community practices of migrants and those they leave behind, to the social and political contexts that characterize sites of origin, transit, and destination."[12] Snyder takes up the specific relationship between migration and the church in her introduction to *Church in an Age of Global Migration*. The church, argues Snyder, exists in and for the world, and thus those forces that shape the broader world will ineluctably shape the church.[13] In the age of migration, "[i]f ecclesiology is going to be responsive—both to the world outside church walls and to the multiple worlds coexisting within the lives of church members—it needs to engage with this developing migratory context in depth and with nuance."[14] A growing body of scholarship examines the impact of migration on the church and the church's roles and obligations in the age of migration, but sustained and further attention is required given the scope and impact of migration on the church. Daniel Groody's decade-old argument remains relevant and prescient today: "The current climate points to the need to move the migration debate to an even broader intellectual terrain, one in which theology not only has something to learn but something to offer."[15]

The context of migration that Snyder and Groody identify as vital to the church and to the work of Christian theology includes the law of migration. The law of migration structures the possibilities, constraints, and conditions of international migration. It profoundly influences the world—from the contours of global consciousness to the composition of local neighborhoods—in which the church and its people seek to live out lives of Christian witness and practice. The law of migration affects the hermeneutics we bring to the stories (and laws) about migration in the Hebrew Bible and the New Testament (Safwat Marzouk, Chapter 8; Raj Nadella, Chapter 9). The law of migration creates and facilitates practices of xenophobia and structures of inequality that require theological responses (Luis N. Rivera-Pagán, Chapter 10; Gemma Tulud Cruz, Chapter 11). And in Christian social ethics and political theology, the law of migration looms large as a central site of challenge, reflection, and critique (Schmiedel, Chapter 12; Heyer, Chapter 13). These are just some of the ways that the theological

---

12　Jennifer B. Saunders, Elena Fiddian-Qasmiyeh, and Susanna Snyder, "Introduction: Articulating Intersections at the Global Crossroads of Religion and Migration," in *Intersections of Religion and Migration: Issues at the Global Crossroads*, eds. Jennifer B. Saunders, Elena Fiddian-Qasmiyeh, and Susanna Snyder (New York: Palgrave Macmillan, 2016), 2.

13　Susanna Snyder, "Introduction: Moving Body," in *Church in an Age of Global Migration: A Moving Body* (Basingstoke, UK: Palgrave MacMillan, 2016), 2–3.

14　Ibid., 3.

15　Daniel G. Groody, "Crossing the Divide: Foundations of a Theology of Migration and Refugees," *Theological Studies* 70, no. 3 (2009): 638–67, at 641.

Introduction 5

contributors to this volume engage the law of migration and open important new avenues for doing theology in the age of migration.

While the law of migration is a vital context for Christian theology in the age of migration, it is not the case that Christian theology simply responds to or operates within that context. Scholars of the law of migration can also have a dialogical encounter with Christian theology. Such a dialogue could be imagined as a normative project of bringing the law of migration in line with Christian theology—in other words, articulating a Christian law of migration.[16] We are interested, however, in a different kind of dialogic potential, grounded in the malleability of law's normative claims and its dependence on extralegal narratives for those claims.

In his essay "*Nomos* and Narrative," Robert Cover famously argued that "[n]o set of legal institutions or prescriptions exists apart from the narratives that locate it and give it meaning."[17] Everyone, according to Cover, lives in a *nomos*—a normative world ordered by law. But it is the narratives that give law meaning and make the *nomos* more than a system of rules. "Every prescription," Cover writes, "is insistent in its demand to be located in discourse—to be supplied with history and destiny, beginning and end, explanation and purpose. And every narrative is insistent in its demand for its prescriptive point, its moral."[18] Cover describes the modern nation-state's mode of jurisgenesis—his term for the creation of legal meaning—as "imperial," because it uses state power to fix legal meaning in the midst of competing narratives.

> The precepts we call law are marked off by social control over their provenance, their mode of articulation, and their effects. But the narratives that create and reveal the patterns of commitment, resistance, and understanding—patterns that constitute the dynamic between precept and material universe—are radically uncontrolled. They are subject to no formal hierarchical ordering, no centralized, authoritative provenance, no necessary pattern of acquiescence.[19]

Thus, for Cover, the modern nation-state uses forms of institutional control and violence to fix legal meaning, but competing narratives continue to contest or resist (as well as affirm) the meaning fixed by state institutions.

The law of migration is not a *nomos* in the way that Cover describes it. The law of migration, rather, names the overlapping *nomoi* that migrants navigate or subvert in the endeavor of migration. Cover's discussion of *nomos* and narrative is useful nonetheless. Cover illuminates how law makes its claim to normativity and how

---

16 Ulrich Schmiedel argues, on the contrary, that the figure of the migrant makes the concept of something like a Christian law of migration impossible (Chapter 12).
17 Robert M. Cover, "Foreword: *Nomos* and Narrative," *Harvard Law Review* 97, no. 4 (1983): 4–68, at 4.
18 Ibid., 5.
19 Ibid., 17 (internal citations omitted).

6   *Silas W. Allard*

that claim is contested by competing narratives, at least within modes of imperial jurisgenesis. A dialogical encounter between scholarship on the law of migration and Christian theology opens when Christian theology offers competing narratives that call into question the purportedly fixed answers to questions such as: Who is admissible into the territory of the state, and on what grounds? Who is removable from the territory of the state, and on what grounds? What rights are owed to people on the spectrum from unauthorized immigrant to citizen?

Cover himself might take a dim view of the efficacy of such a dialogue,[20] but as legal scholars seek to interrogate and challenge the normative claims embedded in the law of migration, they will need access to different kinds of narratives. Dialogue with Christian theology may open new approaches to the classically formulated immigration powers to admit, exclude, and deport (Kanstroom, Chapter 1), as well as the conceptualization and composition of the contemporary categories of migration: labor (Enid Trucios-Haynes, Chapter 2); family (Bill Ong Hing, Chapter 3); and humanitarian (Pistone, Chapter 4). Such a dialogue may destabilize categories that are often taken for granted, such as the border (Allard, Chapter 5), integration (Donald M. Kerwin, Chapter 6), and citizenship (Rose Cuison Villazor, Chapter 7). Like the theological contributors, the legal scholars in this volume take up these central themes, opening new avenues for dialogue between Christian theology and the law of migration.

This volume originated with just such a set of dialogues. In February of 2019, the editors gathered 13 scholars (7 legal scholars and 6 theologians) at Columbia Theological Seminary in Decatur, Georgia. The day-long workshop on draft chapters was a prelude to the conference "Migration and Border Crossings,"[21] during which the contributors continued and expanded conversations begun in the workshop. The workshop was an opportunity for each contributor to engage feedback on an early chapter draft across disciplinary boundaries, to learn about the perspective of the other discipline on the topic of their chapter, and to challenge themselves to move forward in their writing in the spirit of a cross-disciplinary dialogue. The workshop was also an opportunity for contributors to begin conversation on jointly authored chapters. While the editors were interested in exploring how cross-disciplinary dialogue could enrich the scholarship of legal scholars and theologians, we also wanted to explore the possibilities of more literally dialogic scholarship by bringing theologians and legal scholars together to cocreate chapters.

The initial conversations and exchanges rooted in the February 2019 workshop have grown and blossomed in the intervening years to produce the chapters

---

20 "A community that acquiesces in the injustice of official law has created no law of its own. It is not sui juris. The community that writes law review articles has created a law—a law under which officialdom may maintain its interpretation merely by suffering the protest of the articles." Cover, "Foreword," 47.

21 Migration and Border Crossings, Columbia Theological Seminary, Decatur, GA, February 7–9, 2019, www.ctsnet.edu/migration-and-border-crossings/.

in this book. The book is divided into three parts. Parts 1 and 2 provide overviews of the law of migration and the theology of migration. In Part 1, seven legal scholars provide chapters interrogating key themes in the law of migration: admission/expulsion/deportation (Kanstroom, Chapter 1), labor migration (Trucios-Haynes, Chapter 2), family migration (Hing, Chapter 3), humanitarian migration (Pistone, Chapter 4), the border (Allard, Chapter 5), integration (Kerwin, Chapter 6), and citizenship (Cuison Villazor, Chapter 7). In Part 2, six theologians elucidate central aspects of Christian theology from the perspective of migration: the Hebrew Bible (Marzouk, Chapter 8), the New Testament (Nadella, Chapter 9), constructive theology (Rivera-Pagán, Chapter 10), praxis theology (Cruz, Chapter 11), political theology (Schmiedel, Chapter 12), and Christian ethics (Heyer, Chapter 13).

In Part 3, each chapter is coauthored by a legal scholar and a theologian. Each set of coauthors was given a set of themes, which they used to develop a deep interdisciplinary dialogue between law and theology. In Chapter 14, Rose Cuison Villazor and Ulrich Schmiedel explore the themes of citizen, stranger, and migrant by unpacking the implications of a religious freedom defense to charges of aiding immigrants crossing the U.S.–Mexico border. In Chapter 15, Donald M. Kerwin and Safwat Marzouk examine the themes of hospitality, integration, and assimilation by arguing for the importance of an attitude of hospitality in any program of immigrant integration. In Chapter 16, Gemma Tulud Cruz and Enid Trucios-Haynes interrogate labor, inequality, and globalization by explicating the legalized precarity of immigrant laborers and the possibility of a theological response. In Chapter 17, Bill Ong Hing and Raj Nadella explicate the historical and moral reasons why the United States should accept refugees from regions such as Central America and argue that it is in the best interest of the United States to integrate such refugees fully into the society. Finally, in Chapter 18 Kristin E. Heyer and Daniel Kanstroom explore the future of migration through the resonant leitmotifs that emerge from the layers of conversation running throughout this volume.

This book is built on dialogue and designed to encourage further dialogue. As the perceptive reader will already have gleaned, parenthetical references to chapters in the book are employed throughout. These parenthetical references reflect the dialogical development of both the single-author and jointly authored chapters, as well as continue the dialogue through the experience of the reader. The topics covered in this volume are intended to assist those new to the issue of international migration to gain perspective on key legal and theological frameworks; to provide an entry point for scholars in law or theology to begin exploring cross-disciplinary engagement; and to invite further conversation between the two disciplines on this important issue, both through the book's content and by its example. Nor do we believe that this kind of cross-disciplinary conversation is or should be limited to Christianity. As Saunders, Fiddian-Qasmiyeh, and Snyder write, "not all religions are equally represented in studies of migration or in policy responses designed to address these. Importantly, these diverse traditions

8 *Silas W. Allard*

have different positions of power in different geopolitical spheres."[22] Other communities of legal and religious scholars could profitably take up this dialogue in other forms and fora.

Thus, in many ways, this volume aspires to introduce a new conversation. The topics chosen for this volume could not exhaust the vital themes and conversations relevant to law and Christianity (or law and religion) in the age of migration. Thus, we recognize that there will be inevitable limitations. While the volume interrogates globally relevant themes, many of the examples are drawn from the domestic law of the United States. As discussed earlier, the law of migration names a set of overlapping national and international legal regimes, and therefore a thorough interrogation of the law of migration begins with an interrogation of those regimes in their particularity. The benefit to an in-depth exploration of one, national legal regime is that the connections between different aspects of a legal framework—the mutually constitutive regulation of family-based and labor-based migration, for example—can be drawn more clearly. While drawing examples predominately from one national legal regime, the contributors have, where applicable, drawn connections to other national legal regimes or contexts that are illuminated by the discussion. Whether the right balance between a productively national and an exemplary global discussion was achieved must be left to the reader, but the recognition of this limitation is another invitation to productively expand the cross-disciplinary dialogue to other contexts.

I conclude with the recognition that international migration is often a divisive political issue. While the contributors to this volume do not agree on a comprehensive set of normative claims or policy proposals, we do begin our dialogue from two key propositions. First, we believe that migration is a vital factor in the social, economic, political, legal, and theological life of people around the globe. Thus, engaging this issue from the perspectives of law and theology is essential. Second, we recognize that the current conditions of international migration shaped by the law of migration and by the response of social institutions, such as the church, have created enormous suffering for many migrants. If there is a normative perspective that binds the contributors of this volume together, it is the necessity of responding to that suffering and the conditions that give rise to it. Our sincere hope is that this volume will make possible and encourage further cross-disciplinary dialogue that takes up this challenge.

---

22 Saunders, Fiddian-Qasmiyeh, and Snyder, "Introduction," 6.

Part 1
The law of migration

1 Exclusion, admission, and deportation

Categorical evolution and normative challenges

Daniel Kanstroom

I Introduction

Although the law, politics, and mechanisms of migration control vary greatly among nation-states, migration law—since the nineteenth century—has generally been understood to embody three distinct structural characteristics or stages: exclusion, admission, and deportation (also sometimes called "return" or "removal"). This venerable model, derived from ideas about Westphalian sovereignty and developed before the era of international human rights, has some obvious virtues as a heuristic. However, it has become both descriptively inaccurate and normatively inadequate.

The descriptive categories blur as millions of people, including many without legal recognition or with various complex legal statuses, seek to cross borders, often in desperation and fear. States have reacted with increasingly sophisticated modes of governmental (and sometimes privatized) control, including discretionary visa and screening regimes, detention centers, interdiction beyond state territory, outsourcing of physical migration control, bilateral and regional cooperation schemes, so-called voluntary return systems, and fast-track deportation methods.[1]

These evolving phenomena present profound analytic, legal, and normative challenges, which have inspired various attempts to capture new realities.[2] As Ulrich Schmiedel notes in this volume, the figure of the migrant destabilizes

---

1 For a fuller explication of these phenomena, see Daniel Kanstroom, *Deportation World: Dynamic Sovereignty, Human Rights and the Promises of Law* (Cambridge, MA: Harvard University Press, forthcoming).

2 See, for example, Marie-Claire Foblets, Luc Leboeuf, and Zeynep Yanasmayan, "Exclusion and Migration: By Whom, Where, When, and How?" Working Paper 190, Max Planck Institute for Social Anthropology Working Papers, 2018, www.eth.mpg.de/pubs/wps/pdf/mpi-eth-working-paper-0190.

(Aiming toward "a more sophisticated understanding of exclusion mechanisms [and] the interdependencies and interactions among the many facets of this comparatively understudied phenomenon. . . [elaborating] a multi-dimensional research framework that rests on analytically separating the exclusion of migrants into six constitutive elements: actors, acts, moments, representations, areas of exclusion, and reactions against exclusion.")

12 Daniel Kanstroom

rather than stabilizes the separation between insider and outsider implied in the concept of state sovereignty (Chapter 12). In addition, transformations—and attempted transformations—of international and human rights law, as well as international initiatives such as the UN-negotiated Global Compact for Safe, Orderly, and Regular Migration and the Global Compact on Refugees, have inspired creative thinking outside the box of traditional categories and traditional conceptions of state sovereignty. Indeed, as Pope Francis has put it, "It is not just about migrants."[3]

Still, problems abound: How should we understand the evolving relationship between, on the one hand, state sovereign power to control migration and, on the other, multinational cooperation regimes and enforcement outsourcing in, for example, Mexico, Libya, or Turkey? Where do state power and responsibility begin and end? How should we describe and evaluate ostensibly voluntary but actually coercive return systems? How should we best calibrate efficiency and procedural justice in deportation regimes? And so on.

This chapter describes two systems in which the traditional categories of migration study—exclusion, admission, and deportation—are blurred in practice. It considers how these mechanisms (one might call them border cases) offer productive ways to reframe critical (that is, both descriptive and normative) analysis. The systems are (1) a fast-track U.S. deportation system known as expedited removal and (2) the expanding global regime of so-called voluntary returns.

II The traditional categories: exclusion, admission, and deportation

Let us begin with a brief structural explication of the traditional categories.

A Exclusion

The first traditional structural characteristic of nation-state migration control is commonly called exclusion. This may be most simply defined as the basic authority of the nation-state to keep "outsiders" out. Its descriptive validity and normative legitimacy derive from a few fundamental premises. The most obvious are the interconnected Westphalian ideas of state sovereignty and territorial control. A related premise is the fundamental differentiation between citizens and noncitizens, often referred to in U.S. law—albeit with pejorative undertones—as "aliens" (Schmiedel, Chapter 12).

The interactions between these premises can be complex, particularly when legal systems recognize that noncitizens have enforceable rights. In the late

---

3 Pope Francis, "Message of His Holiness Pope Francis for the 105th World Day of Migrants and Refugees 2019," *Vatican*, September 29, 2019, vatican.va/content/francesco/en/messages/migration/documents/papa-francesco_20190527_world-migrants-day-2019.html.

Exclusion, admission, and deportation   13

nineteenth century, however, a formalist model of state sovereignty and a rigid approach to the citizen–noncitizen distinction (combined with a generous dollop of racism and cultural chauvinism) led the U.S. Supreme Court to accept apparently *unlimited* and judicially unreviewable state power to exclude certain noncitizens from physical entry onto U.S. territory. This exclusion authority applied even to those who had long been legally resident in the United States but who had left to visit family. As the U.S. Supreme Court put it, in the infamous "Chinese Exclusion Case" of 1889: "That the government of the United States . . . can exclude aliens from its territory is a proposition which we do not think open to controversy. Jurisdiction over its own territory to that extent is an incident of every independent nation."[4]

The Court limned an absolutist conception of sovereign exclusion power that overrode all rights claims: "The power of exclusion of foreigners being an incident of sovereignty . . . the right to its exercise at any time when, in the judgment of the government, the interests of the country require it, *cannot be granted away or restrained on behalf of any one.*"[5] To be sure, the evolution of U.S. constitutional law and the development of international human rights law have rendered such formulations of absolutist exclusion anachronistic, highly problematic, and subject to important qualifications. However, the basic U.S. exclusion model remains rather stark. As the Supreme Court recently reiterated in *Trump v. Hawaii*: "For more than a century, this Court has recognized that the . . . exclusion of foreign nationals is a fundamental sovereign attribute exercised by the Government's political departments *largely immune from judicial control.*"[6]

Even in legal systems where such absolutist models have yielded to more nuanced approaches, exclusion is generally viewed as a nation-state prerogative power. Such power essentially polices the line between here and there, between inside and outside, and, most important, between rights for citizens and no rights for noncitizens. In its strongest forms, this formulation may lead to what Hannah Arendt poignantly and famously denominated as the "calamity of the rightless." This calamity, we should recall, had two distinct features: first, "they no longer belong to any community whatsoever;" and second, "no law exists for them."[7] As the U.S. Supreme Court put it in 1953, "an alien, standing on the threshold of initial entry," lacks even basic due process rights.[8] Thus, exclusion power may imply not only no right to enter state territory, but a more pernicious notion: no right *even to a fair process to determine if one has the right to enter.* A recent U.S.

---

4 *Chae Chan Ping v. United States*, 130 U.S. 581, 603 (1889).

5 Ibid., at 609 (emphasis added).

6 138 S. Ct. 2392 (2018) (emphasis added). The Court recognized, however, that "this Court has engaged in a circumscribed judicial inquiry when the denial of a visa allegedly burdens the constitutional rights of a U.S. citizen."

7 Hannah Arendt, *The Origins of Totalitarianism* (New York: Harcourt, Brace & World, Inc., 1966), 295.

8 See *Shaughnessy v. United States ex rel. Mezei*, 345 U.S. 206, 213-15 (1953).

14 Daniel Kanstroom

Supreme Court decision unfortunately not only affirmed this model but, still worse, applied it internally to asylum seekers.[9]

The threshold of entry has largely been a territorial concept. Physical entry, even if surreptitious, confers certain rights in many legal regimes. U.S. courts, for example, have long held—with some exceptions—that noncitizens on U.S. soil are entitled to (at least some) due process protections: "aliens who have once passed through our gates, even illegally, may be expelled only after proceedings conforming to traditional standards of fairness encompassed in due process of law" (p. 1328).[10] More recently, the Court reiterated, "once an alien enters the country, the legal circumstance changes" because our Constitution provides due process protections "to all 'persons' within the United States, including aliens, whether their presence here is lawful, unlawful, temporary, or permanent."[11] The rationales behind such a distinction are both implicitly normative and related to legally technical aspects of jurisdiction and the significance of physical presence on territory. Very simply put, people who are here have stronger claims, even if they got here without express legal authorization, because they are now physically within our communities. Internal migration enforcement thus differs in principle from external border control. This is in part because it has been understood to more immediately affect communities and the citizens within them. Still, when ostensibly clear categories overlap—like physical presence and legal status—complex legal and normative problems arise. Thus, the United States legal system has never resolved the particular question of *what* process was due to a noncitizen described by the U.S. Supreme Court as a "clandestine entrant" apprehended on U.S. soil near the border soon after entry.[12]

The absolutist notion of state sovereign power to exclude is powerfully challenged by principles of international law. These include the rights of people entitled to special protection, including refugees, asylum seekers, and victims of torture and human trafficking. Protection does not necessarily include a right to be admitted to state territory, however. As Atle Grahl-Madsen once put it, "[t]he right [sic] of a State to grant asylum flows from its territorial integrity, which is a pillar of international law."[13] The traditional view has thus long been that the right of asylum is that of a state *to grant asylum*, not the right of an individual

---

9 *Department of Homeland Security v. Thuraissigiam*, 140 S.Ct. 1959 (2020) (holding that an asylum seeker, though on U.S. soil, has no constitutional right to habeas corpus review in federal court of his claims that the government violated his constitutional, statutory, and regulatory rights). See the discussion of expedited removal below.

10 *United States* ex rel. *Mezei*, at 212. See Daniel Kanstroom, "Expedited Removal and Due Process: A 'Testing Crucible' in the Time of Trump," *Washington and Lee Law Review* 75, no. 3 (2018): 1323–60, at 1328.

11 *Zadvydas v. Davis*, 533 U.S. 678, 693 (2001).

12 *Yamataya v. Fisher*, 189 U.S. 86, 94 (1903).

13 Atle Grahl-Madsen, *Territorial Asylum* (London: Oceana Publications, 1980), 23. See generally Roman Boed, "The State of the Right of Asylum in International Law," *Duke Journal of Comparative & International Law* 5, no. 1 (1994): 1–34.

Exclusion, admission, and deportation 15

to obtain it.[14] Moreover, as Michele R. Pistone poignantly notes in this volume, the current state of refugee and related humanitarian protection regimes is very much a work-in-progress and, in many respects, a work under siege (Chapter 4).

Still, a refugee clearly has rights not to be *either* returned or expelled. Article 33 of the 1951 Convention Relating to the Status of Refugees states, "No Contracting State shall expel or return ('refouler') a refugee *in any manner whatsoever* to the frontiers of territories where his life or freedom would be threatened on account of his race, religion, nationality, membership of a particular social group or political opinion."[15] As Paul Weis put it many years ago, whereas asylum entails "admission, residence and protection," *nonrefoulement* is a "negative duty, not to compel a person to return to a country of persecution" (p. 166).[16] Specific rights against exclusion or expulsion are also recognized by other protective conventions (including regional instruments),[17] and have been interpreted as a part of more general human rights regimes.[18] Indeed, the United Nations High Commissioner for Refugees (UNHCR) broadly defines refugees as "persons who are outside their country of origin for reasons of feared persecution, conflict, *generalized*

---

14 See Guy S. Goodwin-Gill, *The Refugee in International Law* (Oxford: Oxford University Press, 1983), 121 (the "individual . . . has no right to be granted asylum" as the right of asylum "appertains to states"). The American Convention on Human Rights (article 22(7)) does, however, include both the right to seek and be granted asylum. Secretary-General of the Organization of American States, American Convention on Human Rights art. 22(7), July 18, 1978, 1144 U.N.T.S. 123 ("Pact of San José, Costa Rica").
15 Convention Relating to the Status of Refugees art. 33, July 28, 1951, 189 U.N.T.S. 137 (emphasis added). These provisions connect to article 32: "The Contracting States *shall not expel* a refugee lawfully in their territory save on grounds of national security or public order" (emphasis added); and article 34, entitled "Naturalization."
16 Paul Weis, "The Draft United Nations Convention on Territorial Asylum," *British Yearbook of International Law* 50, no. 1 (1979): 151–71, at 166. The U.S. Supreme Court has interpreted the nonrefoulement provision of the Refugee Convention to have no extraterritorial effect. See *Sale v. Haitian Centers Council*, 509 U.S. 155 (1993).
17 See, for example, Convention Governing the Specific Aspects of Refugee Problems in Africa art. III(3), September 10, 1969, 10011 U.N.T.S. 14691 ("OAU Convention"): "No person may be subjected by a member State to measures such as rejection at the frontier, return or expulsion, which should compel him to return to or remain in a territory where his life, physical integrity or liberty would be threatened for the reasons set out in Article 1, paragraphs 1 and 2." See also American Convention on Human Rights art. 22(8), July 18, 1978, 1144 U.N.T.S. 123 ("Pact of San José, Costa Rica"): "In no case may an alien be deported or returned to a country regardless of whether or not it is his country of origin, if in that country his right to life or personal freedom is in danger of being violated because of his race, nationality, religion, social status or political opinions."
18 Other United Nations documents have been interpreted to provide protection from refoulement. See UN General Assembly, Resolution 2200A (XXI), International Covenant on Civil and Political Rights, art. 7 (December 16, 1966); Secretary-General of the Council of Europe, Convention for the Protection of Human Rights and Fundamental Freedoms art. 3, August 11, 1955, 213 U.N.T.S. 221 ("European Convention on Human Rights and Fundamental Freedoms"). See also Convention against Torture and Other Cruel, Inhuman or Degrading Treatment or Punishment art. 3, 1465 U.N.T.S. 85, December 10, 1984 ("1984 Convention Against Torture").

16 Daniel Kanstroom

violence, or other circumstances that . . . require international protection."[19] Nevertheless, state sovereign power to exclude remains the basic norm, and exclusion remains a basic structural concept. Nonrefoulement is an exception that protects against return to *particular places for particularly defined migrants.*[20]

B Admission

As Michael Walzer famously asserted, the "primary good" that we distribute to one another is *membership in some human community.*[21] This brings us to the second venerable structural component of migration control: admission. With this concept—more complex and nuanced than the physical aspects of exclusion and entry—we find a more dialogical relationship between state power and rights claims. Admission marks the *intersection* between state sovereign power and (tacit, qualified, or complete) membership in the polity. States agree—through laws and discretionary policies—to allow certain noncitizens to enter their territory and perhaps to become members of the polity. The criteria of admission vary tremendously among systems around the world. Some prioritize family. Others aim for wealth, education, or job skills. Some privilege religious affiliations, whereas others allow ethnic/racial/cultural connections to count. Moreover, some, indeed most, admissions are denominated temporary, such as visas for tourists, temporary workers, and students.[22]

Once a state admits a noncitizen in any status, it has relinquished (or at least qualified) some of its exclusion power. It has entered into a more complex relationship with the individual that is governed by domestic legal and basic rights protections, as well as by international legal constraints. A person who is admitted is not, however, completely immunized from exclusion (if they leave state territory and seek to return) or deportation if they are accused of transgressing various legal requirements. Indeed, even persons who attain citizenship status through naturalization remain vulnerable to "denaturalization" in certain circumstances,

---

19 "Definitions," *United Nations Refugees and Migrants,* https://refugeesmigrants.un.org/definitions (emphasis added). See also UN High Commissioner for Refugees, Convention Governing the Specific Aspects of Refugee Problems in Africa art. I(2), September 10, 1969, 10011 U.N.T.S. 14691 ("OAU Convention"): a refugee is any person compelled to leave his or her country "owing to external aggression, occupation, foreign domination or events seriously disturbing public order in either part or the whole of his country or origin or nationality." Similarly, the 1984 Cartagena Declaration includes persons who flee their country "because their lives, security or freedom have been threatened by generalised [sic] violence, foreign aggression, internal conflicts, massive violations of human rights or other circumstances which have seriously disturbed public order." Regional Refugee Instruments & Related, Cartagena Declaration on Refugees, Colloquium on the International Protection of Refugees in Central America, Mexico and Panama art. III(3), November 22, 1984 ("1984 Cartagena Declaration").

20 Weis, "The Draft United Nations Convention on Territorial Asylum," at 166.

21 Michael Walzer, *Spheres of Justice* (New York: Basic Books, 1983), 31.

22 8 U.S.C. § 1101(a)(15) (2012).

Exclusion, admission, and deportation 17

in which case they may be retransformed into "aliens" and then subject to exclusion and deportation.[23]

C Deportation

Migration scholars and legal systems commonly distinguish deportation (aka expulsion, removal, etc.) from exclusion. But the two concepts are clearly related. Deportation is a form of internal state power that is largely justified with reference to the legitimacy of external sovereign border control. It may be defined as *the state-sanctioned, ostensibly legal, forced or coerced removal of a migrant from the territory of a state, generally (but not always) to return to one's country of origin.*[24] Deportation applies to many classes of migrants, ranging from the undocumented who have recently crossed the border, to long-term legal residents and even former citizens. In the United Kingdom, for example, one may lose citizenship if the home secretary determines that holding such citizenship is "not conducive to the public good."[25]

In combination with expanding exclusion practices, large-scale deportation systems have become pervasive global phenomena.[26] Fully accurate deportation statistics remain elusive for many reasons.[27] As one leading researcher notes, "attempting to compare deportation figures across so many jurisdictions has produced not just apples and oranges, but a metaphorical fruit salad" (p. 156).[28] Nevertheless, we can reliably discern a general trend of increasing interior deportations and returns since the mid-1980s, especially from the so-called (if vaguely defined) Global North.[29] From 1987 through 2016, the United States, for

23 See Kanstroom, *Deportation World.*
24 Deportations frequently return people to the places from which they most recently came, even if that is not their country of origin.
25 Immigration, Asylum and Nationality Act of 2006, c. 13 (Eng.); Matthew Gibney, "The Deprivation of Citizenship in the United Kingdom: A Brief History," *Immigration, Asylum, and Nationality Law* 28, no. 4 (2014): 326–35.
26 See Kanstroom, *Deportation World.*
27 Some indeterminacy is due to the variation and complexity of deportation systems. U.S. government statistics, for example, distinguish among removals, deportations, and returns. A removal is "the compulsory and confirmed movement of an inadmissible or deportable alien out of the United States." A return is more informal: the "confirmed movement of an inadmissible or deportable alien out of the United States not based on an order of removal." This phrase was used repeatedly in the DHS Yearbook of Immigration Statistics. See, for example, "2018 Yearbook of Immigration Statistics," *U.S. Department of Homeland Security*, October 2019, www.dhs.gov/immigration-statistics/yearbook/2018/table39.
28 Leanne Weber, "Deciphering Deportation Practices Across the Global North," in *The Routledge Handbook on Crime and International Migration*, eds. Sharon Pickering and Julie Ham (New York: Routledge, 2015), 155–78, at 156.
29 See Ines Hasselberg, "Introduction: An Ethnography of Deportation from the UK," in *Enduring Uncertainty: Deportation, Punishment and Everyday Life* (New York: Berghahn Books, 2016), 1–22.

18 *Daniel Kanstroom*

example, coercively deported, removed, and returned some 34 million people.[30] In many years, removals and returns have substantially exceeded the number of people admitted as immigrants to "legal permanent resident status."[31] A significant rise in deportation has also marked much of Europe in recent years, especially if one includes so-called voluntary departures (after apprehension) and assisted returns. These numbers spiked in 2015, reaching a total of some 2 million apprehensions, with some 500,000 people ordered to leave Europe, and more than 200,000 non-EU nationals physically returned to their countries of origin.[32] One finds similar growth in many other countries around the world. In Mexico, for example, some 7,300 people were deported in 1985, while the number exceeded 156,000 in 2015.[33]

Like exclusion, deportation is particularly problematic when it involves those who have been severely harmed or who reasonably fear serious harm if they are returned to the place from which they have fled. As noted above, states may not legally deport any person to a place where there are substantial grounds for believing that he or she would be in danger of being subjected to torture or ill treatment or other serious human rights violations, or where there would be a real risk of such violations.[34] But international practice regarding refugees varies

---

30 "DHS Releases End of Fiscal Year 2016 Statistics," *U.S. Immigration and Customs Enforcement* (press release), www.ice.gov/news/releases/dhs-releases-end-fiscal-year-2016-statistics#wcm-survey-target-id; "2015 Yearbook of Immigration Statistics," *U.S. Department of Homeland Security*, December 2016, www.dhs.gov/yearbook-immigration-statistics.

31 Daniel Kanstroom, *Aftermath: Deportation Law and the New American Diaspora* (New York: Oxford University Press, 2012); see also Adam Goodman, "Nation of Migrants, Historians of Migration," *Journal of American Ethnic History* 34, no. 4 (2015): 7–16, at 7; Adam Goodman, "Mexican Migrants and the Rise of the Deportation Regime, 1942–2014" (PhD diss., University of Pennsylvania, forthcoming): "[T]he United States has granted permanent residency to 41 million people in the postwar period, it has carried out more than 54 million deportations." See also Tom K. Wong, *Rights, Deportation, and Detention in the Age of Immigration Control* (Stanford, CA: Stanford University Press, 2015).

32 Bridget Anderson, Matthew J. Gibney, and Emanuela Paoletti, eds., *The Social, Political and Historical Contours of Deportation* (New York: Springer, 2013); Weber, "Deciphering Deportation Practices Across the Global North," 155–78; Wesley Dockery, "A Look at Deportation Policy in Germany," *Deutsche Welle*, February 9, 2017, www.dw.com/en/a-look-at-deportation-policy-in-germany/a-37475912; Antje Ellermann, "Deportation Outcomes and the Institutional Embeddedness of Immigration Bureaucracies: The Comparative Cases of Germany and the United States," working paper, ECPR Joint Sessions, 2004, https://ecpr.eu/Filestore/PaperProposal/76b5dfb5-b646-4a8c-876a-5ff8a25f0299.pdf.

33 Vladimiro Valdés Montoya, "El Flujo Centroamericano(1) Irregular Con Destino A Los Estados Unidos: La Construcción Social De La Vulnerabilidad," *El Bordo Magazine*, no. 14 (2004), graphic 4, http://uia-foundation.org/wp-content/el-bordo/14/graficas4. php; Rodrigo Dominguez Villegas and Victoria Rietig, Migrants Deported from the United States and Mexico to the Northern Triangle: A Statistical and Socioeconomic Profile (September 2015), 8, www.migrationpolicy.org/research/migrants-deported-united-states-and-mexico-northern-triangle-statistical-and-socioeconomic.

34 Convention against Torture and Other Cruel, Inhuman or Degrading Treatment or Punishment art. 3(1), 1465 U.N.T.S. 85, December 10, 1984 ("1984 Convention Against Torture"). See also UN Office of the High Commissioner, Human Rights, and Global Migration

Exclusion, admission, and deportation   19

greatly. Indeed, many countries, including India, Pakistan, Malaysia, Indonesia, Thailand, and many Middle Eastern countries, are still not parties to the UN convention and protocol that created the international refugee protection regime (Pistone, Chapter 4).

The term "deportation" may also describe various forms of collective expulsion that are denominated as "ethnic cleansing" or genocide. Such practices have long been illegal under international law. However, the reality on the ground is often complicated. Some group expulsions—such as mass removals of migrant workers from Saudi Arabia and Malaysia—may exhibit *ostensible*, if highly contestable, legality (that is, they are grounded in interpretations of state law). Indeed, one of the most salient features of deportation systems is that many harsh practices are generally *deemed* to be legitimate, and perhaps even just.[35] Deportation, like exclusion, is said to return migrants to their "rightful places of residence and in so doing reinforces the current international order's account of where individuals are entitled to be."[36]

Still, deportation frequently raises poignant and fundamental questions about law and human rights. Therefore, a functional and dynamic approach that asks *how, why, and against whom* state power is exercised is both analytically superior and more protective of basic rights than is a formalistic and static model of state sovereignty or territorial control.

Moreover, as noted above, the lines between exclusion and deportation practices have become quite blurry. An array of emerging practices reflects profound ambiguities of law, sovereign power, rights, and territory. Together with other major aspects of migration control regimes—particularly interdiction in international waters and the building of walls—deportation is thus part of an evolving global model of "dynamic sovereignty" that presents compelling legal and moral challenges.[37] For example, deportations increasingly involve supranational entities such as the European Union, bilateral state cooperation, and various extra-territorial mechanisms, such as current U.S. practices that subsidize, advise, and participate in the removal of hundreds of thousands of Central Americans from Mexico.

Contemporary exclusion and deportation regimes also involve more than just formal state power. They often involve private entities, including major private detention centers. Exclusion and deportation are major aspects of global

---

Group, *Principles and Guidelines Supported by Practical Guidance on the Human Rights Protection of Migrants in Vulnerable Situations*, UN Doc. A/HRC/37/50 (March 2018).

35 For a critique, see Daniel Kanstroom, *Deportation Nation: Outsiders in American History* (Cambridge, MA: Harvard University Press, 2007); Matthew J. Gibney, "Is Deportation a Form of Forced Migration?" *Refugee Survey Quarterly* 32, no. 2 (2013): 116–29, at 118.

36 William Walters, "Deportation, Expulsion, and the International Police of Aliens," *Citizenship Studies* 6, no. 3 (2002): 265–92; Gibney, "Is Deportation a Form of Forced Migration?"

37 See Kanstroom, *Deportation World*.

20   *Daniel Kanstroom*

capitalism,[38] components of legal, quasi-legal, and private regimes that recruit—and often exploit and oppress—lower-skilled workers. Even extremely limited economic and legal possibilities inspire desperate migrants to risk harm or death to obtain poor conditions of irregular stay and exploitative work, "as these are likely an improvement compared with their home situation."[39] Put simply, the global story of exclusion, admission, and deportation is often one of systems that are harsh, punitive, arbitrary, anomalous, discriminatory, and disproportionate. In sum, deportation is an ostensibly legitimate legal system, grounded in state sovereignty—and thus related in complex ways to exclusion and admission regimes. But its legitimacy is particularly unstable and tenuous. To see some of the reasons why this is so, let us now examine border cases.

D *Border case 1: expedited removal*

In the United States in recent years, the distinctions among exclusion, admission, and deportation have notably eroded, especially in regard to people who have entered without legal inspection by immigration agents.[40] This is due to a variety of fast-track removal mechanisms.[41] In particular, in 1996, "expedited removal of arriving aliens" became U.S. law. This system was applied first at the border and, over the years, to an increasingly broad category of people ("undocumented noncitizens") within the United States.[42]

Essentially, expedited removal allows agents of the executive branch to remove certain noncitizens quickly and, in many cases, without any legal proceedings in immigration courts or federal courts.[43] It drastically restricts many due process protections. It imposes mandatory detention and essentially eliminates hearings, appeals, and judicial review for many noncitizens caught in the United States without proper documents. (There are some special protections for asylum

---

38 See Tanya Golash-Boza, *Deported: Immigrant Policing, Disposable Labor, and Global Capitalism* (New York: New York University Press, 2015).

39 Paul de Guchteneire, Antoine Pecoud, and Ryszard Cholewinski, eds., *Migration and Human Rights: The United Nations Convention on Migrant Workers' Rights* (Cambridge: Cambridge University Press, 2009), 30.

40 See, generally, Kanstroom, "Expedited Removal and Due Process," 1323.

41 See Marc. R. Rosenblum, "Shifts in the US Immigration Enforcement System," *Hoover Institution*, July 14, 2015, www.hoover.org/research/shifts-us-immigration-enforcement-system. In the 25 years before 1996, just 3 percent of all people expelled from the United States were formally removed, versus 97 percent who were "informally returned," generally without legal consequences.

42 The term "undocumented noncitizens" refers to persons born abroad—technically and pejoratively referred to under federal immigration statutes as "aliens"—who are deemed "inadmissible" under 8 U.S.C. §§ 1182(a)(6)(C) or 1182(a)(7) because they have not received authorization to come into, or remain in, the United States. For a discussion of how borders function beyond the line of territorial demarcation, see Silas W. Allard's chapter in this volume (Chapter 5).

43 American Immigration Council, "A Primer on Expedited Removal," July 22, 2019, www.americanimmigrationcouncil.org/research/primer-expedited-removal.

Exclusion, admission, and deportation 21

seekers). Noncitizens who have been expeditiously removed are barred from returning to the United States for five years.[44]

An intriguing categorical aspect of this system is that it *deems* certain noncitizens on U.S. soil to be both "unadmitted" and "inadmissible."[45] Prior to 1996, a noncitizen denied admission at a border or port of entry was said to be "excluded."[46] The immigration statutes contained specific exclusion grounds and special exclusion procedures. They also contained more formal deportation procedures. The most critical fact as to which procedures applied (with some technical exceptions) was *where one stood* at the time of arrest. Noncitizens who were expelled from the interior were "deported," regardless of whether they had ever been lawfully present and regardless of how long they had been in the United States. This system dovetailed with prevailing constitutional norms, guaranteeing certain due process protections to those in deportation proceedings.

Expedited removal replaced this conceptual dividing line between exclusion and deportation based on physical entry into the territory with a new approach to admission. Persons present in the interior without having been lawfully admitted are now treated like those denied admission at a port of entry and are thus denied the concomitant due process protections.

The expansion of the expedited removal system has been dramatic. From 1997 to 2002, it applied only at ports of entry.[47] The Bush administration then expanded it to a narrowly defined class of noncitizens caught within the United States.[48] In 2004, the Bush administration further expanded the category to include noncitizens who are encountered by an immigration officer within 100 air miles of the U.S. southwest land border, and who cannot show that they have been physically present in the United States continuously for the 14-day period immediately preceding the date of encounter.[49] In 2006, expedited removal was then further expanded to apply within 100 miles of *all* U.S. borders, and to "illegal alien families" apprehended in areas along the nation's southern, northern, and coastal borders.[50]

Judicial acquiescence, political forces, and efficiency norms have all played roles in the expansion of expedited removal. From a start of 23,242 in 1997, numbers rose steadily over time. In 2016, of some 240,255 removals conducted by

---

44 8 U.S.C. § 1182(a)(9)(A)(i) (2012).
45 Those who had arrived by sea but who had not been physically and continuously present in the country for two years prior to apprehension. See 8 U.S.C. § 1182(6)(A)(i).
46 See David A. Martin, "Two Cheers for Expedited Removal in the New Immigration Rules," *Virginia Journal of International Law* 40, no. 2 (2000): 673–704, at 689.
47 Alison Siskin and Ruth Ellen Wasem, "Immigration Policy on Expedited Removal of Aliens," *Congressional Research Service*, September 30, 2005, http://trac.syr.edu/immigration/library/P13.pdf.
48 Notice Designating Aliens Subject to Expedited Removal Under Section 235(b)(1)(A)(iii) of the Immigration and Nationality Act, 67 Fed. Reg. 68,924, 68,924 (November 13, 2002) (codified at 8 C.F.R. 235.3(b)(1)(ii) (2017)).
49 Siskin and Wasem, "Immigration Policy on Expedited Removal," 2.
50 Ibid., 6–7.

22 Daniel Kanstroom

Immigration and Customs Enforcement (ICE), 174,923 were removals of individuals "apprehended at or near the border or ports of entry," almost 73 percent of all removals.[51] These trends seem likely to continue. Indeed, the Trump administration sought to apply this system everywhere in the United States to any person who cannot prove "to the satisfaction of an immigration officer" that they have been present in the United States for more than two years.[52] Moreover, in a 2020 decision that will undoubtedly have dreadful consequences, the Supreme Court ruled that a Sri Lankan asylum seeker, on U.S. soil, has no constitutional right to habeas corpus review in federal court of his claims that the government violated his constitutional, statutory, and regulatory rights.[53]

Expedited removal raises major concerns about due process and other rights because arrest, detention, and ultimately removal with a five-year ban on return are all in the hands of executive agents. In most cases, a person subject to expedited removal is detained, has no right to counsel, often has no time to communicate with family members or to seek legal counsel, and has no right to appeal. Yet courts have largely acquiesced.[54] As one judge laconically put it in 2014, "[t]he expedited removal statutes are express and unambiguous. The clarity of the language forecloses acrobatic attempts at interpretation."[55] Other courts have similarly declined to intervene due to jurisdictional impediments. As one court noted in 2010:

> The troubling reality of the expedited removal procedure is that a CBP [Customs and Border Protection] officer can create the . . . charge . . . then that same officer, free from the risk of judicial oversight, can . . . find the person guilty of that charge . . . without any check on whether the person understood the proceedings, had an interpreter, or enjoyed any other safeguards.

---

51 U.S. Immigration and Customs Enforcement, "Fiscal Year 2016 Ice Enforcement and Removal Operations Report," 11, www.ice.gov/sites/default/files/documents/Report/2016/removal-stats-2016.pdf. Of these, some 94 percent were apprehended by U.S. Border Patrol agents and then processed, detained, and removed by ICE. Ibid., 11n4.

52 Designating Aliens for Expedited Removal, 84 Fed. Reg. 35,409, 35,409 (July 23, 2019), www.federalregister.gov/documents/2019/07/23/2019-15710/designating-aliens-for-expedited-removal. The proposed expansion was enjoined temporarily by a federal court. *Make the Road, New York, et al., v. McAleenan, et al.,* US District Court for the District of Columbia, Case 1:19cv-02369-KBJ, September 27, 2019, www.aclu.org/legal-document/order-0. But this injunction was subsequently overturned. *See Make the Road New York v. Wolf,* 962 F.3d 612 (D.C. Cir. 2020).

53 *Department of Homeland Security v. Thuraissigiam,* 140 S. Ct. 1959 (2020). See also *Make the Road New York v. Wolf,* 962 F.3d 612, 618 (D.C. Cir. 2020) (upholding the expansion of expedited removal as within the DHS Secretary's "sole and unreviewable discretion").

54 See Apprehension and Deportation of Aliens, Pub. L. No. 104–132, 110 Stat. 1275, 1277, 1279 (1996) (codified as amended at 8 U.S.C. § 1252 (2012)).

55 *Rodriguez v. U.S. Customs & Border Protection,* 2014 WL 4675182, at *2 (W.D. La. September 18, 2014), *vacated by Diaz-Rodriguez v. Holder,* 2014 WL 10965184 (5th Cir. December 16, 2014).

Still, the court concluded,

> To say that this procedure is fraught with risk of arbitrary, mistaken, or discriminatory behavior . . . is not, however, to say that courts are free to disregard jurisdictional limitations.[56]

We are thus left with a system that implicates the particular normative concerns of deportation—fast-track removal of persons from within our communities—while benefitting from categorical analogies to exclusion and admission: the persons who are deported are deemed to be, in effect, applicants for admission standing at the border.

E Border case 2: "voluntary" returns and self-deportation

Force and coercion are of course conceptually central to all exclusion and deportation regimes. However, some forms of deportation are now called voluntary, a label that, if accepted, might free government and government agents from much moral and legal responsibility. The question of voluntariness thus compels one to grapple with both definitional and, ultimately, normative questions about exclusion and deportation. Given space limitations, my purpose here is simply to highlight and frame this issue as exemplifying—like expedited removal—the inevitably normative aspects of categorical labeling.

The International Organization for Migration (IOM) distinguishes voluntary return from forced return. Voluntary return is "[t]he assisted or independent return to the country of origin, transit or another country based on the voluntary decision of the returnee."[57] Voluntary returns can be either "spontaneous" or "assisted." A spontaneous return is "[t]he voluntary, independent return of a migrant or a group of migrants to their country of origin, usually without the support of States or other international or national assistance."[58] Assisted voluntary return is the "[a]dministrative, logistical, financial and reintegration support to rejected asylum seekers, victims of trafficking in human beings, stranded migrants, qualified nationals and other migrants unable or unwilling to remain in the host country who volunteer to return to their countries of origin."[59] When return programs involve additional reintegration support for returnees, these programs are referred to as assisted voluntary return and reintegration (AVRR). On the other hand, forced return is defined as "The act of returning an individual, against his or her will, to the country of origin, transit or to a third country that

---

56 *Khan v. Holder*, 608 F.3d 325, 329 (7th Cir. 2010).
57 International Organization for Migration, *Glossary on Migration* (Geneva: International Organization for Migration, 2019), 229, https://publications.iom.int/system/files/pdf/iml_34_glossary.pdf.
58 Ibid., 205.
59 Ibid., 12–13.

24   Daniel Kanstroom

agrees to receive the person, generally carried out on the basis of an administrative or judicial act or decision."[60]

Voluntary returns implicate *both* the most coercive aspects of the contemporary nation-state *and* the humanitarian aspirations of human-rights agencies. Indeed, in 1992, Sadako Ogata, then UN High Commissioner for Refugees, declared the 1990s the "Decade of Repatriation."[61] A 1996 handbook published by the UN High Commissioner for Refugees averred that "voluntary repatriation" was viewed as "*the most desirable long-term solution* by the refugees themselves as well as by the international community."[62]

IOM's mandate itself reflects these inherent tensions. IOM is "dedicated to promoting humane and orderly migration for the benefit of all." It works for the "orderly and humane management of migration," and it promotes "international cooperation on migration issues."[63] However, IOM also implements well-funded, multifaceted AVRR programs. AVRR is defended as "an indispensable part of a comprehensive approach to migration management aiming at orderly and humane return and reintegration of migrants *who are unable or unwilling to remain* in host countries and wish to return voluntarily to their countries of origin."[64] The size and growth of the program—begun in 1979—have been dramatic. Of some 1.4 million people repatriated since 1979, more than 412,000 were "voluntarily" returned in the past ten years (about 40,000 per year).[65] In 2015, the 81,681 so-called voluntary returns of migrants (including failed asylum seekers) from EU countries exceeded the number of forced returns (72,473).[66]

Though such repatriations may sometimes derive from a bona fide commitment to human rights and humanitarian solutions, we must critically examine the implicit assumptions that have marked this trend. Such framings of voluntariness

---

60 Ibid., 77.
61 Sadako Ogata, "Statement by Mrs. Sadako Ogata, United Nations High Commissioner for Refugees, at the International Management Symposium, St. Gallen, Switzerland, 25 May 1992," May 25, 1992, transcript, www.unhcr.org/en-us/admin/hcspeeches/3ae68faec/statement-mrs-sadako-ogata-united-nations-high-commissioner-refugees-international.html; see also Saul Takahashi, "The UNHCR Handbook on Voluntary Repatriation: The Emphasis of Return over Protection," *International Journal of Refugee Law* 9, no. 4 (1997): 593–612.
62 *UNHCR Handbook: Voluntary Repatriation* (Geneva: United Nations High Commissioner for Refugees, 1996), preface (emphasis added), www.unhcr.org/en-us/publications/legal/3bfe68d32/handbook-voluntary-repatriation-international-protection.html. This is also reflected in the emphasis on durable solutions. As the *UNHCR Handbook* says, "The purpose of international protection is not, however, that a refugee remain a refugee forever, but to ensure the individual's renewed membership of a community and the restoration of national protection, either in the homeland or through integration elsewhere." Ibid.
63 "About IOM," *International Organization for Migration*, www.iom.int/about-iom.
64 Ibid. (emphasis added).
65 "Assisted Voluntary Return and Reintegration," *International Organization for Migration*, www.iom.int/assisted-voluntary-return-and-reintegration.
66 "2015 Global Migration Trends Fact Sheet," *IOM's Global Migration Data Analysis Centre*, February 2017, http://gmdac.iom.int/global-migration-trends-factsheet.

may have pragmatic benefits. But they may also imply acceptance of the legitimacy of many troubling features of contemporary migration, including the Westphalian state system itself; vast global wealth disparities; the inevitability of forced migration resulting from wars, persecution, and climate change, among other factors; and the prevalence of large exclusion and deportation systems. Such understandings of voluntariness also often acquiesce to—rather than confront—troubling political trends. In Europe, for example, the surging number of asylum seekers in recent years has spawned not only general public dissatisfaction with EU and government responses (over 90 percent disapproval in Greece, for example) but also strong general support for deportation systems of various types.[67] Many people who participate in so-called voluntary return clearly have little choice other than to accept the deal.

Another ostensibly voluntary phenomenon related to deportation is much harder to defend. Some nation-states (and, in the United States, states such as Arizona and Alabama) have undertaken to impose harsh conditions of life on noncitizens to induce "self-deportation," a policy once described by William Safire as "make'em so miserable that they leave the country."[68] Similar strategies are called "attrition through enforcement." Such laws have included attempts to forbid undocumented noncitizens from participating in the basics of economic life, such as renting housing or engaging in business. Xenophobic mob violence, often in cooperation with demagogic leaders and with government authorities, is also a feature of some deportation regimes. In a particularly brutal example, Ethiopian migrant workers in Saudi Arabia told Human Rights Watch researchers in 2015 that they were attacked during a government deportation campaign by groups armed with sticks, swords, machetes, and firearms.[69] Similar episodes have been reported around the world, from Hungary to South Africa, from the Dominican Republic to Kuwait, from Greece to Myanmar. When migrants flee from such systems, one can hardly describe such flight as "voluntary."

In sum, the label of voluntariness often obscures the brute structural power that undergirds the traditional approaches to exclusion, admission, and deportation. It relieves governments and legal systems from grappling with harder, more nuanced normative questions about the right relationship between power and rights.

---

67 See, for example, Bruce Stokes, "Euroskepticism Beyond Brexit," *Pew Research Center*, June 7, 2016, www.pewresearch.org/global/2016/06/07/euroskepticism-beyond-brexit/; see also Ana Gonzalez-Barrera and Phillip Connor, "Around the World, More Say Immigrants Are a Strength Than a Burden," *Pew Research Center*, March 14, 2019, www.pewresearch.org/global/2019/03/14/around-the-world-more-say-immigrants-are-a-strength-than-a-burden/. Majorities in most immigrant destination countries surveyed support the deportation of people who are in their countries illegally.

68 William Safire, "Essay: Self-Deportation?" *New York Times*, November 21, 1994, A15, www.nytimes.com/1994/11/21/opinion/essay-self-deportation.html.

69 Human Rights Watch, "Detained, Beaten, and Deported: Saudi Abuses Against Migrations During Mass Expulsions," May 10, 2015, www.hrw.org/report/2015/05/10/detained-beaten-deported/saudi-abuses-against-migrants-during-mass-expulsions.

III Why (and how) to care?

Let me therefore conclude with two most basic questions, to which I will offer tacit answers in the hope of developing further dialogue. The first question is *why* should "we" (by which I mean, in particular, we who are privileged to be citizens of wealthy countries), be concerned about the normative (and the obscuring categorical) problems of exclusion, admission, and deportation? After all, one might say, the very nature of the citizen–noncitizen dichotomy works to insulate one side of this divide from many of the travails of the other.

The most fundamental answers to this question derive from deeply held prior commitments of a moral or, for many, a religious nature. We must, first of all, not accept the citizen–noncitizen line as a wall between those who have rights and those who do not. Simply put, they are we, and we are they. As Pope Francis has powerfully intoned, "It's not just about migrants, but about all of us."[70] From this premise, we achieve something even more powerful than empathy for those who face the frequent harsh consequences of contemporary exclusion, detention, and deportation policies (though empathy is of course a powerful force.) We achieve a deep sense of identity, fraternity, and solidarity. This makes it quite obvious why we should reject "the myth of a progress that benefits a few while built on the exploitation of many."[71]

But law and critical politico-legal discourses also help us to appreciate other, more technical and pragmatic modes of *how* to care. The excluded and deported face a welter of harms, stigma, and legal vulnerabilities upon return, the full scope of which is only beginning to be understood by human-rights activists and researchers.[72] For example, we should think about the implications of categorizing exclusion and deportation as civil, rather than criminal or punitive, regimes. Though often defined by law as a civil mechanism, deportation in particular can be quite punitive in many different ways.[73] Deportation separates families and causes disproportionate hardships. Many of the deported, especially in the United States, are long-term residents with strong family and community ties. Indeed, in recent years, the United States has annually deported approximately 100,000 parents of U.S. citizens.[74] Many, perhaps most, such people have no ties

---

70 Francis, "Message of His Holiness Pope Francis for the 105th World Day of Migrants and Refugees 2019."

71 Ibid.

72 See, for example, Daniel Kanstroom and Jessica Chicco, "The Forgotten Deported: A Declaration on the Rights of Expelled and Deported Persons," *New York University Journal of International Law and Politics* 47, no. 3 (2015): 537–92; Kanstroom, *Aftermath*.

73 See *Fong Yue Ting v. United States*, 149 US 698 (1893) (defining deportation as civil); cf. *Wayne Smith, Hugo Armendariz, et al. v. United States*, Inter-Am. Ct. H.R. (ser. C) No. 81/10, ¶ 5 (July 12, 2010) (describing harsh effects of "civil" deportation).

74 U.S. Department of Homeland Security, "Deportation of Parents of U.S.—Born Citizens," in "Fiscal Year 2011 Report to Congress" (2012); U.S. Department of Homeland Security, "Deportation of Parents of U.S.—Born Children, First Semi-Annual Calendar Year 2013," in "Fiscal Year 2013 Report to Congress" (2014).

whatsoever in the "home" countries to which they are sent.[75] Their job prospects there are bleak; they may not even speak the language, and they are routinely ostracized.[76] In many cases, deportation transforms its targets from members of communities into outcasts without rights, analogous, per Giorgio Agamben, to *homo sacer*: beyond meaningfully protective law, and, for many, beyond political, social, or linguistic community.[77] Others, though they may be seeking entry or be more recent border-crossers, often face profoundly punitive harms from exclusion, strict admission policies, and deportation. These harms include torture and persecution, in addition to desperate poverty, disease, crime, violence, and corruption.

The harms suffered by migrants are often also procedural. Certain government actions against them may have deep implications for the legitimacy of our legal systems and may serve as worrisome or dangerous precedents for other legal arenas. Expedited removal is a classic example. It began as a limited experiment at the border. It has now metastasized far beyond that, applied by the Trump administration throughout the United States to a vast array of people.

Critically rethinking the categories of migration, in sum, allows us to grapple more precisely with fundamental questions, including:

- Should noncitizens caught at the threshold of state territory or migrants who enter or remain in states without the states' consent have rights that those states must respect, especially rights regarding expulsion?
- Can contemporary exclusion and deportation practices be reconciled with the Universal Declaration of Human Rights principle that all human beings are born "free and equal in dignity and rights" and with the Declaration's aspiration to treat noncitizens with "humanity and with respect for the inherent dignity of the human person"?[78]

In sum, exclusion, admission, and deportation as currently understood and as implemented are highly problematic structural components of the global migration system. They implicate much more than abstract Westphalian ideas of state sovereignty and immigration status. They must therefore be critically challenged with analytic precision and normative principle.

Around the world, exclusion and deportation—*as ideas and as systems*— challenge our deepest moral, ethical, legal, and political principles. In many of

---

75 See, generally, Kanstroom, *Aftermath*.
76 See, generally, Ibid.; Anda M. David, "Back to Square One: Socioeconomic Integration of Deported Migrants," *International Migration Review* 51, no. 1 (2018): 127–54.
77 See Giorgio Agamben, *Homo Sacer: Sovereign Power and Bare Life*, trans. Daniel Heller-Roazen (Stanford, CA: Stanford University Press, 1998), 72; Nicholas De Genova and Nathalie Peutz, eds., The Deportation Regime: Sovereignty, Space, and the Freedom of Movement (Durham, NC: Duke University Press, 2010).
78 UN General Assembly Resolution 217A (III), preamble, Universal Declaration of Human Rights, December 10, 1948.

28 Daniel Kanstroom

their prevalent forms they corrode the best ideals of law itself. This is a harsh irony, as proponents of exclusion and deportation regularly cite the rule of law in support of deportation. But the ease with which such laws may be implemented against noncitizen "outsiders"—along with their immense power and flexibility—put tremendous pressure on structural and rights protections within legal systems.

Though sometimes described as a natural, inherent power (or a "right") of national sovereignty, exclusion and deportation are never value neutral. Such laws do more than allow governments to do things to noncitizens that would be much more problematic were they done to citizens. They also tend to support strict compliance with binary, technical legal norms, regulation of demography by race and ethnicity, bureaucratic control of movement, surveillance of foreigners, and ethnic and cultural stasis. They invariably conflict with such values as humanitarian discretion, proportionality, antidiscrimination, antiarbitrariness, social dynamism, and pluralism.

Moreover, in wealthy Western countries, these systems function typically as legal mechanisms of power and control over marginalized outsiders, primarily poor people of color. There is simply no way to think seriously and capaciously about exclusion and deportation without also considering their relationship—*conceptually, as dynamic practice, and as a legal, bureaucratized structure*—to deep questions of power, law, rights, politics, ethics, and morality. Such thinking allows us to escape formalist categories of state power and thus to better appreciate the wisdom of Hermann Cohen's famous (if perhaps apocryphal) aphorism: "*In the alien, therefore, man discovered the idea of humanity.*"[79]

Suggested Reading

Aleinikoff, T. Alexander. *Semblances of Sovereignty: The Constitution, The State, and American Citizenship.* Cambridge, MA: Harvard University Press, 2002.

Benhabib, Seyla. *The Rights of Others: Aliens, Residents and Citizens.* The Seeley Lectures. Cambridge: Cambridge University Press, 2004.

Motomura, Hiroshi. *Immigration Outside the Law.* Oxford: Oxford University Press, 2014.

Neuman, Gerald. *Strangers to the Constitution: Immigrants, Borders, and Fundamental Law.* Princeton: Princeton University Press, 1996.

Ngai, Mae M. *Impossible Subjects: Illegal Aliens and the Making of Modern America.* Princeton, NJ: Princeton University Press, 2004.

---

79 The quote comes from Joseph H. H. Weiler, "Thou Shalt Not Oppress a Stranger: On the Judicial Protection of the Human Rights of Non-EC Nationals—A Critique," *European Journal of International Law* 3, no. 1 (1992): 65. Weiler quotes from *The Pentateuch and Haftorahs: Hebrew Text, English Translation and Commentary*, ed. J. H. Hertz, 2nd ed. (London: Soncino Press, 1980), 313, where the quotation is attributed to Cohen. For Cohen's thought on the stranger, see Hermann Cohen, *Religion of Reason: Out of the Sources of Judaism*, trans. Simon Kaplan (Atlanta: Scholars Press, 1995), chapter 8; see also, Cohen, "Die Nächstenliebe im Talmud: Als in Gutachten dem Königlichen Landgerichte zu Marburg ersttatet," in *Jüdische Schriften*, ed. Bruno Strauss (Berlin: C. A. Schwetschke, 1924), 1:145–50.

2 The institutionalization of inequality

Lower-skilled and undocumented workers in immigration law

Enid Trucios-Haynes

I Introduction

In 2018, nearly two-thirds of the world's 272 million immigrants were workers.[1] The movement of immigrant workers is highly regulated by complex national systems of immigration law that determine what kinds of jobs, education, or experience allow a worker to immigrate—referred to throughout this chapter as labor migration or immigration law systems. These labor migration systems rely on the categorization and stratification of labor, inevitably privileging some immigrants while devaluing others. Furthermore, the underlying principles of many labor migration systems are disconnected from international human rights norms, such as equality, nondiscrimination, and fair treatment, creating systemic inequality and failing to respect the dignity of workers.

Labor stratification in immigration law is connected with and produces social discrimination against immigrant workers. Discrimination against lower-skilled immigrant workers pervades destination countries. Even in countries where immigrant workers can transition to permanent residence, such as the United States, workers face challenges to transition from their perceived status as "disposable" lower-skilled workers to long-term community members. Immigrant workers in lower-skilled and lower-wage jobs find themselves locked in the least regulated industries, working in so-called 3D jobs, defined as dirty, dangerous, and demeaning.[2]

Immigrant workers experience discrimination on multiple grounds, such as race, ethnicity, religion, and nationality. The International Labour Organization has emphasized the importance of taking specific steps to combat the xenophobia and social and cultural stereotypes that contribute to employment discrimination

---

1 International Organization for Migration, *World Migration Report 2020* (Geneva: International Organization for Migration, 2019), 2, www.un.org/sites/un2.un.org/files/wmr_2020.pdf.

2 International Labour Organization, *Labour Migration in Latin America and the Caribbean. Diagnosis, Strategy and ILO's work in the Region* (Peru: ILO Regional Office for Latin America and the Caribbean, International Labour Organization, 2017), 16, www.ilo.org/americas/publicaciones/WCMS_548185/lang-en/index.htm; *World Migration Report 2020*, 173.

30 Enid Trucios-Haynes

against immigrants.[3] In the United States, this labor market segregation and economic disadvantages can result in intergenerational discrimination against the U.S.–citizen children of lower-skilled immigrant workers.[4]

Legal stratification and social discrimination, in turn, create the conditions for the labor market segregation and employment discrimination of lower-skilled workers,[5] who become locked into 3D industries. Nonstate actors of the global migration infrastructure can reinforce inequality, sustain the lack of access to mobility, and deepen the exploitation of poor, lower-skilled people, including contract workers (prevalent in Asia and the Middle East), guest workers (often in Europe and in U.S. agriculture), and undocumented workers (irregular migrants) lacking any immigration status.

Although labor migration also involves people working in another country as managers and executives, scientific researchers, and entertainers, these higher-skilled workers may position themselves as a different kind of immigrant worker. Often referred to as expatriates, to distinguish among labor immigrants, these immigrant workers are privileged in labor migration systems and are less constrained by the global migration infrastructure.[6]

Labor market segregation, then, justifies legal stratification and perpetuates social discrimination. In other words, these three phenomena of stratification, discrimination, and segregation create a mutually reinforcing cycle that results in vulnerability and exploitation of immigrant workers, particularly those deemed lower-skilled. Examining this cycle and its impact on vulnerable immigrant workers, this chapter proposes that an action agenda will resonate most widely if it is premised on core Christian values, a transformational Christian ethics, and a Christian praxis focused on advocacy that centers on the dignity and equality

---

3 International Labour Organization, *Addressing Governance Challenges, in a Changing Labour Migration Landscape* (Geneva: International Labour Organization, 2017), 23, International Labour Conference, 106th Session, April 10, 2017.

4 Jeanne Batalova, Brittany Blizzard, and Jessica Bolter, "Frequently Requested Statistics on Immigrants and Immigration in the United States," *Migration Policy Institute*, February 14, 2020, https://www.migrationpolicy.org/article/frequently-requested-statistics-immigrants-and-immigration-united-states-2019.

5 The higher-/lower-skill dichotomy in the labor stratification of many immigration systems does not account for the multiplicity of external factors that motivate migration, such as unequal access to global mobility for many, or whether the categorical boundaries adequately respond to the current situations of people on the move. The categories also are inaccurate in terms of the knowledge, expertise, and experience of workers. As Bill Ong Hing points out, the distinction is insulting to workers whose occupations demand "a level of ability that requires cultivation and experience" (Chapter 3). The implicit value judgment of these constructed categories itself justifies the exclusion of lower-skilled workers because states adopt policies focused on attracting "desirable" higher-skilled workers. While these terms are endemic to the discussion, they should be recognized as inadequate and demeaning.

6 Sophie Cranston, "Expatriate as 'Good' Migrant: Thinking Through Skilled International Migrant Categories," *Population, Space and Place* 23, no. 6 (2017): e2058, 1–13, at 1, doi:10.1002/psp.2058.

The institutionalization of inequality   31

of all immigrant workers, regardless of their immigration status. The values and praxis drawn from Christian theology and ethics could combine with the new global consensus about incorporating immigrants' human rights into state legal systems. The promise of this social justice advocacy is to break the cycle of stratification, discrimination, and segregation.

II Legal stratification: the example of U.S. immigration law

Globally, immigration law systems operate in tandem with exclusionary practices in destination countries in ways that violate the human rights of vulnerable workers. Lower-skilled immigrant workers are segregated into less regulated industries worldwide. This includes both those with protected immigration status and undocumented immigrants. Immigration law systems reinforce labor market segregation by creating significant barriers to entry and to legal protections. The U.S. system offers an example of this layered inequality. Inequality in the U.S. immigrant labor system is created by extreme differentiation in the immigration opportunities for those categorized as higher-skilled and lower-skilled workers. This differentiation reinforces employment discrimination and other forms of abuse and exploitation of vulnerable immigrant workers. The legal system offers reduced opportunities for lower-skilled workers to transition to permanent resident status open to higher-skilled workers, and it incorporates procedures that violate the principles of fundamental fairness and nondiscrimination.

The categories and preferences in the U.S. labor migration system, as with any immigration program, represent an assessment of the positive or negative effect of immigrant workers on the economic productivity and prosperity of the destination country.[7] Legal barriers that exclude lower-skilled workers also reflect longstanding attitudes, whether based in fact or not, about harmful economic competition, perceived integration challenges based on the race, religion, and culture of prospective workers, and concerns about the impact of global trade on U.S. workers.

The U.S. immigration system uses a two-tier visa system, with one tier for permanent residence (immigrant visas) and another for temporary admissions (nonimmigrant visas). The permanent resident tier dedicates five visa categories to family reunification and five to employment, many with several subcategories.[8] The vast majority of people, however, come to the United States for short, temporary visits under 1 of the 22 temporary visa categories. These temporary visas generally cover family members awaiting a permanent resident visa; long-term employment and business; education in the United States; and survivors

---

7 Immigration and Nationality Act (INA), Pub. L. No. 82–414, 66 Stat. 163 (1952). In 1952, Congress codified immigration law in the INA, which is the basis of current immigration and citizenship laws.
8 INA §§ 203 (a),(b).

32 Enid Trucios-Haynes

of violence.[9] Temporary, long-term work visas are available for individuals with a baccalaureate degree or its equivalent working in jobs requiring such a degree (H-1B); nurses working in shortage areas (H-1C); employment trainees (H-3); intracompany transferees who are managers, executives, or workers with proprietary specialized knowledge (L); individuals with "outstanding" ability, including athletes, entertainers, and performers (O & P); investors or traders working in the United States under a U.S. bilateral treaty with their home country (E); Canadians, Mexicans, and others covered by multilateral free trade agreements (TN); cultural exchange workers (Q); religious workers (R); foreign diplomats (A); and press representatives (I). Other nonimmigrant visa categories may provide limited work authorization for students (F) and exchange visitors (J).

Despite these numerous employment categories, lower-skilled workers have very limited immigration opportunities for *either* temporary admission or permanent residence. Only two, very limited, temporary employment categories are available for lower-skilled work, defined as occupations requiring two years or less of work experience. These categories include agricultural workers (H-2A) and people performing seasonal or intermittent work in other industries (H-2B), often in landscaping and construction.[10] Both visas include a labor market test to certify that no U.S. workers are available and generally permit residence for less than one year. The seasonal/intermittent work category has a numerical limit of 66,000 visas annually, and the cumbersome hiring process requires approvals by the U.S. Department of Labor and the U.S. Department of Homeland Security. These systemic limits on temporary visas for lower-skilled workers often leave unauthorized entry as the only available pathway, creating a subclass of workers who are often poor, living at the margins as a shadow population, and exploited due to their lack of immigration status.

Agricultural workers have some labor protections in the H-2A guestworker program. The Department of Labor establishes a state-by-state minimum wage, and the law requires that employers provide housing, meals or cooking facilities, return transportation, and workers' compensation insurance or its equivalent. Any worker who violates the terms or remains in the United States beyond the approved stay is barred from the program for five years. As a practical matter, these limitations on both employers and workers shift workers into undocumented status because of the complexities of both H-2 temporary labor programs.

By comparison, higher-skilled workers seeking temporary admission may receive an H-1B Specialty Occupation temporary work visa for professionals with college degrees.[11] These temporary work visas are available for up to six years, and there are two corresponding permanent resident worker categories. Amendments

---

9 INA §§ 101(a)(15) (A)-(V).
10 INA § 101(a)(15)(H)(2). Temporary agricultural work may last no longer than one year, except in extraordinary circumstances. For other intermittent or seasonal workers, the employment position must end "in the near, definable future," generally "a period limited to one year or less." 8 C.F.R. §§ 214.2(h)(5)(iv)(A), 214.2(h)(6)(ii).
11 INA § 101(a)(15)(H)(1)(b).

The institutionalization of inequality 33

to the law in 1990 capped the annual number of H-1B visas at 65,000, leading to ongoing frustrations of U.S. business interests because the demand for H-1B visas has far exceeded supply. In recent years, the H-1B visa caps were reached within days of becoming available on the first day of the fiscal year. There are regular calls either to increase the number (particularly from the information technology industry) or to reduce it because of claims of unfair competition with U.S. workers.[12]

The U.S. system, unlike many other state systems, provides a pathway to permanent residence for immigrant workers. In the U.S. this pathway privileges higher-skilled immigrant workers, and effectively is nonexistent for lower-skilled workers.[13] The permanent resident categories also offer a coveted path to U.S. citizenship. Higher-skilled workers fall into five employment categories: (1) priority workers, including managers and executives, as well as individuals with "extraordinary" abilities in the sciences, arts, education, business, athletics, and research; (2) individuals with advanced degrees (equivalent to a U.S. master's degree); (3) individuals with baccalaureate degrees, skilled workers, and "other" (lower-skilled) workers; (4) special immigrants, a category that includes religious workers, abandoned and neglected children, and Afghan and Iraqi translators, among others; and (5) business investors. The 1990 amendments to the permanent resident categories increased the annual visas for employment categories to 140,000 and, at the same time, severely limited the number of visas for lower-skilled "other" workers to 10,000.

Labor stratification is further reproduced in the opportunities or constraints in converting a temporary work visa to a permanent resident visa. For privileged workers, the labor migration system provides a seamless path and limited wait-times for permanent residence. For example, the transition is facilitated if the temporary worker visa provides sufficient time to complete the permanent residence process while working in the United States. The permanent residence application process can be time-consuming, involving an employer's petition for the permanent visa with a labor market test as the first step. The process may include significant delays caused by backlogs in visa availability for different categories and different nationalities. For some higher-skilled workers, the extended period for the H-1B temporary work visa generally provides enough time to complete the permanent residence process and move onto the pathway to citizenship.

The L-1 temporary work category offers another example of the seamless path open to higher-skilled workers.[14] It is available to multinational managers and executives who were employed abroad by a company for at least three years.

---

12 Stuart Anderson, "H-1B Visas All Gone For 16th Straight Year," *Forbes Magazine*, April 23, 2018, www.forbes.com/sites/stuartanderson/2018/04/23/h-1b-visas-all-gone-for-16th-straight-year/#1c7ebbd56b04.

13 INA § 202 (annual allocation of employment permanent resident visas).

14 L-1 nonimmigrant visas for multinational business managers and executives are under INA § 101(a)(15)(L), and immigrant (permanent resident) visas are available, generally without a visa backlog, for multinational business managers and executives under INA § 203(b)(1)(A).

34　*Enid Trucios-Haynes*

Managers and executives must manage other employees or direct a function of the organization before and after the transfer. There are no numerical limits on L-1 temporary work visas, which are available for managers and executives for up to seven years, providing more than enough time to process a permanent resident application. The transition to a permanent resident visa is further eased for these managers and executives by a parallel permanent resident category for "priority workers," which rarely has significant, if any, backlogs.

In contrast, lower-skilled workers face numerous, often insurmountable, road-blocks in seeking employment-based permanent residence. There is no long-term temporary work visa, such as the L-1 or H-1B visa, for lower-skilled work, and therefore no pathway from a temporary work category to a permanent residence category. Further, the "other" worker category is exceptionally limited, and the number of annual visas available was reduced from 10,000 visas worldwide to 5,000 since 1999. This reduction was designed to allocate visas to certain unsuccessful asylum seekers from El Salvador, Guatemala, and former communist countries in Europe—thereby pitting asylum seekers against lower-skilled workers.[15]

Clearly, lower-skilled workers have no meaningful path to seek a permanent residence visa, while they face significant limitations on temporary work visas; thus, many lower-skilled immigrant workers are undocumented. While labor stratification has driven a growth in undocumented workers, Congress has responded by further penalizing undocumented immigration. In 1996, Congress for the first time enacted a ban on unlawful presence in the United States. This dramatic shift made unauthorized presence in the country for more than one year punishable by a ten-year bar to reentry.[16] This change, disproportionately impacting Latinx immigrants, was a major departure from prior policy, which regulated employers rather than vulnerable workers. Before 1996, a person with periods of unauthorized presence in the United States could become a permanent resident by meeting the criteria for either an employment or a family visa. Today, many immigrant workers who satisfy these criteria are ineligible merely because of their unauthorized presence, except in limited cases where a waiver may be available.[17] This change affected many lower-skilled workers who might have been eligible for family permanent residence, and it limited the rights of U.S. citizen spouses in filing petitions for their partners who have periods of unauthorized presence.

An increase in the number of employment visas for permanent residence would allow more workers and their families to reside permanently in the United States. Lower-skilled workers compete for far fewer visas than workers in other employment categories. The current allotment of only 5,000 lower-skilled employment visas annually includes those given to family members of workers, which means

---

15　Nicaraguan Adjustment and Central American Relief Act (NACARA) Pub. L. No. 105–100, 111 Stat. 2160 (November 19, 1997).

16　INA §§ 212(a)(9)(B), 212(a)(9)(C) (creating a permanent bar for anyone who returns after a deportation if they return without a discretionary waiver).

17　§212(a)(9)(B)(v) (discretionary waiver if applicants establish that extreme hardship would exist for their U.S. citizen or legal permanent resident spouse or parent).

The institutionalization of inequality   35

that far fewer than 5,000 immigrant workers become permanent residents annually. Reform of the 1996 ban on unlawful presence would have the greatest impact on undocumented workers, allowing a transition to permanent residence—an essential step to a more humane, inclusive system. Several immigration reform proposals in the past decade have included this specific change, recognizing the harsh reality, but have failed.

The broader U.S. immigration framework further exacerbates the vulnerability of immigrant workers. Fundamental fairness, due process, and nondiscrimination have become, at best, aspirational values in immigration law. Although these values are enshrined in the U.S. Constitution, these constitutional requirements do not limit immigration law or policy. Immigration law remains the only field of U.S. public law that affects both U.S. citizens and immigrants but is exempt from constitutional limits. Often referred to as "immigration exceptionalism," the plenary power doctrine in immigration law makes virtually all law and policy decisions purely political.[18] There is no constitutional right to review, except for review mechanisms provided by Congress in the statute, and no right to judicial process to challenge decisions to exclude or deport, except in a few circumstances. This plenary power extends to all rules and procedures relating to immigrant admissions and deportation.[19] As a practical matter, this doctrine prevents judicial review of most immigration policies, because Congress can determine which decisions in the immigration process are reviewable in court. The executive branch is similarly immune when implementing immigration law, because Congress has delegated its broad discretion to it. Legal challenges in courts generally are based on statutory definitions and procedures, nearly all of which are in the discretion of Congress to create, amend, or eliminate.

III Social discrimination: gender, class, race, and immigration status

The vulnerabilities created by the legal stratification of vulnerable immigrant workers is exacerbated by social discrimination. Gender, class, race, and immigration status have a profound effect on immigrant workers during their migration journeys and in destination countries. The global migration industry also creates and perpetuates power asymmetries and social inequalities with differing experiences across lines of gender, class, race, legal status, and age.[20] Understanding this

---

18 *Mathews v. Diaz*, 426 U.S. 67, 79–80 (1976) (the broad power of Congress over immigration and naturalization allows it to "regularly make rules that would be unacceptable if applied to citizens").

19 *Chae Chan Ping v. United States* (*The Chinese Exclusion Case*), 130 U.S. 581 (1889) (articulating the plenary power doctrine).

20 Sophie Cranston, Joris Schapendonk, and Ernst Spaan, "New Directions in Exploring the Migration Industries: Introduction to Special Issue," *Journal of Ethnic and Migration Studies* 44 (2018): 543–57.

36 *Enid Trucios-Haynes*

social context is important to a full appreciation of the challenges facing immigrant workers across the globe.

A *Gender*

Women constitute about a third of global immigrant workers, although the gender balance differs significantly by industry and destination country.[21] Women are more vulnerable than men before, during, and after migration, particularly in terms of safety and security.[22] For women lacking immigration documents, the opportunities to migrate for work through safe and regular channels are even more limited than for men.[23] Gender affects how skills are constructed and identified for men and women, thereby "deskilling the recruitment channels" for women immigrant workers.[24] Women are more likely than men to experience discrimination on account of their gender, nationality, *and* immigrant status. Young immigrant domestic workers particularly are exposed to physical and sexual violence in the workplace. Such workers

> face a double penalty in terms of labor market segregation and discrimination; they are more likely to work in less-paid and rewarded sectors of the economy because of their sex, and are more likely to work in lower skilled positions in that sector because of their ethnicity and migrant status.[25]

Many women immigrant workers become part of the "global care chain" engaged in paid and unpaid home care work.[26] Domestic responsibilities are transferred from women to other women, perpetuating labor market segregation, gender inequalities, and discrimination.[27] Immigrant domestic workers support other women working outside their homes, and these immigrant domestic workers then must rely on relatives or other low-paid workers to care for their own families. This care chain limits the family members who assist the domestic worker, often mothers or eldest daughters, who can no longer pursue economic or education opportunities.

---

21 IOM, *World Migration Report 2020*, 52. Sixty-eight percent of immigrant workers are male, and there are major geographical differences: Southern Asia (6 million males compared with 1.3 million females) and the Arab states (19.1 million males compared with 3.6 million females). ILO, *Labour Migration in Latin America and the Caribbean*, 15.
22 IOM, *World Migration Report 2020*, 52.
23 ILO, *Labour Migration in Latin America and the Caribbean*, 69.
24 Saskia Bonjour and Sébastien Chauvin, "Social Class, Migration Policy and Migrant Strategies: An Introduction," *International Migration* 56, no. 4 (2018): 5–18, at 9, https://doi.org/10.1111/imig.12469.
25 ILO, *Addressing Governance Challenges*, 24.
26 Ibid., 24. Premilla Nadasen, "Rethinking Care: Arlie Hochschild and the Global Care Chain," *Women's Studies Quarterly* 45 (2017): 124–28.
27 ILO, *Addressing Governance Challenges*, 24.

B Class

Class privilege is reflected in the categories of immigrant workers in most legal systems, although all immigrants are marginalized by their temporary status. For example, Gulf Cooperation Council (GCC) states have relatively open labor migration policies but do not offer a pathway to permanent residence or citizenship. Nationality can be a factor in the class privilege experienced by some immigrant workers. Arab immigrant workers in GCC states may have a privileged migration status because of their work, ranging from business executives to wealthy university students.[28]

Class discrimination in immigration law systems that privilege more "desirable" immigrant workers usually manifests in proxies for exclusion, such as skill level or education.[29] Highly skilled workers, often referred to as "expats," are assumed to integrate easily into the economies of destination countries and to share their core values. Class, tied to economic resources and educational attainment, also determines opportunities and resources available for a migration journey. In some countries, including the United States, class discrimination creates a system of stratified access to citizenship.[30]

C Race, nationality, and xenophobic rhetoric

Discrimination based on race, nationality, and religion often functions worldwide as a proxy for perceived threats to national security. Immigration viewed as a national security issue can be used to justify limitations on employment rights and other immigrant worker protections.[31] In the United States, political rhetoric has characterized Latinx immigrants as criminals and a national security threat and has justified a constant stream of restrictionist measures by the Trump administration.[32] Similarly, in the Netherlands, rhetoric connecting nationality to national security has affected policy debates about Dutch-Moroccan boys and young men, who are perceived as a social and security threat."[33]

Xenophobic discrimination against lower-skilled workers based on race, ethnicity, and nationality is pervasive in destination countries. The ILO has emphasized the importance of combating xenophobia and the social and cultural stereotypes

---

28 Breanna Small, "Book Annotation: *Arab Migrant Communities in the GCC*, Edited by Zahra Babar, Georgetown University Qatar: Oxford University Press, 2017," *New York University Journal of International Law and Politics* 50 (2017): 341–46.
29 Bonjour and Chauvin, "Social Class, Migration Policy and Migrant Strategies," 3.
30 Ibid., 7.
31 Michelle Leighton, "Remarks by Michelle Leighton," *Proceedings of the ASIL Annual Meeting* 112 (2018): 181–83.
32 Gregory Korte and Alan Gomez, "Trump Ramps Up Rhetoric on Undocumented Immigrants: 'These Aren't People. These Are Animals'," *USA Today*, May 16, 2018, www.usatoday.com/story/news/politics/2018/05/16/trump-immigrants-animals-mexico-democrats-sanctuary-cities/617252002/.
33 Bonjour and Chauvin, "Social Class, Migration Policy and Migrant Strategies," 12.

38 *Enid Trucios-Haynes*

that contribute to discrimination.[34] The politicization of migration in elections worldwide is connected to the discrimination, racism, xenophobia, and violence experienced by immigrants in destination countries.[35] This politicization creates public support for excessively restrictive policies bolstered by rhetoric equating immigration with the displacement of national workers and changing demographics.

Enduring intergenerational workplace discrimination exists in destination countries, reinforcing the labor segregation experienced by vulnerable immigrant workers. Discrimination against the citizen children of lower-skilled immigrant workers continues because of their race, nationality, religion, or other perceived difference within destination countries. This discrimination leads to exclusionary practices that prevent long-term integration, which the U.N. identifies as a threat to social cohesion in destination countries.[36] Immigrant integration also is stymied when immigrant workers and their citizen–family members are assumed to be responsible for their own marginalization, "which is no longer understood as a social injustice which should be remedied by the state, but rather as a result of cultural incompatibility and private failure."[37]

D Immigration status

The lack of immigration status creates heightened vulnerability on the migration journey and in destination countries. Workers lacking immigration status often must rely on smugglers. Undocumented immigrants on the journey face extraordinary violence, ranging from demands for bribes to mass kidnapping and extortion. Families at home are targeted for bribes as well.[38] Executions, physical and sexual assaults, torture, and disappearances are common. Women and children without immigration status have perilous journeys. Children who travel alone are particularly vulnerable to dangerous routes and smugglers, who often sell children into exploitation and forms of slavery.[39]

Undocumented workers on the move are best understood as survival immigrants who do not fit into the binary of refugee versus economic immigrant. They travel by way of well-organized smuggling routes across the globe. They also face serious challenges in navigating border control and enforcement systems,

---

34 ILO, *Labour Migration in Latin America and the Caribbean*, 71.

35 IOM, *World Migration Report 2020*, 186–87.

36 Ibid., 343.

37 Bonjour and Chauvin, "Social Class, Migration Policy and Migrant Strategies," 12.

38 James Verini, "How U.S. Policy Turned the Sonoran Desert into a Migrant Graveyard," *The New York Times*, August 18, 2020, www.nytimes.com/2020/08/18/magazine/border-crossing.html?searchResultPosition=1.

39 UNICEF, *A Child Is a Child: Protecting Children on the Move from Violence, Abuse and Exploitation*, May 2017, www.unicef.org/publications/index_95956.html. (Europol estimates that 20 percent of suspected smugglers on their radar have ties to human trafficking: p. 2).

including detention and deportation, as well as border violence. The migration routes to, within, and from North Africa, have immigrant-smuggling operations that are increasingly concentrated among a few organized criminal networks. In Asia, smugglers have migration routes within the region (such as from Cambodia to Thailand) and out of the region (such as from Vietnam to Europe).[40] Immigrant smuggling is a major feature of migration across the United States–Mexico border. Here, smuggling is a profitable industry overseen by international criminal groups taking advantage of people desperate to get to the United States.[41]

IV Market segregation: inequality and the global labor migration infrastructure

The highly regulated and constrained opportunities for labor migration, particularly for lower-skilled workers, creates the conditions for the labor market segregation of these workers and exposes them to particular vulnerabilities as workers. This market segregation is exacerbated by the growth of a global labor migration infrastructure, which both facilitates migration and entrenches the inequalities endemic to lower-skilled labor migration. Both of these aspects of labor migration are covered in this section.

A *The inequality experienced by vulnerable immigrant workers*

Legal stratification and labor market segregation create social vulnerabilities for lower-skilled workers, who may have work authorization and protected immigration status, or may be undocumented and lack work authorization. In the United States, immigrants without work authorization may have applied for immigration benefits or may have an immigration status that does not provide work authorization, such as asylum seekers. Some vulnerable immigrant workers may have protected immigration status *and* work authorization but be unable to find a job in the formal economy because of discrimination. Such discrimination often extends to second-generation immigrants who are the citizen children of immigrants.[42] Self-employed immigrants, who may lack work authorization, often are in lower-skilled and lower-wage jobs.[43]

The intersection of legal stratification and discrimination means that these vulnerable immigrant workers are concentrated in 3D (dirty, demeaning, and dangerous) jobs at a much higher percentage than other workers. They work

---

40 IOM, *World Migration Report 2020*, 62, 78.
41 Ibid., 123, 136. ILO, *Labour Migration in Latin America and the Caribbean*, 22.
42 Batalova, Blizzard, and Bolter, "Frequently Requested Statistics on Immigrants and Immigration." "Second-generation immigrant children" include any U.S.–born child with at least one foreign-born parent. "First-generation immigrant children" include any foreign-born child with at least one foreign-born parent. "Children with immigrant parents" include both first- and second-generation immigrant children.
43 ILO, *Labour Migration in Latin America and the Caribbean*, 71.

40 Enid Trucios-Haynes

in less regulated industries and face unsafe working conditions, significant wage gaps (and even larger gender pay differences), limited enforcement of occupational safety and health, lack of other social protection (such as health care), and lack of recognition of their skills and diplomas.[44] Lower-skilled and undocumented immigrant workers, particularly U.S. Latinx workers, work predominantly in agriculture, construction, gardening, childcare, house cleaning, food processing, manufacturing, and other services. These fields have the highest human-trafficking–related violations and abusive labor practices, particularly in construction, food processing, and cleaning services.[45] Immigrant workers, especially in agriculture and domestic work, are at much higher risk of being victims of forced labor than others, and child immigrants are particularly vulnerable.[46]

Undocumented workers face significant additional challenges. The scarcity of legal means to regularize their status means that people can remain perpetually undocumented despite having lived in the United States for decades. In 2017, about two-thirds of the 10.5 million undocumented individuals had lived in the United States for more than 15 years.[47] Extreme exclusion from the immigration system has targeted primarily Latinx people, who account for 77 percent of this group.[48] Undocumented immigrants are members of our communities, living in the shadows and vulnerable to abuse and exploitation in every aspect of their lives.[49] In the United States, undocumented immigrants include four million tentatively approved for a family permanent residence visa; nearly 4 million who are parents of U.S. citizens and permanent residents; 2 million who have lived in the United States for 20 years or more; 3 million brought to the United States at age 16 or younger; and 8 million workers (see Donald M. Kerwin, Chapter 6).

Undocumented immigrant workers particularly face substantial barriers to labor rights and protections because of their fear of deportation. Employers use the threat of deportation, arrest, and detention to quiet undocumented workers who attempt to protest abuses, organize unions, or file complaints with enforcement agencies.[50] The industries where undocumented immigrant workers are found in higher numbers—such as agriculture, fishery and home care—rely more heavily on undocumented workers, thus deepening the labor segregation in destination countries.

---

44 Ibid., 15.

45 Ibid., 21.

46 ILO, *Addressing Governance Challenges*, 17.

47 Most undocumented people are not new arrivals; more than 65 percent of undocumented adults in 2017 had lived in the United States for more than fifteen years. Batalova, Blizzard, and Bolter, "Frequently Requested Statistics on Immigrants and Immigration."

48 Ibid.

49 In the United States, vulnerable immigrants are subjected to surveillance, racial profiling, and harassment by law enforcement officers who assume people are undocumented solely because of how they look and the language they speak. See Southern Poverty Law Center, "Immigrant Justice," www.splcenter.org/issues/immigrant-justice.

50 Shirley Lung, "Criminalizing Work and Non-Work: The Disciplining of Immigrant and African American Workers," *University of Massachusetts Law Review* 14 (2019): 290–349, at 333.

B The global migration infrastructure

The global migration infrastructure describes the intersecting roles of state actors, nonstate actors, employers, and those who facilitate the migration journey, particularly for lower-skilled immigrants.[51] State agencies provide information and services relating to migration, while nonprofit and humanitarian agencies, as well as their social networks, also share information and make connections to ease the journey. The knowledge and services generated by state and nonstate actors has been commercialized by recruiters, brokers, and traffickers operating in and between legal, gray, and illicit markets to exploit and circumvent the legal regulation of labor migration. Taken together, this global migration infrastructure offers services and knowledge for workers who seek to migrate through either sanctioned means or irregular migration outside of a destination country's legal system.[52] This vast global commercial enterprise is, however, associated with systemic human rights abuses during the migration journey and in destination countries.[53]

As Kristin E. Heyer notes, this "immigrant industrial complex" operates with limited public oversight and accountability (Chapter 13). The migration industry is characterized by the "commodification of migration," and it occupies a pivotal role in negotiating borders within the current context of restrictive migration policies and border control.[54] As a global *mobility* industry, it can be analyzed as "a multitude of activities, practices, and technologies that must be considered in specific contexts," thus requiring an examination of the journeys and trajectories of immigrants as opposed to origins and destinations.[55]

Labor intermediaries, such as temporary staffing agencies, contractors, and recruitment agents, have a role in structuring labor markets. Brokers become actors who "mediate between parties in contexts of structural inequality."[56] These brokers channel lower-skilled immigrant workers into 3D industries, reinforcing labor market segregation in destination countries.[57] Employers often prefer immigrant workers over national workers, given the limited labor protections afforded to immigrants. This preference facilitates "social dumping," which happens when an industry relies on immigrant workers for 3D jobs and reinforces

---

51 Maria Cecilia Hwang, "Review of 'Multinational Maids: Stepwise Migration in a Global Labor Market,' by Anju Mary Paul," *Sojourn: Journal of Social Issues in Southeast Asia* 34 (2019): 215–18.

52 Cranston, Schapendonk, and Spaan, "New Directions," 9.

53 Bassina Farbenblum and Justine Nolan, "The Business of Migrant Worker Recruitment: Who Has the Responsibility and Leverage to Protect Rights?" *Texas International Law Journal* 52 (2017): 1–44, at 2.

54 Cranston, Schapendonk, and Spaan, "New Directions," 5.

55 Sophie Cranston, "Calculating the Migration Industries: Knowing the Successful Expatriate in the Global Mobility Industry," *Journal of Ethnic and Migration Studies* 44 (2018): 626–43 (theorizing the migration industry as part of the knowledge economy).

56 Maybritt J. Alpes, "Papers That Work: Migration Brokers, State/Market Boundaries, and the Place of Law," *PoLAR: Political and Legal Anthropology Review* 40 (2017): 262–73.

57 Cranston, Schapendonk, and Spaan, "New Directions," 6.

labor market segregation and the continued overrepresentation of immigrants in these jobs.[58] This occurs worldwide in specific industries, especially domestic work, agriculture, fishery, electronics, and construction.

Labor intermediaries work in countries of origin to identify workers for labor migration programs, and, in the case of staffing agencies, to complete all of the required visa documents. Immigrant workers pay fees to the recruitment agencies for the cost of the visa, travel, and any side-payments.[59] Intermediaries can also further limit access to available legal protections. In the United States, employers can guarantee their compliance with U.S. immigration regulations by shifting legal requirements to recruiting agencies. Although fees are prohibited in the U.S. temporary worker program, recruitment and staffing agencies can charge excessive fees to workers who depend on the agencies for access to U.S. employers.[60]

Migration brokers facilitate border crossing outside of a destination country's legal system. Labor migration processes segregate workers who lack immigration status, and who must rely on smuggling networks or other alternative means. The broker–immigrant relationship is complex. Aspiring labor immigrants may view brokers as a resource, regardless of their characterization as smugglers or human traffickers. Migration brokers may provide resources for immigrant workers to shape their credentials to meet state labor system criteria, thus providing for greater mobility.[61] A recent study in Cameroon showed that general societal disapproval of labor intermediaries—who were viewed as dangerous criminals, particularly those who facilitate irregular migration—ignored the instrumental ways brokers assisted immigrants.[62] Immigrants often are personally connected with brokers, and brokers may be respected within their home communities. Immigrant workers have greater agency in this narrative, making choices to assume the risks of abuses of power and financial ruin. This raises questions about the legitimacy of specific migration broker services.[63]

V Opportunities and challenges to reform—Christian values and ethics

Advocacy premised on Christian values presents opportunities to break the cycle of legal stratification, social discrimination, and market segregation that create the conditions for the exploitation of immigrant workers. In this section, I examine the kinds of interventions Christian theology and ethics could make in labor migration. Unfortunately, not all religious communities may be allies in

---

58 ILO, *Labour Migration in Latin America and the Caribbean*, 16, 22.
59 Jennifer Gordon, "Regulating the Human Supply Chain," *Iowa Law Review* 102 (2017): 445–505, at 448.
60 Ibid., 480.
61 Bonjour and Chauvin, "Social Class, Migration Policy and Migrant Strategies," 10.
62 Alpes, "Papers That Work," 263.
63 Lisa Åkessona and Jill Alpes, "What Is a Legitimate Mobility Manager? Juxtaposing Migration Brokers with the EU," *Journal of Ethnic and Migration Studies* 45 (2019): 2689–705.

demanding human rights for all immigrants, so I also address the challenges that engagement with Christianity may pose.

A Christian values and ethics: illuminating a path toward equality and human dignity

Pope Francis's speech to the U.S. Congress in 2015 advised us to focus on people and their migration stories, so that we may respond in a "humane, just and fraternal way."[64] Gemma Tulud Cruz emphasizes our shared humanity and interdependence derived from the Christian belief in the inalienable and equal dignity of all persons (Chapter 11). This demands a policy response addressing the needs of the most marginalized immigrants of our time: lower-skilled, lower-wage immigrant workers. As Cruz notes, a praxis theology can motivate an agenda that combines specific attention to the experiences of immigrant workers with transformative action to use this knowledge to achieve "human emancipation" as God's will.

Christian liberation theology focuses on those most marginalized. A Christian response must include not only a relational understanding of immigrant experiences but also a "sense of responsibility for the other, especially the members of the Body of Christ who need support" (Cruz, Chapter 11). Vulnerable immigrant workers have been identified as an iconic representation of the poor in our modern, globalized world. Yet we continue to see epic failures to embrace the equal dignity of immigrants, particularly those denigrated as "undeserving" workers. This is evident in the responses of some European countries to the 2015 mass migration, and in the U.S. response to mass Central American migration in 2018–19.

The complexity of immigrant experiences and state regulatory systems finds an apt parallel in the Hebrew Bible's use of several different terms to represent *the stranger*. Safwat Marzouk helps us understand how ancient biblical practices of "welcoming the stranger" can provide useful guidance today (Chapter 8). He identifies basic theological principles in the Hebrew Bible that apply to all foreigners: judicial fairness and economic protection from host communities; equality of the stranger before God; safeguards to limit any oppression of host community members; and an acknowledgment that exclusion could protect the freedom of the stranger (to be exempt from certain religious practices if desired).

The marginalization of immigrant workers transcends the negotiation of border crossing and the exclusion that borders entail. Once inside destination countries, vulnerable immigrant workers experience profound discrimination. In the United States, people of color experience an imputed foreignness applied to

---

64 Donald M. Kerwin and Elizabeth Kilbride, "Pope Francis and Migrants: Honoring Human Dignity, Building Solidarity and Creating a Culture of Encounter," *Center for Migration Studies*, https://cmsny.org/pope-francis-and-migrants-honoring-human-dignity-building-solidarity-and-creating-a-culture-of-encounter/.

44 *Enid Trucios-Haynes*

immigrants, and their citizen family members are identified as foreign from their "language, accent, clothing, religious practice, or other markers" (Silas W. Allard, Chapter 5). Asian Americans, Latinx Americans, and Arab Americans are racially categorized as foreign-born outsiders, regardless of their citizenship status.[65] This racialized foreignness forces some to "wear the border" at all times, creating a figurative border and making them subject to exclusion by anyone challenging their right to remain.[66] For lower-skilled immigrant workers, this figurative border carries real-world consequences. They have limited job opportunities and are channeled into 3D jobs where they experience hazardous working conditions in less regulated industries. Labor market segregation is exacerbated by employer preferences for hiring immigrant workers, creating the social dumping phenomenon. Finally, their families experience intergenerational discrimination, racism, and labor segregation.

Anxieties about globalization and the economic displacement caused by outsourced production are conflated with immigrant workers in the United States. As Heyer points out, political candidates rely on messaging that capitalizes on economic anxieties, anxieties about terrorist activities, and white people's fears of being overwhelmed by the racial differences of newer immigrants (Chapter 13). This political rhetoric creates fertile ground for the toxic combination of misinformation and racial animus. The dominant discourse about people who lack immigration status has been conflated with Latinx Americans, 67 percent of whom are U.S. citizens.[67] The former U.S. president, Donald Trump, deliberately amplified fears about broken borders and the incorrect correlation of increased criminal activity by people lacking status (Luis N. Rivera-Pagán, Chapter 10).

A praxis theology focused on Latinx community members who lack immigration status and other vulnerable immigrants would help policymakers understand "their stories of suffering, hope, courage, resistance, ingenuity, and, as so frequently happens in the wilderness areas of the American Southwest, death" (Rivera-Pagán, Chapter 10). Inspiration from Christian values could help to "reappropriate concepts like sovereignty, security, and the rule of law that have been used to exclude and marginalize all immigrants." This could be an antidote to the dominant U.S. discourse that relies on inaccurate information about the contributions of vulnerable immigrant workers and demeaning labels such as "illegal immigrant" to manipulate public opinion (Kerwin, Chapter 6).

Christian values can also transform the border from a site for exclusion to a place of engagement (Allard, Chapter 5). This focus invites further consideration of our collective responsibility toward immigrants beyond encounter and connection. However, the traditional version of Christian migration ethics focused

---

65 Terri Yuh-lin Chen, "Hate Violence as Border Patrol: An Asian American Theory of Hate Violence," *Asian Law Journal* 7 (2000): 69–101.

66 Robert S. Chang and Keith Aoki, "Policy, Politics and Praxis: Centering the Immigrant in the Inter/National Imagination," *California Law Review* 85 (1997): 1395–447, at 1411.

67 Luis Noe-Bustamante and Antonio Flores, "Facts on Latinos in the U.S.," *Pew Research Center*, September 16, 2019, www.pewresearch.org/hispanic/fact-sheet/latinos-in-the-u-s-factsheet/.

on hospitality may not be sufficient to spur meaningful change and address the current extreme exclusion (Heyer, Chapter 13).

A radical Christian migration ethics can lead communities and the larger polity to look beyond encounter and connection to focus on the root causes that compel migration. Heyer advocates transformational Christian ethics to achieve this. Radical Christian ethics could move communities beyond welcoming the stranger into instrumental advocacy, and perhaps greater understanding of the communities' complicity in exploiting vulnerable immigrants. This would extend the "covenant of justice and righteousness" that Luis N. Rivera-Pagán notes is an essential attribute of the Christian "ethics of hospitality" to care for the stranger (Chapter 10).

Such radical Christian migration ethics and praxis can surmount what Pope Francis has called the "globalization of indifference" to examine the interests served by exclusionary migration systems and targeted enforcement against the most vulnerable members of our communities. Pope Francis laments the impact of this indifference on the foundation of civil society:

> There has been a tragic rise in the number of immigrants seeking to flee from the growing poverty caused by environmental degradation. They are not recognized by international conventions as refugees; they bear the loss of the lives they have left behind, without enjoying any legal protection whatsoever. Sadly, there is widespread indifference to such suffering. . . . Our lack of response to these tragedies involving our brothers and sisters points to the loss of that sense of responsibility for our fellow men and women upon which all civil society is founded.[68]

Poverty causes many to migrate for a better life. Labor segregation, reinforced by immigration law systems, limits the opportunities available to those deemed to be lower-skilled workers. This cycle of inequality, exploitation, and exclusion requires a solution—one premised on core Christian values, a transformational migration ethics, and a Christian praxis leading to renewed advocacy. Such advocacy can support a meaningful transnational action agenda based on the nearly universal agreement that destination countries must protect the human rights of all immigrant workers. Liberation theology, centering on the concerns of the most vulnerable, shines a spotlight on the experiences of immigrant workers. Christian advocacy therefore can be the impetus for meaningful change.

B Christian values can support a restrictive U.S. immigration policy

There are, however, challenges to a transformational Christian ethics and Christian praxis focused on immigrants' human dignity and on our corresponding responsibility for their migration experiences. Religious affiliation, shared

---

68 Quoted in Kerwin and Kilbride, "Pope Francis and Migrants."

46 Enid Trucios-Haynes

attitudes within religious communities, and the social networks of different Christian denominations shape opinions in favor of, or opposed to, restrictionist U.S. immigration policies. National religious leaders have the capacity to influence broad public opinion through their statements, just as local religious leaders influence their communities. Support for immigration restrictions has been linked to specific religious denominations as well as religiosity, defined as the frequency of religious service attendance. Religious affiliation is useful, although not predictive, in understanding attitudes toward immigration, because other factors influence attitudes as well.[69] Religious affiliation is an important determinant of international policy preferences toward immigration.[70] Globalization in this context is viewed as a challenge to cultural boundaries that forces an awareness of increasing global connectivity.

U.S. public opinion about immigration also is shaped by the shared attitudes within religious denominations that are reinforced by their religious communities. Individuals in liberal and mainline Protestant denominations are more likely to favor increased immigration and are less threatened by secular society, tending to view religious beliefs as more personal and private. More frequent religious service attendance has been linked to opinions favoring immigration, as is membership in a minority religion, such as the Latter-day Saints. Members of more fundamentalist Christian denominations, including pre–Vatican II Catholics, are more likely to support restrictions on immigration. Fundamentalist denominations are defined here as part of a religiously-based social movement built to counteract secularism and modernization, and to protect a traditionalist culture. Denominations in the southern United States also were found to have this stronger sense of separatism.[71]

The social networks of Christian denominations are predictive regarding positive or negative attitudes about immigration.[72] Social networks in more fundamentalist denominations have strong in-group loyalty and generate antagonism toward outsiders. In contrast, liberal and moderate Protestant denominations create bridging networks that are less threatened by modernization, generate relatively more outward trust, and are less likely to be antagonistic toward outsiders.

National religious leaders influence public attitudes about immigration. An analysis of pro-immigration statements in 2010 from the largest U.S. religious

---

69 Joseph P. Daniels and Marc von der Ruhr, "God and the Global Economy: Religion and Attitudes Towards Trade and Immigration in the United States," *Socio-Economic Review* 3, no. 3 (2005): 467–89, at 486, https://doi.org/10.1093/SER/mwi020. Attitudes favoring immigration restrictions are shaped by factors such as negative stereotypes about the Latinx community; perceptions of the economic and/or cultural threat posed by new immigrants; education; labor market vulnerability; and pessimistic evaluations of the economy.

70 Daniels and von der Ruhr, "God and the Global Economy," 486.

71 Tatishe M. Nteta and Kevin J. Wallsten, "Preaching to the Choir? Religious Leaders and American Opinion on Immigration Reform," *Social Science Quarterly* 93 (2012): 891–910, https://doi.org/10.1111/j.1540-6237.2012.00865.

72 Ibid., 892.

The institutionalization of inequality   47

denominations found that their support influenced the preferences of their parishioners.[73] These statements included testimony before a U.S. House of Representatives subcommittee from the U.S. Conference of Catholic Bishops that the current system does not "accommodate migration realities[,] . . . serve our national interests, or respect the basic human rights of immigrants who come to this nation in search of employment for themselves and better living conditions for their children."[74]

National religious leaders also influence political views. Elite-opinion theory shows how people follow elites' cues on political issues. The sway of national religious leaders is bolstered by the rational-ignorance theory, which describes the political judgments of ordinary citizens as relying more on cues from elites than from their own attention to political.[75] These elites include media as well as political and social actors, but local religious leaders also function as elites and influence individual attitudes about immigration policy through sermons, lectures, and discussions in places of worship.

A transformational Christian ethics and praxis is threatened by the politicization of religious doctrine to support or oppose immigration. In 2018 and 2019, U.S. politicians and religious leaders cited religious doctrine to support or oppose increased federal funding for the U.S.–Mexico "border wall." Explicit use of religious doctrine can harden opinions within Christian communities and cause further polarization among religious denominations. The effort to shut down the federal government unless further funding was allocated to build the border wall was extraordinarily contentious. The speaker of the U.S. House of Representatives, Nancy Pelosi, called the entire debate immoral, in response to religious and political leaders who used religious doctrine to support anti-immigration policies. Those invoking biblical verses included the U.S. attorney general at the time, Jeff Sessions, who told the public that God wanted the wall, and that it was divinely ordained.[76]

A more hopeful view of Christian core values influencing a positive attitude toward immigration would focus on the way in which the "teaching about the common origin, dignity, solidarity and destiny of all human beings has been the most enduring constants of the most orthodox Christian tradition of the last 2,000 years" (Cruz, Chapter 11). These core values, together with a

---

73 Ibid. Statements from the United Methodist Church (the largest mainline Protestant church in the United States), the National Association of Evangelicals, the Episcopal Church, the Southern Baptist Convention, the Evangelical Lutheran Church in America, and smaller denominations were analyzed. Support also was expressed by the Conservatives for Comprehensive Immigration Reform, Christians for Comprehensive Immigration Reform, and the Interfaith Statement in Support of Comprehensive Immigration Reform.

74 Ibid.

75 Nteta and Wallsten, "Preaching to the Choir?" 892.

76 "The Moral Question of Trump's Border Wall," National Public Radio, *All Things Considered*, January 27, 2019, www.npr.org/2019/01/27/689191255/the-morality-question-of-trump-s-border-wall.

48 *Enid Trucios-Haynes*

transformational Christian ethics and praxis, could motivate societies to protect vulnerable immigrant workers. In this sense, Christian values can leverage the global consensus that destination countries must establish further protective measures for vulnerable immigrants. A transnational movement premised on these core values aligns well with the consensus for action reflected in the Global Compact for Safe, Orderly and Regular Migration (GCM) and the Global Compact on Refugees (GCR) of 2018.

VI Conclusion: an opportunity to break the cycle

Christian values can be a catalyst for state action to protect immigrant workers' human rights and to widen the global consensus for protections. Christian values can also reveal the complicity of nations and their people in the structure of immigration law systems, the work of labor intermediaries, and national labor markets that create a cycle of inequality, exploitation, and exclusion. Nations and their people have a corresponding responsibility for the migration experiences of vulnerable workers. This understanding offers the promise of an action agenda that centers on the dignity and equality of all immigrant workers, regardless of their immigration status. This challenge to the status quo invites us to move past what Pope Francis called the "globalization of indifference," toward a unified response premised on core Christian values, a transformational Christian ethics, and a Christian praxis focused on renewed advocacy.

Significant global consensus about the dire need to protect immigrants' human rights has been achieved recently. This occurred, however, at the same time as serious migration and displacement challenges emerged.[77] In December 2018, the United Nations finalized two historic agreements on migration, culminating after decades of work: the Global Compact for Safe, Orderly and Regular Migration (GCM) and the Global Compact on Refugees (GCR).[78] This section discusses the GCM, although the compacts together create a common approach to international migration.[79]

Global migration is a transnational phenomenon, yet it is regulated by varied, often competing or conflicting, state systems. The multilateral commitment to safe and orderly migration began in 2016, when the UN General Assembly unanimously adopted the New York Declaration for Refugees and Migrants, recognizing the need for a comprehensive approach to human mobility and enhanced global cooperation. The goal was to protect the safety, dignity, and human rights and fundamental freedoms of all immigrants—at all times, regardless of status. Although nonbinding, the unanimous vote gave the Declaration great weight.

---

77 ILO, *World Migration Report 2020*, 291. This consensus emerged while millions of people were fleeing conflict in Syria, Yemen, and South Sudan; violence in Central America; genocide against the Rohingya people in Myanmar; and political instability in Venezuela.
78 Ibid., 20.
79 The Global Compact for Safe, Orderly and Regular Migration (GCM), www.iom.int/global-compact-migration.

The 2018 GCM was signed by 193 nations, demonstrating a commitment to global implementation.[80] The GCM also is nonbinding.

Several binding international treaties that protect immigrants have wide U.N. member-state support and have changed the behavior of states. The International Covenant on Civil and Political Rights (ICCPR)[81] and the Convention Relating to the Status of Refugees[82] have been widely ratified. The ICCPR enshrines the nondiscrimination principle by ensuring that the rights of all individuals, including migrants, are not nullified or impaired on the basis of "race, colour, sex, language, religion, political or other opinion, national or social origin, property, birth or other status," including migration status.[83] Other migration treaties have not been so widely accepted. For example, the International Convention on the Protection of the Rights of All Migrant Workers and Members of Their Families[84] has not been ratified by many states, and no traditional destination countries have joined the treaty. As a result, the 1990 Migrant Worker Convention has not altered state behavior or changed norms. International human rights norms also provide a body of universal standards and values to bolster human dignity, equality, nondiscrimination, and freedoms. For example, equality and nondiscrimination are foundational norms in the Universal Declaration of Human Rights.[85]

The GCM has the promise to reach *all* actors in the migration infrastructure, including private actors, through the creation of new norms.[86] The GCM pushes to rebalance sovereign state authority to exclude with its human rights obligations to protect all immigrants regardless of status. This rebalancing can be spurred by the radical Christian ethics proposed by Kristin E. Heyer to focus on root causes. One of the GCM's central foci is protecting immigrants' rights and ensuring their well-being. Both of the U.N. compacts demonstrate the current global intent to take action to protect immigrants' human rights. The GCM asks states "to foreground migrants' needs and to provide supports, especially as

---

80 Ibid.

81 International Covenant on Civil and Political Rights, opened for signature December 19, 1966, 999 U.N.T.S. 171 (entered into force March 23, 1976, adopted by the United States September 8, 1992).

82 Convention Relating to the Status of Refugees, July 28, 1951, 189 U.N.T.S. 137.

83 ILO, *World Migration Report 2020*, 291, 344.

84 International Convention on the Protection of the Rights of All Migrant Workers and Members of their Families, December 18, 1990, U.N. Doc. A/RES/45/158.

85 Universal Declaration of Human Rights, G.A. Res. 217A (III), U.N. GAOR, 3rd Sess., Supp. No. 16, U.N. Doc. A/810 at art. 16(3) (1948).

86 The U.N. General Assembly Resolution adopting the GCM was signed by 152 nations. The United States, Hungary, Israel, Czech Republic, and Poland voted against it, and 12 countries abstained. The text of the accord was approved in July 2018 by every member state of the U.N. except the United States. Nick Cumming-Bruce, "U.N. Approves Sweeping Deal on Migration, but Without U.S. Support," *The New York Times*, December 10, 2018, www.nytimes.com/2018/12/10/world/europe/un-migration-deal-morocco.html?searchResult Position=1.

50 *Enid Trucios-Haynes*

they relate to human rights."[87] The GCM explicitly recognizes that immigrants benefit both their destination and home countries, expanding our understanding of their experiences and vulnerabilities. Recent research coupled with Christian advocacy can be the catalyst for states to take action relating to human trafficking, wage gaps with national workers, discrimination in other forms, slave-like working conditions, disparities in access to health care, and the special vulnerabilities of refugees, and women and children.[88]

The hope is that the GCM will strengthen existing rights for immigrants and create new norms to advance social justice.[89] One challenge to GCM implementation is the varied individual state implementations of existing human rights norms and labor standards. States that already avoid local implementation of human rights and international labor standards may similarly avoid action under the GCM because it is nonbinding.

In this context, Christian values, transformational migration ethics, and praxis can amplify advocacy inside destination countries to address the human rights needs of vulnerable immigrant workers. The GCM's promise of meaningful change will occur only if championed by people within destination societies. Christian values can spur the development of action agendas inside destination countries and transnational coalitions to support the GCM. The growing global consensus, along with recognition of our complicity in the systems that create inequality, exploitation, and exclusion, has exciting potential—to permanently disrupt the cycle that is reinforced by immigration law stratification, labor market segregation, and pervasive discrimination of vulnerable immigrant workers.

Suggested Reading

Alpes, Maybritt J. "Papers That Work: Migration Brokers, State/Market Boundaries, and the Place of Law." *PoLAR: Political and Legal Anthropology Review* 40 (2017): 262–73.

Bonjour, Saskia, and Sébastien Chauvin. "Social Class, Migration Policy and Migrant Strategies: An Introduction." *International Migration* 56, no. 4 (2018): 5–18. https://scholar.google.com/scholar?hl=en&as_sdt=0%2C18&q=Social+Class%2C +Migration+Policy+and+Migrant+Strategies%3A+An+Introduction&btnG.

Cranston, Sophie. "Expatriate as 'Good' Migrant: Thinking through Skilled International Migrant Categories." *Population, Space and Place* 23 (2017): e2058. https://onlinelibrary.wiley.com/doi/abs/10.1002/psp.2058.

Cranston, Sophie, Joris Schapendonk, and Ernst Spaan. "New Directions in Exploring the Migration Industries: Introduction to Special Issue." *Journal of Ethnic and Migration Studies* 44 (2018): 543–57.

Gordon, Jennifer. "Regulating the Human Supply Chain." *Iowa Law Review* 102 (2017): 445–505.

---

87 ILO, *World Migration Report 2020*, 340.
88 Ibid.
89 Leighton, "Remarks."

3 In defense of chain migration

Bill Ong Hing

I Introduction

In May 2019, President Trump announced an "immigration reform" plan meant to upend the present "chain migration" immigration system that he and other anti-immigrant groups have come to disdain. At the presentation of his "points-based system," which would favor younger workers with "merit and skill" and advanced education, he complained that "currently 66 percent of legal immigrants come here on the basis of random chance. They're admitted solely because they have a relative in the United States, and it doesn't matter who that relative is."[1] Trump's proposal mimicked an old one promoted by Senator Alan Simpson in the 1980s and a more recent one by Senators Tom Cotton and David Perdue, who introduced the Reforming American Immigration for Strong Employment Act (RAISE Act) in 2017. Cotton and Perdue complained that "chain migration is one of the biggest problems in our immigration system today. [O]ur system prioritizes people based on their family ties, instead of their ability to contribute to our nation's economic well-being."[2] Thus, their bill would eliminate all family sponsorship beyond spouses and minor children of U.S. citizens and lawful permanent residents (reducing the age limit for minor children from 21 to 18), and would lower capped family categories from 226,000 green cards to 88,000.

In this chapter, I defend so-called chain migration, the term used by opponents of family immigration in an attempt to portray family immigration in negative light.[3] Family reunification is certainly at the heart of the U.S. immigration system

---

1 Heather Timmons, "Trump Himself Wouldn't Be an American Under His New Immigration Plan," *Quartz*, May 16, 2019.

2 U.S. Senators David Perdue, Tom Cotton, and Chuck Grassley, "Any DACA Deal Must Include an End to Chain Migration," *The Hill*, January 18, 2018.

3 For example, Jessica Vaughn, director of policy studies at the anti-immigrant Center for Immigration Studies, argues: "Unlike earlier times in our history, when immigration ebbed and flowed in distinct waves, the last several decades have been a time of constantly increasing immigration. Our immigration system allows this growth both through family chain migration and by expanding the number of initiating immigrants through amnesties, humanitarian admissions, employment visas, and the visa lottery, all of which set off new chains of family migration." Jessica Vaughan, "Immigration Multipliers: Trends in

52 *Bill Ong Hing*

today. Consistently, at least 60 percent of new lawful permanent residents to the United States each year are admitted because of family ties. However, the attacks on the family-based categories are either disingenuous or not based on data. Thus, I argue that (1) the attacks on family-based immigration are grounded in xenophobia, and particularly racism, and that in fact, (2) family-based immigration plays an important economic role. Furthermore, (3) family-based immigration is critical to the social structure in immigrant communities, and (4) family-based immigration promotes the moral good of family unity.

While I use the United States as my example, family-based immigration is a large, and often the largest, category of immigration in many other countries, where it is subject to similar efforts at restriction.[4] All immigration systems create tensions between family-based and employment-based immigration and between nuclear and nonnuclear family categories, as well as fears of family migration anchoring demographic change. While none of these tensions are necessary or justified, they occur around the world.

II Background

Family unity is a deeply rooted value, and promoting family reunification has been a major feature of U.S. immigration policy for decades, traceable to the Emergency Quota Act of 1921.[5] In replacing the deeply flawed national-origins quota system with family-based categories under the Hart-Celler Act of 1965,[6] Congress affirmed family reunification as a core value of the United States.[7] The reforms made family the cornerstone of the immigration admission system.

Chain Migration," *Center for Immigration Studies*, September 27, 2017, https://cis.org/Report/Immigration-Multipliers?utm_source=Non-congressional+invite+list&utm_campaign=1cc05af6e8-EMAIL_CAMPAIGN_2017_11_25&utm_medium=email&utm_term=0_ea59261c39-1cc05af6e8-45116721.

4   In OECD countries, family-based immigration accounts for around 40 percent of total immigration and is the largest category. OECD, *International Migration Outlook* (Paris: OECD Publishing, 2019), 23. Recent trends indicate that family-based categories are increasingly subject to restriction. OECD, 61–62.

5   Emergency Quota Act of 1921, Pub. L. No. 67–5, § 2(d), 42 Stat. 5, 6 (1921). ("[P]reference shall be given so far as possible to the wives, parents, brothers, sisters, children under eighteen years of age, and fiancées [of United States citizens and legal residents].")

6   Hart-Celler Act, Pub. L. No. 89–236, §§ 201(b), 203, 79 Stat. 911 (1965) (providing that immediate relatives are not subject to numerical limitations, and that children, spouses and parents of U.S. citizens fall under the "immediate relative" category. The act prioritized the following family relationships that were subject to numerical limitation: unmarried sons and daughters of U.S. citizens; spouses, unmarried sons or daughters, and parents of lawful permanent residents; married sons or daughters of U.S. citizens; and brothers or sisters of U.S. citizens).

7   Representative Harold Ryan testified in support of eliminating the quota system: "It is unfair—it is unjust—it is pure discrimination for us to stamp a 'second best' rating on any individual because of his birthplace." Representative William Barrett testified: "It is perhaps unnecessary for me to reiterate the well-known fact that the national origins quota

In defense of chain migration 53

The 1965 reforms allotted 20,000 immigrant visas for every country not in the Western Hemisphere. Of the 170,000 immigrant visas set aside for Eastern Hemisphere immigrants, about 80 percent were specified for "preference" relatives of citizens and lawful permanent residents, and an unlimited number was available to immediate relatives of U.S. citizens. The category of immediate relative included spouses, parents of adult citizens, and minor, unmarried children of citizens. The family-preference categories were established for adult, unmarried sons and daughters of citizens (first preference), spouses and unmarried children of lawful permanent resident aliens (second preference), married children of citizens (fourth preference), and siblings of citizens (fifth preference). Third and sixth preferences were established for 54,000 employment-based immigration visas.

By 1976, a new worldwide preference system (which now included the Western Hemisphere) was installed with a quota of 270,000 that continued to reserve 80 percent for kinship provisions; the category for immediate relatives of U.S. citizens remained unlimited. The effects of this priority were demonstrated vividly in the subsequent flow of Asian immigration, even though nations such as those in Africa and Asia, with low rates of immigration prior to 1965, initially were disadvantaged. The nations with large numbers of descendants in the United States in 1965 were expected to benefit the most from a kinship-based system. At the time, when the total U.S. population was more than 194 million, fewer than a million Asian Americans resided in the country. Although the kinship priority meant that Asians were beginning on an unequal footing, at least Asians were on par numerically, in terms of the quota of 20,000 visas per country. Gradually, by using the family categories to their fullest extent, along with the employment route, Asians built a family base from which to use the kinship categories more and more. By the late 1980s, virtually 90 percent of all immigration to the United States—including Asian immigration—was through kinship categories.[8] By the 1990s, the vast majority of immigrants in kinship categories were from Asia and Latin America.

III The race-based assault on family begins

Within 20 years of the 1965 reforms, Asian and Latin immigrants began to dominate the family-immigration categories. When that happened, somehow the emphasis on family reunification made less sense to some pundits and

---

system . . . is based upon an infamous lie. . . . This outrageous and untrue theory, and proven to be such by facts, history, and science, is a black mark on the fair face of the United States in the eyes of the world. . . . We must enact statutes which permit families in this country to be united." See Immigration and Nationality Act: Hearing on H.R. 7919 before Subcomm. No. 1 of the H. Comm. on the Judiciary, 88th Cong. 208 (1964).

8 See, generally, Bill Ong Hing, *Making and Remaking Asian America Through Immigration Policy, 1850–1990* (Stanford, CA: Stanford University Press, 1993).

54 *Bill Ong Hing*

policymakers. The kinship system came under attack—revealing the racist intent of many of the critics. Consider the following critique from 1986:

> Nowhere else in public policy do we say not "who are you and what are your characteristics?" but ask rather, as we do in immigration, "who are you related to?" Current policy says: "if you have the right relatives, we will give you a visa; if you don't have the right relatives, well, it is just too bad."[9]

Arguing that the system was nepotistic, or that the country would be better off with a skills-based system, became popular. The following like-minded statement, also from the mid-1980s, about lawful and undocumented migration reveals the racial nature of the complaint:

> If the immigration status quo persists, the United States will develop a more unequal society with troublesome separations. For example, some projections indicate that the California work force will be mostly immigrants or their descendants by 2010. These working immigrants, *mostly nonwhite* will be supporting mostly white pensioners with their payroll contributions. *Is American society resilient enough to handle the resulting tensions?*
>
> The American economy will have more jobs and businesses if illegal alien workers are allowed to enter freely and work in the United States. But the number of jobs and businesses alone is not an accurate measure of the soundness of economic development or *quality of life*. Tolerating heavy illegal immigration introduces distortions into the economy that are difficult to remedy, while imposing environmental and *social costs* that must be borne by the society as a whole.[10]

Apparently, this perception of a good "quality of life" without "environmental and social costs" is one with minimal tension from the presence of "nonwhite" "immigrants or their descendants." As one commentator recognized, "It may be fair to conclude that the problem masquerading as illegal immigration is simply today's version of a continuing American—in fact, human—condition, namely xenophobia."[11]

From the early 1980s to 1996, the leading voice attacking family immigration, especially the sibling category, was Republican Senator Alan Simpson of

---

9 Testimony of Barry R. Chiswick before the Joint Economic Committee, Congress of the United States, S. Hrg. 99–1070, May 22, 1986, at 236. Of course, this statement was factually incorrect; even under the system at the time, prospective immigrants with skills needed by an employer could qualify for a labor employment category.

10 Martin, Philip, "Illegal Immigration and the Colonization of the American Labor Market," *Center for Immigration Studies*, January 1, 1986, at 45 (emphasis added), https://cis.org/Report/Illegal-Immigration-and-Colonization-American-Labor-Market.

11 Annelise Anderson, *Illegal Aliens and Employer Sanctions: Solving the Wrong Problem, Hoover Essays in Public Policy* (Stanford, CA: The Hoover Institution, 1986), 21.

Wyoming. Simpson had been a member of the Select Commission on Immigration and Refugee Policy, which issued a report in 1981 calling for major changes in the immigration laws. However, the commission had overwhelmingly endorsed the policy of keeping brothers and sisters as a preference category.[12]

After the Immigration Reform and Control Act of 1986 (IRCA)[13] was enacted to address the issue of undocumented migration through employer sanctions and legalization, Simpson turned his attention to legal immigration categories. At the time, although 20 percent of preference categories were available to employment immigrants (54,000), when the unrestricted categories of immediate relatives were added to the total number of immigrants each year, fewer than 10 percent of immigrants entering each year were doing so on the basis of job skills.

Simpson wanted the family immigration numbers reduced. The Senate in July 1989 approved his legislation, S. 358, which would establish a ceiling of 630,000 legal immigrants for three years. Of the total, 480,000 would be reserved for all types of family immigration, and 150,000 would be set aside for immigrants without family connections but with skills or job-related assets. However, Democratic Congressman Howard Berman, from Los Angeles, blocked attempts to reduce the number of family-based visas, refusing to "betray . . . the core American value and tradition of emphasizing the integrity of the family."[14]

Enacted on October 26, 1990, a compromise bill turned back attempts to reduce family immigration. Although the main thrust of immigration law continued to be family immigration, the annual number of employment-based visas nearly tripled, from 54,000 to 140,000 per year. With racist overtones, Simpson took some pride by announcing that "we [now] open the front door wider to skilled workers of a more diverse range of nationalities."[15] Of course to Simpson, "diverse" meant something other than Asians, Latinx, or even Africans.[16] Teaming up with Congressman Lamar Smith in 1996, Senator Simpson again took aim at the Asian- and Latin-dominated category of siblings of U.S. citizens as well as the category available to unmarried, adult sons and daughters of lawful resident aliens. Smith and Simpson's efforts ultimately failed, and Simpson retired.

IV The assault on family renewed

Most recently, the attack on family immigration is embodied by President Trump's May 2019 announcement and the introduction of the Cotton-Perdue RAISE Act

---

12 United States Immigration Policy and the National Interest, *Final Report of the Select Commission on Immigration and Refugee Policy* 119 (1981).

13 Pub. L. No. 99–603, November 6, 1986, 100 Stat. 3359.

14 Stewart Kwoh, "Family Unity Ranks First in Immigration," *Los Angeles Times,* September 14, 1989.

15 136 CONG. REC. S17,109 (daily ed. October 26, 1990) (statement of Sen. Simpson).

16 Bill Ong Hing, "African Migration to the United States: Assigned to the Back of the Bus," in *The Immigration and Nationality Act of 1965: Legislating a New America,* eds. Gabriel Chin and Rose Cuison Villazor (Cambridge: Cambridge University Press, 2015), 60–115.

56 *Bill Ong Hing*

in 2017. Slightly more than a million immigrants are granted lawful permanent residence in the United States each year. Family-based immigration comprises about two-thirds of the annual total. The RAISE Act seeks to halve this million by eliminating most categories for family-sponsored immigration, including the categories of parents and siblings of adult U.S. citizens. Senator Perdue admitted that one reason for eliminating the parent category is that someday DACA recipients (who are mostly Latinx) might become U.S. citizens, and "the first thing they're going to do is turn around and sponsor their parents who brought them here illegally. And you can't have that. There's no way that you've got the majority of people in America who want that sight unseen."[17]

The pejorative rhetoric of chain migration is echoed by a slew of others like Senator Charles Grassley, the former chairman of the Senate Judiciary Committee,[18] and, of course, President Trump: "[C]hain migration—think of that. So you come in, and now you can bring your family, and then you can bring your mother and your father. You can bring your grandmother."[19] President Trump's rhetoric readily revealed his racist motivations. He wanted to end the "visa lottery system" as well as chain migration because those programs "hurt our economy and allow terrorists into our country." In particular, he asked rhetorically, why would we want people from Haiti or Africa here: "Why do we want these people from all these [expletive deleted] countries here? We should have more people from places like Norway."[20]

---

17 National Public Radio (2018). "Republican Sen. David Perdue Outlines What He Sees as Immigration Debate Priorities" [podcast], *All Things Considered*, www.npr.org/2018/02/14/585841211/republican-sen-david-perdue-outlines-what-he-sees-as-immigration-debate-prioriti.

18 Chuck Grassley, United States Senator for Iowa (2018). "Op-Ed—Any DACA deal must include an end to chain migration," www.grassley.senate.gov/news/commentary/op-ed-any-daca-deal-must-include-end-chain-migration. ("Chain migration is one of the biggest problems in our immigration system today.") See also Q. Bui and C. and Dickerson, "What Can the U.S. Learn from How Other Countries Handle Immigration?" *New York Times*, February 16, 2018, www.nytimes.com/interactive/2018/02/16/upshot/comparing-immigration-policies-across-countries.html. (The family based system "is far more generous than I think the spirit of the United States is today": quoting Professor Justin Gest of George Mason University); and R. Girduskey, "It's Time For Congress to End Chain Migration and Put America's Working Class First," *FoxNews.Com*, February 23, 2018, www.foxnews.com/opinion/its-time-for-congress-to-end-chain-migration-and-put-americas-working-class-first. ("chain migration . . . is both a national and economic threat [to the] country and [its] working-class.")

19 Meghan Keneally, "8 Times Trump Slammed 'Chain Migration' Before It Apparently Helped Wife's Parents Become Citizens," *ABC News*, August 10, 2018, https://abcnews.go.com/beta-story-container/US/times-trump-slammed-chain-migration-apparently-helped-wifes/story?id=57132429.

20 Josh Dawsey, "Trump Derides Protections for Immigrants from 'Shithole' Countries," *Washington Post*, January 12, 2018, www.washingtonpost.com/politics/trump-attacks-protections-for-immigrants-from-shithole-countries-in-oval-office-meeting/2018/01/11/bfc0725c-f711-11e7-91af-31ac729add94_story.html.

The xenophobic nature of the attacks on family-based migration should appall us theologically as well as out of a sense of justice. In developing a biblical theology of migration, Luis N. Rivera-Pagán reviews the tension between xenophobia and racism, on one hand, and love and welcome for the stranger on the other. Citing passages from Leviticus, Exodus, and Deuteronomy, Rivera-Pagán points out that caring for the stranger became a key element of the Torah, the covenant of justice and righteousness between Yahweh and Israel (Luis N. Rivera-Pagán, Chapter 10; see also Safwat Marzouk, Chapter 8; Raj Nadella, Chapter 9). These and other biblical passages can fairly be read as a command to care for the stranger and to love the sojourners and resident foreigners (Rivera-Pagán, Chapter 10).

Professor Rivera-Pagán also reminds us, however, of biblical passages that display distaste for the alien. For example, "it is from the nations around you that you may acquire male and female slaves. You may also acquire them from among the aliens residing with you, and from their families . . . and they may be your property. . . . These you may treat as slaves" (Leviticus 25:44–46 [NSRV]). The epilogues of Ezra and Nehemiah "demonstrate the beginning of the establishment of a religious tradition that leaned toward traditionalism, conservatism, exclusivity, and xenophobia."[21]

Rivera-Pagán ultimately relies on Jesus's disruptive actions and attitudes to reject nationalistic exclusion and racism. We must "welcome and embrace the immigrant, and those in our midst who happen to be different in skin pigmentation, culture, language, and national origins" (Rivera-Pagán, Chapter 10). Why? Because they are, in their powerlessness and vulnerability, the sacramental presence of Christ. "For I was hungry and you gave me food, I was thirsty and you gave me something to drink, I was a stranger and you welcomed me, I was naked and you gave me clothing, I was sick and you took care of me, I was in prison and you visited me" (Matthew 25:35–36). Thus, these "vulnerable human beings turn out to be . . . the sacramental presence of Christ in our midst" (Rivera-Pagán, Chapter 10; see also Nadella, Chapter 9).

Raj Nadella calls attention to how biblical texts are often employed to perpetuate xenophobia as well as to justify anti-immigrant policies in the United States, and Nadella explores what key biblical texts say about hospitality to strangers and immigrants (Chapter 9). Nadella traces evolving portrayals of the other and the stranger (*xenos*) in the New Testament, primarily in the Gospels, and explores how the Bible forcefully challenges xenophobia. He analyzes several texts—Matthew 1 (the story of Jesus's family fleeing to Egypt), Matthew 8 (Jesus's encounter with the Roman centurion), Matthew 12 (the story of the Gadarene demoniac), Matthew 15 (Jesus's conversation with the Canaanite woman that foregrounds concerns about inclusion of the other), and Matthew 25 (the discourse on hospitality to the stranger that Nadella argues connects with the Greco-Roman concept of

---

21 Naim Stifan Ateek, *A Palestinian Christian Cry for Reconciliation* (Maryknoll, NY: Orbis Books, 2009), 132, as quoted in Rivera-Pagán discussion in this volume (Chapter 10).

58   *Bill Ong Hing*

theoxenia)—and delineates a movement from ambivalence about the stranger to embrace and eventual depiction of the stranger as manifestations of the divine.

Clearly, the xenophobic practices of limiting family reunification globally run counter to a Christian tradition of care for others. Yet while nationalism and racism lie at the core of much of the critique of family immigration, many opponents of family immigration couch their opposition in economic terms instead. Thus, in the next section I more closely consider issues related to economics and labor needs.

V Pitting family visas against employment visas

As the debate over immigration and border enforcement roils much of the world today, family-based immigration is frequently targeted by immigration restrictionists as counter to the interests, particularly the economic interests, of receiving countries. This critique is often presented as a variation on the wouldn't-it-better-to-choose-immigrants-based-on-skills theme, by positioning family visas in opposition to employment-based visas. As Doris Meissner of the Migration Policy Institute has asserted: "There is an *inherent tension* in the immigration system between job and family-based admissions. In allocating visas between family and employment criteria, the goal of family reunification cannot be entirely reconciled with the problem of visas as a scare resource."[22]

Inherent tension? Of course, there is only an "inherent tension" between employment- and family-based visas if we choose to accept the premise that visas are a "scarce resource," and therefore that more visas of one type must mean fewer of the other. If, instead, we view the two systems as complementary ways of achieving and reflecting social goals and values, then we do not have a tension problem. In other words, if, for the sake of argument, governments use immigration to help the economy, promote social welfare, and advance family values, then family and employment categories together can meet those goals.

VI The labor force picture

Placing employment visas in opposition to family visas implies that family immigration represents the soft side of immigration, while employment immigration is more about being tough and strategic. The wrongheadedness of that suggestion is clear from the experience of the United States: family immigration has served the United States well even from a purely economic perspective. The country needs workers with all kinds of skills, and family immigration provides many of the needed workers.

---

22 Memorandum to The Independent Task Force on Immigration and America's Future of the Migration Policy Institute from Doris Meissner, November 30, 2005 (emphasis added).

A Workforce needs

Some policymakers are concerned that the vast majority of immigrants who enter in kinship categories are working class or low skilled. These claims, however, are misleading. In fact, new immigrants to the United States are more highly educated as a group than native-born Americans. About 39 percent of immigrants admitted to the United States in 2015 had a college degree or above, compared to about 31 percent of adult natives. New immigrants are more educated than people realize and are increasingly better educated over time.[23] Beyond that oversight by the complainants, what we know about the country and its general need for workers in the short and long terms is instructive.

The truth is that modern economies need immigrant workers of all skill levels today and will continue to need them in the future. As of 2017, 27.4 million immigrants were in the U.S. labor force, representing 17.1 percent of the total labor force. Latinx immigrants account for 47.9 percent of the foreign-born labor force, and Asians constitute more than a quarter of the immigrant workforce.[24] Roughly 7.8 million of these immigrants are undocumented workers, representing about 4.8 percent of the total U.S. labor force.[25] Both reporting by the Bureau of Labor Statistics and the experience of the disruptive COVID-19 global health pandemic—ongoing as of the writing of this chapter—reveal that many of these immigrant laborers perform essential work in agriculture, supply chain, and medical industries, among others.

Immigrants are also found in jobs that are expected to be important in serving tomorrow's aging population. Seniors are expected to generate increasing demand for medical, home-care, and other services, many of which require workers with only on-the-job training. According to the Bureau of Labor Statistics, 8 of the 15 occupations projected to grow most rapidly—and several of the occupations projected to have the largest absolute growth—are medical-support occupations.[26]

Furthermore, in communities across the country, many employers are having trouble finding enough skilled workers. A large share of immigrant workers are in lower-skilled jobs, but with access to the education and training that they need to advance their careers, many of these workers have the potential to meet these labor force needs. The Urban Institute observes that workforce-development services could help immigrants develop their skills, earn higher wages to support

---

23 Alex Nowrasteh, "The RAISE Act Talking Points Are Deceptive," *Cato Institute*, August 4, 2017, www.cato.org/blog/raise-act-talking-points-are-deceptive.

24 Bureau of Labor Statistics, U.S. Department of Labor, "Foreign-Born Workers: Labor Force Characteristics—2017," May 17, 2018, www.bls.gov/news.release/archives/forbrn_05172018.pdf.

25 Jens Manuel Krogstad, et al., "5 Facts About Illegal Immigration in the U.S.," *Pew Research Center*, November 28, 2018, www.pewresearch.org/fact-tank/2018/11/28/5-facts-about-illegal-immigration-in-the-u-s/.

26 Ibid., 7.

60 Bill Ong Hing

themselves and their families, and meet employer demands.[27] Middle-skilled jobs are an avenue for many of these workers to get good jobs without needing a four-year degree, and employers have expressed a need for workers with bilingual and cultural skills to serve an increasingly diverse public.

In summary, forecasts of occupational growth suggest continued strong growth in occupations requiring better-educated workers. However, substantial growth will also occur in jobs that require little training, and where immigrants are already well represented. Finally, educational forecasts suggest that through-out the next decade, immigrants are likely to play an important role in restructur-ing the U.S. labor force.[28]

B Interrogating the low-skill/high-skill binary

In attacking family-based immigration, opponents frequently trumpet "high-skilled" immigration and claim that the family-based system tends to favor low-skilled laborers.[29] The low-skill/high-skill binary is insulting to work-ers who are not classified as high skilled, and it serves to perpetuate a sys-tem of inequality within the labor-migration system (Enid Trucios-Haynes, Chapter 2). While the rhetoric is pervasive, in truth, the purportedly low-skill occupations—often filled by members of a family—frequently demand a level of ability that requires cultivation and experience (that is, a skill). For example, in his ethnography of migrant farmworkers, Seth Holmes describes the dif-ficulties and skillfulness involved in harvesting fruit.[30] As Silas W. Allard has aptly pointed out:

> The common parlance for this bifurcation is high-skill versus low-skill, but these categories are inaccurate and obfuscate the value determinations implicit in differentiating between these kinds of work. A skill is the ability to do something well, and thus we can speak of highly skilled workers in any field, i.e., those workers who perform well at whatever task they are assigned on the basis of whatever metrics measure success.[31]

---

27 Hamutal Bernstein and Carolyn Vilter, "Upskilling the Immigrant Workforce to Meet Employer Demand for Skilled Workers," *Urban Institute*, July 2018, www.urban.org/sites/default/files/publication/98766/upskilling_immigrant_workforce_to_meet_employer_demand_for_skilled_workers_2.pdf.
28 Ibid., 7–8.
29 See, for example, Ronald Brownstein, "The Purpose of This from the Beginning Has Been to Cut Legal Immigration," *The Atlantic*, January 18, 2018, www.theatlantic.com/politics/archive/2018/01/gop-immigration-bill/550724/.
30 Seth M. Holmes, *Fresh Fruit, Broken Bodies: Migrant Farmworkers in the United States* (Berkeley: University of California Press, 2013), 34, 79.
31 Silas W. Allard, "A Desired Composition: Regulating Vulnerability Through Immigration Law," in *Vulnerability and the Legal Organization of Work*, eds. Martha Albertson Fineman and Jonathan W. Fineman (Abingdon: Routledge, 2017), 177–93, at 188.

Moreover, Allard points out that the work is often "literally disabling" and is often "accompanied by increased risks of both accidental injury . . . and chronic health conditions."[32] As such, interrogating the false binary between high and low skill helps to clarify how family-based immigration has vital economic benefits that are not considered in a points-based system.

C Support for Social Security and Medicare

The aging of the baby boom generation will slow growth of the labor force, increase the burden of older, retired persons on younger workers, and create a potential drag on growth in productivity. The aging of the population will change the dependency ratio—the number of nonworking dependents compared to economically active workers. That ratio is expected to rise as the baby boom generation increasingly enters retirement and as U.S. fertility rates remain low, leaving a greater number of elderly to be supported by each worker—a demographic trend that is widespread across wealthier nations. The decreasing number of taxpaying workers supporting each retiree will strain public assistance programs for the elderly, including Social Security and Medicare.[33] An infusion of young, taxpaying immigrants can help address future shortfalls in these programs. While immigration alone cannot be expected to solve the problem, evidence suggests that greater immigration could aid elderly assistance programs and lessen the burden of Social Security and Medicare on native workers.

D Housing

The foreign-born population in the United States also contributes significantly to the housing market. More than half of the foreign-born population are homeowners. In 2015, 50.7 percent of immigrant heads of household owned their own homes, compared with 65.2 percent of U.S.-born heads of household. Rates of homeownership are comparable between native-born and naturalized immigrants, 64.6 percent of whom owned their own homes in 2015.[34] Immigrants contribute $3.7 trillion to housing markets nationwide.[35]

E Productivity

Immigration also boosts productivity, because immigrant workers tend to be younger and therefore generally more productive than older workers. According

---

32 Ibid., 191.
33 Krogstad, et al., "5 Facts About Illegal Immigration in the U.S."
34 Mark Uh, "Immigration Nation: Homeownership and Foreign Born Residents," *Trulia*, October 13, 2016, www.trulia.com/blog/trends/immigration-nation/.
35 Prashant Gopal, "Why Trump's Immigration Crackdown Could Sink U.S. Home Prices," *Bloomberg*, February 22, 2017, www.bloomberg.com/news/articles/2017-02-22/why-trump-s-immigration-crackdown-could-sink-u-s-home-prices.

62 Bill Ong Hing

to the National Academy of Sciences, the children of immigrants (the second generation) are among the strongest economic and fiscal contributors in the U.S. population, contributing more in taxes than either their parents or the rest of the native-born population.[36] Potential problems created by the aging of the U.S. labor force cannot simply and entirely be solved by more immigration, but budgetary and productivity shortfalls at least will generate demand for generous numbers of skilled immigrant workers. Immigrants can be expected to contribute to meeting the future demand of many industries.[37]

F The labor force summarized

The evidence is clear that immigrants who arrive largely because of family ties have contributed greatly to the U.S. economy. They added an estimated $2 trillion to the U.S. GDP in 2016. They also boost productivity through innovation and entrepreneurship.[38] In 2010, more than 40 percent of Fortune 500 companies had been founded by immigrants and their children. These companies included 90 founded by immigrants and 114 founded by children of immigrants. These companies employ more than 10 million people worldwide.[39] As baby boomers retire en masse over the next 20 years, immigrants will be crucial to filling these job openings and promoting growth of the labor market. From 2020 to 2030, 7 million U.S.-born individuals, on net, are expected to leave the labor force. Two million immigrants and 6.9 million children of immigrants are projected to join the labor force during the same period.[40] Looking further into the future, from 2015 to 2065, immigrants and their descendants are expected to account for 88 percent of U.S. population growth.[41] As such, immigrants and their children will be critical both in replacing retiring workers—preventing labor-market contraction—and in meeting the demands of the future economy.[42] The current family-centered system brings in designers, business leaders, investors, and Silicon

---

36 Francine D. Blau and Christopher D. Mackie, *The Economic and Fiscal Consequences of Immigration, the National Academies of Sciences, Engineering, and Medicine* (Washington, DC: National Academies Press, 2017).
37 Daniel Costa, David Cooper, and Heidi Shierholz, "Facts About Immigration and the U.S. Economy: Answers to Frequently Asked Questions," *Economic Policy Institute*, August 12, 2014, www.epi.org/publication/immigration-facts/.
38 Blau and Mackie, *The Economic and Fiscal Consequences of Immigration*.
39 Partnership for a New American Economy. "The New American Fortune 500," June 2011, www.newamericaneconomy.org/sites/all/themes/pnae/img/new-american-fortune-500-june-2011.pdf.
40 Blau and Mackie, *The Economic and Fiscal Consequences of Immigration*.
41 Pew Research Center, "Modern Immigration Wave Brings 59 Million to U.S., Driving Population Growth and Change Through 2065," September 28, 2015, www.pewresearch.org/hispanic/2015/09/28/modern-immigration-wave-brings-59-million-to-u-s-driving-population-growth-and-change-through-2065/.
42 Dowell Myers, Stephen Levy, and John Pitkin, "The Contributions of Immigrants and Their Children to the American Workforce and Jobs of the Future," *Center for American Progress*, June 19, 2013, www.americanprogress.org/issues/immigration/

Valley–type engineers. And much of the flexibility available to U.S. entrepreneurs in experimenting with risky labor-intensive business ventures is afforded by the presence of low-wage immigrant workers.

VII The benefits of family immigration and the "Corazon" effect

Beyond the obvious economic benefits of the current system, a thorough consideration of the benefits of the family-based immigration system must include the psychological, nonmonetary values of such a system. The psychic value of family reunification is generally overlooked by empiricists, perhaps because of the difficulty in making exact calculations. Yet the inability to make such a calculation is no reason to facilely ignore the possibilities.

Perhaps as a first step in getting a sense of the unquantifiable values of family reunification, we could begin by thinking of our own families and what each one of our loved ones means to us. How much less productive would we be without one or more of them? How much less productive would we be, having to constantly be concerned about their sustenance, safety, or general well-being? How much more productive or emotionally satisfied are we when we know that we can come home at the end of the day and enjoy their company or share our day's events with them?

I call this psychic value the "Corazon" effect, after the name of one of my former clients: Corazon Ayalde. Corazon ("heart" in Spanish) became a U.S. citizen several years after she immigrated to the United States as a registered nurse to work in a public hospital devoted to caring for senior citizens. When her sister Cerissa, who had remained in the Philippines, became widowed without children, the two sisters longed to be reunited—especially after Cerissa became ill. Corazon filed a sibling petition, and after years of waiting, Cerissa received her visa. Corazon felt her "heart being lifted to heaven" as the sisters reunited to live their lives together once again. I think of the Ayalde sisters often in the context of my own mother's inability to successfully petition for her sister's immigration out of mainland China to be reunited when I was a young attorney. First there was the paperwork for the application, complicated by the difficulty in obtaining documents from China; then there were the backlogs in the sibling category; and finally there were the hurdles of getting travel documents out of China in the 1970s. When my mother received word that her sister had passed away, the tears she shed were only a fraction of the pain she had endured being separated from her sister for decades.

Is there truth behind the Corazon effect? Ask Ming Liu, a design engineer from China who works for a U.S. telephone and electronics equipment company. Liu was doing fine, better than his boss expected, and always had his nose to the

---

reports/2013/06/19/66891/the-contributions-of-immigrants-and-their-children-to-the-american-workforce-and-jobs-of-the-future/.

64 *Bill Ong Hing*

grindstone. But he became an even better worker after his wife and child rejoined him following a two-year immigration process. Liu's productivity skyrocketed. His boss observed Liu's personality opening up after his family arrived, and Liu came up with a completely innovative concept that helped the company change direction and increase sales. In Liu's words, after his family immigrated, he could "breathe again."[43]

Or ask Osvaldo Fernandez, a former pitcher for the San Francisco Giants. He had defected from the Cuban national baseball team, leaving his wife and child back in Cuba. After a mediocre first half of the 1996 season, his wife and child were allowed to leave Cuba and join Fernandez in the United States. Overnight, his pitching performance radically improved. He attributed this turnaround to reunification with his wife and child.[44]

One of my students, N. V., was able to petition for her father (one of the categories attacked by the RAISE Act) and experienced the Corazon effect:[45]

> My father immigrated through the family-immigration category. As an adult U.S. citizen, I was able to petition him as my father. I cannot imagine being unable to petition in behalf of my father. He has always been the pillar of both my immediate and extended family. He has particularly been a great support for my mother, my brother, and me. Even though my brother and I are already married and no longer living at home, my father continues to be a big part of our lives. Even now that I am an adult, my father continues to help me in any way that he can, either emotionally or financially, and I know that he does the same for my brother.
>
> For example, ever since I began attending law school and had to leave my job, my father has volunteered to pay for all my textbooks every semester so that I don't have to increase my loans. This has been a huge help for me. I also always go to him for advice because I trust his judgment a lot and have always been very close to him. Now that he has his green card, he is also able to travel and visit my brother, who lives out of state, and he helps babysit my brother's daughter (my father's granddaughter) and in general to be part of his granddaughter's life. Having my father with legal status here in the United States gives me peace of mind, as I no longer need to worry about him being separated from the family.
>
> My mother relies a lot on my father as well. She does not speak English, and he does, so he takes care of any paperwork or finances that need to get done. My mother also does not have any immediate family here, aside from

43 Interview of Ming Liu, San Francisco, CA, May 5, 2006.
44 Nancy Gay, "A Pitch for Togetherness: The Long Road to Reunion for Osvaldo Fernandez's Family," *San Francisco Chronicle,* April 5, 1997, www.sfgate.com/sports/article/A-Pitch-for-Togetherness-The-long-road-to-2846130.php.
45 Stories from my students are used with their permission.

her family through marriage, so not having my dad here would be very difficult emotionally.

My student E. M. talks about the importance of family, particularly about having his aunt in the United States:

> When you look at Latinx heritage, an essential part of the culture surrounds the family unit.
>
> My aunt Alicia, who came in the family-sibling category, is also my godmother, is a mother of five children, works in a factory near her home, and, most importantly, is an essential part of our whole extended family. Through the hard work of herself, her husband, and her now-adult children, she has been able to purchase a home with space large enough to host all family events. My aunt provides a space where her brothers and sisters not only can reminisce about their home country but also can gather to support one another in making new memories in the United States. It is this home where their citizen children learn of their struggles, pass on tradition, and connect with one another. It is my aunt's selflessness and welcoming nature that bring everyone in the family together, and this is how Latinx-American children succeed, with the support of a strong family network. It is because my aunt is in the country that my Mexican American family is able to support one another and provide a safe space when navigating a Eurocentric education system and work force. Family unity is a large part of the Latinx community, and depriving families of pursuing the family immigration visa pathway would hinder the growth of Latinx families in the country. Looking just at citizen children, their parents and older family members are not complete without their siblings, and children without their cousins.

The family fosters productivity after resettlement in the United States through the promotion of activity in the labor force and emotional stability at home. In this regard, the family is a vital "condition of integration" into a new society (Donald M. Kerwin, Chapter 6). The benefits of having parents, siblings, and adult children by your side as you navigate life are obvious. The current family-immigration system recognizes that value to a large extent. The RAISE Act and other challenges to family-based immigration would create real problems for real families, while solving no perceptible problem.

Those who would eliminate family categories contend that family separation is a fact of life (sometimes harsh) that we can get over or live with. Yes, most of us live without someone whom we love dearly, either because of that person's death or because the person lives across the country. Yes, we can get over this separation and perhaps become as productive as ever. Yet to take this ability to recover and place it in the context of immigration policy and say to someone who wants to reunify with a brother, sister, son, or daughter, "No, your relative cannot join you; you cannot reunify with this person on a permanent basis"—this is cruel.

66   *Bill Ong Hing*

That policy choice would remove control from the family and place the burden and challenge of recovery on them unnecessarily. The policy would prevent voluntary choice by adults who are capable of making important life decisions relating to very private family matters.

There are countless reasons why a person may want to petition for a family member to join them. A family unit can provide a stable, solid, supportive foundation for individuals. Families provide support and companionship that positively impact one's quality of life. With family nearby, parents are able to rely on other family members for childcare rather than miss important opportunities. Children are able to stay in school when they have family members who can support them to avoid dropping out to get a job. By helping individuals to be more productive or develop more human capital, the entire nation benefits, not simply the individual. When people have support systems, they are much more likely to succeed. Family provides an inherent safety net that immigrants can rely on, should they need help or assistance.

When a person immigrates to the United States, he or she makes a number of sacrifices to start a new life. Hard work and determination are necessary for success. The decision to petition for family members signals two important realities.

First, the person is taking on the financial responsibility of another family member. They are aware of the time and effort entailed in the immigration process. They know about the public-charge ground of inadmissibility, fully conscious of their legal and moral responsibility for the newcomer. By petitioning for a family member, this person is signaling that they have the ability to support the beneficiary as a result of the work that they have invested.

Second, petitioning for a family member communicates a clear commitment to living in the United States. Petitioning for a relative signals a dedication to living comfortably and peacefully in the adopted country. That commitment is important no matter the class of worker. The commitment tells us that this is the type of person who wants a better life for their family, and that is the type of person who is good for the country. The person wants the country to thrive so that their family will flourish as well. Admitting family members strengthens the ties that the immigrant family has to this country. The people they love and care about are in the same place, helping the family to feel at home in the United States.

VIII Conclusion

Opponents of the current family-based system contend that there has been unending chain migration. They conjure the image of a single immigrant who enters, then brings in a spouse, after which the spouse brings in siblings, who, in turn, bring in their spouses and children, while each adult brings in parents who can petition for their siblings or other children, as the cycle goes on and on. These opponents of the system hope to scare us about an imaginary unending horde.

Certainly, for a period of time, family categories result in the reunification of some relatives. However, the purveyors of the image of limitless relatives forget that, throughout the course of global immigration history, these so-called family

In defense of chain migration 67

chains are invariably broken. For example, although virtually limitless numbers of Western Europeans were permitted to immigrate to the United States throughout the past 200 years, at a given point, decisions were made—often slowly and gradually—by families about who was willing or wanted to come to the new country, and who did not. As a result, immigration numbers from Western Europe eventually dropped. Hundreds of thousands of immigrants from the United Kingdom, Germany, and Ireland immigrated to the United States in each decade of the first part of the twentieth century. The figures continued to be substantial for Germans and British nationals through 1970, but the figures diminished significantly after that.

In an era of promoting family values, proposals to eliminate family-immigration categories seem odd. What values do such proposals impart? What's the message? That parents, brothers, and sisters are not important? Or (in the case of the proposal to restrict older children of lawful permanent residents) that once children reach a certain age, the parent–child bond does not remain strong? Eliminating such categories institutionalizes concepts that are antithetical to the nurturing of family ties, that ignore the strong family bonds in most families, and that discourage ideals that should be promoted among all families. Indeed, the proposals send a strong antifamily message.

Without an empirical foundation for attacking the entry of immigrants with low job skills, critics of the current family-based system simply argue that there is a better way of doing things. They are not satisfied that immigration fills needed job shortages and aids economic growth as a result of the entry of ambitious, hard-working family immigrants and their children, many of whom are professionals as well as skilled workers in lower-paying jobs with a propensity for saving and investment. As we have seen, these claims also carry serious racial overtones. The preference for "high-skilled" migrants is often a pretext for xenophobia, coming at a time when three in four immigrants are from Latin America or Asia.

Family-immigration categories should be retained. Former President Donald Trump and restrictionist leaders have claimed that eliminating certain family-based categories would allow more "quality" immigrants to be admitted. However, a person's worth to their neighborhood and country is not determined solely by what that person earns. Aside from the fact that low-wage workers are also skilled, people can contribute to the greatness of a country and goodness of the community in different ways. That immigrants may not have entered because of high-paying employment skills does not mean that they have not added value to the society.

In this volume, Gemma Tulud Cruz provides a theological framework for understanding our responsibility for the "unwanted" migrants who are victims of forced displacement (Chapter 11). The three parts of the framework—one bread, one body, and one people—guide us in recognizing that the Christian revelation of the unity and common destiny of the human race compels us to welcome the unwanted. Her framework highlights the importance of "social responsibility, especially to those in need, by witnessing to solidarity and the common good from a collective or global perspective" (Cruz, Chapter 11). This responsibility

68 *Bill Ong Hing*

is also helpful in responding to challenges to voluntary family migrants who are mislabeled of "poor quality" or "low skilled." Sponsoring relatives demonstrate responsibility to their family members, and we should recognize our own responsibility to these families. There is no basis for any of the rest of us to judge that migrant relatives are not a worthy part of our collective selves. They come in good grace to be part of our figurative as well as literal family.

The preamble to the Universal Declaration of Human Rights highlights the unity of the family as the "foundation of freedom, justice and peace in the world" for good reason. Our families make us whole. Our families define us as human beings. Our families are at the center of our most treasured values. Our families make us strong.

Suggested Reading

Connor, Phillip, and Neil G. Ruiz. "Majority of U.S. Public Supports High-Skilled Immigration." *Pew Research Center*, January 22, 2019. www.pewresearch.org/global/2019/01/22/majority-of-u-s-public-supports-high-skilled-immigration/.

Gelatt, Julia. "The RAISE Act: Dramatic Change to Family Immigration, Less So for the Employment-Based System." *Migration Policy Institute*, August 2017. www.migrationpolicy.org/news/raise-act-dramatic-change-family-immigration-less-so-employment-based-system.

Hing, Bill Ong. *Deporting Our Souls: Values, Morality, and Immigration Policy.* Cambridge: Cambridge University Press, 2006.

———. *Making and Remaking Asian America Through Immigration Policy, 1850–1990.* Stanford, CA: Stanford University Press, 1993.

Hooper, Kate, and Brian Salant. "It's Relative: A Crosscountry Comparison of Family-Migration Policies and Flows." *Migration Policy Institute*, April 2018. www.migrationpolicy.org/research/crosscountry-comparison-family-migration.

Kamasaki, Charles. *Immigration Reform: The Corpse That Will Not Die.* Simsbury, CT: Mandel Vilar Press, 2019.

Zolberg, Aristide R., and Russell Sage Foundation. *A Nation by Design: Immigration Policy in the Fashioning of America.* Cambridge, MA: Harvard University Press, 2006.

4 The state of the law on refugees, asylees, and stateless persons

Michele R. Pistone

I Introduction

In fear for his or her life, a person leaves home and flees across the border, entering another country. What rights does that person possess? The unfortunate reality of the current international refugee regime echoes Stephen Crane's famous poem:

A refugee said to the government:

"Sir, the law exists!"
"However," replied the government,
"The fact has not created in me
A sense of obligation."[1]

This chapter begins by discussing the laws that *might* give that person the legal right to live lawfully outside of the country of his or her nationality, that is, to gain the protected status of refugee or asylee. The chapter then discusses the many measures nations have adopted in recent years to discourage such persons from exercising their rights. It next addresses the question of why migration-control measures have proliferated recently, then ends with an assessment of whether and when this trend is likely to be reversed.

II The international law of refugee protection

While "refugee" as a concept is of ancient provenance,[2] the current international legal regime governing refugees dates back to 1951. In that year, the United Nations convened in Geneva a Conference of Plenipotentiaries on the Status of

---

1 This poetic allusion was suggested by my husband, John J. Hoeffner, and is a close paraphrase of, "A Man Said to the Universe":
A man said to the universe:
"Sir, I exist!"
"However," replied the universe,
"The fact has not created in me
A sense of obligation."
Stephen Crane, "A Man Said to the Universe," in *The Complete Poems* (Dublin: Honeycomb Press, 2011), 118.
2 See, for example, Karen Musalo, Jennifer Moore, and Richard A. Boswell, *Refugee Law and Policy: A Comparative and International Approach*, 4th ed. (Durham: Carolina Academic Press, 2011), 3–10.

70 *Michele R. Pistone*

Refugees and Stateless People. The goal of the conference was to draft an international treaty that would define the term "refugee" under international law and set out the obligations of nation-states toward refugees. The Convention Relating to the Status of Refugees (Refugee Convention) was the product of those negotiations.

The Refugee Convention, which was initially ratified mostly by European countries, took effect in April 1954. The Convention defines a refugee as any person who:

> owing to well-founded fear of being persecuted for reasons of race, religion, nationality, membership of a particular social group or political opinion, is outside the country of his nationality and is unable or, owing to such fear, is unwilling to avail himself of the protection of that country; or who, not having a nationality and being outside the country of his former habitual residence as a result of such events, is unable or, owing to such fear, is unwilling to return to it.

Once a person is determined to satisfy this definition, the principle of nonrefoulment (or nonreturn) prohibits any signatory state from repatriating the refugee to a country in which his or her life or freedom would be threatened. The refugee's international right to seek protection is triggered once the refugee enters the territory of a signatory nation-state. If a migrant has convinced authorities that he or she is entitled to recognition as a refugee, the refugee is granted status in the destination country, allowing him or her to live and work there without fear of removal. The 1951 Refugee Convention contains several notable limitations. First, its protection was limited to events that occurred prior to January 1, 1951. Second, it was limited to events that took place in Europe.

These limitations were effectively swept away by the 1967 Protocol Relating to the Status of Refugees. Under the Protocol, which has now been ratified by 146 states, the rights of refugees were extended without regard to any geographical limitations and allowed protection for events of persecution that took place after 1951 and into the future. Importantly, the 1967 Protocol maintained the essential substantive requirements for refugee status, that is, that one have a well-founded fear of persecution on account of one of the five protected grounds: race, religion, nationality, membership in a particular social group, or political opinion.

The architects of the 1951 Convention and 1967 Protocol would recognize much of the protection—indeed, most of the protection—offered to refugees today as clearly deriving from their efforts. Some developments they would recognize as new, however, and those developments stem from three sources: (1) other international agreements, (2) judicial interpretations of refugee law, and (3) legislation or regulation that provides new forms of nonpermanent relief from removal.

A International agreements

Other than the 1967 Refugee Protocol's effective elimination of the Refugee Convention's temporal and geographical limitations, as a matter of codified international law, "there have been few formal changes to the refugee rights regime since the entry into force of the Refugee Convention."[3] Refugees have gained additional protections, however, from some international agreements of general applicability, such as the International Covenant on Civil and Political Rights[4] and the International Covenant on Economic, Social and Cultural Rights.[5] The International Covenant on Civil and Political Rights, for example, declares "nearly all internationally recognized *civil rights* . . . to be universal and not subject to requirements of nationality."[6]

B Judicial interpretations of refugee law

Other developments in refugee law that may not have been anticipated by the drafters of the Refugee Convention and Protocol arise from judicial interpretations of the definition of refugee. Probably the greatest expansion of protection in recent years stemming from this source is the recognition that the category of "membership in a particular social group" is broad enough to include women suffering from gender-based violence.

In the United States, the first Board of Immigration Appeals (BIA) precedential decision on gender-based violence was issued in 1996. In *Matter of Kasinga*, the BIA held that Fauziya Kasinga was eligible for asylum protection on the basis of her membership in the particular social group of "young women of the Tchamba-Kunsuntu Tribe who have not had FGM [female genital mutilation], as practiced by that tribe, and who oppose the practice." The BIA also found in *Kasinga* that female genital cutting constituted "persecution" under the definition of refugee.[7]

---

3 James C. Hathaway, *The Rights of Refugees Under International Law* (Cambridge: Cambridge University Press, 2005), 110.
4 UN General Assembly, Resolution 2200A (XXI), International Covenant on Civil and Political Rights (December 16, 1966).
5 Ibid.
6 Hathaway, *The Rights of Refugees under International Law*, 120 (emphasis in original). Ironically, one post-1951 Convention agreement specifically intended to enhance the basic protection rights of refugees—a regional agreement among African nations named the Convention Governing the Specific Aspects of Refugee Problems in Africa—is, in at least one respect, in tension with the International Covenant on Civil and Political Rights. While the latter declares the universality of speech rights, the former prohibits refugees from expressing views "likely to cause tension between Member States." Convention Governing the Specific Aspects of Refugee Problems in Africa, September 10, 1969, 1001 U.N.T.S. 14691 ("OAU Convention"); see also Hathaway, *The Rights of Refugees under International Law*, 119n177.
7 Matter of Kasinga, 21 I. & N. Dec. 357 (B.I.A. 1996).

72 Michele R. Pistone

The *Kasinga* decision is now firmly established and led to other developments based on its logic. I have cited the *Kasinga* case in winning asylum for a number of clients, including: (1) a Middle Eastern woman who fled an abusive spouse; (2) a gay man who fled violence directed at him because of his sexual orientation; (3) a young African woman who was forcibly recruited by an insurgent army to become a child soldier and sex slave; and (4) a Central American indigenous woman who fled abuse by her domestic partner. Other attorneys have brought and won similar cases. In 2014, for example, the Board of Immigration Appeals held in another binding precedential decision, *Matter of A-R-C-G*, that "married women in Guatemala who are unable to leave their relationship" constitute a particular social group for purposes of obtaining asylum.[8] Notably, although the persecutor in these cases was a private actor, asylum was granted because the record reflected that the government in the applicant's home country was either unable or unwilling to protect the applicant from persecution.

The progeny of *Kasinga* are not as firmly established as *Kasinga* itself, however, and in fact have been attacked as too expansive. Indeed, in June 2018, in *Matter of A-B-*, the U.S. Attorney General overruled *Matter of A-R-C-G*. *Matter of A-B-* threatens the continued viability of some asylum claims based on domestic violence, and perhaps even other cases involving persecutors who are private, rather than government, actors.[9]

Nonetheless, the basic principle that gender may play a role in forming a social group is well established both in the United States and elsewhere. Examples are numerous. In 1996, the United Kingdom judicially recognized gender as a particular social group under the refugee definition,[10] as did Australia in 2002.[11] The Immigration and Refugee Board of Canada, albeit administratively, first recognized gender as a basis for protection as early as 1993, when it issued national guidelines on gender-based persecution. Those guidelines, updated in 2003, expressly recognize gender as a social group.[12] In all events, for gender-based and other groups, it is likely that the content of the "membership in a particular social group" category will continue to develop through case law, as it has in the past.[13]

---

8 Matter of A-R-C-G, 26 I. & N. Dec. 388 (B.I.A. 2014).

9 Matter of A-B-, 27 I. & N. Dec. 316 (A.G. 2018).

10 *Islam (A.P.) v. Secretary of State for the Home Department; Regina v. Immigration Appeal Tribunal and Another Ex Parte Shah (A.P.)* (Conjoined Appeals) [1999] UKHL 20, [1999] 2 AC 629 (appeals taken from Eng.).

11 *Minister for Immigration & Multicultural Affairs v Khawar* [2000] FCA 1130 (April 11, 2002).

12 Immigration and Refugee Board of Canada, *Chairperson Guidelines 4: Women Refugee Claimants Fearing Gender-Based Violence* [Ottawa], 1996, https://irb-cisr.gc.ca/en/legal-policy/policies/Pages/GuideDir04.aspx.

13 *Matter of A-B-*, 27 I. &. N Dec. 316 (A.G. 2018) (noting that "a recurring question in asylum law is determining whether alleged persecution [in a particular case] was based on [the applicant's] membership in a 'particular social group.' Over the past thirty years, this

C Legislation or regulation providing new forms of nonpermanent relief from removal

The drafters of the legal definition of "refugee" were well aware that their definition was narrower than the colloquial understanding of the word.[14] In the common understanding, people forced to move from Louisiana to Texas after Hurricane Katrina were "refugees"; the thousands of people displaced from Nicaragua and Honduras after Hurricane Mitch hit Central America in 1998 were "refugees"; and the Haitians forced to evacuate their island nation after it suffered from a devastating earthquake in 2010 were "refugees." But none of these groups satisfy the definition of the 1951 Convention (and of course it wouldn't mean much if the Louisianan victims of Katrina did). The more limited nature of the Convention definition is deliberate and meant to exclude various types of mass influx. General conditions of hardship, whether the source of the hardship is war, economic deprivation, or widespread devastation from a natural disaster, do not qualify one for refugee status under the Convention. A definition that would encompass hardships of these sorts is likely to transcend the bounds of political possibility and even, in some cases, to test the bounds of practical feasibility. People who are refugees in the colloquial sense and who are suffering as much as Convention refugees have suffered are thus denied a remedy available to many Convention refugees. For them, disaster relief programs will have to suffice.

The United States has broken no new ground in dealing with this broader group of refugees,[15] but it has passed domestic legislation to address a derivative issue, namely, what to do with migrants to the United States who do not have permanent immigration status (including those who have no official status) when disaster strikes their homeland. The U.S. solution, created as part of the Immigration Act of 1990, was to establish a new form of temporary protection, known as Temporary Protected Status (TPS). TPS is available to nationals of countries that are experiencing extreme hardship, including an environmental disaster, ongoing armed conflict, or extraordinary or temporary conditions that prevent its nationals from safely returning, provided that the national was physically present in the

---

question has recurred frequently before the Board and the courts of appeals, and the standard has evolved over time.").

14 The Convention definition also is often narrower than the intended meaning of the word when used in nonlegal writings, even in formal documents. See, for example, Michele R. Pistone and John J. Hoeffner, *Stepping Out of the Brain Drain: Applying Catholic Social Teaching in a New Era of Migration* (Lanham, MD: Lexington Books, 2007), 30, 38n11 (noting that "Catholic social teaching considers the term refugee appropriately to include not only people who fear persecution on account of one of the five grounds protected by the Convention, but also individuals who are compelled to leave their home country for such reasons as natural disaster, famine, severe economic deprivation, or war").

15 For a discussion of how the U.S. response to such situations can be improved, see Michele R. Pistone and John J. Hoeffner, "Unsettling Developments: Terrorism and the New Case for Enhancing Protection and Humanitarian Assistance for Refugees and Internally Displaced Persons, Including Victims of Natural Disasters," *Columbia Human Rights Law Review* 42, no. 3 (2011): 613–96.

74   Michele R. Pistone

United States prior to the onset of the crisis. While TPS provides no direct benefits to the people most afflicted by disastrous circumstances, the program relaxes the usual immigration laws and allows nationals already located within the United States to stay, and thus avoids adding fuel to the fire in a country already suffering from a perhaps not entirely metaphorical conflagration.

The Secretary of Homeland Security, after consultation with other government agencies, decides which countries are experiencing the hardships contemplated by the TPS legislation, and the date foreign nationals must have been physically present in the United States to be eligible for TPS. Those with TPS status are not subject to deportation and are eligible to work legally while they are in status. The Secretary can make TPS available for periods of 6, 12, or 18 months. Extensions are possible at the end of each period, based on current conditions in the designated country. There is no limit on the number of extensions that can be granted.

TPS and other forms of temporary humanitarian protection are inferior to refugee status in this respect: they make permanent the sense of instability that resettled refugees are able to shed after defined periods of relatively short duration. Thus, while resettled refugees can apply to become legal permanent residents of the United States after one year's presence in the United States (and asylees can do the same one year after being granted asylum), and both can then apply to become U.S. citizens five years after gaining permanent residency, a person with TPS never possesses certainty beyond 18 months into the future. Rather than provide a gateway to a more permanent relationship, TPS is a dead end. In recent years, that has become especially clear as the Department of Homeland Security has started to roll back the TPS designation for nationals of Sudan, Nicaragua, Haiti, Honduras, and El Salvador, some of whom may have lived with TPS status in the United States for decades.[16]

While TPS is a humanitarian response to situations that do not meet the refugee definition, another type of relief—withholding of removal—is available in the United States when a person establishes a clear probability of persecution based on one of the five protected grounds of the Refugee Convention and yet is denied asylum, which is always a discretionary decision. (Asylum might be denied if, among many other things, required filing deadlines were not met, there is evidence of fraud in the application process, or the petitioner could safely reside in and has ties to a third country). Withholding of removal, like TPS, is an intrinsically insecure status, as it does not provide a pathway to a more permanent status and presupposes the existence of a valid removal order.

In Europe, another nonpermanent status exists, this one called subsidiary protection. Subsidiary protection is available to a non-EU citizen or a stateless person

---

16 D'Vera Cohn, Jeffrey S. Passel, and Kristen Bialik, "Many Immigrants with Temporary Protected Status Face Uncertain Future in U.S.," *Pew Research Center*, May 31, 2020, www.pewresearch.org/fact-tank/2019/11/27/immigrants-temporary-protected-status-in-us/.

who does not qualify as a Convention refugee, but who is likely to "face a real risk of suffering severe harm" if returned to his or her home country or country of last habitual residence.[17] Subsidiary protection can be terminated "when the circumstances which led to the granting of subsidiary protection status have ceased to exist or have changed to such a degree that protection is no longer required."[18]

III Restrictions on the exercise of the right to refuge

The previous paragraphs set out various international agreements and domestic laws that by now have saved the lives and preserved the human dignity of millions of people. Whatever the shortcomings and limitations of these laws, they have long been regarded by most people desirous of a more humane world as, at the very least, a good start. Unfortunately, serious questions have arisen as to whether those laws, in the broader scope of history, will be regarded more as a false start than as a good one. As one leading scholar noted, in 2005:

> [T]he reality today is that a significant number of governments in all parts of the world are withdrawing in practice from meeting the legal duty to provide refugees with the protection they require. . . . [M]any appear committed to a pattern of defensive strategies designed to avoid international legal responsibility toward involuntary migrants. . . . For refugees . . . the increasingly marginal relevance of international refugee law has in practice signaled a shift to inferior or illusory protection.[19]

A much more recent assessment is no less gloomy:

> Restrictive migration policies are today the primary, some might say only, response of the developed world to rising numbers of asylum seekers and refugees. This has produced a distorted refugee regime both in Europe and globally—a regime fundamentally based on the principle of deterrence rather than human rights protection. . . . [M]ost of these countries simultaneously do everything in their power to exclude those [seeking] international protection and offer only a minimalist engagement to assist those countries hosting the largest number of refugees.[20]

---

17 Council Directive 2004/83 of the European Commission of April 29, 2004, on Minimum Standards for the Qualification and Status of Third Country Nationals or Stateless Persons as Refugees or as Persons Who Otherwise Need International Protection and the Content of the Protection Granted, 2004 O.J. (L. 304) 12–23.

18 Ibid.

19 Hathaway, *The Rights of Refugees under International* Law, 998.

20 Thomas Gammeltoft-Hansen and Nikolas F. Tan, "The End of the Deterrence Paradigm? Future Directions for Global Refugee Policy," *Journal Migration and Human Security* 5, no. 1 (2017): 28–56, at 28.

76 *Michele R. Pistone*

Governmental undermining of the international right to seek refuge in another country has taken a number of forms. Collectively, the policies resemble the multiple levels of fencing that line portions of the U.S. border with Mexico,[21] only on a much greater scale. Far too often today, people seeking only to secure the rights bestowed upon them by international law find it necessary to overcome one barrier after another, placed not by the government that would persecute them, but by governments that hold themselves out as the guardians of humanitarian law.

How do wealthy countries deter refugees and asylum seekers from securing their rights? Deterrence strategies take various forms and are used strategically at various points along the route away from persecution. They start with preventing refugees from leaving their home countries and continue throughout the migration route even beyond the physical barriers along the borders of receiving countries. Some of these deterrence policies are discussed below, beginning with the start of the migration route and extending through to the adjudication of claims in destination states (see also Daniel Kanstroom, Chapter 1).

First, countries have adopted policies designed to keep refugees and potential applicants for asylum far away (see Silas W. Allard, Chapter 5). Deterrence policies of these types include various bilateral and multilateral agreements between receiving countries and countries of transit or origin. For example, in the Americas, the United States has been funding enhanced border control efforts along Mexico's southern border with Guatemala for many years. The Merida Initiative, a 2008 bilateral cooperation agreement between the governments of the United States and Mexico, centers on Mexico's agreement to erect "a twenty-first-century border structure" along its southern border. In 2014, an additional initiative, Operation Coyote, was "designed to stem the flow of illegal Central American migration"[22] by deploying Department of Homeland Security investigators to Mexico and Central America. In addition, two years later, "funds also flowed to Mexico's military from the U.S. Department of Defense's (DOD) counternarcotics budget to bolster its capacity to control Mexico's southern border."[23] In 2019 and 2020, the U.S. government negotiated agreements with the governments of Guatemala, Honduras, and El Salvador designed to stem the northward movement of refugees to the southern border of the United States by forcing asylum seekers who travel through those countries to seek asylum there.

---

21 Peter Rowe, "Focus: Border Wall: San Diego's Been There, Done That," *San Diego Tribune*, January 28, 2017, www.sandiegouniontribune.com/news/immigration/sd-me-borderwall-update-20170124-story.html (noting that, in and around San Diego, California, three layers of fencing line some portions of the U.S.–Mexico border).

22 *The Outer Ring of Border Security: DHS's International Security Programs, Before H. Subcomm. On Border and Maritime Security*, 114th Cong. 7–8 (2015) (testimony of Lev. J. Kubiak, Assistant Director, International Operations, Homeland Security Investigations, U.S. Immigration and Customs Enforcement, Department of Homeland Security).

23 Bill Frelick, Ian M. Kysel, and Jennifer Podkul, "The Impact of Externalization of Migration Controls on the Rights of Asylum Seekers and Other Migrants," *Journal Migration and Human Security* 4, no. 4 (2016): 190–220, at 202.

The state of the law 77

Many similar agreements exist. For example, the European Union has reached one such agreement with Ukraine and another with Turkey. In addition, a 2017 Memorandum of Understanding between Italy and Libya[24] calls for Italian assistance to Libya's border patrol forces to stem the "flows of transiting migrants through Libya to Europe" and for securing "Libya's borders and preventing departures."[25] This is only the latest of several agreements negotiated since 2000 by Libya and Italy to prevent irregular migrants from accessing Italian territory.

Countries also act directly to prevent arrivals by sea. The U.S. Coast Guard "conducts patrols and coordinates with federal agencies and foreign countries to detain undocumented migrants at sea and prohibit entry via maritime routes to the United States and its territories."[26] Similarly, the European Border and Coast Guard Agency patrols the Mediterranean Sea as part of its effort to control entry into European Union countries.

The Australian government has provided other examples of interdicting boats to prevent asylum seekers from reaching its territory. Started in 2001 after the highly publicized *Tampa* incident, in which Australia refused to allow 438 refugees to disembark from the Norwegian registered container ship that had rescued them at sea, Operation Relex carried out maritime interdictions into 2007. A similar program, Operation Sovereign Borders, commenced in 2013 and continues to the present. The activities of Operation Sovereign Borders "are shrouded in secrecy," but it is known that the "military-led border security operation . . . focuses on deterrence, interception and forcible turnbacks of boats."[27]

Some wealthy nations, including the United States, have also acted to reduce access of asylum seekers to their countries by air. Under their laws, air carriers are sanctioned when they transport travelers who do not possess properly issued travel documents to destination countries. These carrier sanctions create incentives for private carriers to err on the side of denying travel.[28] The policy is not

---

24 Anja Palm, "The Italy-Libya Memorandum of Understanding: The Baseline of a Policy Approach Aimed at Closing All Doors to Europe?" *EU Immigration and Asylum Law and Policy* (blog), October 2, 2017, http://eumigrationlawblog.eu/the-italy-libya-memoran dum-of-understanding-the-baseline-of-a-policy-approach-aimed-at-closing-all-doors-to-europe/.

25 Ibid.

26 "Enforcing Immigration Laws," *GoCoastGuard.com, United States Coast Guard*, www.gocoast-guard.com/about-the-coast-guard/discover-our-roles-missions/migrant-interdiction.

27 Violeta Moreno-Lax, "The Interdiction of Asylum Seekers at Sea: Law and (mal)Practice in Europe and Australia," *Kaldor Centre for International Refugee Law* (May 2017): 3, www.kaldor centre.unsw.edu.au/sites/default/files/Policy_Brief4_Interdiction_of_asylum_seekers_ at_sea.pdf.

28 In 2016, Sweden "extended carrier sanctions to train and ferry companies operating inside the Schengen area as a means to restrict the otherwise free movement of refugees towards the country." Gammeltoft-Hansen and Tan, "The End of the Deterrence Paradigm?" 36. See also Frelick, Kysel, and Podkul, "The Impact of Externalization of Migration Controls," 195 (noting that "[e]xternalization policies also include . . . carrier sanctions imposed on transportation firms . . . that have the effect of preventing departure or transit of migrants to destination countries").

78   Michele R. Pistone

innocuous, as genuine asylum seekers, by necessity, often travel without proper travel documents. To seek official travel documents, or to show authentic identifying documents to government officials before their flight, could put asylum seekers fleeing government-sanctioned persecution in even greater danger.[29]

Second, for migrants who do manage to approach the border of a destination country, additional barriers now appear as well. Walls and fences combined with modern technologies overseen by militarized border agents are increasingly a feature of border security efforts. The fence built by the Hungarian government along the footpath followed by Syrian and Iraqi refugees en route to Europe in 2015 is one example. That fence is now fortified with heat sensors and cameras and is capable of delivering electric shocks. Asylum seekers must make it to one of two transit zones to submit an asylum application, which zones limit entry to ten migrants each day.[30]

The United States has devoted the greatest amount of resources to these sorts of barriers. From approximately 4,000 border patrol agents in the early 1990s, there are now more than 20,000. From 1997 to 2018, a conservative estimate found that "the U.S. immigration enforcement (actual) budget rose from $1.935 billion ($3 billion adjusted for inflation) to $21.1 billion."[31] Overall funding for U.S. Customs and Border Patrol and Immigration and Customs Enforcement increased another 19 percent from FY 2019 to FY 2020.[32] Much of this increase has been to cover increased personnel costs, the build-out of the 580 miles of U.S. fencing and walls along the border with Mexico, and the military-like and high-tech equipment used by border patrol agents. Such equipment includes airplanes and helicopters, drones, daytime and infrared cameras, night-vision tools, weaponry, video surveillance systems, and ground, tower, and mobile sensors.

29 In this section discussing how states act to keep refugees far from their borders, I have been considering efforts directed at persons who have not had their claims examined and recognized by the UNHCR or other organization used to bring order to the refugee process. States also can and have acted to keep properly vetted refugees away, through the simple expedient of deciding to accept fewer of them for resettlement. The United States, for example, over a ten-year period from 2008 to 2018, accepted for resettlement about 80,000 refugees per year from international refugee resettlement programs. In 2019, however, the yearly number was reduced to 30,000, the lowest refugee ceiling in the 38-year history of the United States Refugee Admissions Program. See U.S. Department of State, *Report to Congress on Proposed Refugee Admissions for FY2020* (November 4, 2019), www.state.gov/reports/report-to-congress-on-proposed-refugee-admissions-for-fy-2020/.

30 Marton Dunai, "Hungary Builds New High-Tech Border Fence—with Few Migrants in Sight," *Reuters*, March 2, 2017, www.reuters.com/article/us-europe-migrants-hungary-fence/hungary-builds-new-high-tech-border-fence-with-few-migrants-in-sight-idUSKBN-1692MH.

31 Donald M. Kerwin, "From IIRIRA to Trump: Connecting the Dots to the Current US Immigration Policy Crisis," *Journal Migration and Human Security* 6, no. 3 (2018): 192–204, at 193.

32 "2020 Budget Fact Sheet: Strengthening Border Security and Immigration Enforcement," *White House*, March 2019, www.whitehouse.gov/wp-content/uploads/2019/03/FY20-Fact-Sheet_Immigration-Border-Security_FINAL.pdf.

A *third* tool of exclusion, which takes two forms, is applied by various entities to migrants who actually succeed in arriving upon the territory of a destination state. Both forms feature deviations from norms of due process and prior understandings of refugee law. The European version applies wholesale dismissal of asylum claims from specified areas. Thus, Hungary has declared that no persons who cross the border from Serbia are eligible for asylum, and the EU induced Turkey to agree to accept the return of persons who passed onto Greek territory from Turkey, with no requirement that the EU hear those persons' claims to refugee status before they were returned to Turkey. These types of decisions have led some scholars to conclude "that externalization is now the main plank of EU migration policy."[33]

The U.S. version of this policy, adopted in 1996 as part of the Illegal Immigrant Reform and Immigrant Responsibility Act (IIRAIRA) is to offer cursory questioning of migrants who arrive at airports or border crossings without valid travel documents, to determine if they have a claim for asylum. A determination, by a single border patrol official, that a migrant has no such claim, will result in "expedited removal" of that migrant, with no further review. Limited examinations of the expedited removal process have revealed a number of problems, including (1) failure to ask required questions, (2) ignoring of answers that should have forbidden a removal, (3) failure to provide adequate interpretative services, (4) lack of adequate officer training, and (5) having applicants sign statements composed by an officer without having the applicant check it first for accuracy.[34] Genuine asylum seekers mistakenly removed pay the price for these failures.

When a claimant for refugee or asylum status overcomes all these obstacles, a *fourth* and final set of policies is activated, with the effect of making it less likely that a claimant will press forward with a claim, as well as making it less likely that a claim will be successful. The harshest of these policies is detention, and the United States is the greatest proponent of detention. The U.S. immigration detention system is the largest in the world, with an average of more than 45,890 people in administrative immigration detention each day,[35] at an average cost of $150 a day per detainee.[36] According to 2015 figures, over the course of that year, more than 59,000 detainees were younger than 18 years of age.[37] Many detention centers lack adequate health care or proper medication, and reports

---

33 Frelick, Kysel, and Podkul, "The Impact of Externalization of Controls," 208.

34 See, generally, Michele R. Pistone and John J. Hoeffner, "Rules Are Made to Be Broken: How the Process of Expedited Removal Fails Asylum Seekers," *Georgetown Immigration Law Journal* 20, no. 6 (2006): 167–211, see especially 175–93.

35 See Emily Kassie, "How Trump Inherited His Expanding Detention System," *The Marshall Project*, February 12, 2019, www.themarshallproject.org/2019/02/12/how-trump-inherited-his-expanding-detention-system.

36 "United States Immigration Detention Profile," *Global Detention Project*, accessed May 2016, www.globaldetentionproject.org/countries/americas/united-states.

37 Emily Ryo and Ian Peacock, "The Landscape of Immigration Detention in the United States," *American Immigration Council*, December 2018, https://americanimmigration-council.org/research/landscape-immigration-detention-united-states.

80 *Michele R. Pistone*

of abuse in detention centers are not infrequent.[38] It is worth noting that the people in the immigration detention system who face these conditions are not being detained because they have been convicted of, or even charged with, any criminal offense.

Not surprisingly, such conditions can deter people from pursuing their claims and can encourage them to elect voluntary departure instead. Further, even hearing about such conditions can act as a deterrent, as some people may choose not to try to seek refuge. It is true that detention can ensure that migrants appear in immigration court for their removal proceedings and do not abscond into the community. Recently, however, more disreputable motivations for detention have moved to the forefront. Indeed, shortly after the Trump administration announced a policy of detaining entering migrants, prosecuting parents for illegal entry, and separating children from their parents, White House Chief of Staff John F. Kelly called family separation a "tough deterrent."[39]

In addition to discouraging the pursuit of claims, detention also has the effect of making it more difficult for people to succeed in the claims they do pursue. It has been very well documented, for instance, that detained asylum seekers have much lower chances of succeeding on the merits of their asylum cases. In detention, immigrants cannot easily find an attorney and may have difficulty meeting with an attorney who has been retained. As a consequence, detained individuals are often left to present their claims and fight their cases alone, with little to no knowledge of the legal process, the language, or the elements of a successful claim.[40]

Sadly, the United States is not alone in its reliance on detention. Rather, as two European scholars have recently noted:

> Mandatory detention of asylum seekers is a widespread practice intended to deter further arrivals. European states including Greece, Macedonia, Malta, and Hungary have recently stepped up systematic detention of asylum seekers. Australia has long had a policy of mandatory detention of asylum seekers arriving by boat. . . . Israel places irregular migrants for up to a year at the Holot detention center located in the desert. . . . [Such] wide-scale detention

---

38 See, for example, "Prisons and Punishment: Immigration Detention in California." *Human Rights First*, January 2019, www.humanrightsfirst.org/sites/default/files/Prisons_and_Punishment.pdf; John Washington, "Here Is Just Some of the Hateful Abuse Immigrants Face in Detention Centers," *The Nation*, June 27, 2018, www.thenation.com/article/just-hateful-abuse-immigrants-face-detention-centers/.

39 Eli Rosenberg, "Sessions Defends Separating Immigrant Parents and Children: We've Got to Get This Message Out," *Washington Post*, June 5, 2018, www.washingtonpost.com/news/post-politics/wp/2018/06/05/sessions-defends-separating-immigrant-parents-and-children-weve-got-to-get-this-message-out/?noredirect=on&utm_term=.40af985ef333. Daniel Kanstroom and Bill Ong Hing also address these policies elsewhere in this volume (Kanstroom, Chapter 1; Hing, Chapter 3).

40 "Prisons and Punishment," 2–3.

policies are not consistent with the prohibition against penalization of illegal entry or stay in Article 31 of the 1951 Refugee Convention.[41]

Other policies that have had the effect of deterring asylum claims from people who are already present in a country are (1) the introduction of short time limits for filing asylum applications,[42] (2) the existence of long backlogs for hearing claims, (3) decreases in public benefits available to refugees and asylum seekers, (4) cutbacks in family reunification rights, and (5) delayed or more limited grants of work authorization. The trend is unmistakable: the world is no longer as welcoming of refugees as it once was. The next section asks the questions, why is this so, and what can be done about it?

IV The certain end of one era; the uncertain start of another

The Danish philosopher Soren Kierkegaard famously noted that while life must be lived forwards, only backwards can it be understood. So it is, too, with the course of modern refugee law: born in 1951 with the Refugee Convention, it came of age with the 1967 Protocol and matured with the widespread acceptance of the Protocol; its incorporation into the domestic law of nations (the United States did so in the Refugee Act of 1980); and the expansion of international organizations dedicated to the administration and explication of the modern refugee regime, such as UNHCR and the International Organization for Migration. During this period, growth seemed only natural, and a continued extension of humanitarian values and a deepening of international solidarity an inevitable development.

In retrospect, it seems this view was in error. Of course, genuine repulsion at the horror of the Holocaust spurred the determination to codify the humanitarian impulse and spread its reach ever wider across the earth. There is no reason to doubt this conclusion. But another motivation, one that sprang from international competition and not from international solidarity, surely played a bigger role in the development of the modern refugee regime than was commonly believed at the time. With the implosion of the Soviet Union in the early 1990s and the ensuing end of the Cold War—which had been the global context for the

---

41 Gammeltoft-Hansen and Tan, "The End of the Deterrence Paradigm?" 39 (citations omitted).

42 In 1996, the U.S. Congress enacted a one-year limit on all applications for asylum, preventing asylum seekers with otherwise legitimate claims from gaining protection. Under this law, subject to a few limited exceptions, applicants for asylum must file within one year of the applicant's last entry into the United States. According to DHS data, from 2003 through June 2009, 35 percent of all applicants for asylum missed the filing deadline. Andrew I. Schoenholtz, Philip G. Schrag, Jaya Ramji-Nogales, James P. Dombach, "Rejecting Refugees: Homeland Security's Administration of the One-Year Bar to Asylum," *William & Mary Law Review* 52, no. 3 (2010): 651–804, at 653.

82 Michele R. Pistone

entire life of the modern refugee regime—the full extent of the role of competition began to become manifest. Only by living through a generation-long era in which the Cold War context was gone have we been able to fully appreciate its importance to the creation, expansion, and sustainability of that refugee regime.

The following few paragraphs briefly sketch this history. To begin at the beginning, the process that led to the 1951 Refugee Convention was initiated by the need for a strategy "to address impending refugee flows from the Communist states of the East bloc."[43] As the Cold War progressed, "international refugee law came to play a crucial role in legitimizing the politics of the West," with grants of asylum to East bloc defectors a way to "scor[e] ideological points."[44]

The policies of the United States illustrate the centrality of this concern. The United States, which did not ratify the 1951 Convention, did consent to the 1967 Protocol, in 1968. Between the 1951 birth of the Refugee Convention and U.S. agreement to the 1967 Protocol, the most prominent refugee-focused laws passed by the U.S. Congress were the Refugee Relief Act of 1953, the Migration and Refugee Assistance Act of 1962, and the Cuban Adjustment Act of 1966. All three laws were intended primarily (or exclusively) to offer protection to refugees from communist regimes. The Refugee Relief Act of 1953, for example, permitted the admission of 214,000 immigrants, almost 90 percent of whom "were to be refugees and escapees from Communist persecution, both in Europe and Asia."[45] In his statement in support of the law, President Eisenhower explicitly adopted the ideological point-scoring rationale, explaining that the law "demonstrate[d] again America's traditional concern for the homeless, the persecuted and the less fortunate of other lands [and provided] a dramatic contrast to the tragic events taking place in East Germany and in other captive nations."[46]

Similarly, both the Migration and Refugee Assistance Act of 1962 (Pub. L. 87–510, 76 Stat. 911) and the Cuban Adjustment Act of 1966 were intended as ideological statements. The former law was intended mainly to assist Cuban nationals who had left Cuba under Fidel Castro by "drastically expand[ing] resources . . . for refugees."[47] The latter, approved "by a 300–25 margin in the House and an unchallenged voice vote in the Senate," offered Cubans arriving in the United States "work authorization and, after one year's presence . . . the right of permanent residency," no matter whether their arrival was legal or illegal.[48] In conjunction with other policies, "the avowed purpose of the [Cuban Adjustment

---

43 Hathaway, *The Rights of Refugees Under International* LAW, 91.
44 Gammeltoft-Hansen and Tan, "The End of the Deterrence Paradigm?" 30.
45 Staff of the S. Comm. On the Judiciary, 85th Cong., Final Rep. of the Administrator of the Refugee Relief Act of 1953, as Amended 3 (Comm. Print 1957).
46 Presidential Statement on Signing the Refugee Relief Act of 1953, 101 Cong. Rec. 12288 (August 7, 1953).
47 John A. Gronbeck-Tedesco, "On Refugees: Remembering the Legacy of John F. Kennedy," *National Memo*, February 8, 2017, www.nationalmemo.com/refugees-remembering-jfk.
48 David Abraham, "The Cuban Adjustment Act of 1966: Past and Future," *LexisNexis Emerging Issues* 7331 (May 2015): 1.

The state of the law   83

Act] was to weaken and, if possible, topple the communist government of Cuban President Fidel Castro while aiding his victims."[49]

Between the U.S. approval of the Refugee Protocol in 1968 and the implosion of the Soviet Union in the early 1990s, the most significant new U.S. laws focusing on refugees were the 1975 Indochina Migration and Refugee Assistance Act and the Refugee Act of 1980. The Refugee Act of 1980 primarily was intended to align U.S. law with its obligations under the 1967 Protocol, and to establish an administrative and judicial process for doing so. It also authorized the entry of Vietnamese refugees, which was the main goal of the 1975 act. As a result of the two laws, over half a million Vietnamese migrated as refugees to the United States before the close of the 1980s.

As is the case with every other major refugee law previously discussed in this section, the connection between these two laws and Cold War geopolitical considerations is strong and obvious. The Vietnam War was regarded in the United States as a proxy battle in the larger Cold War. Once the Vietnam War ended, to abandon people who had fought on the U.S. side and who had been persecuted for it would be to lose the war twice. The perceived necessities of Cold War geopolitics made such an abandonment unthinkable. Consider, in this regard, the tallies on the congressional vote on the 1975 act: in the House, 381–31 in favor, and in the Senate, 77–2.

The Soviet Union formally dissolved at the end of 1991. The resulting demise of the Cold War saw, too, "the demise of ideologically driven refugee protection."[50] Within five years, the policies that are now variously termed deterrence, externalization, and containment—discussed at length earlier in this chapter—had emerged prominently in the United States and elsewhere. In the United States, an early hint of what was to come was a slight tightening of the uniquely permissive treatment of Cuban refugees with the adoption of the "wet foot/dry foot" policy by President Clinton in 1994.[51] Two years later, "IIRAIRA set the stage for the [subsequent] growth of the immense U.S. immigrant enforcement system by authorizing significant funding for border and interior enforcement"[52] and, with expedited removal and the setting of new time limits for filing an asylum claim, severely curtailed refugee rights. Meanwhile, in Europe, at approximately the same time, Italy and Spain were originating the containment model that remains today at the foundation of the European response to irregular migration.[53]

---

49 Ibid.
50 Gammeltoft-Hansen and Tan, "The End of the Deterrence Paradigm?" 29.
51 The fact that Cuban refugees have received uniquely favorable treatment by the United States is, in its origins, certainly a vestige of the Cold War, but the maintenance of that treatment is by now more a nod to Cuban political power in an important swing state than a policy in active service to an anticommunist political agenda.
52 Kerwin, "From IIRIRA to Trump," 2.
53 Maurizio Albahari, "From Right to Permission: Asylum, Mediterranean Migrations, and Europe's War on Smuggling," *Journal on Migration and Human Security* 6, no. 2 (2018): 121–30, 123.

84 *Michele R. Pistone*

The hard truth we must learn from this history is that, in the absence of Cold War geopolitical concerns, "the legal duty to protect refugees is [no longer] understood to be . . . in the national interest of most states."[54] This hard truth emerged plainly in the years following the ending of the Cold War. My view is that the timing is not a coincidence. The implications are significant with respect to which pro-refugee arguments, if any, are likely to gain currency popularly and with political leaders.

For example, the one argument that all refugee advocates make, usually before anything else is mentioned (check any of their websites), is that the size of the refugee crisis compels action. I have made this argument many times myself, including in the original draft of this chapter. But I have finally realized that if the argument is being made to people who do not believe refugee protection is in their country's national interest—and the history of the last 25 years suggests that this is exactly the case—this most common of arguments is completely counterproductive. If you want me to do something that I believe will hurt me, telling me that I will have to do it a lot is the opposite of persuasive. I understand the reluctance to accept this conclusion. *From a purely humanitarian perspective*, the size of the refugee crisis *is* the best argument for taking immediate and substantial action. I think it is apparent, however, that government officials and large swathes of the public typically do not act from a purely humanitarian perspective.

What arguments will work to turn the tide in favor of enhanced refugee protection? I have argued previously that the risk of terrorists using weapons of mass destruction is vastly underestimated, and that a proper assessment of this risk should lead one to favor a much more protective refugee regime.[55] I still believe this to be so, but I am under no illusion that there is, right now, a large political constituency ready to act on this message. I remain, thus, in listening mode, hopeful that some new message to come will spur the action that the old arguments cannot. Perhaps the best that we refugee advocates can do at this point in time is to maintain the status quo. If that is so, we should regard maintaining the status quo as a worthy endeavor. When we prevent things from getting worse, lives are saved.

Finally, in the introduction to this chapter, I promised that I would end by assessing whether and when the trends of deterrence, externalization, and containment are likely to be reversed. I realize now that I may be guilty of having overpromised. I'll simply note this. The era of deterrence, externalization, and containment will end when events conspire to provide an opportunity for positive change, if the people most desirous of that change have adequately prepared themselves to take advantage of the opportunity. *Otiosis nullus adsistit deus*,[56] after all.

---

54 Hathaway, *The Rights of Refugees under International Law*, 1000.
55 See Pistone and Hoeffner, "Unsettling Developments."
56 The translation is "No deity assists the idle."

V Conclusion

Refugee law did not develop in a vacuum, from the minds of Platonic philosophers, free from the influence of all temporary and accidental phenomena. Rather, it sprang from a very specific environment, was expanded in another specific environment, and, as still another environment arose, for almost three decades now has been undermined to such an extent that it remains for an ever-increasing number of people a theoretical protection only. Many preventable tragedies have resulted from this state of affairs. What shall be done?

As uncomfortable as it is for a refugee-and-asylum lawyer to admit, the answer surely extends beyond the clarification, the extension, and the one-thousandth restatement of the law applying to refugees and asylees, for we already have more law than we are willing to apply. That said, *part* of the answer surely is in continuing the good fight: to litigate on behalf of the individual client; to lobby governments to abandon policies that restrict the practical use of refugee rights; to reach new international agreements encouraging national governments to more equally share responsibility for the protection of displaced persons.[57] We also should work to strengthen the nongovernmental institutions of society that are open to acting in solidarity with refugees. Such institutions can harness and multiply the contributions of individuals who themselves are eager to act in solidarity with refugees, even when governments are not. By strengthening such institutions, we could provide a viable path for millions of people moving from "feeling" solidarity with refugees to concretely acting on their behalf (see Ulrich Schmiedel, Chapter 12; Kristin E. Heyer, Chapter 13; Kanstroom, Chapter 1).

As for the remainder of the answer, I fear, we can but see through a glass, darkly. Right now, our laws are better than we are, so productive change is more likely to arise from changing ourselves than from changing the law. Let no one underestimate the magnitude of that task! Yet all is not lost. The experts advise that, when a task seems overwhelming, we should break it down into manageable parts. Figure out the largest part one can manage and work on that, even if it is no larger than the mirror you gazed into earlier this morning. Let us do what we can, in other words, for there is much to do, and many people suffer while waiting for us to exercise what is our privilege to help.

Suggested Reading

Frelick, Bill, Ian M. Kysel, and Jennifer Podkul. "The Impact of Externalization of Migration Controls on the Rights of Asylum Seekers and Other Migrants." *Journal Migration and Human Security* 4, no. 4 (2016): 190–220.

Kerwin, Donald. "From IIRIRA to Trump: Connecting the Dots to the Current US Immigration Policy Crisis." *Journal on Migration and Human Security* 6, no. 3 (2018): 192–204.

---

57 *See* United Nations High Commissioner on Refugees, Global Compact on Refugees, U.N. Doc. A/73/12, at 10 (December 17, 2018).

Pistone, Michele R., and John J. Hoeffner, "Rules Are Made to Be Broken: How the Process of Expedited Removal Fails Asylum Seekers." *Georgetown Immigration Law Journal* 20, no. 2 (2006): 167–212.

Ryo, Emily, and Ian Peacock. "The Landscape of Immigration Detention in the United States." *American Immigration Council,* December 2018. https://americanimmigrationcouncil.org/research/landscape-immigration-detention-united-states.

5 Borders
Sites of exclusion, sites of engagement

Silas W. Allard

I Introduction

Until the Treaty of Guadalupe Hidalgo redrew the border between the United States and Mexico in 1848, much of what is now the western United States was Mexican territory. Following ratification of the treaty, fewer than 2,000 of the 75,000 Mexican citizens living north of the new border repatriated to Mexico or made an affirmative declaration to maintain Mexican citizenship. The remainder became (in theory) American citizens.[1] The presence of these Mexicans‑/‑Americans[2] turned what had been intranational familial and cultural networks into transnational networks. The new border separated former conationals across a new political boundary, thereby creating new identities, but it also sutured[3] together long-standing and ongoing, as well as new, relations that met at, crossed over, and extended beyond the border in both directions. The new border divided and connected communities living across the United States and Mexico.

One expression of the border's dual nature is the deeply ambivalent transnational labor market that exists between the United States and Mexico. Networks of labor migration from Mexico, and from other parts of Latin America through Mexico, are and have long been a vital source of labor for the U.S. economy.[4] The well-being of people in the United States depends on the labor of those who have crossed the southern border to harvest food, build houses, and care for the young and elderly.[5] Despite the vital importance of labor migration to the U.S. economy, Enid Trucios-Haynes shows how U.S. labor migration policy

---

1 Mae M. Ngai, *Impossible Subjects: Illegal Aliens and the Making of Modern America* (Princeton: Princeton University Press, 2014), 50–51.
2 The sutured hyphen attempts to express the ambiguity of identity and citizenship status that the Treaty of Guadalupe Hidalgo created, and which continues to characterize the borderland.
3 Mark Salter, "Theory of the / : The Suture and Critical Border Studies," *Geopolitics* 17, no. 4 (2012): 734–55; see also Gloria Anzaldúa, *Borderlands / La Frontera: The New Mestiza*, 4th ed. (San Francisco: Aunt Lute Books, 2012).
4 See Ngai, *Impossible Subjects*.
5 See Silas W. Allard, "A Desired Composition: Regulating Vulnerability Through Immigration Law," in *Vulnerability and the Legal Organization of Work*, eds. Martha Albertson Fineman and Jonathan W. Fineman (Abingdon, UK: Routledge, 2017), 177–93.

88 *Silas W. Allard*

stratifies workers by class and creates enduring and systemic inequality for many of those who work the essential jobs of social reproduction, such as agriculture, construction, and care-work (Chapter 2). Despite histories of cross-border labor movement that existed before the border itself moved, the crossing of the border for work also subjects people to forms of "institutionalized inequality" (Trucios-Haynes, Chapter 2). The border connects labor and market, but it also stigmatizes, conditions, and criminalizes forms of labor migration (see also Gemma Tulud Cruz and Trucios-Haynes, Chapter 16).

This brief discussion of history and economics reminds us that a border is neither a fixed condition nor a hermetic barrier; borders shift and morph, dividing and connecting landscapes and populations in the process. The poet Alberto Ríos captures this fundamental ambiguity of borders when he writes, "The border is mighty, but even the parting of the seas created a path, not a barrier. The border is a big, neat, clean, clear black line on a map that does not exist."[6] While my example above is drawn from the border between the United States and Mexico, similar dynamics characterize borders around the globe. Many other examples could be given: the borders of contemporary Europe, with their long histories and ongoing disputes; the often diverging precolonial, colonial, and postcolonial borders throughout much of Asia, Africa, and the Americas; or the layered borders that emerge from transnational visions of ethnic identity such as Kurdistan. Nimmi Kurian, for example, has detailed the long social histories of movement and trade throughout the trans-Himalayan borderland connecting India, Tibet, Bhutan, Nepal, China, and Pakistan. "Across the fixed line," Kurian writes of the border, "human geographies have reconstituted social and symbolic practice, transforming landscapes into multiple sites of interaction."[7] Kurian's description of social practices in the trans-Himalayan borderland that form community across borders is descriptive of many border zones around the globe.

This chapter builds on these insights to explore the border as a site of both exclusion and engagement. Legal thought on borders has generally accepted the prior premise: the border is a sight of exclusion, or more particularly, the site of the sovereign's power to exclude. Borderlands scholars have increasingly challenged this one-dimensional understanding of the border, offering up new, multifaceted conceptions that can help us to see the role of the border as a site of engagement as well as exclusion. The border, on close investigation, is less solid and less determinative than often imagined in legal analysis and described in rule-of-law rhetoric. "Rather than neutral lines," Anssi Paasi writes, "borders are often pools of emotions, fears and memories that can be mobilized apace for

---

6 Alberto Ríos, "The Border: A Double Sonnet," in *A Small Story About the Sky* (Port Townsend, WA: Copper Canyon Press, 2015). For an interview with Alberto Ríos reflecting on the border, see "To Arizona's First Poet Laureate, 'The Border Is What Joins Us'," *PBS NewsHour*, March 16, 2018, www.pbs.org/newshour/show/to-arizonas-first-poet-laureate-the-border-is-what-joins-us.

7 Nimmi Kurian, "Re-Engaging the 'International': A Social History of the Trans-Himalayan Borderlands," *Journal of Borderlands Studies* 35, no. 2 (2019): 243–54, at 250.

Borders 89

both progressive and regressive purposes."[8] While the primary goal of this chapter is to complicate the idea of the border as simply a site of legal exclusion, a praxis of engagement implicates the theological task of understanding the relationship to an other. In the conclusion of the chapter, I turn to some of the theological resources and questions implicated in an ambivalent understanding of the border. But to understand the border as an aspect of the law of migration, I begin with the international political and legal order composed of territorial states.

II The border as a site of exclusion: territory, state sovereignty, and jurisdiction

The framework for the international state system emerged in early modern Europe when supreme authority within a defined territory was consolidated under a single ruler. This process of consolidation took place over several hundred years, as forms of governance in Europe that accommodated disaggregated authority among different rulers (including feudal, religious, and imperial authorities) gave way to structures of hierarchical authority consolidated under a single sovereign—the entity holding supreme authority to govern.

The idea of a unitary sovereign authority developed alongside the idea of territorial integrity, whereby a sovereign has exclusive authority over a defined territory. The 1648 Peace of Westphalia marked an important moment in the development of the modern, territorial, sovereign state as the nascent states of Europe recognized the principle of nonintervention, meaning that one state shall not intervene in the sovereign domain (territory) of another.[9] Territory, then, demarcates the zone or landscape of state sovereignty. The border designates one limit of state sovereignty; it divides a space where the state holds sovereign authority from a space where the state does not hold sovereign authority. We might describe the border as one significant indicium of a state's jurisdiction—the authority to make and enforce law in a given domain.[10]

---

8 Anssi Paasi, "Borders, Theory, and the Challenge of Relational Thinking," in Corey Johnson, et al., "Interventions on Rethinking 'the Border' in Border Studies," *Political Geography* 30, no. 2 (2011): 61–69, at 63.

9 The principle of nonintervention is the subject of both theoretical and historical critique beyond the scope of this chapter. While the concept may not be wholly consistent, it remains a foundational and oft-cited cornerstone of modern international law. Cedric Ryngaert, "The Concept of Jurisdiction in International Law," in *Research Handbook on Jurisdiction and Immunities in International Law*, ed. Alexander Orakhelashvili (Cheltenham: Edward Elgar Publishing, 2015), 50–75, at 50.

10 Arash Abizadeh, "Sovereign Jurisdiction, Territorial Rights, and Membership in Hobbes," in *The Oxford Handbook of Hobbes* (Oxford: Oxford University Press, 2016), 397–431, at 400; see also Ryngaert, "The Concept of Jurisdiction in International Law," 50. Territory is not the only indicium of jurisdiction. For example, a state may retain some authority over its citizens abroad, and exceptions to a state's authority may exist within its territory, as in the principle of diplomatic immunity.

90   *Silas W. Allard*

Jurisdiction classically conceived is exclusive and exclusionary. The exclusivity of jurisdiction manifests in several aspects. The first is the international law principle from the Peace of Westphalia that jurisdiction is exclusive within the territory of the state. As Alison Kesby writes,

> Borders . . . demarcate the internal territory over which a state exercises its authority, that is, its territorial sovereignty. Within the limits of its borders, a state is said to have "exclusive territorial control" and on crossing a state's border, all individuals and property fall under the territorial authority of that state.[11]

The idea that jurisdiction is exclusive within the sovereign's territory also undergirds the principle of nonintervention.[12] Jurisdictional exclusivity manifests in the ability to exclude. It is a long-standing legal maxim that one of the inherent aspects of sovereignty is the ability to exclude noncitizens from the territory.[13] "The essence of a border," writes David Newman, "is to separate the 'self' from the 'other.' As such, one of the major functions of a border is to act as a barrier, 'protecting' the 'us insiders' from the 'them outsiders.'"[14] On this conception of the border, two important binaries converge. There is an "us" who belong "inside" the territory of the state, and a "them" who belong "outside" the territory of the state. This "protective" function of the border takes many forms, including physical security against perceived threats of violence or criminality; economic security against perceived threats of competition for wages or production; cultural security against perceived threats to established values and traditions; and demographic security against perceived threats to the power or dominance of particular racial, ethnic, or religious populations.[15] These protective exclusions of the outsider depend, in turn, on a conception of a coherent collection of insiders; there must be, as Rose Cuison Villazor discusses, a set of allegiances among insiders that do not extend to outsiders or outside of the territory (Chapter 7).

---

11 Alison Kesby, "The Shifting and Multiple Border and International Law," *Oxford Journal of Legal Studies* 27, no. 1 (2007): 101–19, at 108, citing Corfu Channel Case, ICJ Rep 1949, 4 at 18.

12 See Corfu Channel Case, ICJ Rep 1949, 4 at 18; UN Charter art. 2, paras. 4, 7.

13 See, for example, *Chae Chan Ping v. United States*, 130 U.S. 581, 603 (1889); *R. v. Immigration Officer at Prague Airport* [2004] QB 811, at para. 12 (opinion of Lord Bingham) [England]. For a more detailed discussion of exclusion, see Daniel Kanstroom's chapter in this volume (Chapter 1).

14 David Newman, "On Borders and Power: A Theoretical Framework," *Journal of Borderland Studies* 18, no. 1 (2011): 13–25, at 14. For additional discussions of the relationship between states, citizens, and noncitizens, see the chapters in this volume by Ulrich Schmiedel (Chapter 12), Rose Cuison Villazor (Chapter 7), and Kanstroom (Chapter 1). Safwat Marzouk offers another perspective on the self-and-other-distinction drawn from the context of ancient Israel (Chapter 8).

15 Newman, "On Borders and Power," 14.

Thus, the border operates as a process of "national formation and re-formation," or as an identity-making process for the nation.[16] The national identity–forming function of the border can be seen clearly in racist policies designed to create or perpetuate a racially homogeneous national identity, such as the White Australia Policy or the Asiatic Barred Zone in the United States. Both policies sought to maintain a racialized national identity by prohibiting entry into the territory of persons from Asia.[17] National identity formation through exclusive border power can also be seen in the process of decolonization, as "postcolonial sovereignty was typically declared with new immigration acts."[18] Alison Bashford has argued that these immigration laws, often modeled on the immigration laws of settler-colonial societies, persisted "not because it was (necessarily) a practice that distinguished between people of certain races or ethnicities, but simply because it was the key practice that identified all aliens, and asserted and displayed new-found sovereignty over both territory and people."[19] The moral valence of identity formation through exclusionary border policy is ambiguous: functioning, on one hand, to maintain racial homogeneity and, on the other hand, to assert self-determination. Borders can be and have been used to support other practices of national-identity formation, but these limited examples illustrate that the border conceived as exclusive and exclusionary aims to protect and not to interrogate or challenge the contours of that national identity.

The border as a site of exclusion collapses the border as a material and symbolic barrier.[20] Even when the border is not guarded by concrete or steel, the border as a site of exclusion is a symbolic wall guarding a defined territory against the outside world and a locus of the legal power to effectuate practices of exclusion. The symbolic wall of the exclusionary border can, of course, manifest in a physical barrier, becoming a saturated symbol of exclusion.[21] Whether symbolic or

16 Paasi, "Borders, Theory, and the Challenge of Relational Thinking," 63; see also Benedict Anderson, *Imagined Communities*, rev. ed. (London: Verso, 2006).

17 There are a vast number of additional examples. For a global history of racial restrictions on immigration, see Marilyn Lake and Henry Reynolds, *Drawing the Global Colour Line: White Men's Countries and the International Challenge of Racial Equality* (Cambridge: Cambridge University Press, 2008). See Bill Ong Hing for a discussion of the sometimes coded and often explicit racialized exclusion of contemporary immigration policies (Chapter 3).

18 Alison Bashford, "Immigration Restriction: Rethinking Period and Place from Settler Colonies to Postcolonial Nations," *Journal of Global History* 9, no. 1 (2014): 26–48, at 29.

19 Ibid., 39.

20 Kesby, "The Shifting and Multiple Border and International Law," 109 ("[T]he emphasis remains on the border as a geographical limit with the issue being whether the border is to be 'permeated' or respected. Moreover, the whole rhetoric of 'permeability' reinforces the notion of borders as pre-existing physical barriers, rather than as an aspect of the institutionalization of public and social policy in relation to immigration control.").

21 Edward S. Casey, "Walling Racialized Bodies Out: Border Versus Boundary at La Frontera," in *Living Alterities: Phenomenology, Embodiment, and Race*, ed. Emily S. Lee (Albany: SUNY Press, 2014), 195–99. For examples of playful reimagining and repurposing of border walls to facilitate engagement, see Ronald Rael, *Borderwall as Architecture: A Manifesto for the U.S.—Mexico Boundary* (Oakland: University of California Press, 2017).

92 Silas W. Allard

physical, the border-as-wall rests on and reinforces the idea that the identity of the nation is natural and given—natural because the border marks a rightful division between *us inside* and *them outside*; given because there is something that connects all of *us inside* that does not connect *us inside* to *them outside*.[22]

III More than a site of exclusion: complicating the border

While the law may conceive the border as a site of exclusion, the border does not function only to exclude; the border is not, in situ, already a wall. "We must not confine ourselves solely to a discussion of the legal aspects here," Étienne Balibar has written regarding borders; rather, he continues, "it is essential that we also undertake a phenomenological description."[23] The law represents one perspective on and function of the border, but the border is also lived and experienced by and through the people, organizations, and institutions that interact with and across it every day.

Scholars, artists, and activists from border communities have long complicated the lifeworld of the borderland and the role that the border plays in that lifeworld. The work of borderlands scholar-artist-activist Gloria Anzaldúa has been particularly influential in this regard. Anzaldúa, who lived in and wrote about the U.S.–Mexican borderland, recognized the violence that the border creates in the borderland. She opens her book *Borderlands/*La Frontera with the image of a wound: "The U.S.–Mexican border *es una herida abierta* where the Third World grates against the first and bleeds. And before a scab forms it hemorrhages again, the lifeblood of two worlds merging to form a third country—a border culture."[24] While the borderland bears the border as a wound, it is also, for Anzaldúa a site of creative possibility. As cultures bleed together, new cultural forms are created and a new form of community is possible. As Anzaldúa writes toward the conclusion of *Borderlands/*La Frontera, "From this racial, ideological, cultural and biological cross-pollinization, an 'alien' consciousness is presently in the making—a new *mestiza* consciousness, *una conciencia de mujer*. It is a consciousness of the Borderlands."[25] In Anazldúa's scholarship and poetry, the borderland is a complicated space of limit, violence, and liminality, but also of creativity and possibility. The work of Anzaldúa and others challenges the definitiveness of the border as a site of exclusion by pointing to the indeterminacy

---

22 Anderson, *Imagined Communities*.
23 Étienne Balibar, *Politics and the Other Scene*, trans. Christine Jones, James Swenson, and Chris Turner (London: Verso, 2002), 83.
24 Anzaldúa, *Borderlands / La Frontera*, 25. "Es una herida abierta" translates as "is an open wound."
25 Ibid., 99. "Una conciencia de mujer" translates as "a consciousness of woman." The new *mestiza* consciousness that Anazldúa writes about is informed by queer and feminist sensibilities that challenge heteronormative and patriarchal aspects of the cultures on both sides of the border.

of the borderland, particularly as the borderland is lived and experienced by its inhabitants. This work has continued to influence scholarship on borders across multiple disciplines.[26]

One place this conversation has been engaged in more recent scholarship focuses on the endurance of political borders in the era of intensified globalization that marks the late twentieth and early twenty-first centuries. Scholars have taken up Balibar's phenomenological task with new perspectives and approaches to the concept of the border that have coalesced under the framework of critical border studies.[27] The concluding decade of the twentieth century saw the end of the Cold War with the literal toppling of the Berlin Wall and the symbolic opening of the Iron Curtain, as well as the establishment of free movement within the European Union. Some scholars and commentators saw these as dual signs of a triumphant cosmopolitanism that would usher in a borderless world. At the same time that some borders appeared to be softening, however, other borders were hardening amid concerns about increasing immigration propelled by the growth of globalization, the potential collapse of fragile states, and movements for political self-determination.[28]

Michele R. Pistone offers an insightful analysis of one critical aspect of these new developments elsewhere in this volume. She discusses how the global opening of borders brought on by the end of the Cold War undermined solidarity with refugees in the United States and Europe (Chapter 4). This solidarity had been built on the antagonism of Cold War rivalries, with refugee policy being an important political and moral instrument in the war of ideology between liberalism and communism. When those rivalries began to dissipate, so did strong commitments to the international refugee regime. While many in the United States and Europe were celebrating a "more free" world after the collapse of Soviet authoritarianism, opportunities for asylum seekers and refugees to seek and find freedom from persecution were becoming more difficult.

These conflicting global realities, like the lived experience of border communities, sparked scholarly reflection on the border as a more complicated phenomenon than a "line in the sand"[29] demarcating the territorial divisions between

---

26 For an analysis of the influence of Anzaldúa and others, as well as a genealogy of border studies and border theory, see Nancy A. Naples, "Borderlands Studies and Border Theory: Linking Activism and Scholarship for Social Justice," *Sociology Compass* 4, no. 7 (2010): 505–18.

27 For a helpful introduction to and overview of critical border studies, see Noel Parker and Nick Vaughan-Williams, "Critical Border Studies: Broadening and Deepening the 'Lines in the Sand' Agenda," *Geopolitics* 17, no. 4 (2012): 727–33. To contextualize critical border studies in a broader literature on border studies and border theory, see Naples, "Borderlands Studies and Border Theory."

28 Corey Johnson, et al., "Interventions on Rethinking 'the Border' in Border Studies," *Political Geography* 30, no. 2 (2011): 61–69, at 61–62.

29 See Noel Parker and Nick Vaughan-Williams, "Lines in the Sand? Towards an Agenda for Critical Border Studies," *Geopolitics* 14, no. 3 (2009): 582–87; Parker and Vaughan-Williams, "Critical Border Studies."

94   *Silas W. Allard*

states. As Noel Parker and Nick Vaughan-Williams wrote in an essay that emerged from early meetings of scholars of critical border studies:

> [R]ather than treating the concept of the border as a territorially fixed, static, line (as paradigmatically depicted by Mercator's map), we begin thinking of it in terms of a series of practices. This move entails a more political, sociological, and actor-oriented outlook on how divisions between entities appear, or are produced and sustained. The shift in focus also brings a sense of the dynamism of borders and bordering practices, for both are increasingly mobile—just as are the goods, services and people that they seek to control.[30]

Among the manifold insights of critical borders studies are three aspects of the border that I want to highlight in this chapter: (1) heterogeneity, (2) performativity, and (3) ambivalence. Taken together, these three categories help to illuminate the border's multivalent character, acknowledging its exclusionary aspects but inviting considerations of how the border functions beyond or in addition to effecting exclusion.

A Heterogeneity

I borrow the term "heterogeneity" from Balibar, who describes the heterogeneity of borders as "the fact that, in reality, several functions of demarcation and territorialization—between distinct social exchanges or flows, between distinct rights, and so forth—are always fulfilled simultaneously by borders."[31] Heterogeneity names the tendency for the border to demarcate not only territorial distinctions but also political, social, economic, and cultural distinctions.[32] The heterogeneity of the border reflects the nation-state's aspiration to a form of total social identity: the nation as a coherent legal and political unit (the state), but also a territorial unit, an economic unit, a social unit, and a cultural unit. The heterogeneity of the border—its ability to demarcate along multiple dimensions of social life—is the possibility of the nation-state's multidimensional integrity.

As Balibar points out, however, increasingly the territorial border is not coextensive with other borders, and it likely never has been (or, perhaps more accurately, the territorial border's relation to other borders has shifted and changed over the course of history). Rather, the territorial border corresponds to only one or some dimensions of any person's or collective's multidimensional social life. In other words, the territorial border is not comprehensive in its capacity to define and differentiate identity and social reality; rather, the territorial border defines and differentiates along some lines of identity and social life—predominately the

---

30 Parker and Vaughan-Williams, "Lines in the Sand?" 586.
31 Balibar, *Politics and the Other Scene*, 79.
32 Ibid., 84.

Borders 95

legal and political—but other borders define and differentiate other forms of social life—such as race, class, ethnicity, religion, labor, family, friendship, and solidarity. People's sense of belonging along these varied axes both exceeds the territorial border and fractures within it. Furthermore, these forms of social belonging are intersectional: race, gender, class, and religion (as examples) intersect to form complex identities and understandings of where and how one belongs to layered social collectives.[33] Furthermore, as Anzaldúa argues, the border might be the condition of a new culture and community, rather than a distinction between cultures and communities.

This heterogeneity of borders exposes the tension between, on one hand, the nation-state's attempt to simplify the social and political lifeworld through comprehensive demarcation via the border and, on the other hand, the complex lived reality of persons' multiple social locations, relationships, and identities, which give rise to what Balibar calls the "ubiquity of borders" or the idea that *borders are everywhere*.[34] Balibar's *borders are everywhere* thesis has been central to the development of critical borders studies, and other scholars have built upon it to further explicate the heterogeneity of borders: "Borders are never to be found only in border areas," Paasi writes, "but are also located in wider social practice/ discourse all around societies"; or, as Chris Rumford has argued, "borders can be anywhere."[35]

What does it mean that, to take Rumford's formulation, borders can be anywhere? Consider the person who experiences suspicion, hostility, and discrimination based on markers of social location such as race, language, accent, clothing, or religious practice wherever that person is in a given territory. In this sense, the person—sometimes an immigrant but often not—is constantly encountering forms of exclusion demarcated by the territorial border even *inside* the territory. Discussing the oft-acknowledged failure of border walls to physically exclude persons, Edward Casey writes: "Even if the manifest failure of the wall to accomplish its designated mission were to be accepted by those who support it in Congress and elsewhere, satisfaction would still be found in the belief that the wall taken as a gesture of excluding racialized others at least keeps most of them safely at arm's length, on the far side of the wall."[36] Casey goes on to point out that the symbolic racial exclusion at the border foments a racialized construction of belonging *inside* the border; the border travels into the interior of the territory. Thus, the

---

33 On belonging generally, and belonging and intersectionality specifically, see Nira Yuval-Davis, "Belonging and the Politics of Belonging," *Patterns of Prejudice* 40, no. 3 (2006): 197–214; see also Mariana Ortega, "Self-Mapping, Belonging, and the Home Question," in Lee, *Living Alterities*, 173–88.

34 Balibar, *Politics and the Other Scene*, 75–86, especially 84. While the idea that *borders are everywhere* comes from Balibar, the phrase is not strictly his.

35 Paasi, "Borders, Theory, and the Challenge of Relational Thinking," 63; Chris Rumford, *Cosmopolitan Borders* (Basingstoke, UK: Palgrave MacMillan, 2014), 13.

36 Casey, "Walling Racialized Bodies Out," 208; see also Balibar, *Politics and the Other Scene*, 78.

96 Silas W. Allard

border is carried by racialized bodies who come under interrogation about their location and belonging inside the border. Like all interrogation, it sometimes takes the form of the interrogative—Where are you from? No, where are you *really* from?[37]—as well as the imperative—Go back where you came from! This social bordering may also resolve through interior enforcement by immigration authorities who act on social markers of "foreignness," such race, ethnicity, language, accent, dress, and community, thereby drawing a clear link between social bordering and legal bordering within the territory.

The heterogeneity of borders also reflects the reality that the effectuation of legal exclusion, what we might call the state's *borderwall power*, increasingly occurs not at the site of the territorial border but beyond and within the territory. As Parker and Vaughan-Willams note, "Borders are increasingly 'off-shored' beyond the physical territory of the state and 'out-sourced' to other state and non-state actors; . . . 'borders between states are increasingly not what or where they are supposed to be according to the [modern] geopolitical imaginary.'"[38]

There are many potential examples of states off-shoring borders or exercising borderwall power beyond the political border. Australia has a long-standing policy of interdicting migrant boats off the Australian coast and detaining migrants on other island nations, such as Nauru. The European Union is increasingly moving its border into Turkey and North Africa, with agreements to halt migrant movements before they reach the Mediterranean and to require asylum applications from outside of EU territory. During the Trump administration, the United States followed suit with the Migrant Protection Protocols (aka the Remain in Mexico policy), requiring asylum seekers to reside in Mexico while their asylum application was pending.[39]

Conversely, borders can also be interiorized. For example, pursuant to a practice known as expedited removal, the U.S. Department of Homeland Security has the power to deport, without a hearing, any person who was not admitted to the United States and who cannot prove continuous presence for the prior two years.[40] The expedited removal law blurs a long-standing distinction in U.S. law that guarantees greater due process protections for those who have entered the territory of the United States than for those seeking admission at the border. Expedited removal treats persons who have entered as though they are at the border seeking admission. Daniel Kanstroom offers a more detailed analysis of expedited removal (Chapter 1), but the clear consequence of the expedited

---

37 For a biting satire of this phenomena, see Ken Tanaka, "What Kind of Asian Are You?" *You-Tube*, May 23, 2013, https://youtu.be/DWynJkN5HbQ.
38 Parker and Vaughan-Williams, "Critical Border Studies," 730 (internal citations omitted).
39 Refugee Council of Australia, *Seven Years On: An Overview of Australia's Offshore Processing Policy* (July 2020); Rumford, *Cosmopolitan Borders*, 60–64; Kirstjen M. Nielsen, "Memorandum: Policy Guidance for Implementation of the Migrant Protection Protocols," January 25, 2019, www.dhs.gov/publication/policy-guidance-implementation-migrant-protection-protocols.
40 8 U.S.C. § 1225(b)(1)(A)(iii).

removal law is the exercise of borderwall power throughout the entire territory; the border zone is everywhere.

B *Performativity*

Building on the heterogeneous and ubiquitous nature of borders, scholars have also developed an understanding of borders as performed, not given. The border is less a fact than an assertion, and it requires continual performance of its claims. Rumford refers to this idea as "borderwork." Borderwork acknowledges that there are many actors who construct heterogeneous borders: the state remains a particularly influential and powerful agent of border construction, but substate actors and citizens also perform borderwork, both individually and collectively. One stark example of nonstate border work is private, parastate activity at the border, including both vigilante border patrols and humanitarian rescue efforts. Borderwork, argues Rumford, "puts people at the centre of the study of borders by allowing for the possibility that they are important not just as crossers of borders but as active borderers as well."[41]

Borderwork is not only about the construction of borders but also about the way in which people work with and play with the idea of the border. Recognizing the performativity of borderwork illuminates how the border is a site of multifaceted work: constructive, evasive, creative, and instrumental. As Salter argues, the different modalities of borderwork are often intertwined as "governments, citizens, and other agents perform the border, by which I mean that they enact and resist the dominant geopolitical narratives of statecraft as they cross, or are prevented from crossing, borders."[42] The ongoing contest between border crossers, border enforcement agents, citizen vigilantes, smugglers, and humanitarian volunteers creates, entrenches, challenges, and moves the border. Salter goes on to suggest that there are "three registers of border performativity [formal, practical, and popular] that share the same assumptions about the need for the constant articulation and rearticulation of the central claim of the sovereign state: that there is an inside/outside division in global politics that has some meaning."[43] Thus, the creation of what Anzaldúa calls the "third country" deconstructs the geopolitical binary asserted by the border and performs the construction of a culture between cultures, a community between communities. But, as Salter notes, this deconstructive performance is challenged by nation-state performances of the border's integrity and reality, such as the construction and militarization of border walls.

The instrumental work of the border is performed by those who can make opportunity from a border. This work may serve to reify or resist the border,

---

41 Rumford, *Cosmopolitan Borders*, 24.
42 Mark Salter, "Places Everyone!" in Johnson, et al., "Interventions on Rethinking 'the Border' in Border Studies," 66.
43 Ibid.

98   *Silas W. Allard*

but it uses the border to the actor's benefit or end. These actors include those for whom the border is an economic opportunity: smugglers and coyotes, but also customs agents, immigration lawyers, and transnational corporations. Such opportunities, however, are not always economic. The border can be a site of recreation, as in the international volleyball games played over the border wall between Naco, Arizona, and Naco, Sonora, in 1979 and 2007.[44] The border can be a site of worship, as it was in the Border Mass at Nogales, Mexico, in 2014 or the weekly communion service performed by United Methodist pastor John Fanestil at the border wall in Friendship Park between Tijuana and San Diego.[45]

The heterogeneity of the border disambiguates the border, so that it is possible to understand the border as occurring and exercising power along multiple lines of distinction, as well as occurring and exercising power beyond its geographic demarcation, both outside and inside the territory it delineates. Performativity complicates the idea of heterogeneity by making clear that wherever and however a border occurs and exercises power, it does so as an assertion, not a fact. Thus, the border is asserted in its integrity and reality by those interested in maintaining its power, undermined and evaded by those seeking to challenge its power, and made use of by many other actors to varying ends. With an understanding of the heterogeneity and performativity of the border, its ambivalence begins to come into focus.

C Ambivalence

I discussed above the idea of borders as sites of exclusion; the border as already a wall metaphorically understood. The third insight of critical border studies, which builds on the prior two, is that borders do not and cannot function solely to exclude. Michael Dear employs the idea of the border zone as a "third nation" to capture the ambivalent nature of the border performing two contradictory functions: dividing and connecting. While the border divides the territory of two nation-states, "[t]he border zone is a permeable membrane *connecting* two countries, where communities on both sides have strong senses of mutual dependence and attachment to territory. The inhabitants of this 'in-between' place—which I call a 'third nation'—thrive on cross-border support and cooperation."[46] David Newman describes the process by which border zones create the conditions for third nations. Newman writes:

> hybridization takes place in contact zones, where people from different groups or territories begin to cross borders and where they experience

---

44 Rael, *Borderwall as Architecture*, 73–75.
45 Ibid., 76. For a theological analysis of the border mass, see Daniel G. Groody, "Fruit of the Vine and Work of Human Hands: Immigration and the Eucharist," in *A Promised Land, A Perilous Journey: Theological Perspectives on Migration*, eds. Daniel G. Groody and Gioacchino Campese (Notre Dame, IN: University of Notre Dame Press, 2008).
46 Michael Dear, "Why Walls Won't Work," in Rael, *Borderwall as Architecture*, 161–62.

processes of mutual adaptation negotiated through daily working relations with each other. The crossing of the border enables differences to be reconciled as part of a more diverse and multi-cultural landscape, although it does not mean that difference is negated altogether.[47]

We see examples of these third nations in border zones or borderscapes around the world. Dear's own example is drawn from the U.S.–Mexico border, where bilingual and bicultural individuals have created binational communities, particularly in the sixteen sister-cities that meet at the border or, perhaps more accurately, overlap one another across the border. Nimmi Kurian gives us the example of "interrelated territorialities" in the Himalayan borderscape of India, Pakistan, Nepal, Bhutan, China, and Tibet. Differentiated national communities in this area have long been drawn together and integrated by local trading networks. "The social reality of the borderlands," Kurian writes, "means that identity and citizenship defy easy categorization and get constantly transformed almost on a daily basis."[48]

Dear also describes the border zone as a connective tissue between the places separated by the border. Anzaldúa invokes similar imagery with her idea of the wound that separates and binds people in the borderland. Mark Salter has used this metaphor of tissue to describe the border not as a severing but as a suturing: "[T]he suture—as a process of knitting together the inside and the outside . . . and the resultant scar—better evokes the performative aspects of borders."[49] The border bears the mark of division, but the mark of that division is also the sinews of connection that draw together a border community. These metaphors of tissue, wound, and scar are also a reminder that the border as a point of connection is not without violence. The performance that constructs the border is often a performance of violent power, and the performance that resists or challenges the border often risks exposure to that violence.

D More than a site of exclusion

Exploring the border from the perspective of border communities and with the tools of critical border studies reveals that the border is not only a site of exclusion; although, it is surely that. The analyses of performativity and heterogeneity reveal that the border is a locus for practices of exclusion, and that those practices occur along multiple lines of distinction and in a wide geographic scope. The phenomenological analysis of the border, however, does not stop at exclusion. The border has an ambivalent function and is a site of competing performances that separate and bind, with the potential to create new forms of spatiality, culture,

---

47 Newman, "On Borders and Power," 18–19.
48 Kurian, "Re-Engaging the 'International'," 8.
49 Salter, "Theory of the /."

100 *Silas W. Allard*

and community.[50] Thus, the notion of the border as a site of exclusion must be rethought through that which exceeds exclusion.

IV Revisiting jurisdiction

The insights of critical borders studies invite us to revisit the exclusive and exclusionary understanding of jurisdiction and the role of the border as the limit of jurisdiction's exclusivity and the site of its exclusionary power. I defined jurisdiction above as the sovereign's authority to legislate and enforce law in a given domain. For the modern, territorial state, this domain is demarcated by geographic borders. But this authority is also a relationship and a responsibility. Jurisdiction marks a relationship to and a responsibility for that which falls within the sovereign's domain of authority.[51] Jurisdiction's relational nature is highlighted when considering premodern jurisdiction. Prior to the rise of territorially delimited states in the early modern period, "sovereignty was conceived of in a more tribal or community sense: people were subject to the laws of the community or tribe to which they *belonged*, rather than those of the territory on which they resided at a given moment."[52] In this regard, jurisdiction—that is, responsibility for and authority over persons—was defined along lines of relationship and, in particular, lines of kinship. Jurisdiction does not cease to be relational when it comes to be demarcated principally by territory; rather, the authority that formerly ran along lines of extended kinship is reconceived in spatial terms, such that the sovereign is related to (and responsible for) all that is or comes within the sovereign's territory.[53]

In an understanding of jurisdiction as relational, the border is not, a priori, a site of exclusion. Rather, the border is a site of engagement that demands a consideration of the question: For whom and to whom are we responsible? Perkins and Rumford describe the relational nature of the border in this way: "[B]orders function as coordinating devices, practical everyday methods for navigating indeterminate pluralities and the extent to which the configuration of borders remains in the practical attitude of everyday life is the extent to which they remain durable, or fixed."[54] The border is the possibility of new pluralities. Every request for admission, demand for asylum, and unauthorized crossing is an opportunity

---

50 While my concern in this chapter is principally with the border in its modern articulation, Marzouk reminds us that the ambivalent nature of border performance can also be seen in the ancient Israelites' use of multiple terms and concepts for the foreigner to mark varying forms and degrees of inclusion and exclusion within Israelite society (Chapter 8).

51 Abizadeh, "Sovereign Jurisdiction, Territorial Rights, and Membership in Hobbes," 400.

52 Ryngaert, "The Concept of Jurisdiction in International Law," 52, citing Shalom Kassan, "Extraterritorial Jurisdiction in the Ancient World," *American Journal of International Law* 29, no. 2 (1935): 237–47, at 240.

53 Kesby, "The Shifting and Multiple Border and International Law," 108 ("on crossing a state's border, all individuals and property fall under the territorial authority of that state").

54 Chris Perkins and Chris Rumford, "The Politics of (Un)Fixity and the Vernacularisation of Borders," *Global Society* 27, no. 3 (2013): 267–82, at 272.

Borders 101

for new relationships. Likewise, every instance of interior enforcement and discriminatory treatment is an opportunity for an assessment of jurisdictional responsibility. The heterogeneous, performed, ambivalent border (the borders we all live with) are performed anew all the time, creating opportunities for a reconsideration of jurisdiction conceived relationally.

Understanding jurisdiction as relational does not mean that jurisdiction cannot be exclusionary. Acts of exclusion are jurisdictional acts, and they speak volumes about how the state conceives of its relationships and responsibilities. But relational jurisdiction does challenge the assumption that the lines of relationship and the scope of state responsibility are clear and fixed. As Casey suggests, perhaps "[t]he exclusivist dyad of us versus them would give way to an open myriad of ourselves-with-others (and they-with-us) in which the perception of bodies might take on alternative and imaginative directions."[55] The border is not a reflection of some fixed reality of inside/outside, here/there, us/them, but a process by which the contours of these dyads are continually challenged and remade.

V Conclusion: theology and the responsibility of engagement

In this chapter, I have argued that the insights on borders drawn from the experience of border communities and the scholarship of critical border studies can help us to recognize the ambivalent nature of borders and reconceive the legal understanding of the border as a site of engagement, not only a site of exclusion. The narrative of the border as an exclusionary legal-political barrier of the modern state is belied by the heterogeneous performance of the border by multiple actors, including the state's own heterogeneous performance. The border is "a big, neat, clean, clear black line on a map that does not exist,"[56] and thus as Tisha Rajendra argues, we must go "in search of better narratives."[57]

As in the case of the border, Rajendra writes that "narratives can be more or less faithful to reality." Fidelity to reality as a form of historicity or facticity, however, is not all that is at stake. Rajendra goes on to clarify the moral implications of inaccurate narratives by drawing on the resources of Christian theology. "When inaccurate narratives that are divorced from reality become the dominant social understanding of a group of people, something more insidious than divergent competing narratives is at play. Liberation theologians would call this structural sin, that is, sin that appears not in the human will alone but in social institutions, ideologies, and practices."[58] Rajendra argues that the better narratives we need would attend to the social, political, and economic histories that shape migration,

---

55 Casey, "Walling Racialized Bodies Out," 208.
56 Ríos, "The Border: A Double Sonnet."
57 Tisha M. Rajendra, *Migrants and Citizens: Justice and Responsibility in the Ethics of Immigration* (Grand Rapids, MI: Eerdmans, 2017), chapter 3.
58 Ibid., 56.

102 Silas W. Allard

or, put differently, migration exists within an existing set of relationships between migrants and residents, as well as between countries of origin, transit, and destination (see, for example, Cruz, Chapter 11; Bill Ong Hing and Raj Nadella, Chapter 17). Inaccurate narratives distort the nature of these relationships and the responsibility they entail, whereas justice is responsibility to those relationships.[59]

Rajendra's call for attention to better narratives and, in particular, narratives that illuminate the social, economic, political, and religious relationships that cross borders before people do, is a theme that recurs throughout this volume (see, especially, Kristin E. Heyer and Daniel Kanstroom, Chapter 18). As Kristin E. Heyer writes, "Relational emphases in Christian ethics can help reorient reductive protectionist analyses to consider the roles historical relationships and transnational actors play in abetting migration, as well as more receptive responses to immigrants that prioritize hospitality over structural justice" (Chapter 13). Not only do the resources of Christian theology point to the moral danger of inaccurate narratives, as Rajendra notes, but the "relational emphases" of Christian theology help illuminate the nature of responsibility embedded in accurate narratives. There is both a moral imperative to find better narratives and a moral imperative embedded in those narratives. It brings to mind the final Sunday sermon of Martin Luther King Jr., "Remaining Awake through a Great Revolution," in which King weaves together into a single strand of moral argument the descriptive reality of an interconnected world and the moral imperative to know and make that world.

> We are tied together in the single garment of destiny, caught in an inescapable network of mutuality. And whatever affects one directly affects all indirectly. For some strange reason I can never be what I ought to be until you are what you ought to be. And you can never be what you ought to be until I am what I ought to be. This is the way God's universe is made; this is the way it is structured.[60]

King's theological cosmology testifies to an empirical description and normative evaluation of a relational universe that is a call to both awareness and action.

Going in search of better narratives means recognizing the witness of border communities and the insights of critical border studies that the border is not a simple, natural, exclusive barrier, but a heterogeneous, performed site of mutual engagement. As Justo González writes, "A border is the place at which two realities, two worldviews, two cultures, meet and interact. . . . A true border, a true place of encounter, is by nature permeable. It is not like medieval

---

59 Ibid., especially chapter 6.
60 Martin Luther King Jr, "Remaining Awake Through a Great Revolution," in *A Knock at Midnight: Inspiration from the Great Sermons of Reverend Martin Luther King, Jr.*, eds. Clayborne Carson and Peter Holloran (New York: Warner Books, 2000), 207–8.

armor, but rather like skin."[61] As Gonzalez points out, however, the border is also not just a concept to be reimagined or a narrative to be retold. It is "a true place of encounter." The border understood as a site of engagement is also the occasion of the search for new narratives; engagements at and occasioned by borders are the possibility of thinking anew about "the inescapable network of mutuality."[62]

Cross-border liturgies offer one sign and instrument of such encounter(s). Since the early 2000s, Catholic Bishops from border dioceses in Mexico and the United States have held an annual border mass at and through the barrier that marks the current border between the United States and Mexico. Reflecting on the 2003 border mass held in El Paso/Ciudad Juarez, Daniel Groody writes:

> We celebrated mass outside, in the open air, in the dry, rugged, and sun-scorched terrain where the United States meets Mexico. . . . Like other liturgies, a large crowd gathered to pray and worship together. Unlike other liturgies, however, a sixteen-foot iron fence divided this community in half, with one side in Mexico and the other side in the United states. To give expression to our common solidarity as a people of God beyond political constructions, the two communities joined altars on both sides of the wall.[63]

The Diocese of El Paso describes the mass as a mourning for and remembrance of those who have died crossing the border, as well as a call for more humane border enforcement. When the officiant passes the sacrament through the border fence to be received by a congregant in another country, the liturgical act performs borderwork of engagement and reimagines the border. The liturgy invokes transcending unity through the Eucharist, but it also invokes the transnational history and reality of these two interdependent nations as families reunite through the fence. The U.S. government has attempted to make a wall of the border outside El Paso, Texas, envisioning it as solely a site of exclusion. The border mass is a profound reminder that the border is not only or necessarily a site of exclusion; it is a site of engagement.

---

61 Justo L. González, *Santa Biblia: The Bible through Hispanic Eyes* (Nashville: Abingdon Press, 1996), 86–87; see also Kristin E. Heyer, *Kinship Across Borders: A Christian Ethic of Immigration* (Washington, DC: Georgetown University Press, 2012), 25; Roberto S. Goizueta, "Beyond the Frontier Myth," in *Hispanic Christian Thought at the Dawn of the 21st Century*, eds. Alvin Padilla, Roberto S. Goizueta, and Eldin Villafane (Nashville: Abingdon Press, 2005), 150–58.

62 See, for example, Silas W. Allard, "Asylum: The Constraint of a Definition and the Agency of a Claim," *Moral Agency Under Constraint*, August 3, 2020, https://scholarblogs.emory.edu/moralagency2019/2020/08/03/claiming-asylum-as-moral-agency/.

63 Groody, "Fruit of the Vine and Work of Human Hands," 386.

104 *Silas W. Allard*

Suggested Reading

Anzaldúa, Gloria. *Borderlands/*La Frontera*: The New Mestiza*. 4th ed. San Francisco: Aunt Lute Books, 2012.

Graziano, Manlio. *What Is a Border?* Stanford, CA: Stanford University Press, 2018.

Heyer, Kristin E. *Kinship across Borders: A Christian Ethic of Immigration*. Washington, DC: Georgetown University Press, 2012.

Rajendra, Tisha M. *Migrants and Citizens: Justice and Responsibility in the Ethics of Immigration*. Grand Rapids, MI: Eerdmans, 2017.

Rumford, Chris. *Cosmopolitan Borders*. Basingstoke: Palgrave MacMillan, 2014.

6 Immigrant integration and disintegration in an era of exclusionary nationalism

Donald M. Kerwin

I Introduction

In *Strangers in the Land: Patterns of American Nativism, 1869–1925*, the historian John Higham credited the success of the United States at integrating immigrants in the nineteenth century to the desire of immigrants "to share" in the nation's life and the willingness of Americans not to demand too high a "level of solidarity" from them.[1] Instead, the nation mostly "trust[ed] in the ordinary processes of a free society" to meld "many peoples into one."[2] The Americanization movement in the late nineteenth and early twentieth centuries, which peaked during World War I, departed from this approach. Driven by fear of divided immigrant loyalties, the United States invested heavily in English and civics classes, insisted that immigrants naturalize, adopted "America First" and other slogans, and embarked on a public–private crusade to instill allegiance to the nation.[3]

A comprehensive 2015 report on integration by the National Academies of Sciences, Engineering, and Medicine (NASEM) recalled the Europeans who immigrated in the early twentieth century with little education and high levels of illiteracy, and whose children entered the labor market in the midst of the Great Depression.[4] Despite these immense challenges, this generation of immigrants and their descendants successfully integrated over time, a process enabled, in large part, by the expanding U.S. economy after World War II.[5] Today's immigrants and their descendants continue to integrate, albeit with variances based on their "starting points and on the segment of American society—the racial and

---

1 John Higham, *Strangers in the Land: Patterns of American Nativism, 1860–1925* (New York: Atheneum, 1975), 234–235.
2 Ibid., 234.
3 Ibid., 242–47.
4 Mary C. Waters and Marisa Gerstein Pineau, eds., *The Integration of Immigrants into American Society: Panel on the Integration of Immigrants into American Society, National Academies of Sciences, Engineering, and Medicine* (Washington, DC: National Academies Press, 2015).
5 Ibid., 248–49.

106   *Donald M. Kerwin*

ethnic groups, the legal status, the social class, and the geographic area—into which they integrate."[6]

The question arises, however: Will the nation's historic genius at integrating immigrants persist? With a record 45 million foreign-born U.S. residents and nearly double that number counting their U.S.-born children, the stakes could not be higher. This chapter explores the integration successes and challenges of U.S. immigrants and their progeny. It examines the conditions in receiving societies that improve and diminish the integration prospects of immigrants. These include, on the one hand, rising nationalism; nativism; and a rapidly changing labor market due to automation, robotization, and artificial intelligence; and, on the other hand, inclusive policies, integration initiatives, and strong mediating institutions.[7]

The chapter begins by exploring different conceptions of integration and concludes by reflecting on how Christianity might inform national and local integration policies. While this chapter focuses on the U.S. context, the issues discussed are pertinent in a wide variety of countries experiencing significant immigration.

II Conceptualizing integration

The European Union (EU) has provided a helpful starting point for conceptualizing integration. In 2004, the EU adopted Common Basic Principles of Integration that define integration as "a dynamic, two-way process of mutual accommodation by all immigrants and residents of Member States."[8] This process creates rights and responsibilities on the part of the immigrant, including respect for the EU's core values and access by immigrants to state institutions and to goods and services "equal to national citizens."[9] In 2011, the EU expanded this definition to reflect the role of countries of origin in facilitating integration through predeparture initiatives, support to their diasporas, and circular migration policies.[10] Several international processes, dialogues, and agreements have underscored the need for integration strategies that foreground human agency and that benefit both immigrants and receiving communities, making these strategies more likely to garner public support.[11]

---

6 Ibid., 3, 268.

7 The chapter also assumes that the well-known drivers of migration and integration dynamics will reemerge after the trauma, economic fallout, and policy restrictions from the COVID-19 pandemic.

8 Council of the European Union, Press Release 14615/04, "Common Basic Principles for Immigrant Integration Policy in the EU," November 19, 2004, § 9.

9 Ibid., § 14.

10 European Commission, "Communication from the Commission to the European Parliament, the Council, the European Economic and Social Committee and the Committee of the Regions: European Agenda for the Integration of Third-Country Nationals," *COM* (2011) 455 final, July 20, 2011, https://eur-lex.europa.eu/LexUriServ/LexUriServ.do?uri=COM:2011:0455:FIN:EN:PDF.

11 These include the processes leading to the Global Compact on Safe, Orderly and Regular Migration (GCM) and the Global Compact on Refugees, as well as the High-Level

While liberal democracies, supranational entities, and regional and international agreements envision integration as a process leading to the full participation of immigrants in their new communities, this view is not universal. A growing number of countries define themselves in terms of a common origin, race, ethnicity, religion, or exclusionary culture. Furthermore, the fundamental character of a country strongly influences the reception of immigrants, their success at integrating, and even the perception of what constitutes integration. Gulf Cooperation Council (GCC) states, for example, have relatively open labor migration policies and immense foreign-born populations. However, they equate integration with the incorporation of foreign workers into their labor markets, without access to the rights, services, or benefits of citizenship.

Christianity's core belief in universal human dignity and its global reach align with a vision of integration that responds holistically to immigrants as human beings and would treat them as fully contributing members to the good of their communities. In that vein, U.S. settlement-house leaders of the late nineteenth and early twentieth centuries believed that each immigrant group should be encouraged to contribute its gifts and the best of its own traditions to its new country.[12] Living with immigrants, these leaders learned that countries could most effectively promote integration by offering immigrants a home and embracing their gifts, rather than seeking to erase their heritages.[13]

Pope Francis understands integration as "neither assimilation nor incorporation," but "rooted essentially in the joint recognition of the other's cultural richness: it is not the superimposing of one culture over another, nor mutual isolation, with the insidious and dangerous risk of creating ghettoes."[14] By this vision, integration is more than socioeconomic advancement over generations. It provides an opportunity to build more just and inclusive societies, promote human flourishing, and unify culturally diverse persons based on their deepest values and longings.

III How immigrants in the United States are faring

Social scientists take a more analytical approach to integration, examining metrics like educational attainment, income, political participation, occupational distribution, residential integration, intermarriage, homeownership, language proficiency, naturalization rates, and sense of belonging.[15] The 2015 NASEM study

---

Dialogues at the United Nations on International Migration and Development and state-led dialogues through the Global Forum on Migration and Development (GFMD).

12 Higham, *Strangers in the Land*, 121, 252.

13 Ibid., 256.

14 Pope Francis, "Address of His Holiness Pope Francis to Participants in the International Forum on 'Migration and Peace'," *Vatican Library*, February 21, 2017, http://w2. vatican.va/content/francesco/en/speeches/2017/february/documents/papa-francesco_ 20170221_forum-migrazioni-pace.html.

15 Even these metrics can seem far removed from integrating experiences like mastering the complexities of a subway system, learning the idioms necessary to negotiate the workplace, participating in school activities, or assuming a leadership role in a faith community.

108 *Donald M. Kerwin*

found "substantial" socioeconomic integration—measured by education, occupation, earnings, and poverty—by immigrants and their U.S.-born descendants, with many qualifications and caveats. In particular, it reported:[16]

- "much more varied . . . skill levels" among the foreign-born than natives of the third generation and beyond, including a "disproportionate share of highly educated workers concentrated in science, technology, engineering, and health fields";[17]
- "[r]emarkably high" socioeconomic integration by the second generation;
- "strong intergenerational progress in educational attainment," albeit with marked "variations between and within . . . ethnoracial groups that reflect the different levels of human capital" of their immigrant parents;
- significant progress by the children of Mexican and Central American immigrants compared to their parents, but not "parity with the general population of native-born";
- an "employment advantage" among immigrant men, particularly the least educated, over comparable native-born men in the second and third generations;
- substantially lower rates of employment among immigrant women compared with native-born women, although the second and higher generation, "regardless of ethnoracial group, approach parity" with the native-born;
- improved earnings of foreign-born workers "relative to the native-born" based on their length of U.S. residence, although earnings "are still shaped by racial and ethnic stratification";
- acute integration challenges for the one in three immigrants without a high school education, who "have a long way to go to reach the middle class"; and
- substantial improvement in "occupational position" in the second generation of those "concentrated in low status occupations," but without reaching "parity with third and later generation Americans."

Moreover, parity with natives does not always translate into positive integration outcomes. In a well-recognized paradox, the well-being of the descendants of immigrants declines by three metrics—health, crime rates, and children in households without two parents—as they come to resemble natives.[18]

The United States is no longer in the vanguard of integration among developed countries. In 2015, the Migrant Integration Policy Index (MIPEX), which measures and compares the integration policies of 38 countries based on 167 policy

---

16 All quotations in the following bullets are from Waters and Pineau, *The Integration of Immigrants into American Society*, 248, 292–95.

17 See also Robert Warren, "The Legally Resident Foreign-Born Population Has the Same Percentage of Skilled Workers as the US-Born Native Population," *Center for Migration Studies*, January 31, 2018, http://cmsny.org/publications/foreign-born-same-skilled-native/.

18 Waters and Pineau, *The Integration of Immigrants into American Society*, 329–30.

Immigrant integration and disintegration 109

indicators, ranked the United States 9th out of 38 developed states. It reported that the United States had created a "slightly favorable path for some immigrants to fully participate in society and become U.S. citizens," but that "disproportionate fees, limited family visas, long backlogs, and insecure rights" denied too many U.S. residents the "dream of citizenship, a secure family life, and a good job."[19] It found that several countries "outperform" the United States in family reunification, allowing workers and students to secure permanent status, facilitating naturalization, and credentialing qualified foreign workers.[20] By 2019, it reported "no positive changes" on MIPEX indicators for the United States and that its international ranking had fallen, citing the "costs, delays and insecurity that defer many from the American dream of citizenship, a secure family, and a good job."[21]

Other studies have found that the United States falls short of many Organisation for Economic Co-operation and Development (OECD), EU, and Group of Twenty (G20) states in metrics such as rates of naturalization; voter participation; homeownership; residential segregation; immigrant poverty; economic self-sufficiency; income inequality; and discrimination based on race, ethnicity, and national origin.[22]

The situation of U.S. immigrants deteriorated from 2017 through 2020, as the Trump administration employed an array of administrative strategies to impede access to permanent residence and citizenship.[23] Even prior to the COVID-19 pandemic, naturalization processing times and backlogs had ballooned.[24] While U.S. family-based immigration policies are generous in many respects, numerical limits on family-based visas have led to backlogs that exceed the life expectancy of many in the queue (see also Bill Ong Hing, Chapter 3). Moreover, once a visa becomes available, most intending immigrants must apply for it through a U.S. embassy or consular office, a process that subjects many to multiyear bars to reentry to the United States based on their prior unlawful presence.[25]

---

19 Thomas Huddleston, Ozge Bilgili, Anne-Linde Vankova, and Zvezda Vankova, *Migrant Integration Policy Index 2015*, www.mipex.eu/.
20 Ibid.
21 Giacomo Solano and Thomas Huddleston, *Migrant Integration Policy Index 2020*, www.mipex.eu/usa (last accessed March 12, 2021).
22 Els de Grauuw and Irene Bloemraad, "Working Together: Building Successful Policy and Program Partnerships for Immigrant Integration," *Journal on Migration and Human Security* 5, no. 1 (2015): 105–23.
23 Donald M. Kerwin and Robert Warren, "Putting Americans First: A Statistical Case for Encouraging Rather than Impeding and Devaluing US Citizenship," *Journal on Migration and Human Security* 7, no. 4 (2019): 108–22.
24 See Miriam Jordan, "Wait Times for Citizenship Have Doubled in the Last Two Years," *New York Times*, February 21, 2019, www.nytimes.com/2019/02/21/us/immigrant-citizenship-naturalization.html; Paul Stern and Sharvari Dalal-Dheini, "AILA Policy Brief: Crisis Level USCIS Processing Delays and Inefficiencies Continue to Grow," *American Immigration Lawyers Association*, February 26, 2020, www.aila.org/advo-media/aila-policy-briefs/crisis-level-uscis-processing-delays-grow.
25 Donald M. Kerwin and Robert Warren, "Fixing What's Most Broken in the U.S. Immigration System: A Profile of the Family Members of U.S. Citizens and Lawful Permanent

110 *Donald M. Kerwin*

IV Conditions that integrate and disintegrate

Scholars have long recognized that the characteristics both of immigrants and of receiving societies influence immigrant integration. A series of papers from 2002, for example, identified the following integration determinants:

> pre-existing ethnic or race relations within the host population; differences in labor markets and related institutions; the impact of government policies and programs, including immigration policy, policies for immigrant integration, and policies for the regulation of social institutions; and the changing nature of international boundaries, part of the process of globalization.[26]

This section examines conditions that particularly influence the reception and integration of immigrants.

A Rising nationalism, nativism, and disintegration

The fundamental character and identity of a nation—defined, for present purposes, as how the majority or a dominant minority of its members conceive of their nation—strongly affect its reception of immigrants and their ability to integrate. Civic nationalists believe that shared civic values and institutions bind the members of a state. Many seminal U.S. texts and speeches have strongly enunciated this vision of the United States as a creedal nation. The Declaration of Independence speaks to the "self-evident" truths of equality and unalienable rights, including the rights to life, liberty, and the pursuit of happiness. In the Gettysburg Address, Abraham Lincoln characterized the United States as a nation "conceived in liberty and dedicated to the proposition that all men are created equal."[27] In his first inaugural address, George W. Bush said that America has "never been united by blood or birth or soil" and called the "American story" one of "a flawed and fallible people, united across the generations by grand and enduring ideals."[28] "The grandest of these ideals," he said, "is an unfolding American promise that everyone belongs, that everyone deserves a chance, that no insignificant person was ever born."[29]

Residents Mired in Multiyear Backlogs," *Journal on Migration and Human Security* 7, no. 2 (2019): 36–41.

26 Jeffrey G. Reitz, "Host Societies and the Reception of Immigrants: Research Themes, Emerging Theories and Methodological Issues," *International Migration Review* 36, no. 4 (2002): 1005–19.

27 Abraham Lincoln, the Gettysburg Address, November 19, 1863, Abraham Lincoln Online, transcript, http://showcase.netins.net/web/creative/lincoln/speeches/gettysburg.htm.

28 George W. Bush, first inaugural address, January 20, 2001, the White House Archives, transcript, https://georgewbush-whitehouse.archives.gov/news/inaugural-address.html.

29 Ibid. U.S. leaders have also long expressed pride in the United States as a "beacon" of freedom, "radiating" its ideals and values to the world. See Ronald Reagan, "Farewell to the Nation," *Ronald Reagan Presidential Foundation and Institute*, January 11, 1989, transcript, www.reaganfoundation.org/media/128652/farewell.pdf; Higham, *Strangers in the Land*, 63.

Immigrant integration and disintegration 111

Civic republicanism is not limited to the United States. At a ceremony commemorating the hundredth anniversary of Armistice Day, French President Emmanuel Macron lauded his nation's defense of universal values during World War I. He argued that nationalism—which he called a "betrayal" of patriotism—threatened to "wipe out what's most valuable about a nation, what brings it alive, what leads it to greatness, and what is most important: its moral values."[30]

By contrast, populist leaders celebrate a core group of "people" within a state—often defined by race, religion, ethnicity, nationality, and ancestry—who alone deserve the rights, benefits, and largesse conferred by state membership. By their telling, the political elite, press, and supranational and international institutions collude to subjugate the "people."[31] Populists intensify political polarization by frequent rhetorical attacks on those they deem to be outsiders, particularly immigrants and refugees. Brazilian President Jair Bolsonaro, for example, has called immigrants "the scum of the earth,"[32] and has charged that the "vast majority of potential migrants do not have good intentions."[33]

The "ideological core of nativism in every form," Higham wrote presciently, is that "some influence originating from abroad" threatens "the very life of the nation from within."[34] Donald Trump regularly regaled his supporters with the lyrics of a 1963 song called "The Snake," which he repurposed as a dehumanizing, nativist anthem.[35] In it, a woman rescues a freezing snake and takes it into her home. Once revived, the snake fatally bites her. In Trump's retelling, refugees and immigrants are the snake that will betray and consume their kindly, but naïve hosts, because that is their very nature. Similarly, Hungary and other Visegrád Group countries opposed the EU's 2015 migrant relocation plan by characterizing asylum seekers as a threat to their security and to European civilization itself.[36]

Nativism does not so much articulate problems with immigrants, as it blames them for a nation's unresolved problems. As such, it often goes hand in hand

---

30 Emmanuel Macron, "Commemoration of the Centenary of the Armistice," *Permanent Mission of France to the United Nations in New York*, November 11, 2018, transcript, https:// onu.delegfrance.org/Emmanuel-Macron-s-speech-at-Commemoration-of-the-centenary-of-the-Armistice.

31 Donald M. Kerwin, "How Robust Refugee Protection Policies Can Strengthen Human and National Security," *Journal on Migration and Human Security* 4, no. 3 (2016): 123–24.

32 "Who Is Jair Bolsonaro? Brazil's Far-Right President in His Own Words," *The Guardian*, October 29, 2018, www.theguardian.com/world/2018/sep/06/jair-bolsonaro-brazil-tro pical-trump-who-hankers-for-days-of-dictatorship.

33 David Gilbert, "Brazil's Far-Right President Jair Bolsonaro Really Wants to Be Trump's Super Best Friend," *Vice News*, March 19, 2019, www.vice.com/en_us/article/j579vx/brazil-jair-bolsonaro-trump-visit.

34 Higham, *Strangers in the Land*, 4.

35 Eli Rosenberg, "'The Snake': How Trump Appropriated a Radical Black Singer's Lyrics for Immigration Fearmongering," *Washington Post*, February 24, 2018, www.washington post.com/news/politics/wp/2018/02/24/the-snake-how-trump-appropriated-a-radical-black-singers-lyrics-for-refugee-fearmongering/.

36 Ashley B. Armstrong, "Nonrefoulement and the Challenge of Asylum," *Columbia Human Rights Law Review* 50, no. 2 (2019): 46–115, at 72–74.

112 *Donald M. Kerwin*

with isolationism, understood as a retreat from the (foreign) source of a perceived threat. As Kristin E. Heyer argues in this volume, isolationism—like nativism—"also betrays a deeper opposition to the common good" (Chapter 13). It represents a failure to recognize the shared humanity of people across borders and rejects the imperative to promote cross-border human flourishing.

Nativism thrives in defensive, inwardly focused countries. It often finds fertile ground in nations and local communities that have low overall immigrant populations[37] but have experienced recent increases in immigration, coupled with the emigration of natives. This combination can lead residents to fear cultural, racial, and religious displacement. In a telling juxtaposition, figure 6.1 highlights 14 African states among the 27 states whose populations are projected to double by 2050, and figure 6.2 lists some of the 37 states whose populations are projected to decline by 2050, some very significantly.

The states with aging populations in figure 6.2 would strongly benefit from an infusion of younger, working-age immigrants. Not coincidentally, however, many of these states have adopted exclusionary policies and are among the states least likely to want or to embrace additional immigrants.

Nativism can flourish in culturally diverse countries, particularly when the majority or a dominant minority population fears racial, cultural, or economic displacement. Such conditions flourished under the administration of Donald Trump, whose strategic use of cruelty to disintegrate immigrant communities became one of its defining features. As a candidate and president, Trump repeatedly stoked these fears: he made bigoted comments, used racist code words and nativist tropes, and championed policies that stereotype and discriminate against persons from certain faiths and countries. Hate groups identified him as a political champion who created space and momentum for their resurgence,[38] and Trump self-identified as a nationalist.[39]

The Trump administration sought to prevent and discourage immigrants from putting down roots by deploying tactics that destabilize and instill fear in immigrant communities, and that impede the path to permanent residence and citizenship. It engaged in indiscriminate deportations, which divide and impoverish mixed-status families and devalue the U.S. citizenship of their members.[40] It sought to remove forms of protected status, such as Deferred Action for

---

37 Higham, *Strangers in the Land*, 168, 181.
38 Owen Daugherty, "Richard Spencer: 'Charlottesville Wouldn't Have Occurred Without Trump'," *The Hill*, May 14, 2019, https://thehill.com/blogs/blog-briefing-room/news/443666-richard-spencer-charlottesville-wouldnt-have-occurred-without.
39 Quint Forgey, "Trump: 'I'm a Nationalist'," *Politico*, October 22, 2018, www.politico.com/story/2018/10/22/trump-nationalist-926745.
40 Donald M. Kerwin, Daniela Alulema, and Mike Nicholson, "Communities in Crisis: Interior Removals and Their Human Consequences," *Journal on Migration and Human Security* 6, no. 4 (2018): 225–41. This study quotes a U.S. citizen, whose father had been deported, asking his mother: "Where are my rights as a U.S. citizen? Where is my right to live with my family and have a home?"

Immigrant integration and disintegration 113

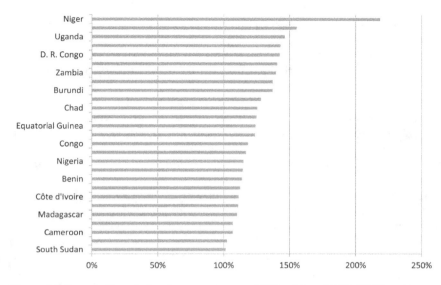

Figure 6.1 Percent Population Increase Among 27 Doublers: 2017–2050

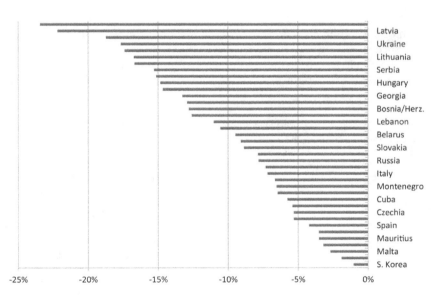

Figure 6.2 Percent Population Decrease Among 37 Decliners: 2017–2050

Source: Calculations for figures 6.1 and 6.2 were made by Joseph Chamie for the Center for Migration Studies based on projections from the United Nations Department of Economic and Social Affairs (2017). Images used by permission of the Center for Migration Studies.

114 *Donald M. Kerwin*

Childhood Arrivals (DACA) and Temporary Protected Status (TPS), from hundreds of thousands of immigrants. Trump proposed limiting family-based immigration to spouses and minor children[41] and endorsed legislation to cut legal immigration (mostly family-based) in half.

On February 21, 2020, the U.S. Department of Homeland Security began to implement the Trump era "public-charge" rule, which sought to exclude large numbers of low-income, working-class immigrants from admission and adjustment to permanent residence.[42] The U.S. Department of Housing and Urban Development issued a proposed regulation that would have denied public housing assistance to families with an undocumented[43] household member. As president, Trump also expressed support for ending (by fiat) birthright citizenship for the children of noncitizens, and his administration prioritized the denaturalization of citizens.

Higham points out the "monotony" of nativist arguments, whose "charges and complaints . . . sounded in endless reiteration," including those of the lawless immigrant bent on disorder and violence.[44] The Trump administration drew from this nativist script to describe Syrian refugees, Central American asylum seekers, and other groups fleeing impossible conditions as a menace to public safety and national security. Such repeated attacks generate hostility toward immigrants and minorities and create an environment that impedes integration. The administration also perfected nativist tactics like guilt by association. If an undocumented immigrant or asylum seeker, for example, committed a violent crime, the administration publicized and treated the offender's status as if it were the cause of the crime. However, it did not ascribe crimes and terrorist acts committed by white citizens to their racial identity or citizenship status. It also established an institutional home for these tactics: the Immigration and Customs Enforcement (ICE) office known as Victims of Immigration Crime Engagement (VOICE), which, among its other stated objectives, sought to study "the effects

---

41 "Fact Sheet: Establish Merit-Based Reforms to Promote Assimilation and Financial Success," *The White House*, October 8, 2017, www.whitehouse.gov/briefings-statements/establish-merit-based-reforms-promote-assimilation-financial-success/.

42 Inadmissibility on Public Charge Grounds, 84 Fed. Reg. 41,292 (2019) (codified at 8 C.F.R. pts. 103, 212–14, 245, 248). In a similar vein, the president issued a proclamation that would have suspended legal immigration by persons who could not prove they would be "covered by approved health insurance" or possessed "the financial resources to pay for reasonably foreseeable medical costs." Donald J. Trump, Presidential Proclamation No. 9945, 84 Fed. Reg. 53,991 (October 9, 2019) ("Suspension of Entry of Immigrants Who Will Financially Burden the United States Healthcare System").

43 The chapter uses the term "undocumented" to describe U.S. residents who lack legal immigration status. This term is factually inaccurate in that many undocumented persons possess identity and other documents. It is also reductive, as it speaks to only one, relatively superficial characteristic of this population. However, it is less offensive than the term "illegal," which implies that human beings can *be* illegal, and it is no worse than the term "unauthorized." In addition, the term "undocumented" is widely understood to refer to persons without legal immigration status.

44 Higham, *Strangers in the Land*, 55, 131.

Immigrant integration and disintegration   115

of the victimization by criminal aliens present in the United States."[45] Yet immigrant crime rates fall well below those of native-born citizens, and high rates of immigration do not adversely affect aggregate crime rates.[46]

B _Public support for nativist policies_

Administrations turn over regularly and, in its first weeks in office, the Biden administration issued a series of executive orders, proclamations, and policy directives that sought to replace Trump era immigration and refugee policies, with policies that promote legal immigration, naturalization, and integration.[47] Despite this change, it remains vitally important to understand the beliefs, needs, and experiences of those who favor nativist policies. Pundits offer a variety of explanations, such as national security fears driven by 9/11 and terrorist attacks in Europe; the economic scarring caused by the Great Recession and lack of accountability for that crisis; and the misperception that the federal government favors undocumented immigrants by poorly enforcing its immigration laws. Several studies, however, have concluded that white voter animus and fears of racial displacement best explain the appeal of such policies.[48]

In an influential 2017 study, the Public Religion Research Institute (PRRI) reported that white working-class residents (not college educated) felt displaced, threatened, and like strangers "in their own" country. The study found that:[49]

- 68 percent of white working class Americans and 55 percent of the general public believe that the American way of life needed to be protected from foreign influence;
- 68 percent of the white working class and 55 percent of the U.S. public think that the United States is at risk of losing its cultural identity;
- 62 percent of the white working class thinks that growing numbers of immigrants threaten U.S. culture;

---

45 "VOICE: Victims of Immigration Crime Engagement," _United States Immigration and Customs Enforcement_, www.ice.gov/voice.

46 Waters and Pineau, _The Integration of Immigrants into American Society_, 326–27.

47 Executive Order No. 14,012, Restoring Faith in Our Legal Immigration Systems and Strengthening Integration and Inclusion Efforts for New Americans, 86 Fed. Reg. 8,277 (February 2, 2021).

48 See Tom Jacobs, "More Evidence That Racism and Sexism Were Key to Trump's Victory," _Pacific Standard_, April 4, 2018, https://psmag.com/social-justice/more-evidence-that-racism-and-sexism-were-key-to-trump-victory; Tom Jacobs, "A New Study Confirms (Again) That Race, Not Economics, Drove Former Democrats to Trump," _Pacific Standard_, April 29, 2019, https://psmag.com/news/new-study-confirms-again-that-race-not-econo mics-drove-former-democrats-to-trump.

49 The following bullet points are taken from Robert P. Jones, Daniel Cox, and Rachel Lienesch, "Beyond Economics: Fears of Cultural Displacement Pushed the White Working Class to Trump," _Public Religion Research Institute (PRRI)_, May 9, 2017, www.prri.org/research/white-working-class-attitudes-economy-trade-immigration-election-donald-trump/.

116 *Donald M. Kerwin*

- just 46 percent believe in the American dream—that is, if you work hard, you can improve your situation and achieve your goals;
- 45 percent who live in their hometown indicate that its quality of life has deteriorated since their childhood, and only 17 percent think it has improved;
- 65 percent believe that the American way of life has deteriorated since the 1950s;
- 40 percent think that efforts to increase diversity almost always come "at the expense of whites";
- 46 percent think that the growing numbers of newcomers threaten "traditional American customs and values."

As Heyer writes, these feelings reflect a sense "of real and perceived loss—and accompanying grief and resentment"—and highlight the importance of rebuilding "public trust and a shared sense of community" (Chapter 13; see also, Gemma Tulud Cruz, Chapter 11). Effectively addressing the underlying conditions that give rise to these concerns, while strongly opposing nativist policies, should be a high national priority, and may lead to greater openness to immigrants.

C *Lack of consensus on national interests and immigration policy*

Immigration policymaking might be conceived as the process of attempting to align a country's interests, values, and diverse needs with its admissions laws and integration policies.[50] Congressional debates, presidential signing statements, and immigration legislation over the last half century reveal a rough consensus on the interests and values—often observed in the breach—that should underlie U.S. immigration laws. These include:

- family reunification and preservation;
- nondiscrimination on the basis of national origin, race, or privilege;
- fairness in admissions policies and due process in removal decisions;
- the responsibility to project values like liberty, freedom, and human dignity;
- economic competitiveness, hard work, self-sufficiency, and the drive to succeed;
- affording all residents access to "the benefits of a free and open society,"[51] and;

---

50 Of course, states should also defend and respect the rights of persons whose concerns for survival or security have led them to migrate, whether or not they fit neatly into legal admissions categories. David Hollenbach, "Borders and Duties to the Displaced: Ethical Perspectives on the Refugee Protection System," *Journal on Migration and Human Security* 4, no. 2 (2016): 148–65. Michele R. Pistone also addresses humanitarian responsibilities of states (Chapter 4).

51 Ronald Reagan, "Statement on Signing the Immigration Reform and Control Act of 1986," November 6, 1986, 22 Weekly Comp. Pres. Doc. 1533–37, transcript.

- respect for the rule of law as reflected in a system characterized by high rates of legal migration.[52]

Yet these values and interests do not resonate as they once did across the political spectrum.

While there has long been consensus on the need to enforce the nation's antiquated immigration laws, absent recognition of the *affirmative* benefits of immigration and refugee protection, meaningful reform will remain elusive. As it stands, the United States has not overhauled its legal immigration system in 56 years. In addition, it has failed for two decades to offer a path to status for its 10.6 million undocumented residents,[53] which include:

- most of the 3.8 million persons waiting in family-based visa backlogs;
- nearly 4 million parents of U.S. citizens and lawful permanent residents;
- 2 million persons who have lived in the United States for 20 years or more;
- 3 million persons brought to the United States at age 16 or younger; and
- 7.4 million workers, nearly three-quarters of whom work in essential critical infrastructure sectors.[54]

The nation's failure to provide a path to citizenship for these groups impedes their integration and that of their families. Along those lines, the NASEM report identified three "causes of concern" regarding immigrant integration in the United States: (1) the effect of policies that seek to block the integration of undocumented and temporary immigrants and their U.S. citizen and lawful permanent resident family members; (2) how race shapes integration outcomes and patterns; (3) and the comparatively low rate of naturalization among immigrants.[55]

D *National and local integration policies*

Federal policies can advance or inhibit integration, but the integration process invariably occurs in local communities. State and local responses range from partnering with federal agencies to enforce immigration laws and denying public services to noncitizen residents, to extending the full benefits of

---

52 Donald M. Kerwin and Robert Warren, "National Interests and Common Ground in the U.S. Immigration Debate: How to Legalize the U.S. Immigration System and Permanently Reduce Its Undocumented Population," *Journal on Migration and Human Security* 5, no. 2 (2017): 297–330.

53 Robert Warren, "Reverse Migration to Mexico Led to US Undocumented Population Decline: 2010 to 2018," *Journal on Migration and Human Security* 8, no. 1 (2020): 32–41.

54 Donald M. Kerwin and Robert Warren, "US Foreign-Born Workers in the Global Pandemic: Essential and Marginalized," *Journal on Migration and Human Security* 8, no. 3 (2020): 282–300.

55 Waters and Pineau, *The Integration of Immigrants into American Society*, 8–12.

118 *Donald M. Kerwin*

membership to immigrants of all statuses and resisting immigration enforcement partnerships with the federal government out of concern that they undermine public safety.[56] Because of variations in state and local integration policies, even within the same state, the integration prospects of immigrants in New York City or Los Angeles differ from those in Atlanta or Minneapolis, which also differ from those in rural Georgia or Minnesota. A particularly positive development has been the expansion of state and local immigrant affairs offices—as well as commissions, task forces, and programs—that celebrate the contributions of immigrants, promote citizenship, and connect immigrant communities to government agencies, the police, and private institutions.[57]

Localities have also increasingly collaborated to advance prointegration policies and to oppose exclusionary federal policies. The Cities of Action Network, for example, consists of 175 U.S. mayors and county executives, representing 70 million persons, devoted to the safety of all of their members, to immigrant rights, and to the participation and inclusion of immigrants in civic life. Welcoming America, a nonprofit, nonpartisan organization, has developed a formal certification process—based on seven requirements and detailed benchmarks—for city and county governments that wish to become certified welcoming communities. Over the course of the COVID-19 pandemic, many states and localities have also offered economic relief and access to health care to immigrants who have been excluded from federal relief and stimulus programs.[58]

The expansion of integration efforts at the local level stands in contrast to federal policies. Throughout much of its history, the U.S. response to concerns about immigration has been to restrict or exclude immigrants, on one hand, and solely to trust in their drive and talent and in the nation's integrative power, on the other.[59] Els de Grauuw and Irene Bloemraad have criticized the modesty of the federal government's "laissez-faire" integration policies, which have mostly supported naturalization and related services. They particularly lament the federal government's failure to connect and build synergies among federal, state, and local government and civil-society integration actors.[60]

A stark example of the federal government's laissez-faire approach to integration can be seen in its provision of social supports. The Global Compact for Safe, Orderly and Regular Migration (GCM), approved by 164 states and endorsed by the UN General Assembly on December 19, 2018, affirmed the need for all immigrants, irrespective of status, to "exercise their human rights through safe

---

56 Roberto Suro, "California Dreaming: The New Dynamism in Immigration Federalism and Opportunities for Inclusion on a Variegated Landscape," *Journal on Migration and Human Security* 3, no. 1 (2015): 1–25, at 15–18.

57 De Grauuw and Bloemraad, "Working Together," 112–15.

58 Roberto Suro and Hannah Findling, "State and Local Aid for Immigrants During the COVID-19 Pandemic: Innovating Inclusion," *Center for Migration Studies*, July 8, 2020, https://cmsny. org/publications/state-local-aid-immigrants-covid-19-pandemic-innovating-inclusion/.

59 As stated, the Americanization movement pursued a third, more proactive track.

60 De Grauuw and Bloemraad, "Working Together."

Immigrant integration and disintegration 119

access to basic services."[61] In the United States, however, immigrant access to public benefits and services is severely restricted.[62] Temporary visa holders (non-immigrants) and undocumented immigrants do not qualify for federal welfare benefits, with exceptions for certain populations and certain benefits.[63] Lawful permanent residents cannot receive "means-tested" federal benefits for five years or more.[64] The federal government extends means-tested benefits to other "qualified" immigrants like refugees, asylees, and other humanitarian migrants, as well as to noncitizen veterans and military personnel, subject to time and eligibility restrictions.[65] Yet U.S. immigrants can face harsh criticism for using the limited benefits and services for which they are eligible.

The U.S. Refugee Admissions Program (USRAP)—which seeks to promote the self-sufficiency of refugees through their early employment—may be the only exception to laissez-faire national integration policies. USRAP operates as a partnership among multiple federal agencies, states, localities, and civil-society institutions. The Population, Refugees, and Migration (PRM) division of the U.S. Department of State (DOS) enters "cooperative agreements" with national voluntary agencies to provide reception and placement services that cover housing, food, and other necessities during refugees' first 30 to 90 days in the nation. The U.S. Office of Refugee Resettlement provides cash assistance, medical assistance, and social service funding through state refugee coordinators. The community-based affiliates of national voluntary agencies provide hands-on resettlement assistance and services. However, funding and severe cuts in refugee admissions have devastated USRAP and its community-based infrastructure.[66]

Despite its limitations, USRAP has saved millions of lives in its 41-year history, and it represents a case study in how modest federal investments can significantly

---

61 United Nations, Global Compact for Safe, Orderly and Regular Migration, UN Doc. A/RES/73/195 (December 19, 2018), § 31. The United States withdrew from the negotiations of the Global Compact for Safe, Orderly and Regular Migration in December 2017.

62 The Trump era rule on the public charge ground of inadmissibility—which led to diminished participation by immigrants and their families in public programs—expanded the list of benefits that could be considered in these determinations. Inadmissibility on Public Charge Grounds, 84 Fed. Reg. 41,292 (2019) (codified at 8 C.F.R. pts. 103, 212–14, 245, 248).

63 Nonimmigrants and undocumented immigrants are eligible for emergency medical care, disaster relief, Medicaid benefits to children and pregnant women, the National School Lunch Program, the Special Supplemental Nutrition Program for Women, Infants, and Children (WIC), and Head Start. Undocumented children can also attend public school through high school.

64 Means-tested benefits include Supplemental Nutrition Assistance Program (SNAP or food stamps), Supplemental Security Income, Temporary Assistance for Needy Families, regular Medicaid, and State Children's Health Insurance Program.

65 Most states, however, use their own funding to supplement coverage to "qualified" immigrants and to extend coverage to those who do not qualify for federal aid.

66 Donald M. Kerwin and Mike Nicholson, "Charting a Course to Rebuild and Strengthen the US Refugee Admissions Program (USRAP): Findings and Recommendations from the Center for Migration Studies Refugee Resettlement Survey: 2020," *Journal on Migration and Human Security* 9, no. 1 (2021): 1–30.

120   *Donald M. Kerwin*

contribute to integration. A study of the socioeconomic advancement of 1.1 million refugees who arrived between 1987 and 2016 found that integration increases dramatically over time. Refugees who arrived between 1987 and 1996 *exceeded* not just later arrivals but also the total U.S. population in median personal income ($28,000 compared to $23,000); homeownership (41 percent compared to 37 percent); income above the poverty line (86 percent compared to 84 percent); access to a computer and the internet (82 percent compared to 75 percent); and health insurance (93 percent compared to 91 percent).[67]

E *The uncertain future of work*

The ability of immigrants to improve their life prospects through work has played a central role in the integration of immigrants to the United States and elsewhere. Work is critical for economic viability (particularly in light of limited access to social safety-net programs), as a point of social connection, and as a framing narrative regarding the contributions of immigrants to the broader society. However, immigrants face a rapidly changing labor market because of advances in automation, robotics, and artificial intelligence. Lower-income, less credentialed immigrant workers occupy a precarious position in the U.S. and global economies since automation will decimate many jobs that they fill at high rates.[68] Several studies point to the potential for immense dislocation and job displacement caused by technological advances. These studies conclude that:

- two-thirds of jobs in developing countries could be "susceptible" to automation in coming decades;[69]
- 30 percent of work activities could be displaced;[70]
- jobs in transportation and logistics, office and administrative support, production and services, sales, and construction are highly susceptible to computerization over the next two decades;[71] and
- at least one-third of the tasks performed in 60 percent of occupations can already be automated.[72]

---

67 Donald M. Kerwin, "The US Refugee Resettlement Program—A Return to First Principles: How Refugees Help to Define, Strengthen, and Revitalize the United States," *Journal on Migration and Human Security* 6, no. 2 (2018): 205–25.

68 Donald M. Kerwin, "International Migration and Work: Charting an Ethical Approach to the Future," *Journal on Migration and Human Security* 8, no. 2 (2020): 111–33.

69 World Bank, *World Development Report 2016: Digital Dividends* (Washington, DC: World Bank, 2016), www.worldbank.org/en/publication/wdr2016, at 23, 126.

70 James Manyika, et al., "Jobs Lost, Jobs Gained: Workforce Transitions in a Time of Automation," *McKinsey & Company*, 2017, www.mckinsey.com/featured-insights/future-of-work/jobs-lost-jobs-gained-what-the-future-of-work-will-mean-for-jobs-skills-and-wages, at 28.

71 Carl Benedikt Frey and Michael A. Osborne, "The Future of Employment: How Susceptible Are Jobs to Computerisation?" working paper, Oxford Martin Programme on Technology and Employment, Oxford Martin School, Oxford University, 2013.

72 Manyika, et al., "Jobs Lost, Jobs Gained," 25–26.

Immigrant integration and disintegration 121

On the other hand, some of the jobs filled by immigrants at high rates, such as nursing, elder care, and domestic work, are expanding,[73] and the greater willingness of migrants to move affords them a competitive advantage in a rapidly changing job market. The availability of sufficient, decent work and its success in promoting social cohesion, despite the disruptions and dislocations in the labor market, will be of overriding importance to immigrant integration into the foreseeable future.

F Mediating institutions and integration fundamentals

Integration occurs, in part, through institutions that nurture, educate, employ, train, and empower immigrants. Family, the workplace, labor unions, political parties, schools, faith communities, the armed forces, and civic associations have traditionally provided immigrants with the resources, tools, and human and social capital to succeed in the broader society. In the immigration field Immigration-focused, U.S. civil-society institutions have also grown in sophistication, number, and ambition over the years.[74]

Integrating institutions, in turn, depend on a broader set of integration fundamentals. The relatively open U.S. labor market, for example, has provided immigrants and their children with abundant opportunities to work, to improve their socioeconomic standing, and to contribute to the U.S. economy. The U.S. Constitution affords rights to "persons," not only to citizens. The Fourteenth Amendment guarantees citizenship by birth, ensuring that immigrant families can never become part of a hereditary underclass of noncitizens.

U.S. immigration policy prioritizes the reunification of families, an institution that provides material, social, and emotional support in the integration process (see Bill Ong Hing, Chapter 3).[75] The U.S. tradition of religious freedom allows faith-based institutions—many created by and for earlier generations of immigrants[76]—to provide refuge, a source of respectability, and resources that facilitate integration.[77] A survey of 170 U.S. Catholic institutions, for example, identified

---

73 "Issue Brief No. 8: Skills Policies and Systems for a Future Workforce," *International Labour Organization*, presented February 15–17, 2018, www.ilo.org/wcmsp5/groups/public/–dgreports/–cabinet/documents/publication/wcms_618170.pdf.

74 Sara Campos, "The Influence of Civil Society in U.S. Immigrant Communities and the U.S. Immigration Debate," in *International Migration, U.S. Immigration Law and Civil Society: From the Pre-Colonial Era to the 113th Congress*, eds. Leonir Mario Chiarello and Donald M. Kerwin (New York: Scalabrini International Migration Network, 2014); Donald M. Kerwin, Roberto Suro, Tess Thorman, and Daniela Alulema, *The DACA Era and the Continuous Legalization Work of the U.S. Immigrant-Serving Community* (New York: Center for Migration Studies, 2017).

75 Zoya Gubernskaya and Joanna Dreby, "US Immigration Policy and the Case for Family Unity," *Journal on Migration and Human Security* 5, no. 2 (2017): 417–30.

76 Donald M. Kerwin and Breana George, *US Catholic Institutions and Immigrant Integration: Will the Church Rise to the Challenge?* (Vatican City: Lateran University Press, 2014).

77 Waters and Pineau, *The Integration of Immigrants into American Society*, 320–21.

122 Donald M. Kerwin

dozens of pastoral, social, health, housing, food, educational, organizing, and legal-service programs provided to immigrants and their families by Catholic parishes.[78]

Yet many of these integration pillars face ideological and political opposition. President Trump, for example, incorrectly argued that he could revoke birthright citizenship for the children of noncitizens by executive fiat.[79] The 1982 U.S. Supreme Court decision in *Plyler v. Doe*, which prohibits states from denying schooling through high school to undocumented children, may be vulnerable in light of the changed composition of the Supreme Court.[80] Participants in the previously mentioned survey of Catholic institutions most frequently identified "fear of apprehension and deportation" as negatively impacting immigrants' access to their services.[81] Thus, while immigrants need robust mediating institutions, many of the institutions that met this need for earlier generations of immigrants face severe challenges.

V Christianity, migration, and integration

In these times marked by such challenges to immigrants' welfare and integration, resources from the Christian tradition can help to restore to the immigration debate concepts such as human dignity, the common good, and reverence for the vulnerable. They can help chart a more life-giving, person-centered approach to a phenomenon that has been "part of the human experience throughout history."[82] A Christian worldview can help to reappropriate concepts like sovereignty, security, and the rule of law that speak to the responsibility to protect and safeguard the rights of all persons, but that have been used to exclude and marginalize immigrants. Christianity can challenge demeaning labels like "illegal aliens" (who are neither illegal nor alien) or "aggravated felons" (a misnomer) or "invading hordes" (a lie) that demagogues use to manipulate public opinion. Religious institutions can prioritize the defense, empowerment, and integration of immigrants in their moments of great need. As in past eras, they can help immigrants to weather ugly nativist periods.

The Judeo-Christian tradition reveres migrants based on its own long experience of exile, exodus, dispersion, and evangelization. In the first five books of the Hebrew Bible, the imperative not to oppress the stranger recurs 36 times. Jesus

---

78 Donald M. Kerwin and Mike Nicholson, "The Effects of Immigration Enforcement on Faith-Based Organizations: An Analysis of the FEER Survey," *Journal on Migration and Human Security* 7, no. 2 (2019): 41–52.
79 Jonathan Swan and Stef W. Kight, "Exclusive: Trump Targeting Birthright Citizenship with Executive Order," *Axios*, October 13, 2018, www.axios.com/trump-birthright-citizenship-executive-order-0cf4285a-16c6-48f2-a933-bd71fd72ea82.html.
80 *Plyler v. Doe*, 475 U.S. 202 (1982).
81 Kerwin and Nicholson, "The Effects of Immigration Enforcement on Faith-Based Organizations."
82 Global Compact for Safe, Orderly and Regular Migration, § 8.

Immigrant integration and disintegration   123

himself identified with newcomers and taught that nations will be judged by their treatment of migrants and others in need.[83]

Administrations that use the law to exclude and marginalize immigrants have found it more difficult to twist scripture for their political purposes. Former U.S. attorney general Jeff Sessions, for example, offered a biblical defense of the Trump administration's policy to separate children from their asylum-seeking parents at the U.S.–Mexico border, without any serious plan to reunite them.[84] He cited Romans 13:1, in which Saint Paul urges: "Let every person be subordinate to the higher authorities, for there is no authority except from God, and those that exist have been established by God" (New American Bible). In fact, the higher authorities also crucified Jesus and, in our era, have perpetrated genocide, slavery, apartheid, the forced displacement of 79 million persons, and the cruel separation of children from their parents. Moreover, they have largely done so under color of law—ruling *by* law but flouting the rule of law.

If Sessions had wanted to draw further from Romans 13, he could have cited: "Love does no evil to the neighbor: hence, love is the fulfillment of law" (Romans 13:10, NAB). The scribes and Pharisees described in the Gospels lived in strict accordance with the laws but failed to live according to its spirit. The Trump administration failed on both counts, as do all those who ignore or endorse cruelty toward immigrants.

Faith leaders are often told that immigrants, particularly those without status, should render unto Caesar what is Caesar's; that is, they should obey the law. This admonition seems selective, if not misplaced, in that lack of access to status exposes persons to all manner of criminality and illegality. More to the point, however, this parable means the opposite of how nativists choose to read it. In Matthew 22:15–22, the Pharisees and the Herodians ask Jesus—as if they want to avail themselves of his wisdom—if it is lawful to pay the census tax to Caesar. They hypocritically praise Jesus for his truthfulness and feign deference to him, but they have found rare common cause in an attempt to entrap him and perhaps have him executed.

To the Pharisees, paying taxes to the pagan occupying government violates the Torah. If Jesus supports paying this tax, he will lose favor with those who have declared him their king. The Herodians, in turn, support Roman rule. If Jesus opposes paying taxes, he could be killed as a political criminal and revolutionary. Jesus ultimately tells them to repay to "Caesar what belongs to Caesar, and to God what belongs to God" (Matthew 12:21, NAB). Yet this reply leads to the question: what belongs to God and what to Caesar? In the Judeo-Christian tradition, everything belongs to God—our love, our allegiance, our land, and our very lives. Thus, Caesar can collect the coins that bear his image, but here

---

83 These themes are explored elsewhere in this volume by Safwat Marzouk (Chapter 8), Raj Nadella (Chapter 9), and Luis N. Rivera-Pagán (Chapter 10).

84 Jeff Sessions, U.S. Department of Justice, "Attorney General Sessions Addresses Recent Criticisms of Zero Tolerance by Church Leaders," June 14, 2018, transcript, www.justice.gov/opa/speech/attorney-general-sessions-addresses-recent-criticisms-zero-tolerance-church-leaders.

124 *Donald M. Kerwin*

is the cosmic punch line: ultimately he will not be able to keep what he collects. Instead, he will be judged by how truly he has loved his neighbor, including the stranger in his midst.

Of course, immigrants should respect their new countries' laws, norms, and institutions. Receiving communities, in turn, should be open to revitalization and renewal by immigrants. Immigrants embody traits that U.S. residents have long thought to be emblematic of their country, like hard work, courage, self-sacrifice, a commitment to family, belief in the American dream, a reverence for freedom, and hope. They can remind the long-settled what it means to be an American, and that what unites the country can be stronger than what divides it. They can be a means of spiritual renewal through their hope, devotion, and religious practices. Finally, in the way the despised foreigner and schismatic models compassion in Jesus's Good Samaritan parable (Luke 17:11–19), immigrants can also be a means of conversion by the way they live their faith. As Pope Francis eloquently put it, they can be "an occasion that Providence gives us to help build a more just society, a more perfect democracy, a more united country, a more fraternal world and a more open and evangelical Christian community."[85]

Suggested Reading

Council of the European Union. "Common Basic Principles for Immigrant Integration Policy in the EU." *European Web Site on Integration*, November 19, 2004. https://ec.europa.eu/migrant-integration/librarydoc/common-basic-principles-for-immigrant-integration-policy-in-the-eu.

De Grauuw, Els, and Irene Bloemraad. "Working Together: Building Successful Policy and Program Partnerships for Immigrant Integration." *Journal on Migration and Human Security* 5, no. 1 (2017): 105–23.

Gubernskaya, Zoya, and Joanna Dreby. "US Immigration Policy and the Case for Family Unity." *Journal on Migration and Human Security* 5, no. 2 (2017): 417–30.

Higham, John. *Strangers in the Land: Patterns of American Nativism, 1860–1925.* New York: Atheneum, 1975.

Jones, Robert P., Daniel Cox, and Rachel Lienesch. "Beyond Economics: Fears of Cultural Displacement Pushed the White Working Class to Trump." *Public Religion Research Institute*, May 9, 2017. www.prri.org/research/white-working-class-attitudes-economy-trade-immigration-election-donald-trump/.

Kerwin, Donald, and Breana George. *US Catholic Institutions and Immigrant Integration: Will the Church Rise to the Challenge.* Vatican City: Lateran University Press, 2014. http://cmsny.org/publications/us-catholic-institutions-and-immigrant-integration-will-the-church-rise-to-the-challenge/.

---

85 Pope Francis, "Message of His Holiness Pope Francis for the World Day of Migrants and Refugees (2014): Migrants and Refugees: Towards a Better World," *Vatican*, August 5, 2013, http://w2.vatican.va/content/francesco/en/messages/migration/documents/papa-francesco_20130805_world-migrants-day.html.

Suro, Roberto. "California Dreaming: The New Dynamism in Immigration Federalism and Opportunities for Inclusion on a Variegated Landscape." *Journal on Migration and Human Security* 3, no. 1 (2015): 1–25.

Waters, Mary C., and Marisa Gerstein Pineau, eds. *The Integration of Immigrants into American Society.* Panel on the Integration of Immigrants into American Society. National Academies of Sciences, Engineering, and Medicine. Washington, DC: The National Academies Press, 2015, doi:10.17226/21746.

7 True faith, allegiance, and citizenship

Rose Cuison-Villazor

I hereby declare, on oath, that I absolutely and entirely renounce and abjure all allegiance and fidelity to any foreign prince, potentate, state, or sovereignty, of whom or which I have heretofore been a subject or citizen; that I will support and defend the Constitution and laws of the United States of America against all enemies, foreign and domestic; that I will bear true faith and allegiance to the same; that I will bear arms on behalf of the United States when required by the law; that I will perform noncombatant service in the Armed Forces of the United States when required by the law; that I will perform work of national importance under civilian direction when required by the law; and that I take this obligation freely, without any mental reservation or purpose of evasion; so help me God.

—Oath of Allegiance[1]

I Introduction

How does the stranger—the noncitizen—become a U.S. citizen and thus a permanent member of the United States polity? In the United States, that process is known as naturalization. This process requires noncitizens who have lawful permanent resident (LPR) status (also known as green card holders) to meet several formal and substantive requirements, which culminate in the taking of an oath of allegiance in a public ceremony or before a court.[2] When taking the oath of allegiance, LPRs must also "renounce and abjure" their allegiance to their native country and give their "true faith and allegiance" to the United States. Upon taking the oath of allegiance along with the oath of renunciation, the applicant for naturalization "shall be deemed a citizen of the United States."[3]

---

1 8 C.F.R. § 337.1 (2019).
2 8 U.S.C. § 1427 (2020) (requirements for naturalization); 8 C.F.R. § 337.1(a) (stating that an applicant for naturalization shall, "before being admitted to citizenship, take in a public ceremony within the United States" the oath of allegiance).
3 8 C.F.R. § 337.9(a) (stating that the naturalized citizen acquires citizenship "as of the date on which the applicant takes the prescribed oath of allegiance").

True faith, allegiance, and citizenship 127

Why does the naturalization process require LPRs to abandon their allegiance to their home country and declare their sole loyalty to the United States? What do these oaths suggest about what it means to become a citizen and a permanent member of the American polity? This chapter seeks to answer these questions and considers their implications for the anthropology of citizenship—what makes a citizen not only formally (such as naturalization requirements) but also substantively.[4]

Specifically, this chapter examines the last step of the naturalization process—the oaths of renunciation and allegiance, which I collectively and interchangeably refer to here as the loyalty oath—to illustrate the disparate expectations of allegiance that the country asks of soon-to-be citizens and those who are *already* citizens. On one hand, the United States demands that LPRs forswear their allegiance elsewhere and declare sole loyalty to the United States. In so doing, the United States mandates that to be a citizen—to be a permanent formal insider of the American polity—is to express faithfulness and devotion to only one sovereign. On the other hand, the United States does not require native-born citizens to take an oath of allegiance or forswear any other allegiance they may have by operation of law. Indeed, it allows millions of U.S. citizens to acquire dual citizenship and thus accepts that the permanent members of the polity may have divided loyalties.[5] Given the different expectations regarding faith and allegiance between those who are about to become naturalized citizens and those who already have U.S. citizenship, the question arises whether the loyalty oath should still be part of the naturalization process.[6]

In answering this question, this chapter employs the theology of hospitality as an overarching theoretical framework. By theology of hospitality, I mean the biblical invocation to welcome, embrace, and care for strangers (see Safwat Marzouk, Chapter 8; Raj Nadella, Chapter 9; Luis N. Rivera-Pagán, Chapter 10). I argue

---

4 For a discussion of this theoretical framework, see Sian Lazar, ed., *Anthropology of Citizenship: A Reader* (Malden, MA: Wiley-Blackwell, 2013).
5 For a discussion of dual nationals, see Stanley A. Renshon, *The 50% American: Immigration and National Identity in an Age of Terror* (Washington, DC: Georgetown, University Press, 2005); Peter J. Spiro, *At Home in Two Countries: The Past and Future of Dual Citizenship* (New York: New York University Press, 2016); Tanja Brøndsted Sejersen, "'I Vow to Thee My Countries': The Expansion of Dual Citizenship in the 21st Century," *International Migration Review* 42, no. 3 (2008): 623–49.
6 Other scholars have examined the ongoing relevance of the oaths of loyalty. See Sanford Levinson, "Constituting Communities Through Words That Bind: Reflections on Loyalty Oaths," *Michigan Law Review* 84, no. 7 (1986): 1440–70; Gerhard Casper, "Forswearing Allegiance" (2008 Maurice and Muriel Fulton Lecture in Legal History, University of Chicago Law School, May 1, 2008). As I explain below, this chapter builds on their work by considering the renunciation and allegiance oaths using the theology of hospitality as a framing device. Additionally, while this chapter focuses on the United States, the questions of loyalty and allegiance are endemic to the modern state (see Daniel Kanstroom, Chapter 1; Ulrich Schmiedel, Chapter 12).

128 *Rose Cuison-Villazor*

that the naturalization law's insistence that noncitizens abjure allegiance to their former countries and declare sole allegiance to the United States is inconsistent with the hospitality tradition. Requiring the oath of loyalty as a condition for acquiring citizenship illustrates the law's distrust of the stranger and perpetuates the exclusionary nature of citizenship and membership.

This chapter begins by discussing the broader history of naturalization as an exclusionary process and then explains the requirements for acquiring citizenship by naturalization today, including the requirement of having to take the oath of allegiance. In the next section, it explores the reasons why the oath of allegiance was included in the naturalization process in the first place. It also examines early revocation cases in which the federal government argued that the oath of allegiance was fraudulently given, highlighting the government's distrust of naturalized citizens. The third section analyzes ways in which U.S. citizens are not required to affirm their allegiance to the United States or renounce any allegiances they might have to other countries, highlighting how U.S. citizens are treated differently from soon-to-be-naturalized citizens. The chapter concludes by raising doubts about the ongoing necessity of the oath of loyalty and contending that a hospitable country not only would treat soon-to-be citizens the same as it treats its existing citizens, but would also welcome them wholeheartedly, even if that meant that the newly minted citizen might have dual allegiances.

II Naturalization

A Story of exclusion

The history of acquiring citizenship in the United States through naturalization can be described as a story of exclusion. The first naturalization statute, which Congress passed in 1790 under the Naturalization Clause,[7] limited the right to naturalize to "free white person[s]" who could establish two years of residency in the United States, possessed good character, and were willing to take an oath to support the Constitution.[8] Since 1790, Congress has amended the naturalization law, although it continued to be racially exclusionary until 1952. In 1795, for example, Congress changed the naturalization law by increasing the required years of residency to five and requiring the noncitizen to show that "he has behaved as a man of good moral character, attached to the principles of the constitution of the United States."[9] The new statute also required the noncitizen to declare before a court, three years before admission to citizenship, an oath of bona fide intent to become a citizen and "renounce forever all allegiance and fidelity" to any foreign sovereign.[10] The mandate of forswearing one's foreign

7 U.S. Const. art. 1, § 8, cl. 4.
8 Act of March 26, 1790, ch. 3, § 1, 1 Stat. 103, 103.
9 Act of January 29, 1795, ch. 20 § 3, 1 Stat. 414.
10 See Ibid., § 1.

True faith, allegiance, and citizenship 129

allegiance would have to be established again at the time of admission to citizenship, when the noncitizen was required to declare an oath to support the Constitution and "absolutely and entirely renounce and abjure all allegiance and fidelity to any foreign prince, potentate, state, or sovereignty whatever."[11]

After the Civil War, Congress amended the statute in 1870 to allow noncitizens of "African nativity and persons of African descent" to be eligible for naturalization, but the law continued to exclude other racial groups from naturalization.[12] The Supreme Court effectively upheld the racial exclusions in naturalization law in *Ozawa v. United States* and *United States v. Thind*, when it held that a Japanese man (Takao Ozawa) and an Indian Sikh man (Bhagat Thind) were not white and thus were racially ineligible for citizenship.[13] Congress did not begin to lift these racial bars to naturalization until the 1940s, when it allowed persons from China, the Philippines, and India to be racially eligible for naturalization.[14] Finally, in 1952, Congress eliminated all racial restrictions to naturalization.[15]

Naturalization laws also excluded persons along gender lines, as illustrated by the 1906 amendment to the 1870 Naturalization Act. Beginning with Section 4 of the 1906 law, the law states that the noncitizen must express "*his* bona fide intention to become a citizen of the United States." That the 1906 law was written with a male noncitizen in mind is further demonstrated by its requirement that if "he is married[,] he shall state the name of his wife and, if possible, the country of her nativity."[16] Indeed, the gendered nature of citizenship laws is further underscored by the 1907 Expatriation Act, which provided that "any American woman who marries a foreigner shall take the nationality of her husband."[17] Upheld by the Supreme Court in *Mackenzie v. Hare*, the 1907 law facilitated the stripping of citizenship from U.S.-born women married to noncitizens.[18] Although the Cable Act of 1922 restored the citizenship of women who had lost their citizenship via the Expatriation Act, as Leti Volpp argued, it did not help American women who had married racially ineligible men, many of whom were Asians.[19]

---

11 See Ibid., § 2.
12 Act of July 14, 1870, ch. 254, § 7, 16 Stat. 254, 256.
13 *Ozawa v. United States*, 260 U.S. 178, 198 (1922); *United States v. Thind*, 261 U.S. 204, 214–15 (1923).
14 Rose Cuison Villazor, "The Other Loving: Uncovering the Federal Government's Racial Regulation of Marriage," *New York University Law Review* 86, no. 5 (2011): 1361–443, 1381 n.113.
15 Immigration and Nationality Act of 1952, Pub. L. No. 82–414, § 311, 66 Stat. 163, 239 (1952) (codified at 8 U.S.C. § 1422).
16 Act of June 29, 1906, Pub. L. No. 59–338, §4, 34 Stat. 596, 596 (1906).
17 Expatriation Act of 1907, Pub. L. No. 59–193, § 3, 34 Stat. 1228, 1228 (1907).
18 *Mackenzie v. Hare*, 239 U.S. 299 (1915); Leti Volpp, "Divesting Citizenship: On Asian American History and the Loss of Citizenship Through Marriage," *UCLA Law Review* 53, no. 2 (2005): 405–84, at 425–31.
19 Cable Act of 1922, Pub. L. No. 67–346, 42 Stat. 1021 (1922); Volpp, "Divesting Citizenship," 432–33.

130   *Rose Cuison-Villazor*

Congress imposed other restrictive requirements for naturalization. It required noncitizens to be able to speak and be literate in English, that they not be anarchists or polygamists, and that they declare an "understanding of and attachment to the fundamental principles of the Constitution."[20] Notably, as the next section discusses, these requirements continue to this day.[21]

B Naturalization requirements today

To be eligible for naturalization in 2020, one must be at least 18 years old, must be a lawful permanent resident (LPR) for at least 5 years, must have lived at least 3 months in the state where applying for naturalization, must demonstrate continuous residency 5 years before filing for citizenship, and must establish physical presence in the United States for at least 30 months out of the 5 years.[22] Additionally, the applicant must demonstrate good moral character and attachment to the "principles of the United States," and must be "well-dispose[d to] . . . the good order and happiness of the United States."[23] Subsequent to submitting a naturalization application and filing fee,[24] the applicant must go through a naturalization interview and show the ability to read, write, and speak basic English, demonstrate an attachment to the principles and ideals of the U.S. Constitution, and pass an examination showing basic understanding of U.S. history and government.[25]

Finally, after successfully passing the interview and examination, the applicant "shall, in order to be and before being admitted to citizenship, take in a public ceremony" an oath of renunciation and allegiance, which contains five requirements: (1) to support the Constitution of the United States; (2) to renounce all allegiance and fidelity to any foreign monarch, state, or sovereignty of "whom or which the applicant was before a subject or a citizen"; (3) to support and defend the Constitution and laws of the United States against "all enemies, foreign and domestic"; (4) to bear "true faith and allegiance to the same"; and (5) to bear arms on behalf of the country when required by the law or to perform noncombatant service in the Armed Forces or perform work of national importance when

---

20 Act of June 29, 1906, Pub. L. No. 59–338, § 8, 34 Stat. 596, 599 [Act of 1906] (speaking requirement); Internal Security At of 1950 tit. 1, Pub. L. No. 81–831, 64 Stat. 987 (literacy requirement); Act of June 29, 1906, § 4, 34 Stat. at 598 (prohibition on anarchists and polygamists); Nationality Act of 1940, Pub. L. No. 76–853, 54 Stat. 1137 (quotation on fundamental principles of the Constitution).

21 See 8 U.S.C. § 1423.

22 8 U.S.C. § 1445(f) (2006) (age requirement); 8 U.S.C. § 1427 (legal permanent residency requirement and domicile requirements). Note that noncitizens who acquired their lawful permanent residency based on marriage to a U.S. citizen are eligible to apply for citizenship in three years. 8 U.S.C. § 1430.

23 8 U.S.C. § 1427.

24 The current filing fee for submitting a naturalization application is $640 plus $85 for a biometrics fee. See U.S. Citizenship and Immigration Services, N-400, Application for Naturalization, www.uscis.gov/n-400.

25 8 U.S.C. § 1423.

required by law.[26] Prior to naturalization, applicants must establish intent, "in good faith, to assume and discharge the obligations of the oath of allegiance," and must show that their attitudes toward the Constitution and laws of the United States render them "capable of fulfilling the obligations" of the oath.[27]

In general, courts have held that there is no right to naturalization unless all the statutory requirements have been met.[28] Exceptions, however, have been made for some individuals. Those who are 50 years old or older and have lived in the United States as LPRs for 20 years or are 55 years old or older and have resided as an LPR for 15 years may be exempted from the English-language test. These individuals must still take the civics test, although they may be able to do so in their native language. Accommodations have also been made for people with physical or developmental disabilities or mental impairments with respect to the English and civics tests and oath of allegiance.[29]

In addition, the Immigration and Nationality Act (INA) allows modifications to the oath for those with religious objections to bearing arms. For example, those who object to bearing arms and/or performing noncombatant service on behalf of the United States because of their "religious training and belief," as shown by "clear and convincing evidence," may take an oath of allegiance without stating their intent to bear arms or to serve as noncombatants.[30] 8 U.S.C. § 1448 defines "religious training and belief" to mean an "individual's belief in relation to a Supreme Being involving duties superior to those arising from any human relation, but does not include essentially political, sociological, or philosophical views or a merely personal moral code."[31] Additionally, for those who prefer not to say the words "on oath" may have those words replaced with "solemnly affirm" and the words "so help me God" may be deleted.[32]

III Allegiance

In 2019, 843,593 individuals took the oath of allegiance as the last legal step to acquire citizenship and became naturalized U.S. citizens.[33] This expression

---

26 8 U.S.C. § 1428.

27 8 C.F.R. § 337.1.

28 *United States v. Ginsberg*, 243 U.S. 472 (1917).

29 8 U.S.C. § 1423 (waivers of English and civics tests); 8 U.S.C. § 1448 (waiver of oath of allegiance for persons with disabilities and mental impairment).

30 8 U.S.C. § 1448(a).

31 Ibid. Those who are seeking an exemption from stating the obligation to bear arms or serve in noncombatant service must still state that they are willing to perform work of national importance under civilian direction. Ibid.

32 8 C.F.R. § 337.1 (oath of allegiance).

33 Department of Homeland Security, *Yearbook of Immigration Statistics* (Washington, DC: Department of Homeland Security, 2020), table 21, www.dhs.gov/immigration-statistics/yearbook/2019/table21 (providing the number of persons naturalized during fiscal year 2019).

132 Rose Cuison-Villazor

of loyalty must be made publicly and may be done administratively or judicially.[34] The INA provides that only after applicants take the loyalty oath do they officially acquire U.S. citizenship.[35] The government thus provides opportunities for public ceremonies that enable thousands of applicants to express loyalty to the United States. Although the COVID-19 pandemic in 2020 initially forced administrative offices and courtrooms to close to the public, the federal government ultimately established socially distant swearing-in ceremonies, including drive-through naturalization ceremonies.[36]

Thus, the oath of allegiance leads to the legal conversion of the noncitizen to U.S. citizen. The loyalty oath, however, not only leads to a legal change of political membership but also signifies what Sanford Levinson referred to as "transformed consciousness."[37] The oath marks the desire of the naturalization applicant to acquire a new identity—the American.

Given the important role that the oath of allegiance plays in the project of understanding what makes a citizen, it is useful to understand the oath's origins. The next section aims to address why the oath of allegiance is necessary to completing the naturalization process.

A Allegiance in the early United States

When Congress passed the first naturalization law, in 1790, it provided that any noncitizen, "being a free white person," who resided in the United States for two years, was a person of "good character," and took an oath to support the Constitution could apply for citizenship.[38] Five years later, Congress amended the statute to require noncitizens to renounce their former allegiance to any sovereign as a prerequisite to becoming a naturalized U.S. citizen.[39] Indeed, Congress seemed to believe this concept of loyalty to be so important that it required noncitizens to affirm their renunciation twice—three years before they sought admission (as

---

34 See U.S. Customs and Immigration Services, Naturalization Ceremonies, www.uscis.gov/citizenship/learn-about-citizenship/naturalization-ceremonies.
35 8 C.F.R. § 337.9(a).
36 See Ethan Nasr and Peggy Gleason, Immigrant Legal Resource Center, *Remote Naturalization Oaths Are Legally Permissible* (San Francisco: Immigrant Legal Resource Center, 2020), www.ilrc.org/sites/default/files/resources/remote_naturalization_oaths_are_legally_per missable.pdf (discussing closure of courthouses for various activities, including oaths of naturalization); U.S. Courts, "Even During Covid, Courts Find Ways to Welcome Americans," *Judiciary News*, July 7, 2020, www.uscourts.gov/news/2020/07/07/even-during-covid-courts-find-ways-welcome-new-americans; U.S. Courts, "A New Road to Citizenship in Detroit," *Judiciary News*, June 18, 2020, www.uscourts.gov/news/2020/06/18/new-road-citizenship-detroit.
37 See Levinson, "Constituting Communities," 1448.
38 See Naturalization Act March 26, 1790, 1 Stat. 103, as amended by Act February 18, 1875, 18 Stat. 318.
39 See Naturalization Act of 1795, 1 Stat. 414.

part of their declaration of intent to become a U.S. citizen) and then again as part of the actual admission for citizenship.

As Gerhard Casper explains, the amendment that added a renunciation requirement to the naturalization act was sponsored by James Madison, who believed that the 1790 Naturalization Act did not guard against "'intrusions and invasions'" of foreigners, including English subjects, who could easily naturalize.[40] As this statement suggests, Madison was concerned about the possibility that naturalized citizens might retain allegiance to another sovereign, such as the English Crown. Indeed, the inclusion of the renunciation of allegiance (and requiring noncitizens to give the oath twice) illustrates the country's general suspicion toward foreigners.

Moreover, the oath of allegiance in the 1795 statute may also have been influenced by British common law regarding land ownership. Under British common law, persons born in England and its possessions acquired birthright citizenship and were thus considered subjects of and owed allegiance to the Crown. Notably, only British subjects were allowed to purchase property.[41] By contrast, "aliens" lacked allegiance and could not own property. To encourage noncitizens to purchase property, Parliament passed naturalization bills for individual noncitizens, which required them to declare their allegiance to the Crown.[42] Naturalization was originally limited to Protestants, but subsequent legislation by Parliament allowed foreign Catholics to disavow Catholicism and declare their allegiance to the Crown and affirm observance of Protestant religious practices.[43] English colonists adopted the same policy—naturalization by private legislation initially— and later, naturalization from the governors of each state.[44]

But the early American settlers, such as the Puritans, also deployed loyalty oaths as measures of willingness to conform to their desired form of local government.[45] During the American Revolution, oaths of loyalty served a crucial role in determining whether an individual was no longer loyal to the English Crown and now devoted to the newly formed United States.[46] As George Washington wrote, an oath of loyalty was necessary to "distinguish friends from foe."[47]

40 See Casper, "Forswearing Allegiance," 2.
41 Jeff E. Pfander and Theresa R. Wardon, "Reclaiming the Immigration Constitution of the Early Republic: Prospectivity, Uniformity and Transparency," *Virginia Law Review* 96, no. 2 (2010): 359–442, at 378 (discussing allegiance under British common law).
42 Ibid., 378–82.
43 Ibid., 382.
44 For further exploration of the relationship between landownership and citizenship, see Polly J. Price, "Alien Land Restrictions in the American Common Law: Exploring the Relative Autonomy Paradigm," *American Journal of Legal History* 43, no. 2 (1999): 152–208, at 157.
45 See Levinson, "Constituting Communities," 1449.
46 Ibid.
47 Ibid., 1450. In this regard, the oath of loyalty partakes in Carl Schmitt's famous friend– enemy distinction (see Schmiedel, Chapter 12).

134 Rose Cuison-Villazor

After the American Revolution, each state had its own system of naturalizing noncitizens, including through state courts. Regardless of how citizenship was acquired (through private legislation, governors, or state courts), the process required noncitizens to renounce former allegiances and declare fealty and allegiance to the state that granted citizenship.[48] Thus, when Congress added an oath of allegiance to the 1795 statute, it was merely codifying a practice already common in many states as part of the common law. Again, the context in which such a requirement was included may have had to do with acquiring citizenship for the purposes of land ownership.[49] That this may have been the case is not surprising given the relationships among loyalty, allegiance, property ownership, and citizenship. No doubt property ownership may have been viewed as a critical mode of establishing connections between homeowners and the land and community, which in turn foster stronger affinity with the state and the nation. Ensuring that landowners are U.S. citizens further embedded these citizens' connections to the nation.[50]

B Allegiance and the revocation cases

As the foregoing discussion highlights, the oath of allegiance had its origins in helping the early republic root out disloyalty to the emerging state and nation. Early cases involving the revocation of naturalized Americans' citizenship[51] further highlight the innate suspicion of noncitizens that the loyalty oath is meant to overcome.[52] Specifically, cases in which the federal government sought to revoke a person's citizenship on the ground that the "oath of allegiance" was false or fraudulently acquired underscore the concept of exclusive allegiance to the United States. Most of these cases took place during the first half of the

---

48 Price, "Alien Land Restrictions," 157.
49 Ibid.
50 Indeed, as I have shown elsewhere, when states exclude landownership from noncitizens, they render noncitizens outsiders and unable to become integrated into the communities where they live. See Rose Cuison Villazor, "Rediscovering *Oyama v. California*: At the Intersection of Property, Race and Citizenship," *Washington University Law Review* 87, no. 5 (2010): 979–1042.
51 In 1906, Congress passed the Immigration and Naturalization Act of 1906, which included a provision that allows the federal government to cancel certificates of citizenship because they were obtained by fraud or were illegally procured. See Act of 1906, at 601.
52 Cases denying naturalization because of the inability to meet the oath of allegiance requirement would be more useful in determining the federal government's understanding of this requirement; however, such cases are not reported. The few reported cases in this area address people with severe mental disabilities who are unable to satisfy this requirement. See Joren Lyons, "Mentally Disabled Citizenship Applicants and the Meaningful Oath Requirement for Naturalization," *California Law Review* 87, no. 4 (1999): 1017–49, at 1020 (discussing how individuals with severe mental disabilities now have the "insurmountable barrier of establishing that one's 'attitude toward the Constitution and laws of the United States renders him or her capable of fulfilling the obligations' of the oath of allegiance").

twentieth century, when naturalized citizens became subject to revocation procedures because evidence suggested that they maintained allegiance to their native countries.[53]

From the outset, the Supreme Court has held that the federal government's power to cancel one's certificate of citizenship on the ground of "fraud" or illegal procurement must meet a high level of proof that such cancellation is warranted.[54] In *Schneiderman v. United States*, the Court recognized that revocation of citizenship is "more serious than a taking of one's property" and explained that "nowhere in the world today is the right of citizenship of greater worth to an individual than it is in this country." Indeed, the Court stated that to many, citizenship "is regarded as the highest hope of civilized men." However, that citizenship retains such an important value in society does not mean that once the government has granted it, it cannot be taken away. The government has the right to revoke naturalized citizenship, but it cannot do so "without the clearest sort of justification or proof." Specifically, the government must establish with clear and convincing evidence that citizenship was "not done in accordance with strict legal requirements."[55]

One of the first cases revoking citizenship on the basis of fraudulent allegiances was *Baumgartner v. United States*.[56] In this case, Baumgartner, an immigrant from Germany, became a naturalized citizen after giving an oath of allegiance to the United States and renouncing his former allegiance to the German Reich. He also swore, as required by the naturalization process, to support and defend the U.S. Constitution. Ten years later, the federal government brought an action to cancel his certificate of citizenship on the grounds that he "did not truly and fully renounce his allegiance to Germany and that he did not in fact intend to support the Constitution."[57] The government submitted evidence of Baumgartner espousing pro-Hitler, pro-Germany, and anti-Semitic statements after he became a citizen.[58] These statements, according to the government, demonstrated that

---

53 For a recent, comprehensive examination of denaturalization actions, see Cassandra Burke Robertson and Irina D. Manta, "(Un)Civil Denaturalization," *New York University Law Review* 94, no. 3 (2019): 402–71. As Professors Robertson and Manta explain, denaturalization was fairly common during the first half of the twentieth century, "with over 22,000 Americans losing their citizenship between 1907 and 1967." Ibid., 422.

54 See *Schneiderman v. United States*, 320 U.S. 118, 122 (1943). The case involved the federal government's efforts to denaturalize a citizen who had been an admitted member of the Communist Party 12 years after he became a U.S. citizen. See Ibid., 120. Although this case ultimately did not center on citizenship on the grounds of fraud but rather illegal procurement, it established the high standard of clear and convincing evidence that the federal government must meet in order to revoke an individual's naturalization certificate. See Ibid., 122.

55 Ibid., 122–23.

56 322 U.S. 665, 672–73 (1944).

57 Ibid., 666.

58 Ibid., 671–72.

136   Rose Cuison-Villazor

he "withheld complete renunciation of his allegiance to Germany," and that he therefore had obtained his citizenship fraudulently.[59]

In rejecting the government's position that Baumgartner was guilty of fraud, the Court emphasized the "importance of 'clear, unequivocal, and convincing proof'" in cases revoking citizenship, and held that the evidence presented failed to meet such an exacting standard.[60] The Court's description of allegiance provides an important starting point for determining the meaning of the concept. Recognizing that Congress in 1795 required the renunciation of foreign allegiance and the swearing of allegiance to the United States as conditions for citizenship, the Court explained,

> Allegiance to this Government and its laws, is a compendious phrase to describe those political and legal institutions that are enduring features of American political society. We are here dealing with a test expressing a broad conception—a breadth appropriate to the nature of the subject matter, being nothing less than the bonds that tie Americans together in devotion to a common fealty.[61]

Here, the Supreme Court emphasizes that allegiance to the United States is a common thread that binds all Americans together: devotion to the country makes one an American citizen.

Such fealty to the United States may be demonstrated best by fighting on behalf of the United States, particularly against one's former country. The court in *United States v. Geisler* makes this point in affirming the revocation of naturalization of a former German citizen.[62] In *Geisler*, the government presented a written affidavit in which the defendant expressed pro-German sentiments. Importantly, in a hearing in which the contents of the affidavit were discussed, the judge asked the defendant whether he had made statements, under oath, that he would rather renounce his citizenship than take up arms against Germany, and the defendant answered that he in fact did not want to fight against Germany.[63] In reviewing the record and ultimately affirming the lower court, the Seventh Circuit held that there was sufficient evidence to support the lower court's findings that the defendant acted fraudulently when he obtained his citizenship.[64] Notably, the court stated,

> [W]hen the defendant took the oath of allegiance to this country in 1940 and renounced his allegiance to the German Reich, he did not do it in good

---

59 Ibid., 666–67.
60 Ibid., 671 (quoting *Schneiderman v. United States*, 320 U.S. 118, 125 [1943]).
61 Ibid., 673.
62 174 F.2d 992, 999 (7th Cir. 1949) (holding that the evidence was sufficient to affirm the lower court's findings that when the defendant "took the oath of allegiance to this country in 1940 and renounced his allegiance to the German Reich, he did not do it in good faith but did it fraudulently").
63 Ibid., 995.
64 Ibid., 999.

True faith, allegiance, and citizenship 137

faith but did it fraudulently. His American citizenship was a thing to be put on or taken off as the fortunes of war might indicate. This record does not reveal the image of a man who was devoted to this country and its institutions when he took the oath of allegiance in 1940, but rather of one whose devotion had always been to Hitler and the Nazi principles.[65]

As this quote evidences, allegiance to the United States means both denying principles that oppose the country's ideals and being willing to take up arms in support of the United States.

Two other cases further demonstrate the Supreme Court's narrative of what makes a noncitizen into a citizen. In *Girouard v. United States*, a Seventh-day Adventist from Canada was willing to take the oath and willing to serve in the army but was not willing to take up arms in defense of the United States.[66] The district court approved his application for citizenship, only to be reversed by the U.S. Court of Appeals for the First Circuit. The Supreme Court, in turn, reversed the appellate decision, holding that "the oath required of aliens does not in terms require that they promise to bear arms." Indeed, the Court noted that "the bearing of arms, important as it is, is not the only way in which our institutions may be supported and defended, even in times of great peril." Notably, the Court explained that the "refusal to bear arms is not necessarily a sign of disloyalty or a lack of attachment to our institutions."[67]

In *Knauer v. United States*, a native of Germany took the oath of citizenship in 1937 but was accused of securing citizenship by fraud because he had not been and was not attached to the principles of the Constitution.[68] Here, the Supreme Court explained that falsely taking the oath of allegiance constitutes fraud, which "connotes perjury, falsification, concealment, [and] misrepresentation."[69] The Court recognized that "citizenship obtained through naturalization is not a second class citizenship."[70] Reviewing the record, the Court held that evidence showed that the noncitizen swore falsely because he still held allegiance to the German Reich.[71] As the Court explained, "[w]hen an alien takes the oath with reservations or does not in good faith forswear loyalty and allegiance to the old country, the decree of naturalization is obtained by deceit."[72]

In sum, the revocation cases emphasize that exclusive allegiance to the United States is a necessary prerequisite of one's eligibility for naturalized U.S. citizenship. This view may be reasonable. As immigration legal scholar Gerald Neuman notes, it might be considered "unproblematic, given that the United States

---

65 Ibid., 999–1000 (stating further that "his early repudiation of his oath of allegiance indicates to us that he at no time acted in good faith").
66 328 U.S. 61 (1946).
67 Ibid., 62, 64.
68 328 U.S. 654, 656 (1946).
69 Ibid., 657.
70 Ibid., 658.
71 Ibid., 660.
72 Ibid., 671.

would 'naturally' desire the undivided loyalty of a new citizen."[73] Citizenship confers rights and duties, and loyalty to one's fellow citizens and the institutions with and through whom such rights and duties are exercised is important for the functioning of the political community. To assume, however, that exclusive allegiance is a condition of such loyalty or that such loyalty is innately suspect among naturalized citizens is not, necessarily, a reasonable extension of those claims. As the next section discusses, it may well be time to revisit the policy of renunciation of one's fealty to a foreign sovereign and being required to take the oath of allegiance.

IV Toward citizenship as hospitality

The mandate of naturalization law that noncitizens must renounce their former allegiance and give sole allegiance to the United States is rooted in the exclusive nature of citizenship that is suspicious of the noncitizen. Such a requirement also illustrates a double-standard, because citizens are not required to give their sole allegiance to the United States. Accordingly, the law of citizenship should adapt and reflect the virtues of hospitality. Reimagining citizenship as hospitality would illustrate a more welcoming naturalization process in which soon-to-be citizens may be accepted as full members of the polity, even though they may continue to have allegiances elsewhere.

A U.S. citizens and dual allegiances

This chapter has largely focused on the acquisition of citizenship through naturalization. The other—most common—way of acquiring citizenship is by birth. Specifically, one can become a U.S. citizen by being born in the United States, as per the Fourteenth Amendment's Citizenship Clause (*jus solis*) or in a U.S. territory by federal statute,[74] or by being born abroad to at least one U.S. citizen parent (*jus sanguinis*).[75] Importantly for purposes of the arguments presented in this chapter, these nonnaturalized U.S. citizens are not required to declare their sole allegiance to the United States. Their loyalty to the country is presumed by virtue of their acquired-at-birth citizenship.

That allegiance is recognized in birthright citizenship is grounded in English common law, which provides the historical underpinnings of the Citizenship Clause. As one court that grappled recently with the meaning of the Citizenship Clause explained, "the fundamental principle of the common law with regard to English nationality was birth within the allegiance" as recognized in the "leading

---

73 Gerald L. Neuman, "Justifying U.S. Naturalization Policies," *Virginia Journal of International Law* 35, no. 1 (1994): 237–78, at 268 (examining renunciation of former allegiance as a qualification for naturalization).

74 U.S. Const., XIV amend.; 8 U.S.C. §1401(a).

75 8 U.S.C. §1401(b)–(g).

True faith, allegiance, and citizenship 139

case known as *Calvin's Case*, decided in 1608."[76] *Calvin's Case* held that persons born in Scotland after the country united with England were not "aliens," but rather English subjects with rights, including the right to land ownership.[77] Notably, the chief justice of the Court of Common Pleas, Lord Edward Coke, who is said to have issued the most "definitive statement of the law," recognized that allegiance is an "incident inseparable to every subject: for as soon as he is born, he oweth by birthright ligeance and obedience to his sovereign."[78] English settlers adopted this rule during the Colonial period in North America.[79]

After the American Revolution and the adoption of the U.S. Constitution, the understanding became implicit, though not explicitly defined in the Constitution, that birth within the United States led to U.S. citizenship.[80] The now infamous decision of the Supreme Court in *Dred Scott v. Sanford*,[81] which created a racial exception to the common-law rule that birth on U.S. soil leads to U.S. citizenship, was overturned by the Fourteenth Amendment's Citizenship Clause. As the Supreme Court held in *Wong Kim Ark v. United States*, under the Fourteenth Amendment, one acquires citizenship if born within and subject to the jurisdiction of the United States.[82] Crucially, the Court noted that allegiance was recognized at birth and recognized Wong's birthright citizenship, commenting that the petitioner, Wong Kim Ark, had not renounced his allegiance to the United States, and that his parents were not foreign diplomats.[83] In brief, based on English common law and the interpretation of the Fourteenth Amendment's Citizenship Clause, citizens do not need to convey allegiance to the United States if they acquired citizenship by being born in the United States.

Moreover, allegiance to the country is also presumed in the case of individuals who acquire citizenship by statute, either because they were born in a U.S. territory or because they were born in a foreign country and at least one of their parents was a U.S. citizen who met the statutory requirements for passing down citizenship. Similar to persons who acquire citizenship through birth in the United States, these statutory citizens are presumed to be loyal to the country from birth.

In other words, birthright citizens need not do anything to demonstrate their sole loyalty to the United States. The expectation of birthright allegiance

---

76 *Fitisemanu v. United States*, 426 F. Supp. 3d 1555, 1160–61 (D. Utah 2019) (discussing *Calvin's Case*). For additional examination of the connection between allegiance and birth, see Polly J. Price, "Natural Law and Birthright Citizenship in *Calvin's Case* (1608)," *Yale Journal of Law & the Humanities* 9, no. 1 (1997): 73–146.

77 *Fitisemanu*, 426 F. Supp. 3d. at 1160 (quoting Price, "Natural Law and Birthright Citizenship," 81).

78 Ibid., 1161 (quoting Lord Coke's opinion in *Calvin's Case*).

79 Ibid.

80 Ibid., 1163.

81 60 U.S. 393 (1857).

82 169 U.S. 649, 653 (1898). On the relationship of territory, sovereignty, and jurisdiction, see Silas W. Allard's chapter in this volume (Chapter 5).

83 *Wong Kim Ark*, 169 U.S. at 654.

140   Rose Cuison-Villazor

articulated in *Calvin's Case* has become a presumption of allegiance in subsequent U.S. citizenship law building on that common-law principle. That presumption would prevail even if a person born on U.S. soil was later raised in a foreign country. That would also be the case for individuals who acquire citizenship by statute and might never step foot in the United States. For these citizens, who acquire citizenship through *jus soli* or *jus sanguinis*, their loyalty to the country is not doubted or questioned. They are not required to take an oath of allegiance to demonstrate their sole fealty to the United States.

Importantly, not only are U.S. citizens not required to take an oath of allegiance, but they may also express loyalty to another country, renounce their allegiance to the United States, and *still* maintain their U.S. citizenship. In *Vance v. Terrazas*, the Supreme Court addressed whether an individual born in the United States (and thus a U.S. citizen) lost his citizenship when he was in Mexico and applied for a Mexican nationality certificate.[84] In his application, Laurence Terrazas, who was also a Mexican citizen at birth, not only expressly renounced his U.S. citizenship but also explicitly renounced his allegiance to the United States. The U.S. Department of State subsequently issued a certificate of loss of nationality, which Terrazas challenged.[85] According to the State Department, Terrazas's voluntary "declaration of his allegiance to Mexico" and repudiation of any loyalty to the United States manifested his intent to abandon his U.S. citizenship.[86] The Supreme Court disagreed and held that expatriation—loss of citizenship— must be supported by evidence showing not only the expatriating act (such as renouncing allegiance) but also the *intent* to terminate one's U.S. citizenship.[87] Evidently, a birthright citizen can verbalize lack of allegiance to the United States but retain U.S. citizenship if not intending to abandon it.

Critical to the Supreme Court's opinion in *Terrazaz* was its prior decision in *Afroyim v. Rusk*, in which the Court held that a naturalized citizen who voted in a foreign country could not be stripped of his U.S. citizenship without his consent.[88] Afroyim, a naturalized U.S. citizen, had moved back to his prior country of nationality, Israel, and had lived there for ten years when he participated in the election there. In this case, a citizen was able to retain citizenship despite being politically engaged in a foreign country where he also had citizenship. Importantly, as Peter Spiro contended, dual nationality became tolerated.[89] Indeed, today millions of U.S. citizens have dual citizenship or claims to dual nationality.[90]

Against this backdrop of case law allowing U.S. citizens to have dual nationality and dual allegiances, the requirement of naturalization law that noncitizens

---

84 444 U.S. 252, 255 (1980).
85 Ibid., 255–56.
86 Ibid., 263.
87 Ibid.
88 387 U.S. 253, 257 (1967).
89 Spiro, *At Home in Two Countries*, esp. chap. 5.
90 See Renshon, *The 50% American*, 9–20; Spiro, *At Home in Two Countries*, 3.

True faith, allegiance, and citizenship 141

must first renounce their prior nationalities and declare their sole allegiance to the United States before attaining citizenship does not seem reasonable or rational. At any point after naturalization, the new citizen may choose to become a citizen elsewhere or keep her prior citizenship. No current law enforces the soon-to-be citizen's promise to carry out the obligations of the oath of allegiance.[91] Coupled with the fact that birthright citizens do not have to provide an oath of allegiance, the requirement for noncitizens to take the loyalty oath seems unnecessary and merely reflective of an exclusionary citizenship system that treats the stranger with a suspicious gaze. It may well be time to stop requiring the oath of loyalty as part of the naturalization process and move citizenship toward the tradition of Christian hospitality.

B *Citizenship as hospitality*

Other scholars in this book have reflected on the meaning of hospitality toward noncitizens. Raj Nadella relies on the New Testament in emphasizing the need to care for and welcome strangers (Chapter 9). Luis N. Rivera-Pagán argues for a theology of migration grounded in xenophilia or love of the stranger (Chapter 10). Donald M. Kerwin and Safwat Marzouk reimagine immigration integration within the tradition of hospitality (Chapter 15).

Here, I build on their work by calling for citizenship as hospitality. Advancing this more welcoming policy of naturalization, I maintain, begins with removing the oaths of loyalty. Abandoning this requirement would be consistent with the current practice of not following through on the obligations of the oath of allegiance.[92] Crucially, it would signal a more inclusive and welcoming policy toward noncitizens and treating them the same way that native-born citizens and other citizens are treated and allowed to have dual allegiances. To be sure and to be clear, current naturalization requirements should still emphasize the importance of being attached to the principles of the Constitution and being "favorably disposed toward the good order and happiness of the United States" and "active support of the Constitution."[93] But removing the renunciation and allegiance oaths would go a long way toward making our country more hospitable to our soon-to-be citizens.

Raj Nadella writes in his chapter in this volume (Chapter 9) that

> [t]he motif of Jesus and God as the stranger offered Christological and theological bases for hospitality to strangers in early Christian communities and allowed them to move from ambivalence about the other to radical welcome of the other. The same motif can undergird Christian hospitality to strangers in our context.

91 See 8 C.F.R. 337.1(c) (obligations of oath).
92 Ibid.
93 8 C.F.R. § 316.11.

142   *Rose Cuison-Villazor*

Removing the renunciation and allegiance oaths would follow in that tradition of hospitality and move the naturalization law from suspicious ambivalence about naturalized citizens to a radical welcome of naturalized citizens in their otherness. Such revolutionary welcome of the naturalized citizen is part and parcel of a broader stance of xenophilia toward migrants (Rivera-Pagán, Chapter 10) or a "subversive hospitality" that imagines citizens and migrants not as fellow and stranger, but as near and distant kin bound together already in relationships of responsibility (Kristin E. Heyer, Chapter 13; see also Bill Ong Hing and Raj Nadella, Chapter 17).[94] The law of naturalization should take such inspiration from the tradition of Christian hospitality.

V Conclusion

In a project that explores the consciousness of citizenship, the oath of loyalty serves as a lens through which to better view the ways in which law defines what makes a stranger a citizen. The oath of allegiance suggests that for noncitizens *to become* American means to have undivided faith and loyalty to the United States. Yet, as this chapter has shown, the exclusionary nature of citizenship has given it an elusive status. That is, requirements for citizenship have long deemed many people suspect, if not unworthy—people of color, women, people with disabilities, immigrants who are poor or illiterate, and people who might not demonstrate the normative view of attachment to the Constitution. There is no longer strong justification for requiring soon-to-be-naturalized citizens to forswear former allegiances while allowing birthright citizens to be able to have dual allegiances. Indeed, if we are to treat naturalized citizens as truly equal and accord them the "same dignity"[95] and respect as other U.S. citizens, then moving toward a more hospitable naturalization process by removing the loyalty oaths would constitute an important step toward that goal.

Suggested Reading

Allard, Silas W. "In the Shades of the Oak of Mamre: Hospitality as a Framework for Political Engagement Between Christians and Muslims." *Political Theology* 13, no. 4 (2012): 414–24.
Casper, Gerhard. "Forswearing Allegiance." 2008 Maurice and Muriel Fulton Lecture in Legal History, University of Chicago Law School, Chicago, IL, May 1, 2008. https://dx.doi.org/10.2139/ssrn.1311584.

---

94 On subversive hospitality, see Kristin E. Heyer, *Kinship Across Borders: A Christian Ethic of Immigration* (Washington, DC: Georgetown University Press, 2012), 145. On justice as responsibility to relationships, see Tisha M. Rajendra, *Migrants and Citizens: Justice and Responsibility in the Ethics of Immigration* (Grand Rapids, MI: Eerdmans, 2017), esp. chap. 6.
95 *Schneider v. Rusk*, 377 U.S. 163, 165 (1964).

Cuison Villazor, Rose. "The Other Loving: Uncovering the Federal Government's Racial Regulation of Marriage." *New York University Law Review* 86, no. 5 (2011): 1361–443.

Levinson, Sanford. "Constituting Communities Through Words That Bind: Reflections on Loyalty Oaths" *Michigan Law Review* 84, no. 7 (1986): 1440–70.

Ngai, Mae. *Impossible Subjects: Illegal Aliens and the Making of Modern America.* Princeton: Princeton University Press, 2014.

Price, Polly J. "Natural Law and Birthright Citizenship in *Calvin's Case* (1608)." *Yale Journal of Law & the Humanities* 9, no. (1997): 73–146.

Volpp, Leti. "Divesting Citizenship: On Asian American History and the Loss of Citizenship Through Marriage." *UCLA Law Review* 53, no. 2 (2005) 405–84.

Part 2
Theology and migration

8 Different kinds of foreignness
The Hebrew Bible's terminology for foreigners

Safwat Marzouk

I Introduction

The Hebrew Bible reflects a complex worldview of how the ancient Israelites negotiated their relationships with the migrants, sojourners, and strangers in their midst. The complex process of discerning different kinds of foreignness is reflected in the use of various Hebrew words to refer to various groups of foreigners. The terms *ger*, *toshav*, *nokhri*, and *zar* are used in different genres and textual traditions throughout the Hebrew Bible to address the legal rights, the economic status, and the inclusion or exclusion of alien residents in religious spaces and practices.

This chapter analyzes how these different terms were employed in the various traditions of the Hebrew Bible to address the phenomenon of migration in ancient Israel. While the discussion of these terms is informed by the historical methods of studying biblical texts (including source and redaction criticisms), this chapter is essentially arranged thematically and organized according to the canonical use of these terms.[1] Furthermore, although the study in this chapter mostly centers on how these terms were used in the Pentateuchal traditions, it occasionally engages other parts of the canon when it seems fruitful for the issue at hand.

This study of the terms explicates the complexity and diversity of what the Hebrew Bible says about migration and migrants. Human relationships are complex, and the way the Israelites negotiated their relationships with the migrants in their midst is no exception. These negotiations varied based on the historical period, power relations, and space of contact (social, legal, religious) between the Israelites and the foreigners. Therefore, the Israelites needed to use different terminology to describe different kinds of foreignness. Furthermore, the complexity

---

1 For a study of the meaning and significance of these terms that reflects a particular historical development of biblical traditions, see Reinhard Achenbach, "*gēr—nåkhrî—tôshav—zår:* Legal and Sacral Distinctions Regarding Foreigners in the Pentateuch," in *The Foreigner and the Law: Perspectives from the Hebrew Bible and the Ancient Near East*, eds. Reinhard Achenbach, Rainer Albertz, and Jakob Wöhrle, BZAR 16 (Wiesbaden: Harrassowitz Verlag, 2011), 29–51.

148 *Safwat Marzouk*

of what the Hebrew Bible says about migration emerges from the fact that these terms were employed by different theological and legal communities in ancient Israel over a long period of time. It should not be a surprise, then, that biblical traditions sometimes differ among themselves on some aspects of the legal and economic rights of foreigners or the inclusion/exclusion of migrants in social and religious circles.

In addition to the historical complexity of the biblical texts, the contemporary reader of the Bible has these texts, which have come from different historical contexts and theological traditions, side by side in one sacred book, and is expected to make an ethical decision based on them toward the phenomenon of migration. Given the diversity of the biblical perspectives on the foreigner, and given the urgency of the phenomenon of migration in our world, this chapter concludes with some reflections on how to hermeneutically discern the disparate biblical traditions and to respond ethically to the migrant, the refugee, and the asylum seeker in ways that address the fear of the other and build trust between people who are different from one another. Before dealing with the hermeneutical question, the chapter proceeds with studying the different terminologies that the Hebrew Bible uses to designate different kinds of foreignness.

II *Zar*

The Hebrew word *zar*, usually translated "foreigner" or "stranger," denotes someone perceived as an outsider from a clearly defined group. The group may be defined by familial ties, by rituals of consecration, or by geography. In Deuteronomy 25:5, only a brother is allowed to establish progeny for his deceased brother; a stranger in this case refers to an Israelite or non-Israelite who does not belong to the family.[2] In other instances, *zar* refers to anyone who does not belong to the priestly line of Aaron. In these cases, the "stranger" could be an Israelite or a non-Israelite; what matters is that the stranger here is someone who does not belong to the group of people whom the God of Israel has chosen and consecrated to this very particular office (Exodus 29:33; 30:33).[3] The term is used by the Assyrian commander while speaking of his military accomplishments and bragging that he drank "foreign" waters (in a reference to subduing Egypt and its Nile, 2 Kings 19:24; Isaiah 37:25).

---

2 In 1 Kings 3:18, the two women explaining to Solomon how one of the infants died use the word *zar* to refer to someone who does not live in the house.

3 In many of these instances, the NRSV translates the word *zar* as "layperson." In some attestations, the word *zar* is used to delineate boundaries between the Levites and the rest of the Israelites (Numbers 1:51), and in other instances it sets boundaries among the Levites themselves in order to set the descendants of Aaron at the center (Numbers 3:10; 16:40). Reinhard Achenbach suggests that the term *zar* in these religious contexts connotes that "The expression does not only mean just lay persons but also people from other levitical clans. The visible expression of this principle was expressed in Hellenistic times in terms of a barrier around the Temple Mount to exclude entry to gentiles." Achenbach, "*gēr—nâkhrî—tôshav—zâr*," 46.

Different kinds of foreignness 149

The foreigner (*zar*) is essentially viewed in a negative light throughout the Hebrew Bible. On the national level, the foreigner is seen as an enemy who seeks to devour, to destroy, and to make the land desolate (Isaiah 1:7; Ezekiel 7:21 and 11:9; Lamentations 5:2). Serving foreign gods (Isaiah 17:10 and 43:12; Jeremiah 2:25 and 3:13) will end up making the people serve foreigners (*zar*) in lands far away (Jeremiah 5:19).[4] This pronouncement of judgment is reversed in prophecies of restoration, which proclaim that "strangers [*zar*] shall no more make a servant of him" (Jeremiah 30:8). The foreigner (*zar*) will serve the Israelites by tending their flocks (Isaiah 61:5). Strangers (*zar*) will not pass through Jerusalem (Joel 4:17 [Hebrew], 3:17 [English]). Thus, according to these prophetic texts, the foreigner represents a national and a religious threat. On an interpersonal level, the feminine form of the word (*zarah*) is used to speak of a foreign woman who should be avoided (Proverbs 2:16). The foreign woman in Proverbs 1–9 "depicts and symbolises 'foreignness' through the identification of זרה [*zrh*] and נכריה [*nkhryh*], and is essentially the way of apostasy."[5] Proverbial wisdom urges its audience to avoid economic and commercial relationships with the foreigner (Proverbs 11:15; 20:16; 27:13).[6] The stranger, in these texts, is portrayed as unreliable and possibly deceitful; therefore, it would be wise to avoid lending or guaranteeing a loan when a foreigner is part of the deal.

III *Nokhri*

In the Deuteronomic law code, the term *nokhri* refers to a group of foreigners who are to be treated differently from the rest of the Israelites. The *nokhri* can be "pressed" to pay any debt they owe to an Israelite. But the *akh*—or "brother," "kin"—is to be released from any debt they owe (Deuteronomy 15:3). The economic distinction between the kin and the foreigner continues with regard to taking interest on loans. The Israelites were prohibited from adding interest on any loans to a fellow Israelite, but they were permitted to take interest on any loans to foreigners. The *nokhri* can receive a loan with interest, while the *zar* would not receive a loan from Israelites (Proverbs 11:15).

---

4 This representation of a foreigner who controls native land is significant, because it addresses a lacuna in migration studies, namely, how do we respond to conquest as a form of "people movement."

5 Nancy Nam Hoon Tan, *The "Foreignness" of the Foreign Woman in Proverbs 1–9: A Study of the Origin and Development of a Biblical Motif*, BZAW 381 (Berlin: De Gruyter, 2008), 104. Nam Hoon Tan argues that "the use of רכנ [*nkr*] is essentially tied up with ideas of 'foreignness,' and רז [*zr*] is a flexible term used to denote the sense of 'otherness,' which is totally dependent on the context for its specific referent. When both terms are used in conjunction, they essentially refer to the 'foreigner' because רכנ [*nkr*] provides the determinant for the context. We also conclude that the OT's idea of 'foreignness' is not bound by geographical proximity or notions of modern definitions of 'nationhood,' but it is essentially tied up with ideas of 'ethnicity.'" Tan, *The "Foreignness" of the Foreign Woman*, 42.

6 N. H. Snaith, *The Meaning of* רז *[zr] in the OT: An Exegetical Study*, OTS 10 (Leiden: Brill, 1953).

150 *Safwat Marzouk*

Similar to the term *zar*, the word *nokhri* has negative connotations. The term is used to describe "foreign" gods (Deuteronomy 31:16; Joshua 24:20, 23), and, according to some biblical traditions, foreigners who worship foreign gods pose a threat to Israel's fidelity to YHWH. Solomon's fall from being a model good king, according to the Deuteronomistic historian, to being an example of infidelity towards YHWH happened in part because he married foreign women (1 Kings 11:1, 8). Solomon's marriage to foreign women (*nokhriah*) was the prime example that Nehemiah used to convince the returnees from exile to divorce their foreign wives (Nehemiah 13:26). Ezra and Nehemiah's program for reforming the Judean community after the exile rested in part on sending away or divorcing the foreign women, who were seen by this ideology as a threat to the "holy seed" of Israel. Marrying foreign wives is described as an act of "unfaithfulness" toward YHWH that has resulted in "increasing the guilt of Israel," and in kindling the divine wrath against the nation (Ezra 10:2, 10, 11, 14).

This negative view toward the foreigner (*nokhri*) is not the only voice found in the Hebrew Bible, however. In his prayer while dedicating the temple, Solomon created a space for foreigners (*nokhri*) who were welcomed as pilgrims in Jerusalem. The Israelite king asked God to heed the prayers of any foreigner, any person who does not belong to the people of Israel who comes to pray in the temple in Jerusalem, because they have heard of God's great name (1 Kings 8:41–43). These foreigners are not forced to go to Jerusalem; rather, they choose to go.

Furthermore, the book of Ruth tells a story of welcoming and integrating a foreign woman, a Moabite, into the Judean community. Interestingly, Ruth uses the same root (*nkhr*) of the Hebrew word (*nokhri*) when she describes how Boaz treats her. After Ruth has moved to Bethlehem with her mother-in-law, and after she has gone to the field, Boaz notices her and allows her to draw from the water of his servants and to eat with them. In their brief exchange in the field, Ruth says to Boaz: "Why have I found favor in your sight, that you should take notice [*nkhr*] of me, when I am a foreigner? [*nkhr*]." The story of Ruth harks back to Ezra and Nehemiah's program of exclusion and asserts another kind of politics, which seeks to include the foreigner and the outsider. Her story shows the positive role the insiders (Naomi and Boaz) can play in integrating foreigners into their destination of migration.[7] Simultaneously, the story shows the resilience, power, and generosity of a migrant like Ruth, who eventually becomes the great-grandmother of King David. Ruth is not just a recipient of hospitality; she has also shown faithfulness to her mother-in-law in Moab and in Judah (Ruth 1:8; 3:10). Although the inclusion of Ruth, the Moabite, happens because she accepts the Israelite God as her God and the people of Judah as her people, it is still a step toward inclusion and acceptance of the other when compared to Ezra's program

---

7 For further discussions of integration in this volume, see Donald M. Kerwin (Chapter 6) and Kerwin and Safwat Marzouk (Chapter 15).

Different kinds of foreignness 151

or Deuteronomy's prohibition of welcoming the Moabites among the people of Israel (Deuteronomy 23:3–4).[8]

In a similar vein, the prophetic tradition of Isaiah, in the postexilic period, presented a countertestimony to that of Ezra and Nehemiah. Isaiah 56 reflects a tension among the community of returnees with regard to the inclusion of the non-Israelites or foreigners. The text captures this tension by ascribing this statement to the foreigners: "Do not let the foreigner joined to the LORD say, 'The LORD will surely separate me from his people'" (Isaiah 56:3). These foreigners (*nokhri*) chose to join (*lwy*) the LORD to serve (*shrt*), but their desire to join and to belong to the people of the covenant was likely disputed by the Zadokite priesthood. Therefore, the prophet asserts their integration and inclusion among the people who belong to the Holy Mountain as long as they keep the covenant, which basically refers to sanctifying the Sabbath (Isaiah 56:6–7). This text shows that the *nokhri* can join the people of God and be integrated into the covenant community regardless of ethnic background or familial ties. It is noteworthy, though, that the religious identity is not forced on the *nokhri*; they choose to join the people of YHWH.[9] At the same time, the boundary that surrounds the people of YHWH is not lost. Rather, it is redefined. It is based not on ethnicity but on religious practices. Inclusion does not mean a loss of boundaries. It means negotiating new boundaries to include more people. Boundaries are porous (compare Silas W. Allard, Chapter 5), and inclusion reflects God's commitment to replace hatred and fear with love and generosity.[10]

---

8 On the comparison between the "ecology of fear" and the "ecology of faith" manifested in the Ezra-Nehemiah reform and the book of Ruth, see the discussion in Susanna Snyder, *Asylum-Seeking, Migration, and Church* (London: Routledge, 2012), 139–96.

9 Inclusion in the Priestly Covenant happened through circumcision (Genesis 17). Ishmael was circumcised (Genesis 17:23, 25, 26). The text goes on to assert that foreigners are to be included in the covenant by way of circumcision: "Throughout your generations every male among you shall be circumcised when he is eight days old, including the slave born in your house and the one bought with your money from any foreigner who is not of your offspring" (Genesis 17:12). At the end of the Priestly Covenant, the text notes, "and all the men of his house, slaves born in the house and those bought with money from a foreigner, were circumcised with him" (Genesis 17:27).

10 In his study of the "Gentile Yhwh-Worshippers," Volker Haarmann discusses various texts (for example, Leviticus 22:25; Isaiah 58:1–8; Ezekiel 44:4–6; 2 Kings 5; Jonah 1) that address the inclusion or the exclusion of outsiders into the worshipping community of YHWH. He writes concerning allowing the gentiles into the temple: "Due to their profaneness (or due to their impurity) gentile access to the Temple obviously was highly controversial in post-exilic times. Both Isaiah 56 and Ezekiel 44, despite their fundamental differences, mirror the controversy that ultimately has led to the general exclusion of gentiles from the temple. However, I have suggested that the exclusion of gentiles from the Temple must not be misunderstood as a general exclusion of gentiles from Yhwh worship in post-exilic texts. In fact, 2 Kings 5 and Jonah 1 speak of gentiles who bound themselves to Yhwh and who offer their sacrifices on 'altars of the Gentiles' (Bickerman) from abroad. . . . The biblical texts analyzed (which presumably are all of post-exilic origin) maintain the differentiation between Israel and gentiles. Neither does Israel vanish into an undifferentiated humanity nor do the

152 Safwat Marzouk

IV Toshav and Ger

Three questions relate to the terms *toshav* and *ger*: (1) Do these terms refer to the same group of migrants or sojourners within Israel, or do they refer to somewhat related yet distinct groups whose legal and religious standings vary? (2) Does *ger* refer to the same group of people with a unified set of legal rights and economic status across the biblical law codes? (3) Does *ger* refer to sojourners and resident aliens who are foreigners, or could it also refer to vulnerable people from within Israel itself?

The terms *toshav* (sojourner, bond servant, tenant, transient) and *ger* (sojourner, alien, resident alien) speak of interrelated yet, in some ways, distinguishable groups of migrants or resident aliens within ancient Israel. Both terms are used by Abraham in his conversation with the Hittites, when he seeks to buy a field to bury his deceased wife, Sarah: "I am a stranger (*ger*) and an alien residing (*toshav*) among you" (Genesis 23:4). The same pair of words is used by the God of Israel in the instructions concerning the Jubilee year: "The land shall not be sold in perpetuity, for the land is mine; with me you are but aliens (*ger*) and tenants (*toshav*)" (Leviticus 25:23). These references do not distinguish between *ger* and *toshav*. Instead, the words are used in apposition and function as a reminder to the Israelite community that their ancestors were strangers in the land of Canaan, and that even when the Israelites possess the land of Canaan, they need to remember that the land essentially belongs to YHWH, and that they are only aliens and tenants. Such a memory binds the people to the land, because they are in a covenant with YHWH, but at the same time it sets the people on the path of empathy and hospitality toward the sojourners or resident aliens in their land.

The terms *toshav* and *ger* refer to related groups of migrants or sojourners since they are used in association in many biblical traditions (Genesis 23:4; Leviticus 25:4, 6, 23, 35, 45, 47; Numbers 35:15; Psalm 39:13; 1 Chronicles 19:15). There are, nevertheless, key differences between the individuals described as *ger* and those described as *toshav*, especially in relation to some religious practices and economic rights. The differences between the *toshav* and the *ger* emerge from the fact that the status of the *ger* changes. While the traditions preserved in Exodus and Deuteronomy use the term *ger* to refer to a dependent sojourner—that is, someone who needs economic support and judicial protection—most of the traditions preserved in the so-called Holiness Code (Leviticus 17–26) use the term *ger* to describe a foreigner who is economically and socially independent. Christophe Nihan notes:

> Contrary to earlier legal collections (the Covenant Code and Deuteronomy) the גר [*ger*], in H [Holiness Code, Leviticus 17–26], is no longer simply viewed as a dependent person. He may still occasionally be included among

---

gentiles have to be incorporated into Israel in order to participate in the worship of Yhwh." Volker Haarmann, "'Their Burnt Offerings and Their Sacrifices Will Be Accepted on My Altar' (Isaiah 56:7): Gentile Yhwh-Worshipers and their Participation in the Cult of Israel," in Achenbach, Albertz, and Wöhrle, *The Foreigner and the Law*, 157–71, esp. 168.

the *personae miserae* (Lev 19:9–10; 23:22), that is, as a person who is unable to subsist himself, although he is never conceived as a client, a category for which H now reserves the term תושב [*toshav*]. In the majority of instances, however, the גר [*ger*] appears to be considered as a free, non-dependent member of the Judean society, who may be the head of a household (Exod 12:48–49) and may even be wealthy enough to own Israelite slaves (Lev 25:47–54).[11]

The change in the usage of *ger* created room for *toshav* to refer to a particular group of sojourners. While in the Holiness Code *toshav* is reserved for the status of a client, *ger*, for the most part, is included in regulations that are applicable to the resident alien and the "native" (אזרח [*'azrkh*]).[12] In summary, then, the Holiness Code distinguishes the *ger* from the Israelites and grants the *ger* more economic and social independence than in Deuteronomy and Exodus. One should not overlook the fact that the *ger* was also mentioned in the Holiness Code (Leviticus 19:9–10; 23:22) among those in need of receiving justice and hospitality—that is, *the ger* may also be vulnerable because of their foreignness.

The identity of the *ger* has been a matter of dispute among interpreters of the Torah. The *ger* has been identified with the "proselyte" who seeks to be integrated into the religious circles of Israel, with the Judahites who returned from exile, with the Samaritans, and with those who remained in the land and tried to join the community of the Judeans who returned to the land.[13] The point underlying this debate is whether the *ger* is a category defined by ethnic affiliation (Israelite or a foreigner) or socioeconomic status (vulnerable, landless). Similarly, the discussion about the identity of the *ger* depends on which legal texts are being discussed. In his treatment of the stranger in the book of Deuteronomy, Mark R. Glanville argues:

> [T]he term *gēr* in Deuteronomy simply designates a vulnerable person who is from outside of the core family. *Gēr* is a legal term that refers to people who have been displaced from their former kinship group and patrimony and from the protection that kinship and land affords and who seek sustenance in a new context. The *gēr* often appears in Deuteronomy as an outsider in relation to a household or a clan within which s/he is seeking protection and sustenance. Many of those designated *gēr* were internally displaced Judahites—some were non-Judahites/non-Israelites and some may have been northerners who had fled Assyrian invasion.[14]

---

11 Christophe Nihan, "Resident Aliens and Natives in the Holiness Legislation," in Achenbach, Albertz, and Wöhrle, *The Foreigner and the Law*, 111–34, esp. 129.

12 Ibid., 119.

13 See the discussion in Christiana de Groot Van Houten, *The Alien in Israelite Law* (Sheffield: Sheffield Press, 1991), 151–57.

14 Mark R. Glanville, *Adopting the Stranger as Kindred in Deuteronomy* (Atlanta, GA: SBL Press, 2018), 267.

154 *Safwat Marzouk*

Christophe Nihan, in his discussion of the *ger* in the Holiness Code, argues that "The גר [*ger*, in the Holiness Code, H, Leviticus 17–26] is a non-Israelite residing in the land of 'Israel'; attempts to identify him with a Yahwist of Samaria, or with a Judean non-exile, are mistaken and cannot be substantiated."[15] Given the diversity of how the biblical materials construct the identity of the *ger* and the ambiguities that surround the specific sociopolitical contexts out of which these diverse texts have emerged, it is best to understand the *ger* as referring to individuals who, for political, social, religious, ethnic, or economic reasons, experience a sense of *foreignness* and *difference* in relation to the community among whom they had to resettle. They are outsiders, with different economic abilities, sojourning in a land that is not theirs.

The biblical laws are quite clear about granting judicial and economic justice to the resident alien (*ger*). The earliest legal code (the Covenant Code, Exodus 21–23) warns against oppressing resident aliens, who are seen as one of the vulnerable groups in the Israelite society: "You shall not wrong or oppress a resident alien" (Exodus 22:21; 23:9; Zechariah 7:10). Not oppressing the resident alien is stated positively in the form of granting judicial justice to the resident alien: "I charged your judges at that time: Give the members of your community a fair hearing, and judge rightly between one person and another, whether citizen or resident alien" (Deuteronomy 1:16). This non oppression is also expressed positively in the sense of guaranteeing economic justice for the resident alien: "You shall not withhold the wages of poor and needy laborers, whether other Israelites or aliens who reside in your land in one of your towns. You shall not deprive a resident alien or an orphan of justice; you shall not take a widow's garment in pledge" (Deuteronomy 24:14, 17). The legal materials in the Torah go beyond equal and just treatments in the judicial system and in economic transactions; the Torah exhorts the people of Israel to show financial generosity and economic solidarity with resident aliens who might be in dire need.[16] The Israelites were commanded to leave grapes, olives, and sheaves for the aliens and the poor (Leviticus 19:10; 23:22; Deuteronomy 24:19, 20, 21).[17]

The call to do justice, judicial or economic, and the rationale for showing generosity and solidarity to resident aliens are grounded in theological principles that are repeated over and over in the Torah. These principles include:

1   Memory shapes a moral identity (you yourselves were aliens in Egypt; Exodus 22:21). This communal memory of the ancient past deepens the people's

---

15 Nihan, "Resident Aliens," 129.

16 For further discussions of solidarity with vulnerable people elsewhere in this volume, see Enid Trucios-Haynes (Chapter 2); Gemma Tulud Cruz (Chapter 11); Kristin E. Heyer (Chapter 13); Cruz and Trucios-Haynes (Chapter 16).

17 Christophe Nihan notes that the גר [*ger*] did not own land (Leviticus 25), "because possession of the land remains the exclusive prerogative of the community of 'Israel,' as well as the mark of their unique, privileged relationship to the patron deity of that community, Yhwh (Lev 20:22–26)." Nihan, "Resident Aliens," 129. This observation is quite different from what we read in Ezekiel's vision of restoration (Ezekiel 47), which suggests that the *ger* was allowed to possess land in an equal way to the native or citizen (Ezekiel 47:22–23).

Different kinds of foreignness   155

sense of empathy toward the resident alien; when the people settle in the land for a long time, they may forget what it means to be an alien, a migrant; therefore, the Torah repeatedly reminds the Israelites of their time in Egypt (you know the heart of an alien, for you were aliens in the land of Egypt, Exodus 23:9). José E. Ramírez Kidd suggests that "After the exile the גר [*ger*] became a mirror" of Israel's own story.[18] The story of the host community became bound to the story of the resident alien.

2   Doing justice for the migrant or resident alien reflects the people's ability to love themselves. Despite the ethnic and religious difference between the Israelites and foreigners who resided in their midst, the Torah asserts that doing justice for the other is grounded in loving the resident alien as oneself. Leviticus 19:34 puts it this way: "The alien who resides with you shall be to you as the citizen among you; you shall *love* the alien as yourself, for you were aliens in the land of Egypt: I am the LORD your God."

3   While Leviticus establishes the case for loving the migrant and doing justice for the resident alien based on memory and empathy, Deuteronomy grounds the commandment of loving the resident alien not only in the notion of empathy but also in the call to mimic God, who loves the stranger and provides for their needs: "For the LORD your God is God of gods . . . who *loves* the strangers, providing them food and clothing. You shall also *love* the stranger, for you were strangers in the land of Egypt" (Deuteronomy 10:17–20). That is, loving the resident alien, which means doing justice and offering hospitality, is essentially a way of mimicking God, who loves the strangers and offers them justice and shows them generosity.[19] Mark Glanville argues that whether in loving the *ger*, showing impartiality, or including them in the pilgrimage festival, Deuteronomy "is nourishing the *gēr*'s inclusion as kindred."[20] It is true that the *ger* is not described as a "brother," an important term that Deuteronomy preserves for the Israelites, yet Deuteronomy speaks of resident aliens as if they are related to the family. Interestingly, the prophetic literature considers the violation of doing injustice to resident aliens and shutting the doors of generosity in their faces as one reason why the people are exiled—that is, their injustice toward the resident alien has led the Israelites themselves to become resident aliens in foreign lands that they have not known before (Jeremiah 7:6; Ezekiel 22:7; Malachi 3:5; Psalm 94:6).

As mentioned above, while Exodus and Deuteronomy present the *ger* as a vulnerable stratum of foreigners who dwelt among the Israelites, the Holiness Code speaks of the *ger* as economically independent individuals. The editorial expansions in Leviticus 25, which are responsible for the laws that follow the Jubilee

---

18 José E. Ramírez Kidd, *Alterity and Identity in Israel: The* גר *in the Old Testament* (Berlin: Walter de Gruyter, 1999), 132.
19 For further discussion of loving the migrant in this volume, see Raj Nadella (Chapter 9); Luis N. Rivera-Pagán (Chapter 10).
20 Glanville, *Adopting the Stranger*, 265–66.

156 *Safwat Marzouk*

statutes, make use of the terms *ger* and *toshav* to address different scenarios of economic deterioration among Israelites or economic flourishing among non-Israelite migrants or sojourners. The norm and standard for the relationship among the Israelites is that they are kin (*akhim* = brothers, Leviticus 25:35, 39). The Israelites were freed by YHWH from slavery in Egypt, and therefore they belong only to YHWH. If an Israelite becomes poor, that person should be offered support, and there should be no interest on the loans they receive. Leviticus 25:35 prohibits turning kin into a slave; instead, they should be treated as resident aliens (*ger* and *toshav*): "If any of your kin fall into difficulty and become dependent on you, you shall support them; they shall live with you as though resident aliens." In another case, if an Israelite has become poor and is sold to another Israelite, they should be treated not as a slave but as any of the resident workers (*sakhir toshav*, Leviticus 25:40). They shall remain in this status until the year of the Jubilee. Israelites should not turn any of their kinfolk into slaves (Leviticus 25:39). Permission is granted, however, for the Israelites to take slaves to themselves from among the resident aliens or their families that dwell as migrants in their midst (*toshav hagirim*, Leviticus 25:44–46). One more law is added in this corpus of laws that follow the statutes of the year of the Jubilee. What happens if the resident aliens (*ger* and *toshav*) flourish economically and one of the Israelite kinsfolks owes them money? In this case, the impoverished Israelite should be treated as a "hired worker" (*sakhir*), not as a slave, until he or she is freed either through a kinsman redeemer or when the Jubilee year comes (Leviticus 25:47–55).

From these cases, one can conclude that according to the laws of Leviticus 25: (1) the resident alien was recognized to be ethnically and economically different from the Israelites; (2) the poor Israelite was treated like a resident alien; but (3) the resident alien is not necessarily a slave; and (4) the sojourners in the land were divided into different economic strata, some with the possibility of becoming rich, some treated as workers, and others becoming poor to the point of being acquired as slaves by the Israelites.

The relationship between the *ger* and *toshav* is complex. In some of the laws mentioned above, the *ger* and the *toshav* were considered to be equal economically (Leviticus 25:35, 47). Furthermore, they were granted the same rights to sanctuary cities as the Israelites (Numbers 35:15). Interestingly, some of the religious regulations distinguish between the resident alien (*ger*) and the sojourner (*toshav*). For example, whoever resides (*toshav*) with a priest as well as any hired worker (*sakhir*) cannot eat from the food consecrated as part of the priestly meals (Leviticus 22:10). Along with the foreigner (*ben nekhar*), the resident alien (*toshav*) and the hired worker (*sakhir*) cannot celebrate the Passover. Yet the sojourner (*ger*) is permitted to celebrate the Passover as long as they get circumcised (Exodus 12:43–50). In contrast to the Deuteronomic tradition, which is silent about the participation of foreigners in the festival of Passover, the priestly tradition creates room for resident aliens to participate in the Passover if they choose to, under one condition—namely, that they be circumcised (Exodus 12:48). Note, though, that Numbers 9:14 speaks of the inclusion of the resident alien in the celebration of the Passover but does not mention the condition of

Different kinds of foreignness 157

circumcision. It is hard to tell if Numbers 9:14 assumes Exodus 12:48 or ignores it altogether. The volition or the desire of the resident alien to participate in the ritualistic life of Israel is also acknowledged in Numbers 15:14–16, 26–30 with regard to offering sacrifices. These laws show that the Israelites distinguished between different kinds of migrants or resident aliens regarding the possibility of being included in religious practices. Furthermore, this distinction also shows that the Israelites did not force the celebration of religious festivals on migrants. If sojourners wished to join the celebration of the Passover, they were required to be circumcised. That is, the Israelites had a sophisticated way of negotiating boundaries between the "citizens" and the "resident aliens" (Exodus 12:50). Inclusion did not mean a loss of boundaries; but it was not coercive either.

The legal texts in the Torah address the issue of integrating the *ger* "sojourner" or "resident alien" in the religious practices of ancient Israel. On one level, the Torah seems clear that the resident alien, like the Israelites, *must* comply with the following regulations: not possessing leaven during the Festival of Unleavened Bread (Exodus 12:19), keeping the Sabbath (Exodus 20:10, 23:12; Leviticus 16:29; Deuteronomy 5:14), offering sacrifices at the tent of meeting (Leviticus 17:8, 22:18), avoiding consumption of blood (Leviticus 17:10–13), purifying after eating hunted animals (Leviticus 17:15; see also Numbers 19:10), following closely laws on sexual purity (Leviticus 18:26), making no offerings to the god Molech (Leviticus 20:2), facing death for blasphemy (Leviticus 24:16), celebrating the Festivals of Weeks and Booths (Deuteronomy 16:11, 14), enjoying the first fruit and bringing tithe to the sanctuary (Deuteronomy 26:11, 12, 13), and participating in the ceremonies of renewing the covenant and reading the Torah (Deuteronomy 29:10–12, 31:12; cf. Joshua 8:33–35). Other priestly laws insist on equality between resident aliens and citizens when it comes to these religious practices: "You and the alien who resides with you shall have the same law and the same ordinance" (Numbers 15:15–16; cf. Leviticus 24:22). Christophe Nihan notes that the גר [*ger*] in the Holiness Code is never commanded to be holy, as is the rest of the Israelite community. The *ger* were expected to preserve "*sacral* legislations," so that they, along with the members of the Israelite community, would not pollute the sanctuary or the land and thus provoke YHWH. Nihan adds:

> [The] גר [*ger*] remains a guest in the sacral community, just as he is a guest on Israel's land: he may access the sanctuary, but he will never become a full member of the holy community defined by that legislation. This observation accounts for the fact that the sacral legislation is more lenient in the case of the resident alien: contrary to the Israelites, the גר [*ger*] may still perform non-sacrificial slaughters, and they may apparently even continue to worship other deities (Lev 24:15b—16a), as long as he does not offer them sacrifices (Lev 17:8–9).[21]

---

21 Nihan, "Resident Aliens," 129–30.

158 *Safwat Marzouk*

Interestingly, in one incident the instructions delineate a specific practice for the Israelites in comparison to the resident alien (*ger*) and the foreigner (*nokhri*): "You shall not eat anything that dies of itself; you may give it to aliens residing [*ger*] in your towns for them to eat, or you may sell it to a foreigner [*nokhri*]. For you are a people holy to the LORD your God" (Deuteronomy 14:21). What is evident is that the Deuteronomic law distinguishes between the religious commitment of the Israelites and that of the non-Israelites who dwell in their midst. Furthermore, this law does not impose the religious conviction of the Israelites on the non-Israelites. The law, rather, creates a space for these different convictions and consumption of meat to coexist.

The previous survey shows that the law negotiated religious boundaries between the sojourners and the Israelites in a way that allowed the sojourners to participate in some religious practices while maintaining a unique place for the Israelites themselves in their relation to YHWH. Does this negotiation of religious boundaries create a hierarchy between the Israelites and the sojourners? Or does it include the sojourners without losing the distinctive identity of the Israelites? Would exemption or exclusion allow the sojourners to maintain some of their own religious traditions?

Religious inclusion or exemption of the resident alien or sojourner in these laws can be viewed in two ways. In a negative sense, these laws impose particular prescriptions on foreigners who might hold different faith or religious identities, practices, and morals. Seen in a positive way, these laws might have been trying to carve a place of equality and inclusion for these foreigners in an environment that sought to exclude and marginalize them.[22] Inclusion does not mean loss of boundaries; rather, boundaries are reformulated to include the ethnic other. And exclusion does not necessarily mean rejection, because it can mean that a particular practice is not forced on the foreigner. The diversity of views about including or excluding the sojourner in the religious practices of ancient Israel, similar to the laws about the economic status of the sojourner, emphasize the importance and the need for hermeneutics and discernment in negotiating the boundaries between insiders and outsiders.

V Hermeneutics and migration

The legal materials in the Torah reflect the complex reality of the stranger in ancient Israel. Not only does the Torah use different terminology to speak of

---

22 Nihan suggests that "the covenantal relationship between Yahweh and Israel thus implies a sacral bond that, for the Israelites, takes the form of several cultic and ritual obligations, among which the necessity that every animal killed be offered to Yhwh as a sacrifice. Resident aliens, on the other hand, are only *indirectly* included in that covenantal and sacral bond. In that respect, the fact that the גר [*ger*] is subject to a limited number of sacral laws in H is not so much an indication of the 'religious freedom' that is granted to him than of the effective hierarchy that operates between Israelites and resident aliens within the sacral community." Nihan, "Resident Aliens," 125.

Different kinds of foreignness 159

different groups of strangers, but also, depending on the historical context and the literary traditions, the same term could be referring to different groups of strangers whose legal, economic, religious, and social status vary. The diversity in how the Israelites related to strangers in their midst as reflected in the Hebrew Bible emerged from diverse ethical commitments, theological reflections, and political and economic circumstances. Given the diversity of the biblical perspectives about the sojourner, therefore, any engagement with these texts that seeks to address the challenges and potential of the phenomenon of migration today must engage hermeneutically with the diverse biblical traditions. As we have seen, biblical traditions are not monolithic with regard to how they viewed the different groups of strangers; hence, they used the terms *zar*, *nokhri*, *toshav*, and *ger*. This means that the Israelites wrestled with different kinds of foreignness. While the texts of the Hebrew Bible emerged from different historical contexts and different theological communities, the contemporary reader is confronted with all of these texts and their discourse about different kinds of foreignness at once, and side by side. The reader of the Bible finds a text that advocates for the exclusion of a particular group of foreigners next to another text that advocates for their inclusion. Such textual diversity, coupled with the contemporary urgency of the phenomenon of migration, highlights the need for a critical and hermeneutical engagement with the biblical texts, so that faith communities can discern an ethical response to migrants at the border and within their communities.

The critical question that faces any community with regard to migration has to do with discernment: how to show solidarity to the migrant, the asylum seeker, and the refugee who are in need, and how to recognize the alien who might pose harm to the host community without falling into xenophobia. Richard Kearney raises the question in this way: "[H]ow do we know . . . when the other is truly an enemy who seeks to destroy us or an innocent scapegoat projected by our phobias?" This is a crucial question for the discussion of migration.[23] Kearney underscores the necessity of a critical hermeneutics capable of distinguishing between different kinds of otherness. For Kearny, this is a process that seeks to distinguish between the "other"—"an alterity worthy of reverence and hospitality"—and the "alien," who is viewed with suspicion. He emphasizes the need for hermeneutics capable of addressing the "dialectic of others and aliens." Kearney writes:

> In short, I am suggesting that we need to be able to critically discriminate between different kinds of otherness, while remaining alert to the deconstructive resistance to black and white judgments of Us versus Them. We

---

23 The formulation of this question in law is addressed by Daniel Kanstroom (Chapter 1), Silas W. Allard (Chapter 5), and Rose Cuison Villazor (Chapter 7), elsewhere in this volume. It is taken up as a question of theology by Nadella (Chapter 9), Rivera-Pagán (Chapter 10), Ulrich Schmiedel (Chapter 12), and Kristin E. Heyer (Chapter 13).

160 *Safwat Marzouk*

need, at crucial moments, to discern the other in the alien and the alien in the other.[24]

The discernment process hinges on how identity is constructed; the identity of those who consider themselves insiders is essentially bound to those who are considered outsiders.

Identity is defined over against the other, and therefore self-understanding and knowledge of the other are always intertwined.[25] For our purposes here, the way the host communities understand themselves in relation to the other, the migrant, the refugee, and the asylum seeker, is crucial for discussions about boundary crossing and boundary maintaining. The Western mindset has been shaped by the Greco-Roman worldview, which favored the Same over against the Different, the Other. This approach, however, has been critiqued by deconstructionists as well as by psychoanalysts. While deconstruction idealizes the other at the expense of the self, psychoanalysis reduces the other to a mere reflection of the self. Whereas the approach of Jacques Derrida and Emmanuel Levinas underscores hospitality and responsibility toward the Other to the point of emptying the subjectivity of the self, psychoanalysis almost diminishes the notion of Otherness by arguing that the Other is merely an unconscious reflection of what is strange to the self—that is, the Other looks external but, in reality, is related to the self. Kearney writes, "If deconstruction too rapidly subordinates the Same to the Other, psychoanalysis may too rapidly subordinate the Other to the Same. . . . [T]he trick would be to try to steer a path somewhere between the polar extremes of alterity and immanence."[26]

Kearney posits a need for a critical hermeneutics that would enable us to discern the different kinds of others. "It is not enough to be simply *open* to the other beyond us or within us. . . . One must also be careful to discern, in some provisional fashion at least, between different kinds of otherness."[27] Kearney seeks to find a place for the other between transcendence and immanence. Others and

---

24 Richard Kearney, *Strangers, Gods, and Monsters: Interpreting Otherness* (London: Routledge, 2003), 67.

25 The background for Kearny's discussion of identity engages with the Greco-Roman background for Western thought. The immediate and most obvious way of defining *Self* is by setting it over against an *Other*. The *Self* is associated with the same and sameness, which signifies what is good and familiar. The *Other* is different, strange; it is what is dangerous and exterior. According to Kearney, the association between self-same and other-alien left us with a moral opposition between good (that is us, same) and evil (that is them, different and alien). Kearney writes: "Evil was alienation and the evil one was the alien." In order to protect one's self, one has to get rid of the evil other. "[T]he national *We* is defined over and against the foreign *Them*." Kearney, *Strangers,* 65. He summarizes his view as he notes, "Most ideas of identity, in short, have been constructed in relation to some notion of alterity." Kearney, *Strangers,* 66.

26 Kearney, *Strangers,* 77. Compare Kanstroom's discussion of how such distinctions are drawn in contemporary immigration law (Chapter 1).

27 Ibid.

Different kinds of foreignness   161

selves are bound in a relationship. Following Paul Ricoeur, who criticizes Levinas, Kearney posits that Levinas's work on the relation between the self and the other almost leaves us with no self: "There can be no relation to the other that does not in some respect transform the absolute other into a relative other—an other for another self."[28] He concludes:

> One of the best ways to *de-alienate* the other is to recognize (a) oneself as another and (b) the other as (in part) another self. For if ethics rightly requires me to respect the singularity of the other person, it equally requires me to recognize the other as another self bearing universal rights and responsibilities, that is, as someone capable of recognizing me in turn as a self capable of recognition and esteem.[29]

The approach that calls for discernment between different kinds of others has been critiqued on philosophical and theological grounds. How would one know if one's judgment of the different kinds of foreignness is correct? Or how would one even know if this other is trustworthy or untrustworthy without coming in contact with this other? Thus, Claudia Welz calls for the judgment of judgment and for trust to trump mistrust.[30] Building on Welz's probing of the notion of trust, Ulrich Schmiedel argues,

> Since one cannot decide whether the other is trustworthy or non-trustworthy *prior* to the relation to the other, the prejudice of trust is indispensable for any encounter with both finite and infinite others. Trust is always already appropriate. The trusting leap towards the other is blind in the sense that the disappointment of trust cannot be avoided without turning from trust to mistrust.[31]

Building trust between migrants and host communities depends on the serious and hard work of listening to the fears of the other and hinges on a deep self-understanding that motivates an ethical responsibility toward the needs of the other informed by empathy (see Ulrich Schmiedel, Chapter 12; Kristin E. Heyer, Chapter 13). Susanna Snyder calls on communities of faith to expand

> their horizon to include those who are anti-asylum and anti-immigration. Engaging with the ecology of fear, rather than dismissing it out of hand— which usually only succeeds in entrenching people further in their views—is

28 Ibid.
29 Ibid., 80.
30 Claudia Welz, "Trust as Basic Openness and Self-Transcendence," in *Trust, Sociality, Selfhood*, eds. Claudia Welz and Arne Grøn (Tübingen: Mohr Siebeck, 2010), 45–64. Cited in Ulrich Schmiedel, "Transcendence, Taxis, Trust: Richard Kearney and Jacques Derrida," *Religions* 8, no. 3 (2017): 1–13.
31 Schmiedel, "Transcendence, Taxis, Trust," 10.

162 *Safwat Marzouk*

vital. Faith communities have the potential to act as a space in which bridges can be built between those who are different.

Ecologies of fear can be transformed into ecologies of faith and trust, argues Snyder:

> facilitating friendly encounters between those who fear one another—creating intentional proximity ecologies of faith—could therefore be an important additional way in which churches could support migrants. Interfaith dialogue is one necessary facet of these encounters. We need to be performing ecologies in which people can learn to take risks and cross boundaries.[32]

The processes of building trust, discerning different kinds of foreignness, analyzing the relation between the self and the other should not be used to delay responding with generosity, compassion, and solidarity in order to alleviate the trauma and suffering of asylum seekers and refugees (see Michele R. Pistone, Chapter 4; Bill Ong Hing and Raj Nadella, Chapter 17). Indeed, despite the complexity of how the Hebrew Bible speaks about migration, doing justice and showing hospitality are the cornerstones of the ethical response to the migrant, refugee, and asylum seeker.

Although study of the different Hebrew terms for foreigners yields a complex picture of how ancient Israel negotiated relationships with migrants and sojourners in their midst—a portrait complicated further by contemporary realities of migration—one can still name theological signposts on the road of discerning how to respond ethically to the needs of refugees and to the fears of host communities. This chapter has shown that some central theological convictions guided the ancient Israelites in their interaction with foreigners who resided in their midst. These theological convictions, coupled with hermeneutical reflections on the biblical texts, can still inform how contemporary faith communities should respond to recent waves of migration. These theological convictions include the following.

First, the Hebrew Bible does not make arguments to deter migrants from coming into Israel, nor does it call for sending migrants or asylum seekers back to their country of origin; the Hebrew Bible assumes that migrants and sojourners are part of the Israelite society (compare Daniel Kanstroom, Chapter 1). The Hebrew Bible is not concerned with the question, "should Israel allow migrants to enter or not?" Rather, it is far more concerned with the migrants' legal, economic, and religious standing in the society. Even with a text like Ezra, the concern has to do with religious and marital boundaries more than territorial boundaries. Sending the foreign women away did not necessarily mean sending them to their home countries. As horrific as it is, the decision is far more concerned with religious and familial boundaries.

---

32 Snyder, *Asylum-Seeking, Migration, and Church*, 200–1.

Different kinds of foreignness 163

Second, the complexity of the portrayal of the stranger in the Hebrew Bible calls for a balanced view that avoids the demonization of the stranger or the idealization of the foreigner. Over and over again, and in many different legal traditions from different historical eras, biblical texts exhort the community to show economic solidarity and judicial justice to the sojourner, migrant, and foreigner. In a few cases, where foreigners (at least according to how they were constructed in some biblical texts), possessed power, we find that the biblical texts try to constrain their economic or political power. These instances cannot be used to deter asylum seekers or refugees from being welcomed or shown justice, because these texts are essentially talking not about powerless or helpless migrants but about powerful and rich migrants. In other words, the basic role in discerning the different kinds of foreignness has to do with managing power relations. If the foreigner is weak, then, the community should show solidarity; if the migrant is powerful, then, the community should make sure that the migrant does not flourish at the expense of the members of the host community. A biblical example of this is Joseph, who enslaved the Egyptians under Pharaoh according Genesis 47:13–26.[33] A contemporary example can be traced in the displacement of Native Americans by European migrants. Thus, because migrants are not of the same socioeconomic stratum, solidarity should be unconditional to the powerless refugee and asylum seekers, while migrants who possess power should be called to be agents of care and generosity toward the powerless (see also Enid Trucios-Haynes, Chapter 2; Gemma Tulud Cruz, Chapter 11; Cruz and Trucios-Haynes, Chapter 16). Migrants are not only recipients of generosity; they can also be agents of justice and kindness.

Third, showing hospitality, economic solidarity, social inclusion, and judicial fairness is grounded in the memory that the Israelites themselves were aliens in Egypt. The biblical texts repeatedly envision that this communal memory will invigorate empathy, which, in turn, forms an ethical relationship of solidarity and mutuality with the other; this ethical posture is also grounded in the commandment of loving the stranger as oneself; of equal importance, the community should do justice to the sojourner because God loves them and manifests love in showing them justice and impartiality.

Fourth, the inclusion/exclusion/exemption of aliens or foreigners from religious practices was fluid and depended on how the different biblical traditions tried to make sense of boundary maintaining and boundary crossing in given contexts and in different historical conditions. Not all forms of exclusion, or rather exemption, should be seen in a negative light; in some cases, being excluded or exempted from a particular religious practice can be seen as a way of protecting the freedom of the foreigner. Asking foreigners to comply with some religious practices can be seen as a way of including them in religious circles. Thus, the integration of the migrant in the religious circles sometimes needs to

---

33 This example is discussed in more detail in later in this volume (Kerwin and Marzouk, Chapter 15).

164 *Safwat Marzouk*

be negotiated in contrast to the extremes of assimilation and segregation. Not to mention that being exempted from a particular religious practice does not mean being expelled from the community or the territory. In contemporary interreligious settings in relation to migration, it's important to emphasize dismantling discrimination based on religious difference and to encourage communities to claim their religious identities in ways that reflect hospitality and build bridges with those who are different religiously.

Fifth, and finally, we hear often these days about rejection of vulnerable migrants and refugees who rely on governmental assistance (see Donald M. Kerwin, Chapter 6), and about a migration point system that would essentially help those who have many qualifications while eliminating less qualified migrants (asylum seekers or refugees) who are the ones that need help and assistance (see Trucios-Haynes, Chapter 2; Hing, Chapter 3). Given the emphasis of the Hebrew Bible on solidarity and justice for the vulnerable sojourner, it is clear that the text does not advocate for "merit-based" migration or "qualified" migrants only. Conversely, the Hebrew Bible warns against migrants who flourish at the expense of the Israelites themselves, which can be seen as a caution against powerful migrants or qualified migrants who might benefit from the economic system at the expense of the vulnerable Israelites. The Hebrew Bible essentially urges faith communities to welcome, integrate, and support the vulnerable migrants in their midst.

Suggested Reading

Achenbach, Reinhard, Rainer Albertz, and Jakob Wöhrle, eds. *The Foreigner and the Law: Perspectives from the Hebrew Bible and the Ancient Near East*. BZAR 16. Wiesbaden: Harrassowitz Verlag: 2011.

Claudia Welz. "Trust as Basic Openness and Self-Transcendence." In *Trust, Sociality, Selfhood*, edited by Claudia Welz and Arne Grøn, 45–64. Tübingen: Mohr Siebeck, 2010.

Glanville, Mark R. *Adopting the Stranger as Kindred in Deuteronomy*. Atlanta, GA: SBL Press, 2018.

Kearney, Richard. *Strangers, Gods, and Monsters: Interpreting Otherness*. London: Routledge, 2003.

Ramírez Kidd, José E. *Alterity and Identity in Israel: The* גר *in the Old Testament*. Berlin: Walter de Gruyter, 1999.

Schmiedel, Ulrich. "Transcendence, Taxis, Trust: Richard Kearney and Jacques Derrida." *Religions* 8 (2017): 1–13.

Snyder, Susanna. *Asylum-Seeking, Migration and Church*. London: Routledge, 2012.

9 Embrace, ambivalence, and theoxenia

New Testament perspectives on hospitality to strangers

Raj Nadella

I Introduction

Migration—both within and across borders—has become the defining phenomenon of the twenty-first century throughout the world, but especially in Western countries like the United States. According to the Pew Research Center, as of 2018, about 44.8 million people living in the country—or roughly 13.7 percent of the total population—had been born in another country.[1] The phenomenon of migration continues to have significant impact on the culture, economy, and politics of destination countries as well as on how people see and relate to each other. As Musa Dube has noted, "The intensity of movements across borders has become a major feature in contemporary times to the extent that theorists have begun to theorize bordercrossing, exile and the Diaspora as a framework of being, seeing, thinking and living."[2]

Many biblical texts feature stories of migration and were written primarily from the perspective of migrants and refugees.[3] Ironically, however, several New Testament texts have often been taken out of their larger literary and canonical contexts and employed to justify unjust laws and policies towards immigrants and to perpetuate xenophobia. Such misuse of biblical texts has lately become more common in the political discourse in the United States. Precisely because of such misuse of texts, it is necessary to explicate New Testament perspectives about hospitality to strangers and foreigners "for the humanization of migrants in broader discourse."[4] Along these lines, this chapter explores, in broad terms, Christological, theological, and ecclesial bases for hospitality to strangers in selected New

---

1 The United States also receives roughly 19 percent of the world's migrant population each year. See "Key Findings About U.S. Immigrants," *Pew Research Center*, August 10, 2020, www.pewresearch.org/fact-tank/2020/08/20/key-findings-about-u-s-immigrants/.
2 Musa Dube, "Intercultural Biblical Interpretations," *Swedish Missiological Themes* 98, no. 3 (2010): 361–88 at 366.
3 Safwat Marzouk (Chapter 8) explores migration, foreignness, and hospitality in the Hebrew Bible elsewhere in this volume (Chapter 8). This chapter focuses primarily on the New Testament.
4 Efrain Agosto and Jacqueline M. Hidalgo, eds., *Latinxs, the Bible, and Migration, Bible and Cultural Studies* (Basingstoke: Palgrave Macmillan, 2018), 2.

166 *Raj Nadella*

Testament texts—primarily in the Gospel of Matthew—and their relevance for current debates on migration.

Matthew portrays Jesus as a frequent border-crosser—literally and figuratively—who undermines borders and includes outsiders in the new community, with the result that disrupting borders, rather than erecting them, forms the basis of the community and marks its identity. Accordingly, the arrival of strangers does not undermine the identity of the community but rather reinforces it. Matthew's Gospel, written primarily for the in-group, gradually moves from embrace of strangers to seeming ambivalence about them to depicting strangers as manifestations of the divine, akin to the concept of *theoxenia*—divine stranger—in Greek mythology, which views the foreigner[5] as a manifestation of the divine and Zeus as the protector of foreigners. New Testament discourse on *philoxenia*—love of the stranger—thus models itself on theoxenia but goes further. The Greek idea of hospitality places similar emphasis on the mutual obligations of the host and the guest, but the New Testament, emerging out of contexts of displacement, puts much greater emphasis on hospitality to strangers. Welcoming and caring for strangers is integrally connected not only to the early church's worship of Jesus, the displaced God, but also to its own identity as displaced people. Such displacement—literal and metaphorical—that underlies New Testament texts, such as 1 Peter, provided—and should continue to provide—theological and ecclesial bases for Christian embrace of strangers in our context.

II Misuse of biblical texts to promote xenophobia

Steve Bannon, President Donald Trump's former political adviser and strategist, who played a key role in shaping Trump's policy on immigration, was known to have suggested often that his worldview was influenced by *The Camp of the Saints*, a 1973 French novel by Jean Raspail.[6] The novel begins with the scene of tens of thousands of Asian immigrants and refugees headed for Europe in pursuit of survival and better economic prospects in a "land of plenty." After a long and arduous journey, they make their way to France, which was politically divided over the question of how best to respond to the arrival of these immigrants and refugees. While many in France were open to receiving them on humanitarian grounds, many others, perhaps a majority, perceived them as invaders who threatened French culture and economic prosperity as well as Western civilization as a whole. In particular, while those in northern France, primarily in Paris, were generally eager to receive the newcomers, people in southern France felt threatened by them and fled to the north. The immigrants eventually overran

---

5 I employ the terms "stranger" and "foreigner" interchangeably in this chapter.

6 Paul Blumenthal and J. M. Rieger, "This Stunningly Racist French Novel Is How Steve Bannon Explains the World," *Huffington Post*, March 4, 2017, www.huffpost.com/entry/steve-bannon-camp-of-the-saints-immigration_n_58b75206e4b0284854b3dc03.

southern France and had no apparent desire to adopt French culture, language, or worldview.

The novel is characterized by three key aspects—xenophobia stemming from misperceptions about the other, depiction of the other as less than human, and use of biblical texts to justify dehumanization of the other. The title *The Camp of the Saints* is from Revelation 20:9, where Satan is released after a thousand-year imprisonment and unleashes hostile nations, which "marched across the breadth of the earth and surrounded the camp of God's people." It suggests that France was "the camp of God's people" about to be taken over by the invading immigrants. The novel highlights the myriad ways in which biblical texts are employed to perpetuate xenophobia and to justify unjust legal practices as well as misinterpretation of laws pertaining to immigrants.

The embrace of Raspail's worldview by Bannon and the Trump administration in general calls attention to the rising anti-immigrant sentiment in the United States and the troublesome rhetoric that demonizes Muslim immigrants and undocumented migrants from Latin America. Reflecting a global trend of increased xenophobic nationalism (see Donald M. Kerwin, Chapter 6), the resulting rhetoric and policies perpetuate the myth that immigrants are invaders and adversely impact "our" culture and economy, just as they did in Raspail's novel. Such a view is also consistent with instances in which anti-immigrant attitudes and policies are fueled by misinterpretation of scriptures in the United States. One might recall the misreading of scriptures by the former U.S. attorney general, Jeff Sessions, who quoted from Romans 13 to justify separation of immigrant/refugee families at the southern border in 2018 and the government's prosecution of everyone who crosses the border illegally.[7]

Is such use of biblical texts by Raspail and Sessions consistent with how border-crossers and strangers are depicted in the New Testament? What do New Testament texts say about hospitality to strangers, and how might that perspective be employed to attenuate xenophobia and misperceptions about foreigners? I begin with an exploration of the themes of border crossing and hospitality in Matthew's Gospel and argue that disrupting borders, rather than erecting them, forms the basis of the community and marks its identity in the Gospel.

III Matthew and strangers: embrace, ambivalence, and theoxenia

Matthew's Gospel, written primarily from the perspective of those within the Jewish community, often features outsiders and includes them in its story of God's engagement with the world. It embraces outsiders, celebrates them, and

---

7 Julia Jacobs, "Sessions's Use of Bible Passage to Defend Immigration Policy Draws Fire," *New York Times*, June 15, 2018, www.nytimes.com/2018/06/15/us/sessions-bible-verse-romans.html.

168 *Raj Nadella*

disrupts boundaries. In stories such as the visit by the Magi (Chapter 2), Jesus's family fleeing to Egypt (Chapter 2), his encounter with the Roman centurion (Chapter 8), his conversation with the Canaanite woman (Chapter 15), and the discourse on hospitality to strangers (Chapter 25), Matthean texts delineate a movement from embrace of strangers to ambivalence about them to eventual depiction of strangers as manifestations of the divine.

In one of the first stories in the Gospel, Matthew offers an account of the Magi arriving in Judea from the East to worship Jesus after his birth (2:1–2). The Magi were originally members of the Persian priestly class and were viewed with suspicion as destabilizing forces in the Roman Empire. They were not kings or necessarily wise men, and their knowledge based on stars was often seen negatively, as Warren Carter has observed.[8] Within this context, "ironically, God reveals something very significant to these magi" rather than to anyone associated with the oppressive regime of Herod the Great.[9] This theme of outsiders crossing borders and being privy to knowledge and benefits not always accessible to the elite within continues in subsequent chapters. Matthew, however, depicts both insiders and outsiders as participants in the process of border crossing—literally and metaphorically.

IV Borders disrupted—literally and metaphorically

While all three Synoptic Gospels record numerous travels of Jesus, Matthew depicts Jesus and his associates as itinerants who frequently cross borders—literal and metaphorical—in the process of including others in the community. Key characters frequently disrupt borders, and it is the blurring of borders, rather than their reinforcement, that forms the basis of the community.

In Matthew's account, hostility from oppressive rulers, such as Herod the Great, leads to Jesus's first instance of crossing borders and entering a foreign territory. Herod the Great learns from the Magi about a new king of the Jews who was just born, and Herod feels threatened by this potential rival to his throne. Joseph—warned by an angel of the Lord that Herod would seek to kill the infant to eliminate threats to his regime (2:13–14)—flees with Mary and Jesus to Egypt to escape the imperial violence unleashed in the vicinity of Bethlehem. The Greek word *horioi*, often translated as "vicinity," literally means "territory," "boundaries," or "borders." For Matthew, then, this is the first instance of Jesus crossing borders. After the death of Herod the Great and a revelation from an angel of the Lord, Joseph, Mary, and Jesus return to Israel in another instance of border crossing. But these border crossings by Jesus and his family occur within their homeland as well. When they learn that Archelaus has succeeded his father as the ruler of Judea in the south, they flee to Galilee in the north.

---

8 Warren Carter, *Matthew and the Margins: A Socio-Political and Religious Reading* (Sheffield: Sheffield Academic Press, 2000), 74–75.
9 Ibid., 77.

Embrace, ambivalence, and theoxenia 169

In the first pericope about Jesus's mission (4:12–17), Matthew notes that, in response to the news of John the Baptist's execution by Herod Antipas— Archelaus's brother, who ruled in Galilee—Jesus made his home in Capernaum, in the region of Zebulun and Naphtali. Capernaum was a border town at the intersection of Galilee and Gaulanitis and was home to Jewish and Gentile populations. It was also a town where borders were porous and often contested. Matthew refers to Jesus's new home as "Galilee of the Gentiles," a synonym for Zebulun and Naphtali, and clarifies that the move to that region occurred as a fulfilment of prophecy. Matthew's use of the Greek _horioi_ in this instance connotes that Jesus is again crossing borders to enter a Gentile territory.[10] The term "Galilee of the Gentiles" had been employed for decades by writers such as Flavius Josephus.[11] The significance of the term pertained to a possible perception of Galilee as the other—culturally, politically, and economically—to Judea in the south, which was the citadel of political and economic power. The prophet Isaiah, from whom Matthew borrows the term "Galilee of the Gentiles," was especially known for his vision of including outsiders in God's community and salvific plan. Within this historical and theological context, Matthew's explicit acknowledgment of Galilee as Jesus's new home and starting point for his ministry amounts to introducing and characterizing Jesus's mission as one that will render borders porous—literally and figuratively.

Consistent with Matthew's characterization, Jesus repeatedly enters Gentile territories to extend his mission to communities outside the borders. Matthew also writes that news about Jesus spread all over Syria, and outsiders from there as well as the Decapolis and other regions crossed borders follow him (4:23–25). As Carter aptly notes, the reference to Syria likely suggests that, from Matthew's perspective, the Gospel itself originated outside the borders of Galilee.[12] The possibility that Syria was the location of the Matthean community at the time Matthew wrote his Gospel reflects their identity and self-perception as a community in the diaspora.

Matthew further undermines the insider-outsider binary in the story of the centurion whose servant Jesus healed (8:5–13). In granting the request of the centurion, an outsider, Jesus further disrupts boundaries and changes the criterion of admission into the community from identity to relationality. The story occurs on the heels of Jesus entering Capernaum, a site where borders were contested, and it amplifies the significance of Jesus allowing the metaphorical borders of his movement to be disrupted by admitting an outsider. The story represents another instance of border crossing—both from within and from outside—that becomes a key aspect of the community's identity.

In his seminal book, _Imagined Communities: Reflections on the Origin and Spread of Nationalism_, Benedict Anderson argued that the phenomenon of

---

10 Matthew is the only Gospel to record this story of Jesus moving to Zebulun and Naphtali.
11 Josephus, _Jewish War_, 2.510; 4.105.
12 Carter, _Matthew and the Margins_, 16–17.

170 *Raj Nadella*

nation is socially constructed and is a product of the imagination of people who see themselves as insiders based on their own criteria. He aptly observes that "nation-ness is the most universally legitimate value in the political life of our time."[13] The universal and often destructive phenomenon of nation is made possible primarily by external borders, which exclude those who do not fit the imagined criteria and give insiders a sense of belonging. As Britt Edelen has noted, "the creation of national identities, then, is not a cause but a result of borders."[14] In short, formation of national identities coincides with and largely depends on establishment of borders. Given the role borders play in defining identities and fostering a sense of belonging, identities become hybridized and less clearly defined where borders are porous or blurred. In Matthew's Gospel, Jesus's proclivity to disrupt borders facilitates deterritorialization of the new movement he has inaugurated and allows outsiders to join the community alongside insiders. The disruption of borders amounts to reimagining a community that defies easy categorizations and includes outsiders who do not fit previously imagined criteria. The movement is now defined not by clearly defined borders but precisely by their disruption.

Throughout these stories, Jesus exhibits a proclivity to disrupt borders. Acceptance of the other does not defile his mission but defines it, just as the arrival of the other does not undermine the identity of the community but rather reinforces it.

V From embrace to ambivalence

A trajectory of disrupting boundaries and welcoming strangers into the community results in resistance on the part of his disciples and ambivalence on the part of Jesus about disrupting boundaries. Such resistance to and ambivalence about outsiders is reflected in Jesus's encounter with the Canaanite woman (Matthew 15:21–28).

Matthew's account of Jesus's encounter with the Canaanite woman begins with Jesus leaving Gennesaret and withdrawing into the region of Tyre and Sidon, which was a foreign territory both politically and culturally. Matthew describes Jesus withdrawing into Tyre and Sidon by employing the same Greek term— *anachoreo*—used with reference to the flight of Joseph, Mary, and Jesus into Egypt (Matthew 2). Jesus is a stranger in Tyre and Sidon, just as his family had been strangers in Egypt. Matthew suggests that the woman, too, came out from the *horioi* (boundaries or regions) of Tyre and Sidon. While the specific location of their encounter is unclear, the pericope depicts both Jesus and the Canaanite woman simultaneously crossing and undermining numerous boundaries— geographical, ethnic, gender, religious. Their act of boundary crossing also brings

---

13 Benedict Anderson, *Imagined Communities: Reflections on the Origin and Spread of Nationalism* (London: Verso, 2016), 3.

14 Britt Edelen, "Borders and Identities," *Brown Political Review*, April 7, 2016, https://brownpoliticalreview.org/2016/04/borders-and-identities/.

Embrace, ambivalence, and theoxenia 171

to the fore the ways in which they are mutual strangers and outsiders. While Jesus is a stranger and an outsider geographically and culturally, the woman is an outsider—metaphorically—in her own space vis-à-vis the new kingdom he has inaugurated.

Although both Jesus and the Canaanite woman cross various boundaries, their initial conversation reinforces those boundaries. Such reinforcing stems largely from Jesus's seeming ambivalence about granting the woman's request to heal her demon-possessed daughter. His twofold initial response—"I have been sent only for the lost sheep of Israel" (15:24), and "It is not right to take what belongs to the children and give it to the dogs" (15:26)—should be explored from the perspectives of tradition of the elders and the competition for "limited" resources.

VI The tradition of the elders and the "other"

At the beginning of Chapter 15, Jesus and his disciples were accused of violating the tradition of the elders, the purity laws, by not washing their hands before they eat (15:1–2). In the literary context of Jesus and his disciples frequently crossing geographical and social boundaries to include outsiders, the accusation is primarily about not maintaining social distance from outsiders. The accusation suggests that his disciples were undermining communal boundaries. As Stanley Saunders has observed, "the charge that Jesus and his disciples are not washing their hands before eating is less about hygiene than social purity, the ritual actions that establish social boundaries and hierarchies."[15]

The motif of maintaining social boundaries with outsiders comes to the fore in Jesus's response to the Canaanite woman's request that characterized her community as "dogs." Gregory Cuéllar's book *Resacralizing the Other at the US–Mexico Border: A Borderland Hermeneutic* helpfully highlights the myriad ways people who cross borders are often treated as the inferior other, denied their humanity, and robbed of their sacredness.[16] By characterizing others as less than human, one justifies denying them what one might be obligated to extend to them. Cuéllar moves the conversation beyond the rhetoric of dehumanizing and desacralizing border crossers and prescribes a liberative hermeneutic for reclaiming the sacredness of border crossers. I will return to this idea later in this chapter.

Jesus's initial response to the woman—"it is not right to take what belongs to the children and give it to the dogs"—reflects the tension between the proclivity to maintain purity laws (metaphorical boundaries) and the commandment to love one's neighbor as oneself as outlined in Leviticus 19. The neighbor here comes in the form of the foreigner who seemingly undermines the welfare of the self. Jesus's initial reluctance to grant a miracle to the other reflects a proclivity to

---

15 Stanley Saunders, *Preaching the Gospel of Matthew* (Louisville, KY: Westminster John Knox, 2010), 149.

16 Gregory Lee Cuéllar, *Resacralizing the Other at the US–Mexico Border: A Borderland Hermeneutic* (New York: Routledge, 2020), 78.

172 Raj Nadella

privilege the insiders over a moral obligation to help the woman's sick daughter.[17] What if granting her a miracle, and thereby admitting her into the new kingdom, undermined a strand of the tradition that set borders between children and dogs? Can benefits of the new kingdom that are meant for children be extended to the dogs, the outsiders? Richard Beck's observation that the "strangeness of strangers makes hospitality hard" especially illuminates the response of Jesus and his followers toward the Canaanite woman.[18] His initial response also foregrounds a perceived concern that, since resources might be limited and competition for them intense, letting dogs share in their resources might invariably result in children being denied access to them. As Musa Dube has observed,

> an ancient biblical contact-zone with other cultures was not always, if at all, a romantic love-zone of kisses in the moonlight. It was a power relation. The Bible thus remains a textual evidence of sites of struggle for power that intercultural readers should highlight and re-read for the liberating interdependence of cultures.[19]

The woman's response—"the dogs eat the crumbs that fall from their master's table"—does not go far enough in terms of challenging the language used to refer to the communities or the perception of competition for resources, but it disrupts the notion that dogs and children occupy clearly demarcated spaces and access vastly different resources. Their cultural and ethnic differences should not prevent them from being able to share space or resources in the new community, because their common need for bread is a stronger identifying marker than their differences. To use Homi Bhabha's words, in this hybridizing process, the woman disrupts homogeneous, simplistic narratives about community formation that invariably exclude "others" who do not meet set criteria.[20] Since the new community has been founded on the ethos of disruption of boundaries and thus far includes many outside its boundaries, allowing dogs and children to share space at the table does not undermine the integrity of its space but rather enhances it. In the woman's response, the table becomes the border space that connects the children and the dogs, even as it seemingly separates them (Silas W. Allard, Chapter 5). As an outsider, the woman also reminds Jesus, and by extension those around him, about the inclusive nature of his mission thus far. Her response

---

17 Miroslav Volf's book *Exclusion & Embrace* explicates the violence caused by the exclusion of the other but does not sufficiently account for power dynamics in the encounter. In this chapter, I explore the motif of ambivalent tensions in the process of encountering the other that ultimately lead to *philoxenia*. Miroslav Volf, *Exclusion and Embrace, Revised and Updated: A Theological Exploration of Identity, Otherness, and Reconciliation* (Nashville: Abingdon, 2019).

18 Richard Beck, *Stranger God: Meeting Jesus in Disguise* (Minneapolis: Fortress Press, 2017), 7.

19 Musa Dube, "Intercultural Biblical Interpretations," 364.

20 Homi Bhabha, *The Location of Culture* (London: Routledge, 2004), 243.

Embrace, ambivalence, and theoxenia 173

suggests that, given the nature of his kingdom, which has been promoting an economy of plenty as evidenced by feeding narratives, a concern about dogs stealing children's bread is misplaced.

At the end of their transformative conversation that moves past his ambivalence, Jesus privileges the commandment to love one's neighbor as outlined in Leviticus 19 over any proclivity to maintain social boundaries. He has already violated numerous boundaries and now violates social boundaries to include her in the kingdom he has inaugurated. A community's identity may be typically based on the similarities its members share with the insiders and their imagined differences vis-à-vis outsiders, but the new community Jesus has been forming is built on disrupting the insider–outsider binary. The disruption of boundaries, rather than their reinforcement, has become the foundation and identity marker of the new community. The text is suggestive of the debates about outsiders during Jesus's mission in the early part of the first century, but on a different level, it reflects the Matthean community's struggles in the process of its identity formation and debates about welcoming outsiders in the late first century. Along those lines, the story of the Canaanite woman prescribes for the Matthean audience how they should engage those outside its boundaries.

VII From ambivalence about strangers to deification of strangers (theoxenia)

In the chapters following the story of the Canaanite woman, the mission of Jesus gradually and consistently extends to the outsiders and includes them alongside insiders. Numerous accounts of Jesus performing miracles in Gentile territories have the significance of embracing and including strangers in the new kingdom. Such a trajectory of inclusion of strangers continues until Matthew 25, where the parable of sheep and goats (Matthew 25:31–46) adds a new dimension to the motif of hospitality to strangers. In this parable of eschatological judgment, God admonishes those who failed to care for the hungry, the naked, the prisoners, and strangers and affirms those who attended to their needs. In a motif similar to the Greek mythological concept of theoxenia—divine stranger—the Matthean parable posits God appearing in the form of a stranger.

Ancient Greeks subscribed to the idea of radical hospitality to strangers predicated on the belief that Zeus often visited people disguised as a stranger to test their hospitality to outsiders.[21] The concept of theoxenia suggested that if God occasionally appeared in the form of *xenos*, every encounter with *xenos* was possibly a site of encounter with the divine, and every *xenos* possibly a manifestation of the divine. Since every stranger was potentially a deity in disguise, people should welcome strangers as they would welcome gods themselves, lest they offend the gods or miss out on divine blessings. The motif of a deity seeking to receive

---

21 John Hall Elliott, *A Home for the Homeless: A Social-Scientific Criticism of 1 Peter, Its Situation and Strategy* (Eugene, OR: Wipf & Stock, 2005).

174   *Raj Nadella*

human hospitality in the tradition of theoxenia—the divine stranger—often had the intended effect of encouraging people to welcome strangers into their homes and extend generous hospitality. In taking the form of a stranger to encourage hospitality toward strangers, Zeus became the protector of strangers and a symbol of radical hospitality. The concept of theoxenia places emphasis on the moral obligation of the host to the guest, but it also highlights responsibilities and obligations of the guest to the host.

Akin to the motif of theoxenia, the parable in Matthew (25:31–46) depicts God as the prisoner, the hungry, and the foreigner who knocks on our doors seeking hospitality and protection. It is by caring for the least privileged—the *elaxistos*—that one cares for God. Conversely, every refusal to care for the hungry, the prisoner, the sick, and the stranger is tantamount to turning one's back on the divine and will entail judgment. The parable suggests that since God takes the form of a stranger, the stranger becomes a site of encountering the divine. Every occasion of caring for the hungry, the prisoner, the sick, and the stranger is an opportunity to experience the divine and expand one's horizons of understanding the divine. The stranger is both the manifestation of and the gateway to the divine. Paradoxically, then, Matthew 25 depicts those with the least power and the most ostracized as the sites of encountering the divine.

The motif of God appearing in the form of a stranger is a return to, and builds upon, the motif of God incarnate, who was frequently rendered a stranger by imperial violence at the beginning of the Gospel (Matthew 2). Whereas Zeus disguised himself as a stranger on occasion, Matthew depicts Jesus as having lived the life of a stranger and refugee in Egypt. Just as God became a stranger and refugee in embodied spaces at the start of the Gospel, God now encounters disciples and members of the community in the form of a stranger. In caring for a stranger, therefore, people care both for Jesus, who was a stranger, and God, who took the form of a stranger. Conversely, any hostility toward strangers becomes an act of offense against God. Seen this way, while the motif of Jesus as a refugee in Matthew 2 provides Christological foundation for hospitality to strangers, the parable of sheep and goats in Matthew 25 provides theological foundation for hospitality to strangers.

Seeing the divine in the other is an acknowledgment of one's respect for, and obligation to, a neighbor who appears in the form of a stranger, a prisoner, the poor, and a foreigner. Cuéllar's insights about engaging in hermeneutics that reclaim the sacredness of strangers, the border-crossers, are especially helpful here.[22] Reclaiming the sacredness of strangers and seeing them as manifestations of the divine are also steps toward acknowledging their humanity. When one acknowledges the sacredness or divinity of strangers, it becomes impossible to deny them the dignity and respect they deserve as humans. The language of hospitality in the parable encourages acts of kindness to the other, but it also

22 Cuéllar, *Resacralizing the Other.*

Embrace, ambivalence, and theoxenia 175

articulates one's moral obligation to ensure the well-being of the stranger beyond individual acts of hospitality.

In short, in a span of less than ten chapters, the Matthean Jesus moves from his seeming ambivalence about admitting a stranger—the Canaanite woman—into the kingdom, to equating the *xenos* with the divine. The text outlines the transformative process of the Jesus figure and in doing so offers similar possibilities and encouragement for its readers. The motif of movement from ambivalence to equating strangers with the divine in this parable was possibly an encouragement to the Matthean community to transform their own ambivalence about the other into a radical welcome of the other.

There is also an ecclesial dimension in the parable of the sheep and the goats. The text mentions several disadvantaged groups of people—the hungry, the sick, the imprisoned, and the stranger—but reserves special welcome and hospitality for strangers. Whereas Jesus's audience are asked to feed the hungry, take care of the sick, and visit the poor, they are specifically asked to invite the strangers in. The Greek word *suneygagete*, which is used to encourage hospitality to strangers and is at the root of the English word "synagogue," occurs four times in the parable. The use of *suneygagete* (literally "welcome or invite in") in this context has ecclesial dimensions and suggests that when someone welcomes a stranger, they are facilitating the synagogue. The use of *suneygagete* with reference to strangers also suggests that welcoming strangers is the responsibility of the synagogue, the community, and central to its identity. Inasmuch as they welcomed strangers, they welcomed Christ among them.

As Luis N. Rivera-Pagán puts it, "this sacramental presence of Christ becomes, for the first generations of Christian communities, the cornerstone of hospitality, philoxenia, toward those needy people who do not have a place to rest" (Chapter 10). The motif of embrace of the other would have been especially relevant to Matthew's community as it faced the dilemma of whether to welcome outsiders into its fold in the late 80s CE, when the Gospel was written. Such a motif of embrace of the marginalized would have had additional significance for the Matthean community, which itself was at the margins of the Roman Empire in Syrian Antioch. A possible Christological implication of the parable is that, inasmuch as the Matthean community accepts strangers and the marginalized into their community, they accept Jesus, who himself lived at the margins as a stranger. The parable has significant relevance in the current American context, when many Christians who worship Jesus actively support government policies that close doors on refugees, deny basic rights to immigrants, and separate immigrants at the borders (see Kerwin, Chapter 6; Kerwin and Safwat Marzouk, Chapter 15).

VIII Theoxenia and philoxenia

One finds a similar motif of theoxenia in Hebrews 13, where kindness to strangers is equated with hospitality to angels—"Keep on loving one another as brothers and sisters. Do not forget to show hospitality to strangers, for by so doing

176   Raj Nadella

some people have shown hospitality to angels without knowing it" (13:1–2). The author of Hebrews suggests that humans often encounter angels in the form of strangers, and that Christians cannot welcome angels or the divine unless they are able to extend radical hospitality to strangers among them. Matthew 25 and Hebrews 13 provide a theological basis for hospitality to strangers by envisioning philoxenia—love of the stranger—as hospitality to the divine and to angels. But the New Testament concept of philoxenia goes beyond the Greco-Roman concept of theoxenia. Theoxenia emphasizes mutual obligations of the host and the guest, but the New Testament, written in the context of displacement and from the perspectives of communities that were displaced by imperial violence, places much greater emphasis on one's obligations toward strangers.

Another aspect of this call for radical hospitality pertains to the identity of various early Christian communities as displaced people, especially in Asia Minor. Along those lines, texts such as 1 Peter 2:11–13 provide an ecclesial foundation for hospitality to strangers.[23] The terms *paroikoi* and *parepideymoi*, which occur frequently in 1 Peter, were terms used in Roman law and are generally translated as resident aliens, foreigners, and exiles, although it is not entirely clear whether the author used them literally or metaphorically.[24] In the literal sense, the terms might have referred to noncitizens or legal aliens who migrated to Asia Minor from other parts of the Roman Empire, likely from distant colonies, and who did not enjoy the full rights of citizenship. Metaphorically, the terms likely referred to the probability that, despite their legal status as Roman citizens and their access to rights afforded by Roman law, many Christians in the late first century were at the margins of the empire in terms of their worldview, commitments, and, more important, the rights and benefits due them. Many Christians were treated as inferior and viewed with suspicion because of their religious beliefs. In either sense, there is the motif of displacement and living outside the boundaries of the mainstream.

The author of 1 Peter likely employed the terms in both of those senses, as many Christians living in Asia Minor at the time were both legal aliens and living at the margins of the society economically, politically, and morally. Such marginality and displacement became the locus of Christian identity in the early church and provides theological, Christological, and ecclesial bases for their embrace of strangers. Christians in the late first century were aliens, just as Jesus and his family were strangers and displaced people, first in Egypt, then in Galilee. Just as Christians were strangers, so, too, God came in the form of a stranger. Their status as aliens formed their identity and should inform their treatment of others who were displaced. Would they welcome strangers into the community and extend them hospitality?

The status of Christians as citizens who could not fully enjoy the rights granted by Roman law in the first century has parallels in the current debate in the United

---

23 Elliott, *A Home for the Homeless.*
24 Ibid.

States about unequal and unjust application of immigration law based on factors of race, religion, language, and nation of origin. In particular, as a Pew Research Center survey indicates, there is increasing evidence that Muslim immigrants are subjected to discrimination because of their religion.[25] In a direct contradiction of U.S. immigration law, President Trump went on record stating that Muslim immigrants from certain countries were not welcome.[26] Ironically, the United States currently subjects Muslim immigrants and refugees from Latin America to the kind of mistreatment that first-century Christians experienced and justifies such treatment by using the very scriptures written from the perspective of marginalized Christians in the first century. Christians have an obligation to care for displaced communities, both because Christians worship a God who was a stranger, and because they claim these biblical texts about displacement as their own sacred texts.[27]

IX Conclusion

Matthew's Gospel depicts Jesus frequently crossing borders and disrupting them—literally and metaphorically—in order to include outsiders in the new community, with the result that disruption of borders becomes the basis of community formation and an identifying marker. The Gospel often embraces strangers, but also at times views them ambivalently as the other that undermines the welfare of the self. There is, however, a clear movement from embrace to ambivalence to seeing the other as manifestation of the divine akin to the Greco-Roman concept by which God becomes both the stranger and the protector of the stranger. The motif of Jesus and God as the stranger offered Christological and theological bases for hospitality to strangers in early Christian communities and allowed them to move from ambivalence about the other to radical welcome of the other. The same motif can undergird Christian hospitality to strangers in our context.

Texts such as Matthew 25 and Hebrews 13 provide a theological basis for hospitality to strangers by envisioning philoxenia—love of strangers—as hospitality to the divine and to angels. Various New Testament texts also provide an ecclesial basis for philoxenia with the recurrent motif of displacement of communities and individuals. Later texts, such as 1 Peter, depict Christians as displaced people, literally and metaphorically. This motif of displacement became an integral aspect of Christian identity in the early church and provided theological and

---

25 David Masci, "Many Americans See Religious Discrimination in U.S.—Especially Against Muslims," *Pew Research Center*, www.pewresearch.org/fact-tank/2019/05/17/many-ameri cans-see-religious-discrimination-in-u-s-especially-against-muslims/.

26 Amy Davidson Sorkin, "Trump's Travel Ban 'Drips with Intolerance' on Its Way to the Supreme Court," *The New Yorker*, May 26, 2017, www.newyorker.com/news/ amy-davidson/trumps-travel-ban-drips-with-intolerance-on-its-way-to-the-supreme-court.

27 Kristin E. Heyer helpfully explicates Christian social responsibility in the context of migration elsewhere in this volume (Chapter 13).

ecclesial bases for embrace of strangers and displaced communities. These texts offer theological, Christological, and ecclesial bases for attenuating contemporary Christian theologies that explicitly or tacitly endorse mistreatment of foreigners. These texts forcefully challenge use of terms such as "illegal" that have become part of the legal lexicon (see Daniel Kanstroom, Chapter 1), and they can serve as an antidote to misuse of biblical texts to justify xenophobia.

Suggested Reading

Agosto, Efrain, and Jacqueline M. Hidalgo, eds. *Latinxs, the Bible, and Migration.* Basingstoke: Palgrave Macmillan, 2018.

Beck, Richard. *Stranger God: Meeting Jesus in Disguise.* Minneapolis: Fortress, 2017.

Carroll R., M. Daniel. *Christians at the Border: Immigration, the Church, and the Bible.* 2nd ed. Grand Rapids, MI: Brazos Press, 2013.

Cuéllar, Gregory. *Resacralizing the Other at the US-Mexico Border: A Borderland Hermeneutic.* New York: Routledge, 2020.

Dube, Musa W. *Postcolonial Feminist Interpretation of the Bible.* St. Louis, MO: Chalice, 2000.

Myers, Ched, and Matthew Colwell. *Our God Is Undocumented: Biblical Faith and Immigrant Justice.* Maryknoll, NY: Orbis Books, 2012.

10 Toward a theology of migration

Luis N. Rivera-Pagán

I Introduction: a homeless migrant Aramean

The Bible's first confession of faith begins with a story of pilgrimage and migration: "A wandering Aramean was my ancestor; he went down into Egypt and lived there as an alien" (Deuteronomy 26:5).[1] We might ask, did that wandering Aramean and his children have the proper documents to reside in Egypt? Were they maybe "illegal aliens"? Did he and his children have the proper Egyptian social security credentials? Did they speak the Egyptian language properly?

We know at least that he and his children were strangers in the midst of a powerful empire, and that as such they were both exploited and feared. This is the fate of many immigrants. In their reduced circumstances they are usually compelled to perform the least prestigious and most strenuous kinds of menial work. Yet, at the same time, they awaken the schizophrenic paranoia typical of empires, powerful and yet fearful of the stranger, of the "other," especially if that stranger resides within its frontiers and becomes populous. More than half a century ago, Franz Fanon brilliantly described the peculiar gaze of so many white French people at the growing presence of Black Africans and Caribbeans in their national midst.[2] Scorn and fear are entwined in that stare.

The biblical creedal story continues: "When the Egyptians treated us harshly and afflicted us, by imposing hard labor on us, we cried to the Lord, God of our ancestors; the Lord heard our voice and saw our affliction, our toil and our oppression" (26:6–7). So important was this story of migration, slavery, and liberation for the biblical people of Israel that it became the core of an annual liturgy of remembrance and gratitude. This quoted statement of faith was to be solemnly recited every year in the thanksgiving liturgy of the harvest festival. It reenacted the wounded memory of the afflictions and humiliations suffered by an immigrant people, strangers in the midst of an empire—the recollection of their hard and arduous labor, of the contempt and disdain that are so frequently the fate of the stranger and the foreigner who possess a different skin pigmentation,

---

1 All biblical quotations are from the New Revised Standard Version.
2 Frantz Fanon, *Peau Noir, Masques Blancs* (Paris: Éditions du Seuil, 1952).

180 *Luis N. Rivera-Pagán*

language, religion, or culture. But it was also the memory of the events of liberation when God heard the dolorous cries of the suffering immigrants and the remembrance of another kind of migration, in search of a land where they might live in freedom, peace, and righteousness, a land they might call theirs.

We might ask: Who today might be the wandering Arameans and what nation might represent Egypt these days, a strong but fearful empire?

II Dilemmas and challenges of migration

The United States has witnessed a significant increase in its Latino/Hispanic population in the past 40 years. In 1975, little more than 11 million Hispanics made up just over 5 percent of U.S. inhabitants. Today they number approximately 58 million, around 16 percent of the nation, its largest minority group. Recent projections estimate that by 2050, the Latino/Hispanic share of the U.S. population might be between 26 and 32 percent. This demographic growth has become the subject of a complex political and social debate because it highlights sensitive and crucial issues, like national identity and compliance with the law. It also threatens to unleash a new phase in the sad and long history of American racism and xenophobia.[3] Possibly a quarter of the Hispanic/Latino adults are unauthorized immigrants. For a society that prides itself on its law-and-order tradition, this development represents a serious breach of its juridical structure.

There are signs of an increasingly hostile reaction to what the Mexican American writer Richard Rodríguez has termed "the browning of America."[4] One can clearly recognize this mindset in the frequent use of the derogatory term "illegal alien." As if the illegality would define not a specific delinquency, but the entire being of the migrant. We all know the dire and sinister connotations that "alien" has in popular American culture, thanks in part to the sequence of four *Alien* films (1979, 1986, 1992, and 1997) with Sigourney Weaver fighting back atrocious creatures.[5]

Let me briefly mention some key elements of this emerging xenophobia:

1   The spread of fear regarding the so-called broken borders, the possible proliferation of Third World epidemic diseases, and the alleged increase of criminal activities by undocumented immigrants.[6] A shadowy sinister specter is

---

3 Pyong Gap Min, ed., *Encyclopedia of Racism in the United States*, 3 vols. (Westport, CT: Greenwood Press, 2005). A classic text on American nativism is John Higham, *Strangers in the Land: Patterns of American Nativism, 1860–1925* (New York: Atheneum, 1968). Donald M. Kerwin (Chapter 6) explores the role of nativism in contemporary immigrant integration elsewhere in this volume.
4 Richard Rodríguez, *Brown: The Last Discovery of America* (New York: Viking, 2002).
5 Robert W. Heimburger, *God and the Illegal Alien: United States Immigration Law and a Theology of Politics* (New York: Cambridge University Press, 2018), 36: "Today the term 'alien' conjures up extraterrestrial life forms, perhaps threatening or monstrous."
6 David Leonhardt, "Truth, Fiction, and Lou Dobbs," *The New York Times*, May 30, 2007, C1.

Toward a theology of migration 181

created in the minds of the public: the image of the intruder and threatening other.[7]

2   The xenophobic stance intensifies the post-9/11 attitudes of fear regarding the strangers, those people who are here but who do not seem to belong here. Surveillance of immigration is now located under the Department of Homeland Security. This administrative merger links two basically unrelated problems: threat of terrorist activities and unauthorized migration.

3   U.S. racism and xenophobia have traditionally had different targets—on one hand, racism targeted people with African ancestry (whether slaves or free citizens), marked by their dark skin pigmentation; on the other hand, xenophobia targeted foreign-born immigrants, distinguished by their particular language, religiosity, and collective memory. In the case of Latin American immigrants and other immigrants of color, both nefarious prejudices converge and coalesce.[8]

4   There has been a significant increase of anti-immigrant groups. According to a report by the Southern Poverty Law Center, " 'nativist extremist groups'— organizations that go beyond mere advocacy of restrictive immigration policy and actually confront or harass suspected immigrants—jumped from 173 groups in 2008 to 309 in 2009. Virtually all of these vigilante groups have appeared since the spring of 2005."[9]

5   Proposals coming from the White House, Congress, states, and counties have tended to be excessively punitive. Some examples include expansion and militarization of the wall along the Mexican border, which leads to harder and deadlier crossings (compare this with Ephesians 2:14, "Christ . . . has broken down the dividing wall"); draconian enforcement priorities prescribing mandatory detention and deportation of noncitizens, even for alleged minor violations of law;[10] and legislation and regulations to curtail access to public services (health, education, police protection, legal services, drivers' licenses) by undocumented migrants (see also Donald M. Kerwin, Chapter 6; Bill Ong Hing, Chapter 3).

---

7   See Patrick J. Buchanan's book with the inflammatory title *State of Emergency: The Third World Invasion and Conquest of America* (New York: Thomas Dunne Books/St. Martin's Press, 2008).

8   George M. Fredrickson, *Diverse Nations: Explorations in the History of Racial & Ethnic Pluralism* (Boulder: Paradigm Publishers, 2006). This convergence can also be observed in the 1882 Chinese Exclusion Act, which is, in many ways, the foundation of modern U.S. immigration law. Stuart Creighton Miller, *The Unwelcome Immigrant: The American Image of the Chinese, 1775–1882* (Berkeley: University of California Press, 1969). Daniel Kanstroom explores the role of exclusion in immigration law in more detail elsewhere in this volume (Chapter 1).

9   Mark Potok, "Rage in the Right," *Intelligence Report*, Southern Poverty Law Center, Spring 2010, no. 137, at www.splcenter.org/get-informed/intelligence-report/browse-all-issues/2010/spring/rage-on-the-right.

10 Daniel Kanstroom, *Deportation Nation: Outsiders in American History* (Cambridge, MA: Harvard University Press, 2007).

182 *Luis N. Rivera-Pagán*

The xenophobia and scapegoating of the "stranger in our midst" has resulted in the chaotic condition that now plagues the immigration system in the United States, judicially, politically, and socially. All recent attempts to enact comprehensive immigration reform have foundered thanks to the resistance of influential sectors that have been able to effectively propagate fear of the alien.[11] This is not, of course, unique to the United States. Such fear of the alien has been mobilized around the world, resulting in similar and distinct forms exclusion and suffering for immigrant communities.

III From a clash of civilizations to a clash of cultures

In this social context tending toward xenophobia and racism, the late Professor Samuel P. Huntington wrote some important texts about what he perceived as a Hispanic/Latino threat to the cultural and political integrity of the United States. Huntington was chair of the Harvard Academy for International and Area Studies and cofounder of the journal *Foreign Policy*. He was also the intellectual father of the "clash of civilizations" theory.[12]

In 2004, Huntington published an extended article in *Foreign Policy* titled "The Hispanic Challenge,"[13] followed by a lengthy book, *Who Are We? The Challenges to America's National Identity*.[14] The former prophet of an unavoidable civilizational abyss and conflict between the West and the Rest (specially the Islamic nations) became the proclaiming apostle of an emerging nefarious cultural conflict inside the United States. Immersed in a dangerous clash of civilizations *ad extra*, this messenger of doom prognosticated that the United States was also entering into a grievous clash of cultures *ad intra*.

American national identity seems a very complex issue, for it involves an extremely intricate and highly diverse history. But Huntington has, surprisingly, a simple answer: the United States is mainly identified by its "Anglo-Protestant culture" and not only by its liberal republican democratic political creed (see also Kerwin, Chapter 6). The United States has been, according to this historical reconstruction, a nation of settlers rather than immigrants. The first British pioneers transported not only their bodies but also their fundamental cultural and religious viewpoints, what Huntington designates as Anglo-Protestant culture. In the formation of this collective identity, Christian devotion—the Congregational pilgrims, the Protestantism of dissent, the Evangelical Awakenings—has

---

11 Matthew Soerens and Jenny Hwang provide a succinct and precise summary of several failed attempts to enact a comprehensive legislative and juridical immigration reform in their book *Welcoming the Stranger: Justice, Compassion & Truth in the Immigration Debate* (Downers Grove, IL: IVP Books, 2009), 138–58.
12 Samuel P. Huntington, "The Clash of Civilizations?" *Foreign Affairs* 72, no. 3 (1993): 22–49; *The Clash of Civilizations and the Remaking of World Order* (New York: Simon & Schuster, 1996).
13 *Foreign Policy* (March/April 2004): 30–45.
14 New York: Simon & Schuster, 2004.

Toward a theology of migration 183

been meaningful and crucial. This national identity has also been forged by a long history of wars against a succession of enemies (from Native Americans to Islamic jihadists). There is a certain romantic nostalgia in Huntington's thesis, an emphasis on the foundations of American culture and identity, in their continuities rather than their evolutions and transformations.

But the main objective of Huntington is to underline the uncertainties of present trends regarding his nation's collective self-understanding. After the dissolution of the Soviet threat, he perceived a significant neglect of the American national identity. National identity seems to require the image of a dangerous adversary, what he terms the "perfect enemy." The prevailing trend is supposedly one of a notable decline and loss of intensity and salience of U.S. awareness of national identity and loyalty.

Then, supposedly, emerges the sinister challenge of the Latin American migratory invasion. It is not similar to previous migratory waves. Its contiguity, intensity, lack of education, territorial memory, preservation of language, retention of homeland culture, national allegiance, and citizenship, its distance from Anglo-Protestant culture, its alleged absence of a Puritan work ethic, make it unique and unprecedented. This immigration constitutes, according to Huntington, "a major potential threat to the cultural and possibly political integrity of the United States."[15] He has discovered and named America's newest "perfect enemy"—the Latin American immigrant!

Huntington's discomfiture is intense regarding the encroachment of Spanish in American public life. He calls attention to the fact that now, in some states, more children are ominously christened José than Michael. This increasing public bilingualism threatens to fragment U.S. linguistic integrity. Linguistic bifurcation becomes a veritable menacing Godzilla. He neglects altogether the economic causes for the Latin American migration, including U.S. intervention in Latin America, as well as its financial and social benefits both for the sending nations (remittances)[16] and the receiving nations (lower wages for manual jobs).[17] He does not seem to have any concern regarding the process whereby immigrants become new *douloi* and *μέτοικοι*, helots at the margins of society, in a kind of social apartheid, cleaning stores, cooking meals, doing dishes, cutting grass, picking tomatoes and oranges, painting buildings, washing cars, staying out of the way.

---

15 Huntington, "The Hispanic Challenge," 33; see also Huntington, *Who Are We?* 243.

16 Dilip Ratha, "Dollars Without Borders: Can the Global Flow of Remittances Survive the Crisis?" *Foreign Affairs* (October 16, 2009), www.foreignaffairs.com/articles/65448/dilip-ratha/dollars-without-borders: "[R]emittances are proving to be one of the more resilient pieces of the global economy in the downturn, and will likely play a large role in the economic development and recovery of many poor countries."

17 This is a serious flaw in many ethnocentric critiques of immigration issues, according to Francisco Javier Blázquez Ruiz, "Derechos humanos, inmigración, integración," in José A. Zamora (coord.), *Ciudadanía, multiculturalidad e inmigración* (Navarra: Editorial Verbo Divino, 2003), 86, 93.

184   *Luis N. Rivera-Pagán*

Obfuscated by Huntington are the consequences of the present trend among metropolitan Third World diasporas toward holding dual citizenship. An increasing number of Latin American nations now recognize and promote double citizenship, a process that leads to multiple national and cultural loyalties and to what Huntington classifies, with a disdainful and pejorative tone, "ampersand peoples." Dual citizenship, he rightly recognizes, leads to dual national loyalties and identities. Huntington perceives this trend toward dual citizenship and national fidelity as a violation and disruption of the Oath of Allegiance and the Pledge of Allegiance, essential components of the secular liturgy in the acquisition of U.S. citizenship.[18]

He seems to suggest stricter policies regarding illegal migration, stronger measures to enforce cultural assimilation of legal immigrants, and the rejection of dual citizenship. This perspective not only would be utterly archaic but also might become the theoretical ground for a new wave of xenophobic white nativism.[19] The train has already left that outdated station. What is now required is a wider acceptance and enjoyment of multiple identities and loyalties and, if religious compassion truly matters, a deeper concern regarding the burdens and woes of displaced peoples. The time has come to prevail over the phobia of diversity and to appreciate and enjoy the dignity of difference.[20] For, as Dale Irvin has asserted, "the actual world that we are living in . . . is one of transnational migrations, hyphenated and hybrid identities, cultural conjunctions and disjunctions."[21]

IV Migration and xenophobia

Migration and xenophobia are serious social quandaries. But they also convey urgent challenges to the ethical sensitivity of religious people and persons of good will. The first step in solving these quandaries is to perceive this issue from the perspective of the immigrants, to pay cordial (that is, deep from our hearts) attention to their stories of suffering, hope, courage, resistance, ingenuity, and, as so frequently happens in border zones such as wilderness areas of the American Southwest, death.[22] Many unauthorized migrants have become *nobodies*, in the apt title of John Bowe's book; *disposable people*, in Kevin Bales's poignant

---

18 Rose Cuison Villazor, however, argues for an alternative view on the connection between citizenship and allegiance (Chapter 7).

19 A substantially more nuanced and intellectually complex analysis of the different aspects of immigration in the United States is provided by Alejandro Portes and Rubén G. Rumbaut, *Immigrant America: A Portrait*, 3rd ed. (Berkeley: University of California Press, 2006).

20 Jonathan Sacks, *The Dignity of Difference: How to Avoid the Clash of Civilizations* (London: Continuum, 2003).

21 Dale Irvin, "The Church, the Urban and the Global: Mission in an Age of Global Cities," *International Bulletin of Missionary Research* 33, no. 4 (October 2009): 177–82, at 181.

22 See the poignant article by Jeremy Harding, "The Deaths Map," *London Review of Books* 33, no. 20 (2011): 7–13.

Toward a theology of migration 185

phrase; or, as Zygmunt Bauman poignantly reminds us, *wasted lives*.[23] They are the Empire's new μέτοικοι, *douloi*, modern servants. Their dire existential situation cannot be grasped without taking into consideration the upsurge in global inequalities in these times of unregulated international financial hegemony (see Enid Trucios-Haynes, Chapter 2; Gemma Tulud Cruz and Trucios-Haynes, Chapter 16).

For many human beings, the excruciating alternative is between misery in their Third World homeland and marginalization in the rich West/North, both fateful destinies intimately linked together.[24] According to Michael Dillon, "the global capitalism of states and the environmental degradation of many populous regions of the planet have made many millions of people radically endangered strangers in their own homes as well as criminalized or anathemized strangers in the places to which they have been forced to flee."[25] The situation has been painfully aggravated, with tens of thousands of children and teenagers fleeing poverty and violence from El Salvador, Honduras, Guatemala, or Mexico, daring to survive the gangs of human traffickers, the so-called coyotes, to face—at the end of that arduous and dangerous pilgrimage—detention, contempt, and deportation in the southern frontier of the United States. Their dreadful situation has truly become a humanitarian crisis of epic dimensions (see also Michele R. Pistone, Chapter 4; Bill Ong Hing and Raj Nadella, Chapter 17).[26]

Will the Latino/Hispanics, during these early decades of the twenty-first century, become the new national scapegoats? Do they truly represent "a major potential threat to the cultural and political integrity of the United States"? This is a vital dilemma that the United States has up to now been unable to face and solve, as well as a dilemma that presents itself, along varying demographic lines, in most immigrant-receiving countries in the world. We are not called, here and

23 John Bowe, *Nobodies: Modern American Slave Labor and the Dark Side of the New Global Economy* (New York: Random House, 2007); Kevin Bales, *Disposable People: New Slavery in the Global Economy* (Berkeley: University of California Press, 2004); Zygmunt Bauman, *Wasted Lives: Modernity and Its Outcasts* (Cambridge: Polity, 2004).

24 Branko Milanovic, "Global Inequality and the Global Inequality Extraction Ratio: The Story of the Past Two Centuries" (The World Bank, Development Research Group, Poverty and Inequality Group, September 2009); Peter Stalker, *Workers Without Frontiers: The Impact of Globalization on International Migration* (Geneva: International Labor Organization, 2000).

25 Michael Dillon, "Sovereignty and Governmentality: From the Problematics of the 'New World Order' to the Ethical Problematic of the World Order," *Alternatives: Social Transformations and Humane Governance* 20, no. 3 (Spring 1995): 323–68 at 357.

26 See Elizabeth Kennedy, *No Childhood Here: Why Central American Children Are Leaving Their Homes, American Immigration Council,* July 2014, www.americanimmigrationcouncil. org/research/no-childhood-here-why-central-american-children-are-fleeing-their-homes; *Mission to Central America: The Flight of Unaccompanied Children to the United States,* Report of the Committee on Migration of the United States Conference of Catholic Bishops, November 2013, www.usccb.org/about/migration-policy/upload/Mission-To-Central-America-FINAL-2.pdf.

186 *Luis N. Rivera-Pagán*

now, to solve it. But allow me, from my perspective as a Hispanic and Latin American Christian theologian, to offer some critical observations that might illuminate our way in this bewildering labyrinth.

V Xenophilia: toward a biblical theology of migration

I began this chapter with the annual creedal and liturgical memory of a time when the people of Israel were aliens in the midst of an empire, a vulnerable community, socially exploited and culturally scorned. It was the worst of times. It became also the best of times: the time of liberation and redemption from servitude. That memory shaped the sensitivity of the Hebrew nation regarding the strangers, the aliens, within Israel. Their vulnerability was a reminder of the Israelites' own past helplessness as immigrants in Egypt, but it was also an ethical challenge to care for the foreigners inside Israel.[27]

Caring for the stranger as well as the orphan and widow became a key element of the Hebrew Bible. Again and again, the Torah—the law of justice and righteous established in the covenant between Yahweh and Israel—reminds Israel that "you were aliens in the land of Egypt" and therefore "shall not oppress the alien" (Exodus 23:9; Leviticus 19:33–34). The Torah proclaims that "the Lord your God . . . loves the strangers," and therefore "you shall also love the stranger" (Deuteronomy 10:17–19). Moses intones the trilogy of orphans, widows, and strangers as privileged recipients of solidarity and compassion when he says, "Cursed be anyone who deprives the alien, the orphan, and the widow of justice" (Deuteronomy 27:19). The prophets constantly chastise the ruling elites of Israel and Judah for their social injustice and oppression of vulnerable people. After condemning in harshest terms the apathy and inertia of temple religiosity in Jerusalem, Jeremiah, in the name of God, commands the alternative: "Thus says the Lord: Act with justice and righteousness. . . . And do no wrong or violence to the alien, the orphan, and the widow" (Jeremiah 7:6). He goes on to warn: "Thus says the Lord: . . . If you do not heed these words, I swear by myself, says the Lord, that this house shall become a desolation" (Jeremiah 22:3, 5). The prophet paid a costly price for those daring admonitions.

The divine command to care for the stranger was the matrix of an ethics of hospitality. As evidence of his righteousness, Job affirms that "the stranger has not lodged in the street" for he always "opened the doors of my house" to board the foreigner (Job 31:32). The violation of the divinely sanctioned code of hospitality led to the destruction of Sodom (Genesis 19:1–25).[28] The perennial temptation is xenophobia. Against it, the divine command, enshrined in the Torah, is

---

27 Cf. José E. Ramírez Kidd, *Alterity and Identity in Israel: The "ger" in the Old Testament* (Berlin: De Gruyter, 1999).

28 Sodom's transgression of the hospitality code was part of a culture of corruption and oppression, according to Ezekiel 16:49—"This was the guilt of your sister Sodom: she and her daughters had pride, excess of food, and prosperous ease, but did not aid the poor and needy." The homophobic construal of Sodom's sinfulness, which led to the term "sodomy,"

Toward a theology of migration 187

xenophilia—love for those whom we may find difficult to love: strangers, aliens, foreign sojourners.[29]

The command to love the sojourners and foreigners in the land of Israel emerges from two foundations. One has already been mentioned—the Israelites had been resident foreigners in another land; they should, therefore, be sensitive to the complex existential stress of communities living in the midst of a nation whose dominant inhabitants speak a different language, venerate dissimilar deities, share distinct traditions, and commemorate different historical events. Love and respect toward the stranger and the foreigner are thus, in these biblical texts, construed as an essential dimension of Israel's national identity. This attitude belongs to the essence and nature of the people of God.

A second source for the command of care toward the immigrant is that such care corresponds to God's way of being and acting in history: "The Lord watches over the strangers" (Psalm 146:9[a]).[30] God takes sides in history, favoring the most vulnerable: "I will be swift to bear witness . . . against those who oppress the hired workers in their wages, the widow, and the orphan, against those who thrust aside the alien, and do not fear me, says the Lord of hosts" (Malachi 3:5). Solidarity with the marginalized and excluded corresponds to God's being and acting in history.

How comforting would it be to stop right here, with these fine biblical texts of xenophilia, of love for the stranger. But the Bible happens to be a disconcerting book. It contains a disturbing multiplicity of voices, a perplexing polyphony that frequently complicates our theological hermeneutics. Regarding many key ethical dilemmas, we often find in the Bible not only different but also conflictive, even contradictory perspectives. Too frequently we jump from our contemporary labyrinths into a dark and sinister scriptural maze.

In the Hebrew Bible we also discover statements with a distinct and distasteful flavor of nationalist xenophobia (see also Safwat Marzouk, Chapter 8). Leviticus 25 is usually read as the classic text for the liberation of the Israelites who have fallen into indebted servitude. Indeed, it is that, as its famed tenth verse so eloquently manifests: "Proclaim liberty throughout all the land unto all the inhabitants thereof."[31] But it also contains a nefarious distinction:

> As for the male and female slaves whom you may have, it is from the nations around you that you may acquire male and female slaves. You may also

---

is a later (mis)interpretation. Cf. Mark D. Jordan, *The Invention of Sodomy in Christian Theology* (Chicago: The University of Chicago Press, 1997).

29 José Cervantes Gabarrón, "El inmigrante en las tradiciones bíblicas," in Zamora, *Ciudadanía, multiculturalidad e inmigración*, 262.

30 This pericope deserves to be quoted in its entirety: "The Lord sets the prisoners free; the Lord opens the eyes of the blind. The Lord lifts up those who are bowed down; the Lord loves the righteous. The Lord watches over the strangers; he upholds the orphan and the widow, but the way of the wicked he brings to ruin" (Psalm 146:8–9).

31 This text is inscribed in Philadelphia's Liberty Bell, a venerated U.S. icon.

188 *Luis N. Rivera-Pagán*

> acquire them from among the aliens residing with you, and from their families . . . and they may be your property. . . . These you may treat as slaves.
>
> (Leviticus 25:44–46)

And what about the terrifying fate imposed on the foreign wives (and their children) in the epilogues of Ezra and Nehemiah? They are thrown away, exiled, as sources of impurity and contamination of the faith and culture of the people of God.[32] In the process of reconstructing Jerusalem, "Ezra and Nehemiah demonstrate the growing presence of xenophobia," as the Palestinian theologian Naim Ateek has highlighted. He immediately adds: "Ezra and Nehemiah demonstrate the beginning of the establishment of a religious tradition that leaned toward traditionalism, conservatism, exclusivity, and xenophobia."[33] Let us also not forget the atrocious rules of warfare that prescribe forced servitude or annihilation of the peoples encountered along Israel's route to the Promised Land (Deuteronomy 20:10–17). These all are, in Phyllis Trible's apt expression, "texts of terror."[34]

The problem with some scriptural approaches to immigration—such as those of Matthew Soerens and Jenny Hwang in *Welcoming the Stranger* and M. Daniel Carroll R. in *Christians at the Border*[35]—is that their hermeneutical strategy evades completely and intentionally those biblical texts that might have xenophobic connotations. Both books, for example, narrate the postexilic project of rebuilding Jerusalem physically, culturally, and religiously under Nehemiah,[36] but they silence the expulsion of the foreign wives, an important part of that project (Ezra 9–10; Nehemiah 13:23–31). The rejection of foreign wives in Ezra and Nehemiah does not seem too different from contemporary anti-immigrant xenophobia: those foreign wives have a different linguistic, cultural, and religious legacy—"half of their children . . . could not speak the language of Judah, but spoke the language of various peoples. And I contended with them and cursed them and beat some of them and pulled out their hair" (Nehemiah 13:24–25).

---

32 For a sharp critical analysis of the xenophobic and misogynist theology underlining Ezra and Nehemiah, see Elisabeth Cook Steicke, *La mujer como extranjera en Israel: Estudio exegético de Esdras 9–10* (San José, Costa Rica: Editorial SEBILA, 2011). Susanna Snyder contrasts what she terms "the ecology of fear," exemplified by the banishment of foreign wives (and their children) in Ezra and Nehemiah, with an "ecology of faith," as expressed in the stories of Ruth, a "Moabite woman," and the Syro-Phoenician mother who implores Jesus to heal her daughter. Susanna Snyder, *Asylum-Seeking, Migration and Church* (Farnham: Ashgate, 2012), 139–94.

33 Naim Stifan Ateek, *A Palestinian Christian Cry for Reconciliation* (Maryknoll, NY: Orbis Books, 2009), 132.

34 Phyllis Trible, *Texts of Terror: Literary-Feminist Readings of Biblical Narratives* (Philadelphia: Fortress Press, 1984).

35 M. Daniel Carroll R., *Christians at the Border: Immigration, the Church, and the Bible* (Grand Rapids, MI: Baker Books, 2008).

36 Soerens and Hwang, *Welcoming the Stranger*, 85, 98; Carroll R., *Christians at the Border*, 83–84.

Toward a theology of migration   189

This conundrum is a constant, irritating *modus operandi* of the Bible. We go to it searching for simple and clear solutions to our ethical enigmas, but its complexity exacerbates our perplexity. Who said that the Word of God is supposed to make things easier? But have I not forgotten something? What distinguishes the Christian tradition is its Christological emphasis. What, then, about Christ and the stranger?

Clues to Jesus's perspective regarding the socially despised other or stranger can be found in his attitude toward the Samaritans and in his dramatic and surprising eschatological parable on genuine discipleship and fidelity (Matthew 25:31–46). Orthodox Jews despised Samaritans as possible sources of contamination and impurity. Yet Jesus did not have any inhibitions in conversing amiably with a Samaritan woman of doubtful reputation, breaking down the exclusionary barrier between Judeans and Samaritans (John 4:7–30). Of ten lepers once cleansed by Jesus, only one came to express his gratitude and reverence, and the Gospel narrative emphasizes that "he was a Samaritan" (Luke 17:11–19). Finally, in the famous parable to illustrate the meaning of the command "love your neighbor as yourself" (Luke 10:29–37), Jesus contrasts the righteousness and solidarity of a Samaritan with the neglect and indifference of a priest and a Levite. The action of a traditionally despised Samaritan is thus exalted as a paradigm of love and solidarity.

The parable of the judgment of the nations in Matthew 25:31–46 is vintage Jesus. It is a text whose connotations I refuse to reduce to a too common and constraining ecclesiastical confinement. As he loves to do, Jesus disrupts the familiar criteria of ethical value and religious worthiness by distinguishing between human actions that sacramentally bespeak divine love for the powerless and vulnerable from those that do not. Who, according to Jesus, are to be divinely blessed and inherit God's kingdom? Those who, in their actions, care for the hungry, thirsty, naked, sick, and incarcerated—in short, for the marginalized and vulnerable. But also those who welcome the strangers, who provide them with hospitality; those who are able to overcome nationalistic exclusions, racism, and xenophobia and are daring enough to welcome and embrace the immigrant and those in our midst who happen to be different in skin pigmentation, culture, language, and national origins. These belong to the most powerless of the powerless, the poorest of the poor—in Frantz Fanon's famous term, "the wretched of the earth," or, in Jesus's poetic language, "the least of these."[37]

Why are we to care for the least of these? Here comes the shocking statement: because they are, in their powerlessness and vulnerability, the sacramental presence of Christ. "For I was hungry and you gave me food, I was thirsty and you gave me something to drink, I was a stranger [ξένοσ] and you welcomed me, I was naked and you gave me clothing, I was sick and you took care of me"

---

37 See Clark Lyda's and Jesse Lyda's moving documentary, *The Least of These* (2009).

190 *Luis N. Rivera-Pagán*

(Matthew 25:35). The vulnerable human beings turn out to be, in a mysterious way, the sacramental presence of Christ in our midst.[38]

This sacramental presence of Christ becomes, for the first generations of Christian communities, the cornerstone of hospitality, philoxenia, toward those needy people who do not have a place to rest, a virtue insisted upon by the Apostle Paul (Romans 12:13) (see also Raj Nadella, Chapter 9).[39] When, in a powerful and imperial nation like the United States of America, its citizens welcome and embrace the immigrants who reside and work with or without some documents required by the powers that be, those citizens are blessed, for they are welcoming and embracing Jesus Christ.[40]

The discriminatory distinction between citizens and aliens is broken down. The author of the Epistle to the Ephesians is thus able to proclaim to human communities religiously scorned and socially marginalized: "So then you are no longer strangers and aliens, but you are citizens" (Ephesians 2:19). The author of that missive probably had in mind the peculiar vision of postexilic Israel developed by the prophet Ezekiel. Ezekiel emphasizes two differences between the postexilic and the old Israel: the eradication of social injustice and oppression ("And my princes shall no longer oppress my people" [Ezekiel 45:8]) and the elimination of the legal distinctions between citizens and aliens ("You shall allot it [the land] as an inheritance for yourselves and for the aliens who reside among you and have begotten children among you. They shall be to you as citizens of Israel" [Ezekiel 47:21–23]). This was not merely theological speculation. Ezekiel experienced himself the tragedy of being an immigrant. He was one of the countless Israelites who suffered forced deportation after the violent invasion of Israel by the Babylonian military forces. Exile and diaspora were the fate of the people of Yahweh and the source of Israel's sacred scriptures.[41]

VI An ecumenical, international, and intercultural theological perspective

The United States and other Western nations must countervail the xenophobia that contaminates public discourse; they must, instead, embrace an

---

38 Regarding Matthew 25:31–46, I agree with scholars like Cervantes Gabarrón ("El inmigrante en las tradiciones bíblicas," 273–75), who interpret "the least of these" as referring to the poor, dispossessed, marginalized, and oppressed, and I disagree with those who, like M. Daniel Carroll R., limit its denotation to Jesus's disciples (*Christians at the Border*, 122–23).

39 Peter Phan, "Migration in the Patristic Age," in *A Promised Land, A Perilous Journey: Theological Perspectives on Migration*, eds. Daniel G. Groody and Gioacchino Campese (Notre Dame, IN: University of Notre Dame Press, 2008), 35–61.

40 There is an instance in which Jesus seems to exclude or marginalize strangers. When a woman, "Gentile, of Syrophoenician origin," implores him to heal her daughter, Jesus declines. But her obstinate, clever, and hopeful response impresses him and leads him to praise her word of faith (Matthew 15:21–28; Mark 7:24–30).

41 Daniel L. Smith-Christopher, *A Biblical Theology of Exile* (Minneapolis: Fortress Press, 2002); James M. Scott, *Exile: A Conversation with N. T. Wright* (Downers Grove, IL: InterVarsity Press, 2017); René Kruger, *La diáspora: De experiencia traumática a paradigma eclesiológico* (Buenos Aires: ISEDET, 2008).

Toward a theology of migration 191

exclusion-rejecting perspective of the stranger, the alien, the "other,"[42] one which I have named *xenophilia*, a concept that comprises hospitality, love, and care for the stranger. In times of increasing economic and political globalization, when, in a megalopolis like New York, Toronto, London, or Berlin, many different cultures, languages, memories, and legacies converge,[43] xenophilia should be our duty and vocation, as a faith affirmation of both our common humanity and the ethical priority in the eyes of God of those vulnerable beings living in the shadows and margins of our societies.[44]

Many public scholars and leaders have a tendency to weave a discourse that deals with immigrants mainly or even exclusively as workers, whose labor might contribute or not to the economic welfare of citizens. This kind of public discourse tends to objectify and dehumanize the immigrants. Those immigrants are human beings, conceived and designed, according to the Christian tradition, in the image of God. They deserve to be fully recognized as such, both in the letter of the law and in the spirit of social praxis. Whatever the importance of the economic factors for the receiving nation (which usually, as in the case of the United States, happens to be an extremely rich country), from an ethical and theological perspective, the main concern should be the existential well-being of the "least of these," of the most vulnerable members of God's humanity, among them those who sojourn far from their homeland, constantly scrutinized by the demeaning gaze of many receiving communities.

One of the key concerns energizing and spreading the distrust against resident foreigners is fear of their possible impact on national identity, understood as an already historically fixed essence. We have seen that anxiety in Samuel P. Huntington's assessment of the Latin American immigration as "a major potential threat to the cultural integrity of the United States." It is an apprehension that has spread all over the Western world, disseminating hostile attitudes toward already marginalized and disfranchised communities of sojourners and strangers. These are perceived as sources of "cultural contamination." What this view forgets is, first, that national identities are historical constructs diachronically constituted by exchanges with peoples bearing different cultural heritages; and, second, that cultural alterity, the social exchange with the other, can and should be a source of renewal and enrichment of our own distinct national self-awareness. History has shown the sad consequences of xenophobic ethnocentrism; there have been too many intimate links between xenophobia and genocide.[45] As Zygmunt Bauman

---

42 Cf. Miroslav Volf, *Exclusion and Embrace: A Theological Exploration of Identity, Otherness, and Reconciliation* (Nashville: Abingdon Press, 1996).

43 William Schweiker, *Theological Ethics and Global Dynamics in the Time of Many Worlds* (Malden, MA: Blackwell, 2004).

44 "Xenophilia is commanded us: the neighbor whom we are to love is the foreigner whom we encounter on the road." Oliver O'Donovan, *The Desire of the Nations: Rediscovering the Roots of Political Theology* (Cambridge: Cambridge University Press, 1996), 268.

45 Amin Maalouf, *In the Name of Identity: Violence and the Need to Belong* (New York: Arcade Publishing, 2000).

192   Luis N. Rivera-Pagán

has so aptly written, "Great crimes often start from great ideas. . . . Among this class of ideas, pride of place belongs to the vision of purity."[46]

The United States tends to play the role of the Lone Ranger. Yet migration and xenophobia are international problems, affecting most of the world community, and have thus to be understood and faced from a worldwide context.[47] The deportation of Roma people (Gypsies) in France and other European nations is an unfortunate sign of the times. Roma communities are expelled from nations where they are objects of scorn, contempt, and fear to other nations where they have traditionally been mistreated, disdained, and marginalized. They are perennial national scapegoats, whose unfortunate fate has for too long been overlooked.[48] It would also serve to compare the American situation with that of several European nations, where the difficult and sometimes tense coexistence of citizens and immigrants resembles the historically complex conflicts between the Cross and the Crescent, for many of the foreigners happen to be Muslims, venerators of Allah, and thus subject to insidious kinds of xenophobia and discrimination.[49]

Migration is an international problem, a salient dimension of modern globalization.[50] Globalization implies not only the transfer of financial resources, products, and trade but also the worldwide relocation of peoples, a transnationalization of labor, of human beings who take the difficult and frequently painful decision to leave their kin and kith searching for a better future. According to some scholars, we are in the midst of an "age of migration."[51] Borders have become bridges, not just barriers (see Silas W. Allard, Chapter 5). For, as Edward Said has written in the context of another very complex issue, "in time, who cannot suppose that the borders themselves will mean far less than the human contact taking place

46 Zygmunt Bauman, *Postmodernity and Its Discontents* (Cambridge, UK: Polity Press, 1997), 5.
47 Malise Ruthven, "What Happened to the Arab Spring?" *The New York Review of Books* 61, no. 12 (July 10, 2014): 74: "Of Qatar's population of 2.1 million, 85 percent are listed as 'foreign residents.' Many of these are construction workers from South Asia who work under poor conditions and suffer high casualty rates."
48 Cf. European Commission, "Roma in Europe: The Implementation of European Union Instruments and Policies for Roma Inclusion (Progress Report 2008–2010)," Brussels, April 7, 2010, SEC (2010), 400 final.
49 Giovanni Sartori, *Pluralismo, multiculturalismo e estranei: saggio sulla società multietnica* (Milan: Rizzoli, 2000). Sartori perceives Muslim immigration as irreconcilable with, and thus nefarious for, Western democratic pluralism. His thesis is a sophisticated reconfiguration of the multisecular adversary confrontation between Christian/Western (supposedly open, secular, and liberal) and Islamic/Eastern (allegedly closed, dogmatic, and authoritarian) cultures, a new reenactment of what Edward Said famously named "Orientalism."
50 A task to which not enough attention has been devoted is the advocacy for the signature and ratification by the wealthy and powerful nations of the 1990 International Convention on the Protection of the Rights of All Migrant Workers and Members of Their Families, 2220 U.N.T.S. 3, which entered into force on July 1, 2003.
51 Stephen Castles and Mark J. Miller, *The Age of Migration: International Population Movements in the Modern World*, 4th ed. (New York: Guilford Press, 2009).

Toward a theology of migration 193

between people for whom differences animate more exchange rather than more hostility?"[52]

The intensification of global inequalities has made the issue of labor migration crucial.[53] It is a situation that requires rigorous analysis from: (1) a worldwide ecumenical horizon; (2) a deep understanding of the tensions and misunderstandings arising from the proximity of peoples with different traditions and cultural memories; (3) an ethical perspective that privileges the plight and afflictions of the most vulnerable, as "submerged and silenced voices of strangers need to be uncovered";[54] and (4) for the Christian communities and churches, a solid theological matrix ecumenically conceived and designed.[55]

We must also keep in mind another crucial factor: streams of migration are diversifying and strengthening Christianity in the Western and Northern Hemispheres. According to Brian Stanley, professor of world Christianity at the University of Edinburgh, thanks to massive migrations, "by the year 2012, it is estimated that within the Catholic archdiocese of Los Angeles alone, the Eucharist was being celebrated in forty-two different languages." He adds:

> the great migration movements . . . both diversified and even strengthened the Christian presence in northern-hemisphere societies. . . . Migration thus brought to Europe and North America not simply marked interreligious plurality but also greatly enhanced Christian denominational and cultural diversity, with a new infusion of spiritual vitality.[56]

The churches and Christian communities, therefore, need to address this issue theologically from an international, ecumenical, and intercultural perspective.[57] The sole or main concern is not and should not be our national society but the entire fractured global order; for as Soerens and Hwang have neatly written:

---

52 Edward W. Said, *The Question of Palestine* (New York: Vintage Books, 1992, orig. 1979), 176.

53 Some scholars, for example, argue that the North American Free Trade Agreement (NAFTA), which came into force on January 1, 1994, created havoc in several segments of the Mexican economy and deprived of their livelihoods approximately 2.5 million small farmers and other workers dependent on the agricultural sector. The alternative for many of them was the stark choice between clandestine and dangerous drug trafficking or paying the "coyotes" for the also clandestine and dangerous trek to the north. Ben Ehrenreich, "A Lucrative War," *The New York Review of Books* 32, no. 20 (2010): 15–18.

54 Snyder, *Asylum-Seeking, Migration and Church*, 31.

55 Gemma Tulud Cruz offers another perspective on the ecumenical, theological response to migration elsewhere in this volume (Chapter 11).

56 Brian Stanley, *Christianity in the Twentieth Century: A World History* (Princeton, NJ: Princeton University Press, 2018), 340, 356.

57 Raúl Fornet-Betancourt, ed., *Migration and Interculturality: Theological and Philosophical Challenges* (Aachen: Missionswissenschaftliches Institut Missio e.V., 2004); Jorge E. Castillo Guerra, "A Theology of Migration: Toward an Intercultural Methodology," in Groody and Campese, *A Promised Land, A Perilous Journey*, 243–70.

194   *Luis N. Rivera-Pagán*

"Ultimately, the church must be a place of reconciliation in a broken world."[58] In an age where globalization prevails, there are social issues, migration one of them, whose transnational complexities call for an international ecumenical dialogue and debate. As Susanna Snyder also has aptly written, "a transnational issue requires transnational responses and transnational, global networks such as churches could therefore be key international players."[59] One goal of that worldwide discursive process is the disruption of the increasing tendency of developed and wealthy countries to emphasize the protection of civil rights, understood exclusively as the rights of *citizens*, vis-à-vis the diminishment of the recognition of the human rights of resident noncitizens.[60]

Suggested Reading

Bales, Kevin. *Disposable People: New Slavery in the Global Economy*. Berkeley: University of California Press, 2004.

Fornet-Betancourt, Raúl, ed. *Migration and Interculturality: Theological and Philosophical Challenges*. Aachen, Germany: Missionswissenschaftliches Institut Missio e.V., 2004.

Groody, Daniel G., and Gioacchino Campese, eds. *A Promised Land, A Perilous Journey: Theological Perspectives on Migration*. Notre Dame, IN: University of Notre Dame Press, 2008.

Heimburger, Robert W. *God and the Illegal Alien: United States Immigration Law and a Theology of Politics*. New York: Cambridge University Press, 2018.

Hing, Bill Ong. *American Presidents, Deportations and Human Rights Violation: From Carter to Trump*. Cambridge: Cambridge University Press, 2019.

Snyer, Susanna. *Asylum-Seeking, Migration and Church*. Farnham, United Kingdom: Ashgate, 2012.

58 Soerens and Hwang, *Welcoming the Stranger*, 174.
59 Snyder, *Asylum-Seeking, Migration and Church*, 205.
60 Fernando Oliván, *El extranjero y su sombra. Crítica del nacionalismo desde el derecho de extranjería* (Madrid: San Pablo, 1998).

11 When the poor knock on our door

A theological response to unwanted migration

Gemma Tulud Cruz

I The humanitarian question of unwanted migration: introduction

The twenty-first century has been called the "age of migration,"[1] essentially because there are more people on the move in the world today than ever before. To be sure, a great number of people who move today are forced to do so by a variety of factors. A comparison of recent figures reveals that the movement of these vulnerable peoples is not easing. The Millennium Development Goals Report 2015 estimated that every day, 42,000 persons, on average, were forcibly displaced and compelled to seek protection due to conflicts.[2] The UNHCR Global Trends 2019 Report, meanwhile, indicates that 1 percent of the world's population—or 1 in 97 people—is now forcibly displaced.[3]

The UN points out that the most prevalent root of migration is underlying disparity in access to safety and livelihood opportunities. One could see the persistence of this "push" factor for migration within the above-mentioned Millennium Development Goals Report, which indicates that 836 million people live in extreme poverty, big gaps exist between the poorest and richest households, water scarcity affects 40 percent of people in the world, and, most worrying of all, conflict remains the biggest threat to human development. For many people suffering from calamities caused by natural disasters and their fellow human beings, migration is the best, if not the only, way out of such poverty and death-dealing conditions.[4] Unfortunately, some transit and destination countries are making it

---

1 Stephen Castles, Hein de Haas, and Mark Miller, *The Age of Migration: International Population Movements in the Modern World*, 5th ed. (New York: Guilford Press, 2013) provides descriptions and comparative analyses of major migration regions in the North and South.
2 United Nations, *The Millennium Development Goals Report 2015* (New York: United Nations, 2015), 7.
3 UNHCR, *Global Trends: Forced Displacement in 2019* (New York: United Nations, 2019), 8.
4 Mary DeLorey shows how there is real obligation to protect persons fleeing from the mortal risks of extreme poverty, economic conditions that generate and drive conflict, and environmental conditions. DeLorey, "Economic and Environmental Displacement: Implications for Durable Solutions," in *Driven from Home: Protecting the Rights of Forced Migrants*, ed. David Hollenbach (Washington, DC: Georgetown University Press, 2010), 231–48.

196 *Gemma Tulud Cruz*

increasingly difficult, if not impossible, to cross borders precisely for those who need to move or are desperate to move.

These people on the move are labeled and treated as "undesirable aliens"—potential burdens on society, threats to cultural identity, and dangers to national security. These undesirable migrants are then forced to take clandestine and dangerous journeys, either on their own or with the help of unscrupulous human smugglers. Making matters worse, the challenges for undesirable migrants occur not only at the border of their country of destination or settlement. Problems also occur in the way they are perceived, treated, and received in transit countries. In the words of a migrant:

> I have stowed away in baggage compartments of buses and almost suffocated in a boxcar; I almost froze to death in the mountains and baked to death in the deserts; I have gone without food and water for days, and nearly died on various occasions. As difficult as these are, these are not the hardest parts of being a migrant. The worst is when people treat you like you are a dog, like you are the lowest form of life on earth.[5]

As the next section elaborates, these migrants are subjected to various indignities that pose questions about what it means to be human and Christian in the context of migration today. Pope Francis's speech to the U.S. Congress in 2015, during the migrant crisis in Europe, draws attention to the problems and possibilities for Christians and calls for a more humane reception of people on the move. This perspective is particularly apt toward forced migrants, whose poverty and vulnerability are often exacerbated by the migration process. The pope pointed out that "we must not be taken aback by their numbers, but rather view them as persons, seeing their faces and listening to their stories, trying to respond as best we can to their situation" in a "humane, just, and fraternal" way and not giving in to the common temptation nowadays "to discard whatever proves troublesome."[6]

This chapter sketches the contours of a framework for a Christian theological response to the treatment of vulnerable migrants, specifically in light of the contemporary legal regime of state-ordered border controls. More specifically, it proposes the tripartite framework of "one bread, one body, one people" as a Christian theological response to the migration of undesirable migrants. It contends that the Christian anthropological conviction regarding our shared humanity and interdependence as God's people and as the Body of Christ, based on the

---

5 As quoted in Daniel Groody, "Passing Over: Migration as Conversion," *International Review of Mission* 104, no. 1 (2015): 46–60, at 49. For a thorough discussion of the challenges migrants face in destination countries see the discussion by Donald M. Kerwin elsewhere in this volume (Chapter 6).

6 "Pope Francis urges Congress to treat immigrants in 'humane and just' way," *The Guardian*, www.theguardian.com/world/2015/sep/24/pope-francis-congress-speech-immigration-climate-change-abortion.

When the poor knock on our door 197

Christian belief in the inalienable and equal dignity of persons, is integral to a transformative Christian response to the phenomenon of migration.

This chapter is an exercise in what Elaine Graham calls "praxis theology,"[7] or what Stephen Bevans considers the "praxis model" of doing theology.[8] Praxis theology has two main characteristics: (1) it prioritizes experience and practice over tradition as a starting point; and (2) its goal is transforming, liberating action.[9] This model of doing theology stems from the recognition that God manifests God's presence in the fabric of history. It is about "discerning the meaning and contributing to the course of social change"; hence, "it takes its inspiration from present realities and future possibilities"[10] and affirms that talk about God cannot take place independent of a commitment to a struggle for human emancipation.[11] Thus, as a first step, this chapter describes the 2015 migrant crisis in Europe, particularly the key events and responses, as the context for the ensuing theological reflections.

II The 2015 migrant crisis in Europe: a snapshot of key events and responses

For weeks in September 2015, gripping images and videos of large numbers of unauthorized migrants from all walks of life and ages and from various countries,[12] traveling by boat or on foot across European borders, captured the attention of people worldwide. By mid-December a million migrants had crossed Europe's borders, and in the course of their journey, more than 3,000 had died or gone missing at sea.[13] The world's attention was drawn to the situation not just by the sheer number of people, the tragic deaths, and the sad stories, but also by the treatment the migrants received from Europeans and their leaders. As various governments were caught off guard by the number of unauthorized migrants crossing their borders, they put in place policies and measures that oscillated from welcome and accommodation to containment and exclusion.

---

7 Elaine Graham, *Transforming Practice: Pastoral Theology in an Age of Uncertainty* (New York: Mowbray, 1996), 7.
8 This way of doing theology is usually identified with liberation theology but has also come to be used in the discipline of practical theology.
9 Elaine Graham, et al., *Theological Reflection: Methods* (London: SCM, 2005), 170.
10 Stephen Bevans, *Models of Contextual Theology*, rev. ed. (New York: Orbis, 2004), 70.
11 Graham, et al., *Theological Reflection*, 170.
12 More than 80 percent of those who reached Europe by boat in 2015 were people fleeing from the conflicts in Syria, Iraq, and Afghanistan. Poverty, human rights abuses, and deteriorating security account for the key reasons for the other migrants who came from various parts of Africa and the Middle East. See "Why Is EU Struggling with Migrants and Asylum," *BBC News*, www.bbc.com/news/world-europe-24583286.
13 "Migrant Crisis: One Million Enter Europe in 2015," *BBC News*, www.bbc.com/news/world-europe-35158769. The estimate does not include those who crossed a border undetected.

198   *Gemma Tulud Cruz*

Indeed, several forms of discrimination, at best, and rejection, at worst, were displayed by a number of European countries. Hungary, for example, received much criticism for stopping train service to the Austrian border at one point, building a fence that closed off its borders, then enacting new border laws that entailed its military patrolling the borders and granted the authority to jail anyone entering the country illegally. Television viewers watched migrants being shunted from border to border as Hungarian entry points were sealed off, and video footage showed food being thrown to people in a Hungarian transit camp. At one point, Germany, the most welcoming of the European countries, increased ID checks at the border and temporarily stopped rail service from Austria. Austria, another country that generally welcomes migrants, also sent 2,200 soldiers to its border to help overwhelmed police.[14] At an EU leaders' emergency summit in September 2015, interior ministers voted to resettle about 120,000 migrants across Europe with binding quotas; however, Romania, the Czech Republic, Slovakia, and Hungary opposed the scheme. Hungary and Slovakia even took legal action at the European Court of Justice to challenge the plan. In Finland, about 40 to 50 protesters—some with flaming torches—confronted up to 50 migrants, and some even threw stones at Red Cross workers.[15] An equally troubling scene captured on video showed a Macedonian police officer beating unarmed and defenseless migrants with a baton.[16] Such responses to the crisis also laid bare other problematic ways in which undesirable migrants could be perceived and received. Slovakia indicated it wanted to take Christian migrants.[17] Similarly, a Hungarian Catholic bishop expressed: "They're not refugees. This is an invasion. . . . They come here with cries of Allahu Akbar. They want to take over."[18]

14 Holly Yan and Tim Hume, "Refugee Crisis: Chaos as Hungary Blocks Migrants at Serbian Border," *CNN*, http://edition.cnn.com/2015/09/15/world/europe-migrant-crisis/index.html.
15 "Migrant Crisis: Finland Protesters Throw Fireworks at Buses," *BBC News*, www.bbc.com/news/world-europe-34358410.
16 See James Reynolds, '"Police Brutality Allegations' at Macedonia Migrant Crossing," *BBC News*, www.bbc.com/news/av/world-europe-35379733/police-brutality-allegations-at-macedonia-migrant-border-crossing.
17 "Christian Refugees from Middle East Should Be Given Priority Says Eric Abetz," *The Guardian*, www.theguardian.com/australia-news/2015/sep/08/christian-refugees-from-middle-east-should-be-given-priority-says-eric-abetz. An Australian archbishop expressed a similar sentiment. See Tess Livingstone, '"Fleeing Christians Should Go to Front of Queue': Archbishop," *The Australian*, September 8, 2015, www.theaustralian.com.au/subscribe/news/1/?sourceCode=TAWEB_WRE170_a_GGL&dest=https%3A%2F%2Fwww.theaustralian.com.au%2Fnation%2Fpolitics%2Ffleeing-christians-should-go-to-front-of-queue-arc hbishop%2Fnews-story%2Fd1733d39bb7fa86fdf9e29345dfb7cc5&memtype=anonymous &mode=premium.
18 "Hungarian Bishop Says Pope Is Wrong About Refugees," *Washington Post*, September 7, 2015, www.washingtonpost.com/world/hungarian-bishop-says-pope-is-wrong-about-refu gees/2015/09/07/fcba72e6-558a-11e5-9f54-1ea23f6e02f3_story.html.

In the midst of all of these inhospitable, sometimes downright hostile responses were numerous expressions of support as well as acts of welcome, empathy, and generosity from the European and global community, including some government leaders. In many bus and train terminals, as well as makeshift and official transit camps, migrants were greeted with essential provisions for the journey, such as water, food, and clothing. Pope Francis himself called on religious communities, monasteries, shrines, and parishes all across Europe—including the Vatican's two small parishes—to "express the concreteness of the Gospel and welcome a family of refugees."[19] Thousands of Europeans also joined promigrant rallies, while Australians held vigils across the country in support of refugees.[20] At the time of the crisis, the United States also increased by 30,000 the number of worldwide refugees it would take each year, while Australia offered to take 12,000 refugees from Syria.[21] There were also positive responses among European leaders. The Finnish prime minister offered his own second home for migrants.[22] Britain, France, and Germany pledged to take in thousands of migrants, while smaller or less prosperous European nations, such as Poland and Romania, offered to take a much smaller number.[23] Germans, particularly through the leadership of Angela Merkel, showed considerable welcome for and solidarity with migrants. Images of Germans with welcome signs as migrants disembarked at railway stations were beamed on television screens across the world. *The Economist* listed some of the other notable responses of European Christians: German churches offered asylum to migrants (including Muslims) by letting them live on church property where the police could not enter and deport them; Secours Catholique provided charitable services to people camped out in the port of Calais; the Catholic Agency for Overseas Development (CAFOD) lobbied the British government to take in more refugees from Syria and elsewhere; the Orthodox archbishop of Athens called for his compatriots to be generous to all newcomers; and a German bishop

19 Joshua McElwee, "Francis Calls on Every Parish across Europe to House Refugee Families," *National Catholic Reporter*, September 6, 2015, http://ncronline.org/news/vatican/francis-calls-every-parish-across-europe-house-refugee-families. There are around 50,000 to 120,000 Catholic parishes in Europe alone.
20 "Light the Dark Vigils Held across Australia to Support Syrian Asylum Seekers," *ABC News*, September 7, 2015, www.abc.net.au/news/2015-09-07/light-the-dark-candlelight-vigils-held-for-asylum-seekers/6756390.
21 Hillary Whiteman, "Australia to Take in 12,000 Refugees, Join Coalition Airstrike in Syria," *CNN*, September 9, 2015, http://edition.cnn.com/2015/09/09/asia/australia-refugees-syria-airstrikes/.
22 "Finland's PM Offers His Home to Migrants amid Crisis," *CNBC*, September 5, 2015, www.cnbc.com/2015/09/05/finland-pm-offers-kempele-home-to-migrants-amid-europe-wide-crisis.html.
23 Romania agreed to take a maximum of 1,785 asylum seekers, significantly fewer than the 6,351 it was expected to shelter under the EU plan. "European Migrant Crisis: Britain and France Join Germany in Vowing to Accept Tens of Thousands of Asylum Seekers," *ABC News*, September 7, 2015, www.abc.net.au/news/2015-09-07/germany-pledges-6-billion-euros-for-refugees/6756508.

200   *Gemma Tulud Cruz*

silenced a priest for speaking at a rally by Pegida, on grounds that xenophobia is not compatible with the Christian message of love, kindness, and inclusion.[24]

The response of European governments to the aftermath and, to a certain extent, continuation of this crisis is ongoing, albeit with even more hostile tone for some. The UK's far-right party, UKIP, campaigned successfully for Brexit on an anti-immigration platform, even igniting controversy with its campaign poster showing a stream of nonwhite migrants walking through the European countryside under the slogan "Breaking Point."[25] Meanwhile, Matteo Salvini, the Catholic leader of Italy's Northern League political party and advocate of a new brand of Italian nationalism, instituted various anti-immigration policies during his brief tenure (June 2018 to August 2019) as interior minister. These included the closure of seaports to rescue vessels carrying migrants, the seizure of NGO boats, and fines for ships that bring asylum seekers to Italy without permission. A more controversial piece of legislation, known as the Salvini Bill, received international attention for a series of hardline measures that include abolishing humanitarian protection, a form of protection for those not eligible for refugee status but who, for various reasons, cannot be sent home. The bill also suspends the refugee application process for those considered "socially dangerous" (that is, those who have been convicted of a crime), expels "fake refugees," and stops giving permits to "crafty migrants not escaping war."[26]

Salvini's party shares anti-immigrant sentiments with Greece's ultraright Golden Dawn political party, whose rhetoric ranges from Christian nativism to neopaganism. Like Italy's Northern League, Greece's Golden Dawn claims to have secret supporters in the ranks of the church.[27] This hardline and hostile reaction to undesirable migrants was also reflected in Denmark's plan to move "unwanted" migrants to a remote, uninhabited island formerly used for seriously ill and contagious animals. According to the spokesperson for the Danish People's Party (DPP), a populist right-wing party with anti-immigration policies, "Our hope . . . is that people outside Denmark will understand that Denmark is not a very attractive place to seek asylum, if you are of refugee background, mean to cause harm, or incite crime."[28] Finally, the continuing opposition among some European states was evidenced in the voting on the formal ratification of the 2018 UN Global Compact for Migration: three states (Poland, Czech Republic,

---

24 Pegida is an anti-Muslim movement in Germany. See Erasmus, "Diverse, Desperate Migrants Have Divided European Christians," *The Economist*, September 6 2015, www.economist.com/blogs/erasmus/2015/09/migrants-christianity-and-europe.

25 "Nigel Farage's 'Vile'Anti-Immigration Poster Criticized," *The Irish Times*, June 19, 2016, www.irishtimes.com/news/world/uk/nigel-farage-s-vile-anti-immigration-poster-cri ticised-1.2690915.

26 See Cristina Abellan Matamoros, "Italy's New Security Decree Clamps Down on Immigration," *Euronews*, November 30, 2018, www.euronews.com/2018/11/29/italy-s-new-security-decree-clamps-down-on-immigration.

27 Erasmus, "Diverse, Desperate Migrants Have Divided European Christians."

28 Susanne Gargiulo and Jack Guy, "Denmark Plans to Isolate 'Unwanted' Migrants on Remote Island," *CNN*, December 5, 2018, https://edition.cnn.com/2018/12/05/europe/den mark-immigrant-island-scli-intl/index.html.

When the poor knock on our door 201

and Hungary) voted against it, five abstained (Austria, Bulgaria, Italy, Latvia, and Romania), and one (Slovakia) did not vote at all. In a way, the two graffiti I saw on a trip to Greece in December 2018 reflect the unsettling rhetoric used for these inhospitable and exclusionary policies and actions: "No Borders, No Nations" and "No Border, No Order."

III One bread, one body, one people: a Christian theological response

The two diametrically opposing ways in which Christians, particularly in Europe, have responded to the migrant crisis cannot be denied. On one hand, European churches and religious charities have played a prominent role in succoring migrants and campaigning for them to be treated decently. On the other, politicians on the nationalist right are beating the drum of Christian nativism and have redoubled their warnings about the threat to the long-established religious culture of Europe (see also Donald M. Kerwin, Chapter 6).[29] In itself, making sharp distinctions between citizens and noncitizens by granting the former freedom to come and go and denying this freedom to the latter effectively negates their fundamental equality as persons.[30] Such an approach and the increasing tendency to limit hospitality and protection are directly challenged by the human rights standards of both global humanitarianism and Christian theology and ethics.

What might a Christian response to these challenges look like? What resources and insights could we draw from the Christian tradition "to keep this broad agenda of concerns from seeming so huge that it paralyses action?"[31] In what follows, I sketch, in broad strokes, a tripartite framework for a Christian theological response to the movement and treatment of undesirable migrants. The three parts of the framework—one bread, one body, and one people—come from the refrain of a Christian hymn titled "We Are One."[32]

A One bread

Undesirable migrants are not the migrants who move in search of a *better* life; they move in search of *bare* life.[33] Their migration is a search for bread literally

---

29 Erasmus, "Diverse, Desperate Migrants Have Divided European Christians."
30 David Hollenbach, "Introduction," in Hollenbach, *Driven from Home*, 6. For more detailed discussions of the role of sovereignty, borders, and citizenship in the exclusion of migrants, see the chapters in this volume by Ulrich Schmiedel (Chapter 12), Daniel Kanstroom (Chapter 1), Silas W. Allard (Chapter 5), and Rose Cuison Villazor (Chapter 7).
31 Hollenbach, "Introduction," 9. For a substantive moral treatment of this question, see Christopher Llanos, "Refugees or Economic Migrants: Catholic Thought on the Moral Roots of the Distinction," in Hollenbach, *Driven from Home*, 249–69.
32 Lyrics and music by Carol Banawa. See www.smule.com/song/carol-banawa-we-are-one-karaoke-lyrics/144322362_596840/arrangement.
33 Saskia Sassen, "The Making of Migrations," in *Living With(out) Borders: Catholic Theological Ethics on the Migrations of Peoples*, eds. Agnes Brazal and Maria Teresa Dávila (Maryknoll, NY: Orbis, 2016), 11.

202   Gemma Tulud Cruz

and figuratively.[34] Thus, while those who move may not always and necessarily be the poorest of the poor, economically or politically, one could agree with Peruvian liberation theologian Gustavo Gutierrez's reference to migrants as icons of the poor in the modern globalized world.[35] We live in one common home; we share in only one planet with limited and dwindling resources. The compelling physical, material, or economic motivation for people who move, in a world that is turning more and more into one global village, reinforces the Christian idea that we share, or ought to share, one bread.

The idea of having one bread and sharing it becomes clearer when one takes into account the Christian teaching on the common good or the universal destination of the earth's goods. In Christian thought, the legitimate right of individuals and groups to seek their own advantage is balanced against the common welfare of all. In fact, within the right to private property lies a primordial sense that private property is under a social mortgage: "All that God gives is a product of grace. We cannot earn what God gives us; we cannot deserve it; what God gives is given out of the goodness of God's heart; what God gives us is not pay, but a gift; not a reward, but a product of love."[36]

The movement of millions of poor and vulnerable peoples shows that the search for a bare life knows no borders. Thus, migration serves as a challenge to share resources, and, in the process, share the bread. Bread is a global secular symbol for survival. It is, however, also very much a religious symbol. The Christian tradition itself is rich with images of bread and sharing the bread as a symbol not just of physical and spiritual nourishment but also of discipleship. The story of Israel receiving manna or "bread from heaven" in the wilderness (Exodus 16:1–21) is not only a potent reminder that we all need nourishment. The story is also a stark reminder of how we must all equally share in God's providence.[37] In the Acts of the Apostles, Luke refers several times to the practice of breaking bread in the Christian community in Jerusalem and mentions how "they went as a body to the Temple every day but met in their houses for the breaking of bread; they shared their food gladly and generously" (Acts 2:46). Paul's rebuke of the Corinthian community for their abuse of the communal meal also highlights the social and spiritual significance of equal access to and sharing of the bread. The wealthy members arrived at the communal meal before the others.

---

34 Daniel Groody, "Fruit of the Vine and Work of Human Hands: Immigration and the Eucharist," in *A Promised Land, A Perilous Journey: Theological Perspectives on Migration*, eds. Daniel Groody and Gioacchino Campese (Notre Dame, IN: University of Notre Dame Press, 2008), 305.

35 Gustavo Gutierrez, "Poverty, Migration, and the Option for the Poor," in Groody and Campese, *A Promised Land, A Perilous Journey*, 76–86.

36 Jose David Rodriguez, "The Parable of the Affirmative Action Employer," *Apuntes* 15, no. 5 (1988): 418–24, at 424. Kristin E. Heyer elaborates on the role and importance of the universal destination of created goods in recontextualizing migration (Chapter 13).

37 In the story, all were instructed to gather only what they needed for the day. Those who hoarded did not benefit from their extra picking, as the manna became rotten and smelly, hence inedible. Such an arrangement ensures that no one goes hungry, no one has an undue advantage by having extra food, and everyone is able to partake of the food.

By the time the working-class members arrived, the food and drink had been consumed (1 Corinthians 11:17–22).

Jesus also shines a light on the idea of sharing in one bread, not only by referring to himself as the "bread of life" (John 6:35) but also by putting a spotlight on eating in his parables—for example, the Parable of the Great Banquet (Luke 14:15–24)—and in the miracle stories—for example, the Feeding of the Five Thousand (Matthew 14:13–21). Even his last act before he was arrested was to break bread with his disciples at the Last Supper. Today, this last act is commemorated by all Christians worldwide through the sacrament of the Eucharist, which is considered the source and summit of Christian worship. The centrality of the communal act of receiving Jesus through the bread (and wine) in the Eucharistic celebration is a reminder of the significance of breaking and sharing bread together as a key experience of, as well as witness to, the Christian faith.

B *One body*

The migration of poor and vulnerable people highlights the Christian teaching of not only sharing (in) one bread but also being one body. As 1 Corinthians 10:17 says, "because there is one bread, we who are many are one body." 1 Corinthians 12:12 affirms that "the body is a unit, though it is made up of many parts; and though all its parts are many, they form one body." From a Christian perspective, every part or member of the body is important, and special attention or consideration is given to the weaker members, because if one is ill, all the other parts or members suffer. In the same manner, undesirable migrants are part of this one body, and they—as icons of the poor in the modern globalized world—deserve special attention. 1 Corinthians 12:13–26 provides such an eloquent description of the significance of seeing and caring for one another as one body that I quote most of the text here:

> For we were all baptized by one Spirit into one body—whether Jews or Greeks, slave or free—and we were all given the one Spirit to drink. Now the body is not made up of one part but of many. If the foot should say, "Because I am not a hand, I do not belong to the body," it would not for that reason cease to be part of the body. . . . But in fact God has arranged the parts in the body, every one of them, just as he wanted them to be. If they were all one part, where would the body be? As it is, there are many parts, but one body. The eye cannot say to the hand, "I don't need you!" And the head cannot say to the feet, "I don't need you!" On the contrary, those parts of the body that seem to be weaker are indispensable, and the parts that we think are less honorable we treat with special honor. . . . [T]here should be no division in the body, but that its parts should have equal concern for each other. If one part suffers, every part suffers with it; if one part is honored, every part rejoices with it.[38]

---

38 This idea is echoed in Romans 12:4–5: "Just as each of us has one body with many members, and these members do not all have the same function, so in Christ we who are many form

204   *Gemma Tulud Cruz*

Treating poor and vulnerable migrants as unwanted indicates that the body—that is, God's people—is not well. Just as "the eye cannot say to the hand, 'I don't need you!' and the head cannot say to the feet, 'I don't need you!'" so we cannot turn our back on undesirable migrants as members of the body of Christ. Neither should these migrants, as the members of the body who need support, be underestimated, for they are vital to the overall health of the body. Migrants not only are sites of need; they also come bearing gifts. Though coming from a more vulnerable position, they are important to the cultural as well as economic health and vitality of destination countries. Not only are they an indispensable part of the functioning of households, businesses, communities, and nation-states worldwide, but their religious faith and practice also provide means and pathways in the building, as well as renewal, of the Churches (especially congregations or parishes) as the body of Christ.

Anselm Min explains what it means to be one body in the context of migration:

> All the central Christian doctrines have to do with the common destiny of all humanity: their common subjection to the sovereignty of the one Creator and the saving providence of the triune God, their fundamental equality as creatures before God, their common redemption through the one mediator, Jesus Christ, their common eschatological call to share in the communion of the triune God as members of the Body of Christ, their social interdependence with one another in sin and grace. . . . The "Body of Christ" is not only a category of ecclesiology but also that of theological anthropology pertaining to all humanity.[39]

Thus, Min says:

> It is fitting to teach the faithful that we are, by virtue of our membership of the Body of Christ, *sons and daughters of the same heavenly Father*, but it is also imperative to teach the corollary, that we are, therefore, *brothers and sisters of one another* in the triune God, and to draw the political conclusion that our global human solidarity in God should determine all our political priorities and concrete choices.[40]

Indeed, perhaps the greatest challenge of being a Christian in the context of undesirable migration is not in the experience of connecting with, but in our

---

one body, and each member belongs to all the others." It is also mentioned or referred to several times in the Bible, for example, Ephesians 1:22–23 and 5:29–30; Colossians 1:18 and 3:15. Raj Nadella provides further discussion of how the New Testament treats the stranger (Chapter 9).

39 Anselm Min, "Migration and Christian Hope," in *Faith on the Move: Towards a Theology of Migration in Asia*, eds. Fabio Baggio and Agnes Brazal (Quezon City, Philippines: Ateneo de Manila University Press, 2008), 190–91.

40 Italics in original. Min, "Migration and Christian Hope," 194–95.

sense of responsibility for, the other, especially the members of the body of Christ who need support. In God's great economy of salvation, there is bread, room, and a place for everyone. Hence, a Christian response to unwanted migration should be rooted in xenophilia, not xenophobia (Luis N. Rivera-Pagán, Chapter 10).[41] Sharing the bread, making room, and providing a place, especially to those in need, is part and parcel of building, becoming, and being one body and one people.

C One people

Flowing from and, at the same time, expanding on the idea of migration as highlighting the Christian belief in one body sharing in one bread is the idea of one people. Contemporary responses to the migration of poor and vulnerable peoples, particularly as reflected in the preceding section, drive home to Christians and all people of goodwill the challenge of being one people. The injustices such migrations lay bare and, at the same time, the intercultural societies and churches they bear help develop a compelling sense of a common humanity with a shared destiny across alienating and separating boundaries. These migrations set the stage and provide resources to more fully respect and recognize our fundamental equality and solidarity as human beings. Unwanted migrations, in other words, provide a way of rediscovering and recovering a sense of universal humanity based on mutual dependence and common destiny as citizens of a single world and children of one God.

From a Christian perspective, we are "one family under God";[42] our neighbor (without any exception) is "another self," and it is our "inescapable duty to make ourselves the neighbor of every individual, without exception, and to take positive steps to help a neighbor whom we encounter, whether that neighbor be an elderly person abandoned by everyone, a foreign worker who suffers the injustice of being despised, a refugee . . . or a starving human being who awakens our conscience."[43] The encyclical *Caritas in Veritate*, issued by Pope Benedict XVI, accentuates the relational and collective dimension of the human quest for well-being. It argues that "the development of peoples depends, above all, on a

---

41 See also Luis N. Rivera-Pagán, "Xenophobia or Xenophilia: Towards a Theology of Migration," *The Ecumenical Review* 64, no. 4 (2012): 575–89.

42 For a more comprehensive treatment of this idea in the context of immigration, see Sister Stephanie Spandl, "One Family under God: A Theological Reflection on Serving Our Immigrant Brothers and Sisters as Christian Social Workers," North American Association of Christians in Social Work (NACSW), Orlando, FL, February 2008, www.nacsw.org/Publi cations/Proceedings2008/SpandlSOne.pdf. See also Grace Yukich, *One Family under God: Immigration Politics and Progressive Religion in America* (New York: Oxford University Press, 2013). Yet, as Bill Ong Hing notes, contemporary immigration policy often seeks to prevent families from reuniting (Chapter 3).

43 Second Vatican Council, *Gaudium et Spes* (Pastoral Constitution on the Church in the Modern World), 27, www.vatican.va/archive/hist_councils/ii_vatican_council/documents/ vat-ii_const_19651207_gaudium-et-spes_en.html.

206 *Gemma Tulud Cruz*

recognition that the human race is a single family working together in true communion, not simply a group of subjects who happen to live side by side" (CV, 53).[44] This point is highly relevant here because one could make a case that the discrimination and exclusion that undesirable migrants experience is rooted in a failure to recognize that migrants are part of the larger human family. The idea of being one people, one human family, is the very same reason why the encyclical insists on international cooperation and the collaborative nature of responses or solutions to problems brought by contemporary migration (CV, 62). The encyclical notes that "the unity of the human family does not submerge the identities of individuals, peoples, and cultures, but makes them more transparent to each other and links them more closely in their legitimate diversity" (CV, 53).

In the Christian tradition, no other image more powerfully drives home the point about relationality and being a family than that of the Trinity.[45] The Trinity is absolute unity, insofar as the three divine Persons are pure relationality. The reciprocal transparency among the divine Persons is total, and the bond among them is complete, since they constitute a unique and absolute unity. Thus, in light of the revealed mystery of the Trinity, true openness means not loss of individual identity but profound interpenetration (CV, 54). This foundational role of unity in Christian life is highlighted in Jesus's prayer at the Last Supper, where he prayed that "all may be one" (John 17:21), and in Paul's exhortation that even in this world, baptized Christians are to live in such a way that "there is no longer Jew or Greek, there is no longer slave or free, there is no longer male or female; for all of you are one in Christ Jesus" (Galatians 3:28).

Theologically, the idea of "one people" also fits well into the mark of the church as catholic. First of all, the true meaning of the catholicity of the church lies in its being an effective sign or sacrament of universal solidarity.[46] Robert Schreiter, for example, argues for catholicity as a framework for addressing migration.[47] In the context of unwanted migration, this is about witnessing to a practical catholicity that gives evidence of the one human family to which we all belong. As Kristin E. Heyer argues, the subversive hospitality invited by a migrant God demands not

---

44 See Benedict XVI, *Caritas in Veritate* (On Integral Human Development in Charity and Truth), http://w2.vatican.va/content/benedict-xvi/en/encyclicals/documents/hf_ben-xvi_enc_20090629_caritas-in-veritate.html (subsequent references are in parentheses).

45 A similar treatment of the Trinitarian dimension of migration is offered by Fabio Baggio, "Diversity in Trinitarian Communion: Pointers Toward a Theology of Migrations," in *Migration in a Global World*, eds. Solange Lefebvre and Luis Carlos Susin, *Concilium* 2008, no. 5 (London: SCM Press, 2008), 74–85.

46 Cunningham and Egan point out that the deepest meaning of catholic spirituality is a discipleship that concerns the universal (catholic) needs of the world, and that our common way of discipleship is best understood as being part of the pilgrim people of God. Lawrence Cunningham and Keith Egan, *Christian Spirituality: Themes from the Tradition* (Mahwah, NJ: Paulist, 1996), 19.

47 Robert Schreiter, "Catholicity as Framework for Addressing Migration," in Lefebvre and Carlos Susin, *Migration in a Global World*, 41–46.

only a reorientation of operative frameworks but also a concrete praxis of kinship with the displaced.[48]

In the context of the divisive dimensions of migration, one could also point to Ephesians 2:19, which reminds us that we "are no longer foreigners and aliens, but fellow citizens with God's people and members of God's household." Min argues that this eschatological reality is the deepest identity of human beings. All other identities based on empirical contingencies, such as nationality, status, class, gender, culture, and religion, are temporal and transient.[49] This teaching about the common origin, dignity, solidarity, and destiny of all human beings has been the most enduring constant of the most orthodox Christian tradition of the last two thousand years, and nothing has been more unchristian than idolatry of class, nation, sect, empire, or gender. It is precisely to this teaching—so central, so enduring, and so essential to the Christian faith—that we are compelled to return by the needs of our globalized world, with all its alienating and degrading contradictions, best exemplified in the figure of poor and vulnerable peoples on the move. Their plight and the responses to the migrant crisis in Europe show how global solidarity may be the most important virtue, individually and collectively, in our time. This is because, ultimately, our eschatological destiny has an incarnational dimension. This incarnational dimension lifts up the imperative to listen and respond to the historically concrete word of God, in this case the experience of undesirable migrants and the need for solidarity with them, without which God would be reduced to silence and irrelevance.

IV Toward transformative action: conclusion

Migration is not just about the experience of moving from place to place; it is also linked to the ability, individually and collectively, to imagine an alternative. This chapter demonstrates that the Christian revelation of the unity and common destiny of the human race presupposes a metaphysical interpretation of the "humanum," in which human dignity, relationality, and solidarity are essential elements.

Unwanted migration presents itself as both a challenge and an opportunity to this Christian anthropological perspective. Realistically speaking, the responsibility for forced migrants, according to U.S. ethicist David Hollenbach, is not simply a free-floating obligation of the whole human race. Hollenbach asserts that responsibility belongs, first and foremost, to the migrant's home state/community, and that if it is unable or unwilling to assume that obligation, the responsibility moves to the international community. He adds that the responsibility will be greater for a country or people whose history and politics have linked it with that of the country generating migrants, especially if the former has gained any form

---

48 See Kristin E. Heyer, "Reframing Displacement and Membership: Ethics of Migration," *Theological Studies* 73, no. 1 (March 2012): 188–206.
49 Min, "Migration and Christian Hope," 191.

of benefit from the latter or has contributed to the causes of the migration[50]—as, for example, the United States did in the Iraq War. At the same time, some forced migrations have deep internal roots and are of such magnitude—for example, the flight generated by the Syrian conflict—that "no country can address the challenges and opportunities . . . on its own."[51] Indeed, the immensely tragic, multifaceted, and complex challenges that characterize forced migrations today bring into sharp focus the need for global solidarity and cooperation or, in the words of Silvano Tomasi, the former permanent observer of the Holy See to the UN in Geneva, global humanitarianism.

On one hand, global humanitarianism is founded on the universal human rights that reach across religious traditions, cultures, and national borders. On the other hand, from the perspective of Catholic social teaching, rights also have an indispensable partner, that is, responsibility, which is often diminished or passed over, if not forgotten, in mainstream rhetoric about unwanted migration. The tripartite framework of one bread, one body, one people is relevant in the sense that it highlights the importance of social responsibility, especially to those in need, by witnessing to solidarity and the common good from a collective or global perspective.

Christianity is not naïve nor indifferent to the real and daunting challenges on the ground for destination countries. It affirms every country's right to sovereignty when it comes to managing its borders. However, it also insists that such sovereignty is not absolute.[52] As Pope Francis contends, the principle of the centrality of the human person "obliges us to always prioritise personal safety over national security."[53] The passionate plea that Italy's former prime minister, Matteo Renzi, made to members of his Christian Democratic Party sums up this higher moral imperative from a Christian perspective: "We need rules, we cannot take in everyone. . . . But nothing will ever stop us trying to save a life whenever possible. This is our challenge."[54]

---

50 Hollenbach, "Introduction," 7. His book *Humanity in Crisis: Ethical and Religious Response to Refugees* (Washington, DC: Georgetown University Press, 2019) sheds further light on this, as he draws on the values that have shaped major humanitarian initiatives over the past century and a half, and the values of religious and ethical traditions, to examine the scope of our responsibilities and practical solutions to the global crises in relation to refugees. Michele R. Pistone provides thorough discussion of the framework for and challenges to international responsibility for refugees elsewhere in this volume (Chapter 4).

51 United Nations, Global Compact for Migration, paragraph 11, https://refugeesmigrants.un.org/sites/default/files/180713_agreed_outcome_global_compact_for_migration.pdf.

52 For additional discussion of the limitations on sovereignty see the chapters in this volume by Schmiedel (Chapter 12) and Allard (Chapter 5).

53 Pope Francis, "Message for the 104th World Day of Migrants and Refugees 2018," www.vatican.va/content/francesco/en/messages/migration/documents/papa-francesco_20170815_world-migrants-day-2018.html.

54 "European Migrant Crisis: Britain and France Join Germany in Vowing to Accept Tens of Thousands of Asylum Seekers," *ABC News*, September 7, 2015, www.abc.net.au/news/2015-09-07/germany-pledges-6-billion-euros-for-refugees/6756508.

When the poor knock on our door 209

It is in living this challenge, which is central to the tripartite framework of one bread, one body, one people, that we understand and witness to what it means to be human and Christian in the context of unwanted migration today. In the face of anti-immigrant sentiments and legislations and the dehumanizing plight of undesirable migrants embodied in the lifeless body of Aylan Kurdi as well as Oscar Alberto Martinez and his 23-month old daughter, Valeria, social responsibility means that the churches need to be a sacrament of (radical) solidarity. They need to speak boldly.[55]

Churches must also go beyond words. They must continue to develop solutions that address immediate needs, such as providing much-needed material and human resources at the border, identifying and declaring certain parishes as sanctuaries, and intensifying the lobbying for more humane immigration reforms.[56] Based on the experience of Europe in 2015 and, to a certain extent, up to the present, the Churches must also summon uncommon courage[57] to compel governments to find long-term, durable, humane solutions and, where necessary, resort to civil disobedience. Italian priests showed how to do this in various ways during the Christmas season in 2018 by calling for, and expressing, conscientious objection to the Salvini Bill. Father Alex Zanotelli launched a change.org petition calling for civil disobedience, such as asking doctors to keep treating migrants, lawyers to challenge the legislation, and citizens to disobey the decree. Father Luca Favarin, meanwhile, posted a Facebook message calling on Christians to boycott the traditional Christmas nativity scene. Favarin argued that it is "hypocritical" to display a nativity scene and also support Salvini, because the message of the Gospel is to welcome the poor, the sick, and strangers. The nativity scene, Favarin points out, is the image of a refugee who seeks shelter and finds it in a stable. Last, but not least, Father Paolo Farinella made headlines for his extraordinary decision to shut his Genoa church over the whole Christmas period as a "conscientious objection" to Salvini.[58] Indeed, radical solidarity with migrants means challenging not just the political and religious authorities but also fellow Christians, especially the silent majority and the vocal minority whose respective sins of omission (the good that they fail to do by their silence and indifference)

---

55 See, for instance, "Editorial: Don't Look Away from the Concentration Camps at the Border," *National Catholic Reporter*, June 19, 2019, www.ncronline.org/news/opinion/editorial-dont-look-away-concentration-camps-border.

56 Dan Morris-Young, "Bay Area Volunteers Head to Border to Learn from, Serve Migrants," *National Catholic Reporter*, June 24, 2019, www.ncronline.org/news/parish/bay-area-volunteers-head-border-learn-serve-migrants. Rose Cuizon Villazor and Ulrich Schmiedel analyze the humanitarian border work of No More Deaths and the possibility of an emergent praxis theology through direct action against state exclusion of and harm to migrants (Chapter 14).

57 See Joan Chittister, *The Time Is Now: A Call to Uncommon Courage* (New York: Convergent Books, 2019), for what is required by uncommon courage.

58 Gianluca Mezzofiore, "Priests Demand 'Civil Disobedience' for Christmas to Protest Anti-Migrant Law," *CNN*, December 18, 2018, https://edition.cnn.com/2018/12/18/europe/priests-civil-disobedience-immigration-intl/index.html.

210 Gemma Tulud Cruz

and commission (the evil that they do by actively supporting anti-immigrant politicians and their inhumane policies) perpetuate dehumanizing treatment of unwanted migrants.

Michael Sean Winters lays out how social responsibility in the form of radical solidarity might look like in the United States, especially for Catholic bishops:

> [Bishops could] go to the site of an ICE raid with a team of lawyers, surrender their passport and ask ICE to apprehend them too. Or if they have a detention center in their diocese, they could lead a group of Catholics in blocking the entrance. . . . [T]he police will remove the protesters and return a bishop but the point will have been made. . . . The bishop could place himself in front of the entrance [of a sanctuary church]. If there is an ICE raid, demand a warrant. If there is a warrant, block the entrance and make them arrest the clergy before they get to the migrants. Retreat houses and seminaries would make excellent sanctuaries, already possessing the capacity to provide shelter and food. Take a special collection at all parishes to provide for these basic necessities. Cling to the oppressed as we cling to the cross: The embrace is one and the same.[59]

As Winters insists these are not normal times. Indeed, the tension between the ideal and the real is an existential reality that confronts the Christian. It is a dynamic tension that should not paralyze but rather encourage the Christian to be courageously persistent in finding ways to respond to the concrete situations that history presents. The world is on the move; "the whole creation has been groaning as in the pains of childbirth right up to the present time" (Romans 8:22). The magnitude of the movement and the collective pain and sorrow, joys and hopes, tragedies and triumphs that accompany it evoke images of a world in childbirth.[60] Juxtaposing grace with sin, in view of the hope and promise of a truly Christian response to the migration of poor and vulnerable peoples, one could posit that migration could very well be not only the source of a renewed Christianity but also the birthplace of a new humanity.[61]

---

59 Michael Sean Winters, "To Defend Immigrants, It's Time for US Bishops to Break the Law," *National Catholic Reporter*, June 21, 2019, www.ncronline.org/news/opinion/distinctly-catholic/defend-immigrants-its-time-us-bishops-break-law.

60 An eloquent representation of this idea in pictures is depicted by internationally renowned photographer Sebastião Salgado in photographs taken over seven years and across more than 35 countries. This 432-page book is a first-of-its kind pictorial survey to extensively chronicle the current global flux of humanity by documenting the epic displacement of the world's people at the close of the twentieth century. See Sebastião Salgado, *Migrations: Humanity in Transition* (New York: Aperture, 2000).

61 Anthony Rogers, FSC, "Towards Globalising Solidarity Through Faith Encounters in Asia," in *The Migrant Family in Asia: Reaching Out and Touching Them*, ed. Anthony Rogers, FSC (Manila: Office for Human Development, 2007), 68–71.

Suggested Reading

Fiddian-Qasmiyeh, Elena, et al., eds. *The Oxford Handbook of Refugee and Forced Migration Studies*. Oxford: Oxford University Press, 2016.

Groody, Daniel, and Gioacchino Campese, eds. *A Promised Land, A Perilous Journey: Theological Perspectives on Migration*. Notre Dame, IN: University of Notre Dame Press, 2008.

Hollenbach, David, ed. *Driven from Home: Protecting the Rights of Forced Migrants*. Washington, DC: Georgetown University Press, 2010.

———. *Humanity in Crisis: Ethical and Religious Response to Refugees*. Washington, DC: Georgetown University Press, 2019.

Mavelli, Luca, and Erin Wilson, eds. *The Refugee Crisis and Religion—Secularism, Security and Hospitality*. Lanham, MD: Rowman and Littlefield, 2016.

Tyler, Imogen. *Stigma: The Machinery of Inequality*. London: Zed Books, 2020.

Yukich, Grace. *One Family Under God: Immigration Politics and Progressive Religion in America*. New York: Oxford University Press, 2013.

12 The theopolitics of the migrant
Toward a coalitional and comparative political theology

Ulrich Schmiedel

I Introduction

Migration is a challenge for democracies. Democracies assume that the citizens who are affected by the law are also its authors and that the citizens who are its authors are also affected by the law. Citizens, then, have clear legal rights and clear legal responsibilities. But what about the migrants who have not acquired citizenship? What are their legal rights? What are their legal responsibilities? *Whose* law applies to them?

Consider the tricky case of three Muslim teenagers in France—Fatima, Leila, and Samira—who were suspended from school for refusing to remove their hijabs. Across Europe, the case that caused what came to be called the "hijab affair" has continued to stir up controversies since the 1980s.[1] These controversies, Seyla Benhabib points out, involve noncitizens affected by laws (namely, laws that ban religious symbols such as the hijab from public places) that they have not authored, and citizens who have authored laws (namely, laws that ban religious symbols such as the hijab from public places) that do not affect them.[2] As French artist and activist Rokhaya Diallo argues in "Hijab: A Very French Obsession," on Al Jazeera:

> Of course, one can legitimately question the . . . patriarchal character of the wearing of the hijab. It is perfectly acceptable to debate the ways in which femininity is expressed; but French hijabi women . . . should be the ones defining the meaning of the hijab in France. However, they are rarely invited to express their opinion.[3]

---

1 Jocelyne Cesari, "*Shari'a* and the future of secular Europe," in *Muslims in the West After 9/11: Religion, Politics and Law*, ed. Jocelyne Cesari (London: Routledge, 2010), 145–75, offers a short overview of the controversies stirred up by the "hijab affair," comparing European and American contexts.
2 Seyla Benhabib, *The Rights of Others: Aliens, Residents and Citizens* (Cambridge: Cambridge University Press, 2004), 183–98.
3 Rokhaya Diallo, "Hijab: A Very French Obsession," *Aljazeera*, www.aljazeera.com/indepth/opinion/hijab-french-obsession-180402135257398.html.

The theopolitics of the migrant 213

Whether it is about migrants, the migrants' children, or the migrants' children's children, the hijab affair exemplifies how migration challenges the very core of the constitution of the law in democracies. Although I cannot cover the "hijab affair" in any depth or detail here, I take it as a point of departure to sketch the contours of political theology in the age of migration.

The constitution of the law is a central concern of political theology. The combination of "political" with "theology" is curious. In the academy, it signifies an increasingly interdisciplinary field of studies concentrating on the intersections of theology with politics.[4] Considering that migration challenges the constitution of the law, it is a core concern for political theologians. Hence, in this chapter, my aim is to confront political theology with the figure of the migrant in order to chart the impact of migration on the constitution of the law. In *The Figure of the Migrant*, Thomas Nail argues that "we need to reinterpret the migrant first and foremost according to its own defining feature: its movement."[5] When "we"— Nail means philosophers, but I see no reason why his "we" could not include political theologians, whether they work in departments of philosophy, theology, or politics—view static political systems from the vantage point of the migrant (rather than the migrant from the vantage point of static political systems), migration comes into view as a "political concept."[6] The figure of the migrant moves insiders to the outside and outsiders to the inside. What happens when the figure of the migrant is introduced into political theology? I argue that the migrant can be characterized as a theopolitical figure that resists the separation of insider and outsider implied in the concept of state sovereignty. Advancing such theopolitical resistance, I advocate for coalitional and comparative political theologies that rattle strong and stable sovereignty. Although my argument remains admittedly abstract, it is intended to offer a theological reflection and a theological rationale for the theopolitics of the migrant that is already practiced where migrants make it onto the beaches and over the borders of Europe.

II The problem of migration

When the Peace of Westphalia ended the wars of religion that had waged across Europe, state sovereignty was established as the cornerstone of both the national

---

4 Overviews are offered from a more philosophical angle by Hent de Vries and Lawrence E. Sullivan, eds., *Political Theologies: Public Religions in a Post-Secular World* (New York: Fordham University Press, 2006) and from a more theological angle by William T. Cavanaugh and Peter Manley Scott, eds., *The Wiley Blackwell Companion to Political Theology* (Chichester: Blackwell, 2019).

5 Thomas Nail, *The Figure of the Migrant* (Stanford, CA: Stanford University Press, 2015), 3. The concept of the figure of the migrant captures both migrants who are and migrants who are not accepted as refugees. Empirically, the distinction between migrants who left their homes involuntarily (and could thus be accepted as refugees) and migrants who left their homes voluntarily (and could thus not be accepted as refugees) is increasingly untenable, because it presumes that one could distinguish between political conditions which do and economic conditions which do not force people to migrate.

6 Nail, *The Figure of the Migrant*, 11.

214   *Ulrich Schmiedel*

and the international order. Each state exerted exclusive and exclusionary authority over its territory. Through the Westphalian order, internal and external politics were strictly separated: subjects belong to "their" state as much as states belong to "their" subjects, so states cannot intervene in each other's affairs. The concept of citizenship as a contract between state and subject is rooted in such exclusive and exclusionary state sovereignty. The border that separates the insider from the outsider is, as Silas W. Allard argues, one of the "significant indicia of a state's jurisdiction" that contribute to the construction of the identity of the nation (Chapter 5). Such jurisdiction characterizes the core of the conception of citizenship in many countries today. "Allegiance" must be to one state only (Rose Cuison Villazor, Chapter 7).

In several field-defining studies, Saskia Sassen has mapped the impact of migration on citizenship in the post-Westphalian order. When migrants arrive in a state, the state becomes responsible for both citizens and noncitizens. Since the Declaration of Human Rights was adopted by the United Nations, all human beings can claim rights, regardless of whether they are citizens or noncitizens: rights are decoupled from states and states are decoupled from rights.[7] But how can state sovereignty be transferred from the Westphalian to the post-Westphalian order? Sassen condenses the changes in the understanding of citizenship, the blurring of the distinctions between citizen and noncitizen, into the concept of "denationalization."[8] Denationalization stresses the transformation of state sovereignty. Under the conditions of migration, sovereignty is still significant for the state, but sovereignty has to shift its shape. The challenge that migration entails for the constitution of the law is a central and critical site for such shapeshifting. Confronted with outsiders on the inside (and insiders on the outside)—which is to say, confronted with migrants—the state is "in search of a normative framework" (Daniel Kanstroom, Chapter 1).

Although its decline has been diagnosed again and again, religion is vital for the reconceptualization of state sovereignty, because it provides such a normative framework. When citizenship has lost its function to distinguish between insiders and outsiders because both citizens and noncitizens can claim rights, religion can step into the breach. It is no accident that the hijab affair accentuates religion: "The hijab does not carry a single meaning that can be used in any given context. . . . But in a country like France, where it is not the norm, the hijab can be a

---

7 Arguably, states have always been responsible for citizens and noncitizens. The existence of slaves is a case in point. The difference between the past and the present is that both citizens and noncitizens can now claim rights regardless of any citizenship status. Hannah Arendt famously formulated the right to have rights with regard to refugees. Arendt, "We Refugees," in *The Jewish Writings*, eds. Jerome Kohn and Ron H. Feldman (New York: Schocken, 1994), 264–74.

8 Saskia Sassen, *Territory—Authority—Rights: From Medieval to Global Assemblages* (Princeton, NJ: Princeton University Press, 2006), 305–9.

The theopolitics of the migrant   215

tool to make the Muslim identity visible."[9] Here, Islam is pitted against the secularized Christian legacy of French laïcité and the secularized Christian legacy of French laïcité is pitted against Islam in the construction of the nation's identity.[10]

According to Wendy Brown, sovereignty becomes explicitly rather than implicitly—"aggressively," as she puts it—*theologized*: sovereignty acquires a "religious aura."[11] "Conflicting sovereign and would-be sovereign powers . . . appear to serve warring godheads."[12] For Brown, the denationalization of state sovereignty demarcates "a potential political-theological crisis."[13] Both Brown and Benhabib stress the significance of political theology for denationalizing discourses.[14] Within the challenge that migration poses to the constitution of the law in democracies, then, political theology becomes a problem: with reference to religion, citizens and noncitizens are kept apart.[15] Under the conditions of the denationalization of the state, Brown concludes, "sovereignty needs God more as its . . . territorial grip falters."[16] Religion is thus construed in a way that justifies the construction of a framework for the law, where the authors are not the affected, and the affected are not the authors. The consequences were captured in the photos of "armed French police confronting a woman on a beach in Nice . . . to remove some of her clothing to make her comply with the 'burkini ban.' "[17] These photos are the epitome of the frenzy of "antiburka" and "antiburkini" discussions fevering across Europe. Although these discussions cannot be reduced to issues of theology, theology is crucial to them.[18]

Overall, Sassen's characterization of the denationalization of citizenship corroborates the significance of religion. Under the conditions of migration, political theology is inextricably interwoven with denationalizing discourses about the state, because religion functions as a marker of identity that separates insiders from outsiders. Yet migration, Sassen suggests, is "a sort of wrench one can throw

---

9   Diallo, "Hijab: A Very French Obsession." See also the account of the history of multiculturalism in France in Rita Chin, *The Crisis of Multiculturalism in Europe: A History* (Princeton, NJ: Princeton University Press, 2019).

10 Seyla Benhabib, "The Return of Political Theology: The Scarf Affair in Comparative Constitutional Perspective," in her *Dignity in Adversity: Human Rights in Troubled Times* (Cambridge: Polity Press, 2014), 166–83.

11 Wendy Brown, *Walled States, Waning Sovereignty* (New York: Zone Books, 2010), 62. See also Wendy Brown, "Subjects of Tolerance: Why We Are Civilized and They Are the Barbarians," in de Vries and Sullivan, *Political Theologies*, 298–317.

12 Brown, *Walled States, Waning Sovereignty*, 63.

13 Ibid., 69.

14 Benhabib, "The Return of Political Theology"; Brown, "Subjects of Tolerance."

15 See the contributions to Ulrich Schmiedel and Graeme Smith, eds., *Religion in the European Refugee Crisis* (New York: Palgrave Macmillan, 2018).

16 Brown, *Walled States, Waning Sovereignty*, 63.

17 Diallo, "Hijab: A Very French Obsession."

18 See Diallo, "Hijab: A Very French Obsession," where she points to the significance of feminism and critiques of feminism for the hijab affair in France. See also Joan Wallach Scott, *The Politics of the Veil* (Princeton, NJ: Princeton University Press, 2007) for a detailed discussion.

216   *Ulrich Schmiedel*

into theories about sovereignty."[19] Building on Sassen, then, my core concern in this chapter is to confront the accounts of sovereignty in political theology with the figure of the migrant. For political theologians, the problem of migration can be either a provocation or a promise—and perhaps it can even be turned from the one into the other.

III   The provocation of migration

Whatever else political theology is, it is contested. Here I concentrate on the decisionist political theology of Schmitt and on the dialectical political theology of the critics of Schmitt. Why Schmitt? The German legal and political theorist Carl Schmitt (1888–1985) was central to the critique of democracy in the Weimar Republic, contested as it was by both the political Right and the political Left. Due to his allegiance to the totalitarian regime under Adolf Hitler, Schmitt rapidly rose in the ranks inside and outside academia. Professor at the University of Berlin, he took up the presidency of the Union of National Socialist Jurists. Dubbed the "crown jurist" of the regime, he offered opinions that justified its internal and external politics. After the liberation of Germany by the Allies, Schmitt spent about a year in internment. He resisted attempts at denazification, which barred him from academic appointments across Germany. Nonetheless, he participated in academic debates through his companions and his correspondence. Whether one agrees or disagrees with him, Schmitt is a classic. He claimed to have coined the curious combination of theology with politics,[20] which makes his political theology a point of departure for scholars past and present. As Jan-Werner Müller argues in *A Dangerous Mind: Carl Schmitt in Post-War European Thought*, "At a time when Left and Right remain confused about their respective identities . . . it is perhaps no accident that Schmitt has also reappeared at the supposed cutting edge of political theory."[21] It is his "double role as a diagnostician and as a danger" that attracts scholarly attention.[22]

According to Müller, Schmitt "had a strong tendency towards constructing myths around his own politics and personality."[23] The reception of Schmitt shows how his "trap . . . sprung shut. The self-mythologization he had put so much effort into paid off after his death. Schmitt's hermetic, self-consciously mythmaking approach led to ever more hermeneutics—the kind of hermeneutics in which the German approach to the history of political thought and theory excels."[24]

---

19 Saskia Sassen, *Losing Control? Sovereignty in an Age of Globalization* (New York: Columbia University Press, 1996), 67.
20 Jan-Werner Müller, *A Dangerous Mind: Carl Schmitt in Post-War European Thought* (New Haven, CT: Yale University Press, 2003), 156.
21 Ibid., 9–10.
22 Ibid., 237.
23 Ibid., 7.
24 Ibid., 203.

The theopolitics of the migrant   217

I aim to avoid Schmitt's trap by taking both the decisionist and the dialectical model of political theology into account, so that the critics can hold the classic in check. To be clear, neither the decisionist model nor the dialectical model of political theology addresses migration; neither Schmitt nor the critics of Schmitt have anything to say about burkas and burkinis. But by charting the key concerns and the key concepts of these models before confronting them with the figure of the migrant, I stress the significance that the decisionist and the dialectical models might have for conceptualizations of political theology under the conditions of migration. If migration is, as Sassen argues, a wrench that can be thrown into the wheels of sovereignty, the figure of the migrant could and should function as a provocation for political theology. The provocation can turn out to be either more destructive or more productive, depending on whether a strict separation of insider and outsider is integral to the concept of sovereignty with which the respective theology works. Tackling the strict insider–outsider separation, then, can come to the fore as *the* task for political theology in the age of migration.[25]

A   Migration in the decisionist model

In *Political Theology: Four Chapters on the Concept of Sovereignty*, published in the 1920s, Schmitt declares: "Sovereign is he who decides on the exception."[26] Schmitt's concentration on the decision is crucial because it positions the sovereign beyond the law. Sovereignty is about the sovereign making the law rather than the law making the sovereign. The sovereign is like God. It is well known that Schmitt argues that "all significant concepts of the modern theory of the state are secularized theological concepts."[27] The concept of God survives secularization as a category for a power which is beyond conditions because it proposes conditions in the first place. Throughout history, theologians have conceived of God as transcendent (and thus outside the world) rather than immanent (and thus inside the world), creator rather than creation. God is the lord of the world. Schmitt's sovereign is similar. He—for Schmitt, the sovereign is a "he" rather than a "she"—is outside rather than inside the law. He makes the law through a decision that "emanates from nothingness."[28] He is the lord of the law. The scriptural "Let there be light: and there was light" equals the Schmittian "Let there be law: and there was law." In their "systematic structure," the sovereign and the sacred are identical.[29]

---

25 For the characteristics of the age of migration, see Stephen Castles, Hein de Haas, and Mark J. Miller, *The Age of Migration: International Population Movements in the Modern World* (New York: Palgrave Macmillan, 2014).
26 Carl Schmitt, *Politische Theologie: Vier Kapitel zur Lehre von der Souveränität* (Berlin: Duncker & Humblot, 2015), 13; Carl Schmitt, *Political Theology: Four Chapters on the Concept of Sovereignty*, trans. G. Schwab (Chicago: The University of Chicago Press, 1985), 5.
27 Schmitt, *Politische Theologie*, 43; Schmitt, *Political Theology*, 36.
28 Schmitt, *Politische Theologie*, 38; Schmitt, *Political Theology*, 32.
29 Schmitt, *Politische Theologie*, 43; Schmitt, *Political Theology*, 36.

218 *Ulrich Schmiedel*

The significance of the sovereign decision is spelled out in the definition of the political. In *The Concept of the Political*, published in the 1930s, Schmitt defines the political via the "distinction between friend and foe."[30] According to Schmitt, this distinction is the "criterion" that allows for the definition of something as political (when it is concerned with distinguishing between friends and foes) or apolitical (when it is not concerned with distinguishing between friends and foes).[31] Schmitt's definition of the political, then, clarifies that the separation of insiders and outsiders is the cornerstone of his political theology. Substantiating the concept of the foe rather than the concept of the friend, Schmitt stresses that the political is about "the other" who "is, in a specially intensive way, existentially something . . . alien, so that in the extreme case conflicts with him are possible."[32] Proposing the distinction between friend and foe as a public rather than a private distinction, undisturbed by the commandment to love your enemy in the Bible, Schmitt points to the example of Islam: "Never in the thousand-year struggle . . . did it occur to a Christian to surrender rather than defend Europe out of love toward the Saracens or Turks."[33] What Schmitt has in mind is "the real possibility of physical killing" in the combat between friend and foe.[34] He concludes: "A world in which the possibility of war is utterly eliminated, a completely pacified globe, would be a world without the distinction of friend and foe and hence a world without politics."[35]

For theology to be political, according to Schmitt, it has to be able to draw the distinction between friend and foe so decidedly that the distinction can cause war. The "litmus test for the political," then, is the intensity of the distinction between insider and outsider: the possibility of mortal combat against the other constitutes the political.[36] Crucially, Schmitt consistently connects the notion of the foe with the notion of the foreign. He contends that the decision about the friend/foe distinction cannot be made from a neutral position.[37] On the contrary, the decision remains the marker and the maker of sovereignty. Schmitt's contemporaries criticized his concept of sovereignty because it is circular: the decision about friend and foe is both the condition and the consequence of what he calls

30 Carl Schmitt, *Der Begriff des Politischen: Text von 1932 mit einem Vorwort und drei Corollarien* (Berlin: Duncker & Humblot, 2015), 25; Carl Schmitt, *The Concept of the Political*, trans. G. Schwab (Chicago: The University of Chicago Press, 1996), 26. The translation of *Freund* and *Feind* is contested. I have decided against the commonly chosen translation with "enemy." Throughout, I translate *Feind* as "foe." See Schmitt, *Der Begriff des Politischen*, 17, 94–102.
31 Schmitt, *Der Begriff des Politischen*, 25; Schmitt, *The Concept of the Political*, 26.
32 Schmitt, *Der Begriff des Politischen*, 26; Schmitt, *The Concept of the Political*, 27.
33 Schmitt, *Der Begriff des Politischen*, 28; Schmitt, *The Concept of the Political*, 29.
34 Schmitt, *Der Begriff des Politischen*, 31; Schmitt, *The Concept of the Political*, 33.
35 Schmitt, *Der Begriff des Politischen*, 33; Schmitt, *The Concept of the Political*, 35.
36 Müller, *A Dangerous Mind*, 33.
37 Schmitt, *Der Begriff des Politischen*, 33; Schmitt, *The Concept of the Political*, 35.

The theopolitics of the migrant   219

the political.[38] His contemporaries' critique returns the political to theology. The sovereign still asserts the sovereign out of nothing.

In *The Nomos of the Earth*, published in 1950, Schmitt returns to his reflections on sovereignty. According to Müller, the study is "the touchstone for all his post-war reflections—not least because it allowed him to shift the level of discussion away from the German past."[39] Schmitt's turn from intrastate to interstate affairs adds the significance of soil to the structural similarity between the sacred and the sovereign. Schmitt explains that *nomos* comes from the Greek νέμειν, meaning both "to partition" and "to pasture," and thus stands for the taking of soil.[40] In *The Nomos of the Earth*, the establishment of the law and the land coincide.[41] Schmitt links *nomos* to "wall" (*Mauer*) because the wall creates the clear inside/outside distinction so central to both sacred and secular containments.[42] While Schmitt's etymology is somewhat strange,[43] his argument is applicable to the European state law that followed from the Peace of Westphalia. Here, sovereignty is achieved through localization and law, through "orientation" (*Ortung*) and "order" (*Ordnung*).[44] Confronting each other on the model of a duel, states that are ordered according to the European state law limit warfare both internally and externally. Although it rests on the distinction between civilized European land, where warfare is limited, and uncivilized un-European land, where warfare is unlimited—thus positioning Europe at the center of the earth—Schmitt praises the limitation as a "humanization of war."[45] However, according to Schmitt, the European state law ceased to exist when the United States entered the stage of world politics toward the end of the nineteenth century. In the world ideology that disconnects the land from the law, the liberalism of the United States has justified interventions across the globe.[46] In spite of all the liberal talk about the avoidance of violence through ethics and economics, the violence of the friend/foe distinction remains in place: the sovereign asserts the sovereign in the end. The political cannot be escaped.

Although Schmitt's decisionism is tamed in as much as sovereignty is tied to soil, the structural similarity between the sacred and the sovereign is still

---

38 See Müller, *A Dangerous Mind*, 33.

39 Ibid., 87.

40 Carl Schmitt, *Der Nomos der Erde im Völkerrecht des ius publicum Europaeum* (Berlin: Duncker & Humblot, 2011), 39; Carl Schmitt, *The Nomos of the Earth in the International Law of the Jus Publicum Europaeum*, trans. G. L. Ulmen (New York: Telos Press, 2003), 70.

41 Schmitt, *Der Nomos der Erde*, 36–47; Schmitt, *The Nomos of the Earth*, 67–78.

42 Schmitt, *Der Nomos der Erde*, 40; Schmitt, *The Nomos of the Earth*, 71.

43 Müller, *A Dangerous Mind*, 88: "Schmitt chose an unorthodox interpretation of the ancient Greek word to avoid what he saw as the positivist connotations of the German word *Gesetz*."

44 Schmitt, *Der Nomos der Erde*, 39; Schmitt, *The Nomos of the Earth*, 70.

45 Schmitt, *Der Nomos der Erde*, 121; Schmitt, *The Nomos of the Earth*, 149. Crucially, this "humanization" rests on the separation of the "civilized world" and the "uncivilized world," which for Schmitt allowed Europeans to take land in Africa and the Americas.

46 Schmitt, *Der Nomos der Erde*, 200–13; Schmitt, *The Nomos of the Earth*, 227–39.

220   Ulrich Schmiedel

significant. Schmitt now reads the scriptural "Let there be light: and there was light" simultaneously as "Let there be law: and there was law" and "Let there be land: and there was land." The disentanglement of the sovereign and the sacred with soil that Schmitt diagnoses in the U.S.-led order that emerged after the war signals the end of political theology. Schmitt rhymes snippily: "verborgen bleibt der liebe gott/die ganze welt wird melting pot."[47] Put more prosaically, when the whole world is turned into a melting pot of cultures and civilizations, God remains hidden.

Overall, the decision about the friend/foe distinction is at the core of Schmitt's concept of sovereignty. The strong and stable sovereign draws the distinction, thus constituting the law of the land and the land of the law. The figure of the migrant, then, is indeed a wrench in the wheels of political theology. Schmitt's political theology cannot cope with migratory movements that blur the boundaries between insider and outsider. Schmitt's conceptualization of the political requires that identity and alterity remain static. For Schmitt, anything that blurs the boundaries between identity and alterity, inside and outside—such as migratory movements—has to be evaluated as depoliticizing. The figure of the migrant, then, allows for the identification of the strict and stable separation of insider and outsider in Schmitt's concept of sovereignty as the core concern for political theology in the age of migration. Can identity be constructed in a way that allows for alterity? Can alterity be constructed in a way that allows for identity? What would a concept of sovereignty look like that overcomes the strict separation between insider and outsider without collapsing the other into the self or the self into the other?

While imprisoned, Schmitt returned to the friend/foe distinction. Asking himself "whom can I recognize as my foe at all?" he answered:

> Obviously only the one who can put me into question. By recognizing him as my foe I recognize that he can put me into question. And who can really put me into question? Only I myself. That's it. The other is my brother. The other turns out to be my brother, and the brother turns out to be the foe.[48]

Although in a somewhat escapist and esoteric way, Schmitt appears to put the image of the strong and stable sovereign into question here.[49] In the reflections on his prison experience, friend and foe are intimately intertwined, so that the decision about who can and who cannot count as other is turned from a public into a personal decision: the self can be found in the foe, and the foe can be found

---

47 It is taken from a poem that Schmitt wrote for Alexandre Kojève, cited in Wolfgang Palaver, "Globalisierung und Opfer: Carl Schmitts Lehre vom Nomos," in *Das Opfer—aktuelle Kontroversen: Religionspolitischer Diskurs im Kontext der mimetischen Theorie*, ed Bernhard Dieckmann (Münster: LIT, 2001), 181–207, at 195.

48 Carl Schmitt, *Ex Captivitate Salus. Erfahrungen der Zeit 1945/47* (Berlin: Duncker & Humblot, 2011), 89 (my translation).

49 See Müller, *A Dangerous Mind*, 55.

The theopolitics of the migrant 221

in the self. Note the slippage from foe to other and from other to foe. What are the consequences for the constitution of the law? As far as I can ascertain, Schmitt has not pursued the questioning of the strong and stable sovereign. It is, however, a core concern in the "new political theology" after Schmitt.

B Migration in the dialectical model

After the war, theology in Germany had to confront its complacency and its complicity with the totalitarian regime under Hitler. A multifaith "theology after Auschwitz" emerged, rigorously and radically rethinking the concept of God after all the classic concepts of a strong and stable sovereign had gone up in the smoke of the crematories in the death camps. For the protagonists of the theology after Auschwitz in Germany, Jürgen Moltmann and Johann Baptist Metz, the rethinking of God required and ran into a "new political theology."[50]

Moltmann refers to the memoirs of Elie Wiesel, a survivor of Auschwitz, in sketching what his new political theology would look like:

"The SS hanged two Jewish men and a youth in front of the whole camp. The men died quickly, but the death throes of the youth lasted for half an hour. 'Where is God? Where is he?' someone asked behind me. As the youth still hung in torment for a long time, I heard the man call again, 'Where is God now?' And I heard a voice in myself answer: 'Where is he? He is here. He is hanging there on the gallows.'" Any other answer would be blasphemy. There cannot be any other Christian answer to the question of this torment.[51]

Moltmann grappled with a concept of God that connected God's sovereignty and God's suffering dialectically in the cross of Jesus Christ. In accordance with Moltmann, the new political theologians concentrated on Christology to open up the classic concept of God as a strong and stable sovereign. The central corollary is the interest of theology in the concept of suffering, both anthropologically and theologically. Suffering, then, is seen as a category that can counter complacency and complicity.[52] Schmitt remains a reference for the new political theologians, albeit implicitly rather than explicitly. In contrast to Schmitt, the new political theologians consider praxis to be crucial. Taken from critical theories and critical

---

50 Johan Baptist Metz, *Zum Begriff der neuen Politischen Theologie* (Mainz: Matthias-Grünewald-Verlag, 1997).

51 Jürgen Moltmann, *Der gekreuzigte Gott: Das Kreuz als Grundlage und Kritik christlicher Theologie* (München: Kaiser, 1973), 262; Jürgen Moltmann, *The Crucified God: The Cross of Christ as the Foundation and Criticism of Christian Theology*, trans. R. A. Wilson and J. Bowden (Minneapolis: Fortress, 1993), 273–74.

52 Moltmann and Metz conceptualized "suffering" differently, the one with a more theological and the other with a more anthropological focus.

222   *Ulrich Schmiedel*

theologies inspired by Marxism, theology itself is interpreted as a praxis that stands with the oppressed rather than the oppressors.

Discussing and drawing on both Moltmann and Metz, Dorothee Sölle argues that Schmitt's political theology insisted on the correlation of theology with the political. According to Sölle, Schmitt aimed for the identification of metaphysics and politics in order to stabilize the one through the other.[53] Countering such identifications, Sölle insists that the promise of Christianity is *never* a criterion to confirm the status quo, but *necessarily* a criterion to criticize the status quo.[54] Sölle's exploration of the political promise of Christianity is exemplary for the eschatological turn of the new political theology. While Schmitt anchored his accounts of politics in the past, Sölle argues that political theology is not about the past but about the present—as seen from the anticipated future of God's promise. New political theology is about a hope that subverts rather than stabilizes the status quo. Political theology is, as Sölle argues, a "hermeneutics" that takes politics as its horizon of interpretation.[55] Politics, then, is the site for Christian *praxis*. As a consequence, political theology aims at liberation—liberation for both the oppressed from being oppressed and for the oppressors from being oppressors.[56] "Political theology," Sölle concludes, "brings humans against their own apathy to new pains. . . . It entices them to look for change."[57]

In the new political theology, then, sovereignty is interrupted by suffering. Suffering rather than sovereignty signifies the sacred. Among the new political theologians, Sölle arguably suggests the most radical rupture of sovereignty by suffering when she positions her political theology "after the death of God." Sölle points to the processes of secularization that dissolved the classic concept of God in a way that prompts theologians to think and talk about transcendence beyond the guarantees of stability and security.[58] She turns to the traditions of mysticism— apophatic or negative theology (stating what God is *not*) rather than cataphatic or positive theology (stating what God is)—to accentuate that after the death of God at Auschwitz, the responsibility for political practice rests on humans.[59] *We* have to live after the death of God. "God has no other hands than ours."[60]

53 Dorothee Sölle, *Politische Theologie* (Stuttgart: Kreuz Verlag, 1971), 73; Dorothee Soelle, *Political Theology*, trans. J. Shelley (Philadelphia: Fortress, 1974). Schmitt, *Politische Theologie*, 50, refers to *Identitäten*. Throughout, I offer my own translation of Sölle's writings in order to stick to the original as closely as possible, while I point to the English translations that are available.

54 Sölle, *Politische Theologie*, 73.

55 Ibid., 75.

56 Ibid., 85–86.

57 Ibid., 89.

58 Dorothee Sölle, *Stellvertretung: Ein Kapitel Theologie nach dem Tode Gottes* (Stuttgart: Kreuz Verlag, 1965), 148–55; 171–75; Dorothee Soelle, *Christ the Representative: An Essay in Theology after the 'Death of God,'* trans. David Lewis (London: SCM, 1967).

59 See Dorothee Soelle, *The Silent Cry: Mysticism and Resistance*, trans. B. Rumscheidt and M. Rumscheidt (Minneapolis: Fortress Press, 2001).

60 Dorothee Sölle, *Leiden* (Stuttgart: Kreuz, 2003), 183; Dorothee Soelle, *Suffering*, trans. E. R. Kalin (Philadelphia: Fortress Press, 1975).

The interruption of the sovereign by suffering blurs the boundaries between insider and outsider. In *The Window of Vulnerability: A Political Spirituality*, Sölle accounts for vulnerability as a window which opens one's self to the other and one's other to the self. Sölle advocates for vulnerability because it is the condition of the possibility of relationality.[61] For Sölle, vulnerability has to do with openness and otherness, which is why it ought to be seen *simultaneously* as a risk and as a resource. Described differently, there can be no relation without vulnerability and there can be no vulnerability without relation: I have to be vulnerable to the other in order to relate to her, and the other has to be vulnerable to me in order to relate to me. The connection between vulnerability and relationality holds both anthropologically and theologically.[62] The interruption of sovereignty by suffering shows the significance of theology for the political: a suffering sacred implies that the insider/outsider distinction is interrupted, and that the insider/outsider distinction is interrupted implies a suffering sacred. When the strong and stable sovereign is dead, there can be a space for relations between insiders and outsiders.

Overall, Schmitt uses theology to think sovereignty and Sölle uses theology to unthink sovereignty. Given that the strong and stable sovereign allowed Schmitt to build the boundary between insider and outsider, the critics of Schmitt blur the boundary by destabilizing the concept of sovereignty. God is not the sovereign that supports the status quo. God's promise subverts the status quo. The figure of the migrant, then, can appear in the terms of the new political theology. Interestingly, the new political theology emerges in a context of migration. After the war, borders were drawn and redrawn, displaced populations were on the move all across the world, and the Declaration of Human Rights was adopted by the United Nations. However, none of the protagonists of the new political theology have worked on migration. Yet the confrontation of the new political theology with the figure of the migrant confirms that migration is a wrench in the wheels of sovereignty. With the new political theology, migration can be perceived as a promise. Theologically, a concept of God that allows for a destabilization of the distinction between identity and alterity would be the concept of a suffering rather than a sovereign God. Vulnerability allows for relations between insider and outsider. What consequences does such a concept of political theology have for the constitution of the law?

IV The promise of migration

To summarize, migration is a challenge for the constitution of the law in democracies that assume that those who are affected by the law are able to author it and

---

61 Dorothee Sölle, *Das Fenster der Verwundbarkeit: Theologisch-Politische Texte* (Stuttgart: Kreuz, 1988); Dorothee Soelle, *The Window of Vulnerability: A Political Spirituality*, trans. L. M. Maloney (Minneapolis: Fortress Press, 1990).
62 Sturla Stålsett, "Towards a Political Theology of Vulnerability: Anthropological and Theological Propositions," *Political Theology* 16, no. 5 (2015): 464–78.

224 *Ulrich Schmiedel*

that those who are able to author the law are affected by it. As Sassen argues, the denationalization of citizenship in the age of migration demonstrates that democracies need to reconceptualize who counts as a citizen and who counts as a noncitizen. Turning from the Westphalian to the post-Westphalian order, the sovereignty of the state is at stake in these reconceptualizations.

I have confronted the accounts of sovereignty in the political theologies of Schmitt and the critics of Schmitt with the challenge of migration. The figure of the migrant is a provocation for political theology because it moves outsiders to the inside and insiders to the outside, thus blurring the boundaries between identity and alterity. Whether a political theology can cope with migration depends on whether it can account for the other in the construction of the self and the self in the construction of the other. Described differently, the strict separation of insider and outsider is the central challenge for political theology today. For the decision-ist concept of sovereignty the challenge is destructive, while for the dialectical concept of sovereignty the challenge is productive. Conceptually, the interruption of sovereignty through suffering, articulated by theologians such as Sölle, makes relations between insider and outsider possible. The interruption of sovereignty through suffering, then, is the conceptual condition of the possibility of a relationality that connects members to migrants and migrants to members of a citizenry.

The contrast between Schmitt and the critics of Schmitt can be captured by the concept of theopolitics. In *Divining History: Prophetism, Messianism and the Development of the Spirit*, Jayne Svenungsson suggests that a "razor-thin" line separates political theology from theopolitics: the one stabilizes and the other destabilizes the political status quo.[63] Svenungsson acknowledges that theopolitical motifs can be found in political theology as much as political theology motifs can be found in theopolitics.[64] Yet theopolitics, she argues, signifies the resistance against the status quo in the name of a prophetic promise.[65] The figure of the migrant, then, can be characterized as a *theopolitical* figure. The migrant allows for prophetic protest against the constitution of a citizenry that closes itself off against the other. What does theopolitics mean for the concrete challenge that migration poses for democracies? *Whose* law should apply to whom? By way of conclusion, I aim to respond to these questions with reference to Benhabib's characterization of the constitution of the law.

Benhabib accepts the challenge that migration poses for the constitution of the law.[66] While the classic solutions of communitarianism and cosmopolitanism would fall on the side of either the democratic self-determination of the members of the state (at the cost of the human rights of the migrant) or the human rights of the migrant (at the cost of the democratic self-determination of the members

---

63 Jayne Svenungsson, *Divining History: Prophetism, Messianism and the Development of the Spirit*, trans. S. Donovan (New York: Berghan, 2016), 13.

64 Ibid., 37.

65 Ibid., 53.

66 Benhabib, *The Rights of Others*, 12.

The theopolitics of the migrant 225

of the state),[67] Benhabib argues for "another cosmopolitanism" that keeps human rights in democracy.[68] The figure of the migrant is central for the mediations between communitarianism and cosmopolitanism that Benhabib conceptualizes as "democratic iterations."[69] By "democratic iterations" she means deliberations in public squares and political spheres through which people or groups of people lay claim to a right that was not addressed to them. These claims are crucial to save and to strengthen these rights.[70] One of Benhabib's examples for such democratic iterations is the affair that the three Muslim teenagers triggered when they wore hijabs in school. The public discourse and the political discussions of the hijab provoked a thinking and a talking about identity and alterity where "universalist rights claims . . . are contested and contextualized, invoked and revoked, posited and positioned"—which is to say, democratic iterations.[71] Benhabib argues that these iterations can initiate a "jurisgenerative politics," a politics that generates laws in a way that prompts members to conceive of membership more and more expansively, thus turning outsiders into insiders, migrants into members of the citizenry.[72] Through jurisgenerative politics, then, the citizenry can become fluid rather than fixed: the sovereign opens the sovereign to the other.

A French court has overturned the ban on the burkini in Nice, arguing that it violated fundamental freedoms. However, the discourse about bans for burkas and burkinis that swirls in the public sphere across Europe implies that the citizenry can also be conceived ever more exclusively rather than ever more expansively. Anything is possible. According to Diallo:

> France decided long ago that Islam has somehow become "problematic," and consequently adopted particular behaviours to hide Islam . . . from

---

67 According to Kristin E. Heyer, the classic communitarian and cosmopolitan models prioritize the individual acts of migrants as sites for policy interventions, thus losing track of the social, structural, and systemic sites of the legalization or the illegalization of migration (Chapter 13).

68 Seyla Benhabib, *Another Cosmopolitanism: The Berkley Tanner Lectures* (Oxford: Oxford University Press, 2006). Sassen points to Benhabib's account, which localizes these tensions in the contrast between universal humanity-based rights, on one hand, and particular nationality-based rights, on the other, to be resolved in a model of "cosmopolitan federalism." While endorsing Benhabib's suggestions, Sassen contends that the argument "is predicated on a binary, whereby the national and the global are mutually exclusive" (Saskia Sassen, "Response," *European Journal of Political Theory* 6, no. 4 (2007): 433–46, at 435), where the grip of the national increases, the global decreases, and where the grip of the global increases, the national decreases. The concept of denationalization, however, casts doubt on such exclusivity. Sassen is thus confirming Benhabib's cosmopolitan federalism: if the universal human rights and the particular national rights are not as exclusive as they appear to be, practices of cosmopolitan federalism might be out there.

69 Benhabib, *The Rights of Others*, 179.

70 Benhabib, "The Return of Political Theology," 182.

71 Benhabib, *The Rights of Others*, 179.

72 Ibid., 171. For a theological account, see Lukas Meyer, *Fremde Bürger: Ethische Überlegungen zu Migration, Flucht und Asyl* (Zurich: TVZ, 2017).

226   Ulrich Schmiedel

> society's field of vision. . . . Today, the concept of "laïcité" is being used by the French state to make expressions of Muslim identity illegal. However, secularism . . . must remain a principle based on equality. . . . Its vocation is to enable every citizen to freely express his or her faith without fear of being stigmatised.[73]

It seems that the critics of Benhabib are correct. They point out that her account of another cosmopolitanism offers no response to exclusive encasements of the constitution of the law.[74] What can be done to make the constitution of the law ever more expansive rather than ever more exclusive? The theopolitics of the migrant might allow for a response.

Whether acknowledged or unacknowledged, political theology plays a part in democratic iterations. One can easily imagine how the identification of Europe with a sometimes secularized and sometimes not so secularized Christian legacy can be claimed against the three Muslims teenagers, so that their bodies (what they can and what they cannot cover) become objects of the state's control. The consequence of such a political theology of a clash of civilizations—it is easily linked to Schmitt—would be the opposite of Benhabib's endorsed outcome: exclusive and exclusionary citizenship.[75] What is needed, then, is a political theology that insists that God cannot be captured conceptually, so that neither the insider nor the outsider can interpret and instrumentalize God for their purposes. The insistence on the promise of God in the new political theology points to such a concept. In a prophetic promise, God appears apophatically rather than cataphatically, as what God is *not* rather than as what God is. Consequently, God is not categorized to stabilize the status quo but categorized to destabilize the status quo. One reason to refer to the death of God is to avoid God's conceptual categorization. For mystics such as Sölle, "God" is a noncategory rather than a category.

Valentina Napolitano clarifies the connections between the figure of the migrant and the figure of the mystic: both have the "apophatic force" that is brought from the margins to the middle in the age of migration.[76] For political theology, the corollary of the apophatic force of the mystic and the migrant is a prophetic theopolitics that resists the figure of a strong and stable self-sufficient

---

73 Diallo, "Hijab: A Very French Obsession."

74 See the comments by Jeremy Waldron, Bonnie Honig, and Will Kymlicka in *Another Cosmopolitanism*, 83–146. See also Reiner Anslem, "Who are the People? Toward a Theological Ethics of Citizenship and Community," in Schmiedel and Smith, *Religion in the European Refugee Crisis*, 227–42.

75 See Ulrich Schmiedel, " 'We Can Do This!' Tackling the Political Theology of Populism," in Schmiedel and Smith, *Religion in the European Refugee Crisis*, 205–24.

76 Valentina Napolitano, "Anthropology and Theology: Notes on Gender and Migration," Keynote at "The Church and Migration: Global (In)Difference? Twelfth International Gathering of the Ecclesiological Investigations International Research Network Conference," Toronto, June 25–27, 2018, www.academia.edu/36938479/Anthropology_and_Theology_Notes_on_Gender_and_Migration.

The theopolitics of the migrant   227

sovereign that structures the sacred through the separation of insider and outsider. As Napolitano argues, the apophatic force that connects mystic and migrant is about openness "to the transformative incarnate processes through which migration poses new possibilities for living together, not contained already by . . . the (written) Law."[77] Such a theopolitics of apophatic force, then, could and should support democratic iterations. It calls neither for absolutizing nor for abolishing the law, but for its continuous and creative transformation. It comes close to what Allard calls the "relational jurisdiction" that continually challenges the exclusive and exclusionary operations of the law (Chapter 5). But how can such a theopolitics be put into practice? Svenungsson cautions against "the theological temptation to replace law with grace."[78] She calls for enactments of grace *through* the law. But what could or what should they look like?

Building on Sölle, I advocate for the cultivation of theologies that make the self vulnerable to the other and the other vulnerable to the self in order to allow for relationships between insiders and outsiders. In contrast to suffering for the sake of suffering, vulnerability is a more pertinent and a more promising category for receptivity toward the other because it retains the agency of the subject, whether migrant or mystic.[79] Vulnerability is at the core of what I call *coalitional and comparative political theology.*

By "coalitional political theology," I mean theologies on the street level. In the context of contemporary Europe, coalitional political theology is practiced where Christians act together with Muslims and Muslims act together with Christians in order to improve the situation of migrants. One example from Europe is Mediterranean Hope, a refugee relief program run by the Federation of Protestant Churches in Italy.[80] In addition to rescue missions in the Mediterranean, the program also includes the Casa delle Culture, the "House of Cultures," located in the small town of Scicli in Sicily. The Casa can accommodate up to 40 migrants who can access a range of support services. The Casa is also a cultural hub for locals, encouraging intercultural encounters between migrants and members. The Casa brings Christians together with Muslims and Muslims together with Christians, both among the migrants and among the members. Given that the Italian government continues to illegalize both refugees and refugee relief workers, the Casa enables citizens and noncitizens to support each other in their resistance against exclusionary and exclusive laws. Such coalitions between different and diverse theological politics are the condition for the possibility of remaining open to the other. In coalitional political theology, the self makes the self vulnerable

77 Ibid.
78 See Jayne Svenungsson, "Law and Liberation: Critical Notes on Giorgio Agamben's Political Messianism," *European Judaism* 50, no. 1 (2017): 68–77, at 76.
79 See the discussion in Judith Butler, Zeynep Gambetti, and Leticia Sbsay, eds., *Vulnerability in Resistance* (Durham, NC: Duke University Press, 2016).
80 See the information available at Mediterranean Hope, www.mediterraneanhope.com.

to the other because she approaches the other as a resource rather than a risk for her political action.[81]

By "comparative political theology," I mean theologies on the scholarship level. In the context of contemporary Europe, comparative political theology is practiced where Christians analyze together with Muslims and Muslims analyze together with Christians in order to improve the theology of migration. What would a theology look like that allows Muslims to think through the role of Christians in running the Casa delle Culture? What would a theology look like that allows Christians to think through the role of Muslims in running the Casa delle Culture? What can these theologians learn about ethics, politics, and liturgy? Such comparisons between different and diverse theological proposals are the condition for the possibility of remaining open to the other. In comparative political theology the self makes the self vulnerable to the other because she approaches the other as a resource rather than a risk for her political analysis.[82]

Vulnerability, then, connects comparative and coalitional political theology. In the continuing hijab affair, vulnerability could be a vital political power. What if Christian teenagers started wearing hijabs where they are banned? By exposing themselves to the ban of the hijab in school, they would interrupt the strong and stable sovereignty in the constitution of the law. Imagine a beach full of people wearing burkinis—Christians and non-Christians, men and women, all dressed alike—to demonstrate solidarity with those who are affected by laws they could not author. In such solidarity, the self would become vulnerable to the other (and the other would become vulnerable to the self).[83] In *Kinship Across Borders: A Christian Ethic of Immigration*, Kristin E. Heyer stresses the significance of solidarity for migration ethics.[84] She insists that "incarnational solidarity calls us into concrete relationship with the marginalized."[85] Relationships with the marginalized can be both incarnational and interruptive.[86] Such incarnational and interruptive solidarity could be at the core of a political theology that is both comparative and coalitional in order to keep sovereignty open to the other.

---

81 For the significance of vulnerability for coalitional politics, see Bernice Johnson Reagon, "Coalition Politics: Turning the Century," in *Home Girls: A Black Feminist Anthology*, ed. Barbara Smith (New York: Kitchen Table Women of Color Press, 1983), 356–68.

82 For the significance of vulnerability for comparative theology, see Marianne Moyaert, "On Vulnerability: Probing the Ethical Dimensions of Comparative Theology," *Religions* 3 (2012): 1144–61.

83 Of course, there are crucial differences between the vulnerability of the member and the vulnerability of the migrant. The concept of vulnerability calls the construction of membership into question. See also Susanna Snyder, "Walking, Wounds and Washing Feet: Pedetic Textures of a Theo-Ethical Response to Migration," *Studies in Christian Ethics* 32, no. 1 (2019): 3–19.

84 Kristin E. Heyer, *Kinship Across Borders: A Christian Ethic of Immigration* (Washington, DC: Georgetown University Press, 2012), 99.

85 Ibid., 119.

86 Ibid., points out that such solidarity is necessarily conflictual.

What runs through my proposal for a comparative and a coalitional political theology is the insistence on the preservation of plurality: in the age of migration, plurality can be preserved when Christian political theology works for the sake of Muslims and Muslim political theology works for the sake of Christians. They would not be required to agree on their theologies, but they would be required to keep their theologies open to the other—to Fatima, Leila, and Samira for instance. Of course, such a political theology should not position the sacred against the secular but should draw believers and nonbelievers into its comparisons and its coalitions. Thus, migration can be turned from a problem into a promise for political theology. According to Nail's *The Figure of the Migrant*, "The migrant is the political figure of our time."[87] The migrant is a problem and a provocation for political theology. But if political theology is pluralized in coalitional and comparative perspective, the migrant is also a promise.

Suggested Readings

Benhabib, Seyla. *The Rights of Others: Aliens, Residents and Citizens*. Cambridge: Cambridge University Press, 2004.

Brown, Wendy. *Walled States, Waning Sovereignty*. New York: Zone Books, 2010.

Heyer, Kristin E. *Kinship Across Borders: A Christian Ethic of Immigration*. Washington, DC: Georgetown University Press, 2012.

Machado, Daisy, Brian Turner, and Trygve Wyller, eds. *Borderland Religion: Ambiguous Practices of Difference, Hope and Beyond*. London: Routledge, 2018.

Nail, Thomas. *The Figure of the Migrant*. Stanford, CA: Stanford University Press, 2015.

Phan, Peter C., ed. *Christian Theology in the Age of Migration: Implications for World Christianity*. Lanham, MD: Lexington, 2020.

Sassen, Saskia. *Expulsions: Brutality and Complexity in the Global Economy*. Cambridge, MA: Harvard University Press, 2014.

Schmiedel, Ulrich, and Graeme Smith, eds. *Religion in the European Refugee Crisis*. New York: Palgrave Macmillan, 2018.

87 Nail, *The Figure of the Migrant*, 235.

13 Migration, social responsibility, and moral imagination

Resources from Christian ethics

Kristin E. Heyer

I Introduction

While immigration to the United States has declined in recent decades, the profile of those arriving at the U.S.–Mexico border has shifted from seasonal workers from Mexico to family units and children from Central America's Northern Triangle countries seeking asylum.[1] This rise in asylum seekers—who by law are permitted to present claims to immigration agents—poses particular challenges to an already taxed administrative system and to the dominant political focus on punitive policies ostensibly aimed at deterrence. In spite of a "security crisis" drumbeat dominating the political scene, the vast majority of asylum seekers peacefully turn themselves over to the U.S. Border Patrol (in southwestern counties with the lowest crime rates in the nation). Asylum seekers face slow procedures and low probability of relief, given recent reversals in grounds for claims of persecution; they increasingly face forcible family separation and inhumane detention conditions as well.

The treatment and characterization of immigrants under the Trump administration address symptoms rather than causes of migration, whether a misconstrued national border emergency or the trauma effected by a "zero-tolerance" policy of forcibly separating thousands of migrant children from their parents. Mechanisms that instill fear in receiving communities and erode the human rights of migrants reflect broader tendencies to approach migration in terms of crisis management, with populist leaders capitalizing on anxieties related to the global economy and to cultural shifts in recent years.

Given the consequent focus on discrete actions of migrants, wherein individuals remain the primary target of enforcement, relational emphases in Christian social ethics can help reorient analyses to consider the roles historical relationships and transnational actors play in abetting migration. While standard communitarian and cosmopolitan models tend to focus primarily on rights to individual freedom of movement and the self-determination of political communities, categories like restorative justice and the global common good contextualize the individual acts of migrants and underscore social dimensions of justice and sinful

---

1 I am grateful to Aimee Hein for research assistance with this chapter.

Migration, responsibility, imagination   231

complicity alike. Such relational frameworks orient analyses toward root causes of displacement and shared accountability. This chapter takes up the manner in which the relational elements of Christian ethics—social anthropology, the universal destination of created goods, social sin, structural justice—help illuminate the complex causes of migration and the responsibilities of receiving communities. Particular attention is paid to how the resources of Christian social ethics help bring into relief the relationship between ideologies and structures of injustice that deny relationality and bring harm to migrants and receiving communities alike.

II Isolationist signs of the times and the ideologies that enable them

The tendency to treat symptoms of migration rather than address underlying causes or contextual complicity is not limited to the U.S. context. A brief overview of U.S. deterrence efforts and the Trump administration's retreat from international collaboration offers a window into the assumptions and impact of such propensities. Given shifts in the populations crossing the U.S. southern border, debates about a wall or threats of retributive trade policy constitute a manufactured crisis that diverts attention from humanitarian needs and U.S. complicity in generating the flow of people, while playing to a political base enchanted not only by law-and-order campaign promises but also by attempts to wall off intrusive outsiders who threaten (further) displacement. Whereas President Donald Trump inherited a broken system in need of comprehensive reform, he instituted policies that constructed a virtual wall against outsiders through impediments to entry (historic cuts to limits on refugees, termination of Temporary Protected Status, travel bans) and internal enforcement policies, which expand the population of those targeted for deportation to include anyone whom immigration officers judge to pose a risk to public safety or national security. These measures are supported by narratives that frame the issues through enduring interpretive lenses and perpetuate myths about responsibility for irregular migration and threats to national security.

Such rhetoric and policies are of a piece with growing tendencies to prioritize isolationist and illusory understandings of national self-interest over global collaboration.[2] The United States increasingly views international agreements with suspicion, refusing to participate on the ostensible grounds that treaty obligations unduly limit U.S. sovereignty, whether related to criminal courts, climate targets, or the rights of the child.[3] This "America First" mentality is evident in the Senate's refusal to ratify United Nations treaties in recent years: none in the

---

2 David Hollenbach, "The Glory of God and the Global Common Good: Solidarity in a Turbulent World," *CTSA Proceedings* 72 (2017): 51–60, at 51–52, https://ejournals.bc.edu/ojs/index.php/ctsa/article/view/10093/8749.
3 Jeffrey D. Sachs, "The High Costs of Abandoning International Law," *Boston Globe*, March 6, 2017, www.bostonglobe.com/opinion/2017/03/05/the-high-costs-abandoning-international-law/OXGzXIJP3th3Fc9EGNsXTN/story.html.

past decade and only one (cybercrime) in the past 15 years. Jeffrey Sachs has diagnosed such disdain for globally shared and negotiated rules as emerging from three commitments: "a founding myth of America as untethered in its fate from the rest of the world"; an "implicit belief that America's security and economic interests—in the sea, or the environment, or armaments—can be achieved largely through American actions alone rather than the sum of the actions of all of the world"; and an "overarching faith in 'US primacy,' the idea that the US can protect its interest through its power alone, without the need to rely on international rules and international law."[4] He emphasizes that, by contrast, from the nation's origins its prosperity and security have depended on a developing body of international law that helps "govern international trade, intellectual property, global health, international financial flows, arms control and nuclear nonproliferation, human rights, environmental protection and other areas," and without which today's global economy could not function. It is worth noting the nation's pre–World War II history of isolationist tendencies, yet Sachs compellingly argues that absent international treaty agreements, few reliable and practical ways to promote peaceful and beneficial behavior of the world's 193 nations remain.[5]

In terms of migration regulation in particular, the United States exited the UN Global Compact on Safe, Orderly, and Regular Migration, stating that it risked undermining the country's sovereign right to enforce its immigration laws and secure its borders.[6] The compact was signed in December of 2018 by 164 governments, with signatories affirming that the significant challenges posed by migration are "best faced through multilateral processes rather than isolationist policies."[7] International compacts share an orientation toward diplomatic removal of ideological and physical barriers to a shared global good and what Pope Francis has called "our common destiny" as citizens of the world. Hence, just as a border wall's impermeability functions as a metaphor for concerns beyond perceived immigration threats, the isolationism that trumpets threats to sovereignty also betrays a deeper opposition to the common good.

Recent years have witnessed a rise in nativist populism fueled, in part, by anxieties about the economic and cultural impact of globalization. Politicians running on populist platforms have capitalized on fears of demographic shifts, terrorist activities, and chaotic border scenes—increasingly disseminated through unvetted new media platforms—asserting that they alone are willing to control borders and restore law and order. Some even reject the premise of integration out of

---

4 Ibid.
5 Ibid.
6 Rex Tillerson, statement on December 3, 2017, as quoted in Peter Jesserer Smith, "US Leaves UN Global Migration Discussions, to Church's Dismay," *National Catholic Register*, December 11, 2017, www.ncregister.com/daily-news/us-leaves-un-global-migration-discus sions-to-churchs-dismay.
7 Edward Pentin, "Vatican, US Diverge on UN's 'Global Compact on Migration'," *National Catholic Register*, December 12, 2018, www.ncregister.com/daily-news/vatican-us-diverge-on-uns-global-compact-on-migration.

Migration, responsibility, imagination 233

hand, dismissing Islam as "incompatible with European values," for example.[8] Despite crisis-oriented, politicized discourse, grievances reflect much longer-term social phenomena than perceptions of migrant surges: concerns about a loss of socioeconomic status, perceived threats to social norms, and significant demographic changes understood as reshaping society and threatening certain received understandings of community.[9] Because some politicians are unable to deliver fully on law-and-order campaign platforms once elected, the rise of populism and nativism has indirectly influenced how immigration and integration issues have been framed (given the fears remain and intensify), moving mainstream political actors toward extreme (right) positions in response.

Across different European countries—even those largely considered to be Christian societies—nationalist parties have capitalized on receiving communities' discomfort with new migrant flows, socioeconomic precarity, and fear of terrorism.[10] After a populist coalition government recently took power in Italy, its ports were closed to humanitarian landings. Brazil's populist, ultraconservative president, Jair Bolsonaro, withdrew the country from the compact on migration.[11] In the U.S. context, these trends played out via the politics of exclusion peddled throughout Trump's campaign and ongoing scripts, where appeals to economic and cultural anxieties remained cloaked in nativist rhetoric and misrepresentations. Such stoking helps make citizens susceptible to fear-based tactics, even when the claims remain counterfactual.[12] Immigration debates in the United States have long been framed by narratives emphasizing security threats and social costs, despite rhetoric about liberty and hospitality.[13] Ongoing efforts to "Make America safe again" follow from the law-and-order mantle that Trump adopted to distinguish his candidacy, even as studies regularly indicate higher rates of immigration correlate with lower rates of violent and property crime.[14]

---

8 Demetrios G. Papademetriou, Kate Hooper, and Meghan Benton, *In Search of a New Equilibrium: Immigration Policymaking in the Newest Era of Nativist Populism* (Washington, DC: Migration Policy Institute, 2018), 1, 14.

9 Ibid., 3.

10 Marianne Heimbach-Steins, "New Nationalisms in Europe and the Ambivalent Role of Religion," *The First,* Catholic Theological Ethics in the World Church, March 31, 2016, www.catholicethics.com/forum-submissions/new-nationalisms-in-europe-and-the-ambivalent-role-of-religion.

11 Kevin Clarke, "While U.S. Fixates on the Border Wall, Populist World Leaders Still Turn Migrants Away," *America,* January 11, 2019, www.americamagazine.org/politics-society/2019/01/11/while-us-fixates-border-wall-populist-world-leaders-still-turn-migrants.

12 Salvador Rizzo, "The Trump Administration's Misleading Spin on Immigration, Crime and Terrorism," *Washington Post,* January 7, 2019, www.washingtonpost.com/politics/2019/01/07/trump-administrations-misleading-spin-immigration-crime-terrorism/.

13 For a further elaboration of these narratives and their impact, see Kristin E. Heyer, "Internalized Borders: Immigration Ethics in an Age of Trump," *Theological Studies* 79, no. 1 (March 2018): 146–64. The discussion of social sin in this chapter also draws in part from "Internalized Borders."

14 Walter Ewing, Daniel E. Martínez, and Rubén G. Rumbaut, "The Criminalization of Immigration in the United States," *American Immigration Council,* July 13, 2015, www.americanimmigrationcouncil.org/research/criminalization-immigration-united-states.

234 *Kristin E. Heyer*

The rule of law rightly occupies a privileged place in the United States, yet a lack of accountability that marks Border Patrol procedures and the lack of due process afforded immigrant detainees belie this rationale.[15] Moreover, young migrants from the Northern Triangle countries flee homes with the world's highest number of homicides per capita, where gang members murder with impunity—the threat driving many such migrants is precisely the breakdown of the rule of law at home.

Another script from Trump's migration and trade platforms casts newcomers as economic threats, a perception historically fueled in times of economic downturn. Beyond studies that show that immigrant laborers provide a net benefit to the U.S. economy, the detention industry profits from irregular migrants, further confounding the frame of economic threat. Share prices for privately held corrections firms rose over 100 percent in the wake of the 2016 election, given Trump's avowed commitment to nearly double the incarceration of immigrants. The combined revenues of CoreCivic and GEO Group, for example, exceeded $4 billion in FY 2017. Such firms spend millions on lobbying and campaign contributions. The burgeoning immigrant industrial complex raises serious questions about the financial stakes in the broken immigration system, diminished public oversight, and accountability.

Finally, the administration has connected economic anxieties with anxieties over cultural shifts, shaping a particular vision of "America First" that casts newcomers as threatening to a nation's identity. Tapping into the related anti-immigrant sentiment has provoked the demonization of racial, ethnic, and religious minorities. Representations of the outsider as a social menace have been reinvented in moments of national crisis, with the general pattern evidencing xenophobia's productive function in the national imaginary; Trump advisers' sympathy for a "clash of civilizations" paradigm illuminates the restrictionist logic that informs his approach to migration policy and international affairs in terms of the importance of threats to culture rather than political ideology.[16] Hence, these fear-mongering

---

15 Legal reform reports have criticized aspects of the U.S. immigration laws at odds with this complement of features: their retroactivity, inconsistent application, lack of proportionality, procedural unfairness (for example, the effects of unavailability of legal counsel), and failure to comport with basic norms of due process. See Donald M. Kerwin, "Illegal People and the Rule of Law," in *Constructing Immigrant Illegality: Critiques, Experiences and Responses*, eds. Cecilia Menjívar and Daniel Kanstroom (Cambridge: Cambridge University Press, 2013), 327–52; Donald M. Kerwin, "Rights, the Common Good, and Sovereignty in Service of the Human Person," in *And You Welcomed Me: Migration and Catholic Social Teaching*, eds. Donald M. Kerwin and Jill Marie Gerschutz (Lanham, MD: Lexington Books, 2009), 93–122, at 111.

16 Todd Scribner, "You Are Not Welcome Here Anymore: Restoring Support for Refugee Resettlement in the Age of Trump," *Journal on Migration and Human Security* 5 (2017): 263–84, at 263, https://doi.org/10.14240/jmhs.v5i2.84. In his chapter for this volume, Luis N. Rivera-Pagán analyzes how Samuel Huntington's arguments regarding a clash of civilization impact migration attitudes today (Chapter 10). See also Samuel Huntington, *The Clash of Civilizations and the Remaking of World Order* (New York: Touchstone, 1996).

Beyond operative national myths, political expediency and self-interest also foster receptivity to false claims and reductive approaches to migration. Privatized detention companies and unscrupulous employers are not the only ones profiting from a broken system that exploits immigrants; the system benefits those in power and, at some level, remains central to the function of the nation-state. Saskia Sassen's latest work links emergent patterns of displacement—the Rohingyas fleeing Myanmar, the migration toward Europe from Middle Eastern and African countries, as well as mass incarceration and the warehousing of able-bodied unemployed persons in ghettos and slums—in terms of thoroughgoing "expulsions" at the hands of geopolitical and economic powers.[18] In an analogous manner, in reflecting on Hannah Arendt's work, Judith Butler notes:

> As such [the disfranchised] are *produced* as the stateless at the same time that they are jettisoned from juridical modes of belonging. This is one way of understanding how one can be stateless within the state, as seems clear for those who are incarcerated, enslaved, or residing and laboring illegally . . . this particular economy in which the public (and the proper sphere of politics) depends essentially on the non-political, or rather the explicitly depoliticized, suggesting that only through recourse to another framework of power can we hope to describe the economic injustice and political dispossessions upon which the official polity depends and which it reproduces time and again as part of its efforts at self-definition.[19]

When populist leaders divert attention from root causes or incite fear of immigrants, they grease the wheels of a certain system that benefits those who wield political power and even the ordinary economic power to underpay for goods and services. These broader systemic dimensions underscore the inadequacy of reductive diagnoses and short-term responses to migration; point to the wider webs of

---

17 For an analysis of U.S. responses to Northern Triangle arrivals that reflects this crisis-management approach, see Renà Cutlip-Mason, "Moving Away from Crisis Management: How the United States Can Strengthen its Response to Large-Scale Migration Flows," *Center for Migration Studies*, essay honoring Juan Osuna, January 23, 2019, https://cmsny.org/publications/cutlip-mason-crisis-management/.
18 Saskia Sassen, *Expulsions: Brutality and Complexity in the Global Economy* (Cambridge, MA: Harvard University Press, 2014).
19 Judith Butler and Gayatri Chakravorty Spivak, *Who Sings the Nation State? Language, Politics, Belonging* (New York: Seagull Books, 2010), 16–17.

236 *Kristin E. Heyer*

interdependence within which migrants and receiving communities interact; and signal ways in which claims to defend sovereignty or preserve law and order raise deeper questions about the functions of empire.

Dominant populist narratives and diversionary tactics generally ignore historical and structural relationships impacting migration. Reducing immigration matters to the locus of border crossers in the Mediterranean or the desert Southwest eclipses from view, much less blame, transnational actors responsible for violent conflict, economic instability, or climate change. Moreover, fear of difference is relatively easy to mass market and shapes societies' imagination in powerful ways. Encounters with reluctant or desperate migrants signal significant dissonance between exclusionary frameworks and the inhumane impact of populist rhetoric and measures alike. At his border mass in Ciudad Juárez, for example, Pope Francis bade listeners to measure the impact of forced migration not in statistics but with concrete names and stories, evoking a counternarrative to those dominating the airwaves.[20] Attentiveness to the human face of expulsions can help unmask operative narratives. Whereas Christian migration ethics typically emphasizes the humanity of migrants in this vein, renewed attention to social dimensions of Christian ethics can expand consideration beyond the dignity of individuals who cross borders to consider the global contexts and operative interests that compel migration.

III Christian immigration ethics

Drawing on traditions of biblical hospitality, social doctrine, and human rights, literature in Christian migration ethics typically focuses on the plight and agency of migrants and the relative duties of reception within a global framework. Susanna Snyder characterizes the landscape of Christian migration ethics as largely deontological in tone, whether rooted in commands to love the neighbor or show hospitality to the stranger, or marked by a Christian cosmopolitanism grounded in an eschatological vision that transcends borders with implications for the treatment of migrants.[21] Some more communitarian approaches suggest that scriptural directives instead call Christians to prioritize duties to kin and deference to governmental authority over duties to outsiders.[22] To a certain extent, then, Christian ethics reflects wider secular tensions between communitarian and

---

20 Pope Francis, "No Border Can Stop Us from Being One Family," *Vatican Radio*, February 18, 2016, http://en.radiovaticana.va/news/2016/02/18/pope_francis__%E2%80%98no_bor der_can_stop_us_from_being_one_family%E2%80%99/1209507.

21 Susanna Snyder, "Walking, Wounds and Washing Feet—Pedetic Textures of a Theo-Ethical Response to Migration," *Studies in Christian Ethics*, October 2018, https://doi. org/10.1177/0953946818807461.

22 In this vein, Snyder points to James R. Edwards, "A Biblical Perspective on Immigration Policy," in *Debating Immigration*, ed. C. Swain (Cambridge: Cambridge University Press, 2007), 46–62; Nigel Biggar, *Between Kin and Cosmopolis: An Ethic of the Nation* (Cambridge: James Clarke, 2014).

cosmopolitan perspectives but integrates insights from scripture and theological commitments.

The story of the Jewish and Christian pilgrim communities is one of migration, diaspora, and the call to live accordingly. Indeed, after the commandment to worship one God, no moral imperative is repeated more frequently in the Hebrew scriptures than the command to care for the stranger.[23] Despite convenient amnesia in our own nation of immigrants, "it was Israel's own bitter experience of displacement that undergirded its ethic of just compassion toward outsiders: 'You shall not wrong or oppress a resident alien, for you were aliens in the land of Egypt' (Ex. 22:21)."[24] When Joseph, Mary, and Jesus flee to Egypt, the émigré Holy Family becomes the archetype for every refugee family.[25] Jesus's praxis of hospitality to outsiders recurs throughout the Gospel texts.

In the Roman Catholic tradition, immigration directives are rooted not only in biblical injunctions to welcome the stranger but also in the social teachings on universal human rights, the understanding of the political community as oriented to serving the common good, and a global rather than nationalistic perspective. Catholic principles of economic and migration ethics protect not only civil and political rights but also more robust social and economic rights and responsibilities. These establish persons' rights not to migrate—and thus to fulfill human rights in their homeland—or to migrate if they cannot support themselves or their families in their country of origin. Hence, in situations where individuals face desperate poverty or pervasive gang violence, the Catholic tradition supports the right to freedom of movement so that persons can live free from credible fears of violence or severe want. Beyond its foundation in social and economic rights, the right to migrate is also rooted in the tradition's commitment to the universal destination of created goods, that is, the idea that the goods of the earth are generally intended for everyone.

Although this tradition recognizes the right of sovereign nations to control their borders, the right is not understood to be absolute; its temperance by conditions of social justice warrants protection for many who remain within U.S. borders or seek entry. In the case of blatant human rights violations, the right to

---

23 William O'Neill, SJ, "Rights of Passage: The Ethics of Forced Displacement," *Journal of the Society of Christian Ethics* 127, no. 1 (2007): 113–36; W. Gunther Plaut, "Jewish Ethics and International Migrations," *International Migration Review: Ethics, Migration and Global Stewardship* 30 (Spring 1996): 18–36, at 20–21. For a comprehensive discussion of New Testament themes related to migration, see Donald Senior, " 'Beloved Aliens and Exiles': New Testament Perspectives on Migration," in *A Promised Land, A Perilous Journey: Theological Perspectives in Migration*, eds. Daniel G. Groody and Gioacchino Campese (Notre Dame, IN: University of Notre Dame Press, 2008), 20–34.

24 Ched Myers and Matthew Colwell, *Our God Is Undocumented* (Maryknoll, NY: Orbis, 2012), 15.

25 Pope Pius XII, *Exsul Familia*, September 30, 1952, in *The Church's Magna Charta for Migrants*, ed. Rev. Giulivo Tessarolo, PSSC (Staten Island, NY: St. Charles Seminary, 1962), introduction.

238 *Kristin E. Heyer*

state sovereignty is relativized by the tradition's primary commitment to protecting human dignity. Once people do immigrate, the tradition profoundly critiques patterns wherein stable receiving countries accept the labor of undocumented workers without offering legal protections of citizenship. Such practices risk the creation of a permanent underclass, leading to both exploitation of laborers and a two-tiered society. In the terms central to Catholic social thought, this dynamic harms human dignity and the common good alike. Hence, its doctrinal body of migration teaching protects the rights to remain and to migrate and protects refugees and asylum seekers.

Beyond contesting harmful political rhetoric and practices, attention to Christian traditions of social injustice may broaden practical concerns on the ground, where hospitality and charity are often stressed among religious NGOs active in humanitarian work, resettlement agencies, and other direct outreach. Just as individualistic models focus on extralegal entries in isolation, models of charity and hospitality risk eclipsing broader complicity in flows and harm as well as risk a paternalistic pastoral orientation. The Christian tradition, with its social anthropology, understanding of social sin, and tempering of sovereignty rights by a commitment to the universal destination of created goods, significantly reorients responsibility for irregular migration beyond individuals who cross borders or overstay visas alone.

IV Relational resources in Christian social ethics: (re)contextualizing migration

Relational emphases in Christian ethics can help reorient reductive protectionist analyses to consider the roles historical relationships and transnational actors play in abetting migration as well as more receptive responses to immigrants that prioritize hospitality over structural justice. If dominant political narratives keep violence and migration flows local and dehumanize newcomers according to convenient (and abhorrent) scripts, the social commitments of the Christian tradition shape a different story, a counternarrative of shared humanity with implications for a justice-oriented immigration ethic. This ethic is not a meek, naïve paradigm that simply condones open borders, but a tradition committed to universal human rights and shared responsibility for the effects of structural injustice. Christian understandings of what it means to be human radically critique pervasive exploitation and prevailing immigration paradigms that enable exclusion and abet division. The tradition's relational elements help illuminate complex causes of migration and the responsibilities of receiving communities.

The Catholic tradition's defense of social, economic, and cultural rights noted above are rooted in a social anthropology that departs from the atomistic monad or *homo economicus* implicit in some approaches to migration policy. An anthropology that joins autonomy and relationality contests both the dehumanizing manipulation and exploitation of migrants as well as the inadequacy of individualistic frameworks in migration ethics. Tisha Rajendra's work effectively critiques the "supply side cures" of neoclassical migration theory and indicates how

Migration, responsibility, imagination   239

migration-systems theory more accurately reflects a social anthropology and the macrostructures that directly impact migration patterns (quasicolonialism, labor recruitment) alongside mesostructures (social networks).[26] Typically, established communities and migrants are "bound together by history, politics and economics even before the act of migration bridges the distance of geography."[27]

Dynamics of employer recruitment, for example, tend to be shaped by prior bonds forged by colonialism, military invasions, or economic ties. The ongoing legacy of nineteenth- and twentieth-century U.S. foreign policy, expansionism, and neoliberal economic strategies—with attendant narratives—has generated migration flows from Latin America to the United States, for example.[28] The connection between freedom and relationality also underscores the intrinsic nature of family relationships to personhood and the necessity of nurturing primary relationships for growth in freedom. Rooted in a Trinitarian anthropology, Catholic social thought integrates a family's intimate communion with its charge to mutually engage the broader social good. If families serve as basic cells of civil society—"schools of deeper humanity,"[29]—social conditions must protect their participation in the demands and benefits of the common good. Conditions that perpetuate family separation undermine human subjectivity and harm the common good.[30]

The emphasis of the Catholic social tradition on the demands of the global common good contextualizes the individual acts of migrants or refugees and underscores social dimensions of justice and complicity alike. The international scope of this understanding of the participatory, shared good underscores the need for structures and practices that can foster the just development of the human family across borders. Understanding immigration dynamics as related to unjust international political and economic divides also requires nations to share accountability in the wake of the "partial eclipse" of the Westphalian model and to convert from opportunistic patterns of interdependence. Structural analyses

---

26   Tisha Rajendra, "Justice Not Benevolence: Catholic Social Thought, Migration Theory, and the Rights of Migrants," *Political Theology* 15 (2014): 290–306, https://doi.org/10.1179/1462317x13z.0000000007; Tisha Rajendra, *Migrants and Citizens: Justice and Responsibility in the Ethics of Immigration* (Grand Rapids, MI: Eerdmans, 2017), chapter 4.

27   Silas W. Allard, "Who Am I? Who Are You? Who are We? Law, Religion, and Approaches to an Ethic of Migration," *Journal of Law and Religion* 30 (2015): 320–34, at 325, https://doi.org/10.1017/jlr.2015.6.

28   Miguel De La Torre, *The U.S. Immigration Crisis: Toward an Ethics of Place* (Eugene, OR: Cascade, 2016), 151–52. He reflects on a personal level: "I am in this country following my sugar, tobacco and rum" (158).

29   Second Vatican Council, *Pastoral Constitution on the Church in the Modern World Gaudium et spes* (December 7, 1965) no. 52.

30   For a discussion of how Christian family ethics challenges exploitative migration practices and how the concrete experiences of migrant families, in turn, contest idealized "family values," see Heyer, "*Familismo* Across the Americas: En Route to a Liberating Christian Family Ethic," in *Living with(out) Borders: Catholic Theological Ethics on the Migration of Peoples*, eds. Agnes Brazal and María Teresa Dávila (Maryknoll, NY: Orbis Press, 2016), 121–32.

240 Kristin E. Heyer

suggest that migration policy should consider receiving countries' economic and political complicity in generating migrant flows rather than perpetuate amnesic and convenient scapegoating. Sassen links deeper dynamics of debt servicing and extraction to new migratory flows, illuminating their complex origins given "predatory" forms of advanced capitalism, opaque transnational networks, and a global governance system geared to aiding corporations.[31]

Given such systemic culpability, some have proposed that an "instability tax" be levied on private and governmental entities that destabilize migrant- and refugee-producing regions—whether hedge funds profiting from commodity-trading in African minerals, or weapons manufacturers profiting from selling arms to the Middle East, or multinationals profiting from degrading or destabilizing poor nations.[32] Drawing on the Kew Gardens principles,[33] David Hollenbach has proposed norms that help account for histories of relationship and complicity. In light of moral proximity to harm, he suggests that countries that have gained economically from their colonies or that have histories of military involvement in another nation "have special obligations to people in flight from that nation."[34] Beyond particular duties to refugees from wars in Vietnam and Iraq, he notes that benefits gained by the United States through its dominant role in nations like Guatemala, Haiti, and the Philippines also lead to particular duties to those countries, in terms of both contributing to their development and admitting migrants in mutually beneficial ways.[35] Existing economic relationships also confer relative duties for Hollenbach, who asserts that guest workers who "contribute through their work to the life and well-being of the society they have entered" should be welcomed as citizens.[36]

31 S. Sassen, "Three Emergent Migrations: An Epochal Change," *SUR File on Migration and Human Rights* 13 (2016): 29–41, https://papers.ssrn.com/sol3/papers.cfm?abstract_id=2838267; S. Sassen, "A Massive Loss of Habitat: New Drivers for Migration," *Sociology of Development* 2 (2016): 204–23, at 211, https://doi.org/10.1525/sod.2016.2.2.204.

32 Ian Almond, "The Migrant Crisis: Time for an Instability Tax?" *Political Theology Today*, September 22, 2015, www.politicaltheology.com/blog/the-migrant-crisis-time-for-an-insta bility-tax/.

33 The Kew Gardens principle argues that an agent has a positive responsibility to help when four conditions are present: (1) there is a critical *need*, (2) the agent has *proximity* to the need, (3) the agent has the *capability* to assist, and (4) the agent is likely the *last resort* from whom help can be expected. See John Simon, Charles W. Powers, and Jon P. Gunnemann, *The Ethical Investor: Universities and Corporate Responsibility* (New Haven: Yale University Press, 1972), 23–25.

34 D. Hollenbach, "Borders and Duties to the Displaced: Ethical Perspectives on the Refugee Protection System," *Journal on Migration and Human Security* 4 (2016): 148–65, at 153 https://journals.sagepub.com/doi/10.1177/233150241600400306.

35 D. Hollenbach, "A Future Beyond Borders: Re-imagining the Nation State and the Church," in Brazal and Dávila, *Living With(out) Borders,* 223–35, at 232–33.

36 Ibid., 232. For additional criteria rooted in historical and social relationships, see William O'Neill, SJ, "The Place of Displacement: The Ethics of Migration in the United States," in Brazal and Dávila, *Living With(out) Borders,* 67–77, at 73.

Migration, responsibility, imagination   241

Hence, becoming a neighbor to the migrant through a social vision of the person and the good requires meeting basic responsibilities of justice, not charity alone, particularly given the role that receiving nations play in shaping conditions that directly contribute to irregular migration.[37] Whereas standard communitarian and cosmopolitan models tend to focus primarily on rights of individuals to freedom of movement and the right of political communities to self-determination, categories like restorative justice and the global common good contextualize the individual acts of migrants and underscore social dimensions of justice. In sharp contrast to dominant discourse, sovereignty and hospitality are understood in the Catholic social tradition to be mutually implicating: legitimate sovereignty must be exercised in reference to the universal destination of created goods and a "requirement to regulate borders according to basic conditions of social justice."[38] Hence, a social anthropology with its attendant rights and robust vision of global responsibilities helps recontextualize migration in the face of tendencies to locate responsibility solely with the migrant's choice to cross borders, absent attention to transnational forces and contexts.

V Social sin: awakening to structural complicity

The Christian category of social sin explicitly connects these structural relationships with their harmful consequences and abetting ideologies.[39] Distinct elements of social sin—dehumanizing trends, unjust structures, and harmful attitudes—shape complex dynamics that perpetuate inequalities and influence receptivity to outsiders. As signaled above, whether in forms of cultural superiority or profiteering, social inducements to personal sin in the immigration context abound. In Reinhold Niebuhr's view, the universal human experience entails the sin of "seeking security at the expense of another life," arguing that the pretensions and claims of collectives far exceed those of the individual.[40] He singles out the expression of group egotism in the nation-state, as the state gives the collective impulses of the nation instruments of power and imaginative symbols of identity, such that "the national state is most able to make absolute claims for itself, to

---

37 John J. Hoeffner and Michele R. Pistone, "But the Laborers Are . . . Many? Catholic Social Teaching on Business, Labor and Economic Migration," in Kerwin and Gerschutz, *And You Welcomed Me*, 55–92, at 74.
38 Anna Rowlands, "After Lesvos and Lampedusa: The European 'Crisis' and its Challenge to Catholic Social Thought," *Journal of Catholic Social Thought* 14, no. 1 (2017): 63–85, at 71–72.
39 I further elaborate connections between social anthropology, social sin, and global solidarity in *Kinship Across Borders: A Christian Ethic of Immigration* (Washington, DC: Georgetown University Press, 2012).
40 Reinhold Niebuhr, *The Nature and Destiny of Man, Vol. 1, Human Nature* (Louisville, KY: Westminster/John Knox Press, 1996; orig. Charles Scribner's Sons, 1941), 182. Consequently, guilt "represents the objective and historical consequences of sin," for which the sinner is held responsible; guilt represents "the actual corruption of the plan of creation and providence in the historical world": 222.

242 Kristin E. Heyer

enforce those claims by power and to give them plausibility and credibility by the majesty and panoply of its apparatus."[41] Historical examples of state repression and national exceptionalism bear out this analysis, and it is difficult to overlook the ways a border wall showdown has functioned as a manifestation of group ego. The temptations of group ego are also evident, however, in efforts to overcome insecurity that only indirectly contribute to migration flows: whether through opportunistic capital investment, material extraction in developing countries, or active recruitment of racialized and gendered immigrant labor.[42]

The concept of social sin, as it has developed in the Protestant and Catholic traditions, draws attention not only to the operations of group egotism but also to the connections between harmful structures and ideologies: for example, how powerful narratives casting immigrants as security threats or "takers" influence individuals' roles in collective actions that impact migration, such as votes in an election. The primacy of deterrence has institutionalized security concerns rather than concerns for human rights in U.S. immigration laws; the nation's economic interests have been institutionalized in uneven free-trade agreements. When concerns about national identity get distorted by xenophobia and fear, anti-immigrant sentiment and ethnic-based hate crimes surge. At a more subtle level, a consumerist ideology shapes citizens' willingness to underpay or mistreat migrant laborers directly or indirectly, through demand for inexpensive goods and services. These interconnected attitudes and institutions then produce the scotosis that lulls citizens into equating "law-abiding" with "just," or into indifference.

Given such nonvoluntary dimensions of social sin, a Christian social ethic calls for not only defending human rights or providing hospitality to strangers but also unmasking the complex structures and ideologies that abet personal complicity, preventing justice for migrants. These entrenched, intertwined patterns of social sin require repentance from idolatries that marginalize and disempower those beyond one's immediate sphere of concern.[43] From repentance and conscientization, a relational ethic invites conversion toward interdependence in solidarity, both at a personal level, evoking new perspectives and receptivity, and at a broader, systemic level, with nations taking more collective responsibility. Converting patterns of global interdependence from ones marked by domination and oppression to ones marked by equality and reciprocity demands structures of institutional accountability and transparency as well as empowered participation (subsidiarity).[44]

---

41 Ibid., 209. Niebuhr describes group egotism in terms of the egotism of racial, national, and socioeconomic groups.

42 Gioacchino Campese, "¿*Cuantos Más*? The Crucified Peoples at the U.S.-Mexico Border," in Groody and Campese, *A Promised Land, A Perilous Journey*, 271–98, at 279.

43 I elaborate the implications of these dynamics for the practical denial of migrants' rights and human rights frameworks of analysis in "Migrants Feared and Forsaken: A Catholic Ethic of Social Responsibility," *Interdisciplinary Journal for Religion and Transformation in Contemporary Society* 6, no. 1 (July 2020): 158–70.

44 David Hollenbach, *The Common Good and Christian Ethics* (Cambridge: Cambridge University Press, 2002), 225.

Beyond identifying structural forces demanding institutional solidarity, a relational migration ethic entails interrogating more ideological dimensions of social sin that harden resistance to newcomers. Pope Francis has drawn attention to the anesthetizing effects of indifference in this regard, calling for a recognition of our fundamental relatedness in light of the harm borders wreak. On Lampedusa, he lamented the pervasive idolatry that facilitates migrants' deaths and robs us of the ability to weep, a theme he revisited in Manila and then Juárez, insisting that "only eyes cleansed by tears can see clearly."[45] The reductive market ethos dominating trade and migration policies has similarly desensitizing effects. Certain attendant ideological currents of neoliberal globalization—fatalistic understandings of the "price of progress" or "market fundamentalism"—configure coordinates for what becomes normal or conceivable.[46] Pope Francis connects this logic of exclusion based on materialism to perceptions and treatment of migrants as disposable.[47] Migrant women's often exploitative caring labor that sustains citizens' wage labor offers one example. The idea that the economy should serve the person raises serious concerns not only about the freedom of markets compared to people but also about the significant financial stakes in broken immigration systems—detained immigrants fill beds, deportations fill private buses. Various commitments to economic growth at all costs can become authentic bondage that contributes to the dynamics of self-interest and empire noted above. These ideologies reinforce international structures that impede accountability to a global common good.

The concept of social sin, then, offers a framework for critiquing histories of unequal relationships between countries, such as histories of proxy wars, as well as harmful ideologies, from xenophobia to meritocracy. Idolatries of security and invulnerability also facilitate susceptibility to exclusionary temptations. Roberto S. Goizueta's reflections on how fear and self-loathing cause individuals to avoid the wounds of others illuminates the depth and lure of such dynamics. He notes that we construct identities, institutions, and belief systems to shield us from the "terrifying truth" that our lives are ultimately not in our control.[48] Susanna Snyder's work has shown how an isolating ecology of fear conditions responses to migration "crises" in virtually every world capital, illuminating the dynamic

---

45 Pope Francis, "No Border Can Stop Us from Being One Family."

46 Timothy Jarvis Gorringe, "Invoking: Globalization and Power," in *The Blackwell Companion to Christian Ethics*, eds. Stanley Hauerwas and Samuel Wells (Malden, MA: Blackwell, 2004), 346–59, at 353.

47 Jorge E. Castillo Guerra, " 'A Church Without Boundaries': A New Ecclesial Identity Emerging from a Mission of Welcome. Reflections on the Social Magisterium of Pope Francis as Related to Migration," *Journal of Catholic Social Thought* 14 (2017): 43–61, at 51, https://doi.org/10.5840/jcathsoc20171415.

48 Roberto S. Goizueta, "To the Poor, the Sick, and the Suffering," in *Vatican II: A Universal Call to Holiness*, eds. Anthony Ciorra and Michael W. Higgins (New York: Paulist, 2012), 62–79, at 73.

244 *Kristin E. Heyer*

via strands in the biblical tradition rooted in ecologies of fear and of faith.[49] Portraying immigration through a lens of individual culpability alone obscures these multileveled dynamics at play. Hence, beyond rights to movement and political self-determination, categories of social sin and transnational solidarity orient migration analyses toward root causes of displacement and shared accountability.

VI Shaping moral imagination in a time of flux

Rooted in a moral anthropology that takes relational agency and sin seriously, Christian contributions to immigration ethics challenge not only economic functionalism and militarization of deterrence but also approaches marked exclusively by hospitality or charity. The nonvoluntary dimensions of social sin outlined above suggest that the field must address the diffuse and complex structures and ideologies that inhibit solidarity with migrants and abet human rights violations. In light of nonrational influences on moral agency, formulating the best moral and political arguments remains necessary but insufficient. Jonathan Haidt's insights about the moral challenges spurring antiglobalist movements as well as about the role nonrational factors play in the apprehension and pursuit of goods more broadly underscore the importance of cultivating civic friendship and healing broken communities.[50]

Religious practices, narratives, and symbols do hold potential to (re)shape believers' moral imagination and counter the collective delusion that we are not responsible. Some religious institutions have embodied commitments by offering sanctuary and education to undocumented immigrants or faith-based community organizing. Calling attention to the urgency and legitimacy of this formation task, which is distinct from humanitarian outreach or advocacy, may help expand efforts in this vein. Cultivating empathy and civic virtue will require that we resist distortions that fog our vision, recontextualize migrations, and draw near to the realities of immigrant communities marked by vitality and precarious vulnerability alike.

Regional inequalities resulting from globalization and rapid technological change have contributed, in part, to the strains of nationalism traced at the outset. Populist leaders do not shy away from difficult conversations about the impact of migration and rising mistrust in government and antielitism. Ignoring cultural and economic anxiety drivers of opposition to migration (as well as to inclusion and human rights more broadly) overlooks how vulnerable to capture such voters may be.[51] Attention to ideological dimensions of social sin, then, entails addressing

---

49 Susanna Synder, *Asylum-Seeking, Migration and Church* (Farnham, UK: Ashgate, 2012), 85–87, chapter 7.
50 Jonathan Haidt, "When and Why Nationalism Beats Globalism," *American Interest* 12 (2016), www.the-american-interest.com/2016/07/10/when-and-why-nationalism-beats-globalism/; Jonathan Haidt, *The Righteous Mind: Why Good People Are Divided by Politics and Religion* (New York: Vintage, 2012).
51 Papademetriou, et al., *In Search of a New Equilibrium*, 8.

Migration, responsibility, imagination 245

persons' willingness to embrace fake news or "tendency to favor information that bolsters their existing views and to be drawn to more emotional narratives over dispassionate factual arguments."[52] If mainstream political leaders increasingly face a challenge in defending core democratic values (impacting receptivity to migrants), they cannot bypass honest engagement with "people's concerns about the pace of cultural and social changes associated with immigration, while making the case for an inclusive national identity."[53] This context also demands that scholars and activists work beyond policy proposals (or social media engagement) to articulate common values connected to "people's everyday concerns and experiences, avoiding undue reliance on abstract or intangible concepts such as human rights."[54] If political leaders ignore longstanding social divisions and economic grievances, they risk further polarization and nativist breeding grounds.[55]

Hence, the appeal of populism suggests that beyond manipulative narratives, senses of real and perceived loss—and accompanying grief and resentment—foster receptivity to exclusionary rhetoric and measures. Addressing not only nativism and debasing rhetoric but also deeply seated fears perhaps complicates the path forward. Given the deepening tribalization of partisanship and segmented social media feeds, the need to rebuild public trust and a shared sense of community cannot be underestimated or bypassed.[56] Robert Jones has argued that President Trump successfully converted white evangelical Protestant "values voters" into "nostalgia voters" by naming and elevating their anxieties about the country's recent demographic and cultural shifts ("Make America Great Again" as restoring cultural displacement and economic displacement alike). Jones suggests that white southern Christians have been vulnerable to the lure of nostalgia as they perceive a loss of unquestioned white power and its attendant hierarchy of social roles and order.[57] He has suggested that for white evangelical Christians who continued to support Trump, the border wall "is an extraordinarily potent totem," given an "embattled minority" view of the world constituted by "chosen insiders and threatening outsiders" at a time when white Christian dominance is waning in the United States.[58]

---

52 Ibid., 14.
53 Ibid., 19.
54 Ibid.
55 Ibid., 2.
56 Ali Noorani, *There Goes the Neighborhood: How Communities Overcome Prejudice and Meet the Challenge of American Immigration* (Amherst, NY: Prometheus Books, 2017), 235.
57 See Robert P. Jones, *The End of White Christian America* (New York: Simon & Schuster, 2016); Jennifer Rubin, "What the End of White Christian America Has to Do with Trump," *Washington Post*, September 16 and 18, 2017, www.washingtonpost.com/blogs/right-turn/wp/2016/09/16/what-the-end-of-white-christian-america-has-to-do-with-trump-part-1/ and www.washingtonpost.com/blogs/right-turn/wp/2016/09/18/what-the-end-of-white-christian-america-has-to-do-with-trump-part-2/.
58 Greg Sargent, "The Walls Around Trump Are Crumbling: Evangelicals May Be His Last Resort," *Washington Post*, January 2, 2019, www.washingtonpost.com/opinions/2019/01/02/walls-around-trump-are-crumbling-evangelicals-may-be-his-last-resort/.

246 *Kristin E. Heyer*

Christian social ethics can serve an unmasking function, then, calling out not only harmful scripts about migrants but also the ambivalent modes in which religion functions in migration discourse and action. Whereas I have attempted to distinguish nationalist ideologies from a Christian ethic of solidarity, the quasireligious status of sovereignty claims or populist visions perhaps complicates monolithic claims about a Christian migration ethic. On one hand, forms of U.S. Christianity that have sanctified nationalism and imperialism (from Manifest Destiny to global colonialism), while intent on gaining social power and winning culture wars, plainly distort gospel values.[59] On the other hand, the civil religious mode of some restrictionist claims invites a closer examination of latent values: not just fear, for example, but also desire for a tight-knit, mutually supportive community—a desire perhaps distinct from nostalgia for a monoculture that willfully ignores the presence of others. At the least, acknowledging this white Christian nostalgia inflecting a demographic protectionism in such terms underscores the allure of its narrative potential as an alternative religious framework. Decrying wrongheadedness with diatribes or data alone remains insufficient, then, given the power of this (alternative) myth for explaining threats to "the good life," if narrowly construed. Yet Christian audiences must be invited to be formed by the tradition's commitments to the outsider and to justice, not primarily by the temptations and totems of nationalism.

Whereas much research in Christian migration ethics focuses more on crafting theological and moral arguments to promote just immigration policy, the task of Christian ethics must also extend to shaping imagination for receptivity: practices of "incarnational solidarity" that bridge divides and debunk misconceptions;[60] encounters with first-person narratives, art, and poetry; subversive hospitality (Bishop Heinrich Bedford-Strohm's public greeting, Pope Francis's foot washing); lament and pubic repentance; witness to boundary transgressing (*posadas* and border fence liturgies); antiracism training. While fear of the other is easily mass-marketed, mutual understanding across difference can be harder to engender and sustain. Hence, civic and religious leaders could help reshape moral imagination by counteracting myths and xenophobic scapegoating, while remembering ways in which everyone's own deep stories can tempt us to select facts. Religious traditions have a significant role to play in countering the ideologies of hatred and fear outlined above. At the same time, in an environment where "instilling the fear of chaos has become the strategy of successful politics," religious and political reflection alike will risk irrelevance if they do not engage the fears of those

---

59 Stephen Mattson, "White Christian Nationalism—Not Secularism—Is Destroying America," *Sojourners*, February 4, 2019, https://sojo.net/articles/white-christian-nationalism-not-secularism-destroying-america.

60 See Christine Firer Hinze, "Straining Toward Solidarity in a Suffering World: *Gaudium et spes* 'After Forty Years'," in *Vatican II: Forty Years Later, College Theology Society Annual Volume 51*, ed. William Madges (Maryknoll, NY: Orbis, 2005), 165–95.

attracted by the fundamentalist culture.[61] Evoking a moral imagination that takes seriously the roots of anxieties, that calls out their harmful expressions, and that builds bridges across difference is a more complicated task than fear-mongering or self-righteous denunciation alone can execute. It entails generating spaces for conversations about who "we" are as a nation that do not begin and end with defining national identity over and against an outsider (or threat from within). Honestly addressing challenges posed by globalization and migration will entail moving some to empathize with the asylum-seeker in three-dimensional terms, and others with those feeling left behind.

Renewing moral imagination is not unconnected to advancing structural change, as the dynamics of social sin reveal in shadow. Moving away from crisis management (much less crisis manufacturing) may demand that nations cede part of their sovereignty to international bodies and cooperation, where warranted, and collaboratively address root causes of forced migration through strategies such as targeted economic development or investment in proven antiviolence programs (see Michele R. Pistone, Chapter 4). Within the United States, procedural reforms that would restore prosecutorial discretion and promote alternatives to detention; restore asylum protections and improve infrastructure at points of entry; limit the collaboration between immigration enforcement and local police; and revisit Temporary Protected Status and limits on numbers of refugees, to begin, would better align legal immigration policies with the nation's economic and humanitarian interests (see Daniel Kanstroom, Chapter 1; Enid Trucios-Haynes, Chapter 2; Pistone, Chapter 4; Donald M. Kerwin, Chapter 6).[62] In terms of politicians' appeals to "family values," comprehensive training to address the particular needs of child migrants, safeguards to prevent abuse of minors, and the elimination of family detention centers would better serve the needs of children and families as the nation awaits more thoroughgoing systemic reforms (see Bill Ong Hing, Chapter 3; Kerwin, Chapter 6).[63]

Fed by increasingly incendiary news, an idolatry of security and a culture of comfort conspire to desensitize and to estrange those settled from those forced from home. Restrictionist measures, reductive rhetoric, and individualistic normative paradigms fail to convey a sense of the complex roles that historical relationships and economic globalization play in contemporary migration. Social responsibility in the Christian tradition reorients analyses to what patterns of migration reveal and what solidarity demands.

---

61 Antonio Spadaro, "Tornare a Essere Popolari: Sette parole per il 2019," *La Civiltà Cattolica* 1 (January 5, 2019): 42–44.
62 Donald M. Kerwin, Daniela Alulema, and Mike Nicholson, *Communities in Crisis: Interior Removals and Their Human Consequences* (Nogales, AZ, New York, NY, and Washington, DC: Kino Border Initiative [KBI], Center for Migration Studies [CMS], and Office of Justice and Ecology [OJE], 2018), https://doi. org/10.14240/rptl118.//http://cmsny. org/wp-content/uploads/2018/11/FINAL-Communities-in-Crisis-Report-ver-5.pdf.
63 See Cutlip-Mason, "Moving Away from Crisis Management."

248   *Kristin E. Heyer*

Suggested Reading

Brazal, Agnes, and María Teresa Dávila, eds. *Living With(out) Borders: Catholic Theological Ethics on the Migrations of Peoples.* Maryknoll, NY: Orbis Books, 2016.

Heyer, Kristin E. *Kinship Across Borders: A Christian Ethic of Immigration.* Washington, DC: Georgetown University Press, 2012.

Hollenbach, David S. J. *Humanity in Crisis: Ethical and Religious Response to Refugees.* Washington, DC: Georgetown University Press, 2019.

Noorani, Ali. *There Goes the Neighborhood: How Communities Overcome Prejudice and Meet the Challenge of American Immigration.* Amherst, NY: Prometheus Books, 2017.

Phan, Peter C., ed. *Christian Theology in the Age of Migration: Implications for World Christianity.* Lanham, MD: Lexington Books, 2020.

Rajendra, Tisha M. *Migrants and Citizens: Justice and Responsibility in the Ethics of Immigration.* Grand Rapids, MI: Eerdmans, 2017.

Sassen, Saskia. *Expulsions: Brutality and Complexity in the Global Economy.* Cambridge, MA: Harvard University Press, 2014.

Part 3
Dialogues

14 "No more deaths."
Religious liberty as a defense for providing sanctuary for immigrants

Rose Cuison-Villazor and Ulrich Schmiedel

I Introduction

After walking through the Sonoran Desert for two days and two nights, two young men from Central America—José Sacaria-Goday and Kristian Perez-Villanueva—crossed the U.S. southern border near Ajo, Arizona, around January 14, 2018.[1] They ended up in a place called The Barn, a humanitarian aid station 40 miles north of the border.[2] While there, they received water, food, fresh clothing, and medical aid from various individuals, including Scott Warren, who volunteers for the organization No More Deaths.[3] This organization promotes the enactment of "Faith-Based Principles for Immigration Reform."[4] Formed in 2004, the organization has been a ministry of the Unitarian Universalist Church of Tucson since 2008.[5]

The two immigrant men stayed in The Barn for three days.[6] On the afternoon of January 17, 2018, U.S. Border Patrol agents and local law enforcement officers arrived at The Barn and arrested Warren and the two men.[7] Federal prosecutors indicted Warren for violating 8 U.S.C. § 1324, which proscribes knowingly harboring and transporting undocumented immigrants.[8] Warren was already known to federal law enforcement officers. A month before his arrest at The Barn, federal

---

1 Bobby Allyn, "Jury Acquits Aid Worker Accused of Helping Border-Crossing Migrants in Arizona," NPR (November 21, 2019), www.npr.org/2019/11/21/781658800/jury-acquits-aid-worker-accused-of-helping-border-crossing-migrants-in-arizona.
2 Ibid.
3 See Criminal Complaint for Violation of Title 8 United States Code § 1324(a)(1)(A)(iii), *United States v. Warren*, No.CR-18–00223–001-TUC-RCC(BPV) (D. Ariz. January 18, 2018) [hereinafter Criminal Complaint].
4 "About No More Deaths," *No More Deaths*, https://nomoredeaths.org/about-no-more-deaths/.
5 No More Deaths–No Más Muertes, *Unitarian Universalist Church of Tucson*, https://uuctucson.org.
6 Allyn, "Jury Acquits Aid Worker."
7 Ibid.; Criminal Complaint.
8 See Indictment, *United States v. Warren*, No.CR-18–00223–001-TUC-RCC(BPV) (D. Ct. Ariz. February 14, 2018) [hereinafter Indictment].

252 *Rose Cuison-Villazor and Ulrich Schmiedel*

authorities had charged Warren with two misdemeanor crimes—operating a motor vehicle in a wilderness area, 50 C.F.R. § 35.5, and abandonment of property, 50 C.F.R. § 27.93.[9] Warren had used roads in a protected wilderness area without authorization to carry jugs of water and canned food, which he and other volunteers left for migrants crossing the Sonoran Desert.[10]

Warren challenged the prosecutions against him by asserting that the Religious Freedom Restoration Act (RFRA)[11] provided him with an affirmative defense.[12] Seeking to have the 8 U.S.C. § 1324 felony case dismissed, Warren argued that he maintained "a sincere belief in the duty to help fellow human beings . . . in distress" and that this "practice of charity and mercy are core to his spiritual values."[13] The government's criminalization of his humanitarian acts, Warren contended, substantially burdened his ability to practice his faith.[14] The case proceeded to trial on June 12, 2019, and ended in a hung jury.[15] The government retried the case in November 2019, and this time, after deliberating for only two hours, the jury found Warren not guilty.[16] Warren similarly used RFRA as an affirmative defense against the two misdemeanor charges. A bench trial on the misdemeanor cases took place in May 2019, but the court did not announce its verdict until after the felony trial. Notably, the court ruled that, although the government proved beyond a reasonable doubt the two misdemeanor charges against Warren, RFRA provided a successful affirmative defense against one of them—abandonment of property (water and food for the migrants).

This chapter examines Warren's prosecution and defense as a case study to explore the legal and theological issues raised by the criminalization of aiding undocumented immigrants when such aid is considered an expression and exercise of one's faith. As Warren asserted, his "spiritual beliefs" compelled him "to act. . . [because] someone is in need."[17] While the work of No More Deaths can

---

9 See Information, *United States v. Warren*, No. 17–00341-MJ (D. Ct. Ariz. December 6, 2017).

10 Affidavit in Support of Summons for Defendant Named in an Information, *United States v. Warren*, No. 17–00341-MJ (D. Ct. Ariz. December 6, 2017).

11 Religious Freedom Restoration Act, 42 U.S.C. §§ 2000bb-2000bb-4 (2018).

12 Motion to Dismiss Counts 2 and 3 at 8, *United States v. Warren*, No.CR-18–00223–001-TUC-RCC(BPV) (D. Ct. Ariz. April 2, 2018 [hereinafter Motion to Dismiss]; see also Brief by Professors of Religious Liberty as Amicus Curiae, *United States v. Warren*, No.CR-18–00223–001-TUC-RCC(BPV) (D. Ct. Ariz. June 21, 2018).

13 Motion to Dismiss.

14 Ibid.

15 Miriam Jordan, "An Arizona Teacher Helped Migrants: Jurors Couldn't Decide If It Was a Crime," *New York Times*, June 11, 2019, www.nytimes.com/2019/06/11/us/scott-warren-arizona-deaths.html.

16 Jasmine Aguilera, "Humanitarian Scott Warren Found Not Guilty after Retrial for Helping Migrants at Mexican Border," *Time*, November 21, 2019, 3:29 p.m., https://time.com/5732485/scott-warren-trial-not-guilty/.

17 Scott Warren, Testimony, Hearing, Motion to Dismiss, *United States v. Warren*, No.CR-18–00223–001-TUC-RCC(BPV) 44 (D. Ct. Ariz. May 11, 2018) [hereinafter Warren Testimony].

"No More Deaths" 253

be traced back to the sanctuary movement of the 1980s and 1990s,[18] Warren was prosecuted in a new context, characterized by a contradiction in the objectives of President Donald J. Trump's administration to expand religious freedom and to enforce immigration law.[19] The government's criminalization of Warren's humanitarian actions reveals this contradiction.

Warren's case provides insight on the use of RFRA in the provision of humanitarian aid to those in need. Warren admitted to assisting migrants by leaving water, food, and medical aid and by assisting them upon their arrival at The Barn. His basis for doing so was his faith. Deploying RFRA as an affirmative defense against his prosecutions, Warren contended that criminalization of his aid substantially burdened the exercise of his beliefs, that his prosecution did not meet compelling government interest, and that the government had less restrictive means of achieving its goals.[20] Warren's partial success in relying on RFRA as a defense offers valuable perspectives on future uses of RFRA in humanitarian cases near the border. Although the facts of the case are limited to circumstances that took place near the southern U.S. border, Warren's case raises questions about the possible reliance on RFRA in cases involving aid to undocumented immigrants already residing in the United States.[21] Additionally, the case arguably has implications for individuals outside the United States who face potential criminal penalties for exercising their religious autonomy to provide humanitarian aid to undocumented migrants.[22]

Theologically, the case draws attention to the significance of public theology for faith-based humanitarian action. Characterizing Warren's volunteering for No More Deaths as a performative public theology that blurs the boundaries between believers and nonbelievers, we argue that fragments of theology can be used to make a case for civil initiatives that claim to uphold the law against a state that breaks it. For public theologians, then, the question is not so much whether such civil initiatives are religious or nonreligious. The question is whether and which fragments of theology can help prevent the deaths of migrants at borders, both inside and outside the United States.

18 For the international spread of the practices of the sanctuary movement, see *Sanctuary Practices in International Perspectives: Migration, Citizenship and Social Movements*, eds. Randy Lippert and Sean Rehaag (New York: Routledge, 2012).

19 See Stephanie Acosta Inks, "Immigration Law's Looming RFRA Problem Can Be Solved by RFRA," *BYU Law Review* 107, no. 1 (2019): 109–65. On the changes to immigration law in the Trump administration see Bill Ong Hing (Chapter 3) and Donald M. Kerwin (Chapter 6) in this volume.

20 See Motion to Dismiss, at 25.

21 There is no legal definition of the term "sanctuary." In this chapter, we use it to refer to the provision of shelter for immigrants who lack lawful immigration status and are removable from the United States.

22 Frances Paris, "Months-Long Dutch Service to Protect Migrants Ends after Policy Shift," *NPR* (January 31, 2019), www.npr.org/2019/01/31/690403074/months-long-dutch-church-service-to-protect-migrants-ends-after-policy-shift.

254 Rose Cuison-Villazor and Ulrich Schmiedel

II Legal landscape

To better understand the legal issues illuminated in the Warren case, we first lay out the legal landscape surrounding the provision of faith-based aid to undocumented immigrants. There are at least two sets of laws governing provision of humanitarian aid for undocumented immigrants by faith-based organizations and individuals with religious beliefs. The first set of laws protects the free exercise of religion. These include the First Amendment[23] and RFRA. RFRA has been used primarily in the civil and not criminal immigration context. Warren was indicted and tried for violating 8 U.S.C. § 1324, the second set of laws, which proscribe and penalize harboring of undocumented immigrants. Courts have interpreted the antiharboring provision of § 1324 narrowly by requiring a showing that defendants intended to help immigrants evade immigration authorities. That is, merely providing shelter, without intending to hide immigrants from immigration authorities, is not per se a violation of § 1324.

An individual's right to exercise religion is protected by various laws, including the U.S. Constitution and federal statutes.[24] The First Amendment's Free Exercise Clause provides that, "Congress shall make no law . . . prohibiting the free exercise" of religion.[25] In addition, RFRA protects religious liberty rights by recognizing "free exercise of religion as an unalienable right," and that laws of general applicability may, in some cases, impose a substantial burden on the religious exercise of some persons.[26] RFRA requires the government to justify the substantial burden on the individual caused by the general law by demonstrating that there is a compelling government interest, and that the means used to achieve that interest are the least restrictive.[27] In passing RFRA, Congress expressly overturned the Supreme Court's opinion in *Employment Division v. Smith*, which held that neutral laws of general applicability that burden the free exercise of religion should be interpreted under the lowest standard of scrutiny—rational basis.[28] Prior to *Smith*, courts used the highest form of review—strict scrutiny—when examining laws that burdened the exercise of faith.[29] Thus, RFRA restored strict scrutiny as the appropriate level of review when examining the impact of a law of general applicability on the free exercise of religion.[30] Applicable case by case, RFRA established a balancing analysis designed to challenge a particular enforcement of a law because it conflicts with a person's religious practice. RFRA is not

---

23 U.S. Constitution, Amendment 1.
24 In addition to federal laws that protect the free exercise of religion, state laws also prohibit state and local governments from prohibiting an individual's freedom to exercise his or her religion.
25 U.S. Constitution, Amendment 1.
26 42 U.S.C. § 2000bb.
27 Ibid., § 2000bb-1.
28 494 U.S. 872, 878 (1990).
29 See John Witte, Jr. and Joel A. Nichols, *Religion and the American Constitutional Experiment*, 4th ed. (Oxford: Oxford University Press, 2016), 121–27.
30 42 U.S.C. § 2000bb.

meant to challenge general application of a law. RFRA's application in the civil immigration context has not been widely tested, and when it has been used, courts have almost always rejected such claims.[31]

The antiharboring provision of the Immigration and Nationality Act (INA) has its origins in early twentieth-century efforts by Congress to proscribe the smuggling of noncitizens to the United States.[32] In 1907, Congress passed a statute that criminalized the transporting of noncitizens into the United States.[33] In *United States v. Evans*, the Supreme Court held that the statute did not provide any penalty for its prohibition of concealing and harboring aliens;[34] Congress expanded the statute in 1917[35] but did not define harboring or concealing.

In 1952, Congress passed the INA and added an explicit penalty for anyone who "willfully or knowingly conceals, harbors, or shields from detection" an unlawfully present alien.[36] Again, however, Congress did not define "harbor." In 1986, Congress changed the antiharboring provision to its current form, keeping the phrase "conceals, harbors, or shields from detection."[37] Titled "bringing in and harboring certain aliens," 8 U.S.C. § 1324(a)(1)(A)(iii) provides criminal penalties for anyone who

> knowing or in reckless disregard of the fact that an alien has come to, entered, or remains in the United States in violation of law, conceals, harbors, or shields from detection, or attempts to conceal, harbor, or shield from detection, such alien in any place, including any building or any means of transportation.[38]

Courts have held that the mere act of providing housing to an undocumented immigrant does not constitute harboring for purposes of § 1324. Specifically, courts have concluded that harboring includes the intentional act of helping an undocumented immigrant evade law enforcement authorities. In *United States v. Vargas-Cordon*, the U.S. Court of Appeals for the Second Circuit examined whether the district court erred in defining the meaning of harboring in its jury

---

31 Iglesia Pentecostal Casa De Dios Para Las Naciones, *Inc. v. Duke*, 718 Fed. Appx. 646 (10th Cir. 2017); Congregation of the *Passion v. Johnson*, 79 F.Supp.3d 855 (N.D. Ill. 2015); *Shalom Pentecostal Church v. Napolitano*, No. Civ. 11–4491 RMB, 2013 WL 162986 (D.N.J. January 15, 2013).

32 The United States experienced a rise in immigration during the early twentieth century. Congress passed the antismuggling law as part of series of reforms intended to restrict immigration.

33 See Immigration Act of 1907, Pub. L. No. 59–96, 34 Stat. 898, 900–1.

34 333 U.S. 483 (1948).

35 See Immigration Act of 1917, Pub. L. No. 64–301, 39 Stat. 874, 880.

36 See Immigration and Nationality Act of 1952, Pub. L. No. 82–414, § 274(a), 66 Stat. 163, 228–29.

37 See Immigration Reform and Control Act of 1986, Pub. L. No. 99–603, § 112(a), 100 Stat. 3359, 3381–82.

38 8 U.S.C. § 1324(a)(1)(A)(iii) (2018).

instructions.[39] The defendant was convicted of concealing and harboring "an unlawfully present alien in violation of 8 U.S.C. § 1324(a)(1)(A)(iii)," for hiring a smuggler to bring a 15-year-old girl, with whom he had a sexual relationship, into the United States and to his residence.[40] Challenging this conviction, the defendant argued that the trial judge erred by instructing the jury that the term "harbor" means, "to shelter, or afford shelter to."[41] Ultimately, the court held that a textual analysis of the term "harbor" unambiguously reveals that it includes "an element of concealment."[42] Although the court recognized that dictionaries had inconsistent definitions of "harboring," it held that both the placement of the term "harbor" in the statute as well as the overall structure of 8 U.S.C. § 1324 indicate that the central meaning of the term "centered around evading detection."[43] Thus, the court held that harboring refers to conduct "intended to facilitate" a noncitizen's ability to remain in the United States "illegally and to prevent detection by the authorities," and the "mere act of providing shelter to an alien, when done without intention to help prevent the alien's detection by immigration authorities or police," is not harboring.[44]

The Second Circuit's adoption of this narrow definition of "harboring" is consistent with other courts that have held that the mere act of giving shelter to a noncitizen does not constitute harboring. For example, in *Del Rio-Mocci v. Connolly Properties*, the U.S. Court of Appeals for the Third Circuit addressed whether a landlord violated the antiharboring provision by actively advertising and renting apartments to immigrants that they knew were undocumented.[45] Acknowledging that the property managers did not bring the noncitizens to the United States, provide them with false documents, help them avoid federal authorities, or pay rent on their behalf so that their names were not listed on the leases, the court held that simply providing housing to immigrants whom the property managers knew were undocumented did not violate § 1324.[46] Likewise, the U.S. Court of Appeals for the Ninth Circuit, which is the circuit for the court that heard Warren's case, similarly required an element of intent to violate the law. In *United States v. You*, the Ninth Circuit held that when a defendant is charged with illegal harboring under 8 U.S.C. § 1324, the jury must be instructed to find that the defendant acted with "the purpose of avoiding [the aliens'] detection by immigration authorities."[47]

One other factor about 8 U.S.C. § 1324 is worth noting. In 2005, Congress amended the statute to protect religious organizations from being prosecuted

---

39 733 F.3d 366 (2d Cir. 2013).
40 Ibid., 370–71.
41 Ibid., 379–80.
42 Ibid., 381.
43 Ibid.
44 Ibid., 382.
45 672 F.3d 241 (3d Cir. 2012).
46 Ibid., 247.
47 382 F.3d 958, 966 (9th Cir. 2004).

under § 1324 under certain conditions.[48] Specifically, § 1324(a)(1)(C) provides that it would not be a violation of the statute "for a religious denomination having a bona fide nonprofit, religious organization in the United States" or their agents or officers "to encourage, invite, call, allow, or enable an alien who is present in the United States to perform the vocation of a minister or missionary" as noncompensated volunteer, as long as the minister or missionary "has been a member of the denomination for at least one year."[49] The exception does not apply if "a person encourages or induces an alien to come and enter the United States."[50] Introduced by Utah Senator Bob Bennett on behalf of the Church of Jesus Christ of Latter Day Saints, the amendment sought to prevent churches from criminal prosecution because of undocumented ministers who do missionary work.[51]

In brief, courts have interpreted 8 U.S.C. § 1324 narrowly and have held that the mere act of providing shelter is not harboring. Instead, courts have interpreted violations of this statute to include the intention to help a noncitizen evade immigration authorities. What, then, happens when one admits to engaging in humanitarian actions consistent with, if not compelled by, one's faith, in ways that the government contends enabled a noncitizen to evade immigration authorities? This tension between exercising one's faith and being subject to prosecution under 8 U.S.C. § 1324 became evident in the federal government's prosecution of Scott Warren.

III United States v. Warren

Warren faced two different types of prosecution: one for the felony charge of 8 U.S.C. § 1324 and the other for the misdemeanor charges of unauthorized use of a vehicle in the wilderness area (50 C.F.R. § 35.5) and abandonment of property (50 C.F.R. § 27.93). We argue that the cases highlight at least two points regarding immigration enforcement. First, they illuminate both the struggles of immigrants, particularly those from Central America (see also Bill Ong Hing and Raj Nadella, Chapter 17), to seek refuge in the United States and the humanitarian efforts by various individuals and organizations—religious and nonreligious alike—to assist immigrants. Warren framed his humanitarian actions squarely within the ambit of RFRA's protection for religious liberty rights. Second, the cases demonstrate the Trump administration's heightened policies of enforcing immigration laws that have been stymied in part by RFRA. As such, the cases

---

48 Agriculture, Rural Development, Food and Drug Administration, and Related Agencies Appropriations Act, 2006, Pub. L. No. 109–97, § 796, 119 Stat. 2120, 2165 (2005).
49 8 U.S.C. § 1324(a)(1)(C) (2018). Although the missionary or minister must not be compensated, he or she can be provided with room, board, travel, medical assistance, and other basic living expenses.
50 Ibid.
51 "Mormons Initiated Protection on Aliens," *The Washington Times*, November 28, 2005, https://m.washingtontimes.com/news/2005/nov/28/20051128-122403-6535r/.

258 *Rose Cuison-Villazor and Ulrich Schmiedel*

show RFRA's potentially effective use in defending humanitarian acts at or near the border and perhaps in advancing immigrants' rights within the country as well.

Warren, a 37-year-old geography teacher in Arizona, had been volunteering for No More Deaths for years prior to his arrest in January 2018.[52] By volunteering for No More Deaths, he took part in an expanded sanctuary movement that emerged after the November 2016 election.[53] The sanctuary movement in the context of immigration law is, of course, not new. It began in the 1980s after church leaders, such as Jim Corbett and John Fife, provided food, water, shelter, and transportation to Central American asylum applicants whose applications were routinely denied by the federal government.[54] Engaging in what Corbett referred to as "civil initiative," these sanctuary leaders provided humanitarian aid because they believed that the government was violating the law, while the sanctuary workers were merely *upholding* the law. Their arguments were unavailing. Eventually, the federal government prosecuted some of these sanctuary leaders and workers for violating 8 U.S.C. § 1324.[55] Similar to Warren, they argued that the government infringed upon their religious liberty rights. Their claim, however, was based on the First Amendment;[56] RFRA would not become law until a few years later. Unlike Warren, these volunteers were convicted,[57] illustrating the challenges of appealing to the First Amendment as a defense for faith-based humanitarian aid that the government deems to flout immigration law.

Nevertheless, the sanctuary movement continued to provide humanitarian aid. It underwent a resurgence in 2005 when other faith-based leaders formed the New Sanctuary Movement in response to President George W. Bush's immigration enforcement policies.[58] The movement continued throughout President Barack Obama's and President Donald Trump's administrations.

Among the faith-based groups that have continued the sanctuary tradition is No More Deaths. Founded in 2004,[59] it encourages members to draw on their religious faith to push for humanitarian immigration policies. The group presents

---

52 Motion to Dismiss, at 2; Allyn, "Jury Acquits Aid Worker."
53 See Rose Cuison Villazor and Pratheepan Gulasekaram, "The New Sanctuary and Anti-Sanctuary Movements," *UC Davis Law Review* 52, no. 1 (2018): 549–69.
54 Ibid., 554–55; Sanctuary Trial Papers, Special Collections, University of Arizona, https://speccoll.library.arizona.edu/collections/sanctuary-trial-papers.
55 Katherine Bishop, "Sanctuary Groups Sue to Halt Trials," *New York Times*, May 8, 1985, A13.
56 Ibid.
57 "6 Convicted, 5 Cleared of Plot to Smuggle in Aliens for Sanctuary," *New York Times*, May 2, 1986, at A19, www.nytimes.com/1986/05/02/us/6-convicted-5-cleared-of-plot-to-smuggle-in-aliens-for-sanctuary.html.
58 See "Fighting Injustice: The New Sanctuary Movement," *Latin America Working Group*, www.lawg.org/fighting-injustice-the-new-sanctuary-movement/.
59 Kristina Campbell, "Humanitarian Aid Is Never a Crime? The Politics of Immigration Enforcement and the Provision of Sanctuary," *Syracuse Law Review* 63, no. 1 (2012): 71–118, at 109–10.

"*No More Deaths*"   259

itself as a ministry of the Unitarian Universalist Church of Tucson.[60] They have adopted Corbett's concept of civil initiative, explaining that their "responsibility for protecting the persecuted must be balanced by accountability to the legal order."[61] Its volunteers, like Warren, offer humanitarian aid to migrants walking the Sonoran Desert and those who have already crossed the border by giving them food, water, medical care, clothes, and shelter, if need be.[62]

Such was the type of aid that Warren provided to the two Central American men. Kristian Perez-Villanueva and José Arnaldo Sacaria-Goday had searched online for the best ways to cross the border illegally.[63] They had heard that they could get food, water, and shelter at The Barn, and they found its address online.[64] They crossed the border on foot[65] and afterwards received a ride to a local gas station.[66] There they used the station's Wi-Fi to locate The Barn, and they obtained a ride to it.[67] They entered The Barn and drank water and rested.[68] About 45 minutes later, Warren arrived and assessed their medical condition.[69] He called two other volunteers, and for the next three days they gave the men food, water, beds, and clothing.[70]

Border agents had been surveilling The Barn for days. On January 17, 2018, two border agents arrived at The Barn and arrested Warren and the two immigrants.[71] The federal government charged Warren with violating three counts of 8 U.S.C. § 1324.[72] Specifically, the government alleged that Warren conspired with others to knowingly transport Perez-Villanueva and Sacaria-Goday and conceal and harbor both of them.[73]

This was not Warren's first brush with federal law enforcement. Approximately six months before his arrest at The Barn, he had encountered authorities with the U.S. Fish and Wildlife Service, Department of the Interior, which patrols the Cabeza Prieta Wilderness Area, including parts of the Sonoran Desert. On June 1, 2017, a federal wildlife officer saw two trucks parked in the Cabeza Prieta Wilderness Area containing "multiple one gallon water jugs, canned food and

---

60 See notes 4 and 5 above.
61 No More Deaths, https://nomoredeaths.org/about-no-more-deaths/civil-initiative/.
62 Ibid.
63 Criminal Complaint.
64 Ibid.
65 Motion to Dismiss, at 3.
66 Criminal Complaint.
67 Ibid.; Motion to Dismiss, at 4.
68 Motion to Dismiss, at 4.
69 Murat Oztaskin, " 'USA v Scott' and the Fight to Prove that Humanitarian Aid Is Not a Crime," *The New Yorker*, July 8, 2020, www.newyorker.com/culture/the-new-yorker-documentary/usa-v-scott-and-the-fight-to-prove-that-humanitarian-aid-is-not-a-crime.
70 Motion to Dismiss, at 4.
71 Ibid., 5.
72 Criminal Complaint; Indictment.
73 Ibid.

green milk crates with food and toiletry items" on their beds.[74] The officer saw Warren with other individuals by the trucks and asked about their purpose in the area; Warren admitted to driving one of the trucks. The officer eventually told Warren and the others to leave. On December 6, 2017, the federal government charged Warren with Class B misdemeanors of unauthorized use of a vehicle in the wilderness area and abandonment of property for leaving behind water, canned goods, and other materials.[75]

Warren sought to dismiss both the felony and misdemeanor cases, arguing, among other things, that his actions were squarely protected by RFRA.[76] First, in his motion to dismiss, he contended that RFRA applies to "any exercise of religion, whether or not compelled by, or central to, a system of religious belief."[77] This religion may include "any moral, ethical, or religious beliefs about what is right and wrong that are sincerely held with the strength of traditional religious convictions."[78] Warren maintained that he holds a sincere belief in a duty to provide care to fellow human beings in distress and holds this "belief with the strength of traditional religious convictions."[79]

Second, Warren argued that criminally prosecuting him for his humanitarian work would substantially burden his practice of his faith.[80] As he pointed out, there is substantial burden when a person is coerced into a "Catch-22 situation: exercise of their religion under fear of civil or criminal sanction."[81] In his case, Warren faced one of two choices: turn away two migrants who needed his help, which would have violated his moral and spiritual beliefs, or face felony prosecution under 8 U.S.C. § 1324.[82] Thus, Warren faced a dilemma, as he explained in the hearing on his motion to dismiss, "[b]ased on my spiritual beliefs, . . . I have to act when someone is in need."[83]

Third, Warren argued that the government could not meet its burden of establishing that his criminal prosecution furthered a particular compelling interest or that it was the least restrictive means of furthering that interest.[84] The government's assertion of the antiharboring provision of immigration law in general

---

74 Affidavit in Support of Summons for Defendant Named in Information, *United States v. Warren*, 4:17–00341MJ, 4 (Dist. Ct. Ariz., December 7, 2017).
75 Information, *United States v. Warren*, 4:17–00341MJ, 4 (Dist. Ct. Ariz., December 7, 2017).
76 Motion to Dismiss. Although the motion to dismiss discussed in this chapter was filed to seek to dismiss the felony, antiharboring charge, the RFRA arguments presented in this motion were similar to his arguments seeking to dismiss the misdemeanor charges.
77 Ibid., 9.
78 Ibid., 9–10 (citing *Welsh v. United States*, 398 U.S. 333, 340 (1970)).
79 Ibid., 9–11.
80 Ibid., 13.
81 Ibid. (quoting *Snoqualmie Indian Tribe v. F.E.R.C.*, 545 F.3d 1207, 1214 (9th Cir. 2008)).
82 Ibid.
83 See Warren Testimony, at 44.
84 See Motion to Dismiss, at 14–15.

was not enough, Warren maintained; rather, the government needed to show a particular government interest to prosecute him, and this particular government interest had to be compelling and "of the highest order."[85] His criminal prosecution for providing food, water, and shelter to two undocumented immigrants, he argued, failed to further a compelling government interest of the highest order. The government could not possibly have a compelling interest in keeping the migrant men dehydrated.[86] In addition, there could be no compelling government interest where an exception exists that would make an analogous action lawful, 8 U.S.C. § 1324 includes a specific exception for religious denominations to provide food and shelter to undocumented immigrants.[87]

Finally, Warren contended that even if the government were able to show a compelling interest, it could not show that the means to achieve that interest was the least restrictive. Specifically, the government's interest in enforcing immigration law could have been met without prosecuting Warren, because Border Patrol agents still could have detained and arrested the migrants.[88]

A hearing on the motion to dismiss the 8 U.S.C. § 1324 indictment took place on May 11, 2018. A few days prior, the court held a bench trial on the misdemeanor charges of unauthorized operation of a motor vehicle in a wilderness area and abandonment of property. The bench trial illuminated Warren's argumentation as to why RFRA offers a defense against his criminal prosecution. At the outset, his testimony reflected his sincerely held belief in helping people suffering in the desert. He emphasized, for example, that all "life is sacred" and "all places are sacred."[89] Warren explained that he works with two different groups, Ajo Samaritan and No More Deaths, which engage in search-and-rescue and search-and-recovery of migrants crossing the desert. Noting the sacredness of the "the sort of life force of people and of the places and the struggle that people undergo in that particular place," he said he believed that in the desert he bore witness to the remains of the dead, thus benefiting their souls and connecting him to them.[90]

Notably, Warren admitted to "putting out water and supply drops," indicating that he knew full well that he was violating the law. As he explained, "we had the maps, the death maps, and we had been out there on foot a few times, so we sort of understood in a general sense of where we needed to go and where we needed to sort of put the water and other kinds of, yeah, humanitarian supplies."[91] He defended his actions by stating that his religious practice tells him to help those

---

85 Ibid., 16–17 (quoting *Gonzalez v. O'Centro Espirtal Beneficiente Uniao Do Vegetal*, 546 U.S. 418, 433 (2006)).
86 Ibid., 17–18.
87 Ibid., 19–20.
88 Ibid., 21–22.
89 See Scott Warren Testimony, Bench Trial, *United States v. Warren*, MJ-17–341-TUC-RCC (JR) 17 (D. Ct. Ariz. May 5–6, 2018) [hereinafter Warren, Bench Trial].
90 Ibid., 17–21.
91 Ibid., 50.

262 Rose Cuison-Villazor and Ulrich Schmiedel

who have died in the desert and those nearby who need supplies.[92] The very act of leaving water is spiritual to him, allowing him to "take a moment to reflect on and to sort of, in [his] own way, bless those things that they put out, those gallons of water and the other kinds of humanitarian supplies."[93] Significantly, Warren contended that his beliefs compelled him to provide humanitarian aid. When asked whether he would still engage in such acts "even if [he knew] that it's a violation of . . . regulations," he replied, "Yes."[94]

Similarly, Warren admitted to driving through the wilderness without authorization from the federal government. But failing to go to the desert would be inconsistent with Warren's beliefs. As he explained, "to neglect that area of greatest need to me would be sort of just engaging in a hollow performance of what's really needed in the witnessing and the practice that I undertake."[95] When asked whether he "could exercise his faith by not putting supplies out for migrants in need," Warren answered, "No, I would say that realistically I cannot do that, can't exercise my faith by not leaving out supplies for people in need."[96] Indeed, in cross-examination, the government asked Warren whether he knew that he needed a special-use permit to drive to the wilderness; Warren replied that he did.[97]

In sum, Warren's testimony at the bench trial for the misdemeanor charges underscored his RFRA argument: that his sincerely held beliefs and practices were substantially burdened by the government's prosecution of his acts, which constituted exercise of his religious beliefs. After the trial, the court decided to "delay its verdict until the conclusion of the felony [8 U.S.C. § 1324] trial" to avoid impacting the "jury's possible verdict in the felony case."[98]

A few days after the bench trial, a magistrate judge presided over the hearing on Warren's motion to dismiss the felony case. Again Warren testified about his religious beliefs and his arguments as to why RFRA offered a defense against his prosecution. At the hearing, Warren and his father testified about their beliefs that "the Earth is their house of worship and they respect the dignity and wishes of all they encounter" and that a "key element of [Warren's] belief system is to help others in distress to the point of being a duty of compulsion."[99]

The court, however, was unconvinced. Commenting that Warren's "belief is a somewhat modified Golden Rule, in that he has a compulsion to help those in their

---

92 Ibid., 23 ("[e]verywhere that we put water is either where somebody died in the immediate vicinity or very close by, so that ground to me is sacred any time we go there").

93 Ibid.

94 Ibid., 39.

95 Ibid., 40.

96 Ibid., 41.

97 Ibid., 50.

98 Order, *United States v. Warren*, No. 17–00341MJ-001-TUC-RCC 1 (D. Ct. Ariz., November 20, 2019).

99 Report and Recommendation, *United States v. Warren*, No. CR-18–00223–001-TUC-RCC (BPV), May 30, 2018, at 2, www.courtlistener.com/recap/gov.uscourts.azd.1081102/gov. uscourts.azd.1081102.81.0.pdf.

"No More Deaths" 263

immediate need," the court noted that Warren believed in helping people "where they are, but not help[ing] them get to their ultimate destination."[100] However, the court explained that Warren did not present testimony that 8 U.S.C. § 1324 compelled him to do "anything in violation of his religious beliefs." Indeed, the court noted that the statute is a law of "a general nature that [applies] to all and [does] not single him or any identifiable group into acting in conflict with their religious beliefs." As the court explained, Warren is "best told not to violate the laws that apply equally to all."[101] Ultimately, the court held that 8 U.S.C. § 1324 did not substantially burden Warren's exercise of his religious beliefs. The court noted that at no time during Warren's testimony did he explain that his "religious beliefs necessitated [that] he aid undocumented immigrants." Instead, the court held that all that Warren claimed was that his religious beliefs compelled him to aid only persons in distress. Indeed, the court specifically explained that "[a]ssisting undocumented migrants is not an expressed objective of his beliefs."[102]

The court's RFRA analysis focused on whether Warren's stated religious beliefs were specific to helping unauthorized immigrants, even if that meant violating immigration law. As the court explicated, Warren had been charged with harboring undocumented immigrants who were unlawfully present in the United States, but he had not "assert[ed] that harboring or concealing people" unlawfully in the country could not be prohibited. Accordingly, the magistrate judge found that there was no substantial burden on Warren's religious beliefs and recommended denying Warren's motion to dismiss with respect to the 8 U.S.C. § 1324 charge.[103]

The district court adopted the recommendation of the magistrate judge,[104] and the government went forward with its felony case against Warren. The trial lasted seven days and ended on June 11, 2019. After deliberating for three days, the jury could not reach consensus on whether Warren violated 8 U.S.C. § 1324,[105] and, the court declared a mistrial. Undeterred, the federal government tried Warren again, beginning on November 15, 2019. The second trial lasted for six days before the government rested and the jury began deliberations. Unlike the jury in the first trial, the jury deliberated only two hours, this time finding Warren not guilty.[106]

---

100 Ibid.
101 Ibid., 3.
102 Ibid.
103 Ibid., 4.
104 Order Adopting Report and Recommendation, *United States v. Warren*, No. CR-18–00223–001-TUC-RCC (BPV), September 17, 2018, www.courtlistener.com/recap/gov.uscourts.azd.1081102/gov.uscourts.azd.1081102.127.0.pdf.
105 Jury Questions during Deliberations, *United States v. Warren*, No. CR-18–00223–001-TUC-RCC (BPV), June 11, 2019, www.courtlistener.com/recap/gov.uscourts.azd.1081102/gov.uscourts.azd.1081102.276.0.pdf.
106 District Judge's Minutes, *United States v. Warren*, No. CR-18–00223–001-TUC-RCC (BPV), November 20, 2019, www.courtlistener.com/recap/gov.uscourts.azd.1081102/

264 *Rose Cuison-Villazor and Ulrich Schmiedel*

That same day, the district court issued its ruling on the misdemeanor case. The judge held that the government had presented "evidence beyond a reasonable doubt" proving the two charges—operating a motor vehicle in a wilderness area and abandonment of property.[107] Further, the court noted that "the Defendant admitted to doing the very acts that the Government charged him with."[108] Nevertheless, the court agreed that with respect to the charge of abandonment of property, Warren met his burden of showing that his "religious beliefs function as a successful affirmative defense." Noting that it is not up to the court to "weigh the sincerity or the validity of" Warren's beliefs, the court nevertheless took Warren's "word that he sincerely holds such beliefs" and was "obliged to leave water jugs because of his religious beliefs." Thus, the government's regulation "imposes a substantial burden on his exercise of his religion."[109] Further, the court held that the regulation concerning abandonment of property "is not the least restrictive means to achieve" the government's interest in protecting the wildlife refuge.[110] The court, however, rejected the RFRA defense of unauthorized driving through the wilderness area, concluding that Warren's "religious beliefs did not compel him to drive his vehicle in the restricted area." Interestingly, on March 4, 2020, the government filed a motion to dismiss the charge of unauthorized operation of a vehicle in the wilderness, which the court granted, ending all criminal cases against Warren.[111]

The foregoing discussion highlights the successful, albeit partial, reliance on RFRA in Warren's defense. Although it is unclear what role RFRA played in the hung jury trial and at his acquittal, RFRA clearly was effective against the misdemeanor charge. Whether RFRA would be useful in other criminal cases involving assisting undocumented immigrants remains to be seen. The facts of Warren's case took place in the desert, where border crossers indisputably need water, food, and shelter. Further, Warren admitted to having engaged in acts that he knew government officials believed violated the law. However, Warren emphasized that his faith compelled him to aid those persons in the desert who were in need despite the law's proscription. Lastly, the court found that the government had a least restrictive means of achieving its interest in protecting the wilderness. These facts are arguably specific to cases involving the border.

Nevertheless, Warren's cases have some implications for cases involving aid to immigrants in the interior of the United States. The answers to some preliminary questions may be useful in determining whether it would be appropriate to use

---

gov.uscourts.azd.1081102.394.0_1.pdf (noting that the jury found the defendant not guilty).

107 Order, *United States v. Warren*, No. 17–00341MJ-001-TUC-RCC 1 (D. Ct. Ariz. November 20, 2019).

108 Ibid.

109 Ibid., 2.

110 Ibid.

111 Order, *United States v. Warren*, No. 17–00341MJ-001-TUC-RCC 1 (D. Ct. Ariz. March 4, 2020).

RFRA. For example, what type of harm is the immigrant experiencing in the United States and is that different from the border cases? How might a person help the immigrant, and what is the relationship between this help and the individual's faith? For instance, might shelter at someone's home offer the assistance that the immigrant needs? Can provision of sanctuary be tied to an individual's faith? Can it be argued that such help constitutes the exercise of religion? What immigration regulation is at issue, and might this regulation substantially burden one's ability to exercise religion by providing assistance? Does the government have a less restrictive means of achieving its interest? Must the government, for example, remove noncitizens for violating the INA, or is there some other, less restrictive means to effect compliance with the INA. In sum, exploring RFRA's application beyond the border-crossing cases may help advocates who want to engage in humanitarian acts but are concerned about criminal and civil penalties.

IV Public theology for a new legal landscape

No More Deaths introduces itself as a humanitarian organization "dedicated to stepping up efforts to stop the deaths of migrants in the desert."[112] Of course, humanitarian efforts can be either religious or nonreligious, but No More Deaths makes clear that it draws on a set of "Faith-Based Principles for Immigration Reform" that were developed by faith leaders from diverse traditions.[113] While it remains an open question whether Warren's volunteering for No More Deaths could and should fall fully under freedom of religion—as mentioned above, the RFRA defense was accepted for one of the three charges—we argue that it can be characterized as a performative public theology that is claiming or reclaiming theological fragments for the public square in order to convince both believers and nonbelievers that deaths at borders must be prevented. This public theology runs through No More Death's civil initiative.

Freedom of religion is a complex concept. In *The Impossibility of Religious Freedom*, first published in 2005, Winnifred Fallers Sullivan asks whether freedom of religion can ever be put into practice.[114] According to Sullivan, a court has to choose what counts as religious and what counts as nonreligious in order to decide whether an action ought to be protected by freedom of religion. Such a choice, she argues, turns a court into a church. It is a theological task—a task for the insiders rather than the outsiders of a religion—to reflect on which actions are in accordance with their theology. Judges lose their neutrality when they take up this theological task.

---

112 The organization's self-understanding, as indicated by its mission statement, is detailed on its website, https://nomoredeaths.org/about-no-more-deaths/.

113 Both preamble and principles are available at https://nomoredeaths.org/about-no-more-deaths/faith-based-principles-for-immigration-reform/.

114 Winnifred Fallers Sullivan, *The Impossibility of Religious Freedom: New Edition* (Princeton, NJ: Princeton University Press, 2018).

Sullivan paved the way for a number of studies that have assessed the significance of religion for the law. In *Beyond Religious Freedom*, Elizabeth Shakman Hurd clarifies how the category of religion continues to escape conceptual control.[115] She draws on "lived religion"—an approach to the study of religion that aims to take account of the muddle and messiness of practices of faith in the private as well as the public sphere:[116] "religion-in-action," as Robert Orsi puts it.[117] Orsi presents lived religion as dynamic rather than static, concerned and connected with everyday life in all of its social, cultural, and political entanglements. Orsi points out that deciding what can or cannot count as religion involves "high-stakes matters that go well beyond issues of scholarly definition, or—put another way—scholarly definitions of religion are implicated in much broader social and cultural agendas."[118] Hurd captures the impact that these agendas have on politics: "Rather than a stable norm . . . that stands above the fray, the development of religious rights is a technique of governance that authorizes particular forms of politics."[119]

Does Warren's case render freedom of religion possible or impossible? While we cannot go into the debate between the defenders and the despisers of the category of freedom of religion,[120] it is crucial to note that all of them insist (albeit from opposing angles) that theology is inescapable. *Theology* is what is at stake with freedom of religion, as Warren claims it. Does No More Deaths have a theology?

The faith practiced by the Unitarian Universalist Church of Tucson is paradigmatic for lived religion in that it prioritizes authenticity over authority.[121] "If you are looking for a place where you can explore your own spiritual truths," the congregation writes on its website, "you have come to the right place!"[122]

---

115 Elizabeth Shakman Hurd, *Beyond Religious Freedom: The New Global Politics of Religion* (Princeton, NJ: Princeton University Press, 2015).

116 Ibid., 13–15.

117 Robert Orsi, "Introduction to the Second Edition: Fieldwork Between the Present and the Past," in *The Madonna of 115th Street: Faith and Community in Italian Harlem, 1880–1950*, ed. Robert Orsi (New Haven, CT: Yale University Press, 2010), xxvii–lvi, at xxxii. Orsi is often credited with inventing the paradigm of lived religion. See also the contributions to *Lived Religion in America: Toward a History of Practice*, ed. Stuart D. Hall (Princeton, NJ: Princeton University Press, 1997).

118 Orsi, "Introduction to the Second Edition," xxxiii.

119 Hurd, *Beyond Religious Freedom*, 17. See also *Politics of Religious Freedom*, eds. Winnifred Fallers Sullivan, Elizabeth Shakman Hurd, Saba Mahmood, and Peter G. Danchin (Chicago: The University of Chicago Press, 2015).

120 For critiques of Sullivan and Hurd, see Joshua T. Mauldin, "Contesting Religious Freedom: Impossibility, Normativity, and Justice," *Oxford Journal of Law and Religion* 5, no. 3 (2016): 457–81; David Decosimo, "The New Genealogy of Religious Freedom," *Journal of Law and Religion* 33, no. 1 (2018): 3–41.

121 Of course, any religion can be studied as lived religion. What is interesting about the Unitarian Universalists of Tucson is that they acknowledge that practice—rather than doctrine—is at the center of the faith of the congregation.

122 See https://uuctucson.org/.

Historically, both Unitarians and Universalists criticized Christian orthodoxy: against the Trinity of God, they argued for the unity of God, so they became known as Unitarians; against the particularity of God, they argued for the universality of God, so they became known as Universalists. God's salvation is for everyone, because God is unitarian and universal.[123]

Today Unitarian Universalists argue for a "concept of a unity in diversity" that rests on the dignity that comes from a "spark of divinity that resides in us all."[124] Regardless of whether you believe in God, then, you are welcome to join the congregation in Tucson. The congregation blurs the boundaries between believers and nonbelievers—that is, between what is classically considered religious and what is classically considered nonreligious. The congregation in Tucson points out that faith encompasses them all, the believers and the nonbelievers. With their faith, they planned to "flood the federal court room at 405 W. Congress St. in Tucson."[125]

Theologically, it is crucial to note that by blurring the boundaries between religious (believers) and nonreligious (nonbelievers), the congregation makes its theological point and maintains its theological profile. The muddle of religion, then, is not madness but method for its theology. Given this conscious blurring, how could a court decide whether freedom of religion applied to Warren's actions?

The "Faith-Based Principles for Immigration Reform" that are central to the campaign of No More Deaths confirm the theology of the congregation. The short but striking preamble to these principles points to "communities of faith."[126] The principles are multifaith, including both religious and nonreligious "people of conscience."[127] The point of the preamble is that the multifaith perspective "transcends borders," including the borders between confessions. It calls for a justice that comes with love and a love that comes with justice for religious and nonreligious people. The ethical and political principles for immigration reform that follow from the preamble criticize the militarization of the border as "ill-conceived policy," contending that it has not been successful. People will continue to cross the borders. Consequently, the principles call for protecting people, whether they have or have not yet entered the United States. People come first. The principles are interested not in problematizing all borders but in the militarization of the current border to the United States that causes deaths. The

---

123 Ibid. See also John A. Buehrens and Forrest Church, *A Chosen Faith: An Introduction to Unitarian Universalism: Revised Edition* (Boston: Beacon Press, 1998).

124 See https://uuctucson.org/.

125 Ibid.

126 The "Faith-Based Principles" are referenced by the Unitarian Universalist congregation of Tucson. As a ministry of this congregation, No More Deaths presents them on its website, https://nomoredeaths.org/about-no-more-deaths/faith-based-principles-for-immigration-reform/.

127 In what follows, we are citing https://nomoredeaths.org/about-no-more-deaths/faith-based-principles-for-immigration-reform/.

268   *Rose Cuison-Villazor and Ulrich Schmiedel*

policy proposal takes the dignity of persons—documented or undocumented—as a point of departure. The root causes of migration to the United States have to be addressed: economic and environmental inequality.

The reports of No More Deaths—the most recent is *Disappeared: How the U.S. Border Enforcement Agencies Are Fueling a Missing Persons Crisis*[128]—point to the failure of the U.S. immigration system.[129] While concentrating on concrete cases, No More Deaths challenges the system altogether.[130] "Civil initiative" is crucial here. Coined by Corbett, the term has been employed by the U.S. sanctuary movement since the 1980s, particularly in Tucson.[131] Civil disobedience calls citizens to break laws they consider unjust. To contribute to change in these laws, disobedient citizens are willing to accept punishment. Civil initiative, however, turns the tables. Barbara Bezdek explains: "The Sanctuary members claimed that they act to serve the law. They also claimed that the U.S. government was the outlaw, acting in violation of national and international provisions of asylum," thereby challenging "premises about what is 'law.'"[132] No More Deaths continues this challenge, contending that practices like the distribution of water to prevent deaths in the desert should not be considered breaking the law.[133] On the contrary, citizens are called to take the initiative to uphold the law that the government violates.

Both the preamble and the proposals of the "Faith-Based Principles" aim at persuading people with or without faith to perform such civil initiative. Again, the theological point and the theological profile that run through the principles blur the boundaries between the religious and the nonreligious. No More Deaths is faith-based, but it is based on a faith that addresses the religious and the nonreligious. This faith is played out in their practice.

128 *Disappeared* is a multipart report authored by No More Deaths and La Coalición de Derechos Humanos. The report is being released in stages, and can be read at www.thedisappearedreport.org/.

129 See https://nomoredeaths.org/abuse-documentation/.

130 See Ananda Rose, "Transcending Borders: No More Deaths and a Higher Moral Law," in *Showdown in the Sonoran Desert: Religion, Law, and the Immigration Controversy* (Oxford: Oxford University Press, 2012), 61–80.

131 The classic account, referenced by https://nomoredeaths.org/about-no-more-deaths/civil-initiative/, is James A. Corbett, "Sanctuary, Basic Rights and Humanity's Fault Lines: A Personal Essay," Plenary Session Address to the Western Social Science Association on April 23, 1987. See also his posthumously published *Sanctuary for All Life: The Cowbalah of Jim Corbett* (Englewood, CO: Howling Dog Press, 2005). For an account of Corbett's role in the sanctuary movement, see Miriam Davidson, *Convictions of the Heart: Jim Corbett and the Sanctuary Movement* (Tucson: The University of Arizona Press, 1988).

132 Barbara Bezdek, "Religious Outlaws: Legality and the Politics of Citizen Interpretation," *Tennessee Law Review* 62, no. 4 (1995): 899–996, at 971.

133 See https://nomoredeaths.org/about-no-more-deaths/civil-initiative/. Bezdek, "Religious Outlaws," 975–76, clarifies that the case rests on the "Nuremberg argument." The Nuremberg court took the position that people have obligations to each other that transcend their obedience to the laws of the state in which they live: not performing these obligations is punished by the law, so performing these obligations is protected by the law.

In his testimony, Warren reflected on how his faith revolved around place: "There's something about a place, that place in particular, about the soul of that place and the spirit of that place."[134] The Sonoran Desert that migrants cross to enter the United States has a spiritual significance for him: "it's the connection to place, it's the connection to land and life."[135] Because of the "struggle" and the "sacrifice" that migrants experience in the desert,[136] this place is "imbued with soul, with life force," characterized by a "deep sense of presence" and a "deep sense of absence" where they died.[137] "Their spirit continues to dwell in that place."[138] Probed to define what he meant by "spirit," "soul" or "life force," Warren pointed to its performative rather than its propositional quality: "To me, it's . . . a bit hard to pin down, but is something that I . . . sense when I'm in these places."[139] Crucially, this spirit compelled his humanitarian work. "For me the sort of ethical or moral relationship to that place comes from that understanding. It comes from that felt sense of everything having a life force there."[140]

Barbara Andrea Sostaita has analyzed the work of No More Deaths.[141] Drawing on ethnographic fieldwork—during the summer of 2019, she joined activists on their tours through the desert—she points to the spiritual significance of the humanitarian work for the volunteers when they encounter migrants or the remains of migrants in the desert. Warren's testimony speaks to both experiences.

Warren has been involved in the discovery and recovery of almost 20 people. He interprets his involvement as "spiritual experience,"[142] which "flows from the interconnection that I have with the place and the people, the land and life of that place."[143] This interconnection, encapsulated in the life force of a place, provokes him to care for people in need.[144] The place connects him to the particular person in need: "that person is us and we are that person."[145] This connection grounds the Golden Rule: "we must . . . do unto others as we would want to have others done onto us."[146] When water and food are put out where somebody has died, the

134 See Warren's Testimony, *supra* note 17, at 35.
135 Ibid., 36.
136 See Warren, Bench Trial, *supra* note 120, at 16.
137 See Warren's Testimony, *supra* note 1, at 36.
138 See Warren, Bench Trial, *supra* note 120, at 15–16.
139 Ibid., 16–17. In their testimonies, both Warren and Warren's father explained that their spirituality was not expressed in propositions so much as in performances, in practice. It cannot be described, but it can be done. See Warren's Testimony, *supra* note 17, at 12–17 (Warren's father's testimony); 47–48 (Warren's testimony).
140 Ibid., 37.
141 Barbara Andrea Sostaita, " 'Water, Not Walls': Toward a Religious Study of Life That Defies Borders," *American Religion* 1, no. 2 (2020): 74–97.
142 Warren's Testimony, *supra* note 17, at 42. "The entire desert is a sacred place. It's a graveyard. And just the act of moving through that space, that place, to me is a . . . spiritual experience." (Warren's Testimony, *supra* note 17, at 41).
143 See Warren Testimony, at 46.
144 Ibid., 44.
145 Ibid., 45.
146 Ibid.

270   *Rose Cuison-Villazor and Ulrich Schmiedel*

place creates a connection between the people who share it, even if they are not physically close. The place is "sacred ground."[147] As a consequence, the water and food are not simply water and food;[148] they witness to the struggle of people suffering in their attempts to cross the desert.[149] Sostaita calls the sharing of water and food "transborder communion."[150] In sharing, the border is overcome in material and spiritual ways.[151] Acting in accordance with the Golden Rule is a consequence of the spiritual connection created through sacred ground.

Sostaita points to a ritual that Warren practices when he encounters the remains of a migrant who has died in the desert. She interprets his practices as a faith that is "performed."[152] Warren argues that to "recover the people who have died is one of the most sacred things that we can do as humanitarian aid workers."[153] He depicts his ritual as follows:

> I personally will face the person or face the remains of the person and offer a kind of silent acknowledgement, and then I turn away from the site, and I will kneel down and pick up two handfuls of dirt and rocks, whatever kind of soil it is, and I'll hold that in my hands, sort of mash it together, let it fall out of my hands. And in my—in my mind, that's the act of holding—holding that ground, holding that place in my hands, holding it, holding it tight, and letting go of it. That is both sort of an act of, like, holding the person and then releasing, releasing them.[154]

Again, it is the place that allows for the connection: "That's the last place that that person would have . . . experienced when they were living, and they would have felt it. . . . And when we—when we come upon those areas, we feel that place as well."[155] Experiencing the place where the person died "is an act of spiritual completion for them."[156] Sostaita suggests that the spirituality performed in this ritual forms communities which "engage in the prefigurative creation of alternative worlds," beyond the coercion and criminalization of migrants. "This," she concludes "is how we access the sacred."[157] Both in their principles and in their practice, then, No More Deaths communicates a spirituality connected to a

---

147 See Warren, Bench Trial, at 24.
148 Ibid., 29.
149 See also Scott Warren, Kevin E. McHugh, and Jason Roehner, "After the Crossing: Afterlives of Found Objects in the Sonoran Desert," *Journal of the Southwest* 57, nos. 2–3 (2015): 503–16.
150 Sostaita, " 'Water, Not Walls,' " 81.
151 Ibid.
152 Ibid., 85.
153 See Warren Testimony, at 43.
154 See Warren, Bench Trial, at 25–26; see also Warren Testimony, at 44.
155 See Warren, Bench Trial, at 20.
156 Ibid., 18; see also Warren Testimony, at 44.
157 Sostaita, " 'Water, Not Walls,' " 96.

"No More Deaths" 271

theology that transcends the boundaries between the religious and the nonreligious in the public sphere. Is it a public theology?

As a field of study, public theology is interested in the significance of theology for the public square. It is often argued that to inject theology into the public square, theologians have to be bilingual: they have to speak in a religious and a nonreligious register at the same time to convince both religious insiders (who might prefer religious language) and religious outsiders (who might prefer nonreligious language).[158] The case for bilingual public theology owes a lot to Jürgen Habermas's suggestion that postsecular societies require translations: from the secular into the religious and from the religious into the secular.[159] Such translations, Habermas insists, are the condition for processes of communication.[160] The practices of religion cultivate "an awareness of what is missing."[161]

Kristin E. Heyer has suggested that the notion of the public is what is at stake in the classic debate between David Tracy and George Lindbeck about the nature of theology.[162] Is it desirable or undesirable for theology to go public? Who decides?[163] For Tracy (a "liberal" theologian), theology goes public to seek a conversation,[164] whereas for Lindbeck (a "postliberal" theologian), theology goes public to seek a conversion—the conversion of the public.[165] Tracy characterizes the public positively, Lindbeck negatively. Heyer argues that two concepts of truth lie behind these characterizations of the public: postliberals assume that truth is particular, while liberals assume that truth is universal. Theologians opting for the particularity of truth will find it inside the Christian community, while theologians opting for the universality of truth will find it inside and outside the Christian community. As a consequence, Tracy can find truth in a conversation between Christians and non-Christians.[166] For Lindbeck, however, there is no point to

---

158 For a survey of the field, see the contribution to Sebastian Kim and Katie Day, eds., *A Companion to Public Theology* (Leiden: Brill, 2017).

159 Jürgen Habermas, *Between Naturalism and Religion: Philosophical Essays*, trans. Ciaran Cronin (Cambridge: Polity Press, 2008).

160 See also the short summary by Jürgen Habermas, "Notes on Postsecular Society," *New Perspectives Quarterly* 25, no. 4 (2008): 17–29.

161 Jürgen Habermas, "An Awareness of What is Missing," in *An Awareness of What is Missing: Faith and Reason in a Post-Secular Age*, eds. Jürgen Habermas, et al. (Cambridge: Polity Press, 2010), 15–23.

162 Kristin E. Heyer, "How Does Theology Go Public? Rethinking the Debate Between David Tracy and George Lindbeck," *Political Theology* 5, no. 3 (2004): 307–27. For a comprehensive overview, see John Allan Knight, *Liberalism versus Postliberalism: The Great Divide in Twentieth-Century Theology* (Oxford: Oxford University Press, 2013).

163 Heyer, "How Does Theology Go Public?" 308.

164 See David Tracy, *Plurality and Ambiguity* (Chicago: The University of Chicago Press, 1987); David Tracy, *Dialogue with the Other: The Inter-Religious Dialogue* (Louvain: Peeters, 1990).

165 George Lindbeck, *The Nature of Doctrine: Religion and Theology in a Postliberal Age* (Louisville, KY: Westminster John Knox Press, 1984); George Lindbeck, *The Church in a Postliberal Age*, ed. James J. Buckley (Grand Rapids, MI: Eerdmans, 2003).

166 Heyer, "How Does Theology Go Public?" 314.

272 *Rose Cuison-Villazor and Ulrich Schmiedel*

a conversation between Christians and non-Christians, where the claims of Christianity are translated in a way that makes them accessible to both Christians and non-Christians. The translation would corrode the way of life that characterizes and centers Christianity. On the contrary, theology seeks to uphold a strong and stable border between the Christian and the non-Christian.

If No More Deaths was rooted in clearly identifiable and coherently interpretable claims of Christianity, it could make a convincing case for its ministry to fall fully under freedom of religion—but it is not. The principles and the practices of No More Deaths communicate theology in a performative rather than a propositional register. The performance of faith is open to religious and nonreligious interpretations. In cross-examination, Warren compared his spirituality to religion: "[I]f you pointed to particular organized religion, say, Catholicism or Judaism, my beliefs aren't strictly in the definitions of those religions. [But] I do think it's fair to say there are commonalties that I certainly share with these traditions."[167]

Comparing the liberal and the postliberal accounts of the nature of theology, Heyer has made a case for complementarity. Although she favors Tracy, she formulates a public theology that can seek both conversation and conversion in the public square, thus enabling a learning process in which Christianity can learn from the public and the public can learn from Christianity. "For if we believe that the Christian story is true, not simply true for Christians," she concludes, "we must not stop at the borders of the confessing community."[168] Arguably, a public theology that seeks both conversation and conversion is played out in the ministry of No More Deaths. According to the "Faith-Based Principles for Immigration Reform," the call to care for the other—to protect the other, regardless of who she is—is true. It is *true*—not just *true for Christians*. The spirit that Warren references repeatedly—comparable to the "spark of divinity that resides in us all," which the Tucson congregation references on its website—could be considered a fragment of theology used to make sense of a public and political issue—people dying at the U.S. border—in a way that is accessible to both religious and nonreligious.

Public theologian Duncan Forrester opens his *Theological Fragments: Essays in Unsystematic Theology* with a programmatic and provocative outline for public theology, titled "Theology in Fragments."[169] Positing the contemporary public square as postmodern—which Forrester characterizes as a situation of competing rather than comprehensive claims to truth[170]—he introduces the idea of a theology

---

167 See Warren Testimony, at 53.
168 Heyer, "How Does Theology Go Public?" 325.
169 Duncan Forrester, *Theological Fragments: Explorations in Unsystematic Theology* (London: T&T Clark, 2005), 1–24. For engagements with Forrester's explorations, see *Public Theology for the 21st Century: Essays in Honour of Duncan B. Forrester*, eds. William F. Storrar and Andrew R. Morton (London: T&T Clark, 2004).
170 Forrester, *Theological Fragments*, 9–11. Forrester draws on Zygmunt Bauman, *Life in Fragments: Essays in Postmodern Morality* (Oxford: Blackwell, 1995).

"No More Deaths" 273

of "fragments of truth."[171] He insists that there are "illuminating fragments which sustain . . . the life of the community of faith" as they make up the story of Christianity.[172] Forrester interprets these as "theological fragments" that can inform both Christians and non-Christians because they are also "in some sense 'public truth.'"[173] He offers no clear-cut definition of theological fragments, though.[174] Since his practical public theology works inductively rather than deductively, he starts with the concrete rather than the conceptual, concentrating on the practitioners who are often forgotten in the academy.[175] Forrester's theology, then, comes close to the approach of lived religion.[176] He is interested in the muddle and the mess of religion in its connection to the practices of everyday life. What is more crucial for him than precise descriptions and prescriptive definitions of these practices is to encourage people to engage with both the fragments and the source of the fragments, the story told and retold by churches.[177] He concludes that "there are clear duties laid upon Christian believers to contribute fragments of what they know to be true, and hope that they may . . . play a significant role in resolving, even if only temporarily, the kind of ethical dilemmas which surround us today."[178]

No More Deaths, then, is what Forrester calls for: the organization contributes fragments of what they know to be true—the "spark of divinity that resides in us all," experienced in places of struggle and sacrifice, such as the desert—to the ethical dilemma of immigration in order to resolve it, even if only temporarily. The ministry of No More Deaths is a case of public theology: it injects theology into the public square in a way that makes it accessible to both religious and nonreligious people. Crucially, the injection is performative rather than propositional, it is less about describing doctrine than about doing doctrine—caring for the other, even if that implies, in terms of civil initiative, being a carrier of the law in a system that fails to uphold it. Such a performative public theology provokes affirmative action to protect the law by enacting the "legal reality, obscured by statist legalism, that . . . communities retain the power . . . to do justice under law,

---

171 Forrester, *Theological Fragments*, 1.
172 Ibid., 8.
173 Ibid.
174 Ibid., 17.
175 See Ibid., 17–18, where he points to the preferential option for the poor. Marcella Althaus-Reid, "In the Centre, There Are No Fragments: Teologías Desencajadas (Reflections on Unfitting Theologies)," in Storrar and Martin, *Public Theology for the 21st Century*, 365–84, criticizes Forrester for not pushing the preferential option for the poor far enough. However, this preference is part and parcel of Forrester's account of public theology. See the chapters on "Political Theology" and on "Public Theology," collected in Duncan Forrester, *On Christian Ethics and Practical Theology: Collected Writings* (Farnham, UK: Ashgate, 2010).
176 See Duncan Forrester, *Truthful Action: Explorations in Practical Theology* (Edinburgh: T&T Clark, 2000).
177 Forrester, *Theological Fragments*, 12.
178 Ibid.

274 *Rose Cuison-Villazor and Ulrich Schmiedel*

especially when the state betrays its trust to do so."[179] The theological fragment is crucial because, as Bezdek argues, "[c]ivil initiative proceeds from a restorative vision of justice that implements the just law."[180]

Of course, analyzing and assessing Warren's work with No More Deaths as a fragment of theology does not help in deciding whether it should fall under freedom of religion. Yet the fragment of theology might make a convincing case for No More Death's public theology: it convinced religious and nonreligious people, thus "resolving, even if only temporarily, the kind of ethical dilemmas which surround us today"—in this case, immigration.

Altogether, then, No More Deaths is faith-based, but it is based on a faith that appeals to both the religious and the nonreligious. It is paradigmatic for a bilingual public theology that is more performative than propositional. The role of such a theology is to contribute theological fragments to the public square. Warren's work with No More Deaths is public theology, but precisely because it is, public theologians in the academy should not monopolize it.

V Conclusion: no more deaths!

This chapter has explored Warren's prosecution from legal and theological perspectives in order to point to the significance of civil initiatives, such as No More Deaths, in the current context marked by the criminalization of humanitarian aid to migrants.

Legally, Warren's case highlights the ways in which the Trump administration's stringent enforcement of immigration law has collided with religion. In the context of providing aid to undocumented immigrants crossing the border, advocates such as Warren have tested the RFRA as a possible defense against prosecution for violating the antiharboring provision of 8 U.S.C. § 1324. Warren's eventual acquittal stands in stark contrast to the convictions of sanctuary leaders of the 1980s, who asserted First Amendment religious liberty rights.

Theologically, Warren's case draws attention to the significance of public theology. As both the defenders and the despisers of the category of freedom of religion have argued, theology is at stake in any and all claims to such freedom. The practice and principles of No More Deaths communicate a theology that blurs the boundaries between believers and nonbelievers by pointing to the "life force" that connects people and place. Yet theologians should not domesticate or dogmatize it. Had Warren drawn on a clear-cut Christian theology—a system of faith that references the concept of the *imago Dei* (Genesis 1:27), a core category for human dignity in Christian theology—there would have been less doubt about his defense. But drawing on such a clear-cut Christian theology would have missed the point. Warren ought not to be "Christianized." No More Deaths uses theological fragments in its principles and practices to address

---

179 Bezdek, "Religious Outlaws," 973.
180 Ibid.

the ethical dilemma posed by unauthorized migration into the United States. These fragments have to be accessible and acceptable to both Christians and non-Christians, believers and nonbelievers. You do not have to be a Christian— indeed, you do not have to be a person of faith at all—to agree with No More Deaths. Nonetheless, the theological fragments that No More Death uses are crucial to their civil initiative because they point to a vision of justice beyond the criminalization of migration and migration aid, a vision of justice that volunteers like Warren put into practice. Warren's volunteering for No More Deaths *is* public theology. For public theologians, then, the core concern is to ask whether and which fragments of theology can help prevent the deaths of migrants at borders, both inside and outside the United States.

Suggested Reading

Brief of and by Professors of Religious Liberty as Amicus Curiae in Support of Defendant's Motion to Dismiss, *United States v. Warren*, No.CR-18-00223-001-TUC-RCC (District of Arizona, June 21, 2018).

Corbett, James. *Sanctuary for All Life: The Cowbalah of Jim Corbett*. Englewood, CO: Howling Dog Press, 2005.

Rose, Ananda. *Showdown in the Sonoran Desert: Religion, Law, and the Immigration Controversy*. Oxford: Oxford University Press, 2012.

Scott-Railton, Thomas. "A Religious Sanctuary: How the Religious Freedom Restoration Act Could Protect Sanctuary Churches." *Yale Law Journal* 128, no. 2 (2018): 408–81.

Sostaita, Barbara Andrea. " 'Water, Not Walls:' Toward a Religious Study of Life that Defies Borders." *American Religion* 1, no. 2 (2020): 74–97.

15 A vision of integration rooted in hospitality

Donald M. Kerwin and Safwat Marzouk

I Introduction: nativism and its consequences

On August 3, 2019, a white nationalist murdered 22 persons at the Cielo Vista Walmart in El Paso, Texas. In a manifesto prior to the act, the shooter spoke of the "Hispanic invasion of Texas," the "cultural and ethnic displacement of whites" in a region settled by Spanish-speaking persons in the mid-seventeenth century and by native peoples in about 40 CE, and the inspiration he took from the murder of 51 persons five months earlier at a mosque and Islamic center in New Zealand. Nativist leaders throughout the world, cynical politicians, extremist media figures, and self-appointed militias have long portrayed border communities as lawless, crime-ridden zones that threaten the nation's security, sovereignty, and culture. They have repeatedly characterized these communities as a kind of beachhead for a national invasion by foreigners and minorities bent on hostile takeover of "their" countries, whether through demographic conquest, cultural transformation, or armed victory. They have used this fiction to justify their own violence against the "Other," which, in the case of El Paso, included mostly native-born Hispanic members of a family-oriented, civic-minded, and patriotic community.

Nativist border mythology and symbolism have been so virulent that white nationalists now support invading border communities to kill their Hispanic members and to halt the putative conquest of their country. After the El Paso shootings—which religious leaders characterized as a *matanza* (slaughter)—El Pasoans were repeatedly quoted as saying that they did not fear people from their local community, but rather U.S. citizens coming into it to do them harm. The attack and its underlying ideology—long familiar to border communities—led to a more unified community, characterized by the slogan "El Paso Strong." Hate groups applauded the shootings and encouraged more of the same.

Hatred, racism, and ideologies that deny the equality and dignity of persons from other places and cultures serve as a hard barrier to integration and, more broadly, to building societies that are marked by hospitality and justice. Ethnoracial or ethnocultural nationalism defines a nation's identity based on superficial social constructs like race and on the misperception that a nation's culture is immutable and unipolar, and should subsume "inferior" cultures. Newcomers and minorities are presumed to have little to offer but their exploitable labor. These ideologies make virtually impossible full integration informed by hospitality ("integration as hospitality") for immigrants who do not share the membership-defining traits—racial, ethnic, religious, cultural, and other—of the dominant native-born population. Immigrants, according to these ideologies, can integrate, but only as denizens and never as equals or to full participation and membership. These ideologies stand in stark contrast to the "biblical tradition and Jesus' missionary vision" of "the gift of a 'home'—a place and space where justice is done and respect and compassion unite everyone."[1]

Judging from biblical narratives, barriers to hospitality have not significantly changed over the centuries. Then, as now, fear of conquest and displacement (Exodus 1:7–10), a preference for the wealthy, historical amnesia, and obduracy underlie these hateful, exclusionary ideologies. In the text from Exodus, Pharaoh views the "Other" (the Israelites) as a threat and perpetuates a hateful ideology that structures reality through rigid categories of Us versus Them. The violence of forced labor and the attempt to kill the first-born boys of the Israelites started with Pharaoh's refusal to *acknowledge* the wisdom of Joseph (a Hebrew migrant) that saved Egypt from famine.[2] Cutting across all of these perceptions is the failure to identify with the "Other." Nor have the modalities, tactics, and language of nativists varied significantly over time or place. These include laws and declarations that seek to destabilize, terrify, defeat, and block the inclusion of disfavored groups into the nativists' country (Donald M. Kerwin, Chapter 6). Nativists endlessly attack refugees and immigrants as lawless, disorderly, violent, and a threat to public safety and national security. Nativist rhetoric evokes what Toni Morrison called the language of "menace and subjugation," which "does more than represent violence; it is violence; it does more than represent the limits of knowledge; it limits knowledge."[3] Undoing this violence and paving the way toward integration starts with creating spaces for different communities to *know* each other and to realize their need not only for what others can contribute to their well-being, but for the "Other" as a human being, a bearer of God's image.

While Christians are called to move away from *xenophobia* (fear of the "Other") and more towards *xenophilia* (love for the "Other") (Luis N. Rivera-Pagán, Chapter 10),[4] large numbers of Christians throughout the world practice a kind of idolatry in supporting political leaders who espouse hateful ideologies, demonize the poor, the stranger, and religious minorities, and adopt cruel strategies to

---

1 Gemma Tulud Cruz, *Toward a Theology of Migration: Social Justice and Religious Experience* (New York: Palgrave Macmillan, 2014), 103.
2 Safwat Marzouk, "Tyranny Is Nothing New (Nor Is Resistance!)," https://politicaltheology. com/tyranny-is-nothing-new-nor-is-resistance/?fbclid=IwAR1YGOaLBH8mfCnBOBkL6p UOa8rRY_rr5WzuaCmSlNVUqaJIiPCXeRZ8kdc.
3 Toni Morrison, Nobel Lecture, The Nobel Prize in Literature, Stockholm, The Swedish Academy, December 7, 1993, www.nobelprize.org/prizes/literature/1993/morrison/lecture/.
4 See also Luis N. Rivera-Pagán, "Xenophilia or Xenophobia: Toward a Theology of Migration," in *Contemporary Issues of Migration and Theology*, eds. Elaine Padilla and Peter C. Phan (New York: Palgrave, 2013), 31–51.

278   Donald M. Kerwin and Safwat Marzouk

marginalize or even drive designated outsiders from the community. This chapter revisits the migrant roots and identity of Christianity, its bedrock belief in the common origin of all persons, and its commitment to hospitality and justice. It describes how the biblical imperative of hospitality, infused with justice, can lead to a deeper understanding of the integration process.

II Integration

In an exhaustive 2015 report, the National Academies of Science, Engineering, and Medicine's Panel on the Integration of Immigrants into American Society used the term "integration" to describe "the changes that both immigrants and their descendants—and the society they have joined—undergo in response to migration."[5] The panel defined integration as a multigenerational process with "both economic and sociocultural dimensions" in which "members of immigrant groups and host societies come to resemble one another" (citations omitted).[6] "Greater integration," continued the panel, "implies parity of critical life chances with the native-born American majority."[7]

Richard Alba and Nancy Foner note that integration refers to the extent to which migrants and their children "are able to participate in key mainstream institutions in ways that position them to advance socially and materially."[8] The integration process takes place in large part through engagement with institutions—like family, the workplace, faith communities, and civic associations—that provide immigrants with the contacts, skills, and knowledge to succeed in the broader society. To play this mediating role, such institutions must be open to the leadership and gifts of immigrants.[9]

In integration, host and migrant communities treat each other as equals in dignity and recognize that culture is porous. Integration walks a fine line between claiming one's culture without being encapsulated by it, and taking on new traits from the surrounding cultures without losing one's identity. Neither host nor migrant communities seek to preserve their culture at the expense of trying to understand and adapt to the other's culture. In integration, the relationship between diverse communities is shaped by giving and receiving. Immigrants are

---

5 Mary C. Waters and Marisa Gerstein Pineau, eds., *The Integration of Immigrants into American Society: Panel on the Integration of Immigrants into American Society*, National Academies of Sciences, Engineering, and Medicine (Washington, DC: National Academies Press, 2015), 19, www.nap.edu/read/21746/chapter/3#19.
6 Ibid.
7 Ibid.
8 Richard Alba and Nancy Foner, *Strangers No More: Immigration and the Challenges of Integration in North America and Western Europe* (Princeton, NJ: Princeton University Press, 2015), 8.
9 Donald M. Kerwin and Breana George, *US Catholic Institutions and Immigrant Integration: Will the Church Rise to the Challenge?* (Vatican City: Lateran University Press, 2014), 37, 47, https://cmsny.org/publications/us-catholic-institutions-and-immigrant-integration-will-the-church-rise-to-the-challenge/.

A vision of integration 279

not swallowed by the host culture(s), but instead they influence the surrounding cultures as much as they are changed by them. Mutuality between the host and migrant, the ability to negotiate boundary maintaining and crossing, and the ability to find meaning in creating something new together represent the key components of healthy, promise-holding integration. The integration process depends heavily on the willingness and the ability of both migrant and host communities to be vulnerable enough to offer and receive, to make mistakes and seek forgiveness, to communicate and share stories, and to be patient in improving their intercultural competencies.

At the heart of the integration process lie questions of identity and agency, such as: Who is integrating into what? Are the culture and identity of the host community well-defined by its members? What roles do the host and the migrant play in this process of integration? Is the host willing to envision a new expression of culture, given the contributions made by migrants? Is the migrant open to the new society? How do host and migrant communities negotiate continuity and change? How do they envision something new, created by connecting diverse cultures? What are the spiritual or communal practices that enable the community to deal with the anxiety and fear of change and loss? What are the practices that enable the community to celebrate newness and creativity?

To gain greater clarity on how integration might be informed by hospitality, the discussion that follows distinguishes the concept of assimilation and the virtue of tolerance from integration. It also addresses the way in which cultural encapsulation can impede integration in this thicker sense.

A Assimilation

Sociologists use both assimilation and integration to describe the process of the inclusion of migrants into the host community. Despite considerable overlap, integration and assimilation differ in significant ways. To one set of scholars, assimilation "holds that those who arrive in a new country, often from very distant places, . . . and who bring with them different cultures, habits and languages, become part of that new society and thus integrated into its key institutions."[10] These scholars helpfully unpack the psychological and systemic difficulties, such as discrimination, that migrants face in assimilating, yet they put the accent of the work of integration onto migrants by using words like "adaptation" and "accommodation."

This approach begs the question of the willingness and responsibility of the host community to celebrate cultural differences and to accommodate or adapt to the migrants in their midst. Assimilation assumes a dominant, nonporous, relatively fixed culture that cannot adapt to or learn from immigrant cultures,

---

10 Thomas Faist, Margit Fauser, and Eveline Reisenauer, *Transnational Migration* (Cambridge: Polity Press, 2013), 88.

but to which migrants must conform.[11] Assimilation envisions a "unidirectional trajectory" for immigrants into the host culture."[12] Under this model, immigrants must leave behind their home cultures, which would otherwise undermine and threaten the host culture. Assimilation can also require that immigrants possess characteristics (like native populations), which have nothing to do with their ability and willingness to contribute to their new societies. In some cases, assimilation is seen as a precondition to accepting the migrant and extending hospitality. By contrast, the term "integration" was introduced in European discourse "to indicate a greater degree of tolerance and respect for ethno-cultural differences."[13]

B Tolerance

Tolerance can be caricatured as taking the path of least resistance, lacking the courage of one's convictions, or adopting a patronizing attitude toward others by granting them the "best" or "most" (mere tolerance) that they deserve. In its fuller sense, however, tolerance is a prerequisite to building community, and thus to the integration process. Grounded in a "commitment to the equal dignity of all persons,"[14] tolerance allows members of diverse groups to engage each other in an open and nonjudgmental way, to build friendships, and to recognize the values expressed through their respective cultures. It demands "*acceptance* of difference"[15] and creates the possibility of unifying people of diverse backgrounds and cultures based on their shared values and commitments.

At the same time, as David Hollenbach argues, tolerance is an "instrumental rather than an ultimate value" whose "purpose is to assure that the common good is truly common, i.e., shared in by all."[16] It does not offer a moral framework to address challenges that require an understanding of "community" that reaches beyond "homogeneous groups" or the "boundaries of existing groups."[17]

C Cultural encapsulation

In contrast to tolerance, sociologists and psychologists use the term "cultural encapsulation" to describe a form of parochialism in which "members of socially

---

11 Kerwin and George, *US Catholic Institutions and Immigrant Integration*, 8.
12 Jill Marie Gerschutz and Lois Ann Lorentzen, "Integration Yesterday and Today: New Challenges for the United States and the Church," in *And You Welcomed Me: Migration and Catholic Social Teaching*, eds. Donald M. Kerwin and Jill Marie Gerschutz (Lanham, MD: Lexington Books, 2009), 125.
13 Alba and Foner, *Strangers No More*, 7.
14 David Hollenbach, SJ, *The Common Good and Christian Ethics* (Cambridge: Cambridge University Press, 2002), 34.
15 Ibid., 40.
16 Ibid., 69.
17 Ibid.

A vision of integration 281

disconnected groups judge all things by their own cultural perspective and cannot easily identify or understand the perspective of members of other groups."[18] Isolation of this kind makes it difficult to empathize, or " 'imaginatively' to enter into and participate in the world of the cultural 'Other' cognitively, affectively, and behaviorally."[19] Instead, it leads to suspicion, stereotyping, and scapegoating, provides tinder for false narratives about unknown outsiders, and can be easily manipulated for political and socioeconomic purposes.

III A Christian vision of integration: hospitality as a guiding principle

A. *Hospitality in the Christian tradition*

Hospitality is a seminal Christian virtue, rooted in Christ's teaching to welcome the stranger and in the intuition that all human beings are created in God's image and belong to the same human family. From this perspective, hospitality is more than "an act of kindness and solidarity": it springs from a belief in the equality and dignity of all persons that "transcends bloodlines and national boundaries."[20] As Saint Paul put it, "[t]here is neither Jew nor Greek, there is neither slave nor free person, there is not male and female; for you are all one in Christ Jesus" (Galatians 3:28, NAB).

In Hebrew scripture and the New Testament, hospitality takes the familiar form of offering food, drink, refuge, and welcome. On a deeper level, it can be seen as a spiritual journey to God through encounter with the "Other." Hospitality allows culturally diverse persons to experience the virtues, values, and presence of God in persons from groups and nations other than their own. Hospitality builds community, a "cloud of witnesses" that encourage members to "persevere" with their "eyes fixed" on God (Hebrews 12:1–2, NAB). Indeed, a significant starting point for showing Christian hospitality lies in the recognition that God is the host. When God is the host, then citizens and migrants are God's guests. Gemma Tulud Cruz develops this point when she writes, "Seeing God as the provider of hospitality destabilizes the usual roles (with the migrant as the usual guest and the citizen as the usual host) and the unbalanced order of relations these roles spawn. God as the host presents, instead, both the migrant and the citizen as guests and,

---

18 Brett Hoover, *The Shared Parish: Latinos, Anglos and the Future of US Catholicism* (New York: New York University Press, 2014), 106.
19 Carolyn Calloway-Thomas, "Empathy: A Global Imperative for Peace" (College Music Symposium Exploring Diverse Perspectives, 2018), https://symposium.music.org/index.php/current-issue/item/11407-empathy-a-global-imperative-for-peace.
20 Donald Senior, " 'Beloved Aliens and Exiles': New Testament Perspectives on Migration," in *A Promised Land, A Perilous Journey: Theological Perspectives on Migration*, eds. Daniel G. Groody and Gioacchino Campese (Notre Dame, IN: University of Notre Dame Press, 2008), 30.

282 Donald M. Kerwin and Safwat Marzouk

consequently, as both strangers."[21] While this is an important theological insight, God's hospitality is usually extended through human agents who have been transformed by their encounter with the generous and loving God. No wonder, then, that Jesus teaches the faithful to show hospitality to the strangers and to meet the needs of the dispossessed, in the knowledge that they will be serving God and may then receive God's hospitality on the judgement day (Matthew 25:31–46). Hospitality, infused by justice, "requires a commitment by all residents (including immigrants) to contribute to the common good."[22]

Hospitality can help to bridge divisions. It can reveal deeper connections between diverse communities, shared aspirations across cultures, and God's will and presence. It is an invitation to create—inspired by God's grace—a more inclusive and faithful community, one rooted in love of God and neighbor, and not based on divisive human hierarchies. Such a community can serve as a "bulwark against an ideology of racial superiority" and "absolute claims of national or cultural boundaries."[23] Hospitality reflects the profound hope for communion with God and neighbor.

1 Hebrew scripture

In its Judeo-Christian sense, hospitality must be provided to social outsiders, particularly those who lack the law's protections, or who suffer marginalization and exploitation under color of law. Hebrew scripture speaks consistently against exclusionary practices and underscores the need to extend protection (akin to what natives receive) to four groups of vulnerable persons—the poor, widows, orphans, and strangers in the land (Exodus 22:21–23; Jeremiah 7:6–7). These groups need protection precisely because they *lack* full membership in the community—the stranger by virtue of being a resident alien, widows and orphans who have lost standing and protection upon the death of a spouse or parent, and the poor because of their marginal status. Israel is taught to emulate their God, who "has no favorites, accepts no bribes, who executes justice for the orphan and the widow, and loves the resident alien, giving them food and clothing" (Deuteronomy 10:17–19, NAB). M. Daniel Carroll R. comments on this biblical perspective as he writes, "There can be no stronger argument to support caring for the foreigner! The people of Israel would be the means by which that food and clothing would reach the sojourner; they were to be God's hand and feet."[24] Indeed, God's love and care for the refugee, asylum seeker, and migrant are the foundation for any form of a faith-based hospitality.

---

21 Cruz, *Toward a Theology of Migration*, 95. Cruz also elaborates on this argument in her chapter in this volume (Chapter 11).
22 Gerschutz and Lorentzen, "Integration Yesterday and Today," 134.
23 Senior, " 'Beloved Aliens and Exiles'," 32.
24 M. Daniel Carroll R., *The Bible and Borders: Hearing God's Word on Immigration* (Grand Rapids, MI: Brazos Press, 2020), 69.

A *vision of integration* 283

Hospitality leads to a deeper understanding of God's providence. Thus, Abraham and Sarah provide hospitality to three strangers who appear on a sweltering day. One informs them that Sarah will bear a child within the year (Genesis 18:1–15: NAB). Abraham recognizes "the grace that resulted from their encounter—a deeper relationship with God, a covenant, a family, a long-awaited heir."[25] This narrative also speaks to the mutually enriching nature of hospitality: the guests receive food and drink, and the hosts learn of God's unexpected plans for them. The hospitality shown by Abraham toward these visitors is to be contrasted with the inhospitality of the people of Sodom in Genesis 19. Hospitality leads to a mutual blessing, while inhospitality leads to violence and destruction. Juxtaposing these two stories in Genesis 18–19 calls the reader to choose between the path of hospitality and the path of coercion and violence.

God's continued blessing and hospitality, in turn, depend on Israel's own obedience and faithful service (Leviticus 25:28). Israel retains a "deep sense of God as its host"[26]: "the land is mine and you are but resident aliens and under my authority" (Leviticus 25:23, NAB). Israel must ensure that the "the Levite who has no hereditary portion with you, and also the resident alien, the orphan and the widow within your gates, may come and eat and be satisfied; so that the LORD, your God, may bless you in all that you undertake" (Deuteronomy 14:29, NAB). Showing hospitality in these passages means extending God's table to include the marginalized and the outcast. Hospitality is showing solidarity,[27] and this ethical stance simply meant showing generosity by sharing the festival food with the stranger and embracing them as if they were kin, as if they were family.[28]

Israel is also charged to remember its history as a pilgrim people, descended from a "wandering Aramean" (Deuteronomy 26:5, NAB). This is Israel's first faith confession. Israel's identity is constituted by the memory of being strangers. This memory is expressed in other parts of the Hebrew scripture to provide the ethical foundation for doing justice to the oppressed sojourners: "you shall not wrong or oppress a resident alien, for you were aliens in the land of Egypt" (Exodus 22:21–22, NAB). It is plausible to posit that the failure of some people to show hospitality to the sojourners in their midst relates to their repression of the memory of their own identity as migrants. Peter C. Phan reflects on the importance of retaining the identity of a migrant even after one becomes a citizen,

---

25 Michael Simone, "Every Good Work Contains the Possibility for an Encounter with God," *America Magazine*, June 28, 2019, www.americamagazine.org/faith/2019/06/28/every-good-work-contains-possibility-encounter-god.

26 John Koenig, "Hospitality," in *The Anchor Bible Dictionary*, eds. David Noel Freedman and John H. Elliott, vol. 3 (New York: Doubleday, 1992), 301.

27 William O'Neill, "Christian Hospitality and Solidarity with the Stranger," in Kerwin and Gerschutz, *And You Welcomed Me*, 149–55.

28 Mark R. Glanville, *Adopting the Stranger as Kindred in Deuteronomy* (Atlanta, GA: SBL Press, 2018).

284 Donald M. Kerwin and Safwat Marzouk

because it is this memory that shapes one's ethical and hospitable posture toward other migrants. He writes:

> The underlying ethical reasoning seems to be as follows: First, being a migrant enables one to know "the heart of a migrant"; second, knowledge of the migrant's heart is cultivated by remembering one's own personal experience of being a migrant; and third, remembering one's past as a migrant provides the ethical grounding for one's just and loving treatment of migrants.[29]

According to prophets like Jeremiah and Ezekiel, Israel's well-being depended on obeying the commandments of the God of Israel, which entailed showing hospitality, justice, and kindness to the sojourner (Jeremiah 7:5–7; Ezekiel 22:7).

2 Teachings of Jesus

Jesus foregrounded hospitality in his teaching and public ministry (see Raj Nadella, Chapter 9). He did not condition hospitality on conversion, as John the Baptist did. Rather, he first practiced "communion as a symbol of acceptance offered" to those he taught.[30]

Over the course of his life, Jesus experienced uprooting and flight. The Holy Family fled to Egypt to escape an evil king bent on Jesus's death (Matthew 2:13–23). His followers consisted of guests—the 12 itinerant disciples and subsequent missionaries—and "a larger group . . . which included residential supporters."[31] Jesus himself both accepted hospitality in his public ministry, including from tax collectors and Pharisees, and experienced its absence, lamenting that he had "nowhere to rest his head" (Matthew 8:20; Luke 9:58, NAB). In order to extend and receive hospitality, Jesus crossed religious, ethnic, and geographical boundaries.

In the Judgment Day passage of Matthew 25, Jesus personally identifies with the stranger in need of welcome, and he conditions passage to the kingdom—God's ultimate hospitality—on mercy to the "least ones," including the stranger. The Beatitudes likewise speak to the reward that the righteous and the merciful will receive in heaven (Matthew 5:2–12). Jesus also repeatedly describes the kingdom of God in the language of hospitality—refuge, food, and drink.[32]

In the Gospel of Luke, he continually upsets his followers' expectations, breaking through "social and religious barriers,"[33] as exemplified by the parable of the

---

29 Peter C. Phan, "'Always Remember Where You Came From: An Ethics of Migrant Memory," in *Living With(out) Borders: Catholic Theological Ethics on the Migrations of Peoples*, eds. Agnes M. Brazel and María Teresa Dávila (New York: Oribis, 2016), 173–86, at 177.

30 John R. Donahue, *Seek Justice That You May Live: Reflections and Resources on the Bible and Social Justice* (New York: Paulist, 2014), 149.

31 Koenig, "Hospitality," 300.

32 Ibid.

33 John R. Donahue, "Companions on a Journey," in *Scripture and Social Justice: Catholic and Ecumenical Essays*, eds. Anathea E. Portier-Young and Gregory E. Sterling (Lanham, MD: Lexington Books/Fortress Academic, 2018), 5.

A vision of integration   285

Good Samaritan. Samaritans represented a threat to the "religious and national" identity of Jews/Judeans.[34] Yet Jesus holds up the Samaritan (the "Other") as the exemplar of love of God and neighbor, compassion and hospitality (Luke 10:25–37).

3 Early Christian community

The Acts of the Apostles might "be read as a collection of guest and host stories depicting missionary ventures that . . . originated in circles associated with the earliest churches."[35] Jesus's followers experienced rejection, even from fellow Christians. In 3 John 1:7–9, the author writes to the Christian Gaius, seeking hospitality for another missionary. However, he criticizes a fellow Christian, Diotrephes, who refuses to acknowledge or "receive the brothers" and hinders those who wish to do so (3 John 2: 9–11, NAB). Sadly, the world remains filled with self-identified Christians, particularly in the public sphere, who love to dominate but neglect to welcome their brothers and sisters, or even to recognize them as such.

To early Christians, hospitality was "more than a social custom": it was also "an expression of gratitude and faithfulness to God."[36] Failure to offer hospitality, in turn, constituted a "serious offense, equivalent to breaching the covenant with God."[37] As a practical matter, early Christians—driven to migrate by persecution and economic necessity—entered close-knit communities, "defined primarily by kinship through blood or marriage."[38] Established members of these communities often viewed the newcomers as a threat, and, as a result, Christians urgently needed "welcome, material assistance, and acceptance as a full member of the community."[39] In these circumstances, "the virtue most highly recommended to the community was philoxenia, literally, love of strangers or hospitality."[40]

Early Christian communities adopted an expansive vision of hospitality. They rejected the sin of "partiality" (James 2:1, NAB), did not favor the wealthy, and did not discriminate against any believers, including the poor (Matthew 5:3; 1 Corinthians 1:27–29, 11:22) and Gentiles (Galatians 2:11–14). They believed that God does not privilege one group over another, and therefore neither should the faithful.

Acts 10 exemplifies how integration requires hospitality and mutuality between the host and migrant. It recounts an encounter between Cornelius, a Roman centurion, and Peter, a Jew and a follower of Jesus who lives under the Roman occupation. This passage highlights Cornelius's piety. God has heard Cornelius's

---

34 Ibid., 6.
35 Koenig, "Hospitality," 301.
36 Peter C. Phan, "Migration in the Patristic Era: History and Theology," in Groody and Campese, *A Promised Land, A Perilous Journey*, 50.
37 Ibid., citing Deuteronomy 23:3–4.
38 Ibid., 49.
39 Ibid.
40 Ibid., 49–50.

286   *Donald M. Kerwin and Safwat Marzouk*

prayers and has instructed him to summon Peter to tell him what he needs to do. While the messengers are on their way, Peter (who is famished) sees a vision three times in which a voice instructs him to eat from a sheet full of animals. However, Peter refuses to obey the command, claiming that he has never eaten unclean food. In response, the voice asserts: " 'What God has made clean, you are not to call profane' " (Acts of the Apostles 10:15, NAB).

When he meets Cornelius, Peter is frank about his encounters with those who are different from him. He tells the Gentiles, " 'You yourselves know that it is unlawful for a Jew to associate with or to visit a Gentile' " (Acts of the Apostles 10:28, NAB). This statement underscores how difference (religious, ethnic, cultural) can function as an obstacle to communion. One could say that the statement even reflects an "us versus them" mindset. For integration to happen in such a case, conversion—a change of mind and heart—must occur. Once in Caesarea, outside his geographical and ideological zone of comfort, Peter changes and finds common ground with those who are different from him.

In his speech, Peter emphasizes the loss of boundaries and difference, as he articulates God's impartiality: "I truly understand that God shows no partiality, but in every nation anyone who fears him and does what is right is acceptable to him" (Acts of the Apostles 10:34–35, NAB). Not only does Peter recognize that difference is not an obstacle to the integration of Gentiles into the fold of God's people, but his companions confess that the Holy Spirit has been poured on the Gentiles, just as it was on the Jews (Acts of the Apostles 10:44–47).[41]

Although the Gentiles integrate through the gift of the Spirit and the ritual of baptism, the author still notes the difference between the Jews (the circumcised) and the Gentiles (the uncircumcised). In other words, integration does not remove difference. It celebrates it. The Jews (Peter and his companions) remained for several days at Cornelius's house (Acts of the Apostles 10:48). Integration in this narrative means creating a space for others at the table. It requires willingness to relate to the "Other" who is different and to receive them as a gift that transforms one's own identity. Finally, Peter and Cornelius experience this integrative relationship for a fundamental reason: they recognize that they are not God, but human beings.

B A case study: Joseph among the Egyptians

The story of Joseph in Genesis 37–50 has a lot to offer in terms of cross-cultural interaction between the host community, the Egyptians, and the migrants, represented initially by Joseph and eventually by all of his family. Some of the episodes of this long story speak about integration (Genesis 39, 41), others about separation between the host community and migrants (Genesis 46–47), and still

---

41 For a full discussion on the encounter between Peter and Cornelius, see Safwat Marzouk, *Intercultural Church: A Biblical Vision in an Age of Migration* (Minneapolis: Fortress Press, 2019).

others about transnational relations in which the migrants are able to maintain relationships with their home culture, while integrating in the destination culture (Genesis 50).[42] The case study in this section focuses on Joseph's experience in Potiphar's house and in Pharaoh's court. Together, these stories exhort readers to imagine themselves as guest and host. They call us to reflect on how to take agency toward integration and how to empower those seeking to be welcomed and integrated.

In the context of migration, integration entails creating the space for the migrant to regain a sense of self, dignity, purpose, and hope. When people migrate, they lose something of themselves and long to find a new purpose, a new meaning for their life, and a sense of agency that can fulfill their hopes. Joseph's brothers sold him into slavery and shattered his dreams. They removed him from his family and placed him at the mercy of foreigners. Yet Joseph found a sense of purpose and hope through his work in Potiphar's house. Eventually, Potiphar entrusted him with all his possessions. Joseph's integration happened because God was with him, Joseph was dedicated to his work, and the Egyptian host welcomed him and recognized the ways God blessed him through Joseph. Joseph was more than an economic asset; he was an agent through whom God blessed the host community.

Yet Joseph's integration was threatened by the abuse of power by Potiphar's wife and the fact that Potiphar did not allow Joseph a hearing. Potiphar's wife repeatedly highlighted Joseph's otherness—"this Hebrew slave" (Genesis 39:14, 17, NAB)—in order to deprive him of justice. Yet integration demands that migrants be granted justice as equals, and it requires that members of host communities use their power and privilege to ensure the equal treatment of the "Other", the foreigner. The abuse of power and privilege by the host community (in this case Potiphar and his wife) is to be contrasted with how Pharaoh empowered Joseph, a Hebrew migrant, to be integrated into the Egyptian culture and society (Genesis 41).

Despite betrayal, injustice, and hardship, Joseph continued to avail himself of any opportunity. He excelled in prison to the point that the chief jailer entrusted him with all the prisoners (Genesis 39:21–23). Again, Joseph succeeded because God was with him, he was resilient, and someone in power trusted him. In prison, he successfully interpreted the dreams of two prisoners and urged Pharaoh's cup-bearer to remember him to Pharaoh. His ability to network and to express his need for others to advocate on his behalf led Joseph not only to be integrated into Egyptian society but also to assume a leadership role that allowed him to save the Egyptians and his family from the pending famine.

---

42 For extended discussion on the story of Joseph as a diaspora narrative, see Hyun Chul Paul Kim, "Reading the Joseph Story (Genesis 37–50) as a Diaspora Narrative," *CBQ* 75 (2013): 219–38; Safwat Marzouk, "Migration in The Joseph Narrative: Integration, Separation, and Transnationalism," *Hebrew Studies* 60 (2019): 71–90.

288 *Donald M. Kerwin and Safwat Marzouk*

As the narrative unfolds, Joseph continues to integrate into the Egyptian culture. This happens because of his continued willingness to accommodate the host culture, and because agents in this culture create a space for him to contribute to the well-being of the community. When Pharaoh has two disturbing dreams that his officials cannot interpret, his cupbearer remembers Joseph, the migrant, not as a dreamer, but as someone who reveals the meaning of other people's dreams.

In the contemporary context, we often speak of migrants as dreamers and, in fact, they *are* dreamers of a better life. However, the Joseph story reveals that the host community also has dreams, and that the dreams of the migrant (Genesis 37) and the host community (Genesis 40 and 41) are intertwined. The ability of the migrant to accommodate to a new environment and the willingness of the host community to create a space of shared power with the migrant lead to a healthy process of integration. Joseph shows willingness to accommodate to Egyptian culture by shaving and changing his clothes before standing before Pharaoh (Genesis 41:14). Pharaoh, for his part, uses his power to incorporate the Hebrew migrant into the royal court.

The episode of Joseph interpreting Pharaoh's dreams unveils three further aspects about the process of integration. The first is that integration can happen in a productive way when those who are involved—host and migrant—are courageous enough to express their needs to each other. Joseph expresses his need for Pharaoh to the cupbearer. Similarly, Pharaoh expresses his vulnerability by repeatedly telling Joseph that there is no one to interpret his perplexing dream. Being able to see one's need for the "Other", having the courage to express one's vulnerable state before the stranger, is an essential posture that makes integration mutual, and thus possible. Integration flourishes when both sides recognize their interdependence.

Not only do Joseph and Pharaoh need each other, they also *contribute* to meeting the needs of each other. Even better, they see each other as agents whom God uses to fulfill their dreams, to give meaning in the midst of disorientation, and to lend a hand in the face of pending disaster. Joseph tells Pharaoh that through his dreams, God has revealed his plans. After Joseph finishes interpreting the dream, Pharaoh asks his officials: " 'Could we find another like him . . . a man so endowed with the spirit of God?' " (Genesis 41:38, NAB). Both Joseph and Pharaoh use the generic word *Elohim*, which means God. Is Joseph referring to the Hebrew God? Is Pharaoh referring to the Egyptian God? We cannot tell, but we can say with certainty that Joseph and Pharaoh see each other as agents through whom God speaks. Through Joseph, God gives Pharaoh a meaning for his dreams, and through Pharaoh, God fulfills Joseph's long-delayed dreams.

Following the interpretation of his dreams, Pharaoh uses his power to integrate Joseph into the Egyptian royal court. He gives Joseph his royal signet, clothes him with fine linen, puts a golden necklace on him, has him ride a chariot, gives him an Egyptian name, and marries him to Asenath, daughter of the high priest. Joseph is integrated well-enough into the Egyptian culture that his brothers do not recognize him when they come to Egypt for food (Genesis 42:8–9). Yet he does not lose his Hebrew identity. This is evident in his giving his children

Hebrew names, embracing his family, and bringing them to live with him in Egypt (Genesis 45). Thus, while Joseph integrates into Egyptian society, he is not fully assimilated. He has taken on Egyptian cultural traits without fully losing his Hebrew identity. Although the text is silent about how Joseph and his community might have influenced Egyptian culture, such an influence remains a possibility, given how Pharaoh recognizes "the spirit of God" in Joseph (Genesis 41:38).

The cross-cultural interaction between Joseph and Pharaoh shows that for integration to happen, migrants should accommodate the host culture but retain aspects of their home culture. In addition, members of the host community must welcome and use their power and privilege to create space for migrants. This occurs when migrant and host communities admit and express their need for each other. Integration is successful when migrants and hosts realize that they are a divine gift to each other. Then and now, agency, the ability to contribute, mutual need, and openness to God's plan through the other are the essential elements in integration.

IV Conclusion: reimagining integration as hospitality

This chapter began with a reflection on nativist and nationalist ideologies that embolden the hateful, inspire violence, and seek to exclude, expel, and marginalize immigrants and the disfavored groups associated with them. In contrast to this vision, the chapter outlines a positive, inclusive view of integration, rooted in the biblical imperative of hospitality. Hospitality as integration could both incorporate and go beyond the standard definitions and metrics of integration—as a multigenerational process, leading to socioeconomic and political parity with the native-born.[43]

The most basic requirement for integration in this sense is "encounter" between native-born and diverse immigrant populations. Only through engagement can diverse groups come to know and understand each other, and build more inclusive communities, rooted in hospitality and justice. As Pope Francis has said,

> A change of attitude towards migrants and refugees is needed on the part of everyone, moving away from attitudes of defensiveness and fear, indifference and marginalization—all typical of a throwaway culture—towards attitudes based on a culture of encounter, the only culture capable of building a better, more just and fraternal world.[44]

---

43 Elsewhere in this volume, Rose Cuison Villazor also argues for rethinking the oath of loyalty and allegiance required of naturalized citizens through the lens of hospitality (Chapter 7).

44 Pope Francis, "Migrants and Refugees: Towards a Better World," *Message of His Holiness Pope Francis for the World Day of Migrants and Refugees, Vatican City,* August 5, 2013, https://w2.vatican.va/content/francesco/en/messages/migration/documents/papa-francesco_20130805_world-migrants-day.html.

290 Donald M. Kerwin and Safwat Marzouk

A particularly promising form of encounter is the "missionary engagement" of largely immigrant congregations in poor, largely abandoned host communities.[45] This type of "witness as *with*ness"—from migrants to the native-born—builds communion rooted in hospitality and justice.[46]

Integration as hospitality would also seek to contribute to the conditions that allow the native-born, immigrants, and their progeny to flourish. It would recognize immigrants as integral and full members of the community, both entitled to its shared "goods" and responsible for contributing to them. It would provide the space and time for immigrants to communicate their needs and to become full participants in their new communities. It would also embrace their myriad gifts—their hope, commitment to family, labor, strong faith, and the values that drive and sustain them.[47] In other words, integration would reflect the reciprocal nature of hospitality. Both migrants and host communities offer and receive; they are the agents through whom God extends God's goodness, healing, and grace. As a result, integration would require hospitality from both the native-born and immigrants, and would move communities beyond the parsing of the "benefits and burdens" of their diverse groups.

Integration as hospitality would not instantiate a power dynamic or paternalistic relationship between givers and takers, native-born and newcomers, hosts and guests. Rather, it would speak to the need to welcome newcomers and to incorporate them fully into communities, which would be transformed and strengthened by their presence

Integration, in this richer sense, places responsibilities on receiving communities and their native-born members. Nations rife with injustice against immigrants would not honor the Christian imperative of love of neighbor, at the root of hospitality; those that exploited immigrant workers would violate commutative justice; those beset by stark inequalities that failed to meet basic needs of immigrants would offend distributive justice; and those that blocked immigrants' social and political participation would violate social justice.[48] Integration as hospitality would treat immigrants with justice, particularly those without legal status and other vulnerable persons. It would model Jesus's "radical hospitality" to those most in need. It would require host communities to protect and empower immigrants "amid the thicket of barriers they confront."[49]

Finally, integration as hospitality would not treat any single culture as ideal but would locate and build upon the important values and customs in each culture. In bringing together culturally diverse persons, integration would work to unify persons based on a deeper understanding of the gifts and shared values expressed in their cultures. While difficult in practice, a Christian view of integration holds out the possibility of more just, inclusive and unified communities.

---

45 Cruz, *Toward a Theology of Migration*, 103.
46 Ibid.
47 Ibid., 5, 127–52.
48 Kristin E. Heyer, *Kinship Across Borders: A Christian Ethic of Immigration* (Washington, DC: Georgetown University Press, 2012).
49 Ibid.

Suggested Readings

Alba, Richard, and Nancy Foner. *Strangers No More: Immigration and the Challenges of Integration in North America and Western Europe*. Princeton, NJ: Princeton University Press, 2015.

Cruz, Gemma Tulud. *Toward a Theology of Migration: Social Justice and Religious Experience*. New York: Palgrave Macmillan, 2014.

Donahue, John R. *Seek Justice That You May Live: Reflections and Resources on the Bible and Social Justice*. New York: Paulist, 2014.

Groody, Daniel G., and Gioacchino Campese. *A Promised Land, A Perilous Journey*. Notre Dame, IN: University of Notre Dame Press, 2008.

Hollenbach, David. *The Common Good and Christian Ethics*. Cambridge: Cambridge University Press, 2002.

Hoover, Brett. *The Shared Parish: Latinos, Anglos and the Future of US Catholicism*. New York: New York University Press, 2014.

Kerwin, Donald, and Breana George. *US Catholic Institutions and Immigrant Integration: Will the Church Rise to the Challenge?* Vatican City: Lateran University Press, 2014. https://cmsny.org/publications/us-catholic-institutions-and-immigrant-integration-will-the-church-rise-to-the-challenge/.

Marzouk, Safwat. *Intercultural Church: A Biblical Vision in an Age of Migration*. Minneapolis: Fortress Press, 2019.

16 Labor, inequality, and globalization

Legal and theological perspectives on vulnerable migrant workers

Gemma Tulud Cruz and Enid Trucios-Haynes

I Introduction

As a social phenomenon, globalization has primarily been associated with the flexibility and movement of the forms of production; the rapid mobility of capital, information, and goods; the denationalizing of capital; the deterritorialization of culture; the interpenetration of local communities by global media networks; and the dispersal of socioeconomic power. While "globalization" as a term emerged fairly recently, when the world economy rapidly evolved new forms of integration and interdependence, the structures of globalization are not new. Whenever these structures of globalization have appeared throughout history, they have almost always resulted from, or resulted in, the wide-scale movement of people. Indeed, one could argue that globalization's strongest and most dramatic stimuli and effects are most deeply illustrated by the ability of a massive number of people to move from place to place at an increasingly faster pace.

In contemporary times, the majority of people on the move are workers, particularly those from the Global South. A confluence of factors, including migrants' ignorance and/or desperation, demand for cheap labor, and the exploitative profits of licit and illicit labor trafficking, mean that millions of migrant workers end up not only in segregated labor markets with the lowest salaries but also in so-called 3D (dirty, disdained, and dangerous) jobs. Furthermore, and of central importance, while the global migration infrastructure and globalized industry are focused on generating profit from lower-wage, lower-skilled migrants, those same migrants are largely unprotected by host-country legal systems.

In this chapter, we explore and critically reflect on the role of inequality in the structures of international labor migration, particularly as it is implicated in contemporary processes of globalization. More specifically, we consider the experiences of vulnerable migrant workers in Asia, who are primarily intraregional migrants, and in the United States, where migrants primarily come from Latin America. We provide a comparison of the similarity of their experiences using legal and theological perspectives. We contend that this vulnerability, which demands justice with mercy, especially for the poor and vulnerable, is a hermeneutical key not only in legally and theologically describing the experience of these workers but also in articulating a (Christian) moral response.

II Labor migration in comparative perspective

Labor migrants represent two-thirds of all people on the move, primarily moving from the Global South to states with more developed economies, such as the United States, France, the Russian Federation, the United Arab Emirates, and Saudi Arabia.[1] India has the largest number of migrants living abroad, followed by Mexico and China.[2] The Americas are experiencing a rising South–South migration similar to the migration trends in Asia. For example, Central Americans are migrating to Costa Rica, Belize, and Panama; and Haitians increasingly are migrating to Brazil.[3] The comparison of South–South (intraregional) migration in Asia, which represents over 50 percent of all Asian migration, and the South–North migration to the United States illustrates the similarities of the experiences of exploited migrant workers.[4]

A migrant worker is defined as any person who will be, is, or has been engaged in remunerated activity in a nation of which he or she is not a national.[5] Vulnerable migrants generally are subject to "intersecting forms of discrimination, inequality, and structural and societal dynamics that lead to diminished and unequal levels of power and enjoyment of rights."[6] Often, they experience exploitation in their home countries, on their migration journeys, and in their final host countries. Vulnerable migrant workers are concentrated in 3D jobs and at a much higher percentage than national workers. They work in less regulated industries and face unsafe working conditions; significant wage gaps, with even larger gender pay differences; limited occupational safety and health enforcement; a lack of other forms of social protection (such as health care); and a lack of recognition of their skills and diplomas.[7] In many cases, immigrant workers must accept jobs for which they are overqualified to support themselves and their families. Undocumented immigrant workers are especially vulnerable to human traffickers

---

1 International Organization for Migration (IOM), *World Migration Report 2020* (Geneva: International Organization for Migration, 2019), 21.
2 Ibid. India has the largest number of migrants living abroad (17.5 million), followed by Mexico and China (11.8 million and 10.7 million, respectively).
3 International Labour Organization (ILO), *Labour Migration in Latin America and the Caribbean. Diagnosis, Strategy and ILO's Work in the Region* (Peru: ILO Regional Office for Latin America and the Caribbean, 2017), 19, www.ilo.org/americas/publicaciones/ WCMS_548185/lang–en/index.htm.
4 IOM, *World Migration Report 2020*, 86. Asian countries represented over 40 percent of all international migrants in 2019 (111 million), and more than half (66 million) were residing in other countries in Asia.
5 Office of the United Nations High Commissioner for Human Rights (OHCHR), "Principles and Guidelines, Supported by Practical Guidance, on the Human Rights Protection of Migrants in Vulnerable Situations," 14, www.ohchr.org/Documents/Issues/Migration/ PrinciplesAndGuidelines.pdf.
6 Ibid., 6.
7 ILO, *Labour Migration in Latin America*, 60.

294 *Gemma Tulud Cruz and Enid Trucios-Haynes*

tied to criminal organizations that take advantage of their status to lock them into cycles of exploitation.[8]

A South–North migration to the United States

Vulnerable immigrant workers in the United States, typically working in lower-skilled and lower-wage jobs, experience exploitation in different ways, although all of these workers are at risk of abuses by employers. Immigration status is a major factor. Workers may have work authorization and a protected immigration status, or may be undocumented and lack work authorization. Those lacking work authorization also can include workers who have applied for immigration benefits or have a protected status without work authorization. For example, asylum applicants have a protected status as applicants but no guaranteed work permit. Vulnerable immigrant workers may have a protected immigration status *and* work authorization but cannot find a job in the formal economy due to discrimination. Discrimination against immigrant workers often includes second-generation immigrants (U.S.-born individuals with at least one foreign-born parent), immigrants with language barriers, or immigrants whose employers refuse to pay employment taxes or Social Security contributions.[9] Self-employed immigrants often are lower-skilled and engage in lower-wage jobs.[10] Undocumented immigrants in the United States are particularly vulnerable to exclusion from the immigration law system because of their status, even if they are longtime residents. These workers generally have crossed a border without a visa or have entered with a visa and stayed beyond their visa term. The estimated number of undocumented immigrants in 2020 was 10.5 million, accounting for 3.2 percent of the total population. Seventy-seven percent are from Latin America (Mexico and Central and South America).[11] Most undocumented people are not new arrivals; more than 65 percent of undocumented adults in 2017 had lived in the United States for more than 15 years.[12] Many are the parents of U.S. citizens.[13]

---

8 IOM, *World Migration Report 2020*, 95.

9 Jeanne Batalova, Brittany Blizzard, and Jessica Bolter, "Frequently Requested Statistics on Immigrants and Immigration," *Migration Policy Institute*, February 14, 2020, www.migrationpolicy. org/article/frequently-requested-statistics-immigrants-and-immigration-united-states.

10 ILO, *Labour Migration in Latin America*. "Second-generation immigrant children" include any U.S.-born child with at least one foreign-born parent; "first-generation immigrant children" include any foreign-born child with at least one foreign-born parent; "child with immigrant parents" includes first- and second-generation immigrant children. Batalova, Blizzard, and Bolter, "Frequently Requested Statistics on Immigrants and Immigration."

11 Abby Budiman, "Key Findings about U.S. Immigrants," *Pew Research Center*, August 20, 2020, www.pewresearch.org/fact-tank/2020/08/20/key-findings-about-u-s-immigrants/; Jeffrey S. Passel and D'Vera Cohn, "Mexicans Decline to Less than Half the U.S. Unauthorized Immigrant Population for the First Time," *Pew Research Center*, June 12, 2019, www. pewresearch.org/fact-tank/2019/06/12/us-unauthorized-immigrant-population-2017/.

12 Batalova, Blizzard, and Bolter, "Frequently Requested Statistics."

13 Ibid.

Labor, inequality, and globalization 295

Inequality in the U.S. immigrant labor system happens in an ecosystem in which racialized and gendered immigrant workers are segregated into the most exploitative industries, experience wide-ranging discrimination, and lack basic legal protections. The key factors creating exploitation and exclusion are: (1) an immigrant labor program that offers permanent residence for privileged workers with escalating barriers to lower-skilled and lower-wage workers; (2) a toxic political and public discourse that rationalizes inhumane and extraordinarily restrictive regulatory policies; (3) racial discrimination against Black and Brown immigrant workers who represent the majority of recent immigrants to the United States; (4) predatory and criminal facilitators of the migration journey who prey on immigrants; and (5) a large group of immigrant workers concentrated in less regulated 3D jobs. This includes workers with protected immigration status *and* undocumented immigrants.

The U.S. labor-migration program institutionalizes the inequality experienced by vulnerable immigrant workers. The system is tailored to facilitate the migration of those deemed to be higher-skilled workers, and features expansive, multilayered barriers to those who are deemed to be lower-skilled workers. The distinction itself is dehumanizing by delegitimizing the significant experience and skill required to perform many jobs that are categorized as lower-skilled.[14] The implicit value judgment contained in these constructed categories itself justifies the structural obstacles that effectively exclude all lower-skilled workers, creates the conditions for undocumented immigration because of the lack of viable migration avenues, and obscures the hazardous working conditions and other abuses in those less regulated industries employing lower-skilled immigrant workers.[15] The lack of any meaningful legislative reform in over two decades has hardened these obstacles.

For lower-skilled workers, the immigration law system does not provide any long-term temporary worker visas or pathways toward permanent residence and, ultimately, U.S. citizenship. The labor-migration system creates numerous seamless paths toward permanent residency for those deemed to be higher-skilled workers. Several higher-skilled temporary worker categories have analogous permanent resident categories, such as the categories for workers with university degrees and multinational managers and executives. These temporary worker categories allow for long-term temporary employment and the simultaneous application for permanent residence. For example, multinational managers and executives receive a temporary worker visa for up to seven years. This unequal access to permanent residency is further compounded by the lack of any long-term temporary visas for lower-skilled workers, and a very limited number of visas

---

14 As Bill Ong Hing points out, the distinction is insulting to workers whose occupations demand "a level of ability that requires cultivation and experience" (Chapter 3).
15 Silas W. Allard, "A Desired Composition: Regulating Vulnerability Through Immigration Law," in *Vulnerability and the Legal Organization of Work*, eds. Martha Albertson Fineman and Jonathan W. Fineman (Abingdon, UK: Routledge, 2017), 177–93, at 190–91.

296 Gemma Tulud Cruz and Enid Trucios-Haynes

allocated to the permanent resident category of "other" worker for lower-skilled workers (Enid Trucios-Haynes, Chapter 2).

The xenophobic, racialized political rhetoric blaming immigrants for job displacement and stoking irrational fears of changing demographics creates the backdrop for enhanced immigration restrictions and the lack of legislative reform. The widespread anti-immigrant rhetoric characterizes migrants—primarily Latinx migrants and other Black and Brown immigrants—as both a danger to and a drain on U.S. society. This toxic political discourse occurs at the highest level, beginning with former President Donald J. Trump, who continually scapegoated Latinx migrants. In 2015, Trump began his presidential campaign by calling Mexicans "rapists and murderers," and has called undocumented people "animals."[16] The prevalence of conspiracy theories about immigration also creates distrust. A 2018 poll found that more than half of U.S. citizens believed their government was withholding information about the real cost of immigration to society and taxpayers.[17]

The hateful rhetoric has been used to justify inhumane policies that demonstrate a complete disregard for the humanity of vulnerable immigrant workers—for example, the Trump administration's indifference to the serious health risks of immigrant workers vulnerable to the COVID-19 global pandemic. Immigrant agricultural workers, primarily Latinx workers, were uniquely harmed after being designated "essential workers" in the spring of 2020, and then expected to continue working in close proximity in fields and packing facilities. Immigrant workers were told to keep working despite stay-at-home directives.[18] They experienced increased exposure to the dangerous disease in an industry where between 50 and 75 percent of the 2 million agricultural workers are undocumented and require a mechanism to regularize their immigration status.[19] Another example affecting Latinx immigrant workers was the 2018 "zero-tolerance policy" applied to anyone seeking admission at the U.S.–Mexican border who lacked documents, primarily Central Americans and some South Americans. They were arrested, and all parents were separated from their children. Touted as an effort to deter undocumented immigration, the policy resulted separating nursing infants from

---

16 Gregory Korte and Alan Gomez, "Trump Ramps Up Rhetoric on Undocumented Immigrants: 'These Aren't People. These Are Animals'," *USA Today*, May 16, 2018, www.usatoday. com/story/news/politics/2018/05/16/trump-immigrants-animals-mexico-democrats-sanctuary-cities/617252002/.

17 IOM, *World Migration Report 2020*, 344.

18 Immigrant agricultural workers received special permission letters to violate the state directives from the U.S. Department of Homeland Security, the government agency that houses immigration enforcement operations.

19 Miriam Jordan, "Farmworkers, Mostly Undocumented, Become 'Essential' During Pandemic Immigration Law and Policies Intersecting with Labor Rights," *New York Times*, April 2, 2020, www.nytimes.com/2020/04/02/us/coronavirus-undocumented-immigrant-farmworkers-agriculture.html?searchResultPosition=1.

Labor, inequality, and globalization 297

mothers, causing a global outcry against the Trump administration, havoc at the border, human rights abuses, and legal challenges.[20]

Vulnerable migrants also experience profound discrimination on grounds of race, ethnicity, religion, and nationality at all stages of the migration process. Once in the United States, discrimination happens both in the workplace and in the larger U.S. society in the form of racial discrimination. Discrimination by denial of basic services is a growing problem for undocumented workers and their families, particularly in terms of access to health care.[21] Workplace discrimination is widespread, affecting second-generation immigrants and those who face language barriers. According to the Southern Poverty Law Center, the children of vulnerable migrants, many of them U.S. citizens, are often denied school enrollment or the educational services required by law. Further, in their communities, they are subjected to surveillance, racial profiling, and harassment by local law enforcement officers, who assume that people are undocumented solely because of how they look and the language they speak.[22]

Xenophobia has led to violence against vulnerable racialized and gendered immigrants. Bias or prejudiced motivated attacks in the United States reached a 16-year high in 2018.[23] The U.S. Federal Bureau of Investigation (FBI) found in November 2019 that anti-Latinx hate crimes, in particular, rose over 21 percent in 2018, with increased levels of violence.[24] This record high in hate violence was reached because of "a toxic combination of political polarization, anti-immigrant sentiment and technologies that help spread propaganda online."[25] The increase in bias-motivated violence further marginalizes vulnerable immigrant laborers, which has led the International Labour Organization (ILO) to emphasize the importance of combating xenophobia and the social and cultural stereotypes that contribute to the discrimination.[26] Violence in multiple forms is widespread. National statistics cover only a fraction of hate crimes and other violence, because state and local authorities are not required to report or

20 Caitlin Dickerson, "Hundreds of Immigrant Children Have Been Taken from Parents at U.S. Border," *New York Times*, April 20, 2018, www.nytimes.com/2018/04/20/us/immigrant-children-separation-ice.html. The policy was reversed only after two children died in government custody. See Nomaan Merchant, "CBP Orders Medical Checks After Second Child's Death," *APNews*, December 25, 2018, https://apnews.com/0a7e7ec16cd743e48 40c321a99e005ef.
21 ILO, *Labour Migration in Latin America*, 70.
22 Southern Poverty Law Center, "Immigrant Justice," www.splcenter.org/issues/immigrant-justice.
23 Adeel Hassan, "Hate-Crime Violence Hits 16-Year High, F.B.I. Reports," *New York Times*, November 12, 2019, www.nytimes.com/2019/11/12/us/hate-crimes-fbi-report.html.
24 Brad Brooks, "Victims of Anti-Latino Hate Crimes Soar in U.S.: FBI Report," *Reuters*, November 12, 2019, www.reuters.com/article/us-hatecrimes-report/victims-of-anti-latino-hate-crimes-soar-in-us-fbi-report-idUSKBN1XM2OQ.
25 Liam Stack, "Over 1,000 Hate Groups Are Now Active in United States, Civil Rights Group Says," *New York Times*, February 20, 2019, www.nytimes.com/2019/02/20/us/hate-groups-rise.html?searchResultPosition=5.
26 ILO, *Labour Migration in Latin America*, 71.

even collect this data, and more than half of all victims of hate crimes never file a complaint.[27] Vulnerable immigrant workers in hazardous, less regulated industries are silenced also by their isolation in these industries, language barriers, and distrust of state and local police, who often work with federal immigration enforcement officials.

Exploitation on the perilous migration journey to the United States is facilitated by immigrant-smuggling operations that prey on vulnerable immigrants. Labor-migration processes managed by commercial intermediaries, such as brokers, recruiters, and staffing agencies, can be predatory. This industry is largely unregulated, and workers are forced to rely on these agencies, which identify workers for labor-migration programs and, in the case of staffing agencies, file all of the required visa documents for the eligible workers. The agencies charge exorbitant fees to the least financially stable workers, who depend on the agency for access to U.S. employers.[28]

Migrant smuggling is a major feature of migration to the United States. Along the U.S.–Mexico border, smuggling networks are a profitable industry overseen by international crime groups.[29] The system of *coyotaje* connected to drug-trafficking operations in recent years takes advantage of desperate people seeking to cross borders who are seen as a commodity by these actors.[30] *Coyotaje* is the activity leading people to enter illicitly and, in some cases, travel through other states to a final host country where people do not have immigration documents. The coyote is the person delivering and charging for such a service.[31] Undocumented immigrants on the journey face extraordinary violence, ranging from demands for bribes to mass kidnapping and extortion. Families at home are targeted for bribes as well.[32] Executions, physical and sexual assaults, torture, and disappearances are common. A major migrant-smuggling corridor runs through Central America. Fears of this dangerous journey have led to alternative migration processes, such as "safer" migrant caravans of large groups of people traveling together through Mexico from Honduras, El Salvador, and Guatemala.[33] In 2018 and 2019, the U.S. government's response was to characterize everyone in the caravans as criminals. The Mexican government also employed similar rhetoric in order to justify its detentions of migrants.[34]

---

27 Hassan, "Hate-Crime Violence Hits 16-Year High."
28 Jennifer Gordon, "Regulating the Human Supply Chain," *Iowa Law Review* 102, no. 2 (2017): 445–505.
29 IOM, *World Migration Report 2020*, 123.
30 ILO, *Labour Migration in Latin America*, 22. James Verini, "How U.S. Policy Turned the Sonoran Desert into a Migrant Graveyard," *New York Times*, August 18, 2020, www.nytimes.com/2020/08/18/magazine/border-crossing.html?searchResultPosition=1.
31 ILO, *Labour Migration in Latin America*, 22.
32 Verini, "How U.S. Policy Turned the Sonoran Desert into a Migrant Graveyard."
33 Eduardo Torre Cantalapiedra, "Migrant 'Caravans' in Mexico and the Fight Against Smuggling," *Forced Migration Review*, no. 64 (2020): 66–67, www.fmreview.org/issue64/torrecantalapiedra.
34 Ibid., 66.

Labor, inequality, and globalization 299

Inequality is reinforced by the labor segregation of lower-skilled immigrant workers into industries with poor labor protections. They work predominantly in agriculture, construction, gardening, childcare, house cleaning, food processing, manufacturing, and other services, where the highest human trafficking–related violations and abusive labor practices are found.[35] Immigrant workers are at much higher risk of being subjected to forced labor, and child immigrant workers are particularly vulnerable, especially in agriculture and domestic work.[36] Exploitative and hazardous working conditions for immigrant workers result in greater exposure to pesticides and other chemicals, workplace abuse, and higher workloads than for national workers.[37] Perilous chemical exposure is common for agricultural workers, although many employed in construction and manufacturing also are exposed.[38] Immigrant workers in these industries often work in isolated, rural locations and depend on employers for access to health care and other services. They lack sufficient training, protective equipment, medical supervision, and insurance against occupational accidents and for their families.[39] The U.S. meat- and poultry-processing industry, where many lower-skilled immigrant workers find jobs, is notoriously dangerous, with very high risks of occupational injury and illness.[40] Employers can become the gatekeepers for healthcare access, forcing workers to wait weeks or even months for a referral to a physician. Large-scale machinery causes traumatic injuries, and production lines require repetitive "forceful motions, tens of thousands of times each day, causing severe and disabling injuries."[41] Every other day, between 2015 and 2018, one worker from these processing plants lost a body part or was sent to the hospital for inpatient treatment.[42] Abusive working conditions abound, including a lack of access to sanitation facilities, and workers being pushed past their physical and mental limits.

35 ILO, *Labour Migration in Latin America*, 60. Forced labor is most common in construction, food processing, and cleaning services.
36 International Labour Organization, *Addressing Governance Challenges in a Changing Labour Migration Landscape*, International Labour Conference, 106th Session, April 10, 2017, at 23, www.ilo.org/ilc/ILCSessions/previous-sessions/106/reports/reports-to-the-conference/WCMS_550269/lang–en/index.htm.
37 Sally Hargreaves, et al., "Occupational Health Outcomes Among International Migrant Workers: A Systematic Review and Meta-Analysis," *Lancet: Global Health* 7, no. 7 (2019): e872–e882, www.thelancet.com/journals/langlo/article/PIIS2214-109X(19)30204-9/fulltext.
38 Emily Q. Ahonen, "Occupational Health Challenges for Immigrant Workers," *Oxford Research Encyclopedia of Global Public Health* (October 2019), https://doi.org/10.1093/acrefore/9780190632366.013.40.
39 ILO, *Addressing Governance Challenges*, 20.
40 Human Rights Watch, *"When We're Dead and Buried, Our Bones Will Keep Hurting": Workers' Rights under Threat in U.S. Meat and Poultry Plants* (September 4, 2019), www.hrw.org/report/2019/09/04/when-were-dead-and-buried-our-bones-will-keep-hurting/workers-rights-under-threat.
41 Ibid., 7.
42 Ibid., 8.

300 Gemma Tulud Cruz and Enid Trucios-Haynes

Immigrant women are particularly vulnerable; they are overrepresented in service jobs and account for nearly 68 percent of all domestic workers and 80 percent of in-home caregivers.[43] They are more likely than men to experience discrimination on account of their gender, nationality, *and* immigrant status. Young immigrant domestic workers are particularly exposed to physical and sexual violence in the workplace.[44] These workers

> face a double penalty in terms of labor market segregation and discrimination; they are more likely to work in less paid and rewarded sectors of the economy because of their sex, and are more likely to work in lower-skilled positions in that sector because of their ethnicity and migrant status.[45]

This feminization of domestic work is part of a "global care chain" linking women across the globe who are engaged in paid and unpaid home care work.[46] Paid domestic workers are needed for young and elderly family members in order to support women working outside of their homes. Reduced government support for child/elder care creates this need. The care chain is created when immigrant women are hired for domestic work, and then must rely on their relatives or other low-paid workers to care for their own families. The care chain then limits the family members who assist the domestic worker—often mothers or eldest daughters—who can no longer participate in available economic or education opportunities. This global care chain transfers domestic responsibilities from women to other women and perpetuates labor-market segregation, gender inequalities, and discrimination.[47]

B South–South migration in Asia

The inequality, exploitation, and exclusion experienced by vulnerable immigrant workers in the United States has parallels in South–South migration. The comparison to intraregional labor migration within Asia illustrates how the labor segregation of lower-skilled workers results in widespread abuses worldwide.

As in the United States, vulnerable migrant workers in or from Asia significantly experience inequality, exploitation, and exclusion on account of their type of work and/or their migration status or background. Contemporary overseas

---

43 Julia Wolfe, "Domestic Workers Are at Risk During the Coronavirus Crisis," *Working Economics* (blog), *Economic Politics Institute*, April 8, 2020, www.epi.org/blog/domestic-workers-are-at-risk-during-the-coronavirus-crisis-data-show-most-domestic-workers-are-black-hispanic-or-asian-women/.

44 ILO, *Addressing Governance Challenges*, 24.

45 Ibid.

46 Ibid.; Premilla Nadasen, "Rethinking Care: Arlie Hochschild and the Global Care Chain," *Women's Studies Quarterly* 45, no. 3/4 (2017): 124–28.

47 ILO, *Addressing Governance Challenges*, 24.

Labor, inequality, and globalization 301

labor migration in and out of Asia could be characterized into four major systems: (1) the Middle East, which has a strong dependency on foreign labor hired through the *khafel/kafala* system;[48] (2) East Asia, which reluctantly admits workers in low-skilled work; (3) Southeast Asia, which is a region of both origin and destination; and (4) South Asia, which is mostly a region of origin of migration. In keeping with the trajectories of international labor migration, particularly as created by the current process of economic globalization, the majority of the Asian migrant workforce are in semi-skilled or low-skilled work and move from less developed to more developed countries. In fact, the 2018 Asian Economic Integration Report from the Asian Development Bank (ADB) asserts that these migrants constitute the majority of Asian migrants.[49]

The three key features of contemporary cross-border labor migration in the Asian Pacific, which were highlighted in a 2017 report from the ILO, point to key challenges embedded in the experience of Asian migrants in semi-skilled and low-skilled work. First, migration occurs primarily under temporary (contractual) migration regimes and for elementary occupations and medium-skilled workers, such as maids, caregivers, and manual laborers, including those working in construction. One distinct face of this type of temporary work in Australia and New Zealand is the seasonal worker. In Australia, this mostly involves Pacific Islanders who come on state-sponsored seasonal worker programs in regional farms. In addition, around 150,000 backpackers, or young people from Europe, North America, Latin America, and Asia, work annually in the agricultural and hospitality industry, mostly in the countryside, on a one- to two-year working holiday visa. Second, migration corridors and sectors of employment are highly gendered. Sri Lanka, Indonesia, and the Philippines, for example, typically have large outflows of women engaged in domestic work, while men dominate or solely comprise the flow to construction in the countries of the Gulf Cooperation Council (GCC), the fishing industry in East and South-East Asia, and seasonal overseas work in agriculture by Pacific Islanders. Third, irregular migration occurs in parallel with regular migration.[50] A 2019 World Bank report indicates four out of ten workers of the approximately 3.055 million foreign workers in Malaysia in 2017 are irregular.[51] These three key features confirm an often-overlooked fact in the highly politicized and xenophobic rhetoric on migration in the West, that is,

---

48 The *khafel/kafala* system is a sponsorship system for recruitment, a form of franchise granted to loyal subjects to import foreign labor, which thrives on bringing in ever-increasing numbers of foreign workers willing to pay money for their jobs.
49 There is also a considerable number of Asian migrants in skilled work, albeit they tend to move to advanced industrial economies outside the region due to higher pay and the possibility for family reunification.
50 Cansin Arslan, et al., *Safeguarding the Rights of Asian Migrant Workers from Home to the Workplace* (Bangkok: International Labour Organization, 2017).
51 World Bank, *Malaysia: Estimating the Number of Foreign Workers* (Washington, DC: The World Bank, 2019), 21.

302 *Gemma Tulud Cruz and Enid Trucios-Haynes*

that South–South migration is increasingly as common as South–North migration. At the same time, these features point to how the dynamics of South–South migration exhibit similarities to those of South–North migration.

Asian migrants in low-skilled work constitute the underclass among migrant workers in their host countries, as they and their children bear the brunt of the three dominant and problematic attitudes toward migrants in key host countries, particularly in Asia: (1) immigrants should not be allowed to settle; (2) foreign residents should not be offered citizenship, except in certain prescribed cases; and (3) national culture and identity should not be modified in response to external influences.[52] The struggle is equally acute for those in the West or in developed countries who—despite having the education, skills, and training as well experience necessary to engage in skilled work—end up in low-skilled or semiskilled work (for example, as taxi drivers) because of racism or lack of recognition of their education and skills.[53]

Not surprisingly, the vulnerable position of these workers makes them easy targets for exploitation and abuse by various actors in the migration process. These actors include states that create or apply laws and/or migration policies that disadvantage these workers[54] and their children. Examples of these restrictive state migration policies, include Taiwan's nonrenewable three-year contract, Hong Kong's Two-Week Rule (upon contract completion or job termination, migrant workers have only two weeks to find a new employer or be deported), and Singapore's mandatory pregnancy test every six months, which applies only to foreign domestic workers. In the Middle East, the *khafel/kafala* system poses serious problems as well, as it prohibits workers from changing employers and requires them to surrender their passports to the sponsor as soon as they enter the country, as well as to get clearance from the sponsor in order to leave the country. Some states, meanwhile, monetize migrant workers by charging excessive fees or making migrants, or their employers, pay a levy as a condition for their (continued) employment.[55] Other state-related actors include corrupt police and

52 Stephen Castles, "The Myth of the Controllability of Difference: Labor Migration, Transnational Communities and State Strategies in East Asia," paper presented at the International Conference on Transnational Communities in the Asia-Pacific Region: Comparative Perspectives, Singapore, August 7–8, 2000.

53 Farz Edraki and Cathy Pryor, " 'Doctors and Engineers End up Driving Taxis': The Uphill Battle Facing Migrants in Australia," *Australian Broadcast Corporation (ABC) News*, October 31, 2019, www.abc.net.au/news/2019-10-31/migrant-experience-of-work-australia-talks/11600862.

54 Hong Kong's exclusion of domestic workers from a rule that allows foreigners to apply for permanent resident status after 7 years of uninterrupted residency is a case in point—for example, the landmark case of Evangeline Vallejos and Daniel Domingo, who have been denied to apply for permanent residency despite having lived in Hong Kong for 17 and 28 years, respectively. See "Hong Kong Court Denies Domestic Workers Residency," *BBC News*, March 25, 2013, www.bbc.com/news/world-asia-china-21920811.

55 Australia, for example, has the "backpacker tax," which requires any foreigner on 417 or 462 visas earning less than $18,200 to pay a 15 percent tax (Australians are not taxed on similar

Labor, inequality, and globalization 303

military personnel, who engage in bribery and extortion and, as in Malaysia and Thailand, serve as accomplices in the trafficking of workers. The so-called Asian boat people crisis in 2015, for example, actually involved hundreds of Rohingyas fleeing oppression in Buddhist-majority Myanmar and Bangladeshis looking for better livelihood abroad, who have been preyed upon by human traffickers. Not clearly relayed in the news was that the boats left drifting on the Andaman Sea had been abandoned by traffickers after a crackdown on human trafficking when mass graves were discovered along the Thailand–Malaysia border and a clampdown by Thailand's military junta made a well-trodden trafficking route into Malaysia too risky for criminals.[56] Another form of state-related abuse, often exhibited by unscrupulous politicians, occurs when migrants are weaponized to score votes or political points by peddling misleading information[57] or outright lies to create, or stoke, anti-immigration sentiments that result in discriminatory, racist, and sometimes violent behavior against migrants.

A second group of actors who exploit migrants in low-skilled work are the employers—sometimes the migrants' own people who are residents or citizens in host countries—who subject their workers to various forms of exploitation and abuse: political (for example, owners of cruise and cargo ships who register their ships in countries with weaker and poorer implementation of maritime laws), economic (underpayment), psychological (poor working conditions), physical (starvation or bodily harm), sexual (harassment, assault, and rape), etc. Torture and death are not uncommon, particularly for trafficked workers whose experience is often described as modern-day slavery.[58] Women, particularly those in the service and hospitality industry, are also vulnerable. This vulnerability is highlighted in the case of Erwiana Sulistyaningsih, an Indonesian domestic worker in Hong Kong who was subjected to severe physical and psychological abuse, and Joanna Demafelis,[59] a Filipina domestic worker in Kuwait, whose tortured, lifeless body was dumped in a freezer allegedly by her Lebanese employer and his Syrian

---

earnings). The policy was overturned in October 2019 by the federal court, but only in the case of backpackers from countries which have a tax treaty with Australia. See Clint. Jasper, Kath Sullivan, and Nassim Khadem, "Holiday Workers May Receive Hundreds of Millions of Dollars after Backpacker Tax Overturned by Federal Court," *Australian Broadcast Corporation (ABC) News*, October 29, 2019, www.abc.net.au/news/rural/2019-10-30/federal-court-rules-backpacker-tax-invalid/11653928.

56 Al-Zaquan Amer Hamzah and Aubrey Belford, "Pressure Mounts on Myanmar Over Asia 'Boat People' Crisis," *Reuters*, May 17, 2015, www.reuters.com/article/us-asia-migrants/pressure-mounts-on-myanmar-over-asia-boat-people-crisis-idUSKBN0O20JB20150517.

57 See, for example, Devana Senanayake, "More Myths About Migrants and Work," *Eureka Street* 29, no. 7, April 11, 2019, www.eurekastreet.com.au/article/more-myths-about-migrants-and-work.

58 See Vannak Prum's story in Vannak Anan Prum, Jocelyn Pederick, and Ben Pederick, *The Dead Eye and the Deep Blue Sea: The World of Slavery at Sea—A Graphic Memoir* (New York: Seven Stories Press, 2018).

59 For details on the cases of Erwiana and others, see Joanna Plucinska, "Two Years after Erwiana: Has Life Improved for Hong Kong's Domestic Workers?" *Time*, December 31, 2015, https://time.com/4138107/erwiana-hong-kong-domestic-workers-helpers-rights/.

wife.[60] Turning to irregular employment, therefore, often becomes a means of escaping abusive situations, resulting in the creation of an "underclass within the underclass," as irregular status puts these workers not only in legal trouble (with deportation hanging over their head) but also in more vulnerable conditions that render them easier prey for further exploitation and abuse. Even when there is no threat of deportation, the precarity of sponsor-linked employment can lead to mental problems and severe economic challenges.[61]

A third group of actors who take advantage of vulnerable migrant workers are the recruiters and placement agencies, who use a range of exploitative tactics, including falsifying workers' ages to circumvent minimum-age requirements, changing the contract's terms and conditions upon arrival in the host country, charging excessive fees, and commodifying workers with practices that treat workers as merchandise—for example, putting them on sale. The worst of these vultures are the members of local and transnational organized crime syndicates who prey on the vulnerability of workers. These include drug traffickers who use unsuspecting migrant workers as drug mules—one of whom, Mary Jane Veloso, is on death row in Indonesia—and human traffickers, who sometimes masquerade as recruiters by offering nonexistent jobs, then passing or selling workers to the highest bidders in industries that engage in practices considered modern-day slavery. Traffickers who keep migrant workers, meanwhile, treat them like goods and commodities. In a case of 31 Vietnamese workers in Taiwan the workers were rotated to a new employer every month (replacing the regular worker who was on holiday or filling in while a new worker was being selected) and did not receive wages. The workers also reported being treated brutally and being threatened and coerced by their broker while two were sexually abused. In addition, they were transported and moved, often in the middle of the night, unexpectedly and against their will.[62]

The experience of vulnerable Asian migrant workers shows the prevalence and intransigence of exploitation. The legal and political frameworks as well as socioeconomic conditions that underpin, or bolster, this persistent exploitation have parallels with the experience of those in the United States.

---

60 Chandrika Narayan, "Suspect Arrested in Death of Filipino Maid Found in a Freezer," *CNN*, February 23, 2018, https://edition.cnn.com/2018/02/23/asia/philippines-domestic-worker-killing-arrest/index.html.

61 In the case of Allan Par, the souring of the relationship with his Canadian sponsor forced him to bounce from one job to another until he ended up penniless and homeless. See "Homeless Filipino in Winnipeg Who Built an Elaborate Shack Flies Back to Manila via Donated Fare," *Inquirer.net*, August 10, 2019, https://usa.inquirer.net/36719/homeless-filipino-in-winnipeg-who-built-an-elaborate-shack-flies-back-to-manila-via-donated-fare.

62 Danielé Belanger, "Labor Migration and Trafficking Among Vietnamese Migrants in Asia," *The Annals of the American Academy of Political and Social Science Society* 653, no. 1 (2014): 87–106, at 98.

Labor, inequality, and globalization 305

C *The persistence of exploitation in labor migration*

Labor migrants worldwide experience inequality, exploitation, and exclusion regardless of their migration journeys or their final host country. The temporary-worker programs or contracts for lower-skilled workers in less regulated industries, such as domestic services or construction, provide significant opportunities for exploitation within intraregional Asian migration and in the South–North migration to the United States. Migrant workers lack legal protections and are segregated into hazardous industries where they face heightened risks from unscrupulous employers. The gendered dimension of migrant labor is a global phenomenon in which women immigrant workers are more likely to experience employer abuse and violence. The migration of people lacking immigration status is common in South–South and South–North migration corridors.

These long-standing conditions facing all vulnerable migrant workers call for enhanced global cooperation. There are challenges to this cooperation, because lower-skilled workers are an underclass of migrant workers. A common thread found in Asian intraregional migration and South–North migration to the United States is that the perceived threat to national culture and identity leads to excessive restrictions endorsed by host nation societies. The xenophobia, racism, and discrimination reported by the ILO are found universally in host countries and are propelled by unscrupulous politicians who conflate immigrant workers with threats to national identity from changing demographics.

Vulnerable migrant workers are dehumanized, and their experiences of exploitation, abuse, and exclusion are submerged by justifications that foreground the economic needs of host countries rather than the humanity of people. Christian values can provide the means to overcome the exclusionary impulses of widely shared anti-immigrant attitudes and practices embedded within host countries, and to explicitly connect to the experiences of migrant workers. The use of Catholic social teaching to focus on immigrant worker experiences can support mutual economic development and a renewed emphasis on the human conditions of migrant workers seeking to "escape from a life with no future."[63]

III A preferential option for the exploited

A. *Justice, mercy, and the crucified people*

The experience of vulnerable migrant workers clearly constitutes violations of human dignity, which requires justice as a moral response.

---

63 John J. Hoeffner and Michele R. Pistone, "But the Laborers Are . . . Many? Catholic Social Teaching on Business, Labor and Economic Migration," in *And You Welcomed Me: Migration and Catholic Social Teaching*, eds. Donald M. Kerwin and Jill Marie Gerschutz (Lanham, MD: Lexington Books, 2009), 55–92, at 71.

306 *Gemma Tulud Cruz and Enid Trucios-Haynes*

From a Christian perspective, justice is a debt that we owe to those who have been denied human flourishing. The reality, however, is that human action can deviate from justice itself even when it is being undertaken in the name of justice. We can deceive ourselves into thinking that we are acting justly, and for this reason, John Paul II suggests that without mercy, justice cannot be established: "Society can become ever more human only if we introduce into the many-sided setting of interpersonal and social relationships, not merely justice but also that of 'merciful love.' "[64] Mercy, according to John Paul II, differs from justice but is not in opposition to it. Rather, mercy conditions justice in the sense that true mercy is the most profound source of justice and is a mark of the whole of revelation.[65]

Justice informed by mercy is important, since legislation may not necessarily keep up with real situations, rendering it insufficient for setting up true relationships of justice and equality. As can be seen in the case of Vallejos and Domingo in Hong Kong as well as Australia's backpacker tax, legislation (or interpretations of legislation) can also further marginalize certain groups of migrants in low-skilled work. Indeed, if there is no adequate respect for, and service to, others beyond legal rules, then even equality before the law—for example, fees collected by host countries from migrant workers or their employers on behalf of "disadvantaged" local workers—can serve as an excuse for flagrant discrimination, continued exploitation, and actual contempt. Mercy, in a sense, is not the opposite of justice or the complement of justice but its very condition. This is because, as Jon Sobrino points out, mercy is a basic attitude toward the suffering of another, whereby one responds to eradicate that suffering for the sole reason that it exists, and in the conviction that, in this response to the ought-not-to-be of another's suffering, one's own being, without any possibility of subterfuge, hangs in the balance.[66] Mercy, in other words, is linked with *metanoia* or conversion. Jesus makes the importance of mercy, as an expression of Christian witness, explicit in Matthew 9:13: "I desire mercy, not sacrifice."

From a Catholic theological perspective, the experience of vulnerable migrant workers renders them "crucified people." Coined by Jesuit theologian Ignacio Ellacuría, and used by migration theologians Gioacchino Campese and Daniel Groody to describe the experience of irregular migrants,[67] the term "crucified people" refers to "that collective body which, as the majority of humanity, owes

---

64 Pope John Paul II, "Dives in Misericordia," November 30, 1980, http://w2.vatican.va/content/john-paul-ii/en/encyclicals/documents/hf_jp-ii_enc_30111980_dives-in-misericordia.html.

65 Ibid., 13–14.

66 Jon Sobrino, *The Principle of Mercy: Taking the Crucified People from the Cross* (New York: Orbis, 1994).

67 Daniel G. Groody, "Jesus and the Undocumented Immigrant: A Spiritual Geography of a Crucified People," *Theological Studies* 70, no. 2 (2009): 298–316; Gioacchino Campese, "¿*Cuantos Mas?* The Crucified Peoples at the U.S. Mexico Border," in *A Promised Land, A Perilous Journey: Theological Perspectives on Migration*, eds. Daniel G. Groody and Gioacchino Campese (Notre Dame, IN: University of Notre Dame Press, 2008), 271–98.

its situation of crucifixion to the way society is organized and maintained by a minority that exercises its dominion through a series of factors which, taken together and given their concrete impact within history, must be regarded as sin."[68] The crucified people, in other words, are "the actual presence of the crucified Christ in history."[69] In this crucified people, Christ acquires a body in history, and we are challenged, in the words of Sobrino, to "take the crucified people from the cross." As illustrated in the experience of vulnerable workers in South–North and South–South migration, crucifixion takes place for migrant laborers not only in and through the exploitation and abuse they encounter as a result of socioeconomic background and conditions but also on account of legal policies in the host country that create or reinforce inequality, such as racism and discrimination.

B When law is a tool of exploitation

The ecosystem in which racialized and gendered immigrant workers are segregated into the most abusive segments of state labor markets is bounded by law that functions to exploit vulnerable workers or enable their exploitation. Immigration law systems structurally exclude vulnerable immigrant workers who are categorized as lower skilled, and these legal systems advance the labor-market segregation of workers. Immigration law systems distinguish between humanitarian migrants, who are guaranteed some state protection, and "economic" migrants, whose exclusion is justified by this distinction; and between lower-skilled and more "desirable" higher-skilled workers. Labor law systems have fewer regulatory interventions into the industries where vulnerable immigrants regularly work, often because governments deprioritize investigations and oversight of hazardous industries. Border enforcement procedures can heighten the exploitation of vulnerable workers through abusive detention and deportation mechanisms.

The international law distinctions between refugees and other migrants are replicated in state immigration law systems. Labor migration is distinguished from humanitarian migration, and these distinctions are used by policymakers to justify the exclusion of immigrant workers. Refugees, viewed as involuntary humanitarian migrants, must receive state protection after asserting a fear of being persecuted if returned to their home countries.[70] "Economic migrants" are

---

68 Ignacio Ellacuría, "The Crucified People," in *Mysterium Liberationis: Fundamental Concepts of Liberation Theology*, eds. Ignacio Ellacuría and Jon Sobrino (Maryknoll, NY: Orbis, 1993), 580–603, at 590.

69 Jon Sobrino, *Jesus the Liberator: A Historical-Theological Reading of Jesus of Nazareth* (New York: Orbis, 1993), 255.

70 Refugees are "deserving" migrants safeguarded under the clear mandate of the 1951 International Covenant on Refugees Convention Relating to the Status of Refugees and the 1967 Protocol, although these protections are increasingly under attack (Michele R. Pistone, Chapter 4). Seth M. Holmes and Heidi Castañeda, "Representing the 'European Refugee Crisis' in Germany and Beyond: Deservingness and Difference, Life and Death," *American Ethnologist* 43, no. 1 (2016): 12–24.

framed as opportunists who voluntarily leave their communities for a better life.[71] Some have referred to this group as "survival migrants."[72] Both groups include people labeled as "undesirable," who are poor and lower skilled (Gemma Tulud Cruz, Chapter 11). These distinctions are reinforced in immigration law systems that do not recognize human rights obligations to economic migrants. A better framework would recognize that these vulnerable migrants face desperate existential situations intensified by global inequality that do not fit into the binary of "voluntary economic migration" and "involuntary humanitarian or refugee migration" (Luis N. Rivera-Pagán, Chapter 10). The United Nations has recognized the dire consequences facing immigrant workers through the historic 2018 Global Compact for Migration, which seeks to advance the human rights protections of vulnerable immigrants.[73] The Office of the High Commissioner for Human Rights has supported this work with the 2018 Principles and Guidelines that identify the range of human rights obligations to migrant workers who lack the protection accorded to refugees.[74]

Host-country immigrant-worker systems harm vulnerable workers with mechanisms such as employment permit and sponsorship systems that severely restrict the ability of workers to change workplaces, employers, or sponsors. These workers face situations in which employers can exert tremendous power by threatening arrest, detention, and deportation to undocumented workers who attempt to challenge abuses, organize unions, or file complaints with enforcement agencies.[75] Restrictions tying workers to specific employers often create employer preferences for migrant workers over national workers, thus facilitating "social dumping."[76] "Social dumping" happens when an industry relies on immigrant workers for lower-skilled and lower-wage jobs, reinforcing labor market segmentation and the continued overrepresentation of immigrants in industries like domestic work and construction.[77] One contributing factor is the worldwide lack of processes for recognizing the skills of low- and medium-skilled immigrant workers, who are forced into these jobs regardless of their skills.

The law in host countries can systematically exclude immigrant workers from many legal protections. Too often, immigrant workers, particularly undocumented immigrants, have no basic legal protections, such as protection against occupational hazards and other unfair working conditions. Inequality continues

---

71 Holmes and Castañeda, "Representing the 'European Refugee Crisis'."
72 Heavan Crawley, and Dimitris Skleparis, "Refugees, Migrants, Neither, Both: Categorical Fetishism and the Politics of Bounding in Europe's 'Migration Crisis'," *Journal of Ethnic and Migration Studies* 44, no. 1 (2018): 48–64, at 48.
73 The Global Compact for Safe, Orderly and Regular Migration (GCM), www.iom.int/ global-compact-migration.
74 OHCHR, "Principles and Guidelines."
75 Shirley Lung, "Criminalizing Work and Non-Work: The Disciplining of Immigrant and African American Workers," *UMass Law Review* 14, no. 2 (2019): 290–349, at 333.
76 ILO, *Labour Migration in Latin America*, 16.
77 ILO, *Addressing Governance Challenges*, 22.

Labor, inequality, and globalization 309

as longstanding worker abuses remain less regulated, and the enforcement of worker protections is not prioritized. For example, the U.S. government has failed to implement workplace safety and health standards in the meat- and poultry-processing industry and, more recently, has rescinded worker safety measures.[78] Under the Trump administration, oversight of meat and poultry companies was weakened when the U.S. Occupational Health and Safety Administration (OSHA) was operating with the fewest safety and health inspectors in its 48-year history.[79]

The use of legal systems as a tool for exploitation shows that while law is necessary as a means of pursuing justice, it cannot by itself achieve justice. This means that we cannot always and necessarily equate the law with justice. Yes, the law can provide a framework for justice, but it should not be regarded as the same thing as justice. The promise of a Christian perspective emphasizing justice and the human dignity of vulnerable immigrant workers can be a means to reimagine legal regimes that reinforce inequality, exploitation, and exclusion.

C *The option for the poor and exploited*

In Catholic social teaching (CST), making an option for the poor is part and parcel of practicing justice with mercy and, consequently, "taking the crucified people from the cross." This CST principle is rooted in the conviction that the basic moral test of a society is how its most vulnerable members are faring. The Christian tradition itself instructs us to put the needs of poor and vulnerable people first. The option for the poor is a conscious choice to be in solidarity with the poor and to work for structural change to transform the causes of poverty and marginalization. Donal Dorr describes it as a choice "freely made by people who are not already poor" but who, because they are aware "that they are relatively wealthy or privileged," decide "to relinquish their privileges (to some degree at least) and to become identified with the underprivileged."[80] For poor or marginalized people, "it means a choice to be in solidarity with other underprivileged people rather than trying to take advantage of them and join the rich and powerful."[81] Dorr identifies an experiential solidarity with the poor—choosing to share their life and seeing the world from their perspective—and working for structural change to transform the causes of poverty and marginalization as essential dimensions of making an option for the poor.[82]

In the context of migration, Michele R. Pistone and John Hoeffner contend, this means "multiple and concrete personal commitments to the poor and an

---

78 Human Rights Watch, *When We're Dead and Buried*, 10.

79 Ibid.

80 Donal Dorr, "Poor, Preferential Option For," in *New Dictionary of Catholic Social Thought*, ed. Judith A. Dwyer (Collegeville, MN: Liturgical Press, 1994), 755.

81 Ibid.

82 Donal Dorr, *Option for the Poor: A Hundred Years of Vatican Social Teaching*, rev. ed. (Blackburn, Australia: Collins Dove, 1992), 2–4.

analysis of structural impediments that is preceded by a personal and concrete commitment to the poor, that is rooted in love."[83] Speaking of migrants in the United States with irregular status, many of whom are workers, Pistone and Hoeffner point out that, given the distinction, or special place, that CST provides for the suffering poor, one can say that undocumented migrants occupy a privileged position in Catholic social teaching.[84] Pistone and Hoeffner, therefore, urge that efforts to find a legal solution must be made for the sake of mutual development, since "the unmistakable point is that by refusing to aid in the development of those trying to escape from a life with no future who even beyond the limits imposed by law legitimately expect our help in fulfilling their human potential we not only guarantee others' lack of authentic human development, we concomitantly reveal distortions in our own development."[85]

Making an option for the poor, therefore, is not simply the result of critical analysis or taking sides in a conflict. It also stems from our capacity to be rendered vulnerable by the vulnerability of others to a degree that compels us to stand in solidarity with them. It is rooted in a solidarity that "is not [simply] a feeling of vague compassion or shallow distress at the misfortunes of many people, both near and far" but "a firm and persevering determination to commit oneself to the common good,"[86] especially for the poor and vulnerable who have a special claim to it. This solidarity with the poor and vulnerable implies a complementary vulnerability, but one that comes with responsibility. Without correlative duty, solidarity becomes sentimental. It requires a sense of interdependence, because "when interdependence is separated from its ethical requirements, it has disastrous consequences for the weakest."[87]

IV Conclusion

Social justice underpinned by mercy, particularly toward the poor and marginalized, is a legitimate and appropriate moral response to the various forms of inequality that contemporary vulnerable migrant workers experience. This option for poor and vulnerable migrant workers is a testimony to the fact that our desire to improve society and the lives of individuals is not born of some purely intellectual, social, or political position. Instead, it is born from a fundamental conviction of every human being's value, including, if not especially, those who are most

---

83 Michele R. Pistone and John J. Hoeffner, "'In All Things Love': Immigration, Policy-Making, and the Development of Preferential Options for the Poor," *Journal of Catholic Social Thought* 5, no. 1 (2008): 175–91, at 187.
84 Pistone and Hoeffner, "But the Laborers Are . . . Many?" 71.
85 Ibid., 72.
86 Pope John Paul II, "Solicitudo Rei Sociali," December 30, 1987, http://w2.vatican.va/content/john-paul-ii/en/encyclicals/documents/hf_jp-ii_enc_30121987_sollicitudo-rei-socialis.html.
87 David J. O'Brien and Thomas A. Shannon, eds., *Catholic Social Thought: The Documentary Heritage* (New York: Orbis, 1992), 17.

Labor, inequality, and globalization 311

vulnerable. CST commands *all* of us in our communities and larger societies to work toward structural change in "experiential solidarity with the poor." Only through this shared responsibility can we meet the challenge to love vulnerable migrants and other marginalized people to move them from the cross. This represents a call to reform legal systems and the myriad ways these reinforce inequality, exploitation, and exclusion. More specifically, this highlights the imperative for law not to function as a tool to exploit, or make possible the exploitation, of immigrants and their labor, as well as the need for it to serve to protect those who are vulnerable, regardless of their immigration status.

Suggested Reading

Holmes, Seth M., and Heidi Castañeda. "Representing the 'European Refugee Crisis' in Germany and Beyond: Deservingness and Difference, Life and Death." *American Ethnologist* 43, no. 1 (2016): 12–24.

Human Rights Watch, *"When We're Dead and Buried, Our Bones Will Keep Hurting"*: *Workers' Rights under Threat in U.S. Meat and Poultry Plants.* September 4, 2019. www.hrw.org/report/2019/09/04/when-were-dead-and-buried-our-bones-will-keep-hurting/workers-rights-under-threat.

Johnson, Kevin R., Raquel Aldana, Bill Ong Hing, Leticia M. Saucedo, and Enid Trucios-Haynes. *Understanding Immigration Law.* Durham: Carolina Academic Press, 2019.

Kerwin, Donald, and Jill Marie Gerschutz. *And You Welcomed Me: Migration and Catholic Social Teaching.* Lanham, MD: Lexington Books, 2009.

Nadasen, Premilla. "Rethinking Care: Arlie Hochschild and the Global Care Chain." *Women's Studies Quarterly* 45, no. 3/4 (2017): 124–28.

Pope John Paul II. *Dives in Misericordia.* November 30, 1980. http://w2.vatican.va/content/john-paul-ii/en/encyclicals/documents/hf_jp-ii_enc_30111980_dives-in-misericordia.html.

Sobrino, Jon. *The Principle of Mercy: Taking the Crucified People from the Cross.* New York: Orbis, 1994.

17 Empire, displacement, and the Central American refugee crisis

Bill Ong Hing and Raj Nadella

I Introduction

During the four years of the Trump administration, the number of refugees and asylum seekers admitted into the United States, especially from south of the border, was reduced drastically. As the former Republican congressman Reid Ribble wrote in the *Wall Street Journal*, while 85,000 refugees were admitted into the country in 2016, only about 8,600 had been admitted by the end of August 2020.[1] Specifically with regard to refugees from south of the border, Ribble reported that "[t]his administration has allowed the resettlement of only 14 Venezuelans and zero Nicaraguans."[2] It also adopted the immoral policy of separating families at the border in order to discourage people from seeking refuge in the United States. Further, the administration demonized refugees and used biblical texts to justify its policies and practices. The government's move to admit fewer refugees came precisely at a time of historic and unprecedented rise in the number of people seeking refuge worldwide (see Michele R. Pistone, Chapter 4). This policy of closing doors on people seeking refuge in the United States has been adopted to varying degrees regardless of administrations and is problematic on both moral and theological grounds.

Morally, the policy is objectionable because of the responsibility the United States bears for creating the conditions that led to the need for refuge. Since the nineteenth century, the United States has been responsible for perpetuating the factors that have fostered political turmoil and economic crisis and have forced many in Central America to flee their homelands and seek refuge in other countries. A key example of this phenomenon is the Western Hemisphere Institute for Security Cooperation (WHISC). Formerly known as the School of the Americas (SOA), WHISC is a military-training program for Central and South American soldiers housed at Fort Benning in Columbus, Georgia. Graduates of SOA and WHISC have repeatedly perpetrated government violence in Latin America,

---

1 Reid Ribble, "The U.S. Admits Too Few Refugees," *Wall Street Journal*, August 24, 2020, www.wsj.com/articles/the-u-s-admits-too-few-refugees-11598308897.
2 Ibid.

Empire, displacement, and refugee crisis   313

especially in the Central American countries of Guatemala, Nicaragua, and El Salvador, against political dissidents and in support of neocolonial and corporate interests seeking to remove people from land those interests coveted. Given the extensive role of the United States in fostering political turmoil and violence over the decades, it is especially disturbing that the United States turns its back on refugees seeking shelter.

Theologically, several biblical texts highlight the link between imperial violence and displacement of vulnerable populations. Many texts explicitly make displaced individuals and communities sympathetic characters in biblical stories in ways that make the motif of displacement central to Christian texts and to the identity of early Christians. Ironically, many politicians in the United States have lately been using the very same Bible to justify and promote policies against refugees and asylum seekers.

In light of these moral and theological realities, this chapter argues that the United States has an obligation to accept refugees from Central and South America because of its role in fostering the refugee crisis in Central America. Drawing insights from the story of the Gadarene demoniac in Luke 8, the chapter challenges problematic depictions of refugees and individuals displaced by the empire and argues that the United States has a lot to lose by demonizing them and much to gain by rehabilitating and integrating them into society.

II U.S. involvement in Central America[3]

In March 1980, news of the assassination of Archbishop Oscar Romero in El Salvador reached the front pages. After the assassination of a fellow Jesuit priest and friend, Romero had become an outspoken social activist who railed against poverty, social injustice, and torture.[4] In 1979, the Revolutionary Government Junta came to power in El Salvador through a wave of human rights abuses by paramilitary right-wing groups and the government; civil war ensued.[5] Romero criticized the United States for providing military and financial aid to the new government that was known for its human rights abuses.[6] Romero's assassination was ultimately attributed to orders from an extreme right-wing politician,

---

3 Some of the material in this section is adapted from Bill Ong Hing, "Mistreating Central American Refugees: Repeating History in Response to Humanitarian Challenges," *Hastings Race and Poverty Law Journal* 17, no. 2 (2020): 359–98.

4 Michael O'Sullivan, "Archbishop Oscar Romero, Martyr," *Spirituality* 21 (March–April 2015), 119–23, reprinted at www.jesuit.ie/news/greatness-of-oscar-romero/.

5 Center for Justice and Accountability [CJA], "El Salvador," https://cja.org/where-we-work/el-salvador/.

6 Patsy McGarry, "Oscar Romero: One-Time Conservative Who Became a Nation's Social Martyr," *The Irish Times*, October 10, 2018, www.irishtimes.com/news/social-affairs/reli gion-and-beliefs/oscar-romero-one-time-conservative-who-became-a-nation-s-social-martyr-1.3657423.

314 *Bill Ong Hing and Raj Nadella*

and the circumstances epitomized the dangers faced by anyone critical of the government.[7]

If Romero's assassination was not enough to focus attention on El Salvador among those of us in the United States who might care, on December 2, 1980, four Catholic churchwomen from the United States working as missionaries in El Salvador were raped and murdered.[8] Five members of the El Salvador National Guard were arrested and convicted for the crimes a few years later,[9] but 17 years passed before they admitted to acting under orders from above.[10] In fact, a U.S. congressional investigation revealed that the massacre was committed by the right-wing militia supported by the U.S. government.[11]

The high-profile tragedies of 1980 were signals of what was already happening in the region and warned of what was to come. Driven by the turbulence of civil war, thousands of migrants fled El Salvador, Guatemala, and Nicaragua in the 1980s. In El Salvador, between 1979 and 1985, an estimated 50,000 people were killed in political violence; most were murdered by government forces who publicly dumped mutilated corpses in an effort to intimidate the population.[12] One group of 70 victims, half of whom were children, had been tortured; others were burned alive. The Salvadoran government employed a fierce counterinsurgency campaign of "draining the sea," or depopulating civilian conflict zones and guerrilla-controlled strongholds.[13] The displacement was carried out by aerial bombing, strafing, mortaring, and military ground operations that terrorized the civilian population and deprived residents of basic foods. Families were forcibly relocated to areas far away, upon threat of death if they returned.

In Guatemala, 38,000 casualties were recorded between 1980 and 1985. By 1987, the U.S. State Department counted more than 300 deaths per month as a result of the war. Most of those deaths were attributed to the Guatemalan army's brutal counterinsurgency campaign, whose victims were primarily unarmed

---

7 CJA, "El Salvador."

8 Steve Dobransky, "Memorialization and Social Justice Transformation: A Case Study of the Four Missionaries Martyred in El Salvador in 1980 and How Their Mission Continues" paper presented at the 23rd Annual International Association of Conflict Management Conference, Boston, MA, June 24–27, 2010, https://papers.ssrn.com/sol3/papers.cfm?abstract_id=1612489.

9 Ibid., 16.

10 Larry Rohter, "4 Salvadorans Say They Killed U.S. Nuns on Orders of Military," *New York Times*, April 3, 1998, www.nytimes.com/1998/04/03/world/4-salvadorans-say-they-killed-us-nuns-on-orders-of-military.html.

11 CJA, "El Salvador."

12 Amnesty International, *Extrajudicial Executions in El Salvador: Report of an Amnesty International Mission to Examine Post-Mortem and Investigative Procedures in Political Killings 1–6 July 1983* (London: Amnesty International Publications, 1984), www.ai-el-salvador.de/files/ai_el_salvador/PDFs/29-14-1984-El-Salvador-Extrajudicial-Executions.pdf; Amnesty International, *Amnesty International Report 1985* (London: Amnesty International Publications, 1985), www.amnesty.org/download/Documents/200000/pol100021985eng.pdf.

13 Brian D'Haeseleer, *The Salvadoran Crucible: American Counterinsurgency in El Salvador, 1979–1992* (Lawrence: University of Kansas Press, 2015), 264, 356.

Empire, displacement, and refugee crisis 315

civilians in the countryside. Massive attacks on Indigenous villages, resulting in massacres of families and the destruction of homes, were common. According to Amnesty International, Guatemalan forces massacred more than 2,600 Indigenous residents and campesino farm workers in March 1982, when the counter-insurgency program was launched. In September 1984, about a thousand people were arrested in raids, tortured, and executed extrajudicially.[14] As a result, tens of thousands of Guatemalans also fled to the United States seeking refuge.

Given the bedlam in Guatemala and El Salvador, the number of migrants forced to flee the crossfire of civil war was staggering. By the mid-1980s, more than a half million displaced El Salvadorans were living in refugee camps within El Salvador. More than 300,000 fled to other Central American countries, while an estimated 500,000 to 800,000 Salvadorans fled to the United States.[15]

Three decades later, there is another exodus of migrants from Central America. In 2014, more than 60,000 unaccompanied minors arrived at the southern border, along with a similar number of women with children traveling as "family units" from the Northern Triangle of Central America (Honduras, Guatemala, and El Salvador). In 2019, the numbers were quite similar, although more migrants were beginning to flee Nicaragua as well.[16]

Discussion in the United States about the causes for the two great surges of refugees from Central America in the 1980s and today has been superficial. In the 1980s, the connection was made between civil wars and forced migration. Today, at best, we hear about gangs, cartels, and domestic violence as well as poverty. To truly understand the root causes of migration from the region, however, we need to dig deeper. When we do, we begin to see how U.S. policies aimed at extending the political, economic, and cultural control of the United States over areas beyond the nation's boundaries—American Empire (or imperialism)—have affected Central America and, in turn, set the stage for migrant flows.

Lost in the headlines on Central American refugees fleeing to the United States are both the historical context that sparked the exodus and the structural transformations through capitalist globalization that have brought the region to where it is today. Some three decades after the wars of revolution and counterinsurgency came to an end in Central America, the region is once again on the brink of implosion. While the mass revolutionary movements of the 1970s and 1980s did

14 Oficina de Derechos Humanos del Arzobispado [ODHAG], *Guatemala: Nunca Mas*, vol. 3, El entorno histórico (Guatemala City: ODHAG, 1998), 132.

15 Susan Bibler Coutin, "Cultural Logics of Belonging and Movement: Transnationalism, Naturalization, and US Immigration Politics," in *The Anthropology of the State: A Reader*, eds. Aradhana Sharma and Anil Gupta (Malden, MA: Blackwell Publishing, 2006), 310–36, at 313.

16 Dara Lind, "The 2014 Central American Migrant Crisis," *Vox*, October 10, 2014, www.vox.com/2014/10/10/18088638/child-migrant-crisis-unaccompanied-alien-children-rio-grande-valley-obama-immigration; Amelia Cheatham, "U.S. Detention of Child Migrants," *Council on Foreign Relations*, October 29, 2020, www.cfr.org/backgrounder/us-detention-child-migrants.

316 *Bill Ong Hing and Raj Nadella*

manage to dislodge entrenched military–civilian dictatorships and open up political systems to electoral competition, they were unable to achieve any substantial social justice or democratization of the socioeconomic order. Thus, the isthmus has been gripped by renewed mass struggle and state repression, the cracking of fragile political systems, unprecedented corruption, drug violence, and the displacement and forced migration of millions of workers and peasants. The backdrop to this second implosion of Central America, reflecting the spiraling crisis of global capitalism itself, is the exhaustion of the newest round of capitalist development, which has marched to the same drumbeat as the neoliberal globalization that spurred the upheavals of the 1980s.

To contextualize the current migrations from Central America, we outline below the historical roles that the United States or U.S. companies have played in Central America (El Salvador, Honduras, Guatemala, and Nicaragua) that disrupted the economies and political conditions there. We present this context in the form of chronological lists to convey the frequency and persistence of U.S. intervention.

A *El Salvador*[17]

1932 The United States sends naval support to quell a largely Indigenous peasant rebellion led by Farabundo Martí. Between 10,000 and 40,000 rebels are killed under the direction of military leader Maximiliano Hernández Martínez.

1944 Martínez is ousted by a peaceful student revolution, but his party is reinstalled through a coup and immediately recognized by the United States.

1960 The United States, fearing a leftist turn, opposes free elections by withholding recognition. Shortly thereafter, a right-wing counter-coup seizes power and elections are canceled.

1980s The MS-13 gang forms in Los Angeles and spreads to El Salvador (and then all of Central America) after gang members are deported from the United States to El Salvador.

---

17 Sources for this data are: Mark Tseng-Putterman, "A Century of U.S. Intervention Created the Immigration Crisis," *Medium*, June 20, 2018, https://medium.com/s/story/time line-us-intervention-central-america-a9bea9ebc148; Julian Borger, "Fleeing a Hell the US Helped Create: Why Central Americans Journey North," *Guardian*, December 19, 2018, www. theguardian.com/us-news/2018/dec/19/central-america-migrants-us-foreign-policy; Deirdre Shesgreen, "How US Foreign Policy in Central America May Have Fueled the Migrant Crisis," *USA Today*, December 25, 2018, www.usatoday.com/story/news/ world/2018/12/21/has-united-states-foreign-policy-central-america-fueled-migrant-crisis-donald-trump/2338489002/; Hing, "Mistreating Central American Refugees." For more on the United States' involvement in El Salvador during this period, see Aldo A. Lauria-Santiago and Jeffrey L. Gould, *To Rise in Darkness: Revolution, Repression, and Memory in El Salvador, 1920–1932* (Durham, NC: Duke University Press, 2008).

Empire, displacement, and refugee crisis 317

1980–92	The United States intervenes in the Salvadoran civil war pursuant to the Cold War containment policy, offering significant military assistance to the right-wing regime and training battalions. The United States essentially funds the entire war effort at a cost estimated to be $1 million to $2 million a day.
1981	The U.S.-trained Atlacatl Battalion massacres civilians at El Mozote, killing between 733 and 1,200 unarmed people.
1984	During the U.S.-funded civil war, only 3 percent of Salvadoran and Guatemalan asylum cases are approved. Meanwhile, the United States funnels $1.4 million to its favored parties in El Salvador's 1984 election.
2006	El Salvador enters the Dominican Republic-Central American Free Trade Agreement (known as CAFTA-DR) despite protests by thousands of unionists, farmers, and workers.
2014	The United States threatens to withhold almost $300 million dollars' worth of Millennium Challenge Corporation (MCC) development aid, unless El Salvador ends all preferences for locally sourced corn and bean seeds under its Family Agriculture Plan.
2015	Under the tariff reduction model of CAFTA-DR, all U.S. industrial and commercial goods begin entering El Salvador duty free, creating impossible conditions for domestic industry to compete. As of 2016, the country had a negative trade balance of $4.18 billion.

B Honduras[18]

1880	American-owned Rosario Mining Company gains economic and political control in Honduras and Nicaragua, along with control of the Interoceanic Railway Company. The firm becomes the largest mining company in Honduras, securing control of the wharf and railway on the Honduran Atlantic coast.
1911	American businessman Sam Zemurray founds the Cuyamel Fruit Company and encourages Honduras to create a railroad connecting the Honduran coast to Tegucigalpa, which ultimately fails and leads Honduras into substantial debt.
1912	Zemurray stages a coup, replacing Miguel Dávila (who supported land reform and restrictions on foreign investors) with Honduran dictator General Manuel Bonilla, who, despite the country's increasing debt, gives generous concessions to Cuyamel Fruit Company and Standard Fruit Company. Cuyamel then joins forces with United Fruit Company (now Chiquita Brands International)

18 Sources for this data are: "Dancing with Monsters: The U.S. Response to the 2009 Honduran Coup," *Harvard Political Review*, April 13, 2015, https://harvardpolitics.com/us-honduran-coup/; Tseng-Putterman, "A Century of U.S. Intervention."

318   *Bill Ong Hing and Raj Nadella*

to dominate all of Central America, along with control of the International Railways of Central America. Bonilla rewards his corporate U.S. backers with concessions that grant natural resources and tax incentives to American companies, including Vaccaro Bros. and Co. (now Dole Food Company) and United Fruit Company.

1914   Because of Bonilla's deal, U.S. banana interests gain ownership of 1 million acres of the nation's best land, which is protected through the frequent deployment of U.S. military forces.

1975   United Fruit Company pays $1.25 million to Honduran officials and is accused of bribing the government to reduce banana export taxes.

1980s   The United States sends thousands of troops to train right-wing Contra rebels in guerilla warfare. Meanwhile, trade liberalization policies open Honduras to global capital interests and disrupt traditional agriculture in the country.

1984   U.S. military aid to Contra rebels reaches $77.5 million.

2005   Honduras enters CAFTA-DR despite protests from unions and local farmers. Honduras rapidly transitions from net agricultural exporter to net importer, leading to job loss for small-scale farmers and increased migration away from rural areas.

2009   Left-leaning, democratically elected president Manuel Zelaya, who pursues progressive policies, such as raising the minimum wage and subsidizing public transportation, is exiled in a military coup led by a graduate of the WHISC. The United States refuses to join international calls for Zelaya's return. Following the coup, the civil conflict is militarized and more than 100 campesinos are murdered. Organized crime spreads through the country's institutions, and the murder rate soars. Within a year, Honduras is the most violent country in the world not actually at war.

2019   Honduran president Juan Orlando Hernández further militarizes the police force. In danger of losing his reelection bid, he unleashes a wave of violence against the opposition and extinguishes the challenge. The United States congratulates him on his victory.

C *Guatemala*[19]

~1901   The Boston Fruit Company comes to Guatemala and joins forces with banana and railroad entrepreneur Minor Cooper Keith to

---

19 Sources for this information are: William I. Robinson, "The Second Implosion of Central America," *NACLA*, January 28, 2019, https://nacla.org/news/2019/01/28/second-implosion-central-america; Borger, "Fleeing a Hell the US Helped Create"; Tseng-Putterman, "A Century of U.S. Intervention."

Empire, displacement, and refugee crisis 319

form the United Fruit Company, which obtains a monopoly over cultivation, exportation, and transport of bananas throughout Central America.

1920   President Manuel Estrada Cabrera, an ally to U.S. corporate interests who had granted several concessions to the United Fruit Company, is overthrown in a coup. The United States sends armed forces to ensure that the new president remains amenable to U.S. corporate interests.

1947   President Juan José Arévalo's self-proclaimed "worker's government" enacts labor codes that give Guatemalan workers the right to unionize and demand pay raises for the first time. The United Fruit Company, the largest employer and landowner in the country, lobbies the U.S. government for intervention.

1954   The CIA overthrows democratically elected President Jacobo Árbenz under the influence of United Fruit propagandist Edward Bernays in response to the Guatemalan government's steps toward agrarian reform. This ends an unprecedented ten years of democratic rule in the country (known as the "ten years of spring"). The United States replaces the deposed president with Carlos Castillo Armas, whose authoritarian government rolls back land reforms and cracks down on peasants' and workers' movements.

1965   The CIA sends counterinsurgency advisers to aid the authoritarian government in its repression of left-wing movements that are recruiting peasants. The State Department's counterinsurgency adviser describes this as the United States' "direct complicity" in Guatemalan war crimes, which he compares to the "methods of Heinrich Himmler's extermination squads."[20]

1971   Seven thousand civilian dissidents are "disappeared" under the U.S.-backed government of Carlos Arana, nicknamed "the butcher of Zacapa" for his brutality.

1981   The United States approves a two-billion-dollar covert CIA program in Guatemala on top of the shipment of $19.5 million worth of military helicopters and $3.2 million worth of military jeeps and trucks to the Guatemalan army for Operation Ceniza. The operation is a response to the growing Marxist guerilla movement. Entire villages are bombed and looted, and their residents executed, with high-grade military equipment received from the United States.

Mid-1980s   One hundred fifty thousand civilians are killed in the U.S.-funded war, while 250,000 refugees flee to Mexico. Military leaders and government officials are later tried for the genocide of the Mayan victims of military massacres.

20 Noam Chomsky, *The Essential Chomsky* (New York: The New Press, 2008), 215.

320 *Bill Ong Hing and Raj Nadella*

1982	A second U.S.-backed military coup installs Efraín Ríos Montt as president. Montt is convicted of genocide in 2013 for trying to exterminate the Indigenous Maya Ixil.
2006	Ten years after a U.N.-brokered peace deal and the resumption of democratic elections, Guatemala enters CAFTA-DR. Ninety-five percent of U.S. agricultural exports enter Guatemala duty free.

D *Nicaragua*[21]

~1912–24	U.S. marines occupy Nicaragua.
1930s	U.S. marines depart and hand over control to the Somoza family dictatorship, whose notoriously brutal, corrupt, and repressive rule continues with U.S. support for 40 years. The Somozas assassinate their commander of the National Guard with the tacit approval of the U.S. ambassador to Nicaragua.
Late 1970s	The Sandinistas oust the U.S.-backed Somoza dictatorship in a popular revolution. Daniel Ortega assumes the leadership of a new government that begins putting more resources into education and health care, helping to increase literacy and reduce child mortality.
Mid-1980s	The CIA organizes a terrorist war against the Sandinistas, backing counterrevolutionary forces (Contras) that try to overthrow the Ortega government. The Contras wage a campaign of terror throughout Nicaragua. The CIA creates a paramilitary force to stop military supplies from entering El Salvador, despite little evidence of this actually occurring. During the 1980s, the force mounts raids on Nicaragua, attacking schools and medical clinics, raping, kidnapping, torturing, committing massacres, and mining harbors. By the late 1980s, the paramilitary force grows to around 50,000.
1982	A state of emergency is declared because of U.S.-backed Contra attacks.
1986	Nicaragua asks the International Court of Justice (ICJ) to end U.S. efforts to destabilize the government. The court rules in Nicaragua's favor, ordering the United States to end its interventionist policy in Nicaragua and pay massive reparations. The United States ignores the court's ruling, not paying a cent and instead escalating the war.
1987	The United Nations General Assembly also calls on the United States to comply with the ICJ's judgment. The United States

---

21 This information is taken from: Fred Hiatt and Jennifer Omang, "CIA Helped to Mine Ports in Nicaragua," *Washington Post*, April 7, 1984, www.washingtonpost.com/archive/politics/1984/04/07/cia-helped-to-mine-ports-in-nicaragua/762f775f-6733-4dd4-b692-8f03c8a0aef8/; "Nicaragua Profile—Timeline," *BBC News*, May 31, 2018, www.bbc.com/news/world-latin-america-19909695; Borger, "Fleeing a Hell the US Helped Create"; Tseng-Putterman, "A Century of U.S. Intervention."

Empire, displacement, and refugee crisis 321

continues to ignore the ruling. The United Nations repeats its demand the following year.

1990 U.S. officials support Ortega's political opponents and help them gain political power in the 1990 election. U.S. officials continue working to keep their political allies in power while preventing Sandinistas from regaining political power.

1997 Nicaragua is crippled by the highest per capita debt in the world. If the United States were simply to honor the ICJ ruling, the debt would be paid off threefold.

2006 U.S. diplomats lead an effort to steer campaign funds to their political allies while discouraging voters from voting for Ortega. The United States does not succeed, and Ortega is elected. Ortega creates a number of popular social welfare programs, providing free education, free health care, and various home-improvement programs. The programs are effective, raising incomes and significantly reducing poverty.

2018 Nicaragua erupts in turmoil in April 2018 after the government announces a plan to cut social security benefits. Widespread protests cause the government to back down on reducing pensions, but demonstrators demand that Ortega step down. More than 300 people are killed. Ortega calls it a U.S.-supported coup attempt. By the beginning of 2019, a flood of migrants begins to leave the country.

E Across the region

While U.S. interventionism has had devastating consequences in each of the Northern Triangle countries, other neoliberal and neocolonial programs have impacted the region at large. The spread of transnational tourist complexes has turned Central America into a global playground. Local Indigenous, Afro-descendant, and mestizo communities have fought displacement, environmental degradation, and the commodification of local cultures by tourist megaprojects, such as the Ruta Maya throughout the region, Roatan in Honduras, San Juan del Sur in Nicaragua, Costa del Sol in El Salvador, and Guanacaste province in Costa Rica. Services, commerce, and finance have also become transnationalized. The arrival of the global supermarket has involved the invasion of transnational retail conglomerates such as Walmart and fast-food chains, which have displaced thousands of small traders, disrupted local economies, and propagated a global consumer culture and ideology.[22] Globalization also brought with it a major expansion of transnational agribusiness. In Honduras, local and transnational capitalist interests have snatched up vast tracts of rural farmland from peasant,

22 Robinson, "The Second Implosion of Central America."

322 Bill Ong Hing and Raj Nadella

Afro-descendant, and Indigenous communities and converted them into palm oil plantations. In Guatemala, too, palm oil planted by local suppliers of global agro-industrial giants ADM and Cargill is uprooting a growing number of peasant communities and driving them to migrate abroad.[23] In Nicaragua, peasants displaced by transnational agribusiness have pushed into and colonized what remained of the agricultural frontier, disrupting Indigenous land.

The interference of the United States in the political, economic, and military realms of several Central American countries remains the primary factor contributing to the increase in the number of refugees coming to the United States. Given the U.S. role in fostering the refugee crisis, its response to those seeking refuge within its borders needs to be examined on both political and moral grounds. In particular, it is worth considering how a Christian ethic informed by biblical hermeneutics would assess the responsibility of the United States toward Central American refugees.

III Theories of migration and Christian theological imperatives

Mark Amstutz highlights three different paradigms that have figured prominently in current international relations, especially as they pertain to questions about how to address the realities of migration and the refugee crisis. The three paradigms are realism, communitarianism, and cosmopolitanism. In the first paradigm—realism—each community or country acts as a sovereign entity and pursues its own interests with little regard for morality or law. In the second paradigm—communitarianism—states make decisions based on transnational interests and moral values that transcend national borders, even as they privilege their borders and work to advance the interests of their populace. In the third model—cosmopolitanism—concern for the well-being of displaced individuals and communities is the primary factor that guides the decisions of states, because there is no moral basis for privileging the existing population of a state over migrant populations.[24] Amstutz argues that the Christian worldview, which is premised on the belief that all people are created in God's image, shares three key beliefs with cosmopolitanism: (1) people's well-being is primary; (2) since people are entitled to dignity and equality, the international community is, or should act as, an inclusive moral society; and (3) given the moral nature of the international society, people have a right to migrate.[25] While critical of cosmopolitanism, Amstutz combines insights from communitarianism and cosmopolitanism to posit what he calls a global communitarian ethic as the ideal paradigm, which entails states being guided by moral values and treating refugees and immigrants

---

23 Borger, "Fleeing a Hell the US Helped Create."
24 Mark R. Amstutz, *Just Immigration: American Policy in Christian Perspective* (Grand Rapids, MI: Eerdmans, 2017), 80–81.
25 Ibid., 97.

Empire, displacement, and refugee crisis 323

with compassion, while also safeguarding the economic and political interests of their citizens.[26] Kristin E. Heyer, whose work informs Amstutz's, draws upon Christian understanding of humanistic kinship to challenge government policies and practices that harm immigrant families. She calls for a shift from exclusionary global dynamics that privilege borders to shared international responsibility that promotes family flourishing and solidarity across borders. In her view, given the lived experiences of migrants and Christian demands of justice, a Christian ethos of subversive hospitality should lead to and guide immigration reform that promotes human flourishing over national borders (see also Kristin E. Heyer, Chapter 13).[27] What Heyer and Amstutz share is the conviction that an ethic grounded in the Christian belief that all people are created in the image of God cannot accept the elevation of one nation's interest through the harm or abandonment of others.

Despite its long history of complicity in perpetuating the refugee crisis in Central America, the United States has increasingly turned its back on people who show up at its borders seeking political and economic security, as the discussion above has shown. It continues to employ, with alacrity, tactics such as putting children in cages and adults in detention centers in order to terrorize and discourage people from seeking refuge within its borders.[28] The Trump administration demonized refugees by depicting them as animals and subjecting them to inhumane treatment. Such policies and practices toward refugees are deeply problematic because, as Amstutz and Heyer point out, the United States has sought to advance its interests through policies that harm people in Central America and then abandon those who are seeking escape from that harm. As we discuss further below, Amstutz's and Heyer's call for Christian compassion to those who have been harmed is further supported by the New Testament's particular concern for those who must withdraw or flee from the violence of empire.

Before turning to the biblical text, however, it is also important to note that, in some instances, members of the Trump administration and others opposed to assisting Central American refugees have employed biblical texts to justify their immoral policies and practices as well as to demonize refugees.[29] While the government's policies remain oppressive, stereotypes about migrants as burdensome and dangerous in some segments of the society have contributed toward fear and

26 Ibid., 98–99.
27 Kristin E. Heyer, *Kinship Across Borders: A Christian Ethic of Immigration* (Washington, DC: Georgetown University Press, 2012), 5–6.
28 Global Detention Project, "United States," www.globaldetentionproject.org/countries/americas/united-states.
29 Julia Jacobs, "Sessions's Use of Bible Passage to Defend Immigration Policy Draws Fire," *New York Times*, June 15, 2018, www.nytimes.com/2018/06/15/us/sessions-bible-verse-romans.html. However, there is increased criticism among Christians, including among several evangelical groups, of Christian nationalism that employs religion to demonize immigrants. Andrew L. Whitehead and Samuel L. Perry, *Taking America Back for God: Christian Nationalism in the United States* (Oxford: Oxford University Press, 2020), 1–22.

324 *Bill Ong Hing and Raj Nadella*

demonization of migrants. Precisely for that reason, it is important to explore biblical texts that challenge such negative depictions of refugees and highlight their dignity as humans. In her book *Revelation in Aztlán: Scriptures, Utopias, and the Chicano Movement*, Jacqueline Hidalgo offers a powerful observation that since scriptures played a role in the displacement of people south of the border, the Chicano movement had to take back the notion of the sacred and the scriptures in order to remake the world better for the displaced.[30] The remainder of this chapter focuses on a different geographical location, but Hidalgo's insights about the role and power of scriptures in public conversations about displaced people is pertinent.

IV Imperial violence and displacement in biblical texts

Motifs of forced migration and displacement resulting from imperial violence occur in both the Hebrew Bible and the New Testament. Several books in the Hebrew Bible are set in the context of foreign occupation and forced migration of Jewish communities that would later come to be described as diasporic. In particular, the book of Jeremiah is set against the backdrop of the Babylonian king Nebuchadnezzar destroying the southern kingdom of Judah, specifically Jerusalem, and taking with him a great number of people as captives to Babylon. Many of the New Testament books were written by diasporic Jews and reflect motifs of diaspora and displacement. Along similar lines, Jean-Pierre Ruiz's book *Readings from the Edges: The Bible and People on the Move* powerfully highlights the ways the Bible features Israel's story as the story of people on the move, as displaced people, and expresses a preferential option for displaced communities.[31] In many of these stories, the displacement was a direct result of imperial violence from successive empires.

In this section, we explore strands of internal and external displacements in the New Testament that result from imperial violence in colonized or targeted countries. We begin by looking at the theme of withdrawal from imperial violence in the Gospel of Matthew and the particular resonances between the story of John the Baptist and Archbishop Oscar Romero. We then turn to the story of the Gadarene demoniac as it appears across the synoptic Gospels to examine the danger of language that demonizes migrants and refugees.

A Practices of withdrawal in Matthew's Gospel

Matthew's Gospel frequently highlights the interconnectedness between imperial violence and displacement. It consistently employs the Greek term *anechowrey-sen* to refer to individuals and communities escaping from situations of violence.

---

30 Jacqueline M. Hidalgo, *Revelation in Aztlán: Scriptures, Utopias, and the Chicano Movement* (New York: Palgrave Macmillan, 2016).
31 Jean-Pierre Ruiz, *Readings from the Edges: The Bible and People on the Move* (Maryknoll: Orbis Books, 2011).

Empire, displacement, and refugee crisis 325

Anechowreysen is often translated as "to withdraw" and is used to describe people departing a place because of various factors, but it often carries the connotation of fleeing for one's life and being displaced. Matthew employs the verb ten times, mostly to describe people taking refuge from danger. Deidre Good has noted that the same verb is used in the Septuagint version of Exodus 2:15 where "in response to Pharaoh's hostile intentions, Moses 'withdrew from Pharaoh and dwelt in the land of Midian.'"[32] Good also notes that the same verb is employed on numerous occasions in 1 and 2 Maccabees to indicate people withdrawing from danger and violent conflicts.[33]

At the outset, Matthew 2 narrates the story of how Herod the Great learned about the birth of a child who is to become the new king of the Jews, a potential threat to his power; Herod seeks information from the magi that he can use to eliminate the threat. The magi, having been warned by the angel, withdraw to their homeland by a different way. Matthew's use of the Greek word *anachowrew*, which has the connotation of fleeing, implies that they perceived a threat not to just to the newborn but also to their lives. Furthermore, by suggesting that Herod, having failed to locate the newborn king, ordered the murder of all infants under two years of age in Bethlehem and its surrounding areas (Matthew 2:16–18), Matthew foregrounds the intensity of imperial violence. Especially revealing is the quote from Jeremiah recorded in this text: "A voice is heard in Ramah, weeping and great mourning, Rachel weeping for her children and refusing to be comforted, because they are no more" (Matthew 2:18, quoting Jeremiah 31:15) Meanwhile, having been warned by the angel, Joseph withdraws with Mary and Jesus to Egypt to escape the violence that Herod unleashes against all infants in the land. As Warren Carter has observed, "the verb withdrew [*anechowreysen*] appears for the third time (2:12, 13) to denote a response to hostility."[34]

This bloody story reveals the destructive actions of a ruthless king who resorts to mass murder because of deep insecurities and irrational fears. Herod the Great, working on behalf of the Roman Empire, undertook massive expansion and rebuilding projects that displaced vast numbers of people. He achieved such expansion by exploiting people at the margins through large-scale violence and threats of violence. But he was also an insecure ruler who was notorious for eliminating members of his own family, whom he perceived as threats to his power. The Jewish historian Josephus describes the extremely violent tactics Herod employed to suppress political dissidence and potential challenges to his power.[35] The story in Matthew about Jesus and his family fleeing to Egypt because

---

32 Deidre Good, "The Verb ΑΝΑΧΩΡΕΩ in Matthew's Gospel," *Novum Testamentum* 32, no. 1 (1990): 1–12, 6.
33 Ibid., 6.
34 Warren Carter, *Matthew and the Margins: A Socio-Political and Religious Reading* (Maryknoll, NY: Orbis Books, 2001), 84.
35 Flavius Josephus, *Jewish Antiquities*, trans. Ralph Marcus and Allen Wikgren, Loeb Classical Library 410 (Cambridge, MA: Harvard University Press, 1963), volume VII, book 16, at 150–57.

326 *Bill Ong Hing and Raj Nadella*

of Herod's violence squarely fits within that pattern of displacement caused by imperial violence.

The Greek word *anehoreysen*, which Matthew employs to characterize the Holy Family's escape, has the connotation of taking refuge from danger and is used interchangeably with *feugw*, which is semantically connected to the English word for refugees. In the context of Matthew, the term *anechoreysen* refers primarily, although by no means exclusively, to people moving to a different place on account of fear. It depicts the incarnate God as a displaced person, the victim of imperial violence. On a different level, the story also calls attention to the brutal tactics that ancient rulers, as well as modern governments, employ to eliminate perceived or actual threats to their power and authority. Matthew builds upon familiar Exodus stories about Pharaoh seeking to harm infants in the Israelite community during the time of Moses, and Matthew thus depicts Jesus as the new Moses, who survives imperial violence as part of the divine plan. Matthew describes the flight to Egypt as a fulfillment of the prophecy found in Hosea 11:1: "When Israel was a child, I loved him, and out of Egypt I called my son" (NIV).

Later in Matthew, Jesus's family returns to Judea after the death of Herod the Great but flees again—this time to Galilee—when they learn that Archelaus, one of Herod's sons, is ruling over Judea (2:22). When Herod's kingdom was divided into three parts following his death, Archelaus, one of his sons, became ruler of Judea and Samaria. Like his father, Archelaus quickly acquired a notorious reputation as a ruthless ruler who employed excessive violence to maintain his rule and advance his economic and political interests. As Good has observed, "Herod's policy of hostility toward Jesus is continued by his son Archelaus in the face of which Joseph, warned in a dream, intentionally withdraws into the city of Nazareth."[36] Matthew again employs the word *anechoreysen* to characterize the departure of Jesus's family as one of withdrawing and fleeing, thus suggesting that Jesus has again become a victim of the threat of imperial violence.

B *John the Baptist and Oscar Romero: prophets and victims of imperial violence*

Matthew 4 again locates Jesus in Judea, where he learns of John's imprisonment and withdraws to Galilee, again apparently fearing for his life. Jesus would have known that John's imprisonment was a precursor to something more ominous. Herod Antipas became the tetrarch in Galilee after the death of Herod the Great and continued his father's practices of economic exploitation and use of excessive violence to suppress opposition to his policies. Matthew 14 describes the story of John the Baptist being beheaded by Herod Antipas. Imperial violence and resultant displacement seem to have been everyday realities in first-century Palestine, rendering Galilee no more safe for Jesus than Judea. While the Gospel accounts tell us that Herod Antipas had John murdered to honor a commitment

---

36 Good, "The Verb ΑΝΑΧΩΡΕΩ in Matthew's Gospel," 2.

Empire, displacement, and refugee crisis 327

to Herodias and her daughter, and because John was criticizing Herod's immoral life, extracanonical sources tell a slightly different story. In particular, the Jewish historian Flavius Josephus suggests that John had been challenging Herod Antipas's oppressive economic practices, which had dealt death to many at the margins of society. Josephus describes John as the leader of an increasingly popular anti-imperial movement that was a growing threat to Herod's grip on power. Josephus suggests that John was calling upon the people to practice righteousness and to repent, which had the connotation of turning their backs on existing socioeconomic structures. John's message increasingly resonated with the masses, and they were, according to Josephus, ready to do anything he asked of them.[37]

Herod was notorious for many things, but what would have adversely impacted ordinary people the most and inspired them to join a revolt were his massive building projects funded through excessive taxes.[38] As Josephus puts it, Herod was afraid that John's message might lead to a revolt, so he decided to have John killed sooner rather than later. As is the case today, the empire did everything in its capacity to eliminate people like John and intimidate potential threats to its ability to maintain power.

When Jesus learned of John's death, he and his disciples left the place and withdrew into the wilderness. Matthew again employs the Greek word *anechowreysen*, which connotes fleeing, but he adds that people followed Jesus and his disciples into the wilderness. In all these instances, people leave their homes because of imperial violence and the possibility of further violence. However, it was not just a matter of people fleeing as a result of imperial violence; rather, violence was often employed to force people to flee their homelands, which could then be appropriated by the occupying forces. Herod the Great and later Herod Antipas were especially known to employ a variety of tactics, such as violence and excessive taxation, to take possession of people's lands for use in building projects or as gifts to military commanders.[39]

The story of John's death at the hands of Herod Antipas parallels the story of Archbishop Oscar Romero, who was assassinated in 1980 for calling attention to economic injustice and political oppression in El Salvador. Similarly, the Roman Empire's support of oppressive rulers like Herod Antipas parallels the American support of oppressive regimes in Central America that carried out such assassinations. Furthermore, both the assassination of John the Baptist and that of Osar Romero participate in the ruthless terror of empire that is intended by those in power to create a culture of fear and discourage others from challenging the regime's hegemonic economic and political practices.

---

37 Flavius Josephus, *Jewish Antiquities*, vol. VII, book 18.5.2.
38 On a related note, Luke 3 makes explicit references to John's preaching about excessive taxation and extortion practices that had become common practice during that time.
39 Richard Horsley, *Covenant Economics: A Biblical Vision of Justice for All* (Louisville, KY: Westminster John Knox Press, 2009), 88–91.

328 *Bill Ong Hing and Raj Nadella*

C *The biblical critique of the demonization of displaced people*

The story of the Gadarene demoniac in the Gospels offers insights that suggest that demonizing refugees is not just immoral but also detrimental to the social and economic interests of host nations. It clarifies that the United States stands to gain by treating refugees as full-fledged individuals and integrating them into the social and economic fabric of the society (see Donald M. Kerwin and Safwat Marzouk, Chapter 15).

All three synoptic Gospels record the story of the Gerasene or Gadarene demoniac, whom Jesus liberates and integrates into the community (Mark 5:1–20; Matthew 8:28–34; Luke 8:26–39). While Mark refers to him as Gerasene, Matthew and Luke call him a Gadarene. Mark and Luke speak of just one demoniac, while Matthew has two in his version of the story. These differences in details do not alter the basic story or its interpretation in significant ways, but there is at least one other difference that has interpretive implications. Jesus asks the demoniac for his name in both Mark and Luke, but not in Matthew. "Legion," the name of the demoniac, was also a term used to refer to a Roman military contingent of about 5,000 soldiers. Richard Horsley, among other New Testament scholars, argues that the demoniac in this story very likely signifies the Roman imperial occupation of the region of Gerasene and the resultant displacement of local people. He observes that "demonic possession, for example, of the manically violent man among the Gerasenes, can be understood as a combination of the effect of Roman imperial violence, a displaced protest against it, and a self-protection against a suicidal counterattack against the Romans."[40] In this reading, this unnamed, naked, chained person who lives among the dead is driven to such extremes by the legion, the imperial forces, which calls attention to the physical and psychological displacement, as well as the various stratagems, colonized people employ to deal with their displacement.

This story is partly about the oppressive effects of empire on displaced individuals and communities. But the story, specifically Luke's version, also calls attention to the ways the society demonized him, subjected him to inhumane treatment, and robbed him of dignity and respect. It highlights the society's mistreatment and perceptions of this individual as a threat to its safety. Although there is little evidence in Gospel accounts that the demoniac had hurt or posed a threat to anyone, the townspeople put him in chains, placed him outside the city among the dead, and kept him under constant guard. In essence, they treated him as a threat and danger to their security, despite the fact that he had harmed no one but himself. They had labeled him a "demon-possessed" person and treated him as an outcast who needed to be kept outside their community. The townspeople undermined his ability as well as his right to participate in society and become a productive member. Within this context, Jesus's intervention in the story is an

---

40 Richard Horsley, *Hearing the Whole Story: The Politics of Plot in Mark's Gospel* (Louisville, KY: Westminster John Knox Press, 2001), 145.

act of liberating the demoniac from his state of trauma and displacement and of bringing him back into the community.

Luke also calls attention to the townspeople's strange response and resistance to Jesus's act of rehabilitating the individual and restoring him to the community as a contributing member. The people of Gerasene ask Jesus to leave the town after he has cast out the legion and remade the demoniac a member of the society. It is possible that they resented the loss of their swine, which the legion was cast into, but it is unclear why they were uncomfortable seeing the healed man in his right mind and having him join the community. When the people see the "demon-possessed" person fully clothed, in his right mind, and at the feet of Jesus (back in their midst), they are terrified. They were much more comfortable keeping him outside the bounds of the city and chained, likely spending a lot to keep him imprisoned. Why object to his being restored to the community and becoming a contributing member of the society, even after the benefits of having him join the workforce have become obvious?

It appears that the people of the town had branded him a threat to the society, despite evidence to the contrary, and were invested in their unfounded fears about him. Acknowledging that he is not the danger he was perceived to be requires them to view him differently and reconfigure their own relationship with him. The text seems to suggest that they were more comfortable continuing with their perception of him as a threat to their society. From their perspective, their ability to be considered normal depended on treating him as less than normal.[41]

The story of the demoniac is relevant in our study of refugees and immigrants from Central America, who are often vilified, demonized, and treated as less than human. In recent years, many of them have been placed in detention centers, treated as dangerous people, and separated from their families. In some cases, the same inhumane treatment has been extended to children, some of whom were placed in cages. Making our neighbors "other" and depicting them as dangerous is consistent with colonial representations of communities in the Global South as violent and uncivilized. As Edward Said forcefully argued, these "representations usually do, for a purpose, according to a tendency, in a specific historical, intellectual, and even economic setting. In other words, representations have purposes, they are effective much of the time, they accomplish one or many tasks."[42] Employing such representations leads to denying refugees basic human rights. Such a treatment of refugees is immoral, given the international conventions protecting refugees (Pistone, Chapter 4), but also in light of the history of the United States as a nation of immigrants fleeing religious and political persecution. Turning our backs on these refugees is problematic and immoral also because the United States has been deeply complicit in perpetuating the political and

---

41 This reading of the Gadarene demoniac story builds upon Raj Nadella's, "Fear and Wisdom in the Immigration Debate," *HuffPost*, June 19, 2013, www.huffpost.com/entry/gospel-of-luke-immigration_b_3462128.
42 Edward Said, *Orientalism* (New York: Vintage Book, 1979), 273.

economic crises in their homelands that had engendered the refugee flight in the first place. In reminding us of our responsibilities to refugees, Matthew Gibney suggests that humanitarianism rests on the "duty incumbent upon each and every individual to assist those in great distress or suffering when the costs of doing so are low."[43]

Finally, as insights from these biblical texts have shown, on economic and social grounds, too, it is in the best interests of the United States to allow refugees to join the society as full-fledged contributing members. It has been proven repeatedly that immigrants and refugees are the backbone of several essential sectors in the United States.[44] Many economists and think tanks on both the left and the right have provided ample data to establish the economic benefits of including refugees and undocumented migrants in the workforce.[45] Following the example of Jesus from the story of the Gadarene demoniac means rejecting the violence of empire and the harm it visits on persons, but embracing and bringing those who have been marked by that violence into the folds of society. When we combine this insight with the emphasis placed on the moral good of withdrawing from violence of empire in the Gospel of Matthew, it is clear that the United States (and other neoimperial powers) needs a new approach to both our neighbors in Central America and our Central American neighbors arriving at the southern border.

V Conclusion

An ethic of fear demonizes migrants, denies their humanity, and excludes them from participation in society. An ethic of fear also robs migrants as well as host communities of an opportunity to interact as humans and benefit—socially, intellectually, and economically—from mutual presence. On the other hand, an ethic of hospitality grounded in the Christian belief that all people are created in God's image actively acknowledges the humanity of migrants and invites them to participate fully in the community in ways that enhance everyone's well-being. Such a new approach to refugees and "illegal" immigrants can become a reality not just, or even primarily, through political intervention and new immigration policies but through society's ability and willingness to reorient itself to displaced individuals and communities. This can happen only when political parties and communities in host nations—the United States in this instance—get past their stereotypes and unfounded fears about refugees and treat them as full, contributing members

---

43 Matthew J. Gibney, "Liberal Democratic States and Responsibilities to Refugees," *American Political Science Review* 93, no. 1 (1999): 169–81.

44 See, for example, Donald M. Kerwin, et al., *US Foreign-Born Essential Workers by Status and State, and the Global Pandemic* (New York: Center for Migration Studies, 2020), https://cmsny.org/publications/us-essential-workers.

45 International Catholic Migration Commission, "Integrating Migrants and Refugees, a Two-Way Road That Benefits Everyone," December 4, 2017, www.icmc.net/2017/12/04/integrating-migrants-and-refugees-a-two-way-road-that-benefits-everyone/.

of communities. A transformation of this nature requires a new way of relating to refugees that would be guided by wisdom, empathy, and vision.

Suggested Reading

Amstutz, Mark R. *Just Immigration: American Policy in Christian Perspective*. Grand Rapids, MI: Eerdmans, 2017.

Hardt, Michael, and Antonio Negri. *Empire*. Cambridge, MA: Harvard University Press, 2000.

Heyer, Kristin E. *Kinship across Borders: A Christian Ethic of Immigration*. Washington, DC: Georgetown University Press, 2012.

Hidalgo, Jacqueline M. *Revelation in Aztlán: Scriptures, Utopias, and the Chicano Movement*. New York: Palgrave Macmillan, 2016.

International Catholic Migration Commission. "Integrating Migrants and Refugees, a Two-Way Road That Benefits Everyone." December 4, 2017. www.icmc.net/2017/12/04/integrating-migrants-and-refugees-a-two-way-road-that-benefits-everyone/.

Robinson, William I. "The Second Implosion of Central America." *NACLA*, January 28, 2019. https://nacla.org/news/2019/01/28/second-implosion-central-america.

18 Empathy, legitimacy, faith, and the dangerously uncertain future of migration

Kristin E. Heyer and Daniel Kanstroom

I Introduction

As this volume amply demonstrates, the legal structures and discourses that govern migration involve apparent tectonic interactions between (indeed, *among*) deep, underlying principles. Liberty may seem to conflict with security, equality may vie with community self-definition, secularity confronts religion, and so on. One of the most basic apparent conflicts is that between what one might generically denominate—with some oversimplification—the *desiderata* of empathy versus legal legitimacy. One would hope that government actors do not *want* to be cruel (or, at a minimum, to be perceived as cruel).[1] But it is also true that no judge or political leader wants to endorse emotional subjectivity or, as some view it, lawlessness or anarchy. A recent, well-known version of this tension appeared during the nomination process for then-judge Sonia Sotomayor to the U.S. Supreme Court. Responding to what amounted to an accusation that empathy was not a legitimate stance for judges to take, Judge Sotomayor conceded, "Judges can't rely on what's in their heart. . . . It's not the heart that compels conclusions in cases, it's the law."[2]

Whatever the merits of this position may be in other legal arenas, this book illustrates how untenable it often is when it comes to migration. Harsh immigration enforcement and frequent life-or-death consequences compel juries, judges, and, indeed, all of us to confront this dilemma. One is reminded of Ronald Dworkin's observation that the best defense of political legitimacy may be found in the "fertile terrain of fraternity, community, and their attendant obligations."[3]

---

1 Certain aspects of U.S. and global migration control that seek to prevent migration by making it unbearable—for example, family separation, refusing to interdict sinking ships, confinement in inhumane detention centers, etc.—are surely cruel by any reasonable definition.
2 Judge Sotomayor was specifically distancing herself from a comment that then-Senator Obama had made in 2005 during the nomination process for John Roberts. Obama had said that in a certain percentage of judicial decisions, "the critical ingredient is supplied by what is in the judge's heart." Ari Shapiro, "Sotomayor Differs with Obama on 'Empathy' Issue," *NPR*, July 14, 2009, www.npr.org/templates/story/story.php?storyId=106569335.
3 Ronald Dworkin, *Law's Empire* (Cambridge, MA: Belknap Press, 1986), 206.

Empathy, legitimacy, faith   333

This is all the more true in the era of COVID-19, which may render much of our thinking about migration and human rights anachronistic.

II Three brief case studies of the tensions between empathy and legitimacy

Let us briefly consider, as a framework for this final chapter, three distinct situations in which we have seen this tension on vivid display.[4]

The first, and most recent, is the U.S. Supreme Court decision in the so-called DACA case.[5] Here we saw implicitly normative arguments cloaked in the garb of legal technicality. The DACA program, from its inception, stood at uneasy intersections between presidential and legislative power. It was always considered, even by its strongest proponents, to be an inferior solution to the comprehensive legislative immigration reform that had failed during the tenure of George W. Bush and, again, during the administration of Barack Obama. Indeed, even as he enacted DACA, President Obama reiterated, "I have said time and time and time again to Congress that, send me the DREAM Act, put it on my desk, and I will sign it right away."[6] Perhaps more than any other presidential order in history, DACA also reflected the powerful dynamic between empathy and legitimacy. As Obama put it:

> These are young people who study in our schools, they play in our neighbor-hoods, they're friends with our kids, they pledge allegiance to our flag. They are Americans in their heart, in their minds, in every single way but one: on paper. They were brought to this country by their parents—sometimes even as infants—and often have no idea that they're undocumented until they apply for a job or a driver's license, or a college scholarship.[7]

The ham-handed[8] repeal of DACA that had been demanded by Donald Trump and engineered by Attorney General Jeff Sessions was challenged immediately and

---

4 For a more technical exploration of these cases, see Daniel Kanstroom, "'Either I Close My Eyes or I Don't': The Evolution of Rights in Encounters Between Sovereign Power and the 'Rightless'," in *Beyond Borders: The Human Rights of Non-Citizens at Home and Abroad*, eds. Molly Land and Kathryn Libal (forthcoming from Cambridge University Press).

5 *Department of Homeland Security, et al., v. Regents of the University of California, et al.*, 140 S. Ct. 1891 (2020). DACA stands for Deferred Action for Childhood Arrivals, a program deferring deportation for certain immigrants who came to the United States as children.

6 Remarks by the President on Immigration, June 15, 2012, https://obamawhitehouse. archives.gov/the-press-office/2012/06/15/remarks-president-immigration.

7 Ibid.

8 Elaine C. Duke, then President Trump's acting Secretary of Homeland Security, has said she faced "an ambush" by Trump and Sessions, after which she drafted a perhaps intentionally insufficient justification for ending DACA. According to the *New York Times*, she "did not include policy reasons in the memo because she did not agree with the ideas being pushed by Mr. Miller and Mr. Sessions: that DACA amounted to an undeserved amnesty and that it

334   *Kristin E. Heyer and Daniel Kanstroom*

ultimately ended up at the Supreme Court. To the surprise of many observers, the court majority upheld the program. As one reads the majority opinion, written by Justice John Roberts, the tensions between empathy and legitimacy loom large. On one hand, the opinion is highly technocratic: "We address only whether the agency complied with the procedural requirement that it provide a reasoned explanation for its action."[9] But when one considers what, exactly, it was that the agency improperly had failed to consider, the normative implications become clear: "Here the agency failed to consider . . . whether to retain forbearance and *what if anything to do about the hardship to DACA recipients.* That dual failure raises doubts about whether the agency appreciated the scope of its discretion or exercised that discretion in a reasonable manner."[10] This, said the court, was "arbitrary and capricious" agency action. Trump, as expected, was unrepentant. As he fumed, "These horrible & politically charged decisions coming out of the Supreme Court are shotgun blasts into the face of people that are proud to call themselves Republicans or Conservatives."[11] Still, any future actions he might take could not avoid grappling with the human consequences of his actions. In other words, legitimacy must incorporate at least a nod to empathy.

Our second example of the interaction between empathy and legitimacy took place in France: the trial of Cédric Herrou, a French olive farmer, who was criminally tried in 2017 for having assisted desperate, unauthorized migrants in France, near the Italian border. Herrou has been an inspirational figure to many; indeed, his work has been analogized to that of the Underground Railroad.[12] However, the reactions to him have reflected the deep tensions discussed above. A French member of Parliament worried, "Who can say with certainty that of the hundreds of migrants that Mr. Herrou has proudly brought across the border, there isn't hidden among them, a future terrorist?"

When asked by a judge, "Why do you do all this?" Herrou responded with a completely different perspective. He offered pure human rights and humanitarian principles: "There are people dying on the side of the road. It's not right. There are children who are not safe." Moreover, the law itself and legal legitimacy were also on trial in Herrou's case. The prosecutor argued that Herrou had

---

would encourage new waves of illegal immigration." See "Leading Homeland Security Under a President Who Embraces 'Hate-Filled' Talk," *New York Times*, July 10, 2020, accessed July 28, 2020, www.nytimes.com/2020/07/10/us/politics/elaine-duke-homeland-security-trump.html?searchResultPosition=1.

9 *Department of Homeland Security*, 140 S. Ct. at 1916.

10 Ibid. (emphasis added).

11 John Wagner, "Trump Lashes Out at Supreme Court," *Washington Post*, June 18, 2020, www.washingtonpost.com/politics/trump-lashes-out-at-supreme-court-calls-decisions-shotgun-blasts-into-the-face-of-conservatives/2020/06/18/e0bd2988-b176–11ea-8758-bfd1d045525a_story.html.

12 Adam Nossiter, "An Underground Railroad in France, Moving African Migrants," *New York Times*, October 4, 2016, www.nytimes.com/2016/10/05/world/europe/france-italy-migrants-smuggling.html. This and subsequent quotations on the Herrou case are taken from Nossiter's article, unless otherwise indicated.

demonstrated a "manifest intention to violate the law. . . . One can criticize it, but it's got to be applied."[13] Though he even admitted that Herrou's cause was one he "totally respects," he concluded, almost apologetically, "I am the prosecutor. I must defend the law."

Herrou was ultimately convicted and given a suspended prison sentence of four months for facilitating the entry and/or circulation of illegal immigrants in France. He appealed, arguing that the criminal statute conflicted with the French constitutional principle of *fraternité*. In July 2018, the Conseil constitutionnel held that fraternity *is*, in fact, a principle endowed with constitutional value in France.[14] The Conseil then concluded that the freedom to help another for humanitarian reasons—*regardless of whether the assisted person is residing legally or illegally within the French territory*—follows from the principle of fraternity. There were limits, to be sure: such freedom does not guarantee a general and absolute right of entry to—or even residence on—French national territory. Indeed, the Conseil said that the legislature has the responsibility to "strike a balance" between freedom and fraternity and a different constitutional objective: that of safeguarding "public order."[15] Simply put, the Conseil invoked liberty and fraternity to limit the state's sovereign authority to control its external borders. Herrou would be exempt from prosecution at least for "humanitarian acts that aimed to facilitate the circulation of illegal immigrants when the latter is ancillary to their residence."[16] In other words, assistance to those with unlawful presence that *has already been achieved* is different for constitutional purposes than is assistance that enables entry. Obviously, this is a fine line, but the invocation of fraternity, even in this limited sense, was profoundly significant. The substantive reliance on the fraternity principle—as a constitutional provision with real bite—is a milestone.[17] Moreover, the assertion by the Conseil of such broad interpretive and constitutional review power is all the more important, in that it occurred in the realms of immigration and asylum, where deference to the government is especially strong.

The third case is that of Scott Warren and the humanitarian group No More Deaths, a case that was explored earlier in this volume by Rose Cuison Villazor and Ulrich Schmiedel (Chapter 14). Here, unlike in the Herrou case, the defendant did not benefit from the invocation of a transcendent legal principle by a higher court. Rather, a jury refused to convict. As one commentator put it, "The government failed in its attempt to criminalize basic human kindness."[18]

13 Ibid.
14 Décision n° 2018–717/718 QPC du 6 juillet 2018, Par. 7.
15 Ibid., Par. 13.
16 Ibid.
17 See François-Xavier Millet and Jan-Herman Reestman, "Fraternité," *European Constitutional Law Review* 15, no. 2 (2019): 183–93, at 190.
18 Jasmine Aguilera, "Humanitarian Scott Warren Found Not Guilty After Retrial for Helping Migrants at Mexican Border," *Time*, November 21, 2019, https://time.com/5732485/scott-warren-trial-not-guilty/.

336 *Kristin E. Heyer and Daniel Kanstroom*

Scott Warren was a geographer and a volunteer with No More Deaths (also known as No Más Muertes), an aid group that leaves water and food for migrants who seek to cross the deadly Sonoran Desert, channeled there by years of harsh exclusion policies and border walls. No More Deaths dropped water and provided medical aid. Its members also documented abuses on the border as "the most aggressive organization to challenge Border Patrol violations of human rights."[19] A local "Samaritan" activist, stunned that some 60 bodies had been found in one small town, observed, "I can't imagine that happening in any town in our country and not having people be up in arms. . . . You have to do something. You don't want to be a cemetery. These are human lives."[20]

Warren was arrested by Border Patrol agents on January 17, 2018. No More Deaths had just published a report that implicated the Border Patrol in the destruction of thousands of gallons of water left for migrants in the desert.[21] It seemed that the Border Patrol was "punching back."[22] The agents caught Warren with two Central American migrants. Warren told the agents that he had given the migrants shelter, food, and first aid. All of this seemed to the agents to clearly violate U.S. law, which bars "harboring" and "transporting" unauthorized migrants. Charged with two counts of harboring undocumented immigrants and one count of conspiracy to harbor and transport, Warren faced some 20 years in prison.

At Warren's first trial, in June 2019, a jury failed to reach a verdict. The government quickly sought a retrial. After a six-day retrial, the jury found Warren not guilty after about two hours of deliberation. Warren's lawyers did not mount an explicit "necessity defense" (that is, arguing that Warren should not be criminally punished for avoiding a greater harm to others). Nor did they argue expressly for jury nullification to override the letter of the law in the pursuit of abstract ideals of higher justice. They simply argued that the government had not proven criminal intent under these circumstances. The government had evidence of Warren pointing the migrants northward. Prosecutors argued that this meant he was guiding the migrants away from the border and deeper into the United States. But Warren testified that he was merely showing them local mountains.[23] He said that the only available highway ran between them. If they needed rescue, that's where they should go.

How should a jury decide such questions? How should they calibrate empathy and legal legitimacy? Warren testified that his work was similar to that of the International Red Cross: neutral provision of aid amid a humanitarian crisis. Such work, he said, *is legal*. The jury accepted this, apparently completely. One juror reportedly said, "He seemed like a humanitarian that was just trying to help. He

---

19 Ryan Devereaux, "Bodies in the Borderland," *The Intercept*, May 4, 2019, https://theintercept.com/2019/05/04/no-more-deaths-scott-warren-migrants-border-arizona/.
20 Ibid.
21 Ibid.
22 Ibid.
23 Ibid.

Empathy, legitimacy, faith   337

seemed very kind and not like he was trying to harbor somebody or do anything illegal at all."[24]

In the end, Warren's jury—through their interpretation of his intent and their implicit understanding of the morally legitimate bounds of criminal law—effectively navigated the border between strict adherence to a narrow idea of law and deep values. It appears that in the minds and hearts of the jurors, the question was not really whether a law had technically been broken. It was whether Warren should be branded a criminal and punished. The answer was a resounding No! Indeed, one juror made this point quite clearly: "I think we all agreed," she said, "what he and these people do is fantastic."[25] However, such resolutions of conflict between the demands of law and those of empathy are generally transitory and almost always contested. Thus, the prosecutor, with apparent disdain for the jury's approach, referenced "a misguided sense of social justice or belief in open borders or whatever."[26]

These three examples demonstrate how the pervasive, inevitable tension between strict adherence to legal rules and the demands of conscience, empathy, and faith may appear in different ways at various phases of legal process. Jury actions are, of course, the most visceral and direct. But sophisticated, technical interpretive approaches, such as that undertaken by the Supreme Court in the DACA case, often reveal similar impulses. Invocations of constitutional principle, such as that of the Conseil constitutionnel, are, of course, the most durable examples, as they reveal new crystallizations of rights themselves.

Dissonance and interplay among the demands of legal legitimacy, empathy, and faith have appeared in many of the chapters within this book. Let us now briefly recapitulate how this volume's chapters have evoked and explored these tensions. Its interdisciplinary reflections have challenged hard-edged categories of legal citizenship and ostensible rationales for enforcement mechanisms that fail to disclose driving ideologies, the operations of power, and meaningful forms of membership exercised "from below." In so doing, the approach unmasks dominant rhetoric and interests and helps pave a path forward for the law of migration in these extremely uncertain and dangerous times. Its approach may indicate ways to bridge the gaps that persist between the demands of public order and commitments to human rights, especially to such concepts as human dignity, equality, fraternity, solidarity, fair process, and proportionality.

As this volume documents, resurgent nativist populism across the globe continues to stoke citizens' fears of outsiders and permeable borders while advancing nationalist, xenophobic leaders' claims about their power to restore law and order. Amid formidable challenges facing global and local populations, such leaders have convinced their populations that immigration poses a grave threat to their communities, more than inequality, climate change, or compromised

24 Ibid.
25 Ibid.
26 Ibid.

338   *Kristin E. Heyer and Daniel Kanstroom*

governance.[27] Scapegoating narratives have given cover to extensive surveillance measures and the implementation of physical barriers, restrictive policies, and expedited removal practices to deter asylum claims (see Michele R. Pistone, Chapter 4).

The intersecting legal and theological perspectives presented in this volume make clear the stakes of irregular migrants' "impossible" subjectivity, as historian Mae Ngai has termed it, given that they are legal and political subjects without rights, "persons who cannot be," and problems that cannot be solved, produced by immigration restrictions.[28] Although the basic human rights reflected in international rights regimes—and presupposed in the Judeo-Christian tradition—are universal in theory, in practice their exercise depends on legally sanctioned membership in a political community.[29] The Christian understandings of what it means to be human, traced in these chapters, radically critique the pervasive exploitation of migrants, whether through protracted family separation, precarious underemployment, or draconian detention policies. A moral anthropology that underscores humans' inherent dignity and sociality, independent of citizenship status, contests this widespread, multifaceted exploitation, and it illuminates the complex causes of migration and the corresponding responsibilities of receiving communities.

Standard models in migration ethics tend to focus primarily on tensions between persons' rights to freedom of movement and political communities' rights to self-determination. In contrast, this volume's chapters illuminate how these dominant approaches sometimes cannot provide meaningful protections for Ngai's "impossible subjects." For example, a global rights regime reflecting a liberal respect for the "generalized other" largely fails to generate substantive obligations of provision for migrants or to protect would-be migrants from systemic deprivation. Within more communitarian models, undocumented migrants are at best owed forbearance, lacking legal claim to the "good of citizenship and its attendant claim-rights."[30] Even in an increasingly globalized society, positive rights claims may remain bound to citizenship, so that the loss of home and political status becomes tantamount to "expulsion from humanity altogether."[31]

Bringing together legal and normative perspectives, this volume thus signals several avenues beyond standard approaches that struggle to resolve these tensions. Taken together, the chapters emphasize: (1) the need to contextualize

---

27 Suketu Mehta, *This Land Is Our Land: An Immigrant's Manifesto* (New York: Farrar, Straus and Giroux, 2019), 115.

28 Mae M. Ngai, *Impossible Subjects: Illegal Aliens and the Making of Modern America* (Princeton, NJ: Princeton University Press, 2004), 4–5.

29 William O'Neill, SJ, "Rights of Passage: Ethics of Forced Displacement," *The Journal of the Society of Christian Ethics* 27, no. 1 (2007): 113–36.

30 Ibid., 115–16. Claim rights entail substantive responsibilities on the part of other parties toward the right-holder beyond immunities from intrusion or coercion.

31 Ibid., 116, citing Hannah Arendt, "The Perplexities of the Rights of Man," in *The Origins of Totalitarianism*, ed. Hannah Arendt (New York: Harcourt, Brace & World, 1966), 297.

migrations and to move ethical and policy considerations beyond individuals as sites of enforcement; (2) the task of unmasking ideological drivers of policy and the role of power; and (3) the opportunity to recognize new understandings of citizenship "from below," that is, as marked by lived practices of membership and resistance. Religious resources can help counter false narratives and shape possibilities for change in light of these shifts, serving migrant and settled communities alike, and fostering hope amid the challenging signs of the times.

III Historical reckoning, exclusionary idols, and structural justice

Integrating perspectives from law, policy, religion, philosophy, and practice helps illuminate how the "production and experience of 'illegality'" are shaped not only by "state-based rules and regulations" but also by broader international processes and local engagement. Illegality is also "stratified by gender, class and race."[32] The chapters in this volume indicate how patterns that instill fear and threaten human rights reflect tendencies to approach migration primarily as a matter of crisis management. They underscore how understanding immigration in terms of the discrete actions of migrants, in which individuals remain the primary site for enforcement and responsibility, neglects transnational political and economic forces as well as histories of relationships between sending and receiving countries (see Kristin E. Heyer, Chapter 13).

In the summer of 2020, symbols of colonial empire were toppled across Europe and the United States. Movements for Black liberation targeted Confederate monuments and police violence; former colonial and settler-colonial societies reckoned with their treatment of colonial subjects, indigenous, and migrant populations. All of these interventions served to focus global attention on the sins of the past. King Philippe of Belgium expressed deep regrets to the president of the Democratic Republic of Congo in "the first public acknowledgment from a member of the Belgian royal family of the devastating human and financial toll during eight decades of colonization."[33] These uprisings and the conversations they have generated show new promise for a much-needed shift around migration as well: toward expanding public understandings of migration beyond individualistic paradigms and amnesic tendencies, and toward confronting obligations in reparative justice beyond narrow legalistic and retributivist tendencies. The attendant protests and discourse have also drawn attention to the tensions between the obsession of many Western nations with, on one hand, restrictionist policies and law-and-order rhetoric and, on the other, their own checkered

---

32 Roberto G. Gonzales, Nando Sigona, Martha C. Franco, and Anna Papoutsi, *Undocumented Migration: Borders, Immigration Enforcement, and Belonging* (Cambridge, UK: Polity Press, 2019), 4.

33 Monika Pronczuk and Megan Specia, "Belgium's King Sends Letter of Regret Over Colonial Past in Congo," *New York Times*, June 30, 2020, www.nytimes.com/2020/06/30/world/europe/belgium-king-congo.html.

340 *Kristin E. Heyer and Daniel Kanstroom*

histories of respect for other nations' borders, including those of indigenous nations on their own soil.[34]

In light of such histories and the broader operations of the global capitalist economy and the impacts of climate change, a structural and interdisciplinary analysis of migration is indispensable for adequately attending to complex causal forces and sites of responsibility. Greater focus on these structural causes may lead to less rigidity about borders and membership and a longer view that emphasizes restorative justice and humane solutions over legalistic legitimacy alone. It also may raise awareness about how receiving countries' contemporary practices continue to build bridges for migrants. Hence, in addition to Ian Almond's "instability tax," Suketu Mehta proposes levying a "migration tax" on polluting nations to parallel the "carbon tax" on polluting industries.[35] He conceives of migration as a form of reparations more broadly, proposing that immigration quotas be based upon host countries' negative impact on others: "Britain should have quotas for Indians and Nigerians; France, for Malians and Tunisians; Belgians, for very large numbers of Congolese."[36] Rather than punishing migrants driven from home, he insists that host nations "[p]ay the costs of colonialism, of the wars [they] have imposed on [refugees], of the inequality [they have] built into the world order."[37] Alternatively, in order to work preventatively and avoid a migration tax, he suggests that wealthy countries refrain from propping up dictators and allowing their corporations to amass profits by bribing local officials, operating polluting factories and mines, or sustaining unjust trade practices.[38]

Several chapters in this volume try to make these broader contexts visible by attending to the ideologies and agendas that drive laws and policies, to broader economic and political structures, and to normative understandings of the links between laws and structures (via categories of structural violence or social sin, for example). The social responsibility underscored in chapters authored by Gemma Tulud Cruz (Chapter 11), Donald M. Kerwin (Chapter 6), and Kristin E. Heyer (Chapter 13) signal this needed shift toward broader complicity and structural justice. Such emphases help reveal the ways in which a reductive ethos both desensitizes persons and incentivizes harm, and the ways isolation allows settled communities to more readily scapegoat and politicize a migrant presence. As Marianne Heimbach-Steins has noted, colonial structures shaped not only long-term international political and economic relationships that have inhibited equal participation, but also culturalist patterns and ideologies of domination that continue to influence migration barriers and power asymmetries.[39]

---

34 Mehta, *This Land Is Our Land*, 31.
35 Ibid., 210. Kristin E. Heyer's chapter in this volume discusses Ian Almond's "instability tax" (Chapter 13).
36 Mehta, *This Land Is Our Land*, 209.
37 Ibid., 208.
38 Ibid., 215.
39 Marianne Heimbach-Steins, "Migration in a Post-Colonial World," in *Religious and Ethical Perspectives on Migration*, eds. Elizabeth Collier and Charles Strain (Lanham, MD: Lexington, 2014), 87–107, at 87, 93.

Empathy, legitimacy, faith 341

Chapters in this volume also indicate how false narratives, ideologies of security, and idols of invulnerability facilitate susceptibility to exclusionary temptations. For example, Luis N. Rivera-Pagán writes of the influence of Samuel Huntington's xenophobic cultural critiques, regularly cited by President Trump and his closest advisers in warning of threats from certain immigrants and a "clash of civilizations" (Chapter 10).[40] Silas W. Allard's chapter suggests how exclusionary borders function to reinforce national identity (without interrogating it) and sustain racial homogeneity (Chapter 5). At root, perhaps, these pervasive tendencies reflect human misgivings about mortality and control: citizens ultimately fear not migrants' "invasion" or even the claims they make, but host community members' own "fragile, vulnerable, wounded selves." As Roberto S. Goizueta has argued, "We avoid risking the act of solidarity, or companionship with the victims of history, not because we hate them but because we hate ourselves."[41] The many idols of security that dominate our newsfeeds today reflect his insight that

> our ultimate powerlessness in the face of death is what drives us to construct personal identities, social institutions, ideologies and belief systems that can make us feel invulnerable and ultimately invincible. . . . [W]e construct a world that will shield us from [the] terrifying truth [that our lives are ultimately not in our control].[42]

These nonrational tendencies often wield a stronger influence on attitudes than do facts about immigrants' presence, contributions, and relative rates of crime. A recent study showed that U.S. residents believe the foreign-born population makes up 37 percent of the nation, whereas in reality it comprises only 13.7 percent (about a third of that imagined). The French surveyed believed that 1 out of 3 people living in France is Muslim, whereas the accurate number is 1 out of 13.[43] The false narratives and ideologies purveyed by unchecked social media outlets maintain a firm grip on the popular imagination; encounters with migrants and their narratives can begin to disrupt fear-based frameworks, however.

IV Law, ideology, and power

The volume's interdisciplinary approach also sheds light on the implicit values underlying law and policy, which do not remain immune to ideologically driven interests, even as governments ostensibly bypass normative considerations. As

---

40 See also Carlos Lozada, "Samuel Huntington, A Prophet for the Trump Era," *Washington Post*, July 18, 2017, www.washingtonpost.com/news/book-party/wp/2017/07/18/samuel-huntington-a-prophet-for-the-trump-era/.

41 Roberto S. Goizueta, "From Calvary to Galilee," *America*, April 17, 2006, www.americamagazine.org/issue/569/article/calvary-galilee.

42 Roberto S. Goizueta, "To the Poor, the Sick, and the Suffering," in *Vatican II: A Universal Call to Holiness*, eds. Anthony Ciorra and Michael W. Higgins (Mahwah, NJ: Paulist Press, 2012), 62–79, at 73.

43 Mehta, *This Land Is Our Land*, 118–19.

342 *Kristin E. Heyer and Daniel Kanstroom*

Allard's introduction and Daniel Kanstroom's opening chapter indicate, the ways in which laws (regarding entry, admission, and removal, for example) function are never value neutral (introduction; Chapter 1). An overdrawn fact/value distinction takes governments off the hook for normative considerations of the relationship between power and rights, however. Other chapters reveal these tendencies by uncovering tensions between types of law. Enid Trucios-Haynes, for instance, analyzes the departure of U.S. immigration law from mainstream U.S. constitutional law and the tensions between immigration and labor law, given the role migration plays in economic development by helping fill labor market shortages. She contrasts international human rights law norms (like the nonsubordination principle) that balance the interests of noncitizen and citizen workers, with "illusory" protections for low-skilled migrant laborers that ensure that they remain perpetual outsiders vulnerable to exploitation, given the focus of labor migration programs on host countries' economic needs (Chapter 2). Receiving countries that rely on migrant labor regularly communicate "No Trespassing" and "Help Wanted" at once by means of border fortification and visa caps out of step with labor needs and employment practices.

In other cases, laws serve to centralize power even if they serve different ends than their ostensible purpose. Kanstroom's chapter reviews the tenuous legitimacy of deportation as a legal system in general, as its systems are often arbitrary, punitive, and disproportionate, especially in cases of so-called expedited removal and "voluntary" return (Chapter 1). Elsewhere he has traced the history of the deportation system of the United States, indicating how, although it has worked poorly in the realm of U.S. immigration control, it has remained a key feature of the national security state, a labor-control device, and a powerful tool of discretionary social control that lives in peculiar equipoise with society's openness to legal immigration and birthright citizenship.[44] Border fortification efforts have likewise evaded their ostensible goals, in many cases. Peter Andreas has described the U.S. efforts to deter irregular migration at the southern border in the 1990s as a "politically successful policy failure," in that they gave the impression policymakers were addressing irregular migration flows yet did not reduce undocumented migration.[45] In his recent volume on migrant detention, César Cuauhtémoc García Hernández makes an analogous argument, noting that in spite of the common lament that U.S. immigration law is broken, the detention system indicates that it is working precisely as designed:

> As a policy, immigration imprisonment is a failure. As a legal principle, it is a sign of virtually unbridled executive power and an example of law's

44 Daniel Kanstroom, *Deportation Nation: Outsiders in American History* (Cambridge, MA: Harvard University Press, 2007).
45 Peter Andreas and Thomas J. Biersteker, *The Rebordering of North America: Integration and Exclusion in a New Security Context* (New York: Routledge, 2003).

Empathy, legitimacy, faith 343

willingness to push migrants into a marginal, by-their-fingernails hold on to recognition inside courtrooms. As a measure of our collective morality, it's a humanitarian catastrophe. But as a sharp-edged political tool, it is a remarkably effective means of dividing workplaces, friendships, families and communities.[46]

Like the function of the deportation system, the immigration prison system reinforces and benefits from a "security-first philosophy" that casts migrants as dangerous threats, even as a nation like the United States does not need to rely on "fitting people into cages" to enforce immigration laws.[47] Hence, the immigration system itself has not malfunctioned; it "was intended to punish, stigmatize, and marginalize—all for political and financial gain."[48] Detention conditions around the world became only more dangerous and punitive during the global coronavirus pandemic; they have become more profitable with the election of leaders funded by privately held corrections firms and committed to increasing detention. Hence, if the morality of the normative project pursued through the law is always subject to critique from other forms of moral discourse, as Allard discusses in the introduction, the volume's themes of dignity, agency, and the common good serve to directly contest the tendencies of these representative admissions, detention, and deportation systems.

V Citizenship, agency, and membership

If law and policy inevitably function to advance value-laden agendas—and often, as in cases examined here, to consolidate power—the legal category of citizenship similarly fails to capture the ways in which immigrants perform membership and belonging in new and longstanding host communities. Several chapters in this volume attune us not only to the ways in which "illegality" is produced but also to how identity is (re)defined and agency exercised in significant ways. The authors' reflections on allegiance, integration, and resistance indicate that there is more porosity, liminality, and promise than a legalistic understanding of citizenship alone discloses. On one hand, the chapters convey "the plurality of scales at which 'illegality' is produced and experienced," reflective of what migration scholars term an "illegality assemblage," to describe the "loose and dynamic system of laws and practices that transcend national borders and in which different interests and agendas find some kind of accommodation."[49] Chapters by legal scholars, in particular, examine the reach and impact of these "configurations of

---

46 César Cuauhtémoc García Hernández, *Migrating to Prison: America's Obsession with Locking Up Immigrants* (New York: The New Press, 2019), 92–93.
47 Ibid., 92, 147.
48 Ibid., 13.
49 Gonzales, et al., *Undocumented Migration*, 5. See, for example, Silas W. Allard (Chapter 5), Donald M. Kerwin (Chapter 6), and Ulrich Schmiedel (Chapter 12).

344   *Kristin E. Heyer and Daniel Kanstroom*

rights, entitlements, constraints, and challenges in places in which migrants' lives unfold."[50]

On the other hand, as Allard's chapter shows, borders are sites of engagement, not just exclusion (Chapter 5). For refugee camps, schools, and congregations also "create new spaces of encounter between migrants, authorities, and activists," with opportunities for "new processes of political subjectification and solidarity."[51] Migrants' claims to community and belonging can move "citizenship from the federal legal sphere to a more local and interpersonal articulation," as cultural citizenship; by "[r]ooting citizenship in the everyday practices of immigrants, this alternative conception underscores and reaffirms their contributions outside of legal frameworks."[52] Kerwin's chapter in this volume draws attention to similar patterns of integration "from below" (Chapter 6), and Bill Ong Hing's chapter indicates the stability that familial and educational networks can provide (Chapter 3). The kinship of religious congregations with migrants, as profiled herein, also highlights gray areas where status and borders become more permeable, revealing how community-level practices interact with structural constraints to shape "the dynamic processes of contemporary membership."[53] Belonging and exclusion are seldom absolute, whether because of the conditional, revocable nature of certain legal protections, marginalization, and discrimination endured by those with formal citizenship status, or because of the unsteady footing of mixed-status families.

Others migrants claim membership via "collective practice," such as immigrant-rights protests or new forms of resistance that make visible those without legal status; contemporary work "theorizes citizenship as practice and performance" in this way or, rather than underscoring cultural citizenship, calls for global or postnational citizenship.[54] Ulrich Schmiedel's chapter indicates the promise of street-level, interfaith "coalitional" theologies in this vein (Chapter 12). The risk-laden activism of undocumented migrants and their allies helps disrupt dominant narratives and empower the agency of migrants, strengthening rights and belonging. Safwat Marzouk's hermeneutical reflections on how memory shapes communal identity reinforce a notion of self-understanding that exceeds standard boundaries of civic belonging (Chapter 8). And as his joint chapter with Kerwin stresses, integration practices marked by mutuality enable migrants to become full members of their community (Chapter 15).

---

50 Gonzales, et al., *Undocumented Migration*, 5. See, for example, Daniel Kanstroom (Chapter 1), Bill Ong Hing (Chapter 3), and Michele R. Pistone (Chapter 4), Rose Cuison Villazor (Chapter 7).

51 Gonzales, et al., *Undocumented Migration*, 152.

52 Ibid., 49.

53 Ibid., 50. Luis N. Rivera-Pagán's chapter in this volume shows how massive migration has strengthened religious traditions themselves, noting the 42 languages celebrating the liturgy in the Roman Catholic Archdiocese of Los Angeles, California, alone (Chapter 10).

54 Gonzales, et al., *Undocumented Migration*, 146–49.

Empathy, legitimacy, faith 345

Akin to Linda Bosniak's distinctions between the hard and soft boundaries of citizenship,[55] this volume analyzes both the former—for instance, enforcement efforts that "exclude, surveil, and expel unwanted migrants" or maintain boundaries through formal laws and policies—and the latter, in the "soft interiors where social relationships are formed, links are developed, and where migrants practice everyday acts of membership through their labor and community participation."[56] For whereas legal citizenship affords claim rights, immunities, and opportunities, social or cultural citizenship indicates how migrants "forge their own paths and make claims to be included [via] . . . daily practices that establish community, networks, and ties."[57] These practices from below—as well as the problematic ways that laws and policy function from above—raise questions about what should define citizenship in the contemporary era, given the weakness of mere moral luck. As Rose Cuison Villazor's chapter points out, even the allegiance requirement is unevenly applied in the United States, much less any requirements for civic contributions or measures of moral desert (Chapter 7). Everyday practices of incarnational solidarity and normative claims about universal human dignity, family values, and the universal destination of created goods put pressure on a legalistic notion of citizenship and its attendant rights and responsibilities.

VI The dangerously uncertain future of migration

The future of citizenship and of migration is uncertain and, for many, extremely dangerous. A new imagination is required to motivate and inspire productive political activism and international solidarity. Given the impact and stakes of ideologically driven policies and exploitative systems, of new waves of nationalist fear-mongering and pandemic-induced border tightening, we must continue to challenge the operations of the sovereign nation-state to meet the demands of justice, fairness, empathy, and legitimacy. Those who have advocated humane alternatives to detention and who call nation-states to reckon with their exploitative histories (for example, connecting the treatment of indigenous peoples within a nation with that of its refugees) offer powerful examples worth following.[58] This volume's composition suggests that Christian resources also have a vital role to play in reshaping imagination around migration, whether via traditions of philoxenia, biblical hospitality, and the global common good, cross-border liturgical rites, or interruptive practices of political theology. The example of Christian

---

55 Linda Bosniak, *The Citizen and the Alien: Dilemmas of Contemporary Membership* (Princeton, NJ: Princeton University Press, 2006). There she also writes about "gradations of effective citizenship."
56 Gonzales, et al., *Undocumented Migration*, 37.
57 Ibid., 38.
58 For example, the Bookends Project is an initiative of the Australian Jesuit Province that expresses its commitment to justice "for Australia's First Nations peoples and for the country's most recent arrivals, refugees and people seeking asylum": http://jesuit.org.au/wp-content/uploads/Bookends-Project.pdf.

346 *Kristin E. Heyer and Daniel Kanstroom*

teenagers donning banned hijabs in solidarity with those "affected by laws they could not author" suggests accessible possibilities for hopeful resistance (Schmiedel, Chapter 12).

Many religious traditions also challenge reigning paradigms that fail to understand social and economic goods as complementary—such as a scarcity model that facilitates pitting citizens against migrants, or family visas against employment visas, as outlined by Hing in this volume. The fidelity of religious NGOs to meeting the needs of the least of these makes more viable growing calls to defund enforcement systems; their aid practices also resist and subvert the surveillance mechanisms of empire, as the Scott Warren case attests. At its best, then, Christianity offers resources both for bringing water into the desert (or rescue vessels into the sea) and for prophetically indicting the inhumane operations of the illegality assemblage. The transcendent *telos* of Christianity can help critique prevailing social imaginaries and political ideologies that prop up exploitative systems, even as religious traditions themselves are never immune to cooptation.

The contributions of congregations and individuals from below often remain anonymous and piecemeal. When religious leaders step up to publicly name exploitative patterns like those traced in this volume, they amplify the slow and steady solidarity of their members and provide a counternarrative to dominant myths. In June of 2020, Bishop Mark J. Seitz of El Paso, Texas, thus lamented the death-dealing impact of the Trump administration's restrictive immigration measures:

> During World War II, the United States thought it had learned after we felt the guilt of having returned a boat filled with Jewish refugees back to the extermination camps of Nazi Germany [referencing the MS *St. Louis*, turned away in 1939]. But today, we send those who have escaped back into the hands of narco-trafficking gangs, ignoring the very laws we had written. Respect for the truth demands that I speak up to say that this fundamental right to asylum here at the border really is effectively over. . . . And we are all responsible. . . . Yesterday, we valued the life of babies, toddlers and youth. Today, we run roughshod over the law and forcibly return unaccompanied children, putting them at risk of exploitation, trafficking and coronavirus.

Michele R. Pistone's chapter in this volume similarly laments the global costs of the gradual undermining of refugee law in recent decades (Chapter 4). Bishop Seitz adds that he finds some hope in the efforts of ecumenical border organizations to meet the needs of asylum seekers and from families on the move themselves: "That hope shows me that the machinery of darkness which our immigration enforcement has become is not permanent," he said. Yet he insisted that the transformation of racism into reconciliation and the "weight of the law" into a merciful end to suffering remains ours to accomplish "in our freedom and responsibility."[59] Hence, greater attentiveness to the structural contexts of migration, ideological influences on policy, and the constrained agency of migrants suggests accountability for the many, not condemnation of the few. It remains to be seen what the long-term effects of the global coronavirus pandemic will be on migration, as nations tighten borders or de facto abandon asylum, as Seitz notes in the United States. In the short term, at least, it has brought to light both the precarious and indispensable nature of migrant labor and has significantly exacerbated economic push factors.[60] In a sense, sadly, COVID-19 has provided an ideal instrument to impose anti-immigration policies, given that governments can connect an actual disease to ostensible disease vectors, even if (as U.S. patterns made apparent, for example) it remains a false connection. Longstanding, dehumanizing language characterizing immigrants as "vermin" who pose such threats readily facilitates such connections.[61] Yet the pandemic may also ultimately provide an opening for the volume's common-good arguments that push back against xenophobic and nationalistic strains and more aptly serve our longstanding global interdependence, for "[v]iruses don't care about border walls" or nationalistic chest-thumping.[62] In sum, through dialogue, introspection, empathy, historical awareness, and a genuine commitment to principles of human dignity, fairness, and equity, we can better define legitimacy as we seek new ways to bend the arc of history toward justice, without which there clearly can be no peace.

Suggested Reading

Benhabib, Seyla. *The Rights of Others: Aliens, Residents and Citizens*. The Seeley Lectures. Cambridge: Cambridge University Press, 2004.

Carens, Joseph H. *The Ethics of Immigration*. New York: Oxford University Press, 2013.

García Hernández, César Cuauhtémoc. *Migrating to Prison: America's Obsession with Locking up Immigrants*. New York: The New Press, 2019.

Gonzales, Roberto G., Nando Sigona, Martha C. Franco, and Anna Papoutsi. *Undocumented Migration: Borders, Immigration Enforcement, and Belonging*. Cambridge, UK: Polity Press, 2019.

---

59 Rhina Guidos, "Asylum at the Border Is 'Effectively Over,' El Paso Bishop Says," *Crux*, June 27, 2020, https://cruxnow.com/church-in-the-usa/2020/06/asylum-at-the-border-is-effectively-over-el-paso-bishop-says/.

60 As Hing notes, the pandemic has underscored how many immigrants perform essential labor in agriculture, supply chains, and medical industries (Chapter 3).

61 Thomas Crea, panelist, "Jesuit Refugee Service" webinar, *The Show @ 6: BC and The Common Good*, Boston College, July 3, 2020, www.bc.edu/bc-web/sites/global-engagement/expand-your-world/Show-at-6.html#archive.

62 John Gehring, "What Do We Learn from This Place Where We Do Not Want to Be?" *National Catholic Reporter*, March 25, 2020, www.ncronline.org/news/opinion/what-do-we-learn-place-where-we-dont-want-be.

Hollenbach, David, ed. *Driven from Home: Protecting the Rights of Forced Migrants.* Washington, DC: Georgetown University Press, 2010.

Mehta, Suketu. *This Land Is Our Land: An Immigrant's Manifesto.* New York: Farrar, Straus and Giroux, 2019.

Ngai, Mae M. *Impossible Subjects: Illegal Aliens and the Making of Modern America.* Princeton, NJ: Princeton University Press, 2004.

Phan, Peter C., ed. *Christian Theology in the Age of Migration: Implications for World Christianity.* Lanham, MD: Lexington Books, 2020.

Index

Note: Page numbers in *italics* indicate a figure on the corresponding page.

admission 7, 11, 16–17, 26, 27
Africa 88, 96; migration from/within 39, 53, 56, 235; states projected to double in population 112, *113*
African Americans 129, 339
Afro-descendant peoples 129, 179, 181, 321–2
Afroyim v. Rusk 140
Agamben, Giorgio 27
agribusiness, transnational 321–2
agricultural workers 30, 32, 40, 42, 59, 60, 296, 299, 301; *see also* immigrant workers
Ajo Samaritan 261
Alba, Richard 278
aliens *see* immigrants; refugees
Allard, Silas W. 60–1, 214
Almond, Ian 340
alterity 159, 160, 191, 220, 223, 224, 225
American Dream 109, 116, 124
Amstutz, Mark 322–3
Anderson, Benedict 169–70
anthropology: moral 244; social 231, 239, 241; Trinitarian 239
antiglobalism 244
anti-immigrant groups 181, 200
antiracism training 246
antiviolence programs 247
Anzaldúa, Gloria 92, 95, 97, 99
Arameans, wandering 179–80
Arendt, Hannah 13, 235
artificial intelligence 106, 120
Asia: immigration in 53; labor migration from 293; labor migration in 300–5; migrant workers in 291

Asian Development Bank (ADB) 301
Asian Economic Integration Report (2018) 301
Asiatic Barred Zone (U.S.) 91
assimilation 7, 164, 279–80
assisted returns 18
assisted voluntary return 23
assisted voluntary return and reintegration (AVRR) 23–4
asylum: applications for 81; dismissal of claims 79; national and international provisions of 268; for victims of persecution 72
asylum seekers 93; alleviating the suffering of 162; from Central America 230; characterized as threat 111; in Europe 25; exclusion of 14; number of 1; protections for 20–1; rights of 14, 22; traveling without documentation 77–8; *see also* immigrants; refugees
Australia: asylum seekers in 77; backpacker tax 302–3n55, 306; immigration policies in 96; labor migration in 301; support for refugees in 199
Austria 201
automation 106, 120
Ayalde, Corazon 63

backpacker tax 304–3n55, 306
Bales, Kevin 184
Balibar, Étienne 92–3, 95
Bangladesh 303
Bannon, Steve 166–7
Bauman, Zygmunt 185, 191–2

350 Index

Baumgartner v. United States 135–6
Beck, Richard 172
Bedford-Strohm, Heinrich 246
Belize 293
Bellwood, Peter 2
belonging 95–6, 107, 170, 235, 343–4;
  see also membership
Benedict XVI (pope) 205
Benhabib, Seyla 212, 224–5, 226
Bennett, Bob 257
Berman, Howard 55
Bevans, Stephen 197
Bezdek, Barbara 268, 274
Bhabha, Homi 172
biblical texts *see* Hebrew Bible; New
  Testament
Black liberation 339
Bloemraad, Irene 118
Board of Immigration Appeals (BIA) 71
Bolsonaro, Jair 111, 233
border control 14, 17, 38, 41, 76, 196
border crossers 27, 97, 166, 171, 174,
  236, 264
border enforcement agents 97
Border Patrol 234, 336
border security 77, 78
border wall 47, 95, 97, 98, 232, 242,
  245, 336
borders/borderlands 7, 88, 92–3, 99;
  ambivalence of 98–9, 101; as bridges
  192; heterogeneity of 94–7; and
  identity formation 91; interiorization
  of 96; militarization of 181, 267;
  performativity of 97–8; as places of
  engagement 44–5, 88, 100–1, 344;
  as process of national formation 91;
  shifting nature of 88; as sites for
  exclusion 44–5, 88–92, 99, 103; as
  sites for inclusion 158; as sites for
  recreation 98; U.S./Mexican 87,
  92–3, 98–9, 103, 181, 230, 298
borderwall power 96
borderwork 97, 103
boundaries *see* borders
Bowe, John 184
Brazil 293
Brexit 200
British common law 133, 138
Brown, Wendy 215
Bulgaria 201
Bush, George W. 110, 258, 333
Bush administration 21
Butler, Judith 235

Cable Act (1922) 129
Calvin's Case 139, 140
Camp of the Saints, The (Raspail)
  166–7
Campese, Gioacchino 306
capitalism: global 19–20, 185, 316;
  predatory 240
carbon tax 340
Caritas in Veritate (Benedict XVI)
  205–6
Carroll R., M. Daniel 188, 282
Carter, Warren 168, 169, 325
Casa delle Culture 227
Casey, Edward 95, 101
Casper, Gerhard 133
Castles, Stephen 1, 2, 3
Castro, Fidel 82–3
Catholic Agency for Overseas
  Development (CAOD) 199
Catholic parishes 121–2
Catholic social teaching (CST) 73n14,
  208, 305, 309–10, 311
Central America: refugees from 257,
  312–31; U.S. involvement in
  313–22; *see also* Belize; Costa Rica;
  El Salvador; Guatemala; Honduras;
  Nicaragua; Panama
chain migration 51–68; opposition to
  66–7
charity 241, 244, 252; Christian 238
children: as immigrant workers 299; of
  migrants 297; migrants as 247; rights
  of 231; undocumented 122
China, labor migration from 293; *see
  also* Asia
Chinese Exclusion Case 13
Christ *see* Jesus Christ
Christian ethics 7, 47–8, 231, 242;
  and immigration 236–8; relational
  resources 238–41; transformational 45
Christian Praxis 47–8
Christian values 305; and the
  exploitation of immigrant workers
  42–8; and human dignity 43–5; and
  immigrant workers 30; supporting
  restrictive immigration polities 45–8
Christianity: and the Eucharist 203;
  and migration 4, 122–4, 193, 246;
  one body 203–5, 208–9; one bread
  201–3, 208–9; one people 205–7,
  208–9; and politics 222; *telos* of
  346; theological imperatives of
  322–4

Index 351

Christians: as aliens 176; conversation with non-Christians 271–2; European 199
Church of Jesus Christ of Latter-day Saints 257
Cities of Action Network 118
citizenship 7, 343–5; access to 37; for African Americans 129; birthright 138–40, 342; cultural 344; dual 127, 138–41, 184; exclusionary 142, 226; gendered nature of laws 129; as hospitality 138–42; for immigrants 109; for lawful permanent residents 126–7; loss of 17; and marriage 129; and migration 214; new understandings of 339; and the oath of allegiance 126, 130–8; revocation of 134–8, 140; and state sovereignty 214
civic republicanism 110–11
civic virtue 244
civil disobedience 209–10, 268
civil initiative 253, 258, 259, 265, 268, 273–5
civil rights 71, 194
clash of civilizations 182, 226, 234, 341
class privilege 37
Clinton, William Jefferson "Bill" 83
Cohen, Hermann 28
Coke, Edward 139
Cold War 81–2
colonialism 239, 246, 339, 340
colonization 339
common good 67, 112, 122, 202, 208, 230, 232, 237, 238, 239, 241, 243, 280, 282, 310, 343, 345, 347
communitarianism 224–5, 230, 236, 322
Conference of Plenipotentiaries on the Status of Refugees and Stateless People (1951) 70
containment 83, 84
contract workers 30; see also immigrant workers
Convention Relating to the Status of Refugees (1951) 15, 49, 81, 82
"Corazon" effect 63–6
Corbett, Jim 258, 259, 268
cosmopolitanism 93, 224–5, 230, 237, 322
Costa Rica 293, 321
Cotton, Tom 51, 55–6
Cover, Robert 5–6
COVID-19 pandemic 59, 109, 118, 132, 296, 333, 347

coyotes (*coyotaje*) 98, 298
Crane, Stephen 69
criminalization 252–3, 270, 274–5
critical hermeneutics 160
crucified people 306–7
Cruz, Gemma Tulud 43, 67, 281
Cuba 82–3
Cuban Adjustment Act (1966) 82–3
Cuéllar, Gregory 171
Cuison-Villazor, Rose 90
cultural encapsulation 280–1
culture(s) 95, 97, 99, 102, 165, 188–9, 191, 207, 208, 220, 276, 278–80, 287, 290; American 180, 183; Anglo-Protestant 182–3; border 92; clash of 182; conflation with religion 235; consumer 321; deterritorialization of 292; Egyptian 287–9; exclusionary 107; French 166; fundamentalist 247; interdependence of 172; Latinx 65; national 302, 305; religious 201; threats to 115, 167, 234, 246; throwaway 289; traditionalist 46
customs agents 98
Czech Republic 198, 200

DACA (Deferred Action for Childhood Arrivals) case 333–4, 337
DACA (Deferred Action for Childhood Arrivals) program 112, 114, 333–4
Danish People's Party (DPP) 200
de Grauuw, Els 118
de Haas, Hein 1, 2, 3
Dear, Michael 98–9
Declaration of Human Rights 214, 223
deconstruction 160
Deferred Action for Childhood Arrivals (DACA) 112, 114, 333–4
Del Rio-Mocci v. Connolly Properties 256
Demafelis, Joanna 303
Democratic Republic of Congo 339
denationalization 114, 214–15
denaturalization 16
Denmark 200
deportation 7, 11, 17–20, 25, 26, 27–8, 39, 231, 343; efficiency and justice in 12; from Europe 18; fast-track 11, 20; involving supranational entities 19; from Mexico 18–19; of parents of U.S. citizens 26; self- 23–5; from the US 17–18; see also removal; return
Derrida, Jacques 160

352 *Index*

detention 39, 343; alternatives to 247, 345; of asylum seekers 79–80; of minors 79
detention centers 19
deterrence strategies 76–7, 84, 231–6, 242
Diallo, Rokhaya 212, 225–6
dignity 27, 29, 30, 43, 45, 47, 48–9, 75, 107, 116, 122, 142, 174, 184, 197, 207, 236, 238, 262, 267–8, 274, 276, 278, 280, 281, 287, 305, 309, 322, 324, 328, 337–8, 341, 345, 347
Dillon, Michael 185
discrimination 109, 305, 307; against immigrant workers 29–31, 35–9, 43–4, 294, 297; intergenerational 30, 44; against migrants 198; against Muslim immigrants 177; racial 295, 297; social 30; xenophobic 37–8
displacement 38, 48, 163, 166, 231, 235, 237, 321; in biblical texts 176–7, 277, 324–30; causes of 244; in Central America 313–14, 316, 321; cultural 112, 245, 276; economic 44, 112, 245; ethnic 276; forced 67, 123; job 120, 296; psychological 328; racial 112, 115; religious 112; *see also* forced migration
domestic workers 36, 40, 121, 299–303, 305, 308
Domingo, Daniel 302n54, 306
DREAM Act 333
Dred Scott v. Sanford 139
drug trafficking 304
Dube, Musa 165, 172
Dworkin, Ronald 332

ecologies of faith and trust 162
ecologies of fear 162
Edelen, Britt 170
education, for migrant children 297
El Paso shootings 276
El Salvador 76, 185, 298; Indigenous peoples in 321; refugees from 314–15; U.S. intervention in 316–17; violence in 313–14, 327
Ellacuría, Ignacio 306
Emergency Quota Act (1921) 52
empathy 244, 332; and legitimacy 333–9
Employment Division v. Smith 254
employment visas *see* work visas

employment-based immigration *see* immigrant workers; labor migration
English common law 133, 138
entrepreneurship 62–3
ethics *see* Christian ethics; migration ethics
ethnic cleansing 19
ethnocentrism 191
Europe: 2015 migrant crisis 197–201; migration to 235; states projected to decline in population *113*
European Union (EU): agreements with Ukraine and Turkey 77; borders with Turkey and North Africa 96; Common Basic Principles of Integration 106; emergency summit on migrants 198; and immigrant integration 106–7, 109
exclusion 11, 12–15, 17, 26, 27–8, 163, 344; racial 95; rights against 15; sovereign power of 13
expansionism 239
Expatriation Act (U.S. 1907) 129
expats 37
expedited removal 20–3, 27, 79, 96–7, 338, 342
expulsion 7; of groups 19; rights against 15
externalization 84

faith-based institutions 121
fake news 245
family-based migration 6, 7, 21, 51–2, 57
family reunification 51–2, 53, 58, 66, 81, 116
family separation 80, 123, 167, 230, 296, 312
family sponsorship 51; *see also* chain migration
family visas 58
Fanestil, John 98
Fanon, Frantz 179, 189
Farinella, Paolo 209
farmworkers *see* agricultural workers
Favarin, Luca 209
Federation of Protestant Churches in Italy 227
female genital mutilation (FGM) 71
Fernandez, Osvaldo 64
Fiddian-Qasmiyeh, Elena 4, 7
Fife, John 258
Finland 199
Flavius Josephus 169, 325, 327
Foner, Nancy 278

forced displacement *see* displacement
forced migration 25, 195–6, 208; in biblical texts 324–6; *see also* migration
forced return *see* return
foreign diplomats 32
foreigners: in Greek mythology 166; in the Hebrew Bible 147–64
Forrester, Duncan 272–3
France: illegal immigration in 334–5; labor migration to 293; migrants in 199; Muslims in 342
Francis (pope) 12, 26, 45, 48, 107, 124, 196, 199, 208, 232, 236, 243, 246, 289
free trade agreements 32

gender issues: defining refugee groups 72; and immigrant workers 36, 307
genocide 19, 191
ger (sojourners/transients/aliens) 147, 152–3, 155, 156, 157, 159
Germany 199
Gettysburg Address (Lincoln) 110
Gibney, Matthew 330
Girouard v. United States 137
Glanville, Mark R. 153
Global Compact for Safe, Orderly, and Regular Migration (GCM) 12, 48–50, 118–19, 200, 232, 308
Global Compact on Refugees (GCR) 12, 48
globalization 2–3, 7, 44, 46, 93, 191, 192, 194, 232, 244, 247, 291; capitalist 315; of indifference 48; neoliberal 243; and transnational agribusiness 321–2
Goizueta, Roberto S. 243
González, Justo 102–3
Good Samaritan parable 124
Graham, Elaine 197
Grahl-Madsen, Atle 14
Grassley, Charles 56
Greece 80, 200–1
Groody, Daniel 4, 306
group egotism 241–2
Group of Twenty (G20) 109
Guatemala 76, 185, 240, 298; refugees from 314–15; transnational agribusiness in 322; U.S. intervention in 318–20; violence in 313, 314–15
guest workers 30; *see also* immigrant workers

Gulf Cooperation Council (GCC) 37, 107, 301

Habermas, Jürgen 271
Haidt, Jonathan 244
Haiti 240, 293
Hanciles, Jehu 2
Hart-Celler Act (1965) 52
hate crimes 297
health care access 40, 50, 79, 118, 293, 297, 299
Hebrew Bible 7, 57, 122, 159, 164; 1 Chronicles 152; Deuteronomy 57, 149, 150, 151, 153, 154, 155, 157, 158, 179, 186, 188, 282, 283; Exodus 57, 148, 153, 154, 155, 156–7, 186, 202, 277, 282, 283, 325; Ezekiel 149, 155, 190, 284; Ezra 150, 188; Genesis 152, 163, 186, 283, 286–9; Holiness Code 152–4; Hosea 326; Isaiah 148, 149, 151; Jeremiah 149, 155, 186, 282, 284, 324, 325; Job 186; Joel 149; Joseph among the Egyptians 286–9; Joshua 150, 157; 1 Kings 150; 2 Kings 148; Lamentations 149; Leviticus 57, 152, 153, 154, 155–6, 157, 171, 186, 283; 1 and 2 Maccabees 325; Malachi 155; on migrants and strangers 43, 162–4; Nehemiah 150, 188; *nokhri* (foreigners) 147, 149–51, 158, 159; Numbers 152, 156–7; Proverbs 149; Psalms 152, 155, 187; Ruth 150; terminology for foreigners 147–64; *toshav* and *ger* (sojourners/transients/aliens) 147, 152–8, 159; *zar* ("foreigner/ stranger") 147, 148–50, 159; Zechariah 154
hermeneutics, and migration 158–64
Herod Antipas 169, 326–7
Herod the Great 168, 325, 327
Herrou, Cédric 334–5
Heyer, Kristin E. 41, 44, 49, 102, 112, 116, 206, 228, 271, 272, 323
Higham, John 105, 111, 114
hijab affair 212–15, 225
Hoeffner, John J. 310
Holiness Code 152–4
Hollenbach, David 207, 240, 280
Holmes, Seth 60
Holocaust 81

354 *Index*

Honduras 76, 185, 298; Indigenous peoples in 321; refugees from 315; transnational agribusiness in 321–2; U.S. intervention in 317–18
Hong Kong 302, 303
Horsley, Richard 328
hospitality 7; biblical 236, 278, 281–6; Christian 141, 177, 238; in the early Christian community 285–6; in Hebrew scripture 282–4; for immigrants 277; integration as 289–90; radical 173, 174, 176, 290; to strangers 165–6, 236, 242; subversive 206–7, 323; in the teachings of Jesus 284–5; theology of 127–8
housing market 61
human dignity *see* dignity
human rights 259; abuses of 18, 41, 237–8, 297; defense of 242; in democracy 225; and deportation 19; of economic migrants 308; and global humanitarianism 208; of immigrants 43, 224–5; and the law 12, 242; of noncitizens 194; protection of 49–50; universal 237, 238
human smuggling 97–8, 256, 298; *see also* human trafficking
human trafficking 14, 39–40, 293–4, 303, 304, 346
humanitarian aid 74, 251, 269, 274, 334–5; criminalization of 253, 260; faith-based 258; as religious imperative 261–2; for undocumented immigrants 254; use of RFRA to defend 257–8
humanitarian law 76
humanitarianism, global 208
Hungary 80, 111, 198, 201
Huntington, Samuel P. 182–4, 191, 341
Hurd, Elizabeth Shakman 266
Hwang, Jenny 188, 193

identity: American 182–3; and citizenship 99; communal 344; cultural 115; formation of 91; Muslim 215; national 182–3, 187, 242, 245; vs. the Other 160; vs. social reality 94–5
idolatry 207, 243, 247, 277
Illegal Immigrant Reform and Immigrant Responsibility Act (IIRAIRA) 79, 83

immigrant smuggling 39; *see also* human trafficking
immigrant workers 19, 121, 242, 243, 342; in 3D (dirty, dangerous, demeaning) jobs 39–42, 291, 293, 295; agricultural 30, 32, 40, 42, 59, 60, 296, 299, 301; Asian 300–5; children as 299; and Christian values 42–8; and class 37; defined 293; discrimination against 29–31, 35–9, 43–4, 294, 297; domestic 36, 40, 121, 299–303, 305, 308; and gender 36, 307; and the global migration infrastructure 41–2; hospitality workers 301; immigration status of 38–9; inequality experienced by 39–40, 308–9; integration of 115; legal protections for 308–9; marginalization of 43–4; pathway to permanent residence 33–4, 37; and race 37–8, 307; segregation of 31, 307; undocumented 30, 35, 40; and U.S. immigration law 31–5; Vietnamese 304
immigrants: ability to improve life prospects 120; access to public benefits and services 119; from Central America 257, 312–31; Christian theological response to 201–7; demonization of 44, 111, 114, 296, 347; and disease 180; from the Eastern Hemisphere 53; incarceration of 234, 235; integration of 105–7, 117, 121–2, 277, 278–81; Latinx 37, 53, 185–6; Muslim 177, 192, 198–9, 227, 233, 341; rights of 175; second-generation 297; undesirable 196; undocumented 253, 258, 294; in the U.S. 107–9; *see also* asylum seekers; migrants; refugees
immigration: Asian 53; from Central America 230; and Christian ethics 236–8; effect on productivity 61–2, 65; family-based 6, 7, 21, 51–2, 57; illegal 334–5; legal 55, 117, 342; national and local integration policies 117–20; and the root causes of displacement 241–4; surveillance of 181; to the U.S. 66–7; *see also* chain migration; migration
Immigration Act (1990, U.S.) 73–4
Immigration and Customs Enforcement (ICE) 22, 114

Index 355

Immigration and Nationality Act (INA) 131–2, 255, 260, 265
immigration ethics *see* migration ethics
immigration law 11, 31, 98, 342; antiharboring provision 255, 260; changes to 55; class discrimination in 37; enforcement of 257; and human rights 242; and humanitarian aid 254–7; and labor stratification 29–35; lack of Constitutional limits on 35; and lower-skilled workers 295–6; and refugees 307–8; and religion 266; and the sanctuary movement 258; U.S. 232; *see also* immigrant workers; refugee law
immigration reform 51, 265
Immigration Reform and Control Act (IRCA, 1986) 55
immigration status: lack of 38–9; lawful permanent resident (LPR) 126, 130–1; of migrant workers 294; nonpermanent 73, 74–5; protected 295; temporary protected (TPS) 73–4, 114, 231
imperialism 246
inclusion 57, 118, 147–8, 150–1, 157–9, 163, 173, 244, 277, 279
India 293
Indigenous peoples 339–40, 345; in Central America 321–2
Indonesia 301
inequality 340; economic 109, 268; environmental 268; experienced by immigrant workers 39–40, 308–9; global 193; institutionalized 88; in labor migration 307; in labor segregation 299; in the U.S. immigrant labor system 295
injustice *see* justice/injustice
instability tax 340
integration 7, 105–7, 117, 121–2, 277–81; and assimilation 279–80; and cultural encapsulation 280–1; economic 278; as hospitality 289–90; sociocultural 278; and tolerance 280
International Convention on the Protection of the Rights of All Migrant Workers and Members of Their Families 49
International Covenant on Civil and Political Rights (ICCPR) 49, 71
International Covenant on Economic, Social and Cultural Rights (ICESCR) 71

international crime 298
International Labour Organization (ILO) 297, 305
international law 13–14; *see also* immigration law
International Organization for Migration (IOM) 23–4, 81
internationalization 2
interventionism 321
Iraq War 240
Irvin, Dale 184
Islam *see* Muslims
isolationism 112, 231, 232
Israel /Israelites 80; as aliens in Egypt 163
Italy 77, 83, 200–1

Jesus Christ 57, 122–3; as border-crosser 166, 168–70; and the Canaanite woman 170–2, 175; cleansing of the lepers 189; Good Samaritan parable 124; as healer 169; liberating the Gadarene demoniac 328–9; on mercy 306; miracles performed by 173; parable of sheep and goats 173; performing miracles in Gentile territories 173; sacramental presence of 175, 190; and the stranger 189, 281; teachings on hospitality 284–5
John the Baptist 169, 284, 324, 326–7
Jones, Robert 245
jurisdiction 89–90, 100–1
justice/injustice 305–6, 347; and Christianity 323; economic 327; and the law 309; structural 231, 340; *see also* social justice/injustice

Kanstroom, Daniel 96
Kasinga decision 71–2
Kearney, Richard 159, 160–1
Kelly, John F. 80
Kesby, Alison 90
Kidd, José E. Ramírez 155
Kierkegaard, Søren 81
King, Martin Luther Jr. 102
kinship priority 52–4
Knauer v. United States 137
Kurdi, Aylan 209
Kurian, Nimmi 88, 99
Kuwait 303

labor intermediaries 41–2
labor law 307, 342

356 Index

labor market: in the U.S. 121; *see also* immigrant workers

labor migration 6, 7, 87–8; in comparative perspective 292–305; cross-border 301–2; exploitation in 294, 298, 302–4, 305, 309; from the Global South 291, 293, 294; international 291; intraregional 291, 293, 305; programs for 42; South-North 293, 294–300, 305; South-South 300–5; to the United States 294–300; *see also* human trafficking; immigrant workers

labor recruitment 239

laïcité 215, 226

Latin America: labor migration from 294; migrants from 167; *see also* Central America; Mexico

Latinx community and culture 44, 65

Latvia 201

law of migration 3, 4–5, 7

lawful permanent resident (LPR) status 126, 130–1

Levinas, Emmanuel 160–1

liberation theology 43, 45

Libya 77

Lincoln, Abraham 110

Lindbeck, George 271

Liu, Ming 63–4

loyalty oath *see* Oath of Allegiance

Macedonia 80, 198

Mackenzie v. Hare 129

Macron, Emmanuel 111

Madison, James 133

Malaysia 301, 303

Malta 80

Manifest Destiny 246

market fundamentalism 243

market segregation 39–42

Martinez, Oscar Alberto 209

Martinez, Valeria 209

Marxism 222

Marzouk, Safwat 43

Matter of A-B 72

Matter of A-R-C-G 72

Medicare 61

Mediterranean Hope 227

Mehta, Suketu 340

Meissner, Doris 58

membership 3, 15–16, 46, 70–2, 111, 118, 128, 132, 204, 225, 277, 282, 337–9, 340, 343–5; *see also* belonging; citizenship

meritocracy 243

Metz, Johann Baptist 221, 222

Mexico: border with U.S. 87, 92–3, 98–9, 103, 181, 230, 298; deportation in 18; detention of migrants by 298; immigrants from 185; labor migration from 293; refugees from 76; and the transnational labor market 87–8

Middle East: *khafel/kafala* system 302; labor migration to 301, 302; migration from 235

migrant caravans 298

Migrant Integration Policy Index (MIPEX) 108–9

migrant labor *see* immigrant workers

Migrant Worker Convention (1990) 49

migrant workers *see* immigrant workers

migrants: Christian theological response to 196–97; demonization of 324; economic 307–8; harms suffered by 27; from Latin America 167, 296; radical solidarity with 209–10; rejection of 164; relocation plans 111; rights of 212, 224–5; survival 308; undocumented 38, 181; and the U.S. economy 234; *see also* immigrants

migration: in ancient Israel 147–8; antielitism 244; barriers to 340; Christian response to 193, 207–10; and citizenship 214; contextualization of 338–9; and economic growth 1–2; family-based 6, 7, 57; forced 195–6, 208; future of 7, 345–7; global 41–2, 48, 236; hermeneutics and 158–64; humanitarian 6, 7, 307; impact on destination countries 165; international 1, 4, 7, 192; involuntary 307–8; irregular 83, 241, 342; from Latin America 183, 239; legal 117; opposition to 244; and political theology 229; regulation of 3; and religion 4; South-South 293; theology of 7, 179–94; theories of 322–4; unauthorized 181; undesirable 204; undocumented 55; U.S. deterrence efforts 231–6, 242; voluntary 308; and xenophobia 184–6; *see also* immigration; labor migration; law of migration

Migration and Refugee Assistance Act (1962) 82

migration brokers 42

Index 357

migration ethics 44–5, 50, 228, 236–8, 244, 246, 338
migration industry 41
migration law *see* immigration law
Migration Policy Institute 58
migration tax 340
migration theology 7, 179–94, 306
migration theory, neoclassical 238
migration-systems theory 239
Millennium Development Goals 195
Miller, Mark J. 1, 2, 3
Min, Anselm 204, 207
Moltmann, Jürgen 221, 222
moral imagination 247
Morrison, Toni 207
Müller, Werner 216
Muslims 177, 192; in Europe 233; in France 341; hijab affair 212–15, 225; in Italy 227; as refugees 198–9
Myanmar 235, 303
mysticism 222

Nail, Thomas 213, 229
Napolitano, Valentina 226–7
National Academies of Sciences, Engineering, and Medicine (NASEM) 105, 107–8, 117
nationalism 1, 110–11; ethnocultural 276; ethnoracial 276; Italian 200; xenophobic 167
nativism 111–12, 114, 115–16, 201, 232–3, 245, 277, 337; consequences of 276–8
naturalization 115, 126–7; and exclusion 128–30; history of 128–31; processing times for 109; requirements for 129–31, 133–4; through state courts 134
Naturalization Act (U.S.): (1790) 133; (1795) 133, 134; (1870) 129; 1906 amendment to 129
Naturalization Clause (U.S. 1790) 128
neocolonialism 313, 321
neoliberalism 243, 321
Neuman, Gerald 137–38
New Sanctuary Movement 258
New Testament 7, 57, 141, 165–6; Acts 202, 285–6; Colossians 203–4n38; Ephesians 1 203–4n38; 1 Corinthians 203, 285; Ephesians 190, 203–4n38, 207; Galatians 206, 281, 285; Hebrews 177, 281; James 285; John 189, 203, 206; 3 John 285; Luke 124, 189, 284–5, 328–29; Mark 328; Matthew

57, 123, 157, 166, 167–68, 169, 170, 171, 173–4, 177, 189–90, 203, 282, 284, 285, 324–26, 328, 330; parable of sheep and goats 175; 1 Peter 177; Revelation 167; Romans 123, 167, 190, 203–4n38, 210; story of the Gadarene demoniac 324, 328–30
New York Declaration for Refugees and Migrants 48
New Zealand 301
Newman, David 90, 98
Ngai, Mae 338
Nicaragua: Indigenous peoples in 321; refugees from 312, 314; transnational agribusiness in 322; U.S. intervention in 320–1; violence in 313
Niebuhr, Reinhold 241
Nihan, Christophe 154
No Más Muertes *see* No More Deaths
No More Deaths 251, 252, 253, 258–9, 261, 265–8, 270–5, 335–6
nokhri ("foreigners") 147, 149–51, 158, 159
Nomos of the Earth, The (Schmitt) 219
noncitizens 20, 21
nongovernmental organizations (NGOs) 85, 200, 346
nonimmigrant visas 31–2
nonrefoulement 15–16
North Africa *see* Africa

Oath of Allegiance 127–8, 130–8, 184, 345; removal of 141–2
Obama, Barack 333
Ogata, Sadako 24
Old Testament *see* Hebrew Bible
Operation Coyote 76
Operation Relex 77
Organisation for Economic Co-operation and Development (OECD) 109
Orsi, Robert 266
Other: discernment of different kinds of 161; fear of 246; identification with 277; responsibility to 160–1; violence against 276
Ozawa, Takao 129
Ozawa v. United States 129

Paasi, Anssi 88–9, 95
Pacific Islanders 301
Panama 293
Panel on the Integration of Immigrants into American Society 278

358 *Index*

Parker, Noel 94
parochialism 280
Peace of Westphalia 89–90, 213–14, 219
Pelosi, Nancy 47
Perdue, David 51, 55–6
Perez-Villanueva, Kristian 251, 259
permanent resident visas 33, 40
persecution 15, 25, 27, 70, 71–2, 74, 76, 78, 82, 93, 230, 285, 329
Phan, Peter C. 283–4
Philippe (king of Belgium) 339
Philippines 240, 301, 303
philoxenia 176
Pistone, Michele R. 93, 310
placement agencies 304
pluralism 28
Plyler v. Doe 122
Poland 199, 200
political theology 4–5, 7, 213, 215–18, 222, 224, 226, 345; Christian 229; coalitional 227–9; comparative 227–9; Muslim 229
Population, Refugees, and Migration (PRM) 119
populism 111, 232–3, 235–6, 245, 246, 337
promigrant rallies 199
Protocol Relating to the Status of Refugees (1967) 70, 82, 83
psychoanalysis 160
Public Religion Research Institute (PRRI) 115

quasicolonialism 239

racism 13, 38, 44, 182, 305, 307, 346; against Asian migrants 302; in immigration policy 53–8; in the U.S. 181
Rajendra, Tisha 101–2, 238
Raspail, Jean 166–7
realism 322
recruitment agents 41–2, 304
Reforming American Immigration for Strong Employment Act (RAISE Act) 51, 55–6, 64
Refugee Act (1980, U.S.) 81, 83
refugee crisis 84, 313, 322–3
refugee law 85, 307–8, 346; judicial interpretation of 71–2; *see also* immigration law
Refugee Relief Act (1953) 82

refugees: alleviating the suffering of 162; from Central America 73, 312–31; defined 70, 71, 73; from Haiti 73; in immigration law 307; international rights of 69–75; Jewish 346; number of 1; protection for 69–75; and the right to refuge 75–81; rights of 14–16; socioeconomic advancement of 120; from Syria 114, 199; from Vietnam 83; *see also* asylum seekers; immigrants
religion: conflation with culture 235; and immigration 45–8; and the law 215, 266; lived 266; loyalty oaths and 132–3; and migration 4; *see also* Christianity; Muslims; theology
religion-in-action 266
religious freedom 7, 254, 265, 266
Religious Freedom Restoration Act (RFRA) 252–5, 257–8, 260, 262–5, 274
religious leaders, influence of 46–7
removal: expedited 20–3, 27, 79, 96–7, 338, 342; nonpermanent relief from 73–5; withholding of 74; *see also* deportation; return
Renzi, Matteo 208
return: assisted 18, 23–4; forced 23–4; spontaneous 23; voluntary 11, 18, 23–5, 342; *see also* deportation; removal
Ribble, Reid 312
Ricoeur, Paul 161
Ros, Albert 88
Rivera-Pagán, Luis N. 45, 57, 175
Roberts, John 334
robotization 106, 120
Rodríguez, Richard 180
Rohingyas 235, 303
Roma people (Gypsies) 192
Romania 198, 201
Romero, Oscar 313, 324, 326–7
Ruiz, Jean-Pierre 324
rule of law 3, 28, 44, 88, 117, 122, 123, 234
Rumford, Chris 95, 97
Russian Federation 293

Sacaria-Goday, José Arnaldo 251, 259
Sachs, Jeffrey 232
Safire, William 25
Said, Edward 192, 329
Salter, Mark 97, 99

Salvini, Matteo 200, 209
Salvini Bill (Italy) 200, 209
sanctuary movement 253, 258, 268
Sassen, Saskia 214, 215–17, 224, 235
Saudi Arabia 293
Saunders, Jennifer 4, 7
Saunders, Stanley 171
scapegoating 159, 182, 185, 192, 240, 246, 281, 296, 338, 340
Schmiedel, Ulrich 235
Schmitt, Carl 216–20, 223, 224, 226
Schneiderman v. United States 135
School of the Americas (SOA) 312
Schreiter, Robert 206
Secours Catholique 199
secularism 226
segregation 164; of immigrant workers 31, 44, 307; residential 109
Seitz, Mark J. 346
Select Commission on Immigration and Refugee Policy (U.S.) 55
self-deportation 23–5; *see also* deportation
Sessions, Jeff 123, 167, 333
Simpson, Alan 51, 54–5
Slovakia 198, 201
Smith, Lamar 55
Snyder, Susanna 4, 7, 162, 194, 236, 243–4
Sobrino, Jon 306
social anthropology 231, 239, 241
social dumping 41–2, 308
social dynamism 28
social ethics, Christian 4, 246
social justice/injustice 31, 50, 238, 310; *see also* justice/injustice
social networks 46, 239
social responsibility 67, 208, 210
Social Security 61
social sin 231, 241–4, 340
Soerens, Matthew 188, 193
Sölle, Dorothee 222–3, 226
Sostaita, Barbara Andrea 269
Sotomayor, Sonia 332
Southern Poverty Law Center 297
sovereignty: and borders 89; of God 221; Schmitt's concept of 220; state 13–14, 16, 20, 213–16, 219, 224, 237–8; and suffering 222; and theology 222–3, 235; Westphalian 11, 12, 25
Soviet Union 81, 83
Spain 83

Spiro, Peter 140
Sri Lanka 301
staffing agencies 41
Stanley, Brian 193
stateless persons 74–5
stereotyping 29, 37, 112, 280, 297, 323, 330
strangers: in ancient Israel 158–9; biblical injunctions to care for 57, 186–7, 189, 236–7, 242, 281; divine 173–4; hospitality to 173–8
student visas 32
subsidiary protection 74–5
suffering 221
Sulistyaningsih, Erwiana 303
Sullivan, Winnifred Fallers 265–6
Svenungsson, Jayne 224, 227

Taiwan 302, 304
Tampa incident 77
technology: causing job displacement 120; and change 244; and innovation 2–3
Temporary Protected Status (TPS) 73–4, 114, 231
Terrazas, Laurence 140
terrorism 115, 181, 233, 276
Thailand 303
theology: after Auschwitz 221; apophatic/negative 222, 226–7; cataphatic/positive 222, 226; Catholic 306; Christian 5–6, 7, 31, 42, 101–2, 274; coalitional 344; constructive 7; of hospitality 127–8; liberal 271; liberation 43, 45; of migration 7, 179–94, 306; nature of 271; performative public 253; political 4–5, 7, 213, 215–18, 222, 224, 226–9, 345; postliberal 271; postmodern 272; praxis 7, 43, 44, 197, 221–2; public 265–74, 275; and religious freedom 266; and the responsibility of engagement 101–3
theopolitics 224, 226–7
theoxenia 58, 173–7
theoxenia (divine stranger) 166
Thind, Bhagat 129
Tomasi, Silvano 208
Torah 57, 154–5; *see also* Hebrew Bible
torture victims 14, 18
toshav (sojourners/transients/aliens) 147, 152–3, 156, 159
Tracy, David 271, 272

360 Index

transborder communion 270
transnational corporations 98, 321–2
transnational networks 2
Treaty of Guadalupe Hidalgo 87
Trible, Phillis 188
Trinity 206
Trucios-Haynes, Enid 87–8
Trump, Donald 44, 51, 56, 67, 111, 112, 114, 166, 231, 233, 245, 258, 296, 341; and DACA 333–4
Trump administration 22, 114, 123, 167, 230–1, 253, 257, 296–7, 309, 312, 323, 346
Trump v. Hawaii 13
Turkey 77

Ukraine 77
undocumented workers *see* immigrant workers
Unitarian Universalist Church 251, 259, 266–7
United Arab Emirates 293
United Nations High Commissioner for Refugees (UNHCR) 15, 24, 81, 308; Global Trends 2019 Report 195
United States: barriers to immigration 78; fertility rates 61; first naturalization law (1790) 132–3; immigrant integration in 107–9; immigration debates in 233; immigration enforcement in 78; immigration policies/system 31–5, 46, 87–8, 115–17, 121, 268; increase in Latino/Hispanic population 180; involvement in Central America 313–22; labor migration to 87–8, 293, 294–300, 305; Migrant Protection Protocols 96; migrant workers in 291; migration deterrence efforts 76–7, 84, 231–6, 242; migration from Latin America to 239; primacy of 232; public opinion about immigration 46; quality of life in 54; refugees in 7; and the social cost of migration 54; wet foot/ dry foot policy 83; *see also* Oath of Allegiance
United States v. Evans 255
United States v. Geisler 136–7
United States v. Thind 129
United States v. Vargas-Cordon 255–6
United States v. Warren 257–65

United States v. You 256
Universal Declaration of Human Rights 27, 49, 68
U.S. Coast Guard 77
U.S. Conference of Catholic Bishops (USCCB) 47
U.S. Constitution 139; First Amendment 254, 258; Fourteenth Amendment 138, 138
U.S. Customs and Border Patrol 78
U.S. Declaration of Independence 110
U.S. Department of Defense (DOD) 76
U.S. Department of Homeland Security 32, 74, 96, 114, 181
U.S. Department of Housing and Urban Development 114
U.S. Department of Labor 32
U.S. Department of State 140; Population, Refugees, and Migration (PRM) division 119
U.S. Department of the Interior 259
U.S. Fish and Wildlife Service 259
U.S. Occupational Health and Safety Administration (OSHA) 309
U.S. Office of Refugee Resettlement 119
U.S. Refugee Admissions Program (USRAP) 119

Vallejos, Evangeline 302n54, 306
Vance v. Terrazas 140
Vaughan-Williams, Nick 94, 96
Veloso, Mary Jane 304
Venezuela 312
Victims of Immigration Crime Engagement (VOICE) 114
Vietnam War 83, 240
vigilantes 97
violence: anti-immigrant 1; border 39, 99; in Central America 234; experienced by undocumented immigrants 38; gender-based 71; generalized 15–16; government 312–13; against immigrants 297; imperial 324–30; institutional 5; against the Other 276; police 339; programs to counter 247; sexual 36; structural 340; survivors of 31–2
visas 31–2; family 58; nonimmigrant 31–2; permanent resident 33, 40; student 32; temporary work 33–4; work 32–4, 58, 60–1, 295
Visegrád Group 111
Volpp, Leti 129

voluntary departures 18
voluntary return 11, 23–5, 342

Walzer, Michael 16
war 25, 73, 83, 188, 200, 208, 218–20, 240, 313–15, 317, 319, 320, 340; culture 246; proxy 83, 243
Warren, Scott 251–3, 257–5, 266, 269, 270, 274, 335–7, 346
Washington, George 133
Weis, Paul 15
Welz, Claudia 161
Western Hemisphere Institute for Security Cooperation (WHISC) 312–13
wet foot/dry foot policy 83
White Australia Policy 91
Wiesel, Elie 221
Winters, Michael Sean 210
women: abuse of 303; citizenship and marriage 129; as immigrant workers 36, 243, 300, 301

Wong Kim Ark v. United States 139
work visas 58; long-term temporary 295; low-skill/high-skill binary 60–1; requirements for 32–3; temporary 33–4
workforce: immigrants in the labor force 62–3; need for skilled workers 59–60; *see also* immigrant workers

xenophilia 141, 142, 186–7, 191, 205, 277
xenophobia 1, 4, 25, 29, 37–8, 54, 57, 58, 178, 181, 182, 186, 190, 191–2, 200, 242, 243, 296, 297, 301, 305, 341; and biblical texts 166–7; and migration 184–6; nationalist 187

Zanotelli, Alex 209
zar ("foreigner/stranger") 147, 148–50, 159
zero-tolerance policy 296

Taylor & Francis eBooks

www.taylorfrancis.com

A single destination for eBooks from Taylor & Francis with increased functionality and an improved user experience to meet the needs of our customers.

90,000+ eBooks of award-winning academic content in Humanities, Social Science, Science, Technology, Engineering, and Medical written by a global network of editors and authors.

TAYLOR & FRANCIS EBOOKS OFFERS:

- A streamlined experience for our library customers
- A single point of discovery for all of our eBook content
- Improved search and discovery of content at both book and chapter level

REQUEST A FREE TRIAL
support@taylorfrancis.com

Printed in the USA
CPSIA information can be obtained
at www.ICGtesting.com
LVHW020558170924
791293LV00001B/37

9 781032 049526